THE SECRET SERVICE
OF THE
CONFEDERATE STATES
IN EUROPE

JAMES D. BULLOCH

THE SECRET SERVICE

OF THE

CONFEDERATE STATES

IN EUROPE

OR,

HOW THE CONFEDERATE

CRUISERS WERE EQUIPPED

Introduction by Philip Van Doren Stern

THE MODERN LIBRARY

NEW YORK

2001 Modern Library Paperback Edition

Published in the United States by Modern Library, a division
of Random House, Inc., New York, and simultaneously in Canada
by Random House of Canada Limited, Toronto.

MODERN LIBRARY and colophon are registered trademarks
of Random House, Inc.

Grateful acknowledgment is made to Marguerite Stern Robinson for
permission to include the Introduction by Philip Van Doren Stern from
The Secret Service of the Confederate States in Europe, Volume 1, by James D. Bulloch
(New York: Sagamore Press, Inc., Thomas Yoseloff, Publisher, 1959). Reprinted
by permission of Marguerite Stern Robinson.

ISBN 0-679-64022-3

Modern Library website address: www.modernlibrary.com

Printed in the United States of America

2 4 6 8 9 7 5 3 1

Contents

Presidents Lincoln and Johnson.—The "reconstruction" of the Southern States.— Political condition of the United States at the present day.

Introduction

Philip Van Doren Stern

To understand the American Civil War one must go far beyond the military maneuvers, the political disputes, and the social history of the period. The sectional conflict was a major event in international affairs, and its great drama was played out not only on American battlegrounds but in Europe and on four of the world's five oceans. In fact, the shooting war began on the Atlantic Ocean when the Confederates drove away the steamer *Star of the West* on January 9, 1861, while she was trying to bring provisions to Major Anderson's garrison in Fort Sumter. And it ended on June 28, 1865, long after Appomattox, when the Confederate cruiser *Shenandoah* captured ten Yankee whaling vessels in the Bering Sea near the Arctic Circle.

Yet the naval phase of the Civil War has been neglected. The battle between the *Merrimac* and the *Monitor* has been well publicized, although it proved nothing more than the obvious fact that iron is harder to penetrate with shot and shell than wood. The sinking of the *Alabama* by the *Kearsarge* is fairly well known; so is Cushing's extraordinary exploit in blowing up the *Albemarle*. And there has been a spate of books about blockade running—the most picturesque and glamorized aspect of Civil War naval history. But that is about all. Aficionados who can give a day-by-day account of the movements of the Army of Northern Virginia, who know what Grant had for breakfast on the morning of the surrender of Vicksburg, or who can describe in detail what various cavalry commanders did as they dashed around the country, are strangely ignorant about what happened in Europe or on the high seas.

Yet it was there that the fate of the Confederacy was determined. Not Antietam or Gettysburg or Vicksburg decided the destiny of the United States as a nation. The decision was made in the chancelleries of Europe, and, except for a few major battles, the outcome was influenced more by what happened on the sea than on the land. The United States and England nearly went to war over the seizure of the Confederate Commissioners Mason and Slidell on the open ocean. Had Brazil been more powerful, she might very well have terminated friendly relations with the United States when the U.S.S. *Wachusett* recklessly disregarded international law and rammed and captured the Confederate raider *Florida* in the neutral harbor of Bahia in 1864. Such far-flung ports as Melbourne, Cape Town, Halifax, Bermuda, Nassau, Havana, Matamoras, Lisbon, Gibraltar, Brest, Calais, Liverpool, Terceira, and Funchal all played parts in this mighty drama of worldwide significance. And, most important of all, was the deadly effect of the Federal blockade which slowly strangled the Confederacy by cutting it off from the rest of the world.

Since the Confederates did not win a single major battle on the high seas, even Confederate historians have tended to underplay naval affairs. Bulloch himself was apologetic when he said: "The officers of the Confederate Navy had so few opportunities to manifest their professional acquirements and personal qualities—indeed, so few of them were employed in strictly naval operations at all—that scarcely more than some half-dozen will find their names recorded in any future history, and the Confederate Navy as a corps will hardly appear as a factor in the Civil War." Yet a brief outline of the influence of this neglected aspect of Civil War history will show how important the sea was in shaping the final outcome of events.

On April 15 (the day after Fort Sumter was evacuated), President Lincoln called for 75,000 volunteers. Reaction was swift and retaliatory in the South. Virginia seceded from the Union on April 17; on the same day, Jefferson Davis, president of the provisional Confederate government in Montgomery, Alabama, issued a proclamation offering letters of marque and reprisal to owners of private vessels who would arm their ships and attack Yankee commerce. The Northern government promptly countered on April 19 by proclaiming a blockade of all Southern ports from South Carolina to Texas. On the 27th the blockade was extended to include North Carolina and Virginia.

Secretary of State Seward, who was known for his impetuous action at the beginning of the war, is generally blamed for two grievous technical errors involved in the Northern government's move. North Carolina had not yet seceded at this time, and did not actually leave the Union until May 20. Her decision to secede was doubtless accelerated by this too-hasty blockade of her ports.

Even more serious, however, was the use of the word "blockade," for, as critics of the Lincoln administration quickly pointed out, a nation *blockades* an enemy's ports but *closes* its own in time of insurrection. This was a major blunder. It paved the way to foreign recognition of the Confederacy as a belligerent and would have led to full recognition of Southern independence if the coolly calculating men who were running the governments of Europe thought the Confederate States of America had a better-than-even chance of winning the war.

Both Northern and Southern governments blundered in their handling of naval and diplomatic affairs at the beginning of the war. The United States had refused to adopt the principles of international maritime law established on April 16, 1856, by the Declaration of Paris. Americans then believed that a nation with a small navy had nothing to gain by subscribing to the declaration. The four principles of international maritime law established by the Paris Convention were: 1. Privateering is and remains abolished; 2. The neutral flag covers enemy's goods, with the exception of contraband of war; 3. Neutral goods, with the exception of contraband of war, are not liable to capture under the enemy's flag; 4. Blockades ... must be effective, that is to say, maintained by a force sufficient really to prevent access to the coast of the enemy.

In 1861, just five years after the unfortunate American decision of 1856, Secretary of State Seward tried to repair the damage. It was to his country's advantage at this time to subscribe to the Paris convention because such a move would outlaw the Confederate privateers in the eyes of the world. He threw out tentative feelers to determine how his offer would be taken.

The discreet answer indicated that, although the United States would undoubtedly be welcomed to the convention, the offer would be received favorably only if it came from a united nation, North and South alike. Seward's counter-reply that the Confederate states in rebellion against the authority of the central government could not be considered an independent nation met with the answer that if the Confederate States of America was not independent then the United States could not impose a blockade of her ports. The full effect of the misuse of the word "blockade" was now felt.

The Confederates, however, were also in trouble. Since the Declaration of Paris outlawed privateering, the sending to sea of armed vessels of non-governmental origin (whose owners were out to make a profit) was naturally frowned upon by the powerful nations which had subscribed to the convention.

When the news of the firing on Fort Sumter reached Europe, Proclamations of Neutrality were issued by England on May 13, and by France on June 10. These moves temporarily discouraged the Confederacy's hope for foreign intervention, but at no time did the South entirely abandon the effort to win active support from abroad. Even while her Army of Northern Virginia was marching to Appomattox in April, 1865, at least two "unofficial" Confederate agents were at work in Europe trying to persuade Napoleon III to aid the dying Confederacy.

———

At the opening of the war, the South had very few ships and even fewer yards or materials for building them. Hasty but not very effective efforts were made to purchase ships in the North and Canada. Half a dozen small Federal revenue cutters were seized and sent out as armed vessels. A few vessels of various origin which were lying in Southern ports were acquired and outfitted.

But the agrarian Confederacy could not arm her soldiers or build an adequate navy without obtaining supplies and ships from abroad. Hardly more than three weeks after the provisional Confederate government had been formed at Montgomery, its new president named three commissioners to go to Europe. In addition to them, Major Caleb Huse was sent to England to buy arms and ammunition; credit was established in London with Fraser, Trenholm and Company, and James Dunwody Bulloch was summoned to Montgomery to be given *carte blanche* to buy and arm ships in Europe for the Confederate Navy. Since Great Britain was then regarded as "the arsenal, treasury, and dockyard of the greater part of the world," Bulloch naturally went there first.

———

The Confederacy was fortunate in obtaining the services of a man with Bulloch's wide experience in naval affairs, merchant shipping, shipbuilding, and naval armament. He was also trained in the ways of business, had many contacts abroad, and, above all, was the soul of integrity. His forthright honesty in insisting on returning the ship he was commanding at the outbreak of the war to her Northern owners may have irritated some of the Southern fire-eaters, but it established Bulloch's reputation for fair dealing beyond dispute.

To his work he brought superb competence, much ingenuity in solving ever-changing problems, and cool courage in the face of danger. It is doubtful whether anyone in the entire Western hemisphere was as well fitted for his special job as Bulloch was. The Confederate government had such faith in him that it entrusted millions of dollars to his care and abided by his decisions in matters which required huge investments and great discretion in negotiating on an international level. His efforts far outshone the combined accomplishments of the better known diplomatic commissioners Mason and Slidell. Yet everything Bulloch tried to do ended in failure, for he had bound his fate to the Confederacy's and had to see his hopes dashed with the downfall of the nation he had pledged himself to serve.

Bulloch's story is the story of the failure of a mission, but that does not detract from its interest. All Confederate missions eventually proved to be failures no matter how brilliantly successful they may have seemed at the time. A hundred successes will not save a war that is going to be lost. Yet Lee and Jackson and many lesser figures who fought for a lost cause are not forgotten. The men who worked to build the Confederate Navy are.

———

The expert in naval affairs whom fate had endowed with such potentialities for success—and then cruelly doomed to failure in the greatest enterprise of his life—was born near Savannah, Georgia, on June 25, 1823. He came from distinguished Scotch ancestors, one of whom settled in South Carolina in 1729. His great-grandfather, Archibald Bulloch, helped found the American nation, for he took an active part in the Revolution and fought in its wars. And James Dunwody Bulloch's father* was among the far-thinking men who backed the *Savannah* on her history-making voyage in 1819 as the first steamship to cross the Atlantic Ocean.

Salt water played an important part in Bulloch's life. At sixteen, six years before the Naval Academy at Annapolis was established in 1845, he

---

* Bulloch's father, Major James Stephens Bulloch, married twice, in 1817 and 1832. Bulloch was the only child of the first marriage. Children of the second marriage were: Anna Bulloch (Mrs. James K. Gracie); Martha Bulloch (Mrs. Theodore Roosevelt, Sr.); and Irvine S. Bulloch, who was on the *Alabama* and the *Shenandoah*. In 1840 Major Bulloch built a pleasant Greek Revival house on the western edge of Roswell, nineteen miles north of Atlanta, Georgia. James D. must have visited there occasionally, but since he was away at sea after 1839, his connection with this place cannot have been close. His half-sister Martha was married there on December 22, 1853; her son was Theodore Roosevelt, President of the United States, who visited the house in 1905. Although no longer owned by the family, the old building, called Bulloch Hall, still stands.

became a midshipman in the United States Navy. For more than ten years, he slowly worked his way up in a branch of the services that had hardly changed since the Revolution and the War of 1812. Wooden ships and clumsy, heavy guns were operated by hard-driven men under a system of such brutal tyranny that mutiny was not unknown. During Bulloch's training he came in contact with some of the officers who were to command the Federal fleets during the Civil War. He was on the *Decatur* under Farragut and succeeded David Dixon Porter to the command of the *Georgia*.

This steamer was the first one subsidized by the United States to carry mail to California when that new state became prosperous as a result of the large deposits of gold discovered there. Bulloch also commanded government mail steamers in the Gulf. Then he resigned from government service in 1853 to devote all his time to private shipping interests in New York.

At the outbreak of the war, he was in command of the steamer *Bienville*, plying between New York and various Southern ports. He was in New Orleans when word of the firing on Fort Sumter arrived. He immediately proffered his services to the Confederate government but explained that he was honor bound to take the *Bienville* to New York to turn her over to her owners there. Refusing all local efforts to buy the ship, he sailed for New York, found a letter summoning him to Montgomery, Alabama, and promptly hurried South.

The Confederacy appreciated his value. He was sent abroad forthwith and given almost limitless powers to buy ships and arm them. The story of his four-year-long struggle with the governments of England and France is told here by Bulloch himself. This record of his efforts is one of the key books of the Civil War, fit to rank in importance with those written by the leading commanders on both sides. And his is a little-known but fascinating tale, involving, as it does, all sorts of cloak-and-dagger operations and behind-the-scenes negotiations carried on on a grand scale.

His account, however, is strictly a personal and partisan one. He does not attempt to write the history of the Confederate Navy. His book contains practically nothing about naval warfare along the coasts and rivers of the North American continent. It is the report of a mission, addressed to the people of the former Confederate states who had never been told the whole truth about the secret efforts to build a navy overseas. One can only wish that all reports of secret missions were as well and as honestly written.

It is seldom that the top man in any major enterprise writes the history of the undertaking that was under his direction. On the Confederate side, Lee planned to write such a history and even began to gather material for it, but apparently did not put down a word. Jefferson Davis wrote a two-volume work which is really an apologia for his administration. Curiously enough, he practically ignored the naval aspect of the war, perhaps because (as Bulloch charitably explains, p. 350) he felt it unnecessary to mention disappointed hopes for a navy that never materialized in any great force.

———

The privateers which put to sea so hopefully as early as May, 1861, soon proved to be of little value because the increasingly vigilant Union blockading fleet made it nearly impossible for them to bring a captured prize of war into a Southern port. And most privateersmen were interested only in capture and sale, for profit was their primary motive. Only government-owned ships could afford to seek out and destroy, ruthlessly burning their captures at sea even though they were sometimes worth hundreds of thousands of dollars. Many of the people who directed this wholesale destruction and sent hundreds of fine ships to the bottom disliked having to do what they did even as a necessity of war. Bulloch explains his own feeling about this and indicates that he was not alone in his attitude (p. 391).

But the three Confederate commerce-raiders which Bulloch managed to get to sea were so effective in harassing Yankee shipping that American vessels either stayed in port, were sold to the Federal government to be armed and become part of the Navy, or were transferred to the flags of other nations. By March, 1864, the much-feared Confederate raiders had swept the oceans of the world so thoroughly of American merchant ships that the commander of the Confederate *Tuscaloosa* reported that out of more than a hundred vessels seen by him in the South Atlantic only one was of American origin. The depredations of the cruisers cost the North untold millions of dollars not only for the actual value of ships destroyed but for the potential value of trade that was lost.

The story of the Confederate commerce-raiders is confusing because the ships often changed names several times or bred new cruisers at sea by arming the vessels they captured. And ships under construction sometimes had to be sold under pressure to other governments. The exploits of the raiders of American origin, like the *Retribution,* the *Nashville,* and Raphael Semmes's first wartime command, the *Sumter,* are fairly easy to follow. But the foreign-built ships had much more complicated histories. The chart (which appears after the Introduction), summarizing what happened to the various Confederate raiders of foreign origin, will help to guide the reader through their tangled careers.

A study of the chart will show that of the nineteen commerce-raiders ordered abroad, only three—the *Florida,* the *Alabama,* and the *Shenandoah*—can be said to have had truly successful careers. (So did the five ships they captured, armed, and commissioned at sea: the *Lapwing* [rechristened the *Oreto*], the *Clarence,* the *Tacony,* the *Archer,* and the *Tuscaloosa.*) Three other ships did some damage. These were: the *Georgia,* which ranged far and wide during her thirteen months at sea, but she was an unlucky vessel from the start; and the two British-built but American-based cruisers, the *Tallahassee* and the *Chickamauga,* which dashed out of Wilmington, N.C., to make many captures along the Atlantic coast, but they spent little time as active cruisers. The *Georgiana* never got to Charleston where she was to be armed, for she was wrecked while trying to enter the harbor. The *Rappahannock* was sealed up in Calais, and the *Stonewall* put to sea only a few days before Appomattox. The other ten ships contracted for in Europe never reached Confederate hands.

The failure to obtain possession of the ironclads (except the *Stonewall,* which was acquired too late in the war to be of any use) was most disappointing of all, for Bulloch had ambitious plans for them. The French-built rams were purposely planned to be short in length and shallow in draught so they could be maneuvered in the Mississippi River to defend that essential waterway for the Confederacy. The Laird rams were larger, but the French rams were more heavily armed and armored. Bulloch wanted to run them into Wilmington to recruit full crews there and then terrorize the Atlantic coast. He hoped to run them up the Potomac, make Washington untenable, and then steam north to Portsmouth, New Hampshire, spouting shot and shell, burn the important navy yard there, and demand a million dollars in gold as ransom for sparing the city from destruction. Boston and New York would also probably have come under the threat of the two ironclads' mighty guns.

These plans are not so far-fetched as they may seem. The *Tallahassee*'s captain planned to take his far less formidable wooden cruiser "up the East River, setting fire to the shipping on both sides, and when abreast of the (Brooklyn) navy-yard to open fire, hoping some of our shells might set fire to the buildings and any vessels that might be at the docks." And he might have done so if he had been able to capture a local pilot who knew the treacherous waters around Hell Gate. Lt. Charles W. Read, whom Maffitt, commander of the *Florida,* had authorized to arm and commission a series of small Yankee ships as cruisers, boldly entered the harbor of

Portland, Maine, to capture the U.S. Revenue Cutter *Caleb Cushing*. Only a dead calm prevented him from running away with his prize during the night.

Even though Bulloch considered his mission a failure, the tiny Confederate Navy inflicted so much damage on Northern commerce that the United States government demanded enormous reparations from Great Britain after the war. These were the famous *Alabama* Claims, which, after protracted correspondence and several meetings, were finally settled by arbitration in Geneva by an International Tribunal that (on September 14, 1872) awarded the United States $15,500,000 in gold as damages. By an odd coincidence this was almost exactly the same amount raised by the Confederate (Erlanger) bond issue of March, 1863.

When the war ended in April, 1865, the Confederate Navy still had two cruisers at sea. One was the armored ram *Stonewall* which entered Nassau on May 6 only to find that the Confederate States of America had ceased to exist as a government. This heavily armed and armored ram might very well have made a difference in the outcome of the war if it had arrived earlier, for no ship—or combination of ships in the United States Navy—could have stood up against it. The Union also was building a super-ram, the giant *Dunderberg,* which was under construction in New York. But this powerful ironclad, nearly 400 feet long with a 50-foot ram, was not ready for launching until July 22, 1865, and therefore could have been of no help.

Far out in the North Pacific, near the Arctic Circle, the *Shenandoah,* cut off from all communication from Richmond, went on burning Yankee whalers until June 28, 1865. Her mass capture of ten ships on that day was the last offensive act of the already extinct Confederacy. Bulloch had notified the *Shenandoah*'s commander on June 19 that Jefferson Davis had been taken prisoner and that the war was over, but copies of his letter, which were sent by Earl Russell to various British consuls in the Pacific, never reached the *Shenandoah.* Her commander hailed the British ship *Barracouta* on August 2, and on being informed that the war had ended, dismantled her guns, and made a 17,000-mile run to Liverpool, where he turned his ship over to the British authorities on November 6, 1865. That day marks the true end of the Confederate States of America as a fighting nation.

———

Besides building and buying vessels intended to be armed and used as commerce-raiders, Bulloch also obtained a number of fast blockade runners for the Confederate government. Some of them were still on the ways in various British yards when the war ended; others got to sea. One of them was the *Bat* which was captured late in 1864, and which Admiral David Dixon Porter then used as his flagship. During the Appomattox Campaign, President Lincoln slept on this ship several times, and it carried General Sherman back to New Bern after the historic council of war at City Point on March 27–28, 1865.

After the end of the war, the United States government tried to seize all Confederate assets in Europe. Years of litigation brought ruin to the house of Fraser, Trenholm and Company, which had handled Confederate funds and credits. As so often happened in governmental financial transactions of this kind during the postwar era, fraud and chicanery drained off the greater part of the money that was obtained, so the American taxpayer gained very little from the long-continued effort to obtain what was left of the Confederate funds in Europe.

Bulloch was embittered by his experiences. Since it seemed unlikely that amnesty and pardon would be extended to him as one of the chief agents of the former Confederate government, he decided to remain in Liverpool permanently. He entered the shipping business there, specializing in the cotton trade, and although he prospered in his new enterprise, he dropped so far out of the public's eye that his postwar career would be practically unknown if it were not for his close connection with the Roosevelt family.

Young Theodore, not quite eleven, first met "Uncle Jimmie" when he went with his family to visit the Bullochs in England in 1867. He was there again in 1872 and also in 1881, when the aspiring twenty-three-year-old author got some help from his uncle on certain nautical problems involved in the history of the War of 1812 which he was then writing.

Bulloch had been married twice—in 1851 and in 1857. He had five children, three boys and two girls. As he grew older, the conservative Southern gentleman became a British Tory with Gladstone (who had succeeded Lord Russell in 1867 as leader of the Liberal Party) as his special *bête noire*.

He sometimes traveled to other countries on business, but he apparently never revisited his native land. He lived on until the twentieth century, and was well spoken of by those who knew him as a kind, affable, and distinguished elderly gentleman who could seldom be persuaded to talk about his wartime experiences. His book is his testament, his autobiography, and his personal account of the secret operation he had masterminded for the Confederacy. Evidently he said in it all that he intended to say. It was published in England in a small edition from which a few hundred sets of sheets were imported into the United States to be published in New York in 1884. Since then the book has become so exceedingly rare that copies of it are seldom offered for sale.

Its author died in England on January 7, 1901. His gravestone, now reportedly overgrown and neglected, should have borne an inscription more impressive than the simple dates of birth and death. A suitable epitaph for the man who tried so hard to build a Confederate Navy would be Seneca's words: "Admire those who attempt great things, even though they fail."

A CHART OF THE NAVAL HISTORIES OF THE CONFEDERATE CRUISERS OF EUROPEAN ORIGIN

Name by which ship is best known. Names of Commanders.	Dockyard or first name.	Date started to build or acquired. Place of origin.	Contract negotiated by —	First sailing date. Names of supply vessels.	Captured ships armed and commissioned at sea.	Eventual fate
Florida J. N. Maffitt J. N. Barney C. M. Morris	*Manassas* and *Oreto*	Built at Liverpool by W. C. Miller & Sons. Work started in June, 1861.	J. D. Bulloch	From Liverpool, Mar. 22, 1862. *Bababia* and *Prince Alfred*	*Lapwig* (*Oreto*), Mar. 28, 1863; com. S. W. Averett; com. R. S. Floyd. *Clarence*, May 6; *Tacony*, May 10; *Archer*, June 15; com. Charles W. Read	Captured by U.S.S. *Wachusett* at Bahia, Brazil, Oct. 7, 1864. Sunk at Hampton Roads, Va., Nov. 28, 1864.
Alabama Raphael Semmes	No. 290 and *Enrica*	Built at Birkenhead by the Lairds. Work started August, 1861.	J. D. Bulloch	From Liverpool, July 29, 1862. *Aggripina*	*Tuscaloosa*, June 21, 1863, (origin, the *Conrad*), com. John Low	Sunk by U.S.S. *Kearsarge* off the coast of France, June 19, 1864.
Georgiana Geo. T. Sinclair	?	Construction ordered in the spring of 1862.	J. D. Bulloch	From Liverpool, Jan. 21, 1863.		Wrecked Mar. 19, 1863, trying to enter Charleston.
"Lt. North's ironclad"	?	Built at Glasgow by G. and J. Thompson May, 1862.	Lt. James H. North			Sold to Denmark
Pampero	*Canton*	Glasgow, July, 1862	George T. Sinclair			Detained by British, Nov. 1863; then retained by builders.
Two Laird ironclad rams	No. 294, No. 295. Temporary names during Egyptian deal: *El Tousson* *El Mounassir*	Birkenhead, July 1862	J. D. Bulloch	Seized by British, Oct. 1863. Bought for their navy.		Became part of British Navy (May 20, 1864), under names *Scorpion* and *Wivern*.
Georgia Wm. L. Maury	*Japan* *Virginia*	Dumbarton, Launched Jan. 10, 1863.	M. F. Maury	From Greenock, Scotland, Apr. 2, 1863. *Alar*		Armament dismantled in Liverpool, May 2, 1864. Ostensibly sold and sent to Lisbon, Aug. 8, 1864. Captured Aug. 15 by U.S.S. *Niagara*.
Alexandra	?	Built at Liverpool by W. C. Miller. Launched Mar. 7, 1863.	Built for Fraser, Trenholm who intended to present her to Confederacy. Though small, Bulloch admits she could have been armed (p. 235).	Seized by British Apr. 5, 1863. Released Apr. 1864.		Name changed to *Mary*. Sailed for Bermuda, etc.; again seized in Nassau, Dec. 13, 1864. Held for trial until end of war.

Four French-built wooden corvettes	Bordeaux corvettes: *Yedda, Osaca* Nantes corvettes: Names: ?		J. D. Bulloch	Two in Bordeaux Two in Nantes, May, 1863	Two (Bordeaux) sold to Prussia. Two (Nantes) sold to Peru. May, 1864. Remained in Prussian and Peruvian Navies.
2 French-built rams. Prussian ram sold to Prussia.	?		J. D. Bulloch	Bordeaux July, 1863	Sold by the French to Prussia.
Danish ram, later *Stonewall* (CSN). Thos. J. Page	*Sphinx* *Stoerkodder* *Olinde*			Sold to Denmark, May 1864. Resold to C.S.A. Dec. 1864; renamed *Stonewall*; sailed from Copenhagen Jan. 6, 1865. Supply ship: *City of Richmond*	In Ferrol, Spain, Feb. 2 to Mar. 24 for repair. Arrived Nassau May 6 to find war over. Surrendered to U.S. May 19, 1865. Later sold to Japan.
Rappahannock Samuel Barron C. M. Fauntleroy	*Victor* *Scylla*	Purchased as former dispatch boat from British Navy, Sept. 14, 1863.	M. F. Maury	From Sheerness Nov. 24, 1863.	Laid up in Calais from Nov. 1863 to Mar. 1865; claimed by U.S. Govt. at end of war.
Tallahassee John T. Wood Wm. H. Ward J. Wilkinson	*Atlanta* *Olustee*	Built at "Millwall below London." Made two trips as blockade runner in spring 1864 between Bermuda and Wilmington, N.C. Fitted out in Wilmington and commissioned as cruiser July 20, 1864.	?	From Wilmington, Aug. 6–25, and Oct. 29–Nov. 7, 1864, to raid Atlantic coast. Transformed into blockade runner *Chameleon*.	Ran to Liverpool near end of war. Claimed there by U.S. and sold to Japan.
Shenandoah J. I. Waddell	*Sea King*	Purchased Sept. 20, 1864. Had made one voyage to Bombay.	J. D. Bulloch	From London Oct. 8, 1864. *Laurel*	Turned over to British at Liverpool, Nov. 6, 1865. Surrendered to U.S. and sold to Sultan of Zanzibar. Sank in storm in Indian Ocean, 1879.
Chickamauga J. Wilkinson	*Edith*	Built in England as blockade runner, and made several trips in spring of 1864. Acted as cruiser from Oct. 29 to Nov. 19, 1864.	?	From Wilmington, Oct. 29, 1864.	Burned after fall of Ft. Fisher in 1865.

CHRONOLOGY

1860

Nov. 6   Lincoln is elected President of the United States.

Dec. 20   South Carolina secedes.

1861

Jan. 9   Mississippi secedes.

Jan. 9   *The Star of the West* is fired on when it attempts to provision Fort Sumter.

Jan. 10   Florida secedes.

Jan. 11   Alabama secedes.

Jan. 19   Georgia secedes.

Jan. 26   Louisiana secedes.

Feb. 1   Texas secedes.

Feb. 4   Delegates from the first six states to secede meet at Montgomery, Ala., to form a provisional Confederate government.

Feb. 9   Jefferson Davis is named president of the provisional Confederate government.

Feb. 18   Davis is inaugurated.

Feb. 27   Davis names three Confederate Commissioners to Europe: William L. Yancey, Pierre A. Rost, and A. Dudley Mann. Yancey and Rost sail on March 16.

Mar. 4   Abraham Lincoln is inaugurated President of the U.S.A.

Mar.   Bulloch's ship, the *Bienville*, is seized in New York. He goes to Washington to see the Secretary of the Treasury, Salmon P. Chase.

Apr. 12   The Confederates fire on Fort Sumter at 4:30 A.M.

Apr. 13   Gen. Anderson hauls down the flag at Fort Sumter at 1:30 P.M.

Apr. 13   Word of the firing on Fort Sumter reaches New Orleans by telegraph while Bulloch is in port with the *Bienville*. He offers his services to the Confederate government. Confederate officials try to purchase the *Bienville*, but Bulloch refuses to sell.

Apr. 14   The *Bienville* sails from New Orleans at 8 A.M. Fort Sumter is evacuated.

Apr. 15   Lincoln calls for 75,000 3-month volunteers.

Apr. 17   Virginia secedes.

1861

Apr. 17	Davis issues a proclamation offering letters of marque to privateers who will capture or destroy Union shipping.
Apr. 18	The U.S. arsenal at Harpers Ferry is burned and abandoned to prevent it from falling into Confederate hands.
Apr. 19	Lincoln proclaims blockade of the Southern coast from Texas to South Carolina. The Sixth Massachusetts Regiment is attacked as it passes through Baltimore to defend Washington.
Apr. 20	The Norfolk (Va.) Navy Yard is burned and abandoned.
Apr. 20	Robert E. Lee resigns from the U.S. Army and offers his services to his native Virginia.
Apr. 22	Bulloch arrives in New York on the *Bienville,* turns the ship back to her owners, and finds a letter from Judah P. Benjamin summoning him to Montgomery.
Apr. 22–25	Washington, D.C., is cut off from communication with the Northern states.
Apr. 27	The Union blockade is extended to North Carolina and Virginia.
Apr. 29	Confederate Commissioners Yancey and Rost arrive in London.
May 1 (?)	Bulloch leaves for the South.
May 3	Lincoln calls for 42,000 3-year volunteers.
May 3	News of the Proclamation of Blockade is published in the London papers.
May 5	Bulloch arrives in Nashville, Tenn.
May 6	Arkansas secedes.
May 7	Bulloch arrives in Montgomery, Ala.
May 8	He sees Benjamin, who asks him to go to Europe.
May 9	He leaves Montgomery by train, goes to Detroit, and takes a steamship from Montreal to Liverpool.
May 13	The British issue a Proclamation of Neutrality.
May 13	Charles Francis Adams, the new American Minister to England, arrives in Liverpool, and goes to London on May 14.
May 16	At noon, Adams takes full charge of the American Legation in London.
May 20	North Carolina secedes.
May 29	Richmond becomes the capital of the Confederacy.
June 4	Bulloch arrives in Liverpool.

1861

June   Construction of the *Oreto* (later the *Florida*) begun.

June 10   The French issue a Proclamation of Neutrality. They are followed on June 16 by the Netherlands; on June 17 by Spain; and on August 1 by Brazil.

June 24   Tennessee secedes.

June 30   Raphael Semmes takes the *Sumter*, the first Confederate warship, out of the Mississippi River and escapes the Union blockading fleet.

July 3   Semmes captures his first prize, the *Golden Rocket* of Maine, and burns her at sea off the coast of Cuba.

July 21   The Battle of Bull Run (First Manassas) is a Confederate victory.

July 27   McClellan replaces McDowell.

July 27   The first remittance for the Confederate Navy reaches England.

Aug. 1   A contract for the construction of No. 290 (later the *Alabama*) is signed.

Oct. 15   Bulloch leaves Holyhead in the newly purchased blockade runner, the *Fingal*. The ship, loaded with arms, ammunition, and supplies, heads for Savannah, Ga.

Nov. 2   After leaving Terceira (in the Azores) the *Fingal* arrives in Bermuda.

Nov. 7   The *Fingal* leaves Bermuda.

Nov. 8   Confederate Commissioners Mason and Slidell are taken from the British steamer *Trent* by Captain Charles Wilkes of the U.S.S. *San Jacinto*.

Nov. 12   The *Fingal* arrives in Savannah.

Nov. 14   Bulloch goes to Richmond to report to the Confederate Navy Department.

Nov. 23   He returns to Savannah.

Nov. 30   Bulloch is ordered to take command of the first cruiser to leave England.

Dec. 24   For the next few weeks Bulloch tries to take the *Fingal* back to England, but Savannah is so closely patroled by the Federal blockading fleet that he has to give up the attempt.

Dec. 26   The State Department admits that the seizure of Mason and Slidell was illegal and allows them to proceed to Europe.

1862

Jan. 1   Mason and Slidell embark on a British gunboat in the harbor of Provincetown, Mass.

Jan. 13   E. M. Stanton replaces Simon Cameron as U.S. Secretary of War.

Jan. 24   Bulloch arrives in Wilmington, N.C., to sail for England.

Feb. 5   He runs the blockade as a passenger in the *Annie Childs*.

Mar. 9   Battle of the *Monitor* and the *Merrimac* at Hampton Roads, Va.

Mar. 10   Bulloch arrives in Liverpool.

Mar. 14   Federals capture New Bern, N.C.

Mar. 21   Bulloch notifies the Confederate Navy Department that he is investigating the possibility of having ironclad ships built in England.

Mar. 22   The *Florida* sails from Liverpool.

Apr. 6–7   The Battle of Shiloh (Pittsburgh Landing).

Apr. 11   Fort Pulaski, commanding the approaches to Savannah, Ga., is surrendered to the Federals after a heavy bombardment.

Apr. 28   The *Florida* arrives in Nassau.

Apr. 29   Farragut runs his fleet past the Mississippi River forts and occupies New Orleans on April 29.

May 4   Maffitt takes command of the *Florida*.

May 11   The Confederates evacuate Norfolk, Va.

May 15   The *Alabama* is launched.

May and   The Peninsular Campaign to take Richmond is unsuccessful.
June

June 15   The *Florida* is seized by the British when her supply ship, the *Bahama*, arrives in Nassau.

July   Work on the two Laird ironclad rams is begun in England.

July 20   Yellow fever strikes the *Florida* in Nassau.

July 29   The *Alabama* sails from Liverpool.

Aug. 2   The British release the *Florida*. She leaves Nassau the next day and goes to Green Cay, about 75 miles south of Nassau, to be armed and fitted out.

Aug. 16   With yellow fever still raging on board, the *Florida* begins her career as a Confederate raider.

Aug. 19   The *Florida* enters the port of Cardenas, Cuba, with nearly everyone on board prostrated by yellow fever.

Aug. 24   The *Alabama* is commissioned at sea.

Aug. 27   The Battle of Second Manassas is a Confederate victory.

1862

Sept. 4   The *Florida* enters Mobile Bay under fire. She remains there, undergoing repair, until January, 1863.

Sept. 16–17   Battle of Antietam (Sharpsburg).

Sept. 20   Bulloch is notified that Commander M. F. Maury is being sent to England on special service.

Sept. 22   Lincoln releases his Emancipation Proclamation to the press.

Nov. 5   McClellan is relieved from command and is replaced by Burnside.

Dec. 13   The Battle of Fredericksburg is lost by Burnside.

Dec. 28   Bravay and Company of Paris start negotiations to purchase the two Laird rams, ostensibly for Egypt.

1863

Jan. 16   The *Florida* runs out of Mobile Bay and escapes the Federal fleet.

Jan. 25   Hooker replaces Burnside.

Jan. 29   A European loan of $15,000,000 is authorized by the Confederate Congress.

Jan. 31   The Confederate ironclads *Chicora* and *Palmetto State* make an unsuccessful attempt to raise the Federal blockade of Charleston.

Mar.   Maury buys the *Japan* (the *Georgia*) to be used as a Confederate cruiser.

Mar. 7   The *Alexandra* is launched.

Mar. 19   Confederate bonds offered for sale in Europe. The issue is oversubscribed.

Apr. 5   The *Alexandra* is seized by the British.

Apr. 11   Mallory directs Bulloch to employ European mechanics and experts for work in Confederacy.

May 2–4   The Battle of Chancellorsville is lost by Gen. Hooker.

May 6   The *Florida* captures the *Clarence* and converts her into a Confederate raider, Lt. C. W. Read commanding.

May 22   The *Alabama* leaves Bahia, Brazil.

June 17   The *Atlanta* is captured by the *Weehawken* near Savannah.

June 20   The *Alabama* captures the U.S. bark *Conrad* and converts her into a Confederate raider under the name *Tuscaloosa,* John Low commanding.

July 1–3   Battle of Gettysburg. After it, Lee retreats to Virginia.

1863

July 4   Vicksburg, Miss., surrenders; on July 8, Port Hudson, La., also surrenders, thus closing the Mississippi River to the Confederacy.

July 13–16   Draft riots in New York.

July 16   Bulloch signs a contract for two ironclad ships to be built in France.

Aug. 16–29   The *Georgia* at Simon's Bay, Cape of Good Hope.

Aug. and Sept.   The Union fleet makes an unsuccessful attempt to take Charleston Harbor.

Sept. 19–20   The Battle of Chickamauga, Ga., except for Thomas's firm stand, is a Union defeat.

Sept. 24   The Russian Atlantic fleet visits New York as a gesture of friendship. On Oct. 12, the Russian Pacific fleet enters San Francisco Bay. The ships remain in American waters for the next seven months.

Oct. 1   Bulloch reports "disappointment in all our British undertakings."

Oct. 9   The British plan to seize the two Laird ironclads before they are completed.

Oct. 27   The British seize the two Laird ironclads and put a marine guard on them.

Oct. 28   The *Georgia* arrives in Cherbourg.

Nov. 23–25   Battles of Chattanooga and Missionary Ridge are Union victories.

Nov. 24   The *Victor* is commissioned at sea as the *Rappahannock*.

Nov. 26   Bulloch begins to doubt that the two ironclad rams being built in France will be permitted to go to sea.

Dec. 27   The Confederate raider *Tuscaloosa* is seized by the British at Simon's Bay, Cape of Good Hope.

1864

Jan. 27   Bulloch goes to France to try to persuade Napoleon III to buy the two Laird rams but is advised that such an appeal would be hopeless.

Feb. 18   Bulloch notifies the Confederate Navy Department that the ships ordered in France have been forbidden to sail.

Mar. 10   U. S. Grant is placed in command of all Union armies.

1864

May   The *Alexandra* is released by the British; her name is changed to the *Mary*; and she sails for Bermuda and Halifax.

May and June   Wilderness, Spottsylvania, and Cold Harbor campaigns.

May 2   The *Georgia* reaches Liverpool, is sold to new owners there, sails for Lisbon on August 8, and is seized by the U.S.S. *Niagara*.

May 20   Preliminary terms for the two Laird ironclad rams (Nos. 294 and 295) to be sold to the British Navy are settled.

June   Bulloch goes to Paris to consult with Slidell on the disappointing status of the French-built rams.

June 7   Lincoln is nominated for President by the Republican (Union) Party.

June 11   The *Alabama* arrives in Cherbourg to refit.

June 14   The U.S.S. *Kearsarge* arrives off the coast of France and watches the port of Cherbourg to prevent the *Alabama* from leaving.

June 19   The *Alabama* leaves Cherbourg and is sunk at sea by the *Kearsarge*.

Aug. 1   Bulloch gives up hope of getting any ships built in France.

Aug. 5   Farragut captures Mobile.

Aug. 31   McClellan is nominated for President by the Democratic Party.

Sept. 2   Sherman takes Atlanta.

Sept. 16   Bulloch tells Richmond he has bought the *Shenandoah*, then named the *Sea King*.

Oct. 7   The *Florida* is captured at Bahia, Brazil, by the U.S.S. *Wachusett*.

Oct. 8   The *Shenandoah* sails from London, while her supply ship, the *Laurel*, sails from Liverpool to meet her.

Oct. 20   The *Shenandoah*, outfitted at sea, goes into action.

Nov. 8   Lincoln is elected President for a second term.

Nov. 15   Leaving Atlanta burning, Sherman marches across Georgia toward the sea.

Nov. 28   The *Florida* is sunk at Hampton Roads, Va.

Dec. 1   William L. Dayton, American Minister to France, dies in Paris; John Bigelow succeeds him.

Dec. 13   The *Alexandra* (now the *Mary*) is again seized by the British, this time in Nassau, and is held under trial until after the end of the war.

1864

Dec. 16   The details of buying the ram *Stonewall* from Denmark are settled.

Dec. 21   Sherman takes Savannah.

1865

Jan. 6   The *Stonewall* sails from Copenhagen.

Jan. 8   The *Stonewall* arrives at Elsinore.

Jan. 15   Fort Fisher is taken by Union assault, closing Wilmington, N.C., the last major Confederate port.

Jan. 24   The *Stonewall* meets the *City of Richmond* at sea to take on crew.

Jan. 25   The *Shenandoah* arrives in Melbourne, Australia.

Jan. 31   The House of Representatives passes the Thirteenth Amendment abolishing slavery.

Feb. 1   No new contracts made in Europe by the Confederate Navy Department after this date.

Feb. 2   The *Stonewall* puts into Ferrol, Spain.

Feb. 3   Lincoln holds a peace conference with the Confederates at Hampton Roads, but it comes to nothing.

Feb. 18   Sherman takes Columbia, S.C.; Charleston, S.C., surrenders to the Federal fleet.

Feb. 18   The *Shenandoah* leaves Melbourne.

Mar. 24   The *Stonewall* sails from Ferrol.

Mar. 29   Grant begins the Appomattox Campaign.

Apr. 1   The Battle of Five Forks. The *Stonewall* sails from Teneriffe (Canary Islands) to attack Sherman's bases in the Carolinas.

Apr. 2   Richmond and Petersburg are evacuated.

Apr. 9   Lee surrenders the Army of Northern Virginia to Grant at Appomattox Court House.

Apr. 14   Lincoln is assassinated and dies the next morning.

Apr. 26   Surrender of Joseph E. Johnston's army.

May 6   The *Stonewall* arrives in Nassau to find that the war is over.

May 10   Jefferson Davis is taken prisoner near Irwinville, Ga.

May 11   The *Stonewall* arrives in Havana and is surrendered there.

May 21   The *Shenandoah* enters the Okhotsk Sea; she leaves there June 13 and sails north.

May 26   Kirby Smith surrenders all the Confederate troops west of the Mississippi River.

June 28   The *Shenandoah*, on the edge of the Arctic Circle, makes her last capture.

1865

Aug. 2   The *Shenandoah*, off the coast of Mexico, learns from the captain of H.M.S. *Barracouta* that the war has ended.

Nov. 6   The *Shenandoah* arrives in Liverpool and is turned over to the British authorities there.

1871

May 8   The Treaty of Washington is signed to arbitrate the *Alabama* Claims.

Dec. 15   An International Tribunal meets in Geneva, Switzerland, to decide the *Alabama* Claims.

1872

June 15   The Geneva Tribunal settles the *Alabama* Claims and awards
to   the United States government $15,500,000 in gold as dam-
Sept. 14 ages.

PREFACE

The American Civil War of 1861–65 will always remain a notable event in history; and its effects upon the character of the American people and the political institutions of the country are questions which have not yet received a final solution. Thus it is probable that every addition to the history of that great struggle which is founded upon facts not hitherto known, will be received with some favour by those who were actors in the events, or who, from their position as statesmen, are led to observe and to carefully note the political disasters which periodically disturb contemporary nations.

But it is, nevertheless, manifest that the subject has already lost its interest with the general public, who are mostly absorbed in practical affairs of present importance, or who seek amusement in literature of a wholly different kind. This work has not, therefore, been written with the expectation of supplying a public demand, but from a sense of duty, and in compliance with the urgent request of many persons who took opposite sides in the Civil War, and who have thought that the future historian should be furnished with the facts relating to the foreign-built navy of the Confederate States.

Many unavoidable hindrances have prevented the steady, continuous completion of the work; and the necessity of reading a very large mass of diplomatic correspondence, official reports, and legal proceedings, not always readily accessible, has added to the difficulty and delay. The Introduction and Chapter I. were written in the autumn of 1881; the greater portion of the remainder was written from April to August, 1882; and two chapters not until April-May, 1883. As it has been impossible to revise the manuscript critically, the foregoing explanation is necessary to account for the apparent discrepancy in the illustrations* taken from current events, which, upon the supposition that the whole work was written at about the date of the opening chapter, would place some of the incidents in the anomalous position of being used for demonstration before they happened. The events thus used had very lately or just occurred, at the time when the chapters in which they appear were in course of composition; and it is hoped that the context will sufficiently mark the time when they transpired, even if the date has not been altered.

A thorough revision of the whole work would have made it necessary to rewrite a large portion of several chapters and to abridge others, in order to bring them all into precise harmony in respect to the dates of those incidental and transitory occurrences which have been chosen for illustrations, and also to avoid the appearance of unnecessary repetition in applying the principles of law and the actions of public officials to the case of each separate ship.

But while the want of a careful revision has left many defects which mar the excellence of the narrative as a literary production, it does not in any way affect the historical accuracy of the statements, and I have had no other purpose than to furnish a truthful record of the efforts made by the Confederate Government to organize a naval force during the Civil War.

The facts connected with the building and equipping of the ships are stated upon my own knowledge. Such incidents in their cruises as involved questions of belligerent or neutral rights and duties are taken from the letters of their commanding officers to me at the time of the occurrences, or have been epitomized from subsequent conversations with them. All that has reference to the origin, armament, and commissioning of the ships has been stated specifically and without reserve.

Their adventures afterwards have not been told with much particularity, because special histories of their cruises have already been published, and because the chief purpose of this work is to explain the naval policy of the Confederate Government, and the controversies which that policy provoked between the United States and some of the neutral Powers.

I would have gladly avoided any allusion to the causes of the war, and

---

* The original edition of this book contained a number of illustrations indirectly depicting the events in Bulloch's narrative.—ED.

criticism of the diplomatic and other correspondence of United States officials on the subject of the Confederate cruisers, but that correspondence was not confined to complaints and remonstrances against the alleged encouragement and facilities granted to the Confederate States by the neutral Powers. It was made the medium for prejudicing those Powers against the South by *ex parte* statements in reference to the causes of the war, and of disseminating charges and insinuations wholly unsupported by evidence, whose manifest purpose was not only to discredit the policy, but the honour of the Confederate Government.

To have pointed out the inaccuracies of the statements affecting the conduct of neutrals, and of those which specifically referred to the equipment of the ships, and to have omitted all reference to the political disquisitions and allegations contained in the same despatches, would have borne the appearance of tacitly admitting their truth and the justice of their application.

I hope it will be understood that the names of official persons are mentioned historically, and that the criticisms are directed against the contents of the documents and not against the writers.

LIVERPOOL, *June*, 1883.

THE SECRET SERVICE
OF THE
CONFEDERATE STATES
IN EUROPE

FOREWORD

Since the end of the great Civil War which convulsed the States of the American Union during the years 1861–65, many partial histories of the causes which produced the struggle, and the events which marked its progress, have been published.

Some of these were written under the influence of the heat and passion aroused and fostered by the magnitude and bitterness of the contest, and cannot therefore be received with the confidence which every narrative must inspire in order to win and to maintain that worthy and lasting credit which distinguishes history from fiction.

Others have been published to defend the writers from charges of neglect or incapacity in military or civil offices, and are too personal and controversial to interest the general reader.

Lastly, there have been many accounts of events both in the field and in the Cabinet which the writers themselves took part in, and they have narrated the incidents with the clearness and precision which are always manifest in the evidence of an eye-witness.

It is now well known that the Confederate Government made great efforts to organize a naval force abroad during the Civil War, and that a few armed cruisers were got afloat, which destroyed many American ships and well-nigh drove the American commercial flag from the high seas.

The almost romantic cruise of the *Alabama*, and the account of her tragic burial in the stormy Norman Sea off Cherbourg, have been graphically narrated by the late Admiral Semmes, who commanded her during her short career; and there have been brief histories of the cruises of the *Florida, Shenandoah,* and other Confederate ships, so that their performances afloat are familiar to all who feel interested in such adventures.

No account, however, has yet been published which even approaches to a correct statement of the building and equipment of those vessels, nor were the real facts brought out in the well-known suit of the Attorney-General *v.* Sillem and others (commonly called the *Alexandra* Case), tried before the Lord Chief Baron of her Majesty's Court of Exchequer in London, nor yet in that of the *Oreto (Florida)* in the Vice-Admiralty Court of Nassau.

When the time comes for some wholly independent and impartial historian to write a full and complete record of the great Civil War, he will perceive that the naval operations of the Confederate States, which were organized abroad, possess an importance and attraction greater than their relative effect upon the issue of the struggle, as compared with the stupendous military movements and the gigantic campaigns which were carried on within the contending States.

He will perceive that they gave rise to many important legal and diplomatic questions, that they gave much occupation to her Majesty's Courts, and employment to many barristers who occupied the very highest positions at the English bar, a list of whose names would include two who have since been Lord Chancellors of England, one a Lord Justice of Appeal, and one a Vice-Chancellor. He will learn that they were the subject of much negotiation and some rather acrimonious correspondence between her Majesty's Secretary of State for Foreign Affairs and the United States Minister; that they created the necessity of a special mission to Washington, and the negotiation of a special treaty between Great Britain and the United States, by which a material change was made in the rules defining the obligations of neutrals; and finally, that they were the cause of that great international suit known as the Geneva Arbitration, by whose judgment the British taxpayer was unhappily mulcted in damages to the substantial amount of £3,000,000 sterling.

When the future historian contemplates these results, he will naturally look for the facts relating to them, and he will look in vain among the records thus far published to the world.

Much misapprehension has heretofore prevailed in reference to the acts of the Confederate Government in the effort to organize a naval force abroad.

The allegations and affidavits collected by the American Consul at Liverpool, upon which the United States Minister founded his complaints, were in almost every particular either inaccurate or greatly exaggerated; and the "Case of the United States" presented to the Arbitrators at Geneva was full of errors and misstatements, many of which could have been disproved by very direct and positive evidence if her Majesty's representatives had called upon the parties concerned for the real facts.

It surely is not to the interest nor to the permanent advantage of the people of this or any other country to form a conclusion or shape a policy upon a hasty consideration or misapprehension of facts; and the time has arrived when it would seem to be advisable for anyone who is in possession of the authentic records to make them public, both as an act of justice to those whose conduct has been misrepresented, and as a trustworthy historical record.

I was the agent selected by the Confederate Government to manage and direct the general naval operations in Europe, and I was the chief representative of the Navy Department abroad, during the whole period of the war. All of the ships that got to sea, except the *Georgia*, were despatched and equipped under my instructions; and all the documents pertaining to their origin and the means adopted to get them to sea as cruising ships are in my possession.

It would be difficult for anyone not personally conversant with every incident to decipher and arrange the documents, or to edit a narrative of the transactions, which extended throughout a period of four years, and were attended with many complications and perplexities, and not a few disappointments.

Often since the end of the war I have been urged to write an account of those interesting adventures, but have heretofore been unwilling to do so, for the following reasons, among others not necessary to mention:

First, it was necessary to have important dealings with a great many persons—shipbuilders, tradesmen, and manufacturers—who probably would not have liked to see their names put in print while the animosities and ill-will aroused by the war continued. I made it a rule never to deal with any but people of the highest character and credit in their respective branches of business. They were never asked, nor did they offer, to do anything inconsistent with the strictest principles of commercial honour; and I have the happiness to feel conscious that every contract I made in England was fulfilled by the contractor with scrupulous fidelity, although it was often quite impossible for me to supervise the work while in progress, or even to inspect the materials before shipment.

In recurring now, after the lapse of sixteen years, to those literally vast transactions, it is a consolatory and satisfactory conviction to feel that the good understanding between us was never once disturbed by doubt or suspicion; and if any of them happens to see his name mentioned in these pages, he will find no record of anything to his discredit, and I pray him to accept my apology for naming him at all without his leave, which I could not very well get.

The second reason for my reticence up to the present time arose from the reluctance most men feel to write of events which must necessarily appear to be largely of the character of personal adventures, and therefore require the frequent and embarrassing use and repetition of the personal pronoun.

I have got over this difficulty by reflecting that every business or enterprise must have an active agent to manage and direct it; and if it is meet and right to publish a history of these naval affairs at all, no mere squeamishness should deter me from giving them publicity, and furnishing the future historian with the facts pertaining to an interesting episode in that great Civil War which set the Western World in painful commotion, and disturbed the repose of Europe as well.

No one who is attracted by the title, and feels disposed to read this book, need be deterred by the fear of being drawn into an exposition of the causes of the war, or the right of secession; nor will he be asked to join in a wail over the mortification of defeat, or the agonies of "Reconstruction." Whatever opinions may now prevail in regard to the constitutional right or expediency of secession, hostile and depreciatory criticism of the Southern people has long ceased to have any influence.

It is admitted that they fought gallantly, and exhibited admirable qualities in attack and defence, in victory and defeat. When the last hope of success was extinguished; when the drain of battle and the combined forces of hunger, toil, and exposure had consumed their energies and exhausted the power of resistance, the remnant laid down their arms, and took to the plough and the pruning-hook with as little murmuring as any reasonable critic could expect.

It was, literally, beginning a new life from the very start. The whole land was impoverished. Towns had been burned and fields devastated. Throughout large districts every corn-mill and implement of husbandry had been destroyed. There was scarcely food for the people to eat, and the only currency in the country was the paper promises of the dead Confederacy.

Sixteen years have passed, and the South is again in blossom. Railways have been reconstructed and towns rebuilt. Milk and honey, corn and wine, can be had in plenteous profusion, and there is money to buy them; and, lastly, in this year of grace 1881, 6,700,000 bales of cotton have been grown on Southern soil, picked and baled by Southern hands, and there is cheery music among the spindles of Lancashire, in place of the silence and gloom which overshadowed them while the people who grow the fleecy staple were fighting for their cotton-fields. Men who can refer to such a record in the past, and point to such a position to-day, need make no plaintive appeals for pity. They had much sympathy during the struggle, and many kind things were said of them. These served to cheer and inspirit them in the day of adversity, and are gratefully remembered now. Those in England and elsewhere who predicted that the South would win, have failed in their prophecy, but they can at least feel that their sympathies were given to no mean people. The South was defeated, and secession from the Federal Union was shown to be inadmissible. That is all that has been determined by the appeal to arms. Wars do not define principles. They neither analyze nor solve political problems. The sword cuts the knot, and does not unravel it. No Southern man can efface from his mind the conviction that among the reserved rights of the States was that of withdrawing from the Union, and to deny that he held that opinion in the year 1861, and to shrink from confessing it to have been an article of his political faith at that time, would prove that with the loss of his cause he had also been bereft of his honour, and he would be without excuse for the part he took in resisting the authority of the United States Government at the bidding of his own State. When the Southern leaders laid down their arms, they admitted the supremacy of the Federal Congress, and surrendered the right of separate State action; but they did not renounce their belief that the Constitution as it stood at, and previous to, 1861, was an agreement between Sovereign States, and that each State had the first claim to the allegiance and service of her citizens. But the South has "accepted the situation," and as a condition of restoration to the political privileges common to all the States, she has relinquished her own interpretation of the Constitution, and has agreed to accept that of the majority. Every Southerner is bound by that compact, and there is no evidence that a single sane or reasonable man wishes to break, to evade, or to modify it. In fact, causes are already at work in the Southern States which are likely to effect very important and notable changes in the political principles of the people. The large increase in the number of cotton mills in the South since the war, and the tendency to embark in other mechanical industries, will probably ere long attach the capitalists of that section to the Union, and its fostering system of protective tariffs, with the same ardour which has in these latter years distinguished the national affinities of the manufacturing States of the North.

Secession was not indigenous to the South. The doctrine was broached in the early days of the Republic by Massachusetts and other New England States, and was very clearly and forcibly enunciated by a Convention of those States which met at Hartford in 1814–15, as the following extract from the Journal of the Convention will prove:

"That Acts of Congress in violation of the Constitution are absolutely void, is an undeniable position.... In cases of deliberate, dangerous, and palpable infractions of the Constitution, affecting the *sovereignty* of the State and *liberties* of *the people,* it is not only the right, but the duty of such State to interpose its authority for their protection, in the manner best calculated to secure that end. When emergencies occur which are either beyond the reach of judicial tribunals, or too pressing to admit of delay incident to their forms, *States which have no common umpire* must be their own judges, and execute their own decisions."

Anyone at all familiar with the political history of the United States from the adoption of the Constitution to the year 1815, must admit that the right of secession was a doctrine which did not originate at the South, and was not peculiar to Southern men. After the purchase of Louisiana in 1803, the Legislature of Massachusetts passed the following resolution: "Resolved, that the annexation of Louisiana to the Union transcends the Constitutional power of the United States. It formed a new *Confederacy,* to which *the States united* by the *former compact* are not bound to adhere."

The speech of the Hon. Josiah Quincy, of Massachusetts, delivered in the Congress of the United States, January 14, 1811, in opposition to the Bill for the admission of Louisiana into the Union as a State, has been often quoted. He said, "If this Bill passes, it is my deliberate opinion that it is virtually a dissolution of the Union; and as it will be *the right of all,* so it *will be the duty of some, definitely to prepare for separation—amicably if they can, violently if they must.*"

The States which withdrew from the Union in 1860–61 merely exercised a prerogative which had been previously claimed as an inherent "State right" by Massachusetts and other New England States, and which had been asserted and defended by many prominent Northern men.*

---

* I might fill pages with extracts from the Journal of the Hartford Convention, the writings and speeches of eminent Northern politicians before the secession of the Southern States, and leading articles from Northern papers published at or about the time of the se-

Georgia, the Carolinas, and Virginia made common cause with the Northern Provinces, and were loyal to the Confederation during the trying times of the Revolution, though they had far less cause for complaint against the mother country.

---

cession, in support of this statement. But I have no wish to recriminate, or to even approach controversial topics, except in so far as may be necessary to repudiate the crime of "treason" which has been so recklessly alleged against the South. Those who wish to test the accuracy of the statement may refer to the following American works: "Is Davis a Traitor?" by Professor Bledsoe; "The Rise and Fall of the Confederate Government," by Mr. Jefferson Davis; and "Buchanan's Administration"; in all of which will be found copious extracts from the speeches and writings of Northern men who occupied high and influential positions, with particular references to the original sources from which the quotations are taken.

I mention the above works, not with the purpose of directing attention to the arguments of the authors in support of "State rights," but solely because they contain indisputable proof that the assumption was not a new doctrine in 1861, but that it was coexistent with the Union itself, and had some of its staunchest supporters among Northern statesmen and expounders of Constitutional law.

It is a just subject for surprise, and is equally a matter of regret, that two such eminent men as Mr. John Lothrop Motley and the late Mr. Alexander Everett, when writing and delivering public addresses during the Civil War, with the purpose to enlighten public opinion at home and abroad in respect to the action of the Southern States, should have suppressed, or at least omitted to mention, those facts which would have tended to diminish the alleged criminal culpability of the Southern people, and a knowledge of which was absolutely necessary to a fair, impartial judgment. No cause is ever benefited in the long run by an overstatement of its merits, or by exaggerated depreciation of the opposite side; and when public opinion has been influenced by appeals founded upon insufficient evidence, whether by assertion of what is false, or by the suppression of essential facts, there is always a reaction in the opposite direction. This has been notably manifest in regard to foreign opinion in the matter of secession. It is now quite exceptional to meet a European among the reading class who does not believe that the Southern States acted within their constitutional rights.

For the opinion of intelligent foreigners in regard to the right of secession, I may refer to De Tocqueville's "Democracy in America", and "The American Union," by Mr. James Spence, published by Richard Bentley, London, 1861. The allusions in "Buchanan's Administration" to the "View of the Constitution of the United States," by William Rawle of Philadelphia, are much to the point; and the extracts from a correspondence between Mr. John Quincy Adams and Mr. Harrison Gray Otis, both of Massachusetts, are worthy of especial notice. Mr. Adams charges the Federal Party in New England with a deliberate purpose to dissolve the Union. He says, "I had no doubt in 1808 and 1809, and have no doubt at this time (December 30, 1828), that it is the key of all the great movements of the Federal Party in New England from that time forward until its final catastrophe in the Hartford Convention." Mr. John Quincy Adams's opinion in respect to the right of secession is very clearly set out in an address before the New York Historical Society in 1839. A very full quotation from that address will be found in "The Rise and Fall of the Confederate Government," p. 190, etc.; and the following extract from a leading article in the *New York Tribune* of November 9, 1860, manifests not the isolated feeling and opinion of Mr. Horace Greeley, its editor and proprietor, but the views and sentiments of a large number of Northern men at that time:

Again, the Southern States were loyal to the Union in the war of 1812–15, although their special interests had not been hurt or interfered with by Great Britain.

When Massachusetts and other Eastern States, through the action of the Hartford Convention, manifested their purpose to dissolve the Union, the country was engaged in a foreign war—namely, in defence of New England commerce, and for the protection of New England seamen.

The right which Great Britain affirmed to the perpetual unalienable allegiance of all natural-born subjects, the repeated and vexatious vindication of that right by the stoppage of American ships on the high seas, and the violent removal of alleged British subjects from them, were the chief causes of that war. The South had neither ships nor seamen, and there was nothing to arouse the interest of the Southern people, or to bind them to a participation in the contest, but the sense of loyal obligation to the Union.

When the Southern States seceded in 1861, the country was vexed by no foreign complications, and their action did not add to any existing troubles. This difference in the conditions under which Massachusetts threatened to secede and the Southern States actually did secede, should, in common fairness, be borne in mind by those who extol the loyalty of New England and have so vehemently denounced the Southern people as traitors and rebels.

But the result of the Civil War has been to produce a general disavowal of the principles so emphatically laid down by the Hartford Convention. The New England States helped with all their energies to force a contrary admission from the South, and the authority of the Federal Congress has now been made paramount from Maine to Texas, from New York to California, by the compulsory, but still by the unanimous, consent of the people of all the States.

The bitterness and the passionate heat of family quarrels are proverbial, and many unhappy incidents of the war between the States of the American Union have confirmed the experience upon which the proverb

---

"The right to secede may be a revolutionary right, but it exists, nevertheless; and we do not see how one party can have a right to do what another party has a right to prevent. We must ever resist the asserted right of any State to remain in the Union and nullify or resist the laws thereof; to withdraw from the Union is quite another matter. And whenever a considerable section of our Union shall deliberately resolve to go out, we will resist all coercive measures designed to keep her in.

"We hope never to live in a Republic whereof one section is pinned to the other by bayonets."

is based. But old associations and the memory of past troubles, tribulations, and triumphs, shared in common, are drawing the people again together; and it will be well for them earnestly to reflect upon the causes of the estrangement, and to devise the means of preventing their repetition, in a spirit of fraternal regard alike for the common welfare and the separate, if not conflicting, interests of the various communities embraced in the vast domain of the Union. Americans have learned from the sad experience of the Civil War that Democratic institutions are not exempt from the dangers which beset other forms of government. History furnishes no record of any people who have been fused into one cohesive and durable nationality without much internal commotion and many internecine struggles.

It is eight hundred years since the last foreign conquest of England; but since the battle of Hastings there have been the bloody Wars of the Roses and the fierce contest between Cavalier and Roundhead, besides lesser revolutions and much border strife. Only within the present century have the three kingdoms been brought into willing union, and even now the unhappy condition of Ireland excites fears for the peace and quiet of the realm.

The United States could not have reasonably hoped to escape the political afflictions which other people have had to suffer, nor could they have expected to grow from their birth into the family of independent Powers to the full maturity of national life without passing through some political convulsions. The territory is vast, and even at the present rate of increase in population it will be many years before the people are brought into as close contact as in the countries of Europe.

Celt and Saxon, Teuton and Scandinavian, are flowing in a seemingly exhaustless stream towards the great prairies of the West, and the problem of amalgamating those divers races with the descendants of the original colonists, and fusing them into one nation, with language, feeling, tastes, and interests in common, must be left for its solution to those laws of nature or of Providence which have united equally variable materials to form the existing European types.

The theory that the late Civil War was a mere insurrectionary movement can deceive no one now. The fact that the secession of the Southern States divided the American Union into two separate Federal Republics, cannot be destroyed by the counter-fact that the Union has been restored. The judgment of every foreign power declared that there was for four years a *de facto* Government at Richmond, which was wholly independent of the power and control of the Congress at Washington, and every department of the United States Government confirmed that judgment by practical acts of recognition.

The Union founded by Washington, Adams, Jefferson, Hamilton, Madison, and the other "Fathers," was a Federal Republic, that is to say, it was a Government constituted of several Constituent Republics, which were united by an agreement or compact between themselves as distinct and separate States. That Union proved to be inadequate to the exigencies of the conflicting forces to which it was exposed. It resisted several severe strains, and was maintained by one or more compromises, which served to demonstrate its imperfection and its inherent weakness.

In 1861 the disintegrating forces prevailed, and eleven of the Constituent Republics withdrew from the Union on the plea that the original conditions of Union had been broken by the others, and they formed a fresh confederation among themselves.

The remaining States or Republics resisted that act of separation, and affirmed that the people of the whole United States were, or should be fused into, one nation, and that the division of the Union into States had, or should hereafter have, no greater political significance than the division of the several States into counties.

The States which remained in the original Union, and supported the foregoing dogma, proved to be stronger than those which clung to the opinions of the "Fathers," and they succeeded, after a long and bloody war, in compelling the latter to admit that "the people of the United States" meant the aggregate population of all the States, and that the majority, as represented in the Congress at Washington, was the true and only Sovereign of the whole country, irrespective of geographical State lines or separate State Constitutions. I am broaching no theory, but am simply stating facts. And they are facts which it behoves every American who wishes to practise a broad and comprehensive patriotism, and hopes to maintain a hearty and brotherly union among the reunited States, to admit and to thoughtfully consider in the future arrangement and policy of political parties. It is folly and ruin for men in trade to act without reference to the clear manifestations of supply and demand; it is equally unwise and disastrous for politicians and statesmen to deny or to take no account of the difference between theories for which it has been thought necessary to strive even to the shedding of blood, and principles which are fundamental and unchangeable.

The Union of 1787 was dissolved in 1861 by the action of ten of the constituent republics. A new Union was formed in 1865 by the military power of the majority of the States, compelling the minority to accept their view of the national compact. The former Union was a confederation of States, and was of course a Federal Republic; the latter Union is founded upon a fusion of the people into one nation, with a supreme centralized executive and administrative Government at Washington, and can no longer be called a Federal Republic; it has become an Imperial Republic. The latter name gives some promise of greater strength and cohesion than the former, but the duration of the restored Union will depend very much upon whether the people of the whole country fully realize, and are really reconciled to, the new dogma that each State is only an aggregate of counties, and that its political functions are only to consist in regulating such purely domestic concerns as the central authority at Washington may leave to its discretion. The principle upon which the new Union is founded may or may not be sound in theory, but there can be no doubt that the increased influence and power granted to the national executive and legislative authorities will make it more than ever necessary for the educated classes in the United States to interest themselves in politics, and to see that the representatives sent to Washington are not the mere creatures of the corrupt organizations commonly known as the "Machine." If the majority who have effected the change in the conditions of the American Union are content to leave the management of public affairs to the professional politicians, the "caucuses," and the "wire-pullers," they will have fought in vain, and will find that to secure the semblance of a strictly national Union they have sacrificed the substance of individual liberty.

Those who are accustomed to closely scrutinize current political events, must perceive the tendency of both North and South towards a reassertion of the doctrine of State rights, and a tacit admission of that claim by the Federal Government.

A specific manifestation of the revival of the principle may be seen in the action of California with reference to Chinese immigration, and the cautious conciliatory treatment of the subject by Congress and the executive authorities at Washington. It is hardly possible to doubt that the pretension of each State to regulate its own affairs without the intervention of any other authority will, before many years, be as rampant as ever, and unless the statesmen and political leaders have the wisdom and prudence necessary to keep national party lines distinct from geographical boundaries, the danger of another secession will be imminent.

It is earnestly to be hoped that the reunion of the States may be cemented and perpetuated; that bickerings and recriminations may cease; that nothing further may be done or spoken on either side through strife or vain-glory, and that neither diversity of interests, discriminating tariffs, nor State jealousies, will again set the hearts of the people against each other. But, whatever may happen in the distant and inscrutable future, it may be safely predicted, that if there should be a second violent struggle for "State rights," the issue will be fought on very different geographical lines from those which separated the contending parties in the Civil War of 1861.

CHAPTER I

Sketch of the anomalous condition of the whole country, North and South, during the period between the election of Mr. Abraham Lincoln as President of the United States and the beginning of hostilities, in theory an undivided Republic, in fact two separate Governments: one at Washington, one at Montgomery.—The organization of the Confederate Navy Department.—The poverty of the South with respect to naval resources.—The naval policy of the Confederate Government.—The necessity of looking abroad for the means to carry on naval operations.—The commencement of hostilities.—The Louisiana "Board of War" and the Bienville.—Personal incidents.—Journey South.—Blocking the Mississippi.

South Carolina was the first of the Southern States to secede from the American Union. Her "Ordinance of Secession" was passed on the 20th of December, 1860, about one month after the election of Mr. Abraham Lincoln to the Presidency of the United States. Mississippi, Florida, Alabama, Georgia, and Louisiana soon followed. Delegates from those States met at Montgomery in February, 1861, organized a Legislative Assembly, and formed a Provisional Government, with Mr. Jefferson Davis, of Mississippi, as President.

Arkansas, Texas, and North Carolina followed at short intervals, and were not long in joining the Confederacy. Tennessee, with Maryland, and the great border States of Missouri, Kentucky, and Virginia, still faltered, not from want of sympathy with the movement, but because they hoped to act as a barrier between the two sections, and to secure a peaceful separation by negotiation. Events moved rapidly. Tennessee and Virginia withdrew in time to save serious complications; but while Maryland, Kentucky, and Missouri hesitated, the "Union men" within their borders, aided by active partizans from without, got partial control of affairs, and the United States authorities were able to arrest the leading Secessionists, to disperse the local Legislatures, and to maintain possession of those States during the war. By withdrawing from the Federal Union in this irregular way, the South demonstrated that there was no concert of action, and no premeditated purpose to break up the Federal Government. The political organization of the seceded States remained intact, although the Union between them had been dissolved. Each preserved its complete autonomy as a Commonwealth, with Executive, Judiciary and Legislative Departments unbroken, and there was, therefore, no confusion and no disturbance of the ordinary routine of civil government. The delegates at Montgomery had no difficulty in settling the terms of a fresh compact between the States represented by them, and the Provisional Government was soon in working order. The chief and most urgent business of the newly created Executive was to prepare for the great struggle which was becoming more and more imminent day by day. The lack of military resources, and the efforts which were made to organize an army, have been described by many previous writers, and especially with much minuteness and effect by ex-President Jefferson Davis in his great exposition of the "Rise and Fall of the Confederate Government," a work which may be called his "Apologia."

My business is with the concerns of the Navy alone. When President Davis arranged his Cabinet, the Navy Department was assigned to the Hon. Stephen R. Mallory, of Florida. Mr. Mallory had much experience in the management of public business.

He had been a Senator in the Congress of the United States, and had served as a Member of the Committee on Naval Affairs in that branch of the National Legislature.

He was well versed in naval usage and naval law, and had a thorough knowledge of the organization, equipment, and general disciplinary rules of the United States Navy. If he had been placed at the head of that service, he would have been a popular and efficient administrator, but at Montgomery he was like a chieftain without a clan, or an artizan without the tools of his art. It would have been comparatively easy to organize and administer, but the task before him was to create, and the means for constructing and equipping a naval force for offensive warfare, or even for a vigorous resistance, were practically *nil.* The pine belts of Georgia and the Carolinas, the live oak groves of Florida, and the forests of other States, contained inexhaustible supplies of what are called "naval stores" and materials for ship-building of the old wooden type, but they were still in the raw state. The masts and frames of navies were there, but they were sprouting and blooming in the green-tree, and there was great lack of skilled workmen to fell and fashion them. Iron, so indispensable in the equipment of ships of war, even at that time, was scarce to the degree of poverty, and before the end there was a famine. Between March, 1861, and January, 1865, the price of iron advanced from $25 to $1,300 per ton, and although this extreme advance was not wholly due to the scarcity of the article, but arose to some extent from the depreciation of the paper currency, yet it is well known that the home product was never equal to the ordinary wants of the country, and during the Civil War the supply could only be supplemented by driblets through the blockade.

At the beginning of the war there was not a mill in the whole country which could roll a 2½-inch plate, and in the entire Confederacy there was but one shop capable of turning out a first-class marine engine. There was pressing need of everything required to build, equip, and maintain a ship of war. Ordnance and ordnance stores, even medical supplies, provisions, and clothing, were scarce from the very outset; and the Tredegar Iron Works, at Richmond, Virginia, was the only establishment south of the Potomac where a gun of large calibre could be cast or wrought; and Virginia, when Mr. Davis and his Cabinet began their labours, was not among the Confederate States.

Norfolk, in Virginia, and Pensacola, in Florida, contained the only public dockyards within the limits of the Confederacy. The Navy-yard at Norfolk before the war was an extensive and efficient establishment. It contained a dry dock, foundry and machine shops, and a fair supply of materials had generally been kept there. But just at the time when Virginia was in the throes of secession, before there was any organized force at Norfolk capable of effective resistance, the United States naval officers were ordered to evacuate the dockyard, which they did hastily, taking ship to Hampton Roads, after setting fire to and scuttling the vessels that could not be carried off, and destroying as much of the property on shore as possible. (See Note, p. 35.)

Pensacola was in an isolated position, and its dockyard was not one of construction, but only of shelter and repair.

But even if these two naval arsenals had been complete in every particular, and there had been no want of material, machinery, and skilled workmen, they would still have been well nigh useless as places of outfit for vessels suited to cruise at sea, because the Federal Government held the fortifications at their entrances, and there was safe and ample anchorage within reach of the guns on shore, so that a thorough and efficient blockade could be, and indeed was, maintained at those points during the whole war, by a powerful combination of ships and land batteries.

If the Confederate Government had been able to build and equip cruisers at Norfolk, they could not have got to sea, unless they had been strong enough in number and armament to defeat the blockading squadron in Hampton Roads, and had remained after their victory in condition to engage and pass the forts.

There was equal deficiency and want in respect to private ship-yards. The conditions of labour, soil, and climate which prevailed in the South had made the people agricultural and not commercial. They produced valuable and bulky staples, and ships chiefly from the Northern States and from England performed the carrying trade. The merchants who lived and did business at the Southern ports owned few if any ships, and as there was no home want for large shipping, there had been no demand for architects to design and build them.

It is quite safe for me to state that at the beginning of the year 1861 there was not, within the whole boundary of the Confederacy, a single private yard having the plant necessary to build and equip a cruising ship of the most moderate offensive power.

When President Davis and his Cabinet contemplated this paucity of supply and poverty of home resources, they did not renounce the purpose or abandon the hope to harass the enemy's commerce, to interrupt his lines of maritime communication, and to break through his blockading fleets, but they perceived that an effective effort to accomplish all or either of those aims must of necessity be made abroad; and as early as April, 1861, it was determined to send an agent to England to set on foot and direct such naval operations as it might be possible to organize beyond the limits of the Confederate States.

At a very early period of the war it became a matter of common conjecture that ships were building in England for the service of the Confederate States, and it was not many months before the depredations of the *Alabama* and *Florida* confirmed those suspicions. To build or even to buy ships suitable for either attack or defence, to get them out of English ports, and then to equip and arm them, were undertakings requiring the utmost secrecy and reserve, the success of every effort depending upon the fidelity and discretion of many subordinate agents, and the precise correspondence of many complicated arrangements. It was necessary, first, to build or buy a ship, and to disguise or omit the semblance of equipment for purposes of war; to obtain the guns from one maker, and often their carriages and gear from another; to get the shot and shells from a third, and the small arms and ammunition from at least two other parties. The large quantity of stores, clothing, hammocks, etc., etc., required for a cruising-ship could not, with prudence, be obtained from one dealer, and a tender was needed to receive and carry abroad the whole of those essential effects, which it was necessary to forward to the port of shipment with quick despatch and at short notice.

When everything was ready, it was no easy matter to so combine movements that ship and tender, sailing from different ports, should meet at the appointed rendezvous; and then, after the meeting, there was always much difficulty and many obstacles to the safe and speedy transfer of stores and the completion of the armament. The necessity for these perplexing and intricate proceedings arose not from the fact that there was the slightest degree of moral criminality in their performance, but because there is in England, as there is in other countries, a statute known as the Foreign Enlistment Act, or other cognate title, which forbids either of two belligerents to equip, furnish, fit out, or arm any vessel within the realm, for the purpose of making war upon the other. A violation of that statute involved the forfeiture of the whole of the property; and, as the Act might also be so interpreted as to bring the parties concerned under its penal provisions, every detail in the fitting of a ship, which could by any possible construction of the law be considered "equipment," was of necessity dispensed with.

During the war, when the partizans of both sides were irritated and excited, and each spoke and wrote about the other with heat and passion, it was common to denounce the secession of the Southern States as an act of criminal rebellion, and the efforts made by their agents to obtain abroad the supplies which the resources of the country at home could not furnish, were condemned in rather strong language.

That view of the subject has been almost universally discarded in Europe, and even in the Northern States there are now but a scant minority, chiefly of the professional politician class, who affect to regard the late Civil War in any other light than that of a revolution justified by innumerable precedents in history. If the Confederate army had been defeated at Bull Run, and General McDowell, by a rapid pursuit, had captured

President Davis, with Johnston and Beauregard red-handed from the fight, those gentlemen would probably have been summarily tried, and possibly executed, as traitors.

With equal probability that would have been the fate of Washington, Hancock, and Adams if General Gage had been able to disperse the "Continental forces" at Cambridge, Massachusetts, at the beginning of the War of Independence, and to obtain possession of their persons. The vicissitudes of the late war often gave to the Confederacy a preponderance of advantage, both as regards success in the field, and the number of prisoners.

Under those conditions it was manifestly impossible to treat the captive Confederates as traitors, and since the two opposing parties negotiated with each other for years upon equal terms, arranged conditions of surrender, and exchanged prisoners in accordance with the universally admitted rules of war, sensible men everywhere have perceived the irrelevancy of such expressions as "treason" and "traitor." They have ceased to be used in dignified and grave discussions, and will not probably be revived in any fair and impartial history which may be written in the future.

It will be my effort in the following pages to demonstrate that nothing was done by the agents of the Confederate Government in Great Britain which was not justified by the rules of fair and honourable warfare, nothing contrary to English law as construed by English jurists, and confirmed by the judgment of English courts, and nothing in abuse of the hospitality and refuge England has ever offered to the exiled and oppressed. But it will be necessary, or at least it will be convenient and proper, to give a brief account of the condition of the country during the period between the election of Mr. Abraham Lincoln to the Presidency of the United States and the beginning of hostilities, and to describe the manner in which the agent was selected, and with what instructions he was sent to Europe.

The personal incidents are neither important nor peculiar. Adventures similar in kind, and involving greater personal risk to the actors, are without doubt preserved in the memories of many, but they have not been narrated in connection with the general course of events.

It is my wish and purpose to mention no circumstance whose interest is of a purely personal character, but only such as may help to illustrate the very peculiar condition of affairs during those eventful months which immediately preceded the great Civil War.

From the date of the formation of the Provisional Government at Montgomery to the beginning of hostilities, the political condition of the country had been anomalous.

There were two Presidents, two Cabinets, two Congresses. The Government at Washington retained all the regalia and prestige of the supreme power. It controlled the army and navy, and held the national treasury and the national domain. The foreign Diplomatic Corps still recognised it as the only national authority, and no foreign Power had yet questioned Mr. Abraham Lincoln's title to be the President of the whole Union in its entirety, both by privilege of law and by right of possession. Notwithstanding all this, there had been for several months a rival Executive and a rival Congress at Montgomery, to whom at least six States had given their adherence, and within the limits of those States no United States writ could run, and no United States soldier could remain.

The Government at Montgomery had, moreover, assumed control of the postal routes within the seceded States, and the Custom Houses throughout their coasts were administered under the same authority.

By a law of the United States, a vessel sailing from one home port to another was required to have a regular Custom House clearance, under penalty of seizure and forfeiture. The authorities at Washington did not, of course, recognise those at Montgomery, and a certificate of clearance from New Orleans, verified by a Collector of Customs appointed by the Confederate Treasury Department, was not admissible at any port in the United States. In spite of this embarrassing condition of affairs, the coasting trade and the postal intercourse between the North and South were not for some months interrupted or seriously disarranged. The Customs officers at New York and elsewhere made some seizures of vessels arriving with irregular Confederate Custom House clearances, but they were released by orders from Washington. As a test case, the mail-steamship *Bienville,* under my command, was seized at New York in March, 1861, for alleged violation of the United States revenue laws, and I was requested to go to Washington, where I had an official interview with the Secretary of the Treasury, the Hon. Salmon P. Chase, on the subject. I pointed out that there was no United States official of any kind at New Orleans, and that I was compelled either to take a clearance from the *de facto* authority or to remain at that port indefinitely.

Mr. Chase perceived the peculiarities and perplexities of the situation, and released the ship from all liability, but he was manifestly puzzled, and asked me if it was the intention of the Company to send the ship back to New Orleans. I replied that it was.

He then said that the right of the so-called Confederate Government to assume control of the Custom Houses at the Southern ports could not be admitted even by implication; but still it was obvious that for the moment those who had usurped the legitimate authority had the power to enforce it against private persons, and he directed me on the next occasion of applying for a clearance to make a formal notarial protest setting forth the precise circumstances. Before the *Bienville* returned again to New York, hostilities had begun, and questions of civil jurisdiction had been silenced by the clamour of war. All thinking men perceived that this dual authority, and this conflict of prerogative, could not continue for an indefinite time. Virginia was still mediating, and a "peace commission" was sent from the South to Washington to treat for a friendly separation. But neither intercession nor negotiation could effect that purpose. The South wanted to withdraw from the Union, peaceably, if possible. The North wished to preserve it, peaceably if possible. The South urged the distinct autonomy and the complete individual sovereignty of each State. The North saw in that doctrine an indefinite extension of the secession movement and a final dissolution of the whole Union.

That was the real issue. None other could have united the Southern people or have nerved them to suffer as they did; none other could have overcome the repugnance of many in the North to engage in a war of conquest against their brethren of the South. The charge often made, that the North fought for empire in the sense of coveting more territory, appears to me to have been as unfounded as the counter-allegation that the South took up arms to extend the area of slavery, or even to preserve that institution in perpetuity.

Political parties had ceased to be divided upon principles and interests common to both sections of the country, and had come to be separated by a geographical line. Thus had arisen a condition which the Fathers of the Republic foresaw might happen, and which they had predicted would be dangerous, if not destructive, to the Union.

There were, unhappily, many men of extreme views in the dominant party at the North who had got control of the party machinery. They appeared determined to force upon the country measures which would have placed the South at the mercy of a sectional majority. But I believe that the great mass of the people on both sides were very desirous to find a peaceful solution of the difficulties. The principles at issue were, however, too antagonistic to be reconciled, and the tension was approaching nearer day by day to the breaking strain. The fuel was laid in order, the kindling materials were abundant. A spark might at any moment light a conflagration, and the spark soon fell. When Louisiana seceded, the Governor of that State, the Hon. Thos. O. Moore, appointed a committee of experienced and influential men to advise and help him to put the State in a condition to meet any emergency that might arise. Among the members were General Braxton Bragg and Colonel J. K. Duncan, both of whom were ex-artillery officers of the United States army, and the committee was called the "Board of War." The board had been sitting for some time at New Or-leans, and State troops had occupied the old forts, built many years before for the protection of the river approaches, and had put them in habitable and fairly defensible condition against a sudden attack. These circum-stances had somewhat accustomed the people of New Orleans to the prospect of a possible conflict. During the early days of April, 1861, there was a general feeling that affairs could not be peaceably arranged, and there appeared to be a nervous solicitude, and a seeming impatience of further delay, together with a suppressed inclination to precipitate a di-rect and immediate issue.

On the 13th day of April, 1861, I was in New Orleans in command of the United States mail steamer *Bienville.* The ship was appointed to sail on the following morning, and a large number of passengers had booked for the voyage, some for their customary migration during the hot months, and some to escape the danger and privations of battle and siege, which they already scented in the air.

Early in the morning of that day there were flying rumours that fight-ing had begun somewhere, and about ten o'clock it was known with cer-tainty that Beauregard had opened fire at Charleston upon Fort Sumter.

The tidings soon spread, and the whole city was alert to learn the particulars and to discuss the consequences. There was no excitement. Groups of men collected about the street corners, at the hotels, and other places of public resort, and talked earnestly, but gravely, about the possi-bilities of the future.

Every man who has had to face extreme danger probably remembers ever afterwards his feelings on the first occasion. There was a tingling of the flesh, a chilliness of the scalp, and a sensation as if each hair was slowly lifting itself on end. It was not fear, because the bravest of the brave are thus affected. It was only the keen consciousness of peril.

It is narrated of the great Henri Quatre, that once, at the beginning of a battle, he felt this premonitory shiver creeping over him, and looking down at his knees, which appeared to be shaking, he addressed them thus: "Ah! you tremble. You would tremble much more if you knew where I am going to take you." New Orleans seemed to be in that sort of tremor.

There was no appearance of bravado, which is never the mark of true self-reliant courage, neither were there any signs of despondency or dis-trust. There was an effervescence among the younger men, and a few talked of arming and marching to the frontier without waiting for a call; but the majority of the people spoke and acted like men who were conscious that a great crisis had arisen, and they were ready to meet it.

The Southern officers of the United States army and navy had, with remarkably few exceptions, resigned their commissions when their respective States seceded, and the Confederate Congress very soon passed an Act to incorporate them into the new service with the same relative rank which they had held in the old. I was one of a small number of lieutenants in the United States navy who had been detailed by the Government to go into the Mail Service some years before the war, with the object to enlarge the school for experience in steam. The Steam Packet and Mail Service increased, and there was a demand for commanders. In the navy promotion was slow, and the certainty of remaining in a subordinate position until age had sapped the energies and ambition had ceased to inspire was depressing.

Private companies offered good positions and satisfactory emolument, and several lieutenants resigned their naval commissions and remained in the private Mail Service. I was one of those who retired, and when Georgia seceded I was only a private individual engaged in the ordinary business of life. I had become completely identified with the shipping enterprises of New York. I had no property of any kind at the South, nor any pecuniary interests whatever in that part of the country.

Many persons thought to the very last that somehow or other an agreement would be come to, and there would be no war, and I did not feel that there was either a necessity or obligation requiring me to give up my occupation and business connections prematurely. All to whom my opinions were of any interest or importance knew what they were. I had never concealed or even disguised the fact that in respect to the issues at stake my heart and my head were with the South. My sympathies and convictions were both on that side, although my personal interests were wholly, and my personal friendships were chiefly, in the North. Whatever had happened, neither friend nor foe could have said with truth that I was not ready to act in harmony with my convictions at the proper time. When Beauregard fired the first shot at Fort Sumter in the early dawn of April 13th, 1861, he sounded a call which summoned every man to fall into line on his own side, and there could no longer be either hesitation or delay. Those officers who had retired from the United States navy to enter the Mail Service, and who still remained in it, were now drawn by a natural law to their own side of the dividing line. Those from the Northern States thought it their duty to offer their services to the Government at

Washington, and were restored to their former positions in the United States Navy. Those from the Southern States were impelled by corresponding motives to offer their services to the Government at Montgomery, and were incorporated into the Confederate Navy. At 10 A.M. on the 13th of April, 1861, all doubt in regard to the condition of affairs at Charleston had vanished, and I wrote a letter to the Hon. J. P. Benjamin, who was then the Attorney-General of the Confederate States, requesting him to offer my services to the Government.

Some members of the Cabinet knew of my naval education and employment in the Mail Service, and I explained to Mr. Benjamin, that being in command of the steamship *Bienville,* it was necessary for me to take her back to New York, and return her to those to whom she belonged, but that on arrival in New York I would be ready for any service. After posting that letter I went on board ship, to hasten the preparations for sailing on the next morning.

In the course of the afternoon two members of the "Board of War" came to the ship with the company's agent, and informed me that it had been thought important to secure the *Bienville* for the naval service of the Confederate States, and if I would name a price, the Governor would order the amount to be paid.

I replied that I had no authority to sell the ship, and therefore could not fix a price, nor could I make any arrangements for transferring her to the Confederate States. We had some further conversation on the subject, the members of the Board urging me to accept the Governor's offer, and I repeating, in substance, what I had said at first. Finally, they told me that if I did not accept the terms offered, it would probably be necessary to take the ship by force, but they would inform me of the Governor's decision at a later hour.

The Governor of the State and the members of the Board of War knew precisely my position, and the proposal for the purchase of the ship was made in a very friendly way to me personally. I felt assured that nothing would be done in a harsh or violent manner, but still I felt that I could neither sell the ship nor give her up without resistance, and it was inexpressibly painful to contemplate the possibility that I might be forced into collision with the Government I was willing and had just offered to serve.

Late in the afternoon, one of the gentlemen who had previously called came again to the ship, and told me that the Governor had decided to refer the matter to the authorities at Montgomery, and he had telegraphed for instructions. The agent of the Mail Steamship Company, Mr. John Fox, spent the evening on board with me. He was a Southern man, and a

Secessionist, and, I believe, in his heart hoped that the ship would be seized; but he was loyal to me and to the New York owners, and said I was quite right in refusing to give her up on any terms.

I told him I could not, of course, fight, but I could run, and I meant to. To that end I had the mooring lines shifted, so that they could be slipped from on board, and I directed the engineer to get up steam. My purpose was to swing off from the pier, or "levee," at the first show of force, and "skedaddle" down the river. There was a good four or five knot current, for the Mississippi was in the spring freshets, and I had no fear of being stopped by the forts; but I felt both grieved and annoyed at the prospect of having to run from my friends, to save the property of those who were constructively my enemies.*

Happily, the necessity for the race did not arise. At about 10 P.M. I had the pleasure to receive a message from the Governor to the effect that the offer for the purchase of the ship was still open, but that nothing would be done to prevent my departure with her in the morning. The two gentlemen who brought me this very agreeable assurance were authorized by the Governor to show me the reply which had been received from Montgomery to his own despatch about the purchase or seizure of the ship.

The reply was from President Davis. I believe I remember the very words. "Do not detain the *Bienville*; we do not wish to interfere in any way with private property." These personal incidents are of no importance in themselves, but they may be of some interest as demonstrating the comparatively trivial circumstances which mark the beginning of great events, and they manifest the purpose of the Confederate authorities to act with prudence, and without the heat and passion which commonly mark the conduct of men when driven into revolutionary enterprises. At 8 A.M., April 14, the *Bienville* sailed from New Orleans for Havana *en route* for New York. As the ship neared the forts, every one on board came on deck to look at them. We saw the sentinels standing at ease on the parapets. At our peak flew the United States ensign. The flag at the staff on Fort Jackson bore the familiar red and white stripes, with blue Union in the corner, but the stars representing the States which still remained in the Union had

---

* The question of the ability of the forts to stop an ascending fleet by their fire, independently of an artificial obstruction in the river, had been frequently discussed in New Orleans after the secession of the State. On the previous voyage of the *Bienville,* I had noted the time required to pass from a position in which the first gun could be brought to bear upon the ship, until she reached a point at which the curve of the river interposed the protection of the shore. I had found it to be fifteen minutes when descending, and twenty-five minutes when ascending, and I had furnished the Board of War with a memorandum to that effect.

been erased. The Confederacy had not yet adopted an entirely distinctive flag. The *Bienville* carried, I believe, the first report to Havana that hostilities had begun, and there was much excitement there in consequence. The United States steamer *Corwin* was in port, and two transports *en route* for New York with a dismounted regiment of United States cavalry on board. The troops had been serving on the frontier of Texas, and when that State seceded, they had been called upon to surrender the public property to the State authorities and to evacuate the State.

Many officers came on board the *Bienville* to learn the news. The officers of neither army nor navy had been fired with the war-fever at that early date, and all expressed regret at the unhappy turn of affairs. They were nevertheless Northern men, who meant to retain their commissions, and fight it out on that side, and I listened to their comments, but maintained a prudent reserve.

In due course the *Bienville* sailed for New York, and arrived there on the evening of April 22. Off the bar we met two outward-bound steamers, standing to the southward. Both were crowded with troops. One of them hailed in passing, and reported that she was bound for Washington.

It was about 9 P.M. when the *Bienville* reached her berth. Off the pierhead there was lying at anchor a large Long Island Sound steamer. She loomed up grandly in the thin mist that lay upon the river. Her lofty tiers of saloons were brilliantly lighted, and she appeared to be swarming with passengers.

As soon as the *Bienville* was berthed, one of the managing directors of the company came on board. The information he had to give was important. "There had been fears that the Confederates would make a sudden dash and seize Washington, and troops were hurrying forward for its protection. There had been a collision between a regiment of United States volunteers and a mob in Baltimore, and some lives had been lost. The steamer off the pierhead was the *Empire State,* with a regiment from Rhode Island on board.

"The Government had chartered the *Bienville* to take troops to Washington, and the Rhode Island regiment must embark as soon as possible."

Of course, I could not go on that enterprise, and I told the director so.

Fortunately I was not pressed for reasons. The directors of the company were friendly to me, and another commander was appointed in such a way that no especial attention was attracted to my retirement. Very shortly afterwards the steamers belonging to the company were bought by the United States Government, and they were soon armed and sent to blockade the Southern ports.

At a later period of the war I recognised the *Bienville* off the port of Savannah, where she formed a part of Admiral Dupont's fleet.

It was only nine days since Beauregard's guns had opened fire upon Fort Sumter, but their echoes had already reached the farthest limits of the country. They had lighted a conflagration which spread with electric speed and burned with consuming energy for four years.

On the morning after the arrival of the *Bienville* at New York, I went at an early hour to the office of the Steamship Company.

I was in some doubt how to act, because I had received no reply to the letter I had written to the Hon. J. P. Benjamin from New Orleans, and it was manifest that postal and telegraphic intercourse between the North and South would not be kept open, even if it had been safe or prudent to communicate by those means. My embarrassment was happily relieved by finding a letter from Mr. Benjamin awaiting me. It must have been among the last to come through the regular United States mail. The letter was brief, but to the point.

> "Department of Justice, C.S.A.
> Montgomery, Alabama.
> "The Secretary of the Navy desires you to come to Montgomery without delay.
> "Yours, etc.,
> "(Signed) J. P. BENJAMIN."

The document was too compromising to be retained about me, and I destroyed it at once. It was necessary to wind up my affairs with the company, and to settle other matters of business, and safety required that I should act without precipitancy. It is probable that my return to New York with the *Bienville* had removed any suspicion of my "loyalty" which the public authorities might have had, and my friends either thought that I intended at least to remain neutral, or else they were too considerate to ask questions or to suggest doubts. I was detained about ten days in New York, and the compulsory sojourn there at that time was not agreeable. Subsequent information has assured me that if I had shown any haste in my movements, I should have been arrested. I mentioned to a few personal friends that I purposed going to Philadelphia, and possibly to Cincinnati, and in the early days of May I started southward with light luggage, as if for a short journey.

In the train to Philadelphia I met a commander in the United States navy, an old shipmate of former days. The war was uppermost in our minds, and we could talk of nothing else. My friend knew that I was a Southerner, and he had the tact and prudence not to ask any embarrassing questions, but he told me that he was going to Washington to apply for a command in the East Indies, and said that he wanted to get on foreign service, where he could not be employed against the South, and wished no professional honour or preferment which might be gained in such a struggle.

This feeling was common to the majority of the regular officers of the United States army and navy whom I met during the memorable period between the election of Mr. Abraham Lincoln and the attack upon Fort Sumter, and there is no doubt that many took up arms, if not with reluctance, at least with the feeling that they were performing a painful duty.

I stopped one night in Philadelphia. In the public squares and parks large bodies of men were drilling, and the streets were thronged with detachments of troops. Everywhere was the din and bustle of preparation. I hurried on *viâ* Pittsburgh to Cincinnati, arriving at the latter place at six o'clock in the morning.

Here it was necessary to take steamer for Louisville, and the boat did not start until 4 P.M. I walked down to the steamboat landing and looked across the Ohio river at the Kentucky hills beyond. Kentucky was still "in the Union," but I knew that the feeling of the people was with the South, and once across the border I should be free from the danger of being asked at any moment to stop and give an account of myself. At the steamboat landing there were a military guard, and two civil officers who examined the packages of freight, and I learned that passengers and their luggage would be searched. When I went to embark in the afternoon, the guards were examining and questioning passengers at the ship's side, but a local gentleman whom I accidentally met told them I was a friend of his, who was going to Louisville on business, and I was permitted to pass without question and without search. There were a number of Kentucky people on board the boat. The elder were grave and silent, but some of the younger men were loud and vehement in denouncing the examination of their luggage. It was a relief to me when the lines were cast off and we moved swiftly down the river. I took the first train after my arrival at Louisville for Nashville, Tennessee, and arrived there at mid-day, May 5th. Tennessee had not yet seceded, but the Convention elected especially to determine the important question of secession was sitting in the State Capitol, and the town was full of volunteer corps and people from the country. There was no doubt about the feeling here; it was intensely Southern, and everyone with whom I spoke, at the hotel and elsewhere, expressed both the hope and belief that the Convention would "vote the State out of the Union." The telegraph was working to Montgomery, and as it was quite safe to communicate, I telegraphed Mr. Benjamin that I was in Nashville *en route* for the Confederate capital.

While waiting for the departure of a train for the South, I walked to the building in which the Convention was sitting, and saw there General Barrow, a prominent citizen, who had been in the diplomatic service of the United States. General Barrow was a member of the Convention. I mentioned to him that I was on my way to Montgomery to report for duty, and he requested me to say to President Davis, confidentially, that although the vote might not be taken for several days, he might feel confident that Tennessee would secede.

In due time the train started, and I got on rapidly through Chatanooga, Atlanta, etc., to Montgomery. It was nearly midnight, May 7th, when I reached the hotel at Montgomery, but no one seemed to think or care about sleeping. Everywhere on the journey from New York I had heard but one topic of conversation, and everywhere I beheld the same feverish excitement, the same hastening to prepare for the now inevitable conflict.

At an early hour next morning I called at Mr. Benjamin's office. He said the Secretary of the Navy had been expecting me from day to day, and would be desirous to see me as soon as possible. He took me at once to the Navy Department, and introduced me to its chief.

Mr. Benjamin was a busy man at that time, and so were all the members of that hastily constructed Provisional Government at Montgomery. No useless phrases were employed in the presentation.

"Mr. Secretary, here is Captain Bulloch."

"I am glad to see you: I want you to go to Europe. When can you start?"

"I have no impedimenta, and can start as soon as you explain what I am to do."

The announcement of this foreign mission took me aback, to use a nautical phrase. I had somehow become possessed with the expectation that I would be sent to New Orleans.

The insufficiency of the forts to prevent the passing of a hostile fleet up the Mississippi had been a frequent subject of discussion by the "Board of War," and among the leading citizens of New Orleans there had been much argument and many suggestions as to the best means of obstructing the channel. The difficulties to be met were the depth and volume of water, the great strength of the current, especially during the spring-freshets, when the Mississippi flows to the sea with the velocity of a mill-race, and the quantity of drift-wood and timber which are borne along by the stream.

The question was thought to lie within the scope of nautical experience, and I had been drawn into the discussion and asked as a naval man to give an opinion. It was manifest, I thought, that no permanent immovable obstruction could stand the strain of flood and drift-wood, and I suggested the following plan:

"Float down to the bight, between Forts Jackson and St. Philip, a large number of logs from 60 to 100 feet long, some with stumps of the branches remaining. Bore large auger holes through the butts of the logs, reeve chains through the holes, and toggel or staple the ends. Anchor a line of the logs a short distance below Fort Jackson, say 20 feet apart, using for this line logs with the stumps of their branches remaining, to form a sort of marine *chevaux de frise.* Anchor a second line a short distance above the first, with about half of each log trailing in the space between two logs of the first line; and a third line trailing in like manner between the openings in the second line, etc., etc. Multiply the lines to any extent that may be thought necessary. Anchors being scarce, stones of suitable weight, which would soon sink in the soft muddy bottom and hold well, can be used, and timber being abundant, the cost of such an obstruction will be moderate, and it will offer no impediment to the current, while the drift timber will cant and pass between the logs. When the attacking fleet enters the lower reaches of the river and appears to be preparing to force a passage, make fast to the ends of the lower line of logs 6- or 8-inch hawsers, so that they will trail down the river. Between the forts the river takes a great curve, and the action of the current will keep the logs constantly sheering from starboard to port, and they will thus be so completely interlaced as soon to bring up ships attempting to force through them, and the hawsers will foul the screws. While the ships are clearing their screws, and trying to drift out of the obstructions, the fire of the forts can be directed upon them with deliberation, and therefore with precision."

I proposed that field-pieces or howitzers, covered by a protecting force, should be masked on the riverbanks opposite the lower line of logs, to prevent the enemy sending boats to cut the hawsers and the log chains. I am not at all sure that the foregoing plan was ever formally submitted to the Governor in Council—indeed, I suspect it was not; but it was unofficially discussed with me by one or two members of the Board, and when I was in New Orleans with the steamship *Bienville* in March, 1861, I was asked to put the suggestion in writing, and would have done so on my next return in April, but the suddenness of the crisis at that time, the rapidity with which events then moved, and my necessary departure from New Orleans, either prevented my doing so, or other pressing questions took precedence.

The military men on the Board probably thought the plan too simple; at any rate, it was not adopted. When Admiral Farragut attempted to pass the forts on the night of April 23–24, 1862, just one year afterwards, he found the passage obstructed by "a chain which crossed the river, and was supported by eight hulks strongly moored."*

Parties were sent in advance to blow up the hulks and break the chain. "This duty was not thoroughly performed, in consequence of the failure to ignite the petards with the galvanic battery, and the great strength of the current." "The vessel boarded by Lieutenant-Commanding Caldwell appears to have had her chains so secured that they could be cast loose, which was done by that officer, thereby making an opening sufficiently large for the ships to pass through."

The fleet does not appear to have been delayed by the obstructions, for Admiral Farragut says, "We soon passed the barrier chains," and the forts could only therefore get flying shots at the ships as they steamed up the river. From Confederate accounts it appears that the obstruction was a raft, the logs and hulks composing it being held together by chains, and the whole kept in position by numerous anchors.

This stationary and rigid structure could not resist the strain of flood and drift-wood, and was frequently broken. Its condition excited both interest and fears at Richmond. A few days before Admiral Farragut's attack, Mr. Secretary Mallory telegraphed to the officer commanding the naval defences at New Orleans, "Is the boom, or raft, below the forts in order to resist the enemy, or has any part of it given way? State condition." Captain Whittle replied (April 18), "I hear the raft below the forts is not in best condition. They are strengthening it by additional lines. I have furnished anchors." The Commanding General at New Orleans had exclusive charge of the construction of the raft, or obstruction, and the Naval Commander was simply required to supply anchors and assistance when asked.

Discussions in respect to the best mode of obstructing the river channel are useless at this late date, and conjectures whether any other mode than the one adopted would have been effectual in stopping the attacking fleet, would seem to imply some reproach upon the defenders, who doubtless did their best with the materials at hand.

---

* Admiral Farragut's report, dated May 6, 1862, in his "Life" by his son, p. 243, etc.

Remembering the discussions on the subject at New Orleans, I got the impression, when summoned to Montgomery, that I was wanted about the Mississippi river defences, and the Secretary of the Navy's laconic query, when could I start for Europe, rather surprised me. There was, however, no time for parley. The Confederate Government had been scarcely three months in existence, and yet it was pressed by the requirements of a great emergency.

The South was outnumbered in population at least five to one. In military and naval resources the disproportion was many times greater. The only hope of success lay in the prompt and energetic use of her whole strength, and it was the bounden duty of everyone to accept the position and employment allotted to him without cavil or remonstrance.

Many of the Southern officers were on foreign stations when their States seceded. They had not only to return to the United States by long routes, but, after arrival, they were compelled to find their way to the South through the Northern States, whose people were daily becoming more and more hostile. They had often to take circuitous and expensive routes, and hence most of them reached their homes with pecuniary resources exhausted, and they had nothing to offer to their country "but their patriotism and their swords." Even their experience and their technical knowledge were at first of little profit, because the Confederacy had no ships for them to serve in, and no seamen to be organized and drilled.

Mr. Mallory briefly touched upon the condition of his Department. Very few of the naval officers who had resigned from the United States Service had found their way to Montgomery, and not many had yet come into direct communication with him. He had been able to buy one small steamer at New Orleans, and Commander Semmes had been ordered to fit her out for a cruise.

A committee of naval officers were examining the few vessels at the different Southern ports, but up to that date had found only the one Semmes had in hand which could be converted into a ship-of-war.

There were no machine shops, nor yards, no shipwrights, and no collection of material for ship-building. It was thought to be of prime importance to get cruisers at sea as soon as possible, to harass the enemy's commerce, and to compel him to send his own ships-of-war in pursuit, which might otherwise be employed in blockading the Southern ports. These were the chief points of Mr. Mallory's explanatory remarks. He then discussed the description of vessel best suited to the requirements of the service, and the possibility of being able to buy or build them in England, and finally he told me to go to my hotel, turn the whole subject over in my mind, and make such notes of the conversation as might be necessary to impress the substance on my memory, and to call on him again the next day. Even at that early date, the blockade of the chief Southern ports had been established more or less rigidly, and it was thought better that I should find my way into Canada through the Western States, and from thence to Europe, than to attempt an exit from one of the home ports in a sailing vessel, the only description of craft then available; besides which, the route *viâ* Canada promised quicker transit, and time was of the essence of the enterprise. This mode of departure manifestly prohibited the carrying of any documents, or even memoranda, which could betray the object of my mission in case of capture; hence the necessity for committing the chief points of the instructions to memory.

In compliance with Mr. Mallory's request I called at the Navy Department on the following morning, May 9. He examined my notes of the previous day's conversation, and enlarged upon the various subjects. He dwelt especially upon the probable course of the European Powers, and expressed the belief that they would recognise the *de facto* Government at Montgomery, and would grant to the commissioned cruisers of the Confederate States the shelter and privileges conceded to all belligerents by the comity of nations. He did not expect a formal recognition of the Confederate Government as an independent Power until the probability of success had been demonstrated by some substantial victories in the field. He warned me to be prudent and heedful, so as not to involve the diplomatic agents of the Confederate States in embarrassing complaints for alleged violation of neutral law or obligation, and he directed me to acquaint myself, as soon as possible after my arrival in England, with the nature and scope of the Foreign Enlistment Act, and the Queen's Proclamation of Neutrality, if one should be issued. Reverting to the special objects of my mission, he impressed upon me the wish of the Government to get cruising ships of suitable type afloat with the quickest possible despatch, and urged me to buy and forward naval supplies of all kinds without delay. He authorised me to practise a wide discretionary power within the limits of his general instructions, and discussed at some length the financial question, and the mode of placing funds in Europe. He informed me that Messrs. Fraser, Trenholm and Co., of Liverpool, would be the bankers or "depositaries" of the Confederate Government, and directed me to communicate with them, and with the Hon. W. L. Yancey and the Hon. Dudley Mann, the Confederate Commissioners, immediately upon my arrival in England. Finally, he requested me to start as soon as possible, and said that written instructions, with anything further he might wish to communicate, would be sent me by the first opportunity through one of the seaports.

I left Montgomery by that night's train. Before reaching the Kentucky line I destroyed all notes and memoranda, and from Louisville I proceeded, without let or hindrance, to Detroit, Michigan.

The whole North appeared to be in military commotion. Volunteer corps in uniform, and large detachments of men without uniform, were seen drilling in every town through which I passed, and "the war" was the one absorbing topic of conversation among the passengers in the trains, and the crowds assembled at the railway stations.

Crossing from Detroit to the Canada side of Lake Erie, I took the Grand Trunk Railway to Montreal, and the Allan Line steamer *North American* to Liverpool, arriving at that port on the 4th of June, 1861.

NOTE TO PAGE 17

The dockyard at Norfolk was at that time under the command of Commodore C. S. McCauley, U.S.N. He had not sufficient force on shore to have held possession of the dockyard if an attack had been made upon it from the land side. But such an attempt was not contemplated by the local authorities—indeed, it was not possible. The *Cumberland,* a powerful sailing corvette, with a crew of 300 men, had lately arrived from sea, and was lying close at hand. Her batteries commanded the neighbouring town, and not only afforded ample protection to the dockyard, but in fact made Commodore McCauley master of the situation. Virginia had not yet seceded, but the Convention to determine that important question was in session at Richmond, and the signs pointed to the expectation that she would soon cast in her lot with the States which had already withdrawn from the Union. General Taliaferro had been appointed to the local military command at Norfolk on behalf of the State of Virginia, but he had no organized force under his control. Confederate accounts state that he had carried on some negotiations with Commodore McCauley in respect to the dockyard, and that it had been agreed that "none of the vessels should be removed, nor a shot fired, except in self-defence." During the night of April 20th the ship-houses in the yard were set on fire, one of which contained the frame of a line-of-battle ship. These, with a long line of store-houses and offices adjoining them, were soon enveloped in flames, and were burned. The ships afloat, including the sailing line-of-battle ships *Pennsylvania* and *Delaware,* the frigates *Raritan* and *Columbus,* and the corvettes *Plymouth* and *Germantown,* were set on fire and scuttled. The above-named vessels were completely destroyed. The screw-frigate *Merrimac* was burned nearly to the water's edge, but the fire was extinguished after the United States forces had evacuated the yard, and she afterwards became famous as the Confederate ironclad ram *Virginia*. While Commodore McCauley was preparing for the work of destroying the dockyard and its contents, Commodore Paulding arrived with the screw-corvette *Pawnee,* having a detachment of troops on board, and the further operations were carried on under his orders. The greater portion of the guns in the parks were spiked, the machinery in the shops was broken, and an attempt was made to blow up the graving-dock, but this failed. Finally Commodore McCauley, with the officers, embarked; and the *Pawnee,* with the *Cumberland* in tow, proceeded down the river. As much of the naval stores as could be got on board the *Cumberland* was carried off; the remainder was either destroyed or greatly damaged. No effort was made by the Virginia State authorities to stop the ships, for the simple reason that there was no military or naval force capable of opposing them.

It will thus be manifest that when Virginia joined the Confederacy she could offer but a small contribution to the naval resources of her allies— only the wreck of her great dockyard.

CHAPTER II

Messrs. Fraser, Trenholm and Co.—The Confederate Commissioners.—Major Huse, the Military Agent.—Early operations.—Restrictions of the Proclamations of Neutrality.—Their effects upon United States and Confederate Cruisers.—The Oreto (Florida).—Messrs. Laird and the Alabama.—The Equipment of the Alabama.—Counsel's Opinion on the Foreign Enlistment Act.—Despatch of the Bermuda with supplies for the Confederate Army.—Second Voyage and Capture of the Bermuda.—The Trial at Philadelphia.—The United States and belligerent rights.—Decree of Court in the Bermuda case.—Contrast between the action of the United States as a belligerent and as a neutral concerning belligerent rights.—The United States and neutral vessels during the Crimean War.—The Bahama Islands "Regulations" of the British Government.—Reasons for the seeming indifference of the British Government.—Precedents established by the United States favourable to Great Britain.—European Naval Armaments.—British Ship-building.—Importance of British Mercantile Marine.—Weakness of the United States as a Naval Power.—Former efficiency of the American Navy.—Seamanship in the Past and the Present.

My first duty after arrival at Liverpool was to communicate with the financial agents of the Confederate Government, but it was already late in the day, and places of business were for the most part closed. At an early hour on the next morning I called at the counting-house of Messrs. Fraser, Trenholm and Co., and went up to London the same afternoon, to see the

Confederate Commissioners, who at that time were the Hon. William L. Yancey and the Hon. Dudley Mann.

I had no credentials, and nothing to prove my personal identity, or the nature of my mission; but when men are moved by a common sympathy, and their minds are earnestly set upon the same object, the powers of discerning seem to be quickened, and they recognise each other by intuitive perception. At any rate, the Commissioners gave me a cordial welcome, and we were soon deep in Confederate affairs. They explained the diplomatic situation. They had not been officially received by Her Majesty's Secretary of State for Foreign Affairs, and did not think the Confederate States would be recognised until they had demonstrated their ability to win and to maintain their independence; nevertheless, the chief European Powers had admitted that there was a *de facto* Government at Montgomery, with power to raise armies and to levy war, and they thought we would be permitted to obtain supplies in England upon the same conditions as any other belligerent, and they encouraged me to set to work with due precaution, but with alacrity, promising their hearty support whenever I might need their intervention.

Messrs. Fraser, Trenholm and Co. received me with equal cordiality and equal trust. No funds had yet reached them, and they had no advice of remittances on behalf of my mission; but Mr. Charles K. Prioleau, the resident partner, perceiving the necessity of prompt action, authorized me to give out such orders as were of pressing importance, and to refer to his firm for the financial arrangements. Captain, afterwards Major Caleb Huse, of the Confederate Army, had preceded me to England, and had already made some large purchases of arms, and still larger contracts, upon the credit of Messrs. Fraser, Trenholm and Co.

Major Huse was a graduate of the Military Academy at West Point, and after serving a number of years in the United States artillery, had retired from active service, and when the Southern States seceded he was superintendent of the Alabama State Military Academy. When the Provisional Government at Montgomery was formed, Major Huse was sent to Europe to buy arms and other ordnance supplies for the army, and he represented the War Department, and especially the Ordnance Bureau, during the whole war. This officer was a man of ability, and of unusual energy, but his services were scarcely known beyond the office of his departmental chief. I have always felt that the safety of Richmond at the time of General McClellan's advance from Yorktown up the peninsula, in the spring of 1862, was largely due to the efforts of Mr. Charles K. Prioleau and Major Huse, because the former furnished the credits, and the latter bought and forwarded the rifles and field artillery without which the great battles of Seven Pines and the Chickahominy, could not have been successfully fought.

It is an unquestionable fact that the Confederate Government had great financial difficulties to meet, and the "depositaries" in England were often under heavy advances to the various Bureaux of the War Department, and on one or two important occasions to the Navy Department also. Major Huse showed both skill and energy in pressing the credit of the Government, and he often made large contracts, and even got delivery of arms and other ordnance stores, when there were no public funds at all in England.

My early operations were greatly helped by the generous confidence of Messrs. Fraser, Trenholm and Co. Within a month after my arrival, I had not only been able to buy a fair quantity of naval supplies on their credit, but had laid the keel of the first foreign-built Confederate cruiser, and she was partly in frame before the Navy Department had found it possible to place any funds in Europe. The vessel thus early begun (June, 1861), was the *Oreto,* afterwards *Florida.*

As it is the purpose of this narrative not only to show that a Confederate naval force was organized abroad during the Civil War, but that the operations were carried on with strict regard to local law, I feel the necessity of being somewhat minute in describing the manner in which all contracts for ships were made.

The great Maritime Powers in Europe issued proclamations of neutrality* at a very early date after the beginning of hostilities, and these proclamations were supplemented from time to time by Admiralty orders and regulations defining the conditions upon which the ships of both belligerents would be allowed refuge in the neutral ports, to make repairs and to obtain supplies. The chief restrictions specified in those orders were, that no ship should reinforce her crew, or make greater alterations and repairs than were necessary to ensure her safety; that the armament should not be changed or increased, and that no ordnance or other description of stores classed as "contraband of war" should be taken on board; that the quantity of coal to be taken should be no more than enough to carry her to the nearest port of her own country, and after receiving that quantity she should not enter any harbour of the same neutral power for another supply until the expiration of three months, except by special permission.

---

* Proclamation of Her Britannic Majesty dated May 13, 1861.

The example of England and France was followed by the minor Powers. Spain and Portugal proclaimed their neutrality, and announced the conditions upon which their ports might be used by the two belligerents. Even Brazil and the South American Republics soon fell to defining their views, and swelled the general chorus of "impartial neutrality" in the great struggle between the North and South which the easterly trade-winds wafted over to them from Europe. If the restrictions thus imposed upon the cruisers of both parties in the Civil War were vexatious and inconvenient to the Federal Government, they were manifestly more burdensome and perplexing to that of the Confederacy.

The United States had four ample and well-found dockyards on the Atlantic coast (Portsmouth, Boston, New York and Philadelphia), at which their ships could be efficiently and completely equipped. In addition to this advantage, the home ports were always open to them for shelter, repair and supply, and everywhere abroad there were diplomatic and consular agents to appeal to for aid in case of difficulty or undue exactions on the part of local authorities. Besides this, the United States Navy Department could furnish each cruising ship with ample credits through bankers whose financial position had long been assured the world over. A Confederate cruiser, on the contrary, had no home port for outfit or retreat. She was compelled to be as nearly as possible self-supporting. Her flag was tolerated only, not recognised. Once upon the seas, she could never hope to re-supply the continual waste of her powers of offence or defence, and could obtain but a grudging allowance of the merest necessaries. Her "military chest" was the paymaster's safe, and her financial resources were the moderate supply of sovereigns with which she began her cruise. In case of difficulty, there was no resident Minister to whom the captain could refer for counsel or support, no consular representative who could set his case before the authorities in the neutral ports.

In the home ports of England and France the Confederate cruisers were fairly and courteously treated—at any rate, the treatment was uniform and consistent—but in the distant colonies, and at the ports of other less powerful and independent countries, the manner in which they were received, and the spirit in which the neutrality regulations were enforced, depended very much upon the individual sympathies and opinions of the local Governor, or the amount of influence the resident United States Consul could exert.

I believe this to be a very moderate statement of the contrast between the conditions under which the United States and Confederate cruisers were kept at sea during the war.

If it had not been for the limitations and restrictions of the "Admiralty orders" previously referred to, many more vessels might have been got to sea under the Confederate flag; but it would have been manifestly improvident, and a purposeless waste of the limited resources of the Navy Department, to commission ships for distant and continuous cruising, unless they could carry ample supplies of all necessaries, especially of ordnance stores, and could sail as well as steam at a good rate of speed. A vessel without good sailing qualities, and without the arrangement and means for lifting her screw, would have been practically useless as a Confederate cruiser. She could only have made passages from one coaling station to another; and as she could only coal at a port of the same country once in three months, her career would soon have been brought to an untimely and not very creditable end.

The necessities of the case, then, dictated the type of the Confederate ship, and the *Oreto* (*Florida*) and the *Alabama* were especially designed to meet those requirements.*

The *Florida* was a wooden vessel. Messrs. William C. Miller and Sons were the builders, and she was built at their yard in Liverpool. That firm was selected to build the hull of the ship, and to supply the masts, rigging, boats, and general sea-outfit, because the senior of the firm had been in the Royal Navy as a shipwright, and had served in her Majesty's dockyards as a naval constructor. He had therefore much experience in the construction of wooden ships designed to carry heavy weights on deck and to berth large crews. Messrs. Miller and Sons were not engineers, and, as it was advisable, for many reasons, that ship and engines should be as near together as possible, Messrs. Fawcett, Preston and Co., of Liverpool, were chosen to design and build the engines. The financial arrangements were made with Messrs. Fawcett, Preston and Co., exclusively. They took the whole contract for both ship and engines, and the preliminary discussions were of the ordinary business character.

Mr. W. C. Miller had a scale drawing of one of her Majesty's gunboats, which we adopted as a base to start from. She was drawn out in the midship section, and the floor was flattened to get greater carrying capacity. The increased length thus obtained admitted of finer entrance and clearance lines, which secured higher speed. The rigging scale was also largely

---

* The two vessels built at Liverpool, and which were afterwards commissioned abroad as Confederate cruisers, are generally mentioned in this narrative as the *Florida* and *Alabama,* to avoid frequent explanation. It will, however, be understood that they were never known by those names in the port of their construction, and were never alluded to in the arrangements with the builders, except as the *Oreto* and *No.* 290.

increased, so as to get a good spread of canvas, especially when close hauled, or with the wind a-beam. The type and rig of ship being satisfactorily adjusted, Messrs. Fawcett, Preston and Co. designed the engines, which were carefully discussed. The contract was made with me as a private person, nothing whatever being said about the ultimate destination of the ship, or the object for which she was intended. It is not usual for building firms to ask questions, or to express opinions as to the motives or purposes of those from whom they take orders. Before the completion of the ship, Messrs. Fawcett, Preston and Co. and the Messrs. Miller may both have had a tolerably clear notion that she would at some future time, and by some subsequent arrangement, pass into the possession of the Confederate Government; but they never mentioned their suspicions, and they undertook nothing more than to build and deliver in Liverpool a screw-steamer, according to certain specified plans and conditions, fitted for sea in every respect, but without armament or equipment for fighting of any kind whatever. To provide an answer in advance for any inquisitive comments or surmises, *Oreto* was chosen as the dockyard name for the ship. It was incidentally mentioned among the workpeople that she would probably be sent to a mercantile firm doing business in Palermo, and a local representative of that firm undertook the details of supervising and despatching her.

While the negotiations for the *Oreto* (*Florida*) were in progress, I went with a friend to visit the Birkenhead Ironworks, and was introduced to the Messrs. Laird. After an interesting examination of their extensive establishment, I led the conversation to the subject of wooden despatch vessels, and described with some minuteness the type which appeared most desirable in my judgment. The subject was naturally of interest to the Messrs. Laird, and they gave me their opinions and the result of their experience with freedom. A few days after, I called again, re-opened the conversation about a screw despatch vessel, discussed the matter somewhat more in detail, and finally told them that I wished to build such a ship, and asked if they would be willing to go into the necessary calculations, draw up specifications, and make drawings and a model, upon my assurance that I meant business and was ready to give them the necessary financial guarantee. They were satisfied with my proposals, and in a very short time all the details of the *Alabama* were settled to our common satisfaction.

The origin of the *Alabama,* her departure from England, and her career afloat, have been much discussed. Probably no single ship has ever given occasion for so much diplomatic correspondence, or has furnished the grounds for so many complaints, and the foundation for so great an alleged international grievance. She has been called a "British pirate"; many persons believed that she was paid for by a subscription among English merchants. The builders were often accused of risking the peace of the realm by supplying a vessel of war to cruise against the commerce of the United States, and they have been openly charged with committing a flagrant breach of the Queen's proclamation of neutrality for their own selfish profit—bartering, as it were, their loyalty as subjects, and their duty as citizens, for a pecuniary consideration, which it has been erroneously alleged they received in an extravagant price for the ship.

The great Commonwealth which forms one of the mighty union of States across the Atlantic is scarcely known in Europe except as the producer of some half-million bales of cotton per annum; but her little namesake of a thousand tons, in a lifetime of barely two years, has spread the name to the uttermost parts of the earth, and has made it familiar to thousands who know nothing of geographical State lines, and at the mention of it now would probably think of the "*Alabama* Claims," and not of the "Alabama State."

This notoriety of the ship, and the long-current misstatements affecting her builders and all who were in any way concerned with her origin, seem to impose upon me the duty of dwelling upon the purely business arrangements with the Messrs. Laird more particularly than would be at all necessary, or even expedient, under ordinary circumstances.

The contract for the vessel afterwards called the *Alabama* was made in my own name as a private individual, and the negotiations were carried on between the members of the firm and myself, without the intervention of any other parties whatever. The Messrs. Laird very properly looked first to the financial security. I did not leave them a moment in doubt on that point, and being fully satisfied that the proposed transaction was in every particular safe and regular, they took it in hand as a part of their ordinary business.

At that time, wood had almost entirely gone out of use as a material for ship-building in Great Britain, and it was suggested, and as readily admitted, that there would be some difficulty in getting suitable timber for the heavy scantling, such, to wit, as the stem, keelson, and especially the sternpost, which would require to be bored to receive the screw shaft. These facts were mentioned and discussed with reference to the cost and time necessary to build the ship, and it was perceived that both would considerably exceed the estimate for an iron vessel.

The general dimensions and other particulars of the *Alabama* were: length 220 feet; breadth, 32 feet; draft, with all weights on board, 15 feet;

tonnage, 1,040; engines, two horizontal, of 300 horse-power nominal, but on trial trip indicated 1,000 horse-power. She was barque-rigged, with very long lower masts, to get large fore and aft sails. Her sails, carried at will, were as follows: fore, fore-topmast staysail and jib; two large trysails, the usual square sails on fore and main masts, with the exception of the main course, which was set flying; spanker and gaff-topsails; all standing rigging wire. She was admirably fitted in every respect: engines equal to Admiralty standard; brass screw, Griffith's pattern, with lifting apparatus, and stowage in iron bunkers for 350 tons of coal. She was provided with a double suit of sails and the usual outfit for an East India voyage. She had five boats, including launch, cutter and whale-boat, and ample ground-tackle. She was well supplied with hawsers, and had spare blocks, running gear, etc., to meet all requirements for at least a year. The engineer's stores and spare engine-gear were on the scale supplied to ships of the Royal Navy intended for long and distant voyages, and she was provided with condensing apparatus and cooling tank to supply fresh water. She was built of the very best materials, copper-fastened and coppered, and was finished in every respect as a first-class ship. I was satisfied in every particular with the manner in which the builders fulfilled their contract, and I believe she was as fine a vessel, and as well-found, as could have been turned out of any dockyard in the kingdom, equal to any of her Majesty's ships of corresponding class in structure and finish, and superior to any vessel of her date in fitness for the purposes of a sea rover, with no home but the sea, and no reliable source of supply but the prizes she might make.

The price paid to the Messrs. Laird, including the outfit, was £47,500, payable by the terms of the contract in five equal payments of £9,500 each; and the last installment was made payable after satisfactory trial and delivery to me on the Mersey in the *port* of *Liverpool*. Everyone who has had experience in the cost of ships will admit that the price named was not in the least degree excessive or unreasonable. I had previously super-intended the construction of vessels of varying types, and I thought at the time, and am of the opinion now, that the contract price for the *Alabama* afforded only a fair commercial profit to the builders.

The foregoing statement will, I trust, be accepted as a complete and final refutation of the charge often made, that the Messrs. Laird were paid a high price for undertaking the exceptional risk of building a vessel of war, and delivering her to an agent of the Confederate Government be-yond British jurisdiction. In point of fact, they delivered to me an un-armed ship in the port of Liverpool. As another simple matter of fact, they did not know for what purpose the ship was intended when they agreed to build her. They were not informed of anything which had reference to the armament, and are to this day ignorant of the manner and place of equipment, excepting in so far as the movements and performances of the ship, after she passed out of their hands, are known to the general public. (See p. 67.)

I feel that I owe to the memory of the late Mr. John Laird, M.P., an explicit and unequivocal denial of the charge so often made that he was concerned in the building and equipment of the ship afterwards called the *Alabama,* a statement which many persons have thought to be confirmed by some inadvertent expressions in Admiral Semmes's narrative of her cruise under his command. At the time when I was negotiating for the *Alabama,* Mr. John Laird had retired from the firm which bore his name, and he was shortly afterwards elected to serve in Parliament as the first member for Birkenhead. My business arrangements, and all the discussions about the design and cost of the ship, were carried on with Messrs. William and John Laird, junr. Mr. John Laird, the subsequent member for Birkenhead, had nothing whatever to do with the transaction, and I am quite sure that he was never even present at any of my interviews with the firm in reference to that subject.

After Mr. Laird took his seat in Parliament, I understood and appreciated his position, and was rigidly reticent about Confederate affairs. Our acquaintance ripened into friendship, and I was his debtor for many acts of kindly social courtesy, but never, in the freedom of friendly and familiar conversation, was the subject of the *Alabama* discussed or even alluded to until she was afloat as a Confederate cruiser, and her acts had become matters of common knowledge, and topics of general comment.

In May, 1874, I had occasion to go to the Brazils on business, and I called to bid Mr. Laird good-bye, and to get a number of letters of introduction which he had kindly obtained for me. We were talking about the Amazon, and a steamship company formed by the Baron de Maua to navigate that mighty river. The conversation turned upon ships in general, and the *Alabama* was incidentally mentioned. I told him how her battery and ordnance stores were shipped from London, and gave him an account of our adventures at the island of Terceira, where she was armed and equipped. He was much interested, and remarked that he had always thought it most fortunate that I had never mentioned the circumstances to him during the war, because his ignorance of them enabled him to say, when attacked in Parliament, without the least mental reservation, that he was not only free from all complicity in the equipment of the ship, but

46 · *James D. Bulloch*

that he knew nothing about her, except what had been revealed to the general public.

Mr. Laird's statements in the House of Commons that he had nothing to do with the building or equipment of the *Alabama* were frequently spoken of with distrust by other members who were ardent partisans of the United States, and the newspapers which adopted and defended the same cause persisted in repeating the original charge, in face of the most distinct and unequivocal denials; but he had the satisfaction to know that her Majesty's Government implicitly believed his disavowal, and he came to feel at last that the repetition of the charges was merely intended for party purposes, and hence he ceased to give much heed to them.

At this late date, when time has softened the resentful temper and the sharp antagonism which seem always to warp the judgment and embitter criticism during periods of great political excitement, I may indulge the hope that my testimony in regard to the building and equipping of Confederate ships abroad will be received without distrust. I can conscientiously say that I have neither the purpose nor the wish to conceal a single fact; indeed, my only fear is that anxiety to tell the whole truth may lead me into the error of too great minuteness of detail, and that I may be seduced into the expectation that incidents and adventures which force of circumstances strongly impressed upon my own mind may be of corresponding interest to others.

The chief object of this narrative is to demonstrate, by a plain statement of facts, that the Confederate Government, through their agents, did nothing more than all other belligerents have heretofore done in time of need—namely, tried to obtain from every possible source the means necessary to carry on the war in which they were engaged, and that in doing so they took particular pains to understand the municipal laws of those countries in which they sought to supply their wants, and were especially careful to keep within the statutes.

The Foreign Enlistment Act, and its bearing upon the naval operations of the Confederate States in England, will be fully explained and discussed in a subsequent chapter; but to preserve a due and relevant connection of subjects, and to keep the record in appropriate relation to the order of events, it seems fitting to mention that at a very early day after my arrival in England I took legal advice.

The object of the Confederate Government was not merely to buy or build a single ship, but it was to maintain a permanent representative of the Navy Department abroad, and to get ships and naval supplies without hindrance as long as the war lasted. To effect this purpose it was manifestly necessary to act with prudence and caution, and to do nothing in violation of the municipal law, because a single conviction would both expose the object and defeat its aim. A fortunate circumstance led me to consult the late Mr. F. S. Hull, a member of a leading firm of solicitors in Liverpool, and he continued to act as my solicitor during the whole period of the war. Mr. Hull was a prudent, cautious, conscientious adviser, and throughout all those troublous times I found him a watchful and safe mentor. I kept him informed of all important transactions, and consulted him with reference to all contracts.

There were many complications, and perplexing questions were constantly cropping up. These he faced with coolness, judgment, and good temper, and never once led me astray or encouraged me to undertake the impracticable. He piloted me safely through the mazes of the Foreign Enlistment Act, in spite of the perplexing ambiguity of its 7th Section, and the bewildering iterations and reiterations of the precept not to "equip, furnish, fit out, or arm" any ship with intent, etc., etc.

Generally Mr. Hull felt and proved himself competent to deal with the legal questions as they arose, without referring to any other authority; but at the time of making the contracts for the *Alabama* and *Florida,* no case involving the forfeiture of a ship had ever been brought to trial under the Foreign Enlistment Act,* and there had therefore been no judicial decision as to its interpretation. If the Act prohibited the building of a ship for a belligerent under all circumstances, and imposed upon the builder the onus of proving that there was no intent to arm her beyond British jurisdiction, it was important to know it, because if that was the law, merely concealing the ultimate purpose from the builder would not protect the property from seizure and forfeiture. Mr. Hull therefore drew up a case for counsel's opinion, and submitted it to two eminent barristers, both of whom have since filled the highest judicial positions. The case submitted was a general and not a specific proposition. It was not intimated for what purpose or on whose behalf the opinion was asked, and the reply was therefore wholly without bias, and embraced a full exposition of the Act in its bearing upon the question of building and equipping ships in her Majesty's dominions.

The inferences drawn from the investigation of the Act by counsel were put into the following form by my solicitor:

* "*Alexandra* Case," speeches of the Attorney-General and Sir Hugh Cairns.

"1. It is no offence (under the Act) for British subjects to equip, etc., a ship at some country *without* her Majesty's dominions, though the intent be to cruise against a friendly State.

"2. It is no offence for *any* person (subject or no subject) to *equip* a ship *within* her Majesty's dominions, if it be *not* done with the intent to cruise against a friendly State.

"3. The mere building of a ship *within* her Majesty's dominions by any person (subject or no subject) is no offence, *whatever may be the intent of the parties,* because the offence is not the *building* but the *equipping*.

"Therefore any shipbuilder may build any ship in her Majesty's dominions, provided he does not equip her within her Majesty's dominions, and he has nothing to do with the acts of the purchasers done *within* her Majesty's dominions without his concurrence, nor *without* her Majesty's dominions even with his concurrence."

The foregoing deductions from the terms of the Act were kept rigidly in view in all contracts for ships in England, and every possible precaution was practised both for the protection of the builders against criminal prosecutions under the Act, and for that of the ships against forfeiture. In no case was any builder or vendor informed what was the purpose of the purchaser. No ship was ever supplied with any portion of her equipment *within* her Majesty's dominions, nor was the builder or vendor of any ship employed to assist in the equipment *without* her Majesty's dominions.

On the 27th of July, 1861, the first remittance on account of the Confederate Navy Department reached England. The *Oreto* (*Florida*) was then partly in frame, and the plans and specifications of the ship afterwards called the *Alabama* being complete, the contract with the Messrs. Laird was closed on the first day of August.

It is very seldom that a particular name is given to a ship until at or about the time of her launch, but a dockyard number is assigned to her, for convenience of reference, and for specification in the accounts of expenditure. The number given to the ship contracted for with Messrs. Laird was "290," which, it will be perceived, had none of the mysterious signification so often ascribed to it, but meant simply that she was the 290th ship built by them.

It was often alleged, after the departure of the *Alabama* from Liverpool, that a peculiar and mysterious secrecy was practised in respect to her, and that no one was permitted to examine her, or even to go into Messrs. Laird's yard while she was building, without a special permit. This is quite a mistake. My intercourse with the builders was only so far secret that I kept my own counsel, and did not communicate to them the purpose for which the ship was intended. They, on their part, asked no questions, and, so far as I know, they adopted no special restrictions with regard to visitors to the works while she was in their hands. Official documents, long since published, have proved beyond doubt that the officers of Her Majesty's Customs had free and unopposed access to her at all times, and the general public were not excluded in a greater degree, nor under more stringent conditions than are commonly enforced in all well-regulated manufacturing establishments.*

When the United States Minister was clamouring at the door of the Foreign Office, and pressing Her Majesty's Government to seize, or at least to detain, the *Florida* and *Alabama*, the Consul at Liverpool supplied him with numerous "affidavits" of persons who subscribed the usual form of oath that they had seen me on board giving instructions and describing the type, arrangements, and ultimate destination of the ships. Either those affidavits were "made to order," or else it was not difficult to get a view of both the ships. By-and-by it will be shown that many of the affidavits were prepared with little regard to actual facts, and that they were generally made either by hired "private detectives," whose chief aim was to earn their pay, or at least to give something in return for it, by self-appointed spies, who found a ready market for their tales, or by that class of persons who are possessed with a mania to spring at a leap to convictions which may or may not prove to be right in the end, but who, unwilling to await the natural and regular fulfilment of events, are impelled by a restless impatience to manufacture the intermediate facts or to mould and distort them so as to confirm their preconceived opinions.

None but an unsophisticated or very impertinent person would think of walking into any business premises and asking the owners what they were doing, and who for. Such inquirers get either evasive replies, or rebuffs more or less courteously expressed. It is probable that the Messrs.

---

* See report of Mr. Morgan, Surveyor of Her Majesty's Customs, Liverpool, dated 28th June, 1862:

"The officers have at all times free access to the building yards of the Messrs. Laird at Birkenhead, where the said vessel is now lying; and there has been no attempt on the part of the builders to disguise what is now apparent to all, that she is intended for a ship-of-war."— "*Alabama* Papers," 24th March, 1863.

That the *Alabama* subsequently left Liverpool unarmed is proved by the official report of the Surveyor of Customs, dated 30th July, 1862:

"I have only to add that your directions to keep a strict watch on the said vessel have been carried out, and I write in the fullest confidence that she left this port without any part of her armament on board. She had not as much as a signal-gun or musket."—"*Alabama* Papers," 24th March, 1863.

Laird had frequently to meet such contingencies, and I have no doubt that they invariably "rose to the occasion," and knew when to be courteously equivocal, and when to maintain a frigid reserve.

About the month of August, 1861, Messrs. Fraser, Trenholm and Co. determined to send a steamer to one of the Southern ports with a cargo, not wholly of arms, but of general supplies suited to the wants of the armies in the field, and their Charleston house, Messrs. John Fraser and Co., had sent over an experienced coast pilot to take her in. Mr. Prioleau told me of this purpose, and informed me that while his firm expected to realize a fair commercial profit from the undertaking, their chief object was to demonstrate that the blockade was inefficient, and thus they hoped to encourage others to embark in like enterprises, by which means the pressing wants of the South could be supplied with more or less certainty.

It was important to keep the destination of the ship secret, but Mr. Prioleau told me of his purpose, as he said, to advise me about the adventure, and also to offer me the opportunity to ship such arms and ordnance stores as Major Huse and I might have ready to forward. The steamer engaged for the purpose was the *Bermuda*. She was fitted out and loaded at West Hartlepool, and I went to that port with Mr. Prioleau to superintend the shipment of the goods especially intended for the Confederate War and Navy Departments, while Major Huse looked after their despatch to the shipping port.

The *Bermuda* was commanded by Captain Eugene Tessier, who had long been employed by the firm in the Charleston trade; and his pilot was Captain Peck, well known on the coast from Charleston to St. Augustine. She sailed from West Hartlepool in August, 1861; got safely into Savannah, September 18th; and ran out again with a large cargo of cotton, which she brought to Liverpool.

Mr. Edwin Haigh, of Liverpool, the registered owner of the ship, in an affidavit presented to the United States District Court of Pennsylvania in October, 1862,* said as follows: "I am informed and believe that the said steamship (*Bermuda*), in the prosecution of her voyage, was not warned off by any of the blockading cruisers; and that she entered the port of Savannah without meeting with any of such cruisers, or having the opportunity of ascertaining whether the said blockade was still in force, and there discharged her cargo."

It will thus be seen that Messrs. Fraser, Trenholm and Co. accom-

---

* See "Report of Proceedings in Admiralty, U.S. *v.* SS. *Bermuda* and Cargo, Philadelphia, August, 1862," p. 448.

plished their purpose of demonstrating that the blockade of the Southern coast, at the time of the *Bermuda*'s voyage (August and September, 1861), was inefficient; and it is probable that their expectation of realizing a commercial profit by the adventure was also fulfilled. Their example undoubtedly stimulated the trade, but the United States soon strengthened and increased the blockading force, and during the last two years of the war the difficulty of getting in and out of the Southern ports was made greater and greater, until only the swiftest vessels stood any chance of success, and they only when favoured by dark nights and suitable weather.

In February, 1862, the *Bermuda* was despatched again from England, but the greater efficiency of the blockade at that time, together with the fear that she was both too large and too slow to promise success, caused the owner to abandon the purpose or attempt to run her into a Southern port. The cargo, laden in England, was intended to be discharged at Bermuda or Nassau, and a return cargo for Liverpool had actually been provided by her consignees at Nassau.

This voyage of the *Bermuda* is interesting and important, because it affords a typical example of the manner in which the United States dealt with neutral vessels captured for real or alleged violation of the blockade, and furnishes also a fitting occasion for some remarks upon the general conduct of the United States towards neutrals during the war, and the precedents that Government persistently laboured to establish.

In pursuance of the owner's purpose, the *Bermuda* sailed from Liverpool, touched at the island of Bermuda, and in due course proceeded towards Nassau, her final port of destination. On the morning of April 27th, 1862, being off the southern point of Great Abaco Island, the Hole-in-the-Wall Light bearing south-west, distant, according to the varying testimony of witnesses, from less than three to over seven miles, the *Bermuda* was stopped by a shot fired across her bows from the United States steamer *Mercedita,* a prize crew was put on board, and she was taken into Philadelphia.

There was some delay in bringing her case to trial; but finally she was arraigned before Judge Cadwalader, of the United States District Court sitting in Admiralty at Philadelphia. The proceedings began August 12th, 1862, and the arguments *pro* and *con* were closed on the 16th of the same month. "At the conclusion of the argument, the judge remarked that he would consider the case very carefully, and deliver his opinion at as early a day as practicable. "* The outline of the case cannot be better stated than

* See "Report of Proceedings," p. 397.

in the words of Mr. George M. Wharton, counsel for the owners, or the "claimants," as they are designated in the legal proceedings. Mr. Wharton said: "It is the case of a British vessel, owned by a British subject, laden at Liverpool by British merchants, and bound for Bermuda, a British colony. After arriving at Bermuda, the ship has directions from those who have the right to control, so far, her movements, to go from Bermuda to Nassau, another British colonial port; and while navigating in the direct line from Bermuda to Nassau, and at the distance of about 415 miles from that portion of the American coast the blockade of which she is alleged to have violated, while sailing among these British islands in a direct line toward her place of destination, she is overhauled by a cruiser of the United States Government, captured, and brought here for trial and consequent condemnation."

The contention of the United States Attorney was to this effect. The voyage to Bermuda and Nassau was only a colourable pretext. The cargo was either enemy's property, or was shipped with the intent to be forwarded to an enemy's port through the blockade, and that even though the *Bermuda* might break bulk at Nassau and land the whole of her cargo there, the purpose was to reship it for Charleston, or some other blockaded port. He furthermore urged the plea that a vessel bound in point of fact from London to Charleston, could not plead in defence an original design to stop at Nassau during the voyage, and that she was sailing at the moment of capture for or in the direction of the intermediate port. In their arguments the counsel for the United States also contended that if the original intention was to run the blockade, and merely to make Nassau a place of call for any purpose whatever, the vessel was liable to capture the moment she got beyond the limit of British jurisdiction, which they specified to be any distance beyond three miles outside of the port of Liverpool.

International law is not an exact science. The highest authorities differ in the construction of its rules, and the most learned judges have variously interpreted its provisions. It is a code which has never received the willing or unanimous consent of all nations, but bears upon its face the impress of having been forced by the stronger upon the weaker, and history furnishes many instances in which during times of war belligerents have set aside or acted in defiance of its apparent and commonly received conditions, whenever their interests required, and their power was sufficient to enforce their purpose. Interference with trade between neutrals and either of two belligerents has always been considered oppressive, and in derogation of a natural right. By the declaration of Paris of 1856, the principle that the neutral flag covered the goods and protected the ship also from search, when on the high sea, was agreed to, and the rules which prohibited a neutral from carrying the goods of a belligerent, or compelled the neutral to submit to "the right of search," were done away with, as between the Great Powers who were parties to that declaration. This did not, of course, abolish the right of blockade.

It is not my purpose to argue or even to comment upon the law points involved in the case of the *Bermuda*. The whole of the proceedings have been published, and have been no doubt carefully examined by the interested parties. The present object is merely to set out the circumstances of the capture, and the facts appertaining to the disposal of the ship and cargo, and thus to demonstrate the manner in which the United States enforced their belligerent rights, and the broad scope they claimed and practised in the exercise of them. It is manifestly difficult to prove an intent, and in the case of the *Bermuda* the only evidence on the part of the United States was purely circumstantial; on the other hand, a number of persons in Liverpool were interested in the shipments by her, and the particulars of the voyage were known to many persons, and were much discussed. It was well understood among the shippers of goods that the vessel would go only to Bermuda and Nassau, and among the documents laid before the Prize Court,* there appears an affidavit by one of the Liverpool agents of the ship, in which there is set out, among others, the following declaration: "That the cargo laden here" (Liverpool) "was intended to be discharged at Bermuda or Nassau, and that a return cargo for this port" (Liverpool) "had been provided by her consignees at Nassau."

The *Bermuda* was no doubt tainted by the alleged previous violation of the blockade, but it has been shown that she was not warned off, nor did she even see a blockading vessel when she entered the port of Savannah in September, 1861, and it is therefore questionable whether that voyage was in reality a breach of blockade. The captain, too, seems to have lost his head, or to have been over-confident in the protecting influence of his flag and register. He should either have got his ship clearly and indisputably within the marine league, and held on to all of his papers, or destroyed every document except his manifest, letter of instruction, and register, or he should have beached the ship and thus have prevented her capture. He did neither, but stopped at the first shot, and then destroyed only the papers in his personal charge, containing those which demonstrated that the ship was to go no further than Nassau, and left on board the private

---

* See "Report of Proceedings," p. 424.

correspondence, for the nature of which neither the owners nor the agents were responsible.

However, the name and previous history of the ship, the nature of the cargo, and the particulars of the voyage, could neither of them have been known without forcible stoppage and search, and the fact remains that the commander of the *Mercedita* enforced an extreme and unusual belligerent pretension against a neutral ship proceeding to a colonial port of her own country, when steering towards that port, and on a course away from, and 415 miles distant from the nearest part of the coast the blockade of which she was alleged to have violated.

Although the arguments in the Prize Court were concluded on the 16th of August, 1862, and the judge announced his purpose to render judgment "as soon as practicable,"* no decision was given up to December 19th, 1862, and the further proceedings in the case may be briefly stated as follows:

December 19th, 1862, the "Attorney of the United States" petitioned the Court for an order directing the Marshal to deliver to any authorized agent of the Navy Department of the United States the said steamer (*Bermuda*), on the payment by the United States into the Registry of the Court of the amount of her appraised value.† The petition showed that the ship had been appraised at the sum of $120,000, that the United States wished to employ her in the naval service of the United States, and had deposited the full amount of the appraisement with the United States Marshal for that district (Philadelphia); that the steamer had been brought to the port of Philadelphia, *May 3rd*, 1862, and had remained there from that time at heavy charges consequent upon her detention; that besides the official compensation allowed the Marshal for the custody of said steamer, special expenses had been incurred in the employment of means necessary for the preservation of the engines, boilers, and other parts of the ship, "and that the expenses incident to said detention which have accrued, and are continually accruing, render the said steamer in a relative sense perishable," etc.

On the same date (December 19th, 1862) counsel for the owners filed protest against the foregoing in due form.‡ *December 23rd* the Court ordered survey and appraisement. Appraisers reported, *December 30th*.§

---

* "Report of Proceedings," p. 397.
† Ibid., p. 458.
‡ Ibid., p. 459.
§ Ibid., p. 461.

"The said steamship (*Bermuda*) has deteriorated in value since the 12*th day* of *September last* at the rate of $800 *per month*, exclusive of interest ... caused mainly by a want of the care and attention of proper officers and crew"; and they fix the value at $120,000. *March 5th*, 1863, the Court decreed as follows:* "It appearing to the Court that the said steamer was, at the time of capture, the property of enemies of the United States, or otherwise confiscable as prize-of-war, it is ordered, adjudged and decreed that the said steamer, her tackle, apparel and appurtenances be, and the same are, condemned as good and lawful prize." In a sort of preamble to the foregoing decree, the judge stated that he was not prepared to give judgment in respect to the cargo, and would therefore defer his "reasons in detail as to the vessel until a decision as to the cargo." On the same day counsel for the owners gave notice of appeal, and the Attorney for the United States moved for delivery of the ship to the United States;† and it was ordered "that, on the deposit of the said sum of $120,000 in the registry of the Court, the said steamer be delivered to the Navy Department of the United States." *March 6th*, 1863, counsel for the owners prayed an appeal in due form,‡ which was allowed; but, nevertheless, the ship was delivered to the United States Navy Department. She was quickly armed and equipped as a vessel-of-war, and was cruising off the Southern coast under the flag of her captors before the appeal was heard.

It can hardly be the deliberate purpose of any Government to exercise its belligerent rights with vexatious stringency as regards neutrals; and when vessels are captured or detained on suspicion of an intent to violate a blockade, or of carrying enemies' property, the least forbearance that can be claimed is that the case should be promptly dealt with, and that the property should be carefully protected from injury pending the judicial proceedings. But a very brief summary will demonstrate that, if the United States were severe in the practice of their rights on the high seas, they were none the less rigorous and unyielding in the treatment of those whose commercial interests were involved in the captures made by their cruisers. The *Bermuda* was captured April 27th, 1862, and reached Philadelphia May 3rd, 1862, where she was suffered to remain until August 12th, deteriorating "at the rate of $800 per month, exclusive of interest, for want of care and attention." Then, when the hearing of the case was concluded, no judgment was rendered for seven months, the deterio-

---

* "Report of Proceedings," p. 462.
† Ibid., p. 463.
‡ Ibid., p. 463.

ration going on at, or in excess of, the above rate; and finally she was handed over to her captors, upon their application, in spite of the owners' protest, and pending an appeal.

It will be perceived from the statement of this case—and many others of like particulars might be mentioned—that the United States asserted and practised the right to stop any neutral vessel anywhere exceeding three miles from her own coast, to take her to a United States port, and there to determine whether there was circumstantial evidence of a purpose or intent to proceed herself, or to re-ship her cargo, to a blockaded port. Manifestly this pretension was a virtual denial of the doctrine that "the flag covers the goods," a principle for which the United States had contended previously to the Civil War, although they had not formally assented to the agreement of the Great Powers at Paris. It was also an assertion of the "right of search," a doctrine which the United States had ever before resisted with vehement earnestness, carrying the opposition so far, in 1812, as to face the cost and peril of a war with Great Britain rather than submit to it.

The commonly admitted principle that there could be no such thing as contraband goods in a neutral vessel bound from one neutral port to another was wholly abolished by the United States during the Civil War, although no country had so strongly contended for its maintenance in regard to its own commerce in past times.

These statements are not now made as matters of complaint or reproach against the United States, but they serve to confirm the truth of the old and somewhat homely phrase, "circumstances alter cases." They demonstrate the fact that when nations are at war they act upon the principle that the end justifies the means, and although the laws of humanity in reference to the treatment of persons are not often violated in these latter days, yet the "sacred rights of property" are seldom treated with reverence, and belligerents limit their encroachments upon the privileges of neutrals, not by abstract principles of law and justice, by respect for treaty stipulations, or sentimental regard for international comity, but by considerations of policy and self-interest. They press their rights and use their privileges to the full measure of forbearance on the part of neutral states, or their own power to enforce and maintain them.

The bitter complaints of the United States Minister against Her Majesty's Government for alleged neglect in permitting the Confederate agents to get a few unarmed ships in England, the querulous despatches of Mr. Secretary Seward on the same subject, and the harsh epithets which were freely showered upon the persons concerned in those undertakings, appear almost ludicrous when the acts of those agents are contrasted with what was done by the American commissioners to France during the War of Independence, the equipment of Paul Jones's ships *within* the French dominions, the capture of the *Florida* by the United States ship *Wachusett* in the neutral port of Bahia; the seizure and search of numerous vessels sailing under neutral flags, and passing on their course many miles away from the blockaded coast during the Civil War of 1861–65, and the enlistment of thousands of men in Europe, and their shipment from Liverpool and elsewhere for service in the United States army, under the thin disguise of labourers for American railways, or an ordinary exodus of emigrants. If there was any blockade-running under the French or Spanish flags, the attempts were too few to attract public notice, and I have no record of any official remonstrances from either Paris or Madrid against the interference of the United States with the commerce of those countries.

It will scarcely be pretended that French or Spanish subjects refrained from engaging in the prohibited trade with the South because they thought the traffic wrong in itself, or because of any high notions of duty or favour to the United States as a friendly power. The Confederate Government confined their operations chiefly to the better and cheaper markets in Great Britain, and the purchases made in France were for the most part sent first to England, or to Havana, Bermuda and Nassau, from whence they were transhipped to a Confederate port. Moreover, maritime adventure of that kind has always been peculiarly attractive to the Anglo-Saxon race, and during the American Civil War many British subjects embarked in the contraband traffic, stimulated alike by the prospect of large profits and the exhilarating effects of the risk and uncertainty. Besides this, all shipments on account of the Confederate Government were made chiefly in English vessels, because it was soon perceived that no vessel under the Confederate flag could load in a British port and hope to escape interference, detention, and perhaps seizure, on suspicion that she was intended for armament as a cruiser.

The United States Government knew that England was the source and fountain of supply for the Confederate States, and that English bottoms were the means of conveyance. They looked with suspicion upon every British ship which ventured to approach the Western World. Their men-of-war policed the waters adjacent to Mexico and the Spanish as well as the English West Indies, and were not particular as to the course a vessel was steering, or the port to which she was bound. A British register, and a British flag, were assumed to be *prima facie* evidence of an "intent" to run the blockade, and many steamers, and even one sailing vessel, the *Springbok,* were captured when bound from Europe, chiefly from England, to a British Colonial port, or to Cuban and Mexican ports. Many of the vessels employed by the United States in blockading the Southern ports during the war were captured blockade-runners, and it has always seemed strange that no fast steamers were built at the North for that special purpose.

A United States naval officer, who was a long time on blockade service, has told me that few of the original blockaders could steam over eight to nine knots, and it is a fact that very few blockade-runners were caught in an open chase with ample sea-room.

During the Anglo-French War with Russia, commonly called the Crimean War, the Russian Government made a large contract with Colonel Samuel Colt for repeating arms of his patent. The arms were chiefly manufactured at Colonel Colt's works, near Hartford, in the State of Connecticut, and they were shipped together with other goods, contraband of war, in large quantities from the United States in American and other neutral vessels to the Prussian port of Memel, on the Baltic, from which they were forwarded to Russia, probably in great part overland.* The British and French Governments either admitted the legality of this traffic between neutral ports in articles contraband of war, and manifestly intended for their enemy, or else they did not care to involve themselves in controversy with the neutral Powers who were engaged in it.

In the same way the Confederate agents and private commercial parties also shipped goods of all kinds from England to English colonial ports, to Havana and to Matamoras during the Civil War. The general purpose was no doubt to use those ports as *entrepots,* and to transship the goods not intended for *bonâ fide* delivery by steamers especially designed to run the blockade. The ships actually engaged in running the blockade were liable to capture whenever they approached the blockaded coast or were in proximity to it, and were legitimate prizes-of-war when thus caught. But neutral vessels on voyages, say from England to Nassau, Havana, and Matamoras, and steering the direct course for those ports, were surely within their rights, and were or should have been as free from interference by either belligerent as American ships trading to the Baltic at the time of the Crimean War were exempt from interference by the cruisers of France and England.

---

* Besides the taking of arms to Memel on behalf of Russia, many American ships were chartered by the French Government, and were employed as transports during the Crimean War.

The United States would have complained most bitterly, and would probably have done something more than remonstrate, if those Powers had so stretched their belligerent rights as to use the Swedish and Danish bays along the shores of the Cattegat as points of observation from which to watch and interrupt American trade with the neutral ports in the Baltic.

It is on record, however, that United States ships kept up a *quasi* blockade of Nassau during the years 1861–65, and that British vessels bound to that port were chased and captured within the Bahama Channels. The British steamer *Margaret Jessie** was chased off the island of Eleuthera by the United States steamer *Rhode Island,* but escaped, though repeatedly fired at with shot and shell when so close to the shore that some of the shell fell upon the land, cut down trees, and did other damage. In fact, the United States Government attempted to establish coal-depôts at both Bermuda and Nassau, and kept cruisers at or in the near neighbourhood of the latter port, especially to intercept vessels, whether inward bound from Europe or outward bound in the direction of the southern coast.†

To prevent this use of the Bahama Islands, and to prevent also the possible collision of United States and Confederate ships within British waters, her Majesty's Government were induced to issue "regulations," in January, 1862, forbidding the vessels of both belligerents alike to enter the port of Nassau except by permission of the Governor or in stress of weather. The United States paid but little heed to the spirit of those regulations. "There were no less than thirty-four visits of United States ships-of-war to the Bahama Islands during the time that the regulations were in force.‡ On four occasions, at least, vessels of the United States exceeded the twenty-four hours' limit, and took in coal by permission; one of them also received permission to repair. Several were engaged in pursuit of vessels suspected of being blockade-runners, and did not in every instance relinquish the chase within British limits. Two prizes appear, indeed, to have been captured by them, one within a mile of the shore, the other almost in port.§

"The use made of the waters of the Bahamas by Federal cruisers, for the purpose of watching and intercepting vessels supposed to be freighted with cargoes for Confederate ports, was so persistent as to induce the Governor on one occasion, when granting permission to coal

---

* "*Margaret Jessie* Debate."
† See "British Counter-Case," pp. 63–65.
‡ See "British Counter-Case," Geneva Arbitration, pp. 109–10.
§ "Appendix to British Case," vol. v., p. 224, for particulars.

to the commander of the *Dacotah,* to accompany it with the condition that the vessel should not, within the next ten days, be cruising within five miles of any of the Bahama Islands."

It will be perceived that the United States adopted the most rigorous means to repress the trade in neutral ships between England and the British and Spanish West Indian Islands; and they did finally almost entirely suppress it by a strict and severe extension of the belligerent rights of visit, search, and capture—an extension previously unknown to International Law.

Before the American Civil War, it had been commonly assumed that a neutral vessel bound to a neutral port was free from capture, and that a prize court would not inquire into the destination of her cargo. The American Courts introduced the principle that if sufficient evidence could be discovered of an intent to transship the cargo for delivery at a port of the belligerent, the cargo itself, and in some cases the ship also, became, as Judge Cadwalader expressed it *in re Bermuda,* "confiscable." The United States Government acted upon the above interpretation of international law. During the Civil War many neutral vessels were captured by their cruisers on the high seas, when bound from one neutral port to another, and were condemned upon evidence of an intended breach of blockade which was often very slight, and, from the nature of the cases, purely inferential.

The course pursued by the United States cruisers among the Bahama Islands, to which her Britannic Majesty's Government opposed no effectual prohibition, and the decisions of the United States Prize Courts, to which no formal objection seems to have been offered, destroyed in a great degree the advantage which the proximity of Nassau to the southern coast afforded to the Confederate Government, because the risk of capture extended over the whole voyage from England, and was not limited to the comparatively short run from the Bahama banks to the blockaded ports; and the only benefit left was that of transferring the cargoes to lighter and swifter vessels at Nassau.

The United States Secretary of State, Mr. Seward, often complained of and denounced the use which the Confederates made of Nassau, and the trade which grew up at that port, in language not always suited to the courtesy of diplomatic correspondence or the dignity of State Papers, and the United States cruisers continued to chase and often to capture the neutral ships within the waters of the Bahamas and Spanish West Indies, or when approaching them from Europe. England, the Power chiefly concerned, submitted, or at least made no effectual protest, and it is both interesting and important to investigate the reasons for her seeming indifference.

No one who remembers the promptness and spirit with which Lord Palmerston's Government resented the taking of the Confederate Commissioners from the Royal Mail steamship *Trent* by Captain Wilkes, and the alacrity with which preparations were made to forward troops to Canada, and to prepare a fleet for offensive operations if the said Commissioners were not given up, can suppose that her Majesty's Government were deterred from protecting British ships engaged in trade between England and the West Indian Colonies, or between the several islands on that side of the Atlantic, from lack of spirit to uphold the national honour, or from a conviction that the trade was in itself contrary to either Municipal or International Law. In the "counter-case" presented on the part of her Britannic Majesty's Government to the Tribunal of Arbitration at Geneva, it is correctly stated that Havana and Cardenas, in the Spanish island of Cuba, were made use of for the same purpose as Nassau, and that Confederate agents were maintained at those ports, and it is then remarked (p. 58): "In this there was nothing that the British Government was bound or legally empowered to prohibit, nor was any such obligation incumbent on the Government of Spain. Persons trading either with the Southern States or with those which adhered to the Union were free to use Nassau, as they were free to use any other port in the British dominions convenient for their purpose." Clearly, then, according to the views of her Majesty's Government, the Confederate transactions at Nassau, so far at least as regarded its use for the purpose of an *entrepot*, were unobjectionable both in equity and law.

I would not venture to say that the British Ministry of that day seriously discussed the conduct of the United States Government in Cabinet Council, and determined to submit to the interruption of British trade, and to the violation of the British flag, with the intent to confirm a new interpretation of International Law and to establish precedents against the United States; but there can be no doubt that a broad construction of belligerent maritime rights would be especially and peculiarly favourable to Great Britain and the other Great Maritime Powers of Europe whenever they may be again engaged in war, and the course pursued by the United States towards neutral ships during the years 1861–65 and tacitly acquiesced in by the European Powers, will at some future day involve the former Government in a dilemma.

It is manifest to those who are acquainted with the British steamship trade at this time, and the class of vessels engaged in it, that at very short notice—say two months after a declaration of war—England could have at sea not less than one hundred steamers taken from the merchant service capable of carrying heavy guns, ample supplies of stores and fuel, and with an average speed of thirteen knots, a good many with much higher speed. So large a marine police, in addition to the powerful fleet of the Royal Navy, would render the transfer of contraband goods across the seas impossible, and it can scarcely be doubted that, if England were engaged in war, she would act upon the example of the United States, and would stop the conveyance of such goods to ports adjacent to those of her enemy, even though covered by the American flag. What would the successor of Mr. Secretary Seward say to that? He could not deny or explain away the precedents. Submission to such an interruption of their trade would not be long borne by the people of the United States. The alternative would be war, probably at a time when the country would be unprepared with ships either for active cruising or for a vigorous defence of the coasting trade.

All the European Powers are steadily increasing their naval forces. They are not only building armour-cased ships and torpedo vessels, but others especially designed to cruise into distant seas. France, Germany, and even Austria and Italy, have dockyard accommodation and stores of material which would enable them to add quickly to their present force of cruising ships. Steamers taken from the British or Continental merchant services would be more vulnerable than vessels constructed especially for war, but at the beginning of hostilities they would be greatly superior in speed, power, and in number to the opposing ships the United States could quickly put afloat—strikingly superior to those commissioned by the United States during the Civil War. It is well known that many British commercial steamers built of late years have been constructed with special reference to future conversion into cruisers or torpedo vessels, under arrangements with the Admiralty, and the great building-yards of the Clyde, Mersey, Thames, Tyne, etc., could turn out any description of vessels with great rapidity.

The aggregate of tonnage built in Great Britain during the year 1881 was not less than a million tons, the Clyde alone having completed 269 vessels, representing a tonnage of 340,823 tons. There was one firm on the Tyne—Messrs. Palmer—who turned out no less an output than 50,492 tons of iron shipping in that year. In reference to the advance which has been made in speed, it is only necessary to mention such ships as the *Britannic, Germanic, Servia, City of Rome, Arizona, Alaska,* all of which have crossed the Atlantic between New York and Queenstown at a speed of not less than 15 knots for every hour they were at sea; and the steamship *Stirling Castle* has actually performed, at sea, with a dead weight of 3,000 tons, 18½ knots in an hour. There would be no insurmountable obstacle in converting the majority of modern steam vessels of the British mercantile marine to war purposes. The chief and most important alterations would be to remove deckhouses, increase pumping power, place additional watertight compartments, and perhaps protect exposed parts of engines. Such alterations as the foregoing would enable most modern British steamers not only to carry batteries sufficient to defend their own cargoes, but would fit them to cruise against commerce and to make raids upon an enemy's coast. The *Hecla,* a private steamship, was bought by the Admiralty in 1878. She has been armed with five 64-pounders and one 40-pounder gun, and without any structural strengthening has proved a decided success.

The figures in respect to increase of tonnage, performance of steamship *Stirling Castle,* and success of *Hecla* are taken from the address of the President of the "Institution of Naval Architects," and from the paper read by Mr. John Dunn, "On Modern Merchant Ships," at the Session, March 29th, 1882. The logs of the Liverpool and New York packets have been published, and their performances are well known to the travelling public and to all who take an interest in steam shipping.

During the Crimean War, and on other occasions of need, the ability of the private shipbuilders of Great Britain to supplement the efforts of her Majesty's dockyards has been fully and satisfactorily demonstrated, and some of the Continental Powers have in late years largely increased their building capacity. American naval officers, and probably the executive naval authorities also, are conscious of the continuous increase of maritime strength abroad, and contemplate with painful misgivings the apathy that prevails at home. The United States do not appear to have any fixed policy in reference to the national armaments or the efficiency of the naval service. Congress doles out a few millions of dollars from year to year, which barely suffices to keep the public dockyards in repair and a few ships of a bygone type at sea, and allows nothing for steady continuous enlargement of the cruising and fighting fleet proportionate to the increasing extent and growing requirements of the country, or the progress and development of naval efficiency abroad.

There is an admirable naval school at Annapolis; the course of study and the scientific training of young officers for the United States Navy is very thorough, and embraces a large range of subjects. Some may and do think that both the education and the training are too strictly theoretical, and too purely military, and that too little attention is now paid to practical seamanship. Some critics also say that the cadet midshipmen are kept so long and so exclusively employed at the pure mathematics, in the study of law, and at artillery and infantry drill, that they are too old when sent afloat for regular cruising to acquire the constitutional aptitude for the sea, and the smart active habit of handling ships, which the officers bred, say, thirty years ago possessed.

This impression is strengthened by the appearance and manœuvring of the United States ships I have seen abroad since the war. In the year 1841–42, I was serving on board the United States sailing sloop-of-war *Decatur,* on the Brazil Station. She was a model man-of-war. Some of her performances would almost seem incredible to the officers brought up in these days of steam. We used to furl sails from a bowline in thirty-five seconds, and shift courses, when at sea with all sail set, in nine minutes from the time the first order was given to "up courses" until the tacks were on board again. Once, while cruising with a squadron of five other ships, off Cape Frio (the late Commodore Charles Morris being in command), the flagship made signal to "shift main topmasts." The squadron, all sailing ships, was standing by the wind in two columns with top-gallant sails set, and the spare main-topmasts were lashed in cranes outside and abreast of the main-chains, and in tidy ships like the *Decatur* were covered with canvas laced tightly round the spar and painted black. The *Decatur* had her spare spar aloft and on end, rigging all set up, and the main top-gallant sail set again, in fifty-two minutes from the time the signal was hauled down on board the flagship. The times of performing all evolutions were entered in the log-books, and I took notes of them in my journal.

The foregoing may be considered fancy performances, when everything was ready, or at least in expectation; but the smart, well-trained crew of the *Decatur* were equal to any emergency. On one notable occasion the ship was lying off Buenos Ayres. She was moored for the winter gales with seventy-five fathoms of chain on the port bower, and one hundred and five on the starboard, the latter backed by the stream-anchor. The top-gallant masts, top-gallant and royal rigging were on deck, the topmasts were housed, the topsail-yards were down from aloft, and the lower yards were lashed across the rails. While in this condition, the captain received orders very unexpectedly to proceed without delay to Montevideo, and in two hours and forty-two minutes the ship was standing down the river La Plata, under top-gallant sails, jib, and spanker, with both bower-anchors fished and the stream-anchor in the fore-hatch. I ought to mention that at the time referred to the *Decatur* was commanded by the late Commander Henry W. Ogden, and her first-lieutenant was John H. Marshall, who was unsurpassed in his day as an executive officer. Before the end of the cruise, Commander Ogden was invalided, and was relieved in the command by the late Admiral David G. Farragut, who did not permit the *Decatur* to fall off in smartness; indeed, while the latter officer was in command, he once, as an experiment, put the ship through the evolution of reefing topsails in stays, a manœuvre immortalized in nautical song and naval poetry, but which I never saw performed except on that single occasion.

Such performances would not be possible with the heavy ironclads of the present day, and as all men-of-war appear now to enter and leave port under steam, and use canvas only with leading winds, or when they can make nearly the desired course, officers and men have but little practice in manœuvring under sail, and it is not surprising that smart handy seamanship should have declined since the universal application of steampower to men-of-war. This lack of smartness is apparent in the ships of all the Maritime Powers. I stood at the George's Pierhead in Liverpool, and saw her Majesty's ship *Defence* man yards on the occasion of the visit of his Royal Highness the Prince of Wales to open the New North Docks in 1881, and such first-lieutenants as used to handle the British frigates and corvettes in olden times would have nearly gone out of their minds to see the slow cautious way in which the men laid out on the yards, and the prudent deliberation with which they clung to the ratlins when laying down from aloft.

Officers of the American navy are now probably, as a class, more carefully and thoroughly educated than those of any other national marine, at least in the theory of their profession, but there is great scarcity of native seamen, and it is not too much to say that there is not now a single ship on the United States Navy List which would be classed at all among the effective naval forces of any European Power, and the United States could not send a squadron to sea upon a sudden emergency equal in the character of the ships to the fleet which even the little Republic of Chili had in commission during the late war with Peru.

In fact, the United States appear to have voluntarily abandoned their claim to be included among the naval, or even the maritime, Powers. The military marine has been suffered to fall below that of almost every other country; and such is the lack of mercantile ships, that the great staples produced in such prolific abundance in the vast territory of the Union would never reach a foreign market if dependent upon American vessels alone for transportation. England has, in fact, appropriated almost the entire carrying trade of the United States; and the splendid steamships which issue from English ports, and the wealth of British steamship companies, furnish a measure of Britain's profit and America's loss from the apathy of the United States Government in respect to its maritime interests.

If this indifference to naval equality with other countries was the result of a well-considered policy of economy, or arose from confidence in the ability to make good the deficiency by a great effort in case of need, it would be intelligible, although of doubtful wisdom; but ships fit to meet the requirements of modern warfare cannot be built hurriedly, and hasty preparation always involves waste of material and extravagant expenditure.

The United States Government, through a combative but indiscreet Secretary of State, has quite lately reannounced its purpose to insist upon the application of the "Monroe doctrine," with special reference to the Panama Canal and the Chileno-Peruvian embroglio. To make remonstrances effective, either at the Isthmus of Darien or on the coast of Chili, would require the presence of a strong fleet of ships fully up to the modern type; and the United States have none of that kind. Governments who persistently keep their naval and military forces at a low point of strength and efficiency should also practise a modest and inoffensive diplomacy, because otherwise their declarations will either be treated with indifference, or they are liable at any time to receive a rebuff which would wound the national pride and bring upon the responsible Ministry the indignant reproaches of the people.

The "Monroe doctrine" as lately enunciated would surprise its author, who probably never dreamed of so broad an application of its meaning. But if the United States seriously purpose to undertake the sole guarantee of the highway between the two great oceans, and aspire to be the only arbiters in matters affecting the interests of the numerous American States, it is indispensable that they be able to place a powerful fleet at the required spot and at the critical moment.

England's right of way through the Suez Canal would not be worth the value of her shares in the capital stock of the company, if it was not thought that she could hold the two ends of the canal against all comers. A British Minister will probably never issue a circular manifesto to inform Europe that no one must attempt to block the way, but the Admiralty continue to lay down and to launch such vessels as the *Northampton, Thunderer,*

Polyphemus, Dreadnought, Edinburgh, Ajax, Colossus, Majestic, etc., and everyone understands that to interfere would involve the absolute consequence of a hard struggle, to say the least.

In these times of great armaments, nations who wish to advance their influence, maintain their prestige or even to take part in international discussions with the expectation of being listened to with respect, must demonstrate that they are prepared for attack as well as for defence, that they can strike as well as parry. Those who are content to make peaceful progress in wealth and domestic comfort, may possibly be left to enjoy their freedom and their gains; but then they must not attempt the *rôle* of dictators, nor challenge attack by a pretence of aggressive strength which they take no pains to develop, and which all the world knows they do not possess.

NOTE TO PAGE 45

After the departure of the *Alabama* from Liverpool and her equipment as a Confederate vessel-of-war was publicly known, it was often stated that the Messrs. Laird had been guilty of a violation of law in building her. In consequence of such reports, those gentlemen published a letter in the *Times,* dated 25th of May, 1869, which contained copies of the following documents and opinions of counsel:

'I am of opinion that Messrs. Laird had a right to build the ship which has since been called the *Alabama* in the manner they did, and that they committed no offence against either the common law or the Foreign Enlistment Act, with reference to that ship. I am of opinion that the simple building of a ship, even although the ship be of a kind apparently adapted for warlike purposes, and delivering such ship to a purchaser in an English port, even although the purchaser is suspected or known to be the agent of a foreign belligerent Power, does not constitute an offence against the Foreign Enlistment Act (59 Geo. III., c. 60, s. 7) on the part of the builder, unless the builder makes himself a party to the equipping of the vessel for warlike purposes. The *Alabama,* indeed, appears to me to have been equipped at the Azores, and not in England at all.

"GEORGE MELLISH.

"3, Harcourt Buildings, 6th February, 1863.

"We entirely concur in the opinion given by Mr. Mellish on the statements laid before him, and our opinion would not be altered if the fact were that Messrs. Laird Brothers knew they were building the *Alabama* for an agent of the Confederate Government.

"(Signed)   H. M. CAIRNS.

"JAMES KEMPLAY.

"17th April, 1863."

Opinion of Lord Chief Baron Pollock on the trial of the *Alexandra,* June, 1863:

"Many allusions in the course of this case had been made to the *Alabama;* but he held that as that vessel left Liverpool unarmed, and as a simple ship, she committed no unlawful act; and we had nothing to do with the fact that at a subsequent period she was armed and converted into a vessel-of-war at Terceira."

Letter from Lord Clarendon to Mr. Adams, 2nd December, 1865, quoted by Earl Russell in his speech, 27th March, 1868:

"It is nevertheless my duty, in closing this correspondence, to observe that no armed vessel departed during the war from a British port to cruise against the commerce of the United States."

Sir Roundel Palmer, Solicitor General, speech in the House of Commons, 27th March, 1863:

"It was not till the *Alabama* reached the Azores that she received her stores, her captain, or her papers, and that she hoisted the Confederate flag. It is not true that she departed from the shores of this country as a ship-of-war."

It will be perceived from the foregoing that Messrs. Laird were well supported in the view that they were acting in strict conformity with law when they built the ship afterwards called the *Alabama,* but this whole subject is dealt with in another chapter.

Mr. George Mellish, Sir Hugh Cairns, and Mr. James Kemplay, are well known to have been leaders of great eminence at the English Bar, and Sir Hugh Cairns (now Earl Cairns) has since been Lord Chancellor of England.

CHAPTER III

Financial embarrassments of the Confederate Agents.—Incomplete organization of the Confederate Executive at this period.—The financial arrangements of the Confederate States in Europe.—Incompleteness of the instructions of the Naval Representative, and insufficiency of the arrangements to meet financial requirements.—Purchase and equipment of the Fingal, *afterwards the* Atlanta.—*Shipment of war material.—Mr. Low, second officer of the* Fingal.—*An unfortunate start.—The island of Terceira.—The crew agree to run the blockade.—Arrival in the Savannah river. The state of the Southern forces.—Correspondence concerning the future operations of the* Fingal.—*Enlargement of powers as Naval Representative in Europe.—Flag-officer Josiah Tattnall.—Conversion of the* Fingal *into the armour-clad* Atlanta.—*Her engagement with and capture by two United States "Monitors."—Return to England.*

The narrative of the *Bermuda's** second voyage, the account of her capture and condemnation by the Prize Court at Philadelphia, and the remarks upon the general policy of the United States in the practice of their maritime rights as a belligerent, which occupy much of the last chapter, have somewhat anticipated the precise order of events. But the naval operations of the Confederate States in Europe were full of complications, and

---

* Captain Tessier, who commanded the *Bermuda* on the occasion of her successful voyage to Savannah in 1861, was not in her at the time of her capture, or the result would probably have been less disastrous.

gave rise to many questions affecting international duties, as well as international comity, and it will save both time and space, and will, I think, be more impressive, and also more systematic and instructive, to treat such questions, as a general rule, subjectively, and to explain and discuss them when they appear to have a natural connection with a special event in the narrative, than to postpone them for more formal and exclusive treatment in separate chapters.

The *Bermuda* made her first and only voyage to a Confederate port in August–September, 1861, and she took to Savannah the first shipment of war material from Europe on behalf of the Confederate Government. I reported to the Secretary of the Navy by that vessel the particulars of the *Alabama* and *Florida*, advised him of the contracts which had been made for general naval supplies, called attention to the financial difficulties, and informed him that it would probably be necessary to buy a steamer and return to the Confederate States in her myself, with military stores, as well as for further consultation and reconsideration of my instructions. There were at that early date numerous agents of the United States in England, who seemed in no way desirous to conceal their operations. They went about their business with the air of men who were sure of their position, and who neither anticipated nor feared interference or opposition. They were well provided with money, or satisfactory bank-credits, and they rapidly swept the gun market of well-nigh every weapon, whether good or bad. The Confederate agents were forced from want of means to be content with moderate purchases; but they made large contracts for forward delivery, at first on the credit of Messrs. Fraser, Trenholm and Co., and then, when remittances began to arrive, upon the confidence they had already won by prompt payment, and the assurance they were able to give that the Government had made suitable arrangements to meet all liabilities, and to place their bankers in funds. There was always, however, much perplexity and embarrassment from lack of ready money. At one time, in September, 1863, I was forced to report to the Navy Department that the outstanding contracts would require £700,000 in excess of the amount held at that date by the financial agents, and the War Department was rarely, if ever, able to keep pace with its requirements. The compulsory sale of ships that could not be got to sea because of the prohibition of her Majesty's Government more than once supplied the means of continuing purchases and shipments of war material which otherwise could not have been bought.

The home authorities pressed us to hurry forward supplies, and I was urged to place and to keep cruisers at sea, but they appreciated the difficulties, and in looking over the correspondence now, I can find no unreasonable complaints, and no insinuations even, that more could have been effected than was being done.

It has been said that the first remittance from the Navy Department was received July 27, 1861. The funds were forwarded in the form of sterling bills and bank-credits, but the aggregate amount was not sufficient to cover the orders for naval stores already placed, and the price of the two ships (*Alabama* and *Florida*), and no additional funds were received, nor any advices on the subject, until October, hence no further contracts could be made at that time. Meanwhile the work upon the ships was progressing rapidly. It was estimated that the *Florida* would be finished in February–March and the *Alabama* in June, 1862, and such arrangements had been made with the builders that my personal supervision was not necessary, and, moreover, frequent personal attendance at the building yards was not prudent.

The Consular agents of the United States had already begun to practise an inquisitive system of espionage, and it was soon manifest that the movements of those who were supposed to be agents of the Confederate Government were closely and vigilantly watched. Men known to be private detectives in the employ of the United States Consul were often seen prowling about the dockyards, and questioning the *employés* of Messrs. Laird and Miller in reference to the two vessels, whose somewhat peculiar type had attracted notice, and at a very early date it became manifest that her Majesty's Government would take a rigid view of the Foreign Enlistment Act, and that there would be very great difficulty and expense in getting ships to sea especially adapted in their construction and general outfit for purposes of war. The financial question was, however, the greatest cause of perplexity at that time. The rapidly advancing rate of exchange clearly indicated that the Confederate Government would soon be compelled to resort to some other mode of placing funds in Europe than by sterling bills. There was also much delay in communicating by letter, and the danger of miscarriage or capture made it hazardous to write fully and clearly upon subjects it was vitally important to explain and discuss without reserve.

Very soon after the beginning of hostilities the policy of buying up the whole of the cotton at the South, on account of the Government, and forwarding it as quickly as possible to Europe, was suggested to the executive authorities, and was no doubt earnestly considered by them. If 200,000 bales of cotton could have been shipped to Liverpool during the first year of the war, the financial position of the Confederate States would no doubt have been infinitely strengthened, and the first levies might have been put into the field in such a state of efficiency, as regards clothing and equipment, as to have greatly affected the results of the struggle. There have been many persons in the South who have severely criticized the Confederate Government for not adopting the above policy at the beginning; but those who were early employed in important offices connected with the supply of the military and naval wants of the country, and whose faculties were keenly aroused and directed to the consideration of the ways and means, are conscious that there were great, if not insurmountable obstacles to the fulfilment of that policy when it was first suggested. During the greater part of the time which intervened from the secession of South Carolina to the beginning of hostilities, not quite five months, there was no general Executive Government at all. The several States withdrew from the Union at different periods. Each in turn was fully occupied with her own internal affairs, and none were at all sure which, if any, of the neighbouring States would secede, or whether after seceding they would be willing to unite in a joint Confederacy for a common purpose. The Provisional Government was not formed at Montgomery until February, 1861.

On the 13th of April, barely two months after, when the Executive Departments were still in the very throes of organization, with the whole machinery of Government new and untried, without a single shipyard or military arsenal in working order, and with no military forces except the State volunteer corps, and those not yet regularly enrolled into the general service, hostilities were precipitated by the events at Charleston.

While affairs were thus coming to a crisis, the ships lying in the cotton ports took in full cargoes and sailed; but they were of course loaded on private account, and when they left, few, if any, came in their places. The mercantile world, more astute than the politicians, foresaw the coming storm, and did not care to expose their ships to its fury; hence the vessels that came to Southern ports immediately before the attack upon Fort Sumter made haste to load and get away.

The authorities at Montgomery did not prevent their departure, and the United States granted some respite before closing the ports by a declaration of blockade. There were several lines of steamers plying between Boston, New York, Philadelphia, and Southern ports, both on the Atlantic coast and the Gulf of Mexico; but their movements were so arranged that at the critical moment they were almost to a ship either at the Northern ports or *en route* for them, and at the time when actual hostilities began, there was scarcely an available ship of any description in Southern waters.

It has already been mentioned that the steamship *Bienville* was permitted to leave New Orleans on the day after the attack upon Fort Sumter, and I know of only three regular sea-going steamships which were still at Southern ports a month after that event. One of the number was bought by the Confederate Government, and was commissioned by the late Admiral Semmes as the *Sumter;* a second, the *Nashville,* was also bought by the Government, and made a short cruise to England *viâ* Bermuda, and back to a Confederate port, under the command of Captain R. B. Pegram; and the third was bought by Messrs. John Fraser and Co., of Charleston, and sailed from Wilmington, North Carolina, for Liverpool, with a cargo of cotton, rosin, etc., on their account. There were two or three paddle-steamers at Richmond, suited to the coasting trade, but not for foreign voyages, and they were taken up by the Navy Department.

I do not state positively that the above were the only steamers remaining in Southern ports at the time mentioned, but I think that if there had been any others suitable for deep-sea voyages, the fact would not be forgotten by me now, and I feel sure that they would have been promptly and eagerly appropriated by the Confederate Navy Department. Whether, therefore, the Provisional Government at Montgomery approved of the proposition to buy and ship the cotton still remaining at the plantations and other interior points or not, there can be no doubt that the means for shipping it in large quantities were wholly wanting. Private persons and several mercantile firms made many ventures to the Bahamas and Havana during the first six months of the war with no better craft than the ordinary river steamer, but undertakings quite in keeping with mercantile usage, and justified by the ordinary commercial considerations of profit and loss, are inadmissible—indeed, they are impracticable—as State enterprises, for the sufficient reason that the public Departments are enveloped in legal as well as traditional routine. National funds can only be applied in accordance with legislative appropriation, and therefore schemes which may be put in course of effectual progress at the moment of suggestion by a private firm or corporation, can only be executed by the State after due consideration by two or more branches of the Government, which necessarily involves delay, and often such modifications of the original project as to lessen the chances of success, or at least to increase the difficulties to be overcome. Many persons will remember how quickly, and on what a stupendous scale, the Government at Washington hastened to prepare for the invasion of the Confederate States when the surrender of Fort Sumter ended the period of suspense and the state of war began.

The so-called Democratic Party at the North had been generally favourable to the Southern view of "State rights," and was strongly opposed to that party which, by a division among its opponents, had succeeded in electing Mr. Abraham Lincoln to the Presidency. There had been also a strong minority of the dominant or Republican Party, who, while reprobating the action of the South, and denouncing the principle of secession as revolutionary and unauthorized, were yet opposed to the exercise of any coercive measures for the maintenance of the Union.

The Cabinet at Washington, the party leaders and the party press, combined to arouse and direct public sentiment, and to bring the people of the North to the conviction that the right of secession, if once admitted, would logically and inevitably tend to complete dissolution. They addressed themselves to the fears, the prejudices, and the patriotism of the North, and with such success that, when President Lincoln issued his proclamation calling for troops to "avenge the insult to the national flag at Charleston," and to "restore the Union" (to use the phraseology of the period), there was a prompt and ample response. Party distinctions and party principles ceased to restrain men from joining together for the common purpose of restoring and maintaining the Union, and large masses of troops were soon gathering around Washington, along the Potomac and the northern frontier of Virginia. To prepare for the threatened attack, and to provide the means for an adequate resistance, must have strained the resources and taxed the administrative faculties of the Provisional Government of the Confederate States to the fullest tension.

Those who wish to form just and impartial opinions of public men, and who aspire to write the history of great public events, must first look for the facts; then they must give a fair, judicial consideration to all the circumstances. They must be careful not to infer that a course of action which commends itself when viewed in the light of accomplished events was practicable; or, if practicable when first suggested, whether something else of more pressing and essential importance did not necessarily demand precedence. The people of the South will probably admit that it was of more vital consequence to keep the Federal armies out of Richmond in 1861 than to effect even the important purpose of transferring the cotton crop to Europe. An equitable investigation of the facts, and due consideration of all the circumstances, the insufficient means of transport by land, and the still greater lack of means of transport by sea—will demonstrate that both enterprises could not have been accomplished at the same time, and the project of perfecting the financial arrangements abroad was unavoidably delayed. At a later period of the war the Government made great efforts to forward cotton and other products of the South to Europe. The Confederate Congress passed an Act authorizing the Treasury Department to buy and ship whatever staples were readily convertible into money in the European markets, and agents were sent into the interior, and were stationed at the seaports to carry out that purpose. A special agent of the Treasury was sent to Europe, with power to make contracts with banking or commercial houses to supply the money necessary to build steamers suitable for blockade running; and he brought over orders from the Navy Department directing me to look after the designing and construction of the ships, and to see that they were properly fitted for the proposed work. The Treasury agent was Mr. Colin J. McRae, and he made capital contracts with two or more firms, who agreed to advance the money for a commission of ten per cent., and to be recouped from the proceeds of the cotton or other products brought out by the ships themselves. The precise arrangement was that the ships were to be employed in running the blockade, the inward cargoes to be exclusively on Government account, and the outward cargoes half for the Government, and half to go towards payment of the ships, until the whole amount advanced, together with the stipulated commission, was cleared off. Until paid for in full, each steamer was to be registered in the name of a nominee of the firm who had advanced the money, and then she was to become the property of the Confederate Government. Time being of incalculable importance, four paddle-steamers, the best that could be found, were bought to begin with; and ten were laid down, carefully designed to get high speed on a light draft of water. Afterwards several larger and powerful screw-steamers were designed, but these latter were not finished in time to perform any service. One of the smaller class of paddle-steamers brought out on her first voyage 700 bales of unpressed cotton, on a draft of six feet, which was a very satisfactory performance, with cotton at two shillings and sixpence per pound.

Those who have most sharply criticized the Executive Departments of the Confederate Government, and have especially charged them with want of foresight and promptness in the management of the finances, are chiefly Southerners, who must have been impelled by their impatience to expect striking results without taking due heed of the pressure upon the several Departments, and the extreme efforts they were so suddenly called upon to make. Although the Confederate Government was never recognised by any foreign Power, yet when the Treasury Department made a bid in Europe for a loan of £3,000,000, five times that amount was subscribed. There was for a short time what is called a "spurt" in Confederate Bonds, and they actually rose to a premium of five per cent. upon the price at which the loan was placed, and they stood for several months at a higher figure than the bonds of the United States. This is an interesting fact, although it is of no financial importance now; at any rate, it may be fairly taken as an offset to the allegations of the grumblers. Reverting now to the actual state of the finances at the beginning of the operations in Europe, it is proper to remark, *en passant,* that before I was sent from Montgomery the difficulties were foreseen in kind, but not in degree, and it soon became evident that the full purposes contemplated in my original instructions could not be accomplished without a modification of plans and a well-arranged system for providing funds with certainty and regularity. After considering all the circumstances as they were at the time when the first remittance arrived (July, 1861), and taking also into account the fact that personal supervision of the ships under construction was neither necessary nor advisable, it was thought that I should communicate personally with the Government at Richmond, and in September, 1861, I submitted a proposal to the officers representing the War Office, that we should contribute equally from the funds of the two Departments, buy a fast steamer, and that I should go into a Confederate port with her myself, in order to report the precise condition of affairs, as well as to take in the war supplies which were then ready for delivery, and which we knew were greatly needed. We had a consultation with the financial agents, and the proposal was not only approved, but I was urged to carry it out at once. Going upon such an expedition was a deviation from my instructions, and it was also a diversion of a considerable sum of money from the original purpose to which it had been appropriated; but the position of affairs was critical, and I had been authorized to exercise a wide discretion when it appeared necessary to effect an important purpose. However, before taking any decisive course, the proposition was referred to the Commissioners, who expressed their full concurrence, and one of them, the Hon. Dudley Mann, wrote me spontaneously an official letter, virtually offering to assume the responsibility, so far as he could. I immediately bought the screw-steamship *Fingal,* built on the Clyde for the Highland trade. She was a new ship, had made but one or two trips to the North of Scotland, was in good order, well found, and her log gave her speed as thirteen knots in good steaming weather. I had to take her as she stood, with all outfit on board, and was amused to find, in the inventory of cabin-stores, six dozen toddy glasses, with ladles to match. Each glass had the capacity of about a half-pint, and they were hard and thick and heavy enough to serve for grape-shot, in case of need. The ship was placed on a loading-berth at Greenock, and the goods were forwarded to her as rapidly as possible, partly by rail, and partly by a steamer from London. It was necessary to act with caution and secrecy, because the impression had already got abroad that the Confederate Government was trying to fit out ships in England to cruise against American commerce, and during the whole period of the war all vessels taking arms on board, or cases supposed to contain arms or ammunition, were closely watched by agents and spies of the United States Consuls, who frequently sent affidavits to the Customs authorities, affirming the belief that the ships receiving such materials were intended to be armed, and thus often effected their detention, and on several occasions their seizure.

Colonel Edward C. Anderson, of the Confederate army, had been sent to England in July, 1861, to communicate with Major Huse, and to look generally into the affairs of the War Department. Colonel Anderson was directed to remain in Europe if his services seemed to be necessary; but he found that Major Huse had everything in good working train, and was manifestly capable of conducting the operations alone, so he determined to return to the Confederate States, and the *Fingal* expedition afforded a favourable opportunity. Two Charleston gentlemen (Messrs. Charles Foster and Moffat), detained in Europe at the beginning of the war, and unable to return through the United States, had consulted me about the best means of getting to their homes, and I arranged to take them in the *Fingal;* and Dr. Holland, a spirited Texan, who had served in the United States army during the Mexican War, and wished to go to Richmond, was notified to be ready for a move at short notice, and was requested to prepare a big medicine-chest and a case of surgical instruments to take with him. As the *Fingal* was the first ship that ran the blockade solely on Government account, and her subsequent fate as the Confederate ironclad *Atlanta* gives her some historical importance, the particulars of her cargo, and the incidents of her voyage, will probably be of some interest. In 1861 the English army weapon was still the muzzle-loading Enfield rifle. Prussia was adopting the needle-gun, and France was preparing to exchange her old arm for the *chassepot,* but no breech-loaders could be got either in England or on the Continent, except as samples, and the purchases for the Confederate States were of the muzzle-loading type.

The shipment *per Fingal* was:

On account of the War Department—10,000 Enfield rifles, 1,000,000 ball cartridges, and 2,000,000 percussion caps; 3,000 cavalry sabres, with suitable accoutrements, a large quantity of material for clothing, and a large supply of medical stores.

On account of the Navy Department—1,000 short rifles, with cutlass bayonets, and 1,000 rounds of ammunition per rifle; 500 revolvers, with suitable ammunition; two 4½-inch muzzle-loading rifled guns, with traversing carriages, all necessary gear, and 200 made-up cartridges, shot and shell, per gun; two breech-loading 2½-inch steel-rifled guns for boats or field service, with 200 rounds of ammunition per gun; 400 barrels of coarse cannon-powder, and a large quantity of made-up clothing for seamen.

For the State of Georgia—3,000 Enfield rifles.

For the State of Lousiana—1,000 Enfield rifles.

No single ship ever took into the Confederacy a cargo so entirely composed of military and naval supplies, and the pressing need of them made it necessary to get the *Fingal* off with quick despatch, and to use every possible effort to get her into a port having railway communication through to Virginia, because the Confederate army, then covering Richmond, was very poorly armed, and was distressingly deficient in all field necessaries.

Shortly before the *Fingal* was ready for sea, I was joined by Mr. John Low, who was a Liverpool man by birth, but he had lived several years in Savannah, and was there at the beginning of the war. His purpose at that time was to remain permanently in Savannah; he was ardently attached to the South, and at the beginning of hostilities he went to Virginia in a cavalry corps from Georgia, but subsequently came over to England to join me for special service. Mr. Low had been bred to the sea in the British mercantile marine, and as he arrived at a very opportune time, I sent him instanter to Greenock to ship as second officer of the *Fingal*.

The *Fingal* was kept under the British flag for obvious reasons, and it was therefore necessary to employ a captain holding a Board of Trade certificate to clear her outward, and to ship the crew in accordance with the Merchant Shipping Act. Some pains were taken to engage good engineers and a few leading men, but no hint was given that the ship would go further than Bermuda and Nassau. Mr. Low proved to be an able seaman, a reliable and useful officer in every situation. The character of his services, and his advancement in the Confederate navy, will often have conspicuous and commendatory mention in this narrative. The *Fingal* was ready for sea about October 8th. Messrs. Foster and Moffat joined her at Greenock, and the captain was ordered to sail as soon as possible, and to call off Holyhead to take Colonel Anderson, Dr. Holland, and myself on board, it not being thought prudent to show ourselves at or about the ship until she was clear of the Custom House.

On the 11th we went to Holyhead, and learned by telegram that the *Fingal* was off from Greenock.

During the night it came on to blow a hard gale, which continued for two or three days, with thick weather and much rain. We could get no tidings of the ship, and although I felt reasonably satisfied that she had put into some harbour of shelter, yet the uncertainty and delay were perplexing. During the 14th the gale broke. Towards evening the weather was fine, and we had hopes of seeing or hearing from the missing ship on the next day. At about 4 A.M. on the 15th, I was aroused by a loud knock at my bedroom door, and a house-porter came in with a dark lantern, followed by Mr. Low. It had been raining, and Low had on a "sou-wester," and a long painted canvas coat, which were dripping with wet. I was only half awake. In the dim light of the lantern the figure before me loomed up like a huge octopus, or some other marine monster, and I was startled by a sepulchral voice which seemed to be mumbling under the breast of the peajacket like the last tremulous quivering of a thunderclap. But my ear caught the sound of a few articulate words, among which *"Fingal,"* "brig," "collision," "sunk," were fearfully jumbled together. It is astounding with what electric velocity the mind acts in the few seconds of awaking when one is suddenly aroused from sleep. Before I could leap out of bed a painful scene of wreck and disaster passed vividly through my brain, and I fancied the *Fingal* at the bottom of Holyhead harbour, with the fishes swimming among the shattered Enfields, sipping the mixture of sea-water and gunpowder through their gills, and wondering what it all meant. Low was, however, steady, cool, and unimpassioned, and put the facts into my mind without waste of words, and they may be briefly summarized thus: The *Fingal* was creeping cautiously round the breakwater when she suddenly came upon a brig at anchor, with no light up. The steamer had barely steerage way, and the engines were quickly reversed, but her sharp stem took the brig's starboard quarter. There was just a slight sound, like the quick snap of a gun-hammer upon the uncapped nipple, then a shout from the deck of the unhappy craft, and before a boat could be lowered she went down all standing. This is what usually happens when an iron steamer comes in contact with a wooden ship.

We roused up Colonel Anderson and Dr. Holland and got afloat as soon as possible.

Day was just breaking when we got alongside of the *Fingal*, and in the dim twilight we could see the upper spars of the brig standing straight up out of the water, with the bunt of the main top-gallant sail just a-wash. The vessel proved to be the Austrian brig *Siccardi*. She was loaded with coal, which accounts for her going down so quickly and standing upright afterwards.

It was manifestly out of the question to remain where we were. Customs officers would soon be on board; the *Fingal* would be detained to settle, or give security for a satisfactory settlement, with the consignees of the *Siccardi*; Colonel Anderson and I could hardly hope to escape notice; affidavits would be prepared by the United States Consul affirming the *Fingal* to be a suspicious vessel, and then there would surely be inquiry, further detention, and perhaps a final breakup of the voyage. I thought of the rifles and sabres in the hold, and the ill-armed pickets on the Potomac, waiting and longing for them, and told the captain to weigh anchor at once.

There was no wish to defraud the owners of the *Siccardi* of any compensation they were entitled to. I wrote a hasty letter to Messrs. Fraser, Trenholm and Co., briefly reporting the circumstances and asking them to find out the consignees of the brig and make the best possible arrangement with them.* The letter was despatched on shore by a boat we had engaged to bring our luggage off, and the *Fingal* was round the point of the breakwater, and steaming down Channel, before the accident at the mouth of the harbour was known to anyone who would have had authority to stop her.

For several days after leaving Holyhead we had fine weather, and were well satisfied in most respects with the ship. She was staunch, comfortable, and well-fitted in all particulars, but in the anxiety to get as much in her as possible, she had been loaded too deep, and I found that we could not get a higher speed than nine knots, which was rather disappointing, in view of a possible chase between Bermuda and the coast. About the 19th of October we caught a gale from the south-west veering to north and north-east. The sea was so heavy that we were compelled to ease the engines, and in a measure lay-to under fore and aft sails. While the gale was still blowing, the steward informed me that the fresh water seemed to be very low in the big iron tank which held the main supply. Upon examination it was found that we had only one or at most two days' supply left. It seems that after filling up the water-tank at Greenock, the ship continued

---

* Messrs. Fraser, Trenholm and Co. communicated with the consignees very promptly. A friendly arbitration was agreed to, and the affair was satisfactorily settled.

to load for some days, and the crew, as well as a large number of stevedores employed in stowing the cargo, were permitted to use and to waste the water at will. When ready for sea, it did not occur to the captain to sound the tanks and fill them up. I do not wish to injure the captain by mentioning his name. He probably acted according to his lights, which were dull. He was very inefficient, and was of no use to us except as a medium of communication with Customs and other officials. The *Fingal* had no separate condensing apparatus, but fortunately the gale was moderating, and the wind was hauling to the north and east, and so we bore up for Praya, a bay and village on the north-east side of the island of Terceira, where we found good water, fruit, vegetables, fresh meat, etc.

This necessary deviation from our direct voyage, and the consequent delay, were not in the end without a compensating advantage. The bay afforded good anchorage, and the whole neighbourhood was so quiet and retired, so isolated from Europe, that I could not fail to note its fitness for a place of rendezvous at which to collect our cruisers with their tenders. Subsequently the *Alabama* was brought to this very spot and armed without hindrance. Perhaps if it had not been for the captain's forgetfulness in the matter of the *Fingal*'s water supply, we might have gone to some less favourable place with the *Alabama* and failed in our purpose. The efforts of life in all undertakings are made up of alternate failure and success, and all that can be hoped for is a favourable balance-sheet at the end.

The *Fingal* proceeded on her voyage from Terceira, and arrived at Bermuda on the 2nd of November. Here we had the pleasure to find the Confederate States ship *Nashville,* Captain R. B. Pegram, from whom we learned much about the state of affairs in the beleaguered Confederacy. The *Nashville* was a paddle-steamer, built for the coasting trade between New York and Charleston. It has been already mentioned that she was bought by the Navy Department, and her appearance abroad was probably intended as a mere demonstration to prove the inefficiency of the blockade, and to make an exhibit of the Confederate flag upon the high seas and in Europe, because she was weakly armed and dependent upon her engines alone for motion. Nevertheless, she captured and burned the American ship *Harvey Birch* in the English Channel. There had been an original purpose to send the Confederate Commissioners, Messrs. Mason and Slidell, to Europe in the *Nashville,* but this intention was abandoned, and those gentlemen, with their suites, ran the blockade in a small steamer from Charleston, and proceeded to Havana. Captain Pegram handed me a despatch from the Hon. S. R. Mallory, Secretary of the Navy, acknowledging my reports sent *per* steamship *Bermuda* in August. He approved my contracts for the *Florida* and *Alabama,* and for naval ordnance stores, and also the proposition I had suggested of buying a steamer and returning in her to the Confederate States with supplies and for consultation. He furthermore informed me that he had sent out by the *Nashville* several pilots, and that Captain Pegram would let me have any one or more of them I might require. Mr. John Makin, a pilot for Savannah and the inlets to the southward, was transferred to the *Fingal.*

We were detained several days at Bermuda. The United States Consul suspected the ultimate object of the *Fingal's* voyage, and he did his best to put obstacles in the way of our getting coal and other supplies, and employed men to tamper with the crew and alarm them, and persuade them to leave the ship. However, the local merchants and the people generally were very friendly, and we got at last all that was wanted, and sailed for the coast on the afternoon of the 7th of November.

Up to the time of our departure from Bermuda, not a word had been said to a member of the crew, nor even to the captain, about the purpose to run the blockade, and the ship was cleared out from St. George's for Nassau. We had, however, several very active intelligent men forward, among them one named Freemantle, who followed me back to Europe and made the cruise in the *Alabama* as captain's coxswain. During the passage from England I had kept an eye to the men, and Low had been much with them as an officer of the ship, and we felt pretty sure that "Jack" had his suspicions. That they should have resisted the persuasions and warnings of the United States Consul at St. George's was therefore a gratifying evidence of their willingness to take part in a little exciting adventure.

It was especially important to know whether the "engineer department" could be relied upon, and I had often gone into the engine-room to have a talk with the chief. His name was McNair, a silent, steady, reliable Scot, immovable and impassive as the Grampian Hills when it was proper to stand fast, prompt, quick, and energetic when it was necessary to act. He was one of that thoughtful class of men who seem to be always thinking that something unexpected may happen, and to be preparing for the difficulty. From the very first I felt sure of McNair, and never parted from him until the *Alabama* was off on her cruise. In fitting out that ship he was of great service, and he had charge of her engines until she was joined at Terceira by Captain Semmes and his regular staff of officers.

The day after leaving Bermuda it was necessary to put the ship's head in the direction of the actual port of destination, and of course the men at the wheel, and in fact all on board, would soon perceive that we were not steering the course for Nassau. It would not have been fair to conceal the object of the voyage from the men until a critical moment, and it would also have been imprudent to go on to the coast without knowing their minds, because they had not agreed to undertake any such risk.

I determined, therefore, to settle the matter there and then, and sent for all hands to come aft to the bridge. I told them very briefly "that they had shipped in a British port, to make a voyage in a British ship to one or more British islands and back again to England; that I had no right to take them anywhere else without their consent, and I did not mean to use either force or undue pressure to make them do anything not set out in the shipping articles, but I thought they must have suspected that there was some other purpose in the voyage than a cruise to Bermuda and the Bahamas, and the time had arrived when it was both safe and proper for me to tell them the real port of destination, which was Savannah, and of course this meant a breach of blockade, with the risk of capture and some rough treatment as prisoners-of-war." I added, "If you are not willing to go on, say so now, and I will take the ship to Nassau and get other men who will go; but if you are ready and willing to risk the venture, remember that it is a fresh engagement and a final one, from which there must be no backing out."

I had thought over what to say, and was prepared with a few exhilarating and persuasive phrases; but I caught Freemantle's eye and saw that several of the men were whispering together. It flashed across my mind at once that no further talk was necessary, and I put the question plainly, "Will you go?" to which there was a prompt and unanimous consent. I thanked them, but said there was still something to explain, which I did to the following effect:

"The United States have been compelled to buy up steamers from the merchant service for blockaders. Many of them are neither so strong nor so efficient in any way as this ship, and they are not heavily armed. If we should fall in with any blockaders off Savannah at all, they are likely to be of that class, and Colonel Anderson and I, who represent the Confederate Government, and the gentlemen passengers, who are Southern men, do not feel disposed to give up this valuable and important cargo to a ship not strong enough to render resistance useless, or to open boats that may attempt to board us. So long as the *Fingal* is under the British flag, we have no right to fire a shot, but I have a bill of sale in my pocket, and can take delivery from the captain on behalf of the Confederate Navy Department at any moment. This I propose to do, if there should appear to be any likelihood of a collision with a blockader, and I want to know if you are willing under such circumstances to help in defending the ship?"

They answered "Yes" to a man. These preliminaries being satisfactorily settled, all hands were set briskly to work to arm the ship. We mounted the two 4½-inch rifled guns in the forward gangway ports, and the two steel boat-guns on the quarterdeck. We got up a sufficient number of rifles and revolvers, with a good supply of ammunition, and converted the "ladies' saloon" into an armoury, shell-room, and magazine.

The cases containing the made-up cartridges for the guns were stowed out of easy reach, so we hoisted out of the hold a few barrels of powder and a bale of flannel, and made ten or fifteen cartridges for each gun. Colonel Anderson had passed a good many years of his early life in the United States navy, and although he had been long out of the service, his "right hand had not forgot its cunning." He and I cut out the cylinders, the other passengers helped at the sewing, and the *Fingal* was on the next day ready to beat off a boat attack, or even to exchange shots with an impromptu blockader on a dark night, and thus perhaps prevent her closing. Freemantle and two or three others of the crew were old naval men, and took the leading positions at the guns. We had two or three drills, and found that we could handle the "battery" satisfactorily.

I had a talk with McNair after settling everything with the men. Although he did not say so, I felt sure from his manner that he had been expecting the information, because he received it quite as a matter of course, and told me that he had been putting aside a few tons of the nicest and cleanest coal, and if I could give him time just before getting on the coast to haul fires in one boiler at a time, and run the scrapers through the flues, he thought he might drive the ship, deep as she was, at the rate of eleven knots for a spurt of a few hours. These preparations seemed to put all hands in good spirits; indeed, the men were quite jolly over the prospect.

On the 11th McNair got the chance to clean his flues. It was my purpose to make the land at the entrance to Warsaw Sound, through which Makin said he could take the ship by inland creeks into the Savannah river, and the course was shaped so that at noon on the 11th we should be on the parallel of Warsaw. From that position we steered in on a due-west course, and timed the speed to make the land about 3 A.M., or at any rate before daylight.

The moon set early, but the night was clear, and there was an unusually good horizon line. Several suitable stars passed the meridian between dark and 1 A.M., and Polaris was of course available, so we were able to get the latitude every half hour, and thus to check the course. At about 1 A.M. on the 12th we got along-shore soundings inside the Gulf Stream. Up to this time it had been uncomfortably clear, with a light south-east breeze, but it now fell calm, and we could see a dark line to the westward. Makin said it was the mist over the marshes, and the land-breeze would soon bring it off to us. In half an hour or so we felt a cool damp air in our faces, then a few big drops of moisture, and we ran straight into as nice a fog as any reasonable blockade-runner could have wanted. There was not a light anywhere about the ship except in the binnacle, and that was carefully covered, so that the man at the wheel could barely look at the compass with one eye, and the engine-room hatches were well-hooded. Not a word was spoken, and there was not a sound but the throb of the engines and the slight "shir-r-r" made by the friction of the ship through the water, and these seemed muffled by the dank vaporous air.

When we got into six fathoms the engines were eased to dead slow, and we ran cautiously in by the lead, straight for the land, the object being to get in-shore of any blockaders that might be off the inlet. We supposed the ship to be drawing fifteen or sixteen feet, and we stood on into three and a quarter fathoms, when we turned her head off to the light easterly swell, and stopped the engines. The fog was as thick as, and about the colour of, mulligatawny soup, and the water alongside looked of a darkish brown. From the bridge it was just possible to make out the men standing on the forecastle and poop. We could not have been in a better position for a dash at daylight.

While we were thus lying-to and waiting, every faculty alert to catch the slightest sound, and every eye searching the fog for the first glimpse of land, or of an approaching ship, there burst upon our ears a shrill prolonged quavering shriek. The suddenness of the sound, coming upon our eagerly expectant senses, and probably much heightened in volume and force by contrast with the stillness, was startling. I am afraid to venture upon a superlative, but I may safely say it was unearthly. None of us could conceive what it was, but all thought that it was as loud and as piercing as a steam-whistle, and that it must have been heard by any blockader within five miles of us. In a moment the sound was repeated, but we were prepared, and it was this time accompanied by a flapping and rustling noise from a "hencoop" in the gangway. "It is the cock that came on board at Bermuda," said some one. Several men ran to the spot. Freemantle thrust his arm into the coop, drew out an unhappy fowl, and wrung off its head with a vicious swing. But it was the wrong one, and chanticleer crowed again defiantly. "Try again," came up in an audible whisper from under the bridge; but Freemantle's second effort was more disastrous than the first. He not only failed to seize the obnoxious screamer, but he set the whole hennery in commotion, and the "Mujan" cock, from a safe corner, crowed and croaked, and fairly chuckled over the fuss of feathers, the cackling, and the distracting strife he had aroused. At last the offending bird was caught. He died game, and made a fierce struggle for life; but Freemantle managed to catch him with a firm grip by the neck, and fetching a full arm-swing, as if heaving a twelve-pound lead, the body fell with a heavy thud upon the deck, and we were again favoured with a profound stillness.

By this time daylight began to break. Makin said the fog would settle and gather over the low marshes towards sunrise, and gradually roll off seaward before the light land-wind. I went aloft to look out for the first sight of the "inlet." Makin was right. In less than half an hour I could see the bushy tops of the tall pine-trees, then their straight slender trunks, then the brushwood, and finally the pale yellow streak of sand which formed the foreshore.

I reported this to Makin, who could not see it all from the deck, and he asked me to come down and consult. I assured him we were right abreast of Warsaw Inlet, and of this he was satisfied, but he said the buoys would all be up, and the low-lying fog would probably cover the distant leading marks, and we might go wrong in the intricate channels. He thought it would be some time before the fog would clear off to seaward, but as it was settling over the land and we would soon have a tolerably clear view in-shore, he proposed making a dash for Savannah, about 17 miles to the north and east, where he felt sure we could get in, buoys or no buoys.

In a few moments the engines were doing their best, and the ship's head was laid for the outer bar of the Savannah river. McNair fulfilled his promise, for the *Fingal* was making a good eleven knots. Meanwhile the fog continued to settle and roll off the land, and the low sandy beach, with the tall pines in the background, and a gentle surf just creaming its outer edge, was soon in full view from the deck. We skirted the shore in the least water the ship's draft permitted, and were much favoured. The land breeze dropped, and about half a mile off shore the fog hung heavily, a great grey mass, almost black at the water's edge. It served as a veil between us and any blockaders that might be enveloped in it.

We bowled along at a steady pace, and before long the beach and the line of pines trended abruptly away to the westward; we caught sight of the high brick walls of Fort Pulaski, and were off the estuary of the Savannah. In another quarter of an hour Makin had his marks on: "Starboard," "Steady at north-west by north," and the *Fingal* was over the bar and ploughing up channel, "a big bone in her mouth," the favouring fog still to the eastward, and the sheltering fort on the port bow. Before getting in range we fired a gun and hoisted the Confederate flag at the fore, which was answered from the fort. The parapet of the main works and the *glacis* of the outer were lined with men, and as we drew near we saw the caps waving, although we could not hear their cheers.

The entrance to the Savannah river is through a broad estuary, but though the expanse of water is wide, the ship channel is narrow and comparatively shoal. Nearly opposite Fort Pulaski two large wooden sailing ships had been sunk right in the fairway; but Makin thought with our draft we could probably squeeze by on either side, and he ported the helm to pass off shore of them, but just abreast of the outer ship we brought up in an oyster bank.

The tide was ebb, but the bottom was soft oozy mud, and as the ship could take no harm, we determined to let her lie as she was until we could find how it was possible to get round the obstructions. Colonel Anderson was a Savannah man, and he went on shore immediately to learn the news and to telegraph our arrival up to town.

Colonel Olmstead, the commandant of the fort, sent a boat off to the ship as soon as he perceived that we were aground, to inform us that a few days previously a large United States fleet, under Admiral Dupont, had attacked and driven the Confederate troops out of the batteries protecting Port Royal, and that place had been occupied by a strong land force. We were further informed that the Federal fleet was still at Port Royal, and that as there was interior water communication with the Savannah river, the enemy might send over small vessels or boats to cut us out; but the boarding officer was directed to say that a good look-out would be kept on the ship, and a sufficient number of men to defend her would be sent off if any such attempt should be made.

The distance from Port Royal, however, was much too far for us to be seen, and no danger was looked for from that quarter. The blockading vessels had probably been drawn off to assist in the operations at Port Royal. At any rate, we saw nothing of them, although later in the day several appeared off the outer bar. We had thus been able to effect a "breach of blockade" with no graver incident than the scrimmage with the Bermudan cock, and the men appeared to be a little disappointed at the pacific and commonplace termination of the adventure.

At about 1 P.M. three river steamboats, being the main portion of Flag-officer Tattnall's so-called fleet, came down to look after us. Lieutenant-Commanding Johnston sent us a hawser from his ship, the *Savannah,* and dragged us out of the mud. After some pulling and hauling they got the *Fingal* above the obstructions, and escorted her up to the city, abreast of which we anchored at about 4 P.M., November 12th, 1861. The same afternoon I telegraphed my arrival to the Secretary of the Navy, and next day received orders by telegraph to go on to Richmond as soon as arrangements for the discharge of the arms, etc., could be made. On the 14th Flag-officer Tattnall detailed an officer to attend to the business of the ship, and I started in company with Colonel Anderson, who was also going to Richmond to report to the War Department.

I knew from statistics and from personal knowledge of the country that the South was poor in military and naval resources, and that there had been no preparation for war, and no collection of material. But figures never carry to the senses full and clear impressions. When it is said that the drought in India has destroyed so many million tons of rice, the mind is at once impressed with the conviction that there will be a great deficit of food in Bengal; but it is only those who witness the sufferings of the famishing people who fully comprehend the melancholy import of the statement. On the route to Richmond I had ample and painful evidence of the strain which the sudden outburst of war had put upon the South, and the inadequate means to meet it.

The railways having only one line of metals, and the rolling stock barely able to satisfy the ordinary passenger and goods traffic, were already yielding to the increased wear and tear, and the heavy trains, filled with troops moving towards Virginia, and loaded with stores and supplies for the army, were dragged slowly along by the over-worked engines. The troops in the train with me were irregularly and indifferently armed, and were without uniformity of dress or equipment; but they were full of spirit, and laughed and sang songs around the impromptu fires which were quickly kindled wherever the train stopped, for we frequently waited for some purpose or other many miles from a station, often in the woods.

At a place called Goldsborough, in North Carolina, we remained for an hour or more, and while the passengers were getting dinner I heard loud singing in the street, mingled with the music of a band, and going out of the hotel I saw a long line of uncovered railway freight-trucks, with rough cross-benches uncomfortably close together, and each bench was filled with men. There was an engine at the end of the line, and I learned that the men were a regiment of North Carolinians from the Buncombe district, on the way to join the forces at Wilmington.

The troops were remarkably fine-looking men, mostly young and well-proportioned, but they were dressed in their ordinary clothing, and many had no greatcoats, although it was November, and the air was keen and at night frosty. I walked along the whole line of trucks and spoke to some of the men, and asked about their arms. Some had old-fashioned flintlock muskets, some had only double-barrel sporting guns, of course without bayonets, and a few had percussion-lock muskets. I believe twenty or thirty had the old heavy small-bore weapon called the "Mississippi rifle," but I did not see a single modern military rifle in the whole battalion. In about half an hour the train moved on, the men singing "Dixie," and the people in the street cheering.

It would hardly be possible to exaggerate the discomforts and privations to which the Southern troops were exposed during the war. At first they were wholly destitute of camp equipage, and were compelled to bivouac in the open air without tent shelter or even the comfort of covered field hospitals, and these deficiencies were never more than partially supplied. The best manhood of the South, young men of spirit and good wiry constitutions, flocked into the army, and thousands were carried off by diseases always more or less prevalent in camps, but whose virulence and fatal effects are greatly lessened by good food and suitable protection from wet and cold.

No one will suppose that I depreciate the efforts or the services of those who held high commands, or occupied responsible positions, whether in the field or in the Cabinet, but I have always thought that the true heroes of the "lost cause" were the rank and file—the men who, while in no sense responsible for the political events which produced the struggle, and the great majority of whom had not the least personal interest in that domestic institution which many assert to have been the underlying cause of the antagonism between the North and South, yet answered quickly and loyally the appeal of their States, and formed that splendid infantry which, though ill-armed and equipped, poorly clad, and often insufficiently fed, marched and countermarched, toiled in trenches, and fought in line of battle, with admirable patience and courage for four years, and who, in the depressing retreat to Appomattox Court House, when it was manifest that there was no longer a hope of final success, turned upon their pursuers with all the *élan* of Chancellorsville. No one can have witnessed what those men endured, or can know what they performed, without feeling impelled to speak a word of admiration; but the subject is one for the military historian of the war, and I have no space for more than a passing tribute.

After frequent delays *en route*, the train reached Richmond, and I lost no time in reporting at the Navy Department.

It would be both uninteresting and useless to record in detail the consultations with the Secretary of the Navy. I reported fully upon the state of affairs abroad, and the object of my return to the Confederate States was explained. The wants of the Department and the naval policy of the Government—how to supply the one and to carry out the other—were the chief considerations, and they were amply discussed. Finally it was decided as a first step that the *Fingal* should be filled up with cotton, on account of the Navy Department, and that I should return to Europe with her to carry out the further purposes of the Government; and while the ship was loading, my original instructions and powers would be revised, and the mode of furnishing funds would be arranged with the Treasury Department.

Messrs. John Fraser and Co., of Charleston, were instructed to buy in the interior and forward to Savannah the quantity of cotton necessary to fill up the *Fingal,* and the naval paymaster at that station was ordered to supply the coals required for the outward voyage. I got back to Savannah about November 23rd. The situation of affairs was interesting, and I think it will afford a better picture of passing events if I give the official correspondence which was carried on from that place, than if I continue the account in the narrative style.

"Savannah, *November* 25, 1861.

"Sir,—

"I have the honour to report that the steamship *Fingal* has been discharged, and now lies in the Savannah river ready to receive freight. Paymaster Kelly has written to Columbus to have the necessary quantity of coal sent down at once, and expects it to be here tomorrow or next day. I cannot refrain from urging the necessity of getting the ship off without delay. Yesterday five of the enemy's gunboats stood cautiously in, and after throwing a number of shell upon and over Tybee Island, a force was landed without opposition.

"This morning the Federal flag is flying from the lighthouse, and they will doubtless soon have a battery upon the point of the island. The only egress left for the *Fingal* is through Warsaw Inlet, and it can scarcely be supposed that the enemy will permit it to remain open many days…. The small quantity of naval stores and cotton required for the *Fingal* could be got on board in a couple of days if they were brought here on the spot.

"I am, etc.,

"(Signed)   JAMES D. BULLOCH.

"Hon. S. R. Mallory,
"Secretary of the Navy."

The railways were so fully occupied with the transport of troops and material of war for Virginia, and other frontier points, that the local traffic was almost wholly stopped, and the cotton and coals for the *Fingal* were brought forward in the merest driblets. On the 4th of December I received the following letter of instructions:—

"Confederate States of America, Navy Department, "Richmond, Virginia, *November* 30, 1861.
"Sir,—
"You will take command of the *Fingal*, receive on board so much cotton and rosin, to be delivered to you under the orders of the Secretary of the Treasury, as your judgment may approve, together with your coal, and proceed to such port in Great Britain as you may deem expedient, delivering your cargo as you may be requested by the Secretary of the Treasury. You will select two coast pilots to aid in bringing the *Fingal* safely back. On your arrival in Great Britain you will transfer the command of the *Fingal* to Lieutenant G. T. Sinclair, whom you will receive on board at Savannah."

Then follows information in regard to funds, and instructions as to the articles most needed, which I was to buy, if not already included in the outstanding contracts, and ship back to a Confederate port in the *Fingal*.

"So soon as either of the vessels under contract in England shall be completed and delivered, you will adopt such measures as you may deem best to arm and equip her as a vessel of war, without infringing the laws of Great Britain, or giving to that Government just cause of offence; and having obtained a crew and all things necessary for an extended cruise, you will leave England in command, and proceed against the enemy in whatever quarter of the ocean circumstances may then indicate as affording the best chances of success. Lieutenant-Commanding Pegram (of the *Nashville*) is instructed to detail such officers from his vessel as you may require, and you are authorized to confer acting appointments upon such others as you may deem necessary. The Department, the speed and qualities of your vessel being unknown, is unwilling, so far in advance, to assign any particular locality for your operations, but desires to impress upon you the importance of rendering your vessel as formidable, and your cruise as destructive, as practicable, leaving to you entire freedom of action. Should your judgment at any time hesitate in seeking the solution of any doubt on this point, it may be aided by the reflection that you are to do the enemy's commerce the greatest injury in the shortest time. A speedy recognition of our Government by the Great European Powers is anticipated, and I have no reason to doubt that if you shall seek their ports, you will receive the consideration and treatment due from neutrals to an officer of a belligerent Power with which they desire to establish close commercial relations. The strictest regard for the rights of neutrals cannot be too sedulously observed; nor should an opportunity be lost of cultivating friendly relations with their naval and merchant services, and of placing the true character of the contest in which we are engaged in its proper light. You will avail yourself of every opportunity of communicating with your Government, using, when you may deem it expedient, a cipher for this purpose. The Department relies with confidence upon the patriotism, ability, and conduct of yourself, officers, and men, and with my earnest wishes for the prosperity of your cruise, and your triumphant return to your country,

"I am, etc.,

"(Signed)   S. R. MALLORY,

"Secretary of the Navy.

"Captain James D. Bulloch,
"Savannah, Georgia."

In a subsequent letter the Secretary of the Navy directed me to arm the *Fingal* for the outward voyage, and I replied to the main points as follows:

"Savannah, *December* 5, 1861.

"Sir,—
    "I have the honour to acknowledge, etc.... The greatest obstacle will be met at the very outset in the difficulty of arming and equipping a cruiser in a neutral port; for even if Great Britain should have acknowledged the independence of the Confederate States, unless she has become a party to the war, her obligations under the International Code would force her to prohibit the equipment of an armed ship under a belligerent flag in her ports. You are better informed as to such contingencies than I can be, and I only allude to the subject to show that I am fully prepared to submit to the disap-

pointment of not at once getting upon that element which is free to any flag when properly defended.

"Such portions of your instructions as are specific shall be carried out as strictly to the letter as possible, and in the exercise of the large discretion granted me, I will endeavour to act with as much caution and prudence as will be consistent with promptness and vigour. I particularly note your remarks in reference to neutrals, and will bear constantly in mind your suggestions upon this and other points. There has been much delay in getting the cotton forward, but I think the *Fingal* will be ready for sea on Saturday night.... I have not deemed it necessary to arm the *Fingal* for the return voyage, as it is important to preserve her original character as an English ship. This course will ensure her less trouble and annoyance in getting another cargo on board. If, on our arrival in England, the Confederate Government has been acknowledged, the flag can be changed....

"I am, etc.,

"JAMES D. BULLOCH.

"Hon. S. R. Mallory,
"Secretary of the Navy."

Owing to the continued difficulty of inland transportation and the delay in getting the cotton for the *Fingal* to the shipping port, she was not loaded until December 20th, and the following copies of the correspondence will best explain the attempts to get her to sea, as well as the condition of affairs at Savannah:

"Steamship *Fingal,* off Thunderbolt Battery,

"Near Savannah, *December* 24, 1861.

"Sir,—

"On Saturday morning the barometer and the general appearance of the sky indicating a favourable state of weather, I made preparations for sea, and on Sunday morning early dropped the ship down to a bight in Wilmington Island, where she can lie concealed from the enemy's ships at Warsaw as well as at Tybee. This bight is about one mile above a seven-gun battery on Skidaway Island, from which point there is a clear view of the opening to Warsaw Sound. Immediately after anchoring, the captain of this battery informed me that three blockading vessels were off the bar, and that one of them had chased his boat in on the afternoon before. Still, as all appearances indicated a dark and squally night, it was determined to get under weigh on the first quarter of the flood, so as to get down to the bar before the moon rose. At early dark a fog set in over the marshes, concealing the leading marks, and the pilots were unwilling to move the ship. This circumstance, sufficiently annoying at first, probably saved us from capture, as it appears that the enemy were keeping an especial look-out that night.

"No vessel could have seen to cross the bar before half-past seven o'clock, yet at 8 A.M. one of their small vessels appeared in full sight of the battery below us, and actually steamed up to within half a mile of its guns, turned, and steamed down channel again without receiving a shot. I am informed that the approach of this vessel was not reported to the commander of the battery until she was in the act of turning.

"Ignorant of the incident above mentioned, I sent an experienced pilot in an eight-oared boat with good sails, kindly furnished by Lieutenant-Commanding Kennard, of the Confederate States steamer *Samson,* to examine the bar and the coast north and south of the point of Warsaw Island, and to report as quickly as possible, so that if all was clear we might go to sea on the afternoon tide. In the meantime two additional gun-vessels had joined the first, and the three coming rapidly up channel with the young flood, cut off our boat, compelling her, as it is now thought, to go into one of the creeks running through the Romerly Marsh, from which I trust she has been able by this time to reach Green Island. The enemy's three vessels took up an anchorage just opposite the main passage through Romerly Marsh, thus effectually closing all communication with Savannah from the sea, through any inlet. As the enemy could easily have discovered the position of this ship by landing upon Wilmington Island, and could have cut her out with boats at night, I took advantage of last night's flood to bring her up to this place, where there is another battery. For some time before last Saturday the enemy had not entered Warsaw Sound, their vessels simply cruising up and down the coast in very regular order. This movement, therefore, would seem especially intended to prevent the escape of this ship, and would indicate treachery somewhere. It may, however, only be the development of a general plan of attack upon Savannah, which place I consider far from being safe. The batteries are weak in guns and gunners, and whatever the gallantry of the men may be, which is undoubted, they could not withstand a vigorous attack from the ships which could be brought over Warsaw bar.

"I will remain in a position to take advantage of any change in the enemy's plans, and will lose no opportunity of getting to sea.

"I am, etc.,

"(Signed) JAMES D. BULLOCH.

"Hon. S. R. Mallory,
"Secretary of the Navy."

"Savannah, *December* 26, 1861.

"Sir,—

"On the 24th inst. I addressed you from the anchorage at Thunderbolt, reporting my failure to get the *Fingal* to sea, and informing you that the enemy had effectually sealed up all the approaches to Savannah from Warsaw Inlet and the other channels leading from the southward. The position of the *Fingal* below the battery at Thunderbolt was not safe, as the enemy might at any time cut her out with boats. I therefore, by the advice of Flag-officer Tattnall sent her back to the city on the afternoon of the 24th, and went down to Warsaw Island myself in search of the boat I informed you had been cut off by the sudden approach of the enemy's gun-boats on the day before. I returned to Savannah last night, and have the satisfaction to report that the men (with Mr. Low and two midshipmen who were of the party) were found and brought safely to Skidaway, and are now here, with the exception of two of the crew of the *Samson,* who I regret to say deserted, and it is feared got on board the blockading vessels. Yesterday morning, while I was on Warsaw Island, a large paddle-wheel steamer joined the three vessels already anchored below Skidaway, and late in the afternoon a screw-steamer, barque rigged and pierced for eight guns, came in. There are thus five ships-of-war at the entrance to the Romerly Marsh, a force too powerful for the simple blockade of the *Fingal,* and this assembling of the enemy's fleet can only be regarded as preliminary to an attack in force upon the city. It is impossible to conjecture what chance may occur to open a passage for the *Fingal....* If the *Fingal* is irretrievably locked up for the war, I presume you would desire me to get to England by some other means, etc.

"I am, etc.,

"(Signed) JAMES D. BULLOCH.

"Hon. S. R. Mallory."

From the date of the foregoing letter I continued to report the condition of affairs at Savannah, and the position of the enemy's ships at the main entrance to the river, as well as in Warsaw Sound, and received various letters from the Department, increasing the orders for purchase of supplies in England, and enlarging the general scope of my duties there, and especially instructing me to "examine into the subject of constructing iron and steel clad vessels in England and France."

On the 3rd of January, 1862, I reported as follows:—

"Since my last letter there has been no change in the position of the blockading vessels off Tybee, but the enemy seems to have changed the design indicated by the first appearance of his squadron near Skidaway battery. On the 30th ultimo, three old sailing ships, probably part of the much-talked-of 'Stone Fleet,' were brought in and anchored at the entrance to the Romerly Marsh, and have since been stripped to their lower masts. If these vessels are sunk in their present position, the inland communication would of course be closed between Savannah and the more southern ports of Georgia; but should the enemy, content with this interruption of local trade, remove the men-of-war for other operations, or for outside cruising, the *Fingal* might yet be got to sea through the regular ship channel leading between Warsaw Island and little Tybee. Up to the present moment no opportunity has offered to pass the blockading ships. By way of Warsaw they occupy the entire channel with five ships, sometimes seven; and at the anchorage near Tybee there have never been less than four ships, frequently as many as eleven."

January 13th I again reported:—

"I regret to say that this letter must be of the same tenor as the last. The enemy are fully informed of the *Fingal*'s position and the intention to get her out if possible," etc. "Unless there be some changes in the political relations of the United States with the courts of Europe, I consider the port of Savannah as completely closed to commerce for an indefinite time; consequently my detention here with any hope of getting the *Fingal* to sea is not only unnecessary, but will occasion much delay and confusion in the settlement of the business for which I was originally sent to Europe. I therefore respectfully suggest that you order me to proceed at once to England for the purpose of completing that business, and of still further carrying out your instructions of November 30, 1861."

In continuation I pointed out the effect of the delay, and the probable impossibility of completing or even fairly setting on foot the various duties with which I was charged, in time to go to sea in the first ship, which would probably be ready by the date of my arrival in England, and suggested that I should be transferred to the second ship, which would be finished three to four months later. In reply, my orders were modified in the above particular, and the Secretary of the Navy directed me to turn over the *Fingal* to Lieutenant G. T. Sinclair, and to proceed to England by any feasible route.

Mr. John Low, upon my recommendation, was appointed a master in the Confederate Navy, and was ordered to accompany me to Europe. Two midshipmen, E. C. Anderson, junior, and Eugene Maffitt, were ordered to join me, and also Mr. Clarence R. Yonge, an assistant in the paymaster's office at Savannah, the last named to act as clerk, and then to be appointed acting paymaster in one of the cruising ships.

Mr. Yonge afterwards left the *Alabama* when at Jamaica, somewhat unexpectedly, and as he took service on his return to England under the United States Consul at Liverpool, and afterwards took the prominent part of chief witness in the "*Alexandra* Case" (which will be dwelt upon in a subsequent chapter), his conduct was much criticised at the time.

The official correspondence quoted above has not been included in the body of this narrative merely to illustrate the movements of the *Fingal,* but chiefly to demonstrate the views of the Government in respect to the proposed naval operations abroad, and to make a fair representation of the enemy's operations and the condition of affairs at Savannah in December–January, 1861–62. My duties at that time compelled me to be much and often at both entrances to the Savannah river, and to examine carefully and critically the movements and force of the blockading fleet, and the strength and number of the Confederate defensive works.

The main approach to Savannah, *viâ* Tybee, was defended by two old brick forts, very inefficiently armed, chiefly with smooth-bore 32-pounders. The approach from Warsaw Sound, through Wilmington Creek, was protected by a battery of seven guns on Skidaway Island, and another battery of six or seven guns at Thunderbolt, further up the creek, and quite out of range of the first. Both of these fortifications were newly made earthworks, entirely open in rear, and the guns were mounted in barbette.

The United States ships at anchor off the entrance to Romerly Marsh were just out of gunshot from the Skidaway battery. They lay there for days, and so far as I could discover, never made a reconnaissance. There was no sleeping accommodation for the garrison inside the works at Skidaway, and the men lived in tents and huts some distance in the rear, a guard only being actually in the battery night and day. Among the blockading vessels was one fine steamship of the *Iroquois* class, and I often wondered why they did not come inside some dark night with boats, get round the flank of the battery, and spike the guns. The garrison were sturdy fellows, and would have been formidable in a stand-up fight, but the attacking party always have the advantage in a night surprise, and the ships could not only have chosen their time, but could have greatly outnumbered the guard.

The blockading squadron at Tybee was also very apathetic, and never, while I was there, came within range of Fort Pulaski. Among the vessels off Tybee, I recognised my old ship the *Bienville,* or it might have been the *De Soto*—they were sister ships. The gun-boats could have run past the batteries on Wilmington Creek at any time, and so have got into the rear of Fort Jackson, driven the men out of it, and then gone on into the Savannah river, completely isolating Fort Pulaski. The men, working the guns in barbette, could not have stood a rapid fire from the ships; grape and canister would have swept them off the parapet.

I do not know who commanded the United States blockading squadron at that time. Either Farragut or David Porter would have tried to get inside, if they had been there; at least, they would have made some effort to discover the means of resistance. The Confederate naval forces at Savannah were commanded by Flag-officer Josiah Tattnall, as gallant a seaman as ever trod a plank. I suppose no officer of his rank and quality was ever doomed to the indignity of such an inefficient command. His flag-ship, the *Savannah,* was a paddle river-boat, with engines and boilers on deck, and her battery consisted of one smooth-bore 32-pounder gun, on a traversing carriage. A rocket exploding among the flimsy joiner-work of her deck cabins would have set her on fire, and a single shell from one of the gun-boats outside would have blown her up. When Tattnall would come down the river, as he often did, with his so-called "Musquito fleet," and flaunt his flag as a seeming challenge to the formidable ships of the enemy at Tybee, nothing saved the display from the appearance of bravado, or the manœuvre from ridicule, but the natural grace and dignity with which the fine old gentleman performed every act of his life.

Josiah Tattnall was a man out of the common, the *beau idéal* of a naval officer of what must now be called the old school, "the sublime of Jack-tar." He was punctilious on a point of honour, and rigid in the practice of official propriety; but he was genial, modest and unassuming in his private intercourse with friends, and his manners were courtly, yet easy and unrestrained. He was charmingly fluent and entertaining in conversation, and had a very special gift for telling a story with liveliness and spirit, always illustrating the sense and point of his narrative with appropriate action and gesture. In positions of command fully testing his tact, judgment, courage, and professional skill, he almost invariably exhibited higher faculties than the occasions required, and no one can therefore fix the limit of his ability. He possessed all the traits which are found in heroic characters, and, with suitable opportunities, would have set his name among the great naval worthies who are historic. He was a high type of human nature—a "perfect" man in the Scriptural sense—that is to say, complete in all his parts. He died in Savannah, his native place, and was buried near there in a grove of old live-oak trees planted to commemorate the wedding of the first of his ancestors who settled in the Colony of Georgia. A couplet from the touching requiem to "Tom Bowling" would be a fitting epitaph to one who has been called the "Bayard of the sea":—

> "Though his body's under hatches
> His soul has gone aloft."

The prediction that Savannah would be sealed up for the remainder of the war was fulfilled, and the *Fingal*'s proposed voyage to Europe was definitely abandoned. She was not, however, lost to the Confederate States. The Navy Department took her into the service, and she was converted into an armour-clad, and christened *Atlanta*. To effect this conversion she was first cut down to her deck, which throughout about 150 or 160 feet amidships was widened (6 feet on each side, widest part, but tapering towards the ends) by a "heavy solid overway of wood and armour," sloping from a point several feet below the water-line to the edge of the deck. Upon this widened portion of the deck a casemate was built, the sides and ends inclining at an angle of about 30°. The top of the casemate was flat, and the house to cover the steersman and officer directing the fire rose above the roof about three feet. The sloping sides and ends of the casemate were covered with two layers of iron plates, each being two inches thick, screwed to a backing composed of three inches of oak upon fifteen inches of pine. The bolts were one and a quarter inch, countersunk on the outside of the plates, and drawn up by nuts and washers on the inside. She was provided with a beak or ram at the bow; and a pole and lever, which could be lowered at will, was also fitted at the bow, long enough to project beyond the ram. The pole was intended to carry a percussion torpedo. Her armament consisted of two 7-inch rifled guns on bow and stern pivots, and two 6-inch rifled guns in broadside. The 7-inch guns were so arranged that they could be worked in broadside, as well as for fore and aft fire, and the *Fingal* could therefore fight three guns (two 7-inch and one 6-inch) on either side. The guns were cast-iron with wrought iron bands, and were of the "Brooke" pattern.

As soon as the *Atlanta* was finished, the Navy Department was desirous that she should be tried against the enemy's ironclads, eight or nine of which were known to be in the neighbourhood, off Charleston and the entrances to Savannah, or at Port Royal. The senior officers of the Confederate navy at Savannah did not think that she would be a match for the United States *Monitor* class at close quarters, and they did not think it prudent to take her out into Warsaw Sound, where two "Monitors" were lying, except under favourable circumstances of spring-tide, because her draft had been increased by the weight of armour, ordnance, and necessary stores, and the channels were not only intricate, but the depth of water very scant at best, and besides this, the ship steered badly in consequence of the increased draft and the alteration of form caused by the projecting overway, which extended several feet below the water-line.

Flag-officer Tattnall's advice was to wait until the enemy collected his ironclads for a second attack upon Charleston, and then to send the *Atlanta* out on the first spring-tide, when she could be got to sea without the risk of being taken at a disadvantage in the narrow and shoal waters of the Romerly Marshes and Warsaw Sound. Once fairly afloat, and with ample sea-room, he thought she could strike a telling blow, either at Port Royal, where the enemy had a large collection of transports, or at some other point. This wise counsel was unhappily overborne by the weight of public clamour, and the Navy Department yielded to the outside pressure.

Commander Wm. A. Webb, a clever and spirited officer, was ordered to the *Atlanta*, and the condition of his appointment appeared to be that he should at once "do something." Before daylight on the morning of June 17, 1863, Webb got under weigh, and steaming past the old batteries on Skidaway Island, which had ere this been abandoned, entered Warsaw Sound. The United States "Monitors" *Weehawken* and *Nahant* were at anchor in the sound. They made out the *Atlanta* at about 4 A.M., and the *Weehawken* immediately slipped her cable and steamed towards her, followed closely by the *Nahant*. At about 600 yards from the *Weehawken* the *Atlanta* grounded, but was backed off with some difficulty. Shortly after, the *Atlanta* took the bottom again, and stuck fast. The *Weehawken* approached to within about 300 yards, and choosing a position so that "the *Atlanta* could bring her guns to bear with difficulty," opened fire. The engagement, if it can be called one, lasted about fifteen minutes. The *Nahant* did not fire a shot, but the *Weehawken* hit the *Atlanta* four times, twice with 15-inch "cored shot," and twice with 11-inch solid shot. The *Atlanta*'s pilot-house was knocked off, and one of the port-stoppers, or shutters, was driven in; the armour was crushed in at several points, although not pierced, and the backing was much damaged. One 15-inch shot struck fairly on the inclined side of the *Atlanta*, breaking the armour plate and driving a shower of splinters from the backing into the ship. Captain Webb has told me that the concussion knocked down about forty men, and sixteen were more or less wounded by the splinters.

Webb was in a sad plight. It can hardly be said that he was fighting his ship—he was simply enduring the fire of his adversary.

It was manifest that a few more concussions, and a 15-inch shot, perhaps a shell, would find its way into the casemate, and there would be great and useless slaughter among his men. When further resistance ceases to hold out any hope of final success, the dictates of humanity extort an acknowledgment of defeat, and the *Atlanta*'s flag was hauled down.

The foregoing brief statement has been made up almost exclusively from the Confederate accounts. I have before me, while writing, a copy of the report of the commander of the *Weehawken*, and if it contained anything in conflict with the above, I would either mention the fact or give the report in full. Captain John Rodgers, of the *Weehawken* (I hope I may still speak of him in the present tense), is an able officer. He accepted with promptness the *Atlanta*'s invitation to battle, and handled his ship with skill and judgment. He took up a good position, awkward for his adversary and advantageous to himself, which he was bound to do, for it is clearly the duty of a commander so to dispose his force as to defeat the enemy with as little loss to himself as possible, and finally he reported the result of the engagement in a plain, manly, straightforward document, without the least brag or unbecoming elation. As a pleasing but somewhat unique feature in the report of Captain Rodgers, I may mention that he called the *Atlanta* the "enemy," and not the "rebel," an epithet chosen by the politicians at Washington for a purpose, and used by them as a reproach. It crept into the military and naval phraseology of the war, and was thrown broadcast over the correspondence of civil functionaries and United States Consuls;

but the old officers of the army and navy, for the most part, either avoided it, or at any rate seemed to use it as a technical phrase, without opprobrious meaning.

The encounter between the Federal "Monitors" and the *Atlanta* illustrates no general principle applicable to engagements between iron-cased ships. The 15-inch guns of the *Weehawken* were superior in battering power at close quarters to the 6-inch and 7-inch guns of the *Atlanta,* and the only chance of success for the latter would have been to get into deep and broad waters, where she could manœuvre, and thus use her guns efficiently, and choose her distance as well as position. Lying helplessly aground, she was at the mercy of her opponent, who was able to come within the most effective range for her own guns, and to avoid almost entirely the return fire of her adversary. Captain Rodgers does not mention that his ship was hit, or that she received any injury whatever, except by collision with his own consort, the *Nahant,* after the surrender of the *Atlanta.*

When the Secretary of the Navy directed me to turn over the *Fingal* to Lieutenant G. T. Sinclair, and to proceed to England by any practicable route, I communicated at once with Messrs. John Fraser and Co., of Charleston, and they kindly offered me and my party passage in either of two steamers they were about to despatch, one from Charleston and one from Wilmington. The Charleston steamer would try the blockade first, but she was small, and would only go as far as Nassau, from which place I would have to find my way to Havana, and thence round by St. Thomas to Southampton, a circuitous route, and very uncertain as regards connection with packets, etc. The Wilmington steamer was larger, having been built for the coasting trade to Boston, and the purpose was to send her direct to Liverpool, only stopping at Fayal in the Azores to replenish her coals. I chose the latter ship and route, and went on to Wilmington, arriving there January 24, 1862. The steamer's name originally was *North Carolina,* but it had been changed to *Annie Childs.* She was coaling and taking in cotton, rosin, tobacco, and other cargo, until February 1st, when her commander, Captain Hammer, took her down to Orton Point, about twelve miles above the mouth of the river, from which position the ship was concealed from the blockaders.

General J. R. Anderson, commander of the Confederate forces at Wilmington, kindly put a small screw tug-boat at my disposal, and Captain Hammer and I went down to Fort Caswell, at the mouth of the river, every day to reconnoitre. The New Inlet bar was too shoal for the *Annie Childs,* and the only possible egress was by the main ship channel. Two gun-boats were generally lying at anchor during the day about one mile west-south-west from the bar, and were sometimes joined by another from New Inlet. We learned from the coast-guard pickets that they did not get under weigh at night. The nights continued to be clear until February 5th, and there was no chance for a run. I find the following entry in my diary under February 5th, 1862:

"Early part of the day clear, but wind north-east, with passing clouds towards noon. In the afternoon got ready for a start. At 10 P.M. under weigh, moon shining, but light haze. Full tide at 12.7; moon set at same time. Timed the ship's speed so as to reach the bar just after the setting of the moon. Crossed 12:15; low fog, stars over head, smooth sea, calm, might have heard the dip of an oar or the swash of the screw a long way. Block-aders must have been fast asleep. Scarcely clear of the bar when the heating of a bearing made it necessary to stop the engine for at least half an hour. Fortunately it began to rain. The bearing being all right, we started again, and were soon safe in a thick drizzle, which lasted until we got to the eastward of the Gulf Stream."

The *Annie Childs* had a single engine, one inverted cylinder, and was badly found for a voyage across the North Atlantic in the month of February, but she was a capital sea-boat and behaved admirably in a heavy north-west gale which we caught in the "roaring forties." At Fayal the American Consul gave a great deal of trouble, and if it had not been for Lloyds' agent we should not have got any coal at all. As it was, we had to be content with a scant supply. At 2:30 P.M. on the afternoon of March 8th, 1862, we made the Old Head of Kinsale, took a Cork pilot on board, and went into Queenstown that night, burning the sweepings of the bunkers mixed with rosin, and the spare spars cut into short lengths. The next day I took train for Liverpool *via* Dublin and Holyhead, and arrived there at 4 P.M. on the 10th.

CHAPTER IV

Before leaving England with the *Fingal* in October, 1861, I drew up very particular and specific instructions with reference to the outfit of the *Oreto* (*Florida*), with the purpose of preventing any possible violation of the Foreign Enlistment Act, as it had been explained to me by counsel, and to ensure that the ship when delivered to me should be prepared to fulfil the conditions essential to a sea-going steamer of her class and nothing more.

On my arrival in Liverpool from the Confederate States (March 10th, 1862), the *Oreto* (*Florida*) was ready to take the sea. She had made a satisfactory trial trip, and was already provisioned for her outward voyage. I made a thorough investigation, and satisfied myself that not a single article contraband of war was on board the ship—not a weapon, not an appliance for mounting a gun. In this condition I was advised that according to the Municipal Law of Great Britain, she was a perfectly lawful article of traffic, that the builder could deliver her, and I could pay for and receive her, without infringing any statute, or transgressing any requirement of commercial propriety.

Captain James Alexander Duguid, a duly certificated master mariner, was appointed to command the ship, and the crew and engineer's staff were engaged in strict conformity with the conditions of the Merchant Shipping Act, signing articles for a voyage from Liverpool to Palermo, and thence, if required, to a port or ports in the Mediterranean Sea, or the West Indies, and back to a port of discharge in the United Kingdom, the voyage not to exceed six months. Not a single officer or man was enlisted for the service of the Confederate States, nor was a hint thrown out to the crew that the voyage would be other than the route specified in the shipping articles. Captain Duguid and the chief engineer were informed that the ship would go first of all to Nassau, but they knew perfectly well that a shipowner has the right to vary the order of visit to the ports specified in the shipping articles, and that it is not unusual to exercise that privilege when his interests or the special circumstances of the voyage suggest or require a variation within the general limits of the original engagement. Neither the captain nor the engineer were, however, employed, nor in any way pledged to depart from the general conditions set out in the articles, and they did not at any future time enter the service of the Confederate States, so far as I know.

In "The Case of the United States," laid before the Tribunal of Arbitration at Geneva, it is affirmed, on the authority of a despatch from the United States Consul at Liverpool, to Mr. Seward, that the *Oreto* "took her gun-carriages on board at Liverpool," and it is furthermore stated that she sailed with "a crew of fifty-two men and *some* guns."[*] In refutation of the foregoing, the evidence of the Customs officers at Liverpool was that they kept "watch on the proceedings of the vessel *Oreto* from the time she left the Toxteth Dock, on the 4th of March last (1862), till the day she sailed, the 22nd of the same month.... we did not see at any time any arms, or warlike ammunition of any kind, taken on board, and we are perfectly satisfied that none such was taken on board during her stay in the river."

One of the statements was very specific.

"I am one of the Surveyors of Customs at this port (Liverpool). Pursuant to instructions I received from the Collector on the 21st February in the present year (1862), and at subsequent dates, I visited the steamer *Oreto* at various times, when she was being fitted out

[*] "United States Case," p. 65.

in the dock, close to the yard of Messrs. Miller and Sons, the builders of the vessel. I continued this inspection from time to time until she left the dock, and I am certain that when she left the river she had no warlike stores of any kind whatever on board. After she went into the river she was constantly watched by the boarding officers, who were directed to report to me whenever any goods were taken on board; but, in reply to my frequent inquiries, they stated nothing was put in the ship but coals.

"(Signed)   EDWARD MORGAN,
"Surveyor."

The foregoing and other statements of like import will be found in the evidence laid before the Tribunal of Arbitration at Geneva.* They are confirmatory of my own declarations to the same effect, and the fact is therefore established beyond dispute that the *Oreto* left the Mersey wholly unarmed, and without any portion of her outfit which could render her liable to seizure or detention for violation of the Foreign Enlistment Act. As she lay in the river off the Egremont Ferry, she looked a comely craft, as much within her legal rights as a hundred cases of Birmingham rifles, or as many tons of gunpowder, about to start for New York in any other ship. This is not the rash assertion of an interested party, pronounced in a spirit of bravado, or by way of a retort; it is founded upon the decision of one of the highest Courts in the realm, as will be shown in due course.

It will be remembered that the orders of the Navy Department, dated November 30th, 1861, directed me to take personal command of the first ship completed in England, and to proceed to cruise against the enemy's commerce. But other duties assigned to me in Europe were largely increased before my departure from the Confederate States, and I was also instructed to examine into the subject of ironclads, and report whether vessels of that class could be built in England or France. When I called the attention of the Navy Department to the fact that the first ship would probably be ready for sea by the time I could reach England (I have already mentioned that the original orders were modified to suit the new conditions), I was directed to set in train the general business of the Navy Department in Europe, and to take command of the second ship (the *Alabama*).

It was not anticipated that this change would occasion any perplexity, because the *Nashville* (Captain R. B. Pegram) was supposed to be in En-

---

* See "British Case," p. 58, etc.

gland at that time, and thus a commander, with a complete staff of officers, could be provided for the *Oreto* with little or no trouble. The two vessels could be cleared for an appointed rendezvous, and the transfer easily and safely effected. The Secretary of the Navy informed me that he had written Captain Pegram to order such officers to the *Oreto* as I might require, and that officer would have been only too happy to find that under the changed circumstances he would have the opportunity to command the *Oreto* himself. Unhappily, the instructions did not reach Captain Pegram, and when I arrived in Liverpool I learned with regret that he had sailed for a Confederate port, and was far beyond reach. The situation was perplexing. The ship was an object of suspicion and disquietude to the United States Minister, who was pressing her Majesty's Government to detain her, and his importunities might prevail. No inquiries could discover that she was thus far in default—of this I felt assured; but still, the Confederate Government had no acknowledged advocate, and the Government might "strain the law," as the Attorney-General admitted they did at a later period.

It was imperative to send the ship away. Lieutenant (afterwards Commander) J. N. Maffitt had been sent to Nassau on special duty, and I had reason to believe he was there at that time. I knew Maffitt well. He was a man of great natural resources—self-reliant, and fearless of responsibility. I determined to despatch the ship to him at once, and I ordered Low to go in her. The *Oreto* sailed from Liverpool on the 22nd of March, and Mr. Low's instructions were as follows:—

"Liverpool, 21st March, 1862.

"Sir,

"You will take passage in the steam vessel* *Florida*, now about to sail for the Bahamas. This vessel, for reasons already explained to you, is sent out under the British flag, and in command of an English captain, and it is of the utmost importance that nothing shall be done to compromise her character as a neutral vessel until she is safely delivered to an officer of the Confederate navy, or some agent especially appointed by the Confederate Navy Department. You are hereby charged with the care of all public property on board, a

---

* The *Florida*'s dockyard name was *Oreto*; the name first assigned to her by the Navy Department was *Manassas,* by which she is mentioned in some of the correspondence, but to avoid confusion, or frequent explanation, she will hereafter be mentioned in this narrative as the *Florida.*

duplicate list of which is herewith furnished you, and the captain has been instructed after arrival at the first port of destination to be governed by your orders as to the movements and disposal of the ship. As soon as you arrive at the Bahamas, you will communicate with Captain J. N. Maffitt, Confederate States navy, whom you will hear of through Messrs. Adderley and Co., of Nassau, and you will forward the accompanying despatch to the Hon. Secretary of the Navy, reporting also your arrival to him in writing. If Captain Maffitt or any other commissioned officer of the Confederate States navy is at Nassau, give him all the information you have in reference to the ship, hand him the invoice of stores, with the enclosed letter addressed to Captain Maffitt, and make the best of your way back to this country as quickly as possible, as I have duties of great importance for you here. Should you not find Captain Maffitt in Nassau, put yourself in communication through Mr. Adderley with Major Charles J. Helm or Mr. Louis Heyleger, one of whom will doubtless be in Nassau. Consult with those gentlemen as to the propriety of keeping the ship in Nassau, and remain with her until you hear from the Navy Department. You must be careful to appear always as a private gentleman travelling on his own affairs, and let your intercourse with all persons known to be connected with the Confederate Government be very guarded and cautious. With the gentlemen mentioned above, you can of course speak freely, but let your interviews be private, so as to escape notice as much as possible.

"It is impossible to give you instructions to cover every emergency. I have had experience of your discretion and judgment, and must rely upon them now. You will be furnished with money to pay your personal expenses, and to meet any small demands against the ship. As the *Florida* has an extra quantity of coal on board, and the captain has been ordered to make the passage mostly under canvas, it is presumed no material outlay will be required for some time. Should there be absolute need of additional funds, you will apply to Messrs. Adderley and Co., or to either of the aforementioned gentlemen, pledging the Navy Department, through me, for the amount. You will, however, under all circumstances, practise the most rigid economy. You will keep a careful memorandum of the ship's performances, under steam and sail, noting her steering, working, stability, and all particulars of the speed under different circumstances, and the degree of pitching and rolling under various conditions of sea and weather. Furnish information on these points to the officer who may relieve you, and keep a copy for me.

"Among the papers are drawings to show how the sweeps and traverses for the pivot guns are to be put down. These, with the guns and all necessary equipments, are on board the steamship *Bahama*, now about to sail for Nassau. If the officer who will take charge on the part of the Navy Department needs your services for a short time, you are at liberty to remain with him, but unless otherwise directed by the Hon. Secretary of the Navy himself, after he has received the enclosed letter, you will return to England at latest by the first day of June, as your services will then be indispensable to me.

"Wishing you a safe and speedy passage, and a satisfactory consummation of the purposes of your voyage,

"I am, etc.,

"(Signed)   JAMES D. BULLOCH.

"Master John Low,
"Confederate States Navy."

The following letters were given to Mr. Low, along with his instructions, to be delivered to Captain Maffitt, and to be forwarded to the Secretary of the Navy from Nassau:—

"Liverpool, 21*st March*, 1862.

"Sir,—

"Day after to-morrow I despatch for Nassau a gun-vessel, built in England under contract with me for the Confederate navy. In all sailing and steaming equipment she is very complete, but I have been forced to dispense with all outfit suited to her true character. It has been with much difficulty, and only by the most cautious management, that she has escaped seizure or indefinite detention here, and I send her as she is, the first regularly built war-vessel for our navy, to your care. Mr. Low, Master, Confederate States navy, goes in her to take charge of the public property on board, and to place her in the hands of any Confederate officer who may be in the West Indies on her arrival. I hope it may fall to your lot to command her, for I know of no officer whose tact and management could so well overcome the difficulties of equipping her, or who could make better use of her when in cruising order.

"It has been impossible to get the regular battery intended for her on board, but I have sent out four 7-inch rifled guns, with all necessary equipments in the steamship *Bahama*, bound to Nassau, and Mr. Low will give you all particulars as to her probable time of arrival, and will also hand you a list of everything on board the gun-vessel, as well as an invoice of the shipment by the *Bahama*. Another ship will be ready in about two months, and I will take the sea in her myself by some means or other, although I perceive many difficulties looming in the future.

"The country seems to be hard pressed, but I hope no one at home despairs of the final result. Two small ships can do but little in the way of materially turning the tide of war, but we can do something to illustrate the spirit and energy of our people, and if we can arrange to meet, may yet repay upon the enemy some of the injuries his vastly superior force alone has enabled him to inflict upon the States of the Confederacy. Write me as soon as you receive this, and give me full information of the state of affairs on the other side of the Atlantic, and if you get to sea in the little cruiser I send out, appoint a rendezvous. I am too much pressed for time, and have too lately arrived, to write more fully now, but will communicate with you again soon.

"I am, etc.,

"(Signed)　　JAMES D. BULLOCH.

"Captain J. N. Maffitt,
"Confederate States Navy."

"Liverpool, *March* 21, 1862.

"Sir,—

"On the 14th inst., in a necessarily short letter, I informed you of the safe arrival of myself and party in England, and will now report more in detail upon the matters which relate to my especial duties here.... Although arrangements have been made by which correspondence with the Confederate States can be carried on with more freedom than formerly, yet as there is always a probability of letters going astray, such as treat of public affairs must obviously be worded with caution, and names of persons and places be suppressed....

"The *M.* (*Florida*) is ready for sea, with crew, provisions, and all boatswains', carpenters', and sailmakers' stores necessary for several months on board, and I will despatch her on the day after tomorrow to a West Indian port, the exact locality of which will be reported to you in a subsequent letter, as well as from the ship as soon after her arrival as possible. It is hoped that she will be able to communicate immediately upon arrival with the officer you have already detailed for duty between the southern coast and the Bahamas, and for this purpose I will send in her the very trusty and prudent officer you appointed especially to assist me in such affairs as require me to keep in the background.

"It has been found impossible to place any munitions of war on board the *M.* She has been twice inspected by the Custom House authorities, in compliance with specific orders from the Foreign Office, to see that nothing contraband of war has been placed in her, and notice has been given that any attempt to smuggle such articles on board would at once be followed by her seizure. The hammock-nettings, ports, and general appearance of the ship sufficiently indicate the ultimate object of her construction, but there is nothing to compromise the pacific character she must necessarily assume for this voyage. Registered as an English ship, in the name of an Englishman, commanded by an Englishman, with a regular official number, and her tonnage marked upon the combings of the main-hatch, under the direction of the Board of Trade, she seems to be perfectly secure against capture, or even interference, until an attempt is made to arm her, or to change the flag, and this, it appears to me now, can only be effected at sea. The late unseemly conduct of the captain of the Federal ship *Tuscarora* has caused the British Admiralty to issue very stringent orders in reference to the treatment of United States and Confederate vessels in English ports, whether home or colonial."

Here follow specifications of the Admiralty Orders, which have been already mentioned in a previous chapter, and some details in reference to the shipment *per* steamship *Bahama,* sending out officers, pay of crews for the cruising ships, etc.

> "I am, etc.,
>
> "(Signed)   JAMES D. BULLOCH.

"Hon. S. R. Mallory,
"Secretary of the Navy."

The *Florida* arrived at Nassau on the 28th of April, and the subjoined letter is Mr. Low's report:

"Nassau, 1*st May*, 1862.

"Sir,—

"I have the honour to report to you the safe arrival at this port of the Confederate States steamer *Florida,* on the morning of the 28th of April, after a passage of thirty-seven days, which, in compliance with your instructions, has been made principally under canvas. We wished to be as economical as possible in regard to the consumption of fuel, but were rather unfortunate in having light winds and frequent calms, more especially in the Trades. During the latter we thought it prudent to steam, thinking that if we made too long a passage the steamship *Bahama* would be here some time before us. The amount of coal, as you are aware, was one hundred and seventy-five tons, including Welsh and English. Our consumption of the former was eighteen tons per day, and of the latter twenty-four. We have now on board good two days' coal, so I trust you will find, after taking into consideration the weather, and our reasons for not making a long passage, that we have been as economical as possible, not only as regards fuel, but with everything on board.

"I took particular notice of the vessel as regards her speed under steam and canvas, and am happy to report most favourably of her in all respects. Our average steaming is nine knots and a half; her sailing averages, with the wind abeam or quarterly, so that the fore and aft canvas will draw, twelve knots. The above is the average; I now give you what I have seen her do during the passage. Under steam, with smooth water, ten and a half knots, and under canvas alone, with quartering wind, so that we could carry main topgallant studding-sail, thirteen and a half good.

"As regards stability, I do not think there is a stronger vessel of her class afloat; when pitching, you could not see her work in the least, not so much as to crack the pitch in the waterway planks, where I believe a vessel pitching is as likely to show weakness as anywhere else.

"I am, etc.,

"(Signed)   JOHN LOW.

"Commander J. D. Bulloch."

In the concluding portion of the above letter, Mr. Low reported that Captain Maffitt was not at Nassau when he arrived, but was expected shortly, and by the advice of Mr. Heyleger he determined to keep the ship there, but moved her to "Cochrane's" or the "New Anchorage," about six miles from the town, where there was deeper water, and where the ship would be less conspicuous. I received several reports from Mr. Low while he was detained at Nassau, and the subjoined extract from one of them will be interesting as evidence of the rigorous "blockade" which the United States cruisers had established over the British Bahama channels, even at that early date:—

"The steamer *Stettin* arrived here on the 30th of April from Falmouth. A short distance off the island she was chased and fired at several times by a United States gunboat, but the *Stettin* being a faster vessel, she ran away from her. The gunboat fired twelve shot and shell at the *Stettin*—several, as the passengers inform me, came very near. During the firing the *Stettin* had the English ensign flying, but it appears they have no respect for that."

On the 13th of May Low had the happiness to advise me of Maffitt's arrival, and that he had taken charge of the *Florida;* he reported that although everything had been kept as quiet as possible, yet there had been many surmises in reference to the movements of the ship, and he feared there would be trouble if she was detained much longer at Nassau. Fearing this myself, I had advised that she should be run into a Confederate port at once, if there seemed likely to be any difficulty, and there equipped, and this was eventually done; but Maffitt, on the spot, was encouraged to hope that he might get her guns shipped to some neighbouring Cay or some point on the banks, and there complete the equipment without the delay and risk of running the blockade.

I never permit myself to criticize the action of an intelligent energetic officer when he is present on the scene and I am not. Throughout all the trying difficulties Maffitt showed great patience, astonishing endurance, and unflinching pluck. He wrote me a number of letters about the troubles and delays, but the details of the seizure of the ship and the proceedings against her in the Vice-Admiralty Court at Nassau are fully reported in the proceedings before the Tribunal of Arbitration at Geneva, and need not be repeated here. A short summary will suffice.

The United States Consul at Nassau had his suspicions aroused very shortly after the arrival of the *Florida*, and began at once to press the authorities to examine and then to detain her. She was several times inspected by officers of the Royal Navy, who reported, what was quite manifest, that she was in all respects suited for the purposes of a vessel-of-war, but that she was not armed, and had no warlike stores on board. On the 15th of June some of the crew of the *Florida* (she was still called *Oreto*) went on board of her Majesty's ship *Greyhound*, and stated to Commander Hinckley that they had left the *Oreto* because they were not able to ascertain her destination, and that she was endeavouring to ship another crew. Thereupon Commander Hinckley seized the vessel, but on the morning of the 17th she was released, the Attorney-General being of the opinion that there was not evidence sufficient to justify a seizure. Notwithstanding this opinion, however, she was again seized on the same day (June 17th) by orders of the Governor, and proceedings were forthwith instituted against her in the Vice-Admiralty Court of the colony for violation of the Foreign Enlistment Act. Many witnesses were examined, and the trial was continued until August 2nd, when the judge pronounced judgment. After reviewing the evidence, he declared it to be insufficient, and made a decree for the restoration of the vessel "to the master claiming on behalf of her alleged owner."

Under date of August 1st, 1862, Maffitt wrote me from Nassau: "The arguments (*in re Oreto*) were brought to a close last evening, and the judge reads in court to-morrow his decree. We have a clear case, but if the decision is favourable to us, I fear the Governor will order an appeal. Notwithstanding all I say, the *O.* may be released; in that event, six hours will not find her here."

Having been released by the decree of the Vice-Admiralty Court, Maffitt, acting always through the consignees of the ship, cleared the *Florida* outward as a vessel in ballast for St. John's, New Brunswick, and went out of the harbour to a position near Hog Island, to try the machinery and to refit. The ship had been much neglected while under seizure, and many articles had been taken out of her which could not be recovered. At this time vessels were loading daily at Nassau for the purpose of running the blockade. The schooner *Prince Alfred* was engaged by the consignees of the steamship *Bahama,* and was loaded with the armament and other stores intended for the *Florida,* but unfortunately Maffitt was not able to personally supervise the transshipment, and many essential articles were overlooked.

This was one of the great difficulties the Confederates had to encounter during the whole war. Agents of the United States Government could ship war material of every description without disguise or the fear of interference. There were no Confederate Consuls to make up and forward affidavits affirming that the vessels thus loading were intended to be armed as cruisers, and the statement that many vessels were loaded in British ports with rifles, cannon, ammunition, and military equipments for the United States, expressly for use in the war against the Confederate States, requires no proof at this late date.

Maffitt's open personal interference with the *Florida* would have resulted in further detention, probably in another seizure. Every detail was necessarily left to agents, who in this case acted certainly with absolute good faith, but who did not comprehend the full extent of his necessities. About August 9th the *Prince Alfred* cleared out for St. John's, and proceeded to sea as if with the purpose to run the blockade. The *Oreto* (*Florida*) being already outside near Hog Island, soon followed her, and both vessels proceeded in company to Green Cay, a small desert island on the edge of the great Bahama Bank, about sixty miles from Nassau. The United States ships *Adirondack* and *Cuyler* were in the neighbourhood, and they were informed of the *Prince Alfred's* movements and her probable connection with the *Florida,* as appears from a despatch from the United States Consul at Nassau to Mr. Seward, dated August 12th,* but they either kept an indifferent look-out or Maffitt gave them the slip. At Green Cay the armament and other stores were transferred from the *Prince Alfred* to the *Oreto,* the Confederate flag was hoisted for the first time, but not until she was quite clear of the Bank. The ship was then regularly commissioned, and the name was finally changed to *Florida.*

Although Maffitt was now afloat in a Confederate ship-of-war, he was in no condition to begin a cruise. The necessarily quick departure from Nassau after escaping from the clutches of the Vice-Admiralty Court had made it impossible to engage a sufficient number of men to work the ship, far less to fight a battery. He had, moreover, only one officer of experience, Lieutenant J. M. Stribbling.

The work of transferring the armament was very laborious. The hot August sun, combined with night exposure and general want of physical comforts, told upon them all, and the much-dreaded yellow fever, that scourge of the West Indies, broke out among the men. There was no surgeon on board, and the care of the sick was added to Maffitt's other responsibilities. United States cruisers were following him; he himself was ill; it would have been folly to keep the sea—indeed, it was impossible. He succeeded in evading the United States ships which were blockading the Bahama channels, and finally found his way to the port of Cardenas, in the island of Cuba, where he was kindly received by the citizens, and the authorities made no objection to his obtaining such supplies as were needed. From Cardenas Maffitt wrote me the subjoined hasty note:—

---

* The letter is among the documents laid before the Tribunal of Arbitration at Geneva.

"Cardenas, *August* 20, 1862.

"My dear Bulloch,

"I took on board at sea all my battery, but many things in the haste and confusion were forgotten, such as rammers, sponges, etc. Had but two firemen and eleven men; have run the gauntlet splendidly, my Coast Survey experience being of great service. Where I went the Federal ships dared not follow, and here I am, with prospects of filling up my crew and obtaining what is necessary. The *'prize-crew'* committed many acts of robbery, and left the vessel in a terrible plight.... I hope to give a good account of myself soon, if I get the men. I write in great haste. Have Lieutenant Stribbling— good officer; acting-master Bradford, acting-midshipmen Bryan, Floyd, Sinclair—young men of no nautical experience. No doctor, no paymaster. I have now three cases of yellow fever; have had seven. Am doing well in that line. You remember my fondness for doctoring the crew. I was fortunate enough to avoid any connection with the *Oreto* until the day before we gave the Yankees the slip. Semmes was looked upon as the person ordered to command her, and after he left, that Stribbling was to take her to him at a rendezvous.... This is written in extreme haste, to catch a chance to send it to Helm at Havana. Good luck, and a God's blessing.

"Yours affectionately,

"(Signed)   J. N. MAFFITT."

In the foregoing letter Maffitt complained bitterly of the heedless conduct of a Confederate officer to whose indiscreet and uncontrollable looseness in conversation he attributed the seizure of the *Oreto* and her subsequent troubles. It would be as painful to my own feelings as to those of Maffitt to mention any name in such a connection, because the loyalty and good intentions of the person to whom he alluded were beyond suspicion; indeed, it may be fairly said that he was probably unconscious of his failings, and a secret leaked through his mind and found expression from his lips just as the breath permeating through the lungs passes by its natural channels to the open air. There are some men who are wholly without the faculty of concealment, who cannot disguise or suppress their knowledge of important events which are in course of secret preparation, who have not the patience to await results and then to take their share in the credit of having contributed to success, but who are irresistibly impelled to manifest by their manner and speech that weighty concerns have been confided to them, and that the issues thereof are likely to be momentous. Many carefully laid schemes were frustrated during the late war by lack of prudence and for want of self-control on the part of men who were devoted to the South, and from whom nothing to its injury could have been wrung by violence.

From Cardenas Maffitt sent Lieutenant Stribbling to Havana, to communicate with Major Charles J. Helm, who was the Confederate agent at that place, and to see what could be done there in the way of engaging men. In three or four days Stribbling returned with twelve men, and on the 28th of August Major Helm telegraphed that the Captain-General desired that the *Florida* would come round to Havana. On the 30th Maffitt got under weigh and proceeded to Havana, where he arrived on the 31st, but finding the restrictions so severe that it was impossible for him either to increase his crew or to make good his other deficiencies, he resolved to run the ship into Mobile.

While the *Florida* was at Cardenas Maffitt himself was forced to succumb to the fever, which had already more than decimated his small crew. His strong constitution, and the hourly demand upon all his faculties, had kept him up until the ship was safe, but with the rest and relief from incessant care there came a reaction, and the fever took advantage of his relaxed energies and made a well-nigh fatal attack. Dr. Gilliard, a surgeon in the Spanish navy, kindly volunteered his services, and Maffitt probably owes his life, partly at least, to the skill and benevolent efforts of that philanthropic gentleman.

Dr. Barrett, of Georgia (I wish I knew his Christian name), was at that time in Cuba. He heard of the *Florida*'s helpless condition, volunteered his services as surgeon of the ship, and joined her, thus facing all the perils of her hapless condition, with no visible motive, except the wish to be helpful to those in distress, and no expectation of reward except the "answer of a good conscience."

The object of the Captain-General in requesting Major Helm to get the *Florida* away from Cardenas, and to induce Maffitt to bring her to Havana, is not fully apparent. He may have thought that she could be better protected from violence on the part of the United States ships at the latter than at the former port; or he may have wished to have her more completely under his own eye, and where he could with more certainty prevent her obtaining any supplies or reinforcement of her crew which would constitute a violation of Spanish neutrality.

The stringent orders Maffitt found in force on his arrival at Havana suggest that the latter object was the reason; and finding that he could neither refit nor obtain men at Havana, he promptly determined to run into

Mobile. On the afternoon of September 1st, the *Florida* was clear of the Moro Castle, and was steering boldly across the Gulf, which was then the highway for United States transports she had not the power to attack, and which was swarming with United States cruisers she was helpless to resist.

At 2 P.M. on the 4th the lighthouse on Sand Island, and then Fort Morgan, at the entrance to Mobile Bay, were made; but between the sheltering port and the devoted little craft lay three of the enemy's warships. Maffitt had no purpose to retire and draw off the blockaders, and then endeavour to double and get inshore of them. His determination from the first was to dash straight in whenever he made the land. But he hoped to get fairly among them, or even a little beyond, before they suspected his true character or purpose. With this object in view, he hoisted the British ensign and pennant, and stood on directly for the blockading squadron.

Commander Preble was the senior officer of the blockading force, and he placed his ship, the *Oneida*, directly in the *Florida*'s course, the other ships taking up good supporting positions. When the *Florida* got close to the *Oneida*, Preble hailed and ordered her to stop. Maffitt perceived that he must either obey or draw upon the British flag an indignity, and he hauled it down and steered so direct for the *Oneida* that Preble was forced to reverse his engines to avoid a collision. There was no longer any disguise; the *Florida* was recognised, and Maffitt pushed on past the *Oneida*, taking her broadside at little more than pistol-shot. There is, so far as I know, no record of such a scramble as followed. The *Florida* stood steadily on for the bar, receiving broadside after broadside from the three United States ships.* She did not even cast loose a gun, because there were no men to fight them, and as there was nothing to distract the enemy's fire, it is marvellous they did not literally blow her to pieces. For nearly two hours the *Florida* stood this pelting *feu d'enfer*, drawing away little by little from her relentless pursuers, and at last the poor little crippled craft limped like a wounded stag into the friendly port, and anchored under the protection of Fort Morgan.

No shot or shell had got among the *Florida*'s machinery, but she was much cut up. The fore-topmast, and fore-gaff were shot away, all the boats were cut to pieces, the hammock-nettings were nearly all swept off on one side, the main rigging was cut adrift, and she was hulled in many places. One 11-inch shell had passed clean through her just above the water-line,

---

* Two of the blockaders, the *Winona* and the *Rachel, Seaman* did not get to very close quarters, but still they had a good chance for gun practice at the *Florida*.

and another had entered the captain's cabin, fortunately without exploding.

During this unparalleled chase and escape, Maffitt sat most of the time on the quarter-rail, and steered straight for the bar; Stribbling was cool and self-possessed, and not one of the young officers or men flinched. Every man of true courage will say that this was a gallant deed, and will feel a generous regret that men of so much fortitude should have had no opportunity to show their metal except in the test of passive endurance.

It is not the purpose of this history to narrate in detail the cruises of the several vessels which were built or bought in Europe for the Confederate States. The late Admiral Semmes published before his death a full account of his adventures in the *Sumter* and *Alabama*, the journals of the *Florida* have been also published, and there have been accounts more or less complete of the performances of the other ships. I shall therefore give mere summaries of their movements, limiting my remarks upon their cruising careers to such incidents as suggest general reflections in respect to maritime warfare, or which have some special bearing upon the question of belligerent rights and practices.

The *Florida* needed extensive repairs and almost a new outfit, to make good her losses and injury at Nassau, and the terrible punishment she had received from the *Oneida* and her consorts; but at Mobile there was no dock, not even a slip upon which she could be placed, and almost everything required for outfit and armament had to be brought from a distance, the ordnance stores from far-away Richmond.

It was not until December that all necessary work was finished, and the *Florida* did not get to sea until some time in January, 1863. The blockading force had meanwhile been largely increased, with the special purpose to prevent the *Florida*'s escape, and she had to wait some weeks before there was a favourable opportunity. The bold run into Mobile was justifiable only on the ground of its seeming necessity. An attempt to pass outward through the blockaders in the same daring manner would have been reckless and unworthy of Maffitt's reputation for prudence as well as courage. The opportunity came at last. One day, January 15th, 1863, there were signs of a "norther" and everything was got ready for a run. At nightfall the gale began. There was no sheltering rain, but the wind was almost dead off-shore, the dark-blue surface of the Gulf was lashed into foam, and the spume of the sea was flying half-mast high. These northers in the Gulf of Mexico are spiteful, but no good well-found ship need fear leaving the weather-shore in one of them. The blockaders were no doubt doing their best to hold on to the land, for they must have thought the *Florida* would make the attempt to escape. She did, and got clear, although she was seen, and chased nearly across to Havana.

Maffitt did not remain long in the confined waters of the Gulf, but reappeared at Nassau, the scene of his first troubles, on the 25th of January, 1863,* where he remained only one day. From Nassau he cruised down to the southward through the West Indian Islands, touching at Barbadoes, February 24th, and Pernambuco, in Brazil, May 8th. At the last named place he stopped four days to get fresh provisions and make some repairs to his engines. Getting away from Pernambuco, May 12th, he cruised for a short time off the coast of Brazil, and worked his way up to St. George's, Bermuda, where he arrived July 16th, 1863.

During the *Florida's* run through the West Indies, Rear-Admiral Wilkes, of *Trent* notoriety, was commanding the United States naval forces in those latitudes, and he seems to have been looking especially after Maffitt, and to have had some inkling of his necessities, although not particularly well informed in regard to his whereabouts. On the 26th of February Admiral Wilkes wrote to his Government thus: "The fact of the *Florida's* having but a few days' coal makes me anxious to have our vessels off the Martinique, which is the only island at which they can hope to get any coal or supplies, the English islands being cut off under the rules of her Majesty's Government for some sixty days yet, which precludes the possibility, unless by chicanery or fraud, of the hope of any coal or comfort there."† Two days before the date of Admiral Wilkes's letter, *i.e.,* February 24th, 1863, the *Florida* went into Barbadoes, and got what coal she required without practising either "chicanery" or "fraud," but upon Captain Maffitt's simple statement that his fuel had been exhausted from stress of weather. In the "British Case, Geneva Arbitration," p. 68, it is stated on the authority of the Governor that both the United States ship *San Jacinto* and the Confederate ship *Florida* had been permitted to obtain coal at Barbadoes within a less period than three months after they had respectively coaled at another British colonial port, the commander of each vessel having alleged that his supply of fuel had been exhausted by stress of weather.

In the "Case of the United States" it is demonstrated by official documents that the Governor of Barbadoes was mistaken in the supposition that the *San Jacinto* had received a supply of coal at a British port within three months; but it is not pretended that he had reason to doubt the fact

* "British Case," p. 68.
† See "United States Case, Tribunal of Arbitration," p. 96.

at the time of the occurrence, because he mentioned it in a subsequent conversation with Admiral Wilkes, as the precedent which he had followed in extending a like privilege to the *Florida*. The Governor did not construe the regulations as applicable to cases of distress, and in his report he states that both vessels were "dealt with as being in distress."* The *Florida* was, however, only permitted to take on board about ninety tons of coal, which act of grace nevertheless offended Admiral Wilkes, and afforded the occasion for an indiscreet and intemperate protest. It is surprising to perceive how quickly a certain class of the United States naval officers adopted the phraseology of the politicians at Washington, and soiled their reports and marred the dignity of their official correspondence by the use of inelegant and opprobrious epithets in describing the conduct of their opponents, whose only offence was that they had conscientiously, and manifestly to their own injury, taken a different view of a great political question.

The *Florida's* short cruise in the West Indies and on the coast of Brazil caused much uneasiness in the commercial ports of the United States. The war premium advanced, and merchants hastened to register their ships in the names of British subjects, and to put them under the British flag. The *Alabama* was also by this time at sea and actively at work, as will afterwards appear, and her operations added to the panic.

The principal ships captured and destroyed by the *Florida* during the cruise above mentioned were the *Aldebaran, Commonwealth, General Berry, Crown Point, Lapwing, M. J. Colcord, Southern Cross, Oneida, Star of Peace, Rienzi, William B. Nash, Red Gauntlet* and *Henrietta*. I have before me, at the moment of writing, the ransom bonds of four other vessels which were taken by Maffitt from their respective captains, it appearing upon investigation that they were loaded on account of neutrals. Ship *Sunrise,* $60,000,† ship *Kate Dyer,* $40,000, ship *F. B. Cutting,* $40,000, schooner *V. H. Hill,* $10,000. The *Florida* left Bermuda July 25th, 1863, and arrived at Brest August 23rd. On the passage she captured the American ships *F. B. Cutting* and the *Avon,* but released the former.

Besides the vessels above mentioned which Maffitt captured with the *Florida,* he captured the *Clarence* off the coast of Brazil, and fitted her out as a tender, and with her destroyed the *Kate Stuart,* the *Mary Alvina,* the *Mary Schindler,* and the *Whistling Wind.* On May 10th, 1863, he captured the *Tacony,* and finding her better suited to his purpose than the *Clarence,*

---

* "British Appendix," vol. i., p. 92.
† See p. 136 for copy of bond.

he burnt the latter, and transferred her crew and armament to the *Tacony*. In conjunction with this vessel he captured the *Ada, Byzantian, Elizabeth Ann, Goodspeed, L. A. Macomber, Marengo, Ripple, Rufus Choate*, and *Umpire*.

On June 25th, 1863, he captured the *Archer*, transferred guns and crew from *Tacony* to *Archer*, and burned the former, and a few days after the boats of the *Archer* went into the harbour of Portland, Maine, and destroyed the United States revenue cutter *Caleb Cushing*.*

The *Florida*'s arrival at a European port at that time was wholly unexpected by me, for I had received no communication from Captain Maffitt since his escape from Mobile, and had no advice of his intended movements. Maffitt, on his part, was ignorant where I was, although he knew that Liverpool was the most likely place to find me. Immediately upon the *Florida*'s arrival at Brest, Maffitt reported to the Préfet Maritime, Vice-Admiral Count de Gueyton, the necessity which had compelled him to seek the shelter of a French port; and the first reply of the Admiral was that the ship might receive coals and other supplies, and effect necessary repairs on the same conditions as any "merchant ship." But the *Florida* needed a thorough refitting. On the 3rd of September Maffitt sent an officer to Liverpool to see me personally, and to report defects and requirements, which were many and important. The officer brought me a letter from Maffitt, from which the following is an extract:

> "We must dock, relieve our shaft, which has got out of line, and replace some of our copper. We want also a blower to get steam with the bad coal we are often obliged to put up with. While in Mobile we did all that could be done, and that was but precious little, for we lay in the middle of the bay, and the poverty of the city was painful in the extreme. Since leaving Mobile we have been under a constant pressure, without a friendly port in which to overhaul or give ordinary attention to the engines."

I immediately sent a competent representative of the builders of the ship and engines to Brest to examine the *Florida*, and to report her condition. There was no commercial dock at Brest, but after some demur permission was given to use a Government dock. The *Florida* remained in dock five or six weeks, and the French authorities, when they became sat-

---

* The officer who commanded the *Florida*'s tenders and who executed the dashing affair at Portland was Lieutenant C. W. Read. The whole number of prizes taken during Maffitt's cruise was fifty-five.

isfied of her real wants, permitted them to be supplied in full. The rough handling to which the *Florida* had been subjected had told upon her armament as well as upon her general equipment. Permission was given to land the small arms to be overhauled by a local gunsmith, upon a guarantee through the Customs authorities that they would be re-shipped without any addition in quantity. Application was made to land some of the gun-carriages for the same purpose, but this was refused. However, two carriages and the necessary gear were made at Nantes for the pivot guns, and were delivered to the ship off the island of Belle Isle, together with some fusees and other articles contraband of war, without in any way violating the neutrality of France.

The repairs at Brest occupied several months, because applications had to be frequently made to the authorities for leave to do what was necessary as the need was discovered; and the requests had not only to be considered by the local authorities, but often referred to Paris. But there was difficulty, embarrassment, and delay from circumstances relating to the *personnel* of the *Florida,* as well as from the wear and tear of her hull, machinery, and armament. On the 3rd of September Captain Maffitt informed me officially by letter that he had been compelled to discharge a large number of his men at Brest, and had supplied each of them with money sufficient to carry him to Liverpool. He said that he had informed the men that they would not be entitled to be paid their wages in full unless they returned to the Confederate States, but they would be directed on the subject by me.

In writing an historical narrative it is necessary to record events which are often not of especial moment in themselves, but which in their consequences cause difficulties and create obstacles to the achievement of purposes with which they seem at first to have no connection, and they cannot therefore be omitted.

It will appear in a subsequent chapter that the *Florida*'s arrival and delay in Brest, but especially the discharge of a portion of her crew there, caused infinite embarrassment, and contributed to the failure of an enterprise which would have been of incalculable advantage to the Confederate cause. Maffitt, of course, knew only of his own necessities, and his duty was therefore to do his best under the circumstances in which he was placed. His ship required overhauling, and he brought her to a port at which the defects could be made good, and from which he could communicate with the agent of the Confederate Navy Department, and he did not anticipate, neither could he have foreseen, that he would thus cause any trouble elsewhere.

The discharge of the men referred to above left the *Florida* so weak-handed that she would not have been fit to resume her cruise, and it was necessary to replace them. Application was made to the French authorities for leave to fill up the vacancies. There was at first some hesitation, and the application was referred to Paris. It appears from the proceedings before the Tribunal of Arbitration at Geneva that there was a good deal of correspondence on the subject between Mr. Dayton, the United States Minister, and M. Drouyn de l'Huys, the French Minister of Foreign Affairs, of which at the time we could know nothing. Mr. Slidell (the Confederate Commissioner), however, knew that the matter had been discussed by the Imperial Cabinet, and after due process of gestation the application was granted. M. Drouyn de l'Huys stated to Mr. Dayton that the Government had caused inquiries to be made, and had ascertained that seventy or seventy-five men had been discharged from the *Florida* at Brest, because the period for which they had been shipped had expired, and that the Government had concluded not to prohibit "an accession to the crew, inasmuch as such accession was necessary to her navigation."*

This, it must be admitted, was a strange and somewhat unusual proceeding, but we Confederates had no concern with the matter as a diplomatic controversy, or as a question of international law. The *Florida* wanted a number of seamen, and the only question with Maffitt was, how to get them without violating the municipal laws of France, or imposing upon the credulity and friendly consideration which he had received from the local authorities at Brest. It would seem to be an easy matter to engage and get on board seventy seamen in a maritime port, but there was very great difficulty, and much time was consumed in accomplishing that apparently simple purpose. The permission to replace the discharged men did not carry with it the right to enlist them for the Confederate service even in France, and of course it gave not the semblance of a right to do so in England. The *Florida* wanted English-speaking seamen, and these had to be sought for chiefly across the channel. The men were engaged in small groups wherever they could be found, and were forwarded to Calais and other French channel ports, and then taken by rail to Brest. This was the only possible arrangement, and it required the employment of several agents, whose discretion was not always reliable. Manifestly the men could not be told what they were wanted for until they got on board the

---

* See "British Case," "North America," (no. 1), 1872, pp. 71, 72. Correspondence of Mr. Dayton.

Florida. The mystery of the proceedings attracted notice, the suspicion of several of the United States Consuls was aroused, and they did their best to discover the true purpose of the unusual but systematic movement of nautical-looking men, with conductors in charge, and to defeat it.

With so much to accomplish, and by such indirect and tedious means, it is not surprising that the *Florida* was detained a long time in Brest; in fact, she was not ready for sea until February, 1864. All that the *Florida* required could have been completed satisfactorily in a few weeks, if she could have gone to any of the large English building-yards—say on the Clyde or Mersey—and there have done the work openly and in the ordinary commercial way, and the expense would have been moderate. But the constant peril of being stopped for an alleged violation of neutrality, the necessary applications to official personages on every small matter of detail, the hesitations, references to Paris, and general circumlocution, caused great loss of time, and a large increase in the expenditure. The local authorities were most considerate and courteous, and for that very reason it was imperative to scrupulously respect their instructions and limitations, so as not to involve them in any trouble.

I have given the simplest possible synopsis of the cost and labour of refitting a Confederate ship. Full details would, I really think, astonish the reader, but the foregoing will suffice to suggest, if it does not abundantly demonstrate, the immense disadvantages under which the Confederate Government laboured in the effort to keep a small naval force at sea.

Very shortly after the arrival of the *Florida* at Brest, Maffitt's health completely gave way. The attack of yellow fever at Cardenas had left him in a weak state. Subsequent exposure brought on rheumatism of the heart. When at Bermuda in July, 1863, he had informed the Secretary of the Navy that he would feel bound to obtain a relief on the arrival of the ship in Europe, if he did not get much better, and as soon as the arrangements for the repairs were fairly in train, he resigned the command. Several Confederate naval officers were then in Paris, for purposes which will be subsequently explained. One of these, Commander J. N. Barney, relieved Maffitt, and he had much of the worry and labour of refitting the ship, but his health was not strong, and in January it became so feeble that he was compelled to retire, and he was relieved in the command by Lieutenant C. Manigault Morris, about January 4th.

The *Florida* was still short-handed, but there were men enough to handle the ship and work her pivot guns, and the Confederate cruisers were always able to recruit from prizes.

Morris got to sea from Brest on the 12th of February, 1864, took his new gun-carriages on board off Belle Isle, February 19th, and then proceeded to cruise through the West Indies, and up to the northward in the direction of the American coast. He touched at Martinique, April 26, for coal and supplies, called at Bermuda, May 12th, merely to communicate and land a sick officer, and went to that island again on June 18th, where he was permitted to make some necessary repairs and take in a small supply of fuel. July 27th he was off again, and made a bold dash straight in for the enemy's coast, which took him across the track of outward-bound ships. On the 10th of July, thirty miles off the Capes of the Delaware, he captured the United States mail steamer *Electric Spark*, bound from New York to New Orleans, with the mails and a number of passengers on board. Morris transferred the crew and passengers to a passing English schooner, which he chartered for the purpose, and then cut the steamer's pipes, opened her valves and ports, and thus permitted her to sink. During the run in shore from Bermuda the *Florida* captured and burned the following ships:—*Harriet Stevens, Golconda, Margaret Y. Davis,* and *Mondamin*. Manifestly the little Confederate cruiser could not remain in that neighbourhood long. The purpose was to alarm the enemy by a "raid" on the line of his coasting trade, and having struck the blow, Morris ran across to Teneriffe, and then cruised leisurely across the line towards the north-eastern coast of Brazil, burning whatever prizes he made (in all about thirteen), including those captured during the run in and off the American coast.

On the 4th of October, at 9 P.M. the *Florida* anchored at Bahia, the purpose being to get supplies, make some slight repairs, and refresh the crew after a long and active cruise; for, in point of fact, there had been no chance to give the men a run on shore since the departure from Brest on the 12th of February. By this time the *Florida* was in good condition to fulfil the objects of those for whose service she was built. Officers and crew were in fine spirits, and hoped to accomplish a good deal of work still, although American ships were fast disappearing from the high seas, or at least they were rapidly sheltering from capture under the British mercantile flag. But there was another fate in waiting for the gallant little ship. She had braved and survived the lawful, though murdering, attack of the United States ships off Mobile; she surrendered to the treacherous and illegal assault of another United States ship at Bahia. The first encounter was a fair open "stand and deliver," the second was an assassination. This is a harsh word. It has been forced from me. The English language does not offer a milder phrase to fitly distinguish the occurrence, or I would gladly adopt it, but I feel, nevertheless, bound to justify the epithet.

It was dark when the *Florida* anchored, on the evening of October 4th. At an early hour on the morning of the 5th the customary visit of ceremony and inquiry was paid to her by the Brazilian naval authorities, and it was perceived that a United States ship-of-war was at anchor not far off, which proved to be the United States steam corvette *Wachusett,* Commander N. Collins. At about noon of the same day Morris had an interview with the President of the Province, by special appointment, to explain his wants, and to get a reply to the request he had made to the Brazilian Admiral for permission to remain the necessary time to make some repairs to the engine, which request the Admiral had referred to his Excellency. The Admiral was present at the interview, and the result was very satisfactory to Morris. The President promptly consented to his remaining the customary forty-eight hours, to which time all belligerent vessels were limited, but added that if upon the report of a marine engineer, who would be sent on board to inspect, it should appear that the repairs could not be completed in that time, he would grant an extension sufficient to meet the requirements of the case.

The President, in the course of further conversation, remarked upon the presence of a United States ship-of-war in the bay, and impressed upon Morris that he would expect and rely upon him to do nothing that might occasion a hostile collision with her. He added that the United States Consul had given him a solemn assurance on behalf of Captain Collins that the *Wachusett* would do nothing while in the port which was contrary to the laws of nations, or in violation of the neutrality and sovereignty of Brazil, and expressed the desire that Morris would give him a corresponding promise, which he did. At this point the Admiral remarked that the *Florida* and *Wachusett* were lying in close proximity, and he suggested that Morris should move the *Florida* to a position between his (the Admiral's) ship and the shore. After the interview with the President, Morris went immediately on board and shifted his berth to the anchorage suggested by the Admiral. The marine engineer spoken of by the President had preceded him, and soon reported that the repairs would require four days.

Morris now being quite easy in mind with regard to the privilege of remaining in port, and feeling no apprehension of an unpleasant, and certainly believing that there could be no hostile, collision with the *Wachusett,* or any of her belongings, determined to give his crew "liberty." The ship was put in usual harbour trim, the guns were unloaded, the running gear was flemished down, the awnings spread, and the port watch (one half the crew) were permitted to go on shore. The next day, October 6th, the "liberty men" began to return on board at an early hour, and when most of them had returned, the starboard watch was sent on shore, Captain Morris and a party of the officers going at the same time.

When night set in on that 6th of October, 1864, the state of affairs was this: The *Florida* was lying inshore of the Brazilian Admiral's ship (a small wooden sailing sloop-of-war), and the *Wachusett* was some distance off, and on the other or off-shore side of the Admiral. The first-lieutenant, J. K. Porter, with ten officers of all grades, and about seventy men, most of whom had just returned from "liberty," were on board the *Florida*, and Captain Morris, four officers, and the remainder of the crew were on shore. At about 3 A.M. on the morning of the 7th, Lieutenant Porter was aroused by the officer of the deck, Acting-master T. T. Hunter, who reported to him that the *Wachusett* was under weigh, and was standing towards the *Florida*. Lieutenant Porter had not turned in, but was asleep on a sofa in the commander's cabin, and being dressed, he got very quickly on deck, when he saw the *Wachusett* close aboard, and steering directly for them. Before he could give an order, or even hail the approaching ship, she ran violently into the *Florida*, striking her on the starboard quarter. The force of the collision crushed in the bulwarks, started several beams, broke the main-yard, and carried away the mizen-mast, which came down in three pieces. The *Wachusett* at or about the same time fired two shots from her battery, and opened a musketry fire upon the startled crew of the *Florida*, who, thus unexpectedly aroused, could have made no effective resistance, even if they had been armed, being embarrassed, and indeed prevented from even seeing the attacking ship, by reason of the awning, which, borne down by the wreck of the mizen-mast and its gear, covered and confined them as if in a net.

In the confusion of the collision, Lieutenant Stone managed to get clear of the awning, and standing upon a gun, he fired one shot from his revolver. About fifteen of the crew jumped overboard, but only six reached the shore. Those who succeeded in swimming safely to the shore reported to Captain Morris that they had been fired at while in the water by the men on the forecastle and in the boats of the *Wachusett*, and that the missing men had probably been killed or drowned. Immediately after the collision the *Wachusett* backed off a short distance and hailed the *Florida*, demanding an immediate surrender, on pain of being sunk there and then. After a moment's hesitation, and a hasty consultation with Lieutenant

Stone, Lieutenant Porter replied that he would surrender. The *Florida* was then boarded, a hawser was made fast to her, and the *Wachusett* towed her to sea.

I have condensed the foregoing statement into the smallest possible space and into the briefest possible phrases, because I have thought it would be best and fairest to all parties to let them give their own version, and the official reports and statements with reference to the whole occurrence, together with the correspondence between the Brazilian Legation at Washington and the United States Secretary of State, will be found in full at the end of the chapter.

That portion of Captain Morris's report which refers to what took place on board the *Florida* during the attack was, as he himself says, gathered from the six men who succeeded in swimming ashore, and I am satisfied they were mistaken in saying that there was repeated firing on either side. From personal inquiry I feel assured that not more than two pistol-shots were fired from the *Florida*. I am inclined to think there was only one, by Lieutenant Stone, in the manner related above; on the other hand, I cannot learn that the *Wachusett* fired into the *Florida* after backing clear, although the men who escaped asserted that they were fired at in the water.

My object in giving a brief summary of the circumstances attending the capture of the *Florida* is to supply the text for the general remarks I feel called upon to make upon the whole occurrence, in order to justify the use of the word "assassination" which I have applied to it, without being forced to refer frequently to the official documents, which the reader can consult at his convenience. There could hardly be a more flagrant and offensive violation of national sovereignty than that which Captain Collins committed upon the Empire of Brazil; but it is no part of my purpose to discuss the incident with reference to its diplomatic or legal bearings. I have no sentimental notions in regard to the precepts of public law, or the demands of international comity. I know full well that strong Powers have treated such considerations with indifference and contempt, whenever it suited their purpose to do so. Nelson sailed into Copenhagen and destroyed a great part of the Danish fleet without orders, even if not in violation of them, when England and Denmark were not at war, and he set up no pretence in justification, but simply affirmed that the safety and interests of his own country required him to act in that energetic way.*

* "Pictorial History of England," vol. vi., book x., p. 162. When asked by the Crown Prince of Denmark why the British fleet had forced its way up the Baltic, Nelson replied, "To crush and annihilate a confederacy formed against the dearest interests of England."

Captain Hillyar, with the British ships *Phœbe* and *Cherub,* followed the United States ship *Essex* into the harbour of Valparaiso, attacked, and after a desperate resistance captured her under the very guns of a Chilian battery, but both of those acts were done openly in the light of day, and in bold defiance of all consequences. When Buenos Ayres was fighting her war of independence with Spain, a ship-of-war of the "so-called" insurgents, the *Federal,* boarded an American vessel on the high seas, and took out of her some goods alleged to be Spanish property. The *Federal* put into the Swedish island of St. Bartholomew soon after, and found there, or was followed in by, the United States ship *Erie,* Captain Daniel Turner. Captain Turner made a demand upon the Governor for the surrender of the *Federal* to him, she having done violence to the American flag. The Governor refused, on the ground that the ship in question was a commissioned vessel-of-war, belonging to a recognised belligerent Power, and Captain Turner sent in the *Erie's* boats, under command of his first-lieutenant, Josiah Tattnall, and cut her out from under the guns of the fort. The acts of the two Captains Hillyar and Turner were indefensible upon the principles of international law and comity as generally understood, but in neither case was the commander under a personal engagement, implied or otherwise, to respect the neutrality of the countries in whose waters the offences were committed. They simply acted in defiance of law, and were prepared to take the consequences.

There is no evidence that Captain Collins gave any personal assurance to the President of Bahia in reference to his conduct while in that port. He makes no allusion to the subject in his official report; but that is not conclusive either one way or the other. I think those who read the various reports will not doubt that the Consul, Mr. Thomas F. Wilson, did give the assurance required by the President on behalf of the *Wachusett*, and it was his business, his imperative duty, to inform Captain Collins what he had done.

But apart from all technicalities and quibbles, it is perfectly well known that the regulations under which the Neutral Powers permitted the ships of the two belligerents in the American Civil War to enter and remain in their ports, were founded upon the assumption that in return for the hospitalities and shelter granted, there was an honourable and unqualified undertaking to respect the neutrality of the ports. Whenever a United States or a Confederate ship let go her anchor in a neutral port and asked leave to remain, her commander could only accept the privileges he asked under the above conditions, and when the alternative of compliance or departure was not directly and specifically proposed, it was from a feeling of delicacy on the part of the local authority, and of confidence in the good faith of the individual commander.

We come, then, to this final proposition. In stating it I hope to avoid the appearance of exaggeration. The United States ship *Wachusett* lay in the harbour of Bahia, in company with the Confederate ship *Florida* two days, both ships being under an obligation to keep the peace as the condition of their leave to remain. But when the *Wachusett,* by her quiet demeanour, had dispelled all doubt and apprehension, not only in the mind of Captain Morris, but in the minds of the Brazilian authorities as well, she crept stealthily, under cover of night, and struck her adversary a foul blow when there was no power to ward it off, and no possible ground for suspecting it. If Captain Collins had dashed into the harbour in the full light of day, and had made his attack upon the *Florida* without fear of the consequences, the proceeding would not have been more offensive to Brazil, nor would it have been a greater violation of her sovereign rights than the course he adopted, and he would have been equally sure of capturing, or at least destroying his enemy, because she would have been quite unprepared to make effective resistance, and the whole transaction demonstrates that the Brazilian Admiral's ship was too weak and inefficient to exercise any preventive force.* If the *Wachusett's* assault upon the *Florida* had been in the above manner, it could have been classed with that of the *Phœbe* and *Cherub* upon the *Essex,* or the boats of the *Erie* upon the *Federal,* and I should have been spared the pain of denouncing it as an assassination.

Captain Collins offers in justification, or at least in palliation of his offence against the sovereign rights of Brazil, the allegation that the *Alabama* had been permitted to burn some American ships near the island of Fernando de Noronha, within the jurisdiction of the Empire without remonstrance, and he therefore thought it "probable" that his attack upon the *Florida* would be treated with the same leniency. Captain Collins could have had no personal knowledge of the occurrence he mentions, and probably got the alleged fact from the United States Consul, who also put it in his letter to the President, requesting, or rather "claiming," that the *Florida* should in effect be treated as a pirate.† Admiral Semmes, in his history of the *Alabama's* cruise, writing from his diary, and without any knowledge of Captain Collins's counter-allegation, gives the true version,

* See "Admiral's Report," p. 210.
† See "British Case," p. 74.

which is that he burned the *Louisa Hatch* and the *Kate Cory,* "taking the pains to send them both beyond the marine league, that I might pay due respect to the jurisdiction of Brazil."*

The letter of Mr. Thomas F. Wilson to the President of Bahia is a fair example of the diplomatic literature with which the consular agents of the United States tried the patience and vexed the polite sensibilities of the local authorities to whom they were accredited during the Civil War. Brazil, in common with all the other Powers, great and small, had acknowledged the Confederate States as a belligerent, with a *de facto* Government, which conceded to them the same right to commission ships-of-war as the United States had; and yet Mr. Thomas F. Wilson was apparently unconscious of the incivility and impolicy of asserting in an official communication to a high civil officer of the empire that the *Florida* was "not commissioned by any recognised Government whatever," that her officers and crew were "not subject to any international or civilized law," and were consequently "not entitled to the privileges and immunities conceded to vessels navigating under the flag of a civilized nation," and then in conclusion setting up a "claim" that the "piratical cruiser" should be "detained to answer," etc.,† by which the writer probably meant that the officers and crew should be looked upon as Malay pirates, and treated accordingly.

The Brazilians are a very polite race. They are punctilious in the practice of official propriety and decorum. Their officials are easily conciliated by deferential treatment and outward forms of respect. They are very affable and obliging when approached with complaisance and frankness, but are reticent, suspicious, and unyielding at the slightest approach to rudeness or duplicity. I can well imagine the mingled feelings of surprise and repulsion with which his Excellency Antonio Joaquim da Silva Gomes, President of the Province of Bahia, read the letter of Thomas F. Wilson, Consul of the United States, and the effort it must have cost him to suppress his feelings within the limits of the mild and gentlemanly rebuke contained in the last paragraph of his reply.

When the *Wachusett* steamed out of the bay of Bahia with the *Florida* in tow, the Brazilian Admiral pursued her with the force at his disposal; but his three vessels were so small and so inefficiently armed, that he could have had no expectation of compelling the release of the *Florida,* and his demonstration was therefore only a spirited protest against the act of vio-

---

* "My Adventures Afloat," by Admiral Raphael Semmes. London: Bentley, 1869.
† Letter, p. 200.

lence which had been committed under his eye. The *Wachusett*, towing the *Florida*, and with sail on both vessels, had no difficulty in getting away from her pursuers, and she finally arrived at Hampton Roads with her prize on the 12th of November.

On the arrival of the two ships at Hampton Roads the Secretary of State, Mr. William H. Seward, must have been promptly informed of the occurrence, and he must have known that the act of Captain Collins was wholly indefensible. His duty as a statesman, careful and jealous for the honour of his country as well as for its safety, would seem to have been quite clear. He admits, in his reply to the complaint of the Brazilian Minister at Washington, that "the capture of the *Florida* was an unauthorized, unlawful, and indefensible exercise of the naval force of the United States within a foreign country, in defiance of its established and duly recognised government." It is hardly possible to conceive that he should have hesitated one moment in deciding to release the *Florida*, and in offering an apology to Brazil, which would have been so much more gratifying to the recipient, and honourable to the giver, if promptly and spontaneously tendered. But Mr. Seward waited to see what the Brazilian Government would do. He knew that it would be some time, probably two or three months, before that Government could instruct their Minister at Washington, and he seems to have preferred yielding to a demand rather than to proffer a frank explanation.

At last the demand came, on the 12th December, through the Brazilian Legation at Washington, and Mr. Seward made the *amende*, in a despatch hardly ever paralleled in its tone of arrogant and offensive recrimination.

Brazil was too weak to protect the *Florida*. She was equally powerless to resent the injury this ungracious apology must have inflicted upon her pride. Diplomatically, her demands were complied with, but the *status quo* was never restored. Pending the arrival of the anticipated complaint from Rio de Janeiro, the *Florida* was permitted to founder in Hampton Roads, by a judiciously managed oversight in examining her valves, so Mr. Seward could not restore the ship. There were twelve or thirteen thousand dollars in gold in the paymaster's safe when the *Florida* was captured, a part of which belonged to the officers' mess. Mr. Seward did not mention that fact to the Brazilian Minister, nor was a single penny of it supplied to the officers when they were discharged from Fort Warren, after a rigorous confinement of about three months.*

---

* See Lieutenant Porter's official letter to Mr. Secretary Gideon Welles, p. 158.

The treatment of those officers is one of the most painful and discreditable incidents in this unhappy affair. When the *Wachusett* arrived in Hampton Roads the prisoners were sent *en masse* to the military prison at Point Look-out, where the officers and men were separated, and the officers were in a few days transferred to the "Old Capitol Prison" at Washington. After three or four days' confinement in that gaol, they were sent back to the *Wachusett* at Hampton Roads, and were all conveyed by her to Fort Warren, a fortress on an island in the harbour of Boston, which had been converted into a "lock-up" for prisoners-of-state as well as of war. In this cheerless place, and under the trying conditions specified in Lieutenant T. K. Porter's official report,* they were imprisoned until February 1st, 1865, which was nearly seven weeks after Mr. Seward had stated, in an official despatch to the Brazilian Minister at Washington,† that "the capture of the *Florida* was an *unauthorized, unlawful,* and *indefensible* exercise of the naval force of the United States," and that the crew of the *Florida* were "*unlawfully* brought into the custody of this Government," namely, the Government of the United States.

But this is not all. When the officers were set at liberty, they were forced to sign an undertaking that they would leave the United States within ten days from the date of their release. They were without any means to pay their expenses, and Lieutenant Porter wrote an application to Mr. Gideon Welles, the Secretary of the United States Navy, for a return to him of the money which had been captured in the *Florida,* and which, to the extent of the amount of pay due them, was as much the private property of the captured officers as Mr. Gideon Welles's watch was his, to say nothing of the obligation, under the conditions of the *amende* to Brazil, to restore the whole of it to Lieutenant Porter as the senior officer of the *Florida.*

To that application Mr. Gideon Welles did not see fit to reply; he did not even practise the commonplace courtesy of acknowledging its receipt, and the officers were turned into the streets of Boston, and among a population which was then hostile, with no means to pay their way out of the country, and yet under a forced engagement to depart within ten days. Lieutenant Porter was able to arrange for a passage for himself and party to England in the Cunard steamship *Canada,* by giving a draft on the Confederate financial agent, and they reached Liverpool about the middle of

* See Report, p. 219.
† Letter, p. 216.

that month, and came to me very much in the condition of distressed seamen sent home under consular certificate.

I submit the foregoing without comment, as a plain unvarnished statement of the manner in which Mr. Secretary Seward made the *amende* to Brazil for what he himself denounced as an "*unauthorized, unlawful,* and *indefensible* defiance" of her neutral rights, and of the spirit in which he affected to restore the *status quo*.

An historical narrative cannot be limited to a mere record of events in the form of a diary. The occurrences must be illustrated sometimes by explanatory comments, and by comparing or contrasting them with events or with actions upon which public judgment has already been pronounced. A military or naval officer in command of a national force loses, to a certain extent, his personal identity. He is merged in his office, and may thus be criticized without reference to his individuality or the personal qualities which make up his private character. Captain Collins was always looked upon as an honourable and truthful man in his intercourse with friends and acquaintances. If a proposition of doubtful propriety were suggested to him, I should feel sure that, if left to himself, he would come to a fair and just resolution, and that he would not leave it in the power of friend or foe to charge him with bad faith. With reference to his conduct in the adventure with the *Florida,* upon which it has been my painful office to comment, it seems to me that he made the mistake of placing himself in the hands of Mr. Consul Thomas F. Wilson, who appears to have imbibed the acrimonious temper of his departmental chief, and to have adopted the harsh epithets and the opprobrious phrases which that high officer of State did not think it unbecoming to introduce into his diplomatic correspondence when it was necessary to mention those who were opposed to him in the great Civil War.

Since Mr. Seward has thought it proper and dignified to maintain in an official despatch* that "that vessel (the *Florida*), like the *Alabama,* was a pirate," and to further state in the same document that "the crew," among whom he contemptuously includes the officers, "were enemies of the human race," it seemed imperative upon me, as the historian of the little craft's origin and adventures, not only to relate the closing events of her brief career, but to comment upon the manner of bringing them about. I have no feeling of enmity against anyone. It would grieve me to know that I had wounded the feelings of one who was, in former years, a brother

* See p. 151.

officer, or that I had cast an aspersion upon the service in which I once held a commission, by heedless statements or ill-digested comments. I confidently believe that in what I have felt it my duty to write there has been no warping of the facts, but that I have kept faithfully to the record. But the reader himself can judge, because I have annexed the official reports of all the persons involved in the affair.

DOCUMENTS ABOVE REFERRED TO.

FORM OF RANSOM BOND TAKEN FROM PRIZES WHEN RELEASED (SEE P. 121).

This bond, made and entered into this seventh of July, one thousand eight hundred and sixty-three (A.D. 1863), by and between Richard Luce, master and commander of the American ship *Sunrise* of the first part, and John N. Maffitt, lieutenant-commanding in the navy of the Confederate States of America of the second part, witnesseth:

That the said party of the first part is held and firmly bound (for himself, the ship and her owners) unto Jefferson Davis, President of the Confederate States of America, or his successors in office, in the full and penal sum of sixty thousand dollars ($60,000), to be well and truly paid, in gold or its equivalent, within six calendar months after the ratification of a treaty of peace between the Confederate States and the United States.

The condition of this bond is such that the aforesaid party of the first part has this day been captured on the high seas, while in command of the ship aforesaid, by the Confederate States sloop-of-war *Florida*, whereof the party of the second part is commander, and has been allowed to proceed on his voyage without injury or detriment to the ship or cargo, and has been guaranteed against molestation during the present voyage from any and all armed vessels in the service of the Confederate States of America.

Done in duplicate on board the Confederate States sloop-of-war *Florida*, the day and date above written.

Witness: THOMAS BARRY,
First Officer.
Witness: G. D. BRYAN,
Mdn. C.S.N.

RICHARD LUCE (*seal*),
Master-Comdg.
J. N. MAFFITT (*seal*),
Lieut.-Comdg. C.S.N.

[*Copy.*]

THE UNITED STATES CONSUL TO THE PRESIDENT OF THE PROVINCE OF BAHIA.

To his Excellency Antonio Joaquim da Silva Gomes, President of the Province of Bahia.

Consulate of the United States of America,
Bahia, *October 5th*, 1864, 9 A.M.

Sir,—

This morning a steamer anchored in this port, bearing the flag adopted by those who are involved in the rebellion against the Government of the United States of America, and I am informed that the said vessel is the *Florida*, which is engaged in capturing vessels navigating under the flag of the United States of America, and in destroying them by making bonfires of them and their cargoes.

The vessel in question is not commissioned by any recognised Government whatever, and her officers and crew are composed of persons of various nationalities, who are not subject to any international or civilized law, and are consequently not entitled to the privileges and immunities conceded to vessels navigating under the flag of a civilized nation. I therefore protest, in the name of the United States of America, against the admission of this vessel to free practice, by which she might be enabled to supply herself with coal, provisions, tackle, or utensils of any kind whatever, or receive on board any persons whatever; finally, against any assistance, aid or protection which might be conceded to her in this port, or in any other belonging to this province.

I likewise claim that the piratical cruiser, which in combination with the pirate *Alabama* violated the sovereignty of the Imperial Government of Brazil, by capturing and destroying vessels belonging to citizens of the United States of America within the territorial waters of Brazil, near the island of Fernando de Noronha, in April, 1863, be detained, with all her officers and crew, in order to answer for so flagrant a violation of the sovereignty of the Government of Brazil, and of the rights of citizens of the United States within the jurisdiction of the Brazilian Government.

I avail, etc.,

(Signed)   THOMAS F. WILSON,
Consul of the United States.

THE PRESIDENT OF THE PROVINCE TO MR. WILSON.

Palace of the Government of the Province of Bahia,
October 5th, 1864.

In a note dated this day, Mr. Thomas F. Wilson, Consul of the United States, claims that the steamer *Florida*, now anchored in this port, shall not be admitted to free *pratique*, nor obtain permission to provide herself with coal, provisions, supplies, and utensils of any kind whatever, nor receive on board any person whatever; he likewise requests that, as the cruiser, in combination with the *Alabama*, violated the sovereignty of the Imperial Government of Brazil by capturing and destroying vessels belonging to citizens of the United States of America within the territorial waters of the Empire, near the island of Fernando de Noronha, in April, 1863, she may be detained, with all her officers and crew, in order to answer for this flagrant violation of the sovereignty of the Government of Brazil, and of the rights of citizens of the United States, within the jurisdiction of the Brazilian Government.

In reply to the Consul, I have to inform him that, as the said vessel belongs to the Confederate States, in whom the Imperial Government recognised the character of belligerents, all the assistance required by humanity may be furnished her, which does in no wise constitute assistance for warlike purposes, as laid down by international law, and does not conflict with that neutrality which this Government studiously seeks to preserve, and has always preserved, in the contest between the States of North America. The undersigned cannot, therefore, admit the first portion of the claim of the Consul, in the general manner in which it was presented, and particularly in relation to those articles considered as contraband of war, in conformity with instructions issued on that subject by the Imperial Government, and according to which the said vessel will only be permitted to remain in this port for the length of time absolutely indispensable.

In regard to the second part of his note, it is my duty to observe to the Consul that, even if it were fully established that the *Florida* had previously violated neutrality, such a proceeding would scarcely authorize us to refuse her permission to enter the ports of the Empire, and would never warrant us to commit the acts required by the Consul, which would be equivalent to a hostile rupture, without the intervention of the supreme Government of the State, which is alone competent to authorize such a rupture.

I renew, etc.,

(Signed)   Antonio Joaquim da Silva Gomes.

To Mr. Thomas F. Wilson, Consul of the United States.*

[*Copy.* No. 38.]

To the Honourable Gideon Welles, Secretary of the Navy.

United States steamer *Wachusett,*
St. Thomas, W. I., *October* 31*st,* 1864.

---

* For the letter from the United States Consul to the President of Bahia and the reply of the President, see "British Case," pp. 74, 75.

Sir,—

The following is a detailed report of the capture of the rebel steamer *Florida* in the bay of San Salvador, Brazil, by the officers and crew of this vessel, without loss of life:—

At three o'clock on the morning of the seventh day of October instant, we slipped our cable and steered for the *Florida,* about five-eighths of a mile distant. An unforeseen circumstance prevented us from striking her as intended; we, however, struck her on the starboard quarter, cutting down her bulwarks, and carrying away her mizen-mast and mainyard. This ship was not injured.

Immediately upon striking we backed off, believing she would sink from the effects of the blow.

In backing clear we received a few pistol-shots from the *Florida,* which were returned with a volley, and contrary to my orders two of our broadside guns were fired, when she surrendered.

In the absence of Captain Morris, who was on shore, Lieutenant Thomas K. Porter, formerly of the United States Navy, came on board and surrendered the *Florida,* with fifty-eight men and twelve officers, making at the same time an oral protest against the capture.

Five of the *Florida*'s officers, including her commander, and the remainder of her crew, were on shore.

We took a hawser to the *Florida* and towed her to sea.

In contemplating the attack on the *Florida* in the bay, I thought it probable the Brazilian authorities would forbear to interfere, as they had done at Fernando de Noronha, when the rebel steamer *Alabama* was permitted to take into the anchorage three American ships, and to take coal from the *Louisa Hatch* within musket-shot of the fort, and afterward, within easy range of their guns, to set on fire those unarmed vessels.

I regret, however, to state that they fired three shotted guns at us while we were towing the *Florida* out.

Fortunately we received no damage. After daylight a Brazilian sloop-of-war, in tow of a paddle gun-boat, was discovered following us. With the aid of sail on both vessels we gradually increased our distance from them.

We had three men slightly wounded; one only of the three is now on the sick report.

I enclose a list of the prisoners. Those who have a star opposite their names were formerly in the United States navy.

This vessel is ready for service. The *Florida* will require repairs of machinery, a new mizen-mast, etc.

The officers and crew manifested the best spirit. They have my thanks for their hearty co-operation, in which I beg to include Thomas F. Wilson, Esq., United States Consul at Bahia, who volunteered for any duty.

> I am, sir, very respectfully
> Your obedient servant,
> N. COLLINS, Commander.

[*Copy*. No. 39.]
To the Honourable Gideon Welles, Secretary of the Navy, Washington City.

> United States Steamer, *Wachusett,*
> Hampton Roads, Va., *November* 14*th*, 1864.

Sir,—

The following is a supplement to my report, No. 38, dated October 31st, 1864:—

1. On the morning of the 7th of October last, I directed to be cast adrift one of our whale-boats, just returned from reconnoitring the rebel steamer *Florida,* rather than attract attention of outside persons by the noise of hoisting her.

2. At the time of starting to run into the rebel steamer *Florida* on the 7th day of October last, I ordered thirty fathoms of our cable to be slipped without a buoy, as I feared the rope of the latter might possibly foul the propeller.

3. Our second cutter swamped alongside the prize steamer *Florida* while we were towing the ship to sea, and was cut adrift to avoid detention in range of the Brazilian guns. As the tide was flood, both the whale-boat and cutter will probably be recovered by the United States upon the payment of salvage.

Their probable value was, for the cutter, one hundred and fifty, and for the whale-boat, fifty dollars.

4. Thomas F. Wilson, United States Consul at Bahia, desired to remain on this ship during the nights of the 5th and 6th October last, in anticipation of a probable conflict at sea with the rebel steamer *Florida,* and was on board at the time of the capture of the latter vessel. As it was not convenient to land him, I brought him to this place.

5. At the island of St. Bartholomew, West Indies, where we called for supplies, every facility was granted us, although we had one case of varioloid on board. I trust the Department may make some official acknowledgment to the Governor of that island for his civility to us.

6. Walter Dulany, a citizen of Baltimore, a passenger on the American ship *Mondamin,* and captured by the rebel steamer *Florida* with the former vessel, was found on the *Florida* when we captured her, occupying such a position among the *Florida*'s officers, some of whom were former friends and acquaintances, that I would suggest the policy of either holding him as a prisoner or of compelling him to take the oath of allegiance to the United States.

7. The authority to discharge such of our crew as have served out their period of enlistment is respectfully requested. Some have been on increased pay since June last, consequent upon having been detained beyond the time for which they shipped.

8. We touched at St. Bartholomew, West Indies, on the 29th October ult., and at St. Thomas on the 30th, where we remained till the 2nd inst., sailing on that day, and arrived here on the 12th.

I have the honour to be, very respectfully,

Your obedient servant,

N. COLLINS, Commander.

THE SEIZURE OF THE *FLORIDA.*
LIEUTENANT-COMMANDING MORRIS'S OFFICIAL STATEMENT.

Bahia, *October* 13*th,* 1864.

Sir,—

It is with great pain that I have to report the seizure of the Confederate States steamer *Florida,* lately under my command.

I arrived at this port on the 4th inst., at 9 P.M., to procure coal and provisions, and also to get some slight repairs after a cruise of sixty-one days. Just after anchoring, a boat passing around us asked the name of our vessel, and, upon receiving our reply, stated that the boat was from her Britannic Majesty's steamer *Curlew.* Next morning I found that the United States steamer *Wachusett* was at anchor near us, but no English steamer, so I at once concluded that the boat which had hailed us the evening before was from the *Wachusett.*

We were visited on the morning of the 5th by a Brazilian officer, to whom I stated my wants, and was informed by him that he would report the same to the President, and that until his answer was received we could hold no communication with the shore. At noon I received a communication—which was left on board the *Florida*—from the President, stating that he was ready to receive me. At our interview he informed me that forty-eight hours would be allowed me to fit and repair, but that, should his chief engineer, whom he would send on board to examine the machinery, deem the time too short, he would grant the necessary extension. He was most urgent in his request that I should strictly observe the laws of neutrality, at the same time stating to me that he had received the most solemn assurance from the United States Consul that the United States steamer would do nothing in port contrary to the laws of nations and of Brazil; and that he desired the same from me, which I unhesitatingly gave.

The Brazilian admiral, who was present at the interview, suggested that I had better move my vessel in between his ship and the shore, as our proximity to the *Wachusett* might cause some difficulty. My assurance to the President seemed to set his mind at rest on the score of any collision between the two vessels, and upon leaving him I immediately repaired on board and moved the *Florida* close inshore to the position suggested by the Admiral. I found the Brazilian engineer on board and was informed by him that it would require four days to repair the pipe of the condenser. Feeling now no apprehension of any difficulty occurring while in port, and wishing to gratify the crew with a short liberty, not only on the score of good conduct, but also of health, I determined to permit one watch at a time to go ashore for twelve hours, and sent the port watch off that afternoon. About 7:30 P.M. a boat came alongside, stating that she was from the United States steamer *Wachusett*, with the United States Consul, who had an official communication for the commander of the *Florida*. The letter, with the card of the Consul, was handed to First-Lieutenant Porter, who, after examining it, and finding it directed to Captain Morris, "sloop *Florida*," returned it unopened to the Consul, stating that it was improperly addressed; that the vessel was the Confederate States steamer *Florida,* and that when the letter was so directed it would be received. The next day (6th) a Mr. de Vidiky came on board, having received a letter from the United States Consul, enclosing one for me. He requested me, before receiving my letter, to permit him to read to me the one sent to him.

It was a request of Mr. de Vidiky to carry a challenge to the commander of the *Florida,* and in case of its acceptance, to offer his (the Consul's) influence in having the repairs of the *Florida* speedily finished. I informed Mr. de Vidiky that I had heard quite enough, and, finding the letter to me improperly addressed, declined receiving it; but at the same time said to him that I had come to Bahia for a special purpose, which being accomplished, I should leave; but I would neither seek nor avoid a contest with the *Wachusett*, but should I encounter her outside the

Brazilian waters, would use my utmost endeavours to destroy her. That afternoon, the port watch having returned, I sent the starboard watch, the other half of the crew, ashore on liberty, going also myself, in company with several of the officers. From our nearness to the *Wachusett*, persons on board that vessel could well see these men leave the ship. At 3:30 A.M. I was awakened by the proprietor of the hotel at which I was staying, and told that there was some trouble on board the *Florida*, as he had heard firing and cheering in the direction of the vessel, but on account of the darkness was unable to discern anything. I immediately hastened to the landing, and was informed by a Brazilian officer that the United States steamer *Wachusett* had run into and seized the *Florida*, and was then towing her out of the harbour. I hurried off to the Admiral's vessel, and was told by him that he was at once going in pursuit, which he did as soon as steam was raised on board a small steamer belonging to the fleet.

The Admiral's ship, being a sailing sloop-of-war, was taken in tow by the steamer and went out of the harbour. He returned in the afternoon with all his vessels, having been unable to overtake the *Wachusett*. Upon mustering the officers and crew left on shore, I found there four officers, viz., Lieutenant Barron, Paymaster Taylor, Midshipman Duke, and Master's-Mate King, and 71 men, of whom six escaped by swimming from the *Florida* after her seizure. Of the actual occurrences and loss of life on board the *Florida,* I have been able to find out very little. The substance of what I have gathered from the six men who escaped is as follows: That at 3:15 A.M. on October 7th, Master T. T. Hunter, Jr., being in charge of the deck, the *Wachusett* left her anchorage, and taking advantage of the darkness, steamed for the *Florida,* from which she was not seen until close aboard, when she was hailed by Mr. Hunter, who, receiving no answer, called "all hands" to quarters. Before the officers and crew were all on deck the *Wachusett* struck the *Florida* on her starboard quarter, cutting her rail down to the deck and carrying away her mizenmast, at the same time pouring a volley of musketry and a charge of canister from her forecastle pivot gun upon our decks. The *Wachusett* then backed off and demanded our surrender, to which demand Lieutenant Porter declined to accede. The enemy then fired again and again into us, which was returned by the officers and crew of the *Florida*.

Another demand was then made for our surrender, and Lieutenant Porter answered, "I will surrender conditionally." The enemy then stopped firing, and the commander called for Captain Morris to come on board; Lieutenant Porter answered that Captain Morris was on shore, and that he, as commanding officer, would come on board as soon as he could get a boat ready. The enemy then sent a number of armed boats to take possession of the *Florida*. As soon as Lieutenant Porter was heard to surrender, fifteen of our crew jumped overboard to escape capture, of whom only six succeeded, the remaining nine having been shot in the water by the men on the forecastle and in the boats of the *Wachusett*. Mr. Hunter was wounded and a number of men killed. The enemy made fast a hawser to the foremast of the *Florida*, and, after slipping her cable, towed her out to sea.

I called in person on the President as soon as possible, but could get no further information from him. On the 8th I sent a protest to the President, of which I send you a copy, marked 2. On the 10th our agent was informed by the interpreter that the President did not intend to answer my protest, as the Confederate Government had not been recognised by Brazil, and that I could find all the official correspondence in the newspapers.

I then wrote a letter marked 3, in which reference is made to a letter marked 4. Just before leaving Bahia, having received no answer, I sent our agent, Mr. James Dwyer, to the President. The result of his visit is contained in his letter, marked 5. The Bahia papers contain a number of reports as to the killed and wounded on board the *Florida*, all of which I have thoroughly sifted, and find no foundation for the same.

At the time of her seizure there was about twenty-five tons of coal on board, most of which was dust. The list of officers captured is contained in the report of Paymaster Taylor, marked 6.

The enclosed newspaper is an official extract containing all the Brazilian correspondence in reference to the *Florida*.

I am, very respectfully,
Your obedient servant,
(Signed)   C. MANIGAULT MORRIS,
Lieutenant-Commanding, Confederate States Navy.

[*Copy.*]

LETTER OF THE PRESIDENT OF BAHIA TO THE AMERICAN CONSUL.
To Mr. Thomas Wilson.

Bahia, *October 7th*, 1864.
Palace.

Sir,—

Having reached this Presidency the grave attempt committed by the steamer *Wachusett*, of the United States of North America, and which, violating the neutrality of the Empire, treasonably and disrespectfully during the night set at defiance the respect due to the Empire, and in the harbour took prisoner the steamer *Florida,* setting aside the most sacred rights of people and civilized nations, that guards between nations belligerent any such acts, having this Presidency received the word of honour of the Consul, Mr. Wilson, to preserve the neutrality, that in explicit terms promised that the Commander of the steamer *Wachusett* should confine himself to his duties, and respect the neutrality due to the Empire, and not practise any hostile act in these territorial waters. The President cannot refrain from solemnly protesting against the act referred to, the more so that the Consul is therein implicated, seeing that, spite of his formal promise, he has not taken any measure to withdraw from the responsibility of this action. And as this fact and the silence preserved up to this date evidently prove that the President cannot confide in his endeavours to preserve the neutrality and sovereignty of the Empire, it is resolved to at once interrupt all official relations with him until further orders from the Government, where this unexpected and deplorable act will be related, and where, in its higher knowledge, final decision will be given. The Consul is in the meantime duly informed that orders are given to the respective authorities that in no "harbour" of the Province the steamer *Wachusett* will be allowed entrance, resorting, if necessary, to force for this end. According to the terms of the instructions promulgated on the 23rd of June past by the Minister for Foreign Affairs, this, if the steamer obstinately and criminally persists in continuing in this manner, to infringe the rights imposed by the dignity of its own flag.

(Signed)   Antonio Joachim da Silva Gomes.

LETTER FROM THE COMMANDER OF THE
2ND NAVAL DIVISION TO THE PRESIDENT OF BAHIA.

To the President.

Steamer *Paraense*, Bahia, *October 7th*, 1864.

Illus. e Ex. Senhor,—

It is my duty to state to your Excellency that to-day at daybreak the United States of America steamer *Wachusett*, without having previously given any symptom of moving, suddenly left the anchorage where she was, and approached the Confederate States steamer *Florida*. When she passed by the poop of the corvette *D. Januaria,* where I was, I intimated that she should anchor, and not doing so, sent an officer on board to give notice that all the ships of the division, as well as the forts, would fire if she attacked the *Florida*. To this intimation the commander replied that he should comply, and do nothing further, and that he would return to his anchorage, as your Excellency will see by the paper annexed signed by the officer who gave this notice.

Notwithstanding, the corvette, to ratify the intimation, fired a gun loaded with ball. Following, notwithstanding, her way outside, as it appeared to me to return to her anchorage, I observed as she passed by the bow that she was tugging the *Florida*. Immediately this steamer fired in the direction of the steamer *Wachusett* cannon loaded with ball; but escaping this attack, sailing in the direction of the bow, thus rendering useless the fire from the corvette, and I therefore ordered to cease firing. Having previously ordered that the *Paraense* should be made ready to move, I immediately that this was possible sailed, and went after her, seeing that the breeze was light, and made signal to the yacht *Rio de Contes* to follow us to the waters, which she did with all possible speed, sailing in our wake.

We chased the *Wachusett* outside the harbour as she tugged the *Florida*, both of which were little more than three miles off. I trust your Excellency will believe that when I left this port it was with the decided determination of sacrificing every consideration present and future to fight her, notwithstanding the small amount of force on which I could reckon, in order to vindicate the insult offered to the sovereignty of the country, thus taking by main force the steamer *Florida*; and this thought I expressed to the officers on leaving the harbour as they were united in the cabin, showing them the requirement in which we found ourselves to sacrifice every consideration without a thought to consequences, seeing that the proceeding of the commander of the *Wachusett* was of a nature to arouse the indignation of every Brazilian. A general and enthusiastic manifestation of complete adhesion to my opinion was the reply given by all the officers; and I am convinced that the other ships that accompanied me felt the same noble sentiments.

At seven o'clock in the morning the *Paraense*, tugging the yacht, gained considerably on the two American steamers, and I began to nourish the hope that we should satisfy our desires, when the wind calming, which the *Wachusett* soon perceived, always tugging the *Florida*, began steaming, increasing gradually the distance between our ships and their steamers flying before our bow, and being of considerably superior swiftness. Nevertheless, we chased them until eleven o'clock and forty-five minutes, when disappearing, I determined on returning to the port, returning to the *Paraense*, leaving outside the corvette and the yacht, with orders also to return to this harbour, where I dropped anchor at a quarter past three.

Before finishing this communication, I ought to give notice that a few moments before leaving this harbour I received offers from the Inspector of the Arsenal and Captain of the Port of assistance, or anything in their power, which I accepted, begging them to send me as many armed sailors as was possible. But it being necessary to use the greatest possible urgency in order to catch the flying steamers, I believed I ought not to wait, and immediately quitted without waiting for the offered help, also failing to wait on your Excellency for the same motive, according to the message I received.

God preserve your Excellency.

(Signed)   GERVASIO MACEBO,

Commander of the Division.

NOTE.—The two foregoing letters are printed *verbatim* from the translations made by the public interpreter at Bahia, at the time of the occurrence. They were given in the above form to Captain Morris, and handed by him to me on his arrival in England. It has been thought best to reproduce them without putting the phraseology into better idiomatic English, for fear that the precise meaning of the writers might be inadvertently altered in the effort to express the sense in an easier and more graceful flow of language.

[*Copy.*]

LETTER FROM THE BRAZILIAN MINISTER AT WASHINGTON
TO THE UNITED STATES' SECRETARY OF STATE.

(*Translation.*)

To his Excellency the Hon. William H. Seward.

Imperial Legation of Brazil,

Washington, *December* 12*th*, 1864.

The undersigned, Chargé d'Affaires *ad interim* of his Majesty the Emperor of Brazil, has just received orders from his Government to address himself without delay to that of the United States of North America about an act of the most transcendent gravity done on the morning of the 7th day of October last, in the port of the capital of the Province of Bahia, by the war steamer *Wachusett,* belonging to the navy of the Union, an act which involves a manifest violation of the territorial jurisdiction of the Empire, and an offence to its honour and sovereignty.

On the 4th day of the month referred to, there entered that port, where already had been lying for some days the *Wachusett,* the Confederate steamer *Florida,* for the purpose declared by her commander to the President of the province, to supply herself with alimentary provisions and coal, and to repair some tubes of her machinery.

The President, proceeding in accordance with the policy of neutrality which the Empire resolved to adopt on the question in which unfortunately these States are involved, and in conformity with the instructions in this respect issued by the Imperial Government on the 23rd of June of the year last past, assented to the application of the *Florida,* and fixed the term of forty-eight hours for taking in supplies, and fixing, in dependence on the final examination by the engineer of the Arsenal, the determination of the residue of the time which, peradventure, should be deemed indispensable for the completion of the repairs.

The same authority at once took, with the greatest impartiality, all the measures necessary to avoid any conflict between the two hostile steamers.

The *Florida* was placed under cover of the batteries of the Brazilian corvette *D. Januaria,* on the inshore side, at the request of her commander, who, reposing on the faith with which, without doubt, the chief authority of the province could not fail to inspire him, considered himself sheltered from any attack of his adversary, and in this confidence not only stayed a night on shore, but gave liberty to a great part of the crew of his vessel.

It behoves me to say that, as soon as the Confederate steamer entered the port of Bahia, the American Consul, Wilson, addressed to the President a despatch claiming that the *Florida* should not be admitted to free pratique, and that on the contrary she should be detained, alleging for this, that that vessel had, in concert with the *Alabama,* violated the neutrality of the Empire by making captures in 1863, near the island of Fernando de Noronha.

Such exaggerated pretensions, founded on facts not proven, which had already been the subject of discussion between the Imperial Government and the legation of the United States, could not be even listened to.

If the President should have refused the hospitality solicited by the commander of the *Florida,* he would have infringed not only the duties of neutrality of the Empire, but also those of humanity, considering that steamer, coming from Teneriffe, had been sixty-one days at sea, was unprovided with food, and with machinery in the worst condition.

Afterwards, the President having stated to the same Consul that he hoped, from his honour and loyalty toward a friendly nation, that he would settle with the commander of the *Wachusett* that he should respect the neutrality and sovereignty of the Empire, he was answered affirmatively, the Consul pledging his word of honour. Things were in this condition, the term of forty-eight hours being to expire at one o'clock of the afternoon of the 7th, when, about dawn of that day, the commander of the steamer *Wachusett*, suddenly leaving his anchorage, passed through the Brazilian vessels-of-war and approached the *Florida*.

On passing across the bows of the Brazilian corvette *D. Januaria*, he was hailed from on board that he must anchor; but, as he did not attend to this intimation, and continued to approach the *Florida*, at the same time firing a gun and some musketry, the Commander of the Naval Division of the Empire stationed in those waters sent an officer to board the *Wachusett* and inform her commander that the ships of the division and the forts would open fire upon her if she should attack the *Florida*. The Brazilian officer was not allowed to make fast to the *Wachusett*, but the officer of the deck hailed him, saying in reply that he accepted the intimation given, that he would do nothing more, and that he was going to return to his anchorage. The commander of the Brazilian division then thought proper to ratify his intimation by firing a gun, upon which a complete silence followed between the two ships *Wachusett* and *Florida*. At the time this was passing the corvette *D. Januaria*, on board which the commander of the division had hoisted his flag, lay head to flood, the steamer *Florida* anchored B. B., side by side of her, and quite close to the shore, and between her and the corvette the *Wachusett* stopped her wheels.

The Commander of Division then observing—notwithstanding the darkness of the night—that the *Wachusett*, from the position in which she was, kept moving onward, and was passing ahead of the corvette, in a course E.B., became convinced that, in fact, she was steering for her anchorage, thus complying with the promise made.

But a few moments afterwards, perceiving that the *Florida* was in motion, the commander discovered that the *Wachusett* was taking her off in tow by means of a long cable.

Surprised at such an extraordinary attempt, the commander immediately set about stopping this, and redressing, at the same time, as behoved him, the offence thus done to the dignity and sovereignty of the Empire.

But availing himself of the darkness of the night and other circumstances, the commander of the *Wachusett* succeeded in carrying his prize over the bar, and escaping the just punishment he deserved.

The Consul, Wilson, preferred to abandon his post, withdrawing on board the *Wachusett.*

The Government of his Majesty, as soon as it had official information of the event, addressed to the legation of the United States at Rio Janeiro a note, in which, giving a succinct exposition of the fact, it declared that it had no hesitation in believing it would hasten to give to it all proper assurances that the Government of the Union would attend to the just reclamation of the Empire as promptly and fully as the gravity of the case demanded.

In correspondence with this expectative note, the worthy representative of the United States was prompt in sending his reply, in which he declares he is convinced that his Government will give to that of the Empire the reparation which is due to it.

Such are the facts to which the undersigned has received order to call the attention of the Honourable William H. Seward, Secretary of State of the United States.

The principles of international law which regulate this matter, and in respect of which there is not the least divergence among the most distinguished publicists, are common, and known to all. The undersigned would fail to recognise the high intelligence of the Honourable Mr. Seward, if, perchance, he should enter in this respect into fuller developments.

He limits himself then only to recall a memorable example, in which these principles, invariably sustained by the United States, had entire application. In 1793, the great Washington then being President of the United States, and the illustrious Jefferson Secretary of State, the French frigate *L'Embuscade* captured the English ship *Grange* in Delaware Bay, thus violating the neutrality and the territorial sovereignty of the United States. The American Government remonstrated energetically against this violation, and required from the Government of the French Republic, not only the immediate delivery of the captured vessel, but also the complete liberation of all the persons found on board. This reclamation was promptly satisfied. Much more grave, certainly, is the occurrence in the port of the province of Bahia which makes the subject of the present note. By the special circumstances which preceded and attended it, this act has no parallel in the annals of modern maritime war.

The commander of the *Wachusett* not only gravely offended the territorial immunities of the Empire, passing beyond the laws of war by attacking treacherously, during the night, a defenceless ship, whose crew, much reduced, because more than sixty men were on shore with the commander and several officers, reposed unwary beneath the shadow of the protection which the neutrality of the Empire guaranteed to them; and so open was the violation, so manifest the offence, that the enlightened American press was almost unanimous in condemnation of the inexcusable proceeding of Commander Collins.

On this occasion, remembering the United States, whose antecedents are well known and noted in history by the energetic defence and respect for neutral rights, of these unshaken principles, the undersigned cannot consider the event which occurred at Bahia otherwise than as the individual act of the commander of the *Wachusett* not authorized or approved by his Government, and that it will consequently give to the Government of his Majesty the Emperor the explanations and reparation which in conformity with international laws are due to a power which maintains friendly and pacific relations with the United States.

The just reclamation of the Imperial Government being thus presented, the undersigned awaits the reply of the Honourable Mr. Seward, and fully confiding in his exalted wisdom, and in the justice of the Government of the United States, he has not even for a moment doubted but that it will be as satisfactory as the incontestable right which aids the Empire, and the vast gravity of the offence which was done to it, may require.

The undersigned, etc.,

(Signed)   IGNACIO DE AVELLAR BARBOZA DA SILVA.

MR. SEWARD TO MR. BARBOZA DA SILVA.

To Senhor Ignacio de Avellar Barboza da Silva, etc.

Department of State,
Washington, *December* 20*th*, 1864.

Sir,—

I have the honour to acknowledge the receipt of your note, which sets forth the sentiments of the Imperial Government of Brazil concerning the capture of the *Florida* by the United States war-steamer *Wachusett* in the port of Bahia.

You will, of course, explain to your Government that owing to an understanding between you and myself, your note, although it bears the date of the 12th December, was not submitted to me until the 21st inst.

Jealousy of foreign intervention in every form, and absolute nonintervention in the domestic affairs of foreign nations, are cardinal principles in the policy of the United States. You have, therefore, justly expected that the President would disavow and regret the proceedings at Bahia. He will suspend Captain Collins, and direct him to appear before a court-martial. The Consul at Bahia admits that he advised and incited the captain, and was active in the proceedings. He will therefore be dismissed. The flag of Brazil will receive from the United States navy the honour customary in the intercourse of friendly maritime powers.

It is, however, not to be understood that this Government admits or gives credit to the charges of falsehood, treachery, and deception which you have brought against the captain and the Consul. These charges are denied on the authority of the officers accused.

You will also be pleased to understand that the answer now given to your representation rests exclusively upon the ground that the capture of the *Florida* was an unauthorized, unlawful, and indefensible exercise of the naval force of the United States within a foreign country in defiance of its established and duly recognised Government.

This Government disallows your assumption that the insurgents of this country are a lawful naval belligerent; and, on the contrary, it maintains that the ascription of that character by the Government of Brazil to insurgent citizens of the United States, who have hitherto been, and who still are, destitute of naval forces, ports, and courts, is an act of intervention in derogation of the law of nations, and unfriendly and wrongful, as it is manifestly injurious, to the United States.

So, also, this Government disallows your assumption that the *Florida* belonged to the afore-mentioned insurgents, and maintains, on the contrary, that that vessel, like the *Alabama,* was a pirate, belonging to no nation or lawful belligerent, and therefore that the harbouring and supplying of these piratical ships and their crews in Brazilian ports were wrongs and injuries for which Brazil justly owes reparation to the United States, as ample as the reparation which she now receives from them. They hope, and confidently expect, this reciprocity in good time to restore the harmony and friendship which are so essential to the welfare and safety of the two countries.

In the position which I have assumed, the Imperial Government will recognise an adherence to rights which have been constantly asserted, and an enduring sense of injuries which have been the subject of earnest remonstrance by the United States during the last three years. The

Government of Brazil is again informed that these positions of this Government are no longer deemed open to argument.

It does not, however, belong to the captains of ships-of-war of the United States, or to the commanders of their armies, or to their consuls residing in foreign ports, acting without the authority of Congress, and without even Executive direction, and choosing their own time, manner, and occasion, to assert the rights and redress the wrongs of the country. This power can be lawfully exercised only by the Government of the United States. As a member of the family of nations, the United States practise order, not anarchy, as they always prefer lawful proceedings to aggressive violence or retaliation. The United States are happy in being able to believe that Brazil entertains the same sentiments. The authorities at Bahia are understood to have unsuccessfully employed force to overcome the *Wachusett* and rescue the *Florida,* and to have continued the chase of the offender beyond the waters of Brazil, out upon the high seas. Thus, in the affair at Bahia, subordinate agents, without the knowledge of their respective Governments, mutually inaugurated an unauthorized, irregular, and unlawful war. In desisting from that war on her part, and in appealing to the Government for redress, Brazil rightly appreciated the character of the United States, and set an example worthy of emulation.

The disposition of the captured crew of the *Florida* is determined upon the principles which I have laid down. Although the crew are enemies of the United States, and, as they contend, enemies of the human race, yet the offenders were, nevertheless, unlawfully brought into the custody of this Government, and therefore they could not lawfully be subjected here to the punishment which they have deserved. Nor could they, being enemies, be allowed to enjoy the protection of the United States. They will, therefore, be set at liberty, to seek a refuge wheresoever they may find it, with the hazard of recapture when beyond the jurisdiction of this Government.

The *Florida* was brought into American waters, and was anchored under naval surveillance and protection at Hampton Roads. While awaiting the representation of the Brazilian Government, on the 28th November, she sank, owing to a leak which could not be seasonably stopped. The leak was at first represented to have been caused, or at least increased, by a collision with a war transport. Orders were immediately given to ascertain the manner and circumstances of the occurrence. It seemed to affect the army and the navy. A Naval Court of Inquiry and 'also a Military Court of Inquiry were charged with the investigation. The Naval Court has submitted its report, and a copy thereof is herewith communicated. The Military Court is yet engaged. So soon as its labours shall have ended, the result will be made known to your Government. In the meantime it is assumed that the loss of the *Florida* was a consequence of some unforeseen accident, which cast no responsibility upon the United States.

I avail, etc.,

(Signed)   WILLIAM H. SEWARD.

NOTE.—The two foregoing letters, Senhor Barboza da Silva to Mr. Seward, and the reply of Mr. Seward, will be found in the "British Case," pp. 75–78.

COPY OF REPORT OF LIEUTENANT T. K. PORTER ON THE CAPTURE OF THE CONFEDERATE STATES STEAMER *FLORIDA* BY THE UNITED STATES STEAMER *WACHUSETT.*

To Lieutenant-Commander C. M. Morris, Confederate States Navy.

Liverpool, *February 20th,* 1865.

Sir,—

In obedience to orders I submit the following report of the capture of the Confederate States steamer *Florida* at Bahia, Brazil, on the 7th of October, 1864, by the United States steamer *Wachusett,* the treatment of the officers and crew while prisoners; and the manner of our release. But before commencing I beg to call your attention to the fact that before entering the harbour our shot were withdrawn from the guns; that after our being requested by the Brazilian naval commander to anchor in-shore of his squadron we let our steam go down and hauled fires.

At about 3 A.M. on the morning of the 7th October, the officer of the deck, Acting-Master T. T. Hunter, sent the quarter-master down to call me, and tell me that the *Wachusett* was under weigh and standing towards us. I immediately jumped on deck, when I saw the *Wachusett* about twenty yards off, standing for our starboard quarter. A moment after she struck us abreast the mizen-mast, broke it into three pieces, crushed in the bulwarks, knocked the quarter-boat in on deck, jammed the wheel, carried away the mainyard, and started the beams for about thirty feet forward. At the same time she fired about two hundred shots from her small arms, and two from her great guns. She then backed off about one hundred yards, and demanded our surrender. I replied to the demand that I would let them know in a few moments. The reply from the

Wachusett was to surrender immediately, or they would blow us out of the water. As more than half our crew were ashore, and as those on board had just returned from liberty, I believed that she could run us down before we could get our guns loaded. But as I did not like to surrender the vessel without knowing what some of the other officers thought of it, I consulted Lieutenant Stone, the second officer in rank; and finding that he agreed with me that we could not contend against her with any hopes of success, I informed the commander of the *Wachusett* that under the circumstances I would surrender the vessel. I then went on board, and delivered to Commander Collins the ship's ensign and my sword. He immediately sent a prize-crew on board the *Florida,* and towed her out of the harbour. During the day he transferred about two-thirds of those captured to the *Wachusett.* He then paroled the officers, and put the men in double irons. As there were so few men compared to the *Wachusett*'s crew, and those divided between the two ships, I tried to get Captain Collins to allow the irons to be taken off of all, or a part of them, during the day, but he refused to do so. Beyond keeping the men in double irons for nearly two months, there were but two cases of severity towards them that were reported to me. Henry Norman (cox) was ironed to a stanchion with his hands behind him for having the key of a pair of the *Florida*'s irons in his pocket. He, as well as all the other men on the *Wachusett,* was ironed with the irons belonging to her (the *Wachusett*). John Brogan (fireman) was kept in the sweat-box. Dr. Emory reported to me that he was sick and could not stand such treatment. I asked Captain Collins to tell me why he was so treated. His reply was that Brogan was seen talking, and that when his master-at-arms came up he stopped. He also said that Brogan had, the day the *Florida* was captured, cursed one of his engineers, who tried to get him to show him something about our engines. He said, though, that he had ordered his release two days before, and thought he had been taken out. This was about three weeks after our capture. Brogan informed me afterwards that he had been confined there for several days, and eighteen nights. A few days before going into St. Thomas, I went to Captain Collins, and told him that on a previous occasion he had informed me that he was going to put our men ashore at Pernambuco, and that as we would be in port a few days, I would like to know if he still intended to put them ashore, at the same time telling him that I thought the *Florida* would be given up by his Government, and that I thought any honourable man would try to return the ship and crew as nearly in the condition in which he found her as he could. His reply was, "I have not thought of it—I have not thought of it to-day." After further conversation I left him, believing that he would not try to break up the crew. But before leaving St. Thomas our men were informed that all of them who wished to go ashore could do so, and that Master George D. Bryan and one other officer would meet them to look out for them. They asked what was to become of their money, which had been taken for them, and were told that Mr. Bryan would take it ashore for them. A number of them thought this was a trick to get rid of them, and would not go, but eighteen were foolish enough to believe it, and had their irons taken off on the berth-deck, and were put in a boat from the bow port, and allowed to go ashore. The first Mr. Bryan heard of his part of the affair was when we left the *Wachusett* and had an opportunity of talking to the other men. After the men had time to get ashore, the commander of the *Wachusett* called away his boats, and sent an armed force after the boat in which our men had left. So anxious was he to get them ashore, that he sent them when the quarantine flag was flying at his fore in consequence of having the small-pox on board. The United States steamer *Keasarge* left St. Thomas while we were there, and Dr. Charlton and the eighteen men on the *Florida* were transferred to her. When we arrived at Fortress Monroe, we were sent up to Point Look-out Prison, and there the officers were separated from the men, and sent to the Old Capitol Prison in Washington. But in three or four days we were sent back to the *Wachusett* at Fortress Monroe to go to Fort Warren, Boston. On our return to Fortress Monroe, I heard that the *Florida*'s money-chest had been opened, and I went to Captain Collins and reminded him that soon after we were captured, I informed him that there were three hundred and twenty dollars in it which belonged to the wardroom mess, which I had given to the paymaster the evening before we were captured, to keep till the caterer, Lieutenant Stone, should return from shore. He told me that he had mentioned it to Rear-Admiral Porter, but that the Admiral refused to give it to us. We saw the *Florida* before we left. She had lost her jibboom by a steam-tug running into her. A lieutenant-commander told me that if the United States Government determined to give her up, the officers of the navy would destroy her. Several other of our officers were told the same. Whilst in Fort Warren we heard these threats were carried out.

From Hampton Roads we were carried in the *Wachusett* to Boston, but before we were sent to Fort Warren, Lieutenant-Commander Beardsly went to the men and informed them that he was sent by Cap-

tain Collins to tell them that if they would take the oath of allegiance to
the United States Government they would be released. He, meeting
with no success, was succeeded by the master-at-arms of the vessel, and
a sergeant from the fort, who told them that all the men but five of those
who had come from St. Thomas on the *Keasarge* had taken the oath. I do
not know by whose orders this was told them; but we found on arriving
at the fort that it had no more truth in it than the report they gave the
men at St. Thomas, that Mr. Bryan was to meet them on shore. I am
happy to say that but one of the crew deserted his flag, and he did it the
day we were captured. When we arrived at Fort Warren, the men were
all put in one room, and the eleven officers were put into one with
thirty-two other prisoners. These rooms were casemates, and were fifty
feet long and about eighteen feet wide. At sunset we were locked up in
these casemates, and released after sunrise, and allowed to promenade
the extent of five such rooms. At 8 A.M. we were marched around to the
cookhouse, and were all given one loaf of bread each, weighing fourteen ounces. After 12 we were marched around again, and were given
our dinner, which consisted of about eight ounces of cooked meat, with
half a pint of thin soup, three days, and two potatoes, some beans or
hominy the other days. This was all we received each day. Many of the
prisoners by economizing found this enough to appease their hunger,
but a great many others were hungry all the time. If we had been allowed to buy sugar and coffee, and bread and cheese, a great many
would have been able to do so, and divide with some of their friends
who had no means, but we were allowed to buy nothing to eat without a
certificate from the Post surgeon that we were sick. There is an arrangement between our Government and that of the United States, that
prisoners-of-war may be allowed to receive boxes of provisions and
clothing from their friends at home, but the United States Government
now interprets this to mean that all boxes must come by a flag of truce.
As half of the Confederate prisoners have their homes within what is
now the United States military lines, this agreement works almost entirely for the Federals and against us. Half of the *Florida*'s officers were
in this situation, and they were compelled to decline the offers of their
friends. On the 24th December all the *Florida*'s officers except Dr. Charlton and fourteen other prisoners were locked up in a casemate, and kept
in close confinement both day and night. We were not allowed to go out
under any circumstances, except that for the first four days we were
marched under a heavy guard to the cookhouse twice a day. After that

our dinner was brought to us, and two of us were marched around to get the bread for all of those confined. This was for discussing a plan to capture the fort, which one of the prison spies, who pretends to be a lieutenant-colonel in our army, and a lieutenant in the English army, revealed to the authorities. We were kept in close confinement until the 19th of January, when Lieutenant Woodman, of the United States army, sent for me, and told me that he had an order from the Secretary of the Navy to release the officers and crew of the *Florida* from Fort Warren, and that as such was the case he would release all of us from close confinement. He showed me the order from the Secretary of the Navy, which was that we would be released on condition that we signed a parole to leave the United States within ten days. I asked him if we would be given the money and our swords, and other articles captured on the *Florida*, which had not been sunk with her. He said that he knew nothing about them, but that if I wished to write to Mr. Welles, he would send the communication. I then gave him a copy of the following note, which he assured me was sent the same day:

"To the Hon. Gideon Welles, Secretary of the Navy.
"Fort Warren, *January* 19*th*, 1863.
"Sir,—

"I have just been informed by the commanding officer of this fort that the officers and crew of the Confederate States steamer *Florida* will be released on condition of leaving the United States within ten days. We will accept a parole to leave at any time when we are put on board any steamer going to Europe, but we would prefer to go to Richmond. We would call your attention to the fact that there were somewhere about thirteen thousand dollars in gold on the *Florida* when she was captured, which was taken out of her by order of Rear-Admiral Porter. And to leave the United States it will be necessary to have that to take us out, unless the United States Government send us away as they brought us in. If you will give us our money we would prefer remaining here till a steamer leaves here for Europe, or we would ask for a guard till we are put on one in New York, as so many of us being together might be the cause of an unnecessary disturbance, of which we would be the sufferers.

"Very respectfully,
"Your obedient servant,
"THOMAS K. PORTER,
"First-Lieutenant, Confederate States Navy."

Mr. Welles made no reply to this. After waiting a week and finding that the United States Government neither intended to pay our passage away, nor to give us the money belonging to our Government, and not even our private money, I sent Lieutenant Stone to Boston with directions to procure a passage in the British and North American steamer *Canada*, or if he failed in that, to get us out of the United States in any manner possible. He succeeded in getting passage for all of us on the *Canada*, by my giving a draft to be paid at Liverpool. And on the 1st of February we signed the following parole: "We, the undersigned officers and crew of the steamer *Florida*, in consideration of being released from confinement in Fort Warren, do jointly and severally pledge our sacred word of honour that we will leave the United States within ten days from date of release, and that while in the United States we will commit no hostile act," and I left the fort for the steamer *Canada*. It may be of importance to state that we were officially informed by Major Gibson, commanding the Post part of the time we were there, that we could hold no communication with the Brazilian authorities.

Very respectfully,
Your obedient servant,
THOMAS K. PORTER,
First-Lieutenant, Confederate States Navy.

CHAPTER V

The building of the Alabama.—*Suspicions of the United States Consul at Liverpool.—*
Captain Butcher.—The equipping of the Alabama.—*Quitting Liverpool.—Bond,*
the Pilot.—Official Correspondence.—Captain Semmes.—The Alabama *handed*
over to his charge.—Some matters connected with the clearance of the Alabama *from*
Liverpool.—Mr. Price Edwards, the Collector of Customs at that Port.—The
Alabama*'s first engagement.—The* Alabama *a legitimate vessel-of-war.—Action*
of the United States in regard to commissioning vessels at sea.—Influence of the
cruisers on the United States carrying trade.—The Alabama*'s action with the*
Keasarge.—*Mr. Seward and Earl Russell.*

———

Writing subjectively, and following the career of the *Florida* from her birth
on the busy but peaceful shores of the Mersey to her violent seizure in
Bahia, and thence to her final resting-place among the oyster-beds in the
estuary of the River James, the narrative has been carried far beyond the
regular course of events, and we must now return to March, 1862, and
pick up that thread of the history which was woven into the general occurrences of the period by the *Alabama.*

At the time of the *Florida*'s departure from Liverpool, her still more famous consort had not yet been dignified by any other name or title than
the dockyard number "290." Her comely frame had been covered in by the
binding grip of the outside planking, which had developed the graceful
curves of her counter and the delicate wave-lines of her bow; but, nevertheless, I was disappointed to find that she was hardly up to specified time.

The builders were determined to turn out a first-class ship, and feeling perhaps that their obligation to do so was, if possible, increased by my absence, and the fact that there was no one to look after the interests of the owner, they were especially critical and hard to please in the selection of the timber for the most important parts, and had discarded two or three stern-posts* after they had been partly fitted and bored to take the screw shaft, because of some slight defect. This creditable, satisfactory, and punctilious care had caused some delay in completing the hull, but all the other work was in an advanced state, and the engines were ready to go into the ship as soon as she was off the ways.

The Birkenhead Ironworks lie some distance above the chief commercial parts of Liverpool, and being on the opposite side of the Mersey, they do not attract especial notice from persons engaged in business, or passing to and fro by the Woodside Ferry, and the boats plying to the lower landings on the river. But the large number of people passing up river to Tranmere, Rock Ferry, and Eastham, would often pass along the dock-walls of Messrs. Laird's establishment, and they could not fail to observe the gradual development of the graceful craft that stood out in bold relief at the extreme south end of the yard, and to contrast her with the large iron structures they were accustomed to see upon the adjoining building slips and ways.

The departure of the *Florida* without being called upon to give a particular account of herself and her intentions had grieved and vexed the United States Consul, and his suspicions having been once aroused, his mind was kept in a wakeful and agitated condition during the remainder of the war. The voluminous correspondence submitted to the Geneva Arbitrators, and which appeared from time to time in the Parliamentary Blue-books, gives proof of his nervous activity and the irritable and sometimes irritating persistency with which he pressed the local authorities to seize, or at least to detain, ships which he affirmed "it was quite notorious were intended to be armed and equipped as privateers" for the "so-called"—which latter appellation came to be a common designation of the Confederate States among those United States officials who were sometimes willing to drop the still more common epithets of "rebel" and "insurgent," to which, however, the Liverpool Consul generally adhered.

The people who saw the "290" on the building-slip, and were attracted by her appearance, naturally talked about her, and no doubt remarks were often made in respect to her fitness for a cruiser, and it is not therefore

* The single piece of timber finally used for the stern-post cost £100.

surprising that she should have aroused the suspicions of those whose business it was to keep watch over the interests of the United States. I soon learned that spies were lurking about, and tampering with the workmen at Messrs. Laird's, and that a private detective named Maguire was taking a deep and abiding interest in my personal movements; but my solicitor assured me that there was nothing illegal in what I was doing, and there was nothing therefore to be done but to maintain a quiet reserve, to hasten the completion of the ship, and to get her away as soon as possible.

On the 15th of May "290" was launched, and as a matter of fact left that numerical title on the signboard at the top of the slip when she slid off into the Mersey, although it stuck to her some time, and continued to be the term used when mentioning her in the Consular affidavits, and in the diplomatic correspondence, until the frequent reports of her performances afloat gave greater notoriety and distinction to her now historical name of *Alabama.*

But this ship, like the *Florida,* bore more than one name in passing through the various phases of her life, from a mere entity in a dockyard to the position of a commissioned ship-of-war. It is one of the peculiar anomalies of our nautical English grammar that a man-of-war is feminine, and we should say of a frigate whose name was *Ajax,* or which bore the still more harsh and masculine appellation of *Polyphemus,* "*She* is a fine sea-boat." The office of christening a ship is almost invariably performed by a lady, which is an aggravation of the anomaly about the sex, because if custom justifies a sailor in calling his ship "she," and if there is any propriety in his passionate affirmation, "my barque is my bride," the function of handing her into her natural element would be more fittingly, though not so gracefully done, by one of the "opposite sex." I could not take the liberty of introducing the name of the lady who christened "290" into this narrative. She graciously consented to perform the office, and fulfilled it in a comely manner, little knowing that she was constructively taking part in a great Civil War, and wholly unconscious that she was helping to make work for five eminent statesmen at Geneva ten years after. I hope her conscience has never upbraided her since, and that she has not felt in any way responsible for the bill of £3,000,000, which her Most Gracious Majesty had to pay on account of the "*Alabama* Claims."

When "290" was to be launched, it was necessary to provide an appellation for her. The Spanish language furnished a flexible and mellifluous equivalent for the Christian name of the lady who served the office, and when the ship got free of the blocks and glided down the ways, she had been christened *Enrica.* The Spanish name gave rise to another alleged mystery, and it was often asserted that there was a purpose to affect that the ship was intended for the Spanish Government, or at least for a Spanish firm in Spain; but I now state that there was no attempt to deceive anyone by any pretence whatever in the business of building and despatching the *Alabama* from Liverpool. I have already described the negotiations with Messrs. Laird for the building of the ship. There was no mystery or disguise about them, and it will be seen that all the further management of the transaction was conducted in the same ordinary commonplace way. A great effort was made by the United States Minister to induce her Majesty's Government to seize the ship, but no satisfactory evidence was produced that any violation of the Foreign Enlistment Act had been committed, and it appears from what is now known that the Government were not willing to "strain the law" at that early date, or "to seize a vessel which it would have been the duty of a court of law to restore."

I have always attributed the success of getting the *Alabama* finished as a sea-going ship, and then despatched, to the fact that no mystery or disguise was attempted. I was well advised as to the law, and had the means of knowing with well nigh absolute certainty what was the state of the negotiations between the United States Minister and her Majesty's Government. For the rest, I merely practised such ordinary business prudence and reserve as a man would be likely to follow in the management of his private affairs. I never told any *employé* more than was necessary for him to know, and never gave any reason for an order having reference to the outfit or movements of the ship. Everything was done quietly, without any excitement or appearance of haste. At the last moment she was hurried off with some precipitancy, but this will be explained in due course.

The Messrs. Laird, conscious of being somewhat behind time with the hull, appeared desirous to make up the loss by quick work in setting up the engines and completing the outfit. The ship was no sooner in the water than two tugs took her to the entrance of the graving-dock, and she was warped into it, and placed over the blocks at once. The engineer department at the Messrs. Laird's is especially efficient. Before the *Enrica* was fully secured in her berth the great derrick was swinging over her decks, and the first heavy pieces of the machinery were going on board. The work was now rapidly pushed forward, and the progress was satisfactory. On about June 15th the ship was taken out for a trial trip, and was run over the usual course until all parties were satisfied.

As the ship approached completion, it was necessary to appoint a captain who held a Board of Trade certificate, to superintend the preparations for sea, to engage the crew, and transact all such business as by law and custom falls within the office of the commander of a vessel. The selection of the right man was a matter of grave consideration. The requirements were professional competency, prudence, control over the tongue, and absolute integrity. I consulted a friend, and he soon brought to me Captain Mathew J. Butcher, a gentleman who was then serving as first-officer in a Cunard steamship; but he held a master's certificate, and was therefore eligible.

It turned out that I had met Captain Butcher two or three years before in Havana, he being then chief-officer of the Cunard steamship *Karnak,* and thus he was not wholly unknown to me. A conversation of a half to three-quarters of an hour brought us to a satisfactory understanding, and we went across to Messrs. Laird's yard, and I introduced Captain Butcher as the commander of the *Enrica,* through whom I desired them to receive all further instructions with reference to the outfit of the ship. To prevent repetition hereafter, I will take this occasion to say that Captain Butcher fulfilled all the requirements of the offices he engaged to perform, not only with tact, judgment and discretion, but with that nice and discriminating fidelity which marks the man of true honesty. He was engaged merely to take the ship to an appointed place without the United Kingdom; and he was especially warned that no men must be engaged under any pretence whatever, except to navigate the ship to a port or ports in the West Indies, with the privilege of stopping at any intermediate port.

It may be stated here, once for all, that no men were hired or engaged for any other purpose than that of navigating an unarmed ship, and no man was enlisted to enter the Confederate service, nor was a word said to any man to induce him to enter that service, by anyone having the slightest authority to make any such proposition, until after the ship had passed far beyond British jurisdiction. It would have been quite easy to prove that the affidavits obtained by the United States Consul at the time were either the fictitious conceits of the men who made them, or else that the men had been themselves deceived. But while Captain Butcher was only engaged to take out an unarmed ship, and he never did enter the Confederate Service, yet it was manifestly necessary to confide to him more than what appeared on the surface. He therefore knew enough before the arrival of the ship at Terceira to place the success of the whole enterprise in his power. An indiscreet remark, or a hint from him to a careless gossiping acquaintance, would have spoiled all of our well-laid plans. I shrink from seeming to suggest that there might have been a possibility of such a catastrophe; but there can be no doubt that the United States would have given a considerable sum to frustrate the departure of the ship, and a much larger sum still to have got possession of her. There was a time when the commander might have handed her over to an agent of the United States, or for that matter he might have taken her to New York, instead of to Terceira. I mention this to demonstrate the prodigious trust it was necessary to repose in Captain Butcher. But I never had the least uneasiness; men who have had much to do with their fellows, if observant, learn to understand them, and after our first interview I never hesitated to tell Captain Butcher all that was necessary for him to fully comprehend the actual state of affairs, although I never ceased to abide by the rule of burdening no one with more of a secret than it seemed good for him to know.

I was fortunate in having held on to my old friend McNair, the engineer of the *Fingal*, and he took charge of that department on board the *Enrica*, so that I was quite sure nothing would be neglected in the way of proper outfit.

About the 1st of July the *Enrica* was so nearly ready for sea, that I began to make preparations for my own departure in her. Lieutenant J. R. Hamilton had arrived in England from the Confederate States at the end of April, and reported to me for duty as first-lieutenant of the *Alabama* (still *Enrica*). When I was in Savannah with the *Fingal* in February, 1862, Lieutenant Hamilton had expressed an earnest desire to get afloat, and asked if I could bring it about that he should be detailed to serve with me. There appeared to be some difficulty at the time, but the Secretary of the Navy bore it in mind, and I was much gratified by Hamilton's unexpected arrival. He entered with much spirit into the arrangements for our cruise.

In the original instructions the Navy Department had left me a large discretion, and I had fully arranged and planned what, and in what direction, my operations should be. Maffitt and I had both served together on the United States Coast Survey. Both of us could find our way into about every harbour from Boston to the Mississippi. I had proposed a rendezvous with him, and a joint dash at a given point; but, failing the rendezvous, I had sketched out my own course separately. Just about this time, when in another week I should have been off, I received two despatches from the Navy Department of great length, the contents of which greatly disappointed my hopes and expectations in reference to getting afloat, but at the same time added largely to the sphere of my general duties.

The first despatch notified me that it had been thought advisable to order Captain Semmes to return to England from Nassau, and directing me to put him in command of the *Alabama*. That this change may be fully understood, I will just briefly mention that Captain Semmes, in the progress of his cruise in the *Sumter*, had found his way to Gibraltar, and finding it impossible to make at that place the repairs necessary to fit her for further cruising, and being also unable to obtain a sufficient supply of fuel to fetch the ship to a French or English port, he had laid her up and was *en route* with his staff of officers for the Confederate States when the fresh orders of the Secretary of the Navy met him at Nassau.*

The *Sumter* was for some time a *bête noire* to me. She was much in the way at Gibraltar, but having been turned over to me as Confederate property, there was both the necessity and the obligation to look after her. The United States kept two vessels in the neighbourhood to watch her, which was some offset to the inconvenience and expense, but when it became apparent that she could not be got away, and we began to have better and more efficient vessels for cruising, I sold her, and she was put under the British flag by her new owners, and was brought round to Liverpool and converted into a blockade-runner. She was never caught, but ended her days in the natural and ship-shape way by foundering somewhere in the North Sea.

The views of the Navy Department at this time will be best explained by quoting from the second of the afore-mentioned despatches: "Captain Semmes returns to England to assume the command of the *Alabama*, and you will please afford him all possible assistance in getting her to sea and maintaining her as a cruiser."

The Secretary then goes earnestly into the question of ironclads; directs me to build, if possible, two more vessels of the type of the *Alabama*, advises in what way he hopes to provide funds, adds orders for various supplies, and notifies me of some large contracts he has made with private parties, and instructs me to supervise them on behalf of the Government.

It may be interesting to the reader to know the opinion of a member of the Confederate Cabinet in *June–July*, 1862, in respect to the possible intervention of Great Britain and France, and I give it in the following extract:—

"We are all astonished here at the evident apprehension of the Government of Great Britain of a war with the United States. Mr. Seward's gasconades upon this subject excite but the contempt of his own people.... Should Great Britain and France acknowledge our independence, and send their products in their own ships to our

---

* A full account of all this will be found in "My Adventures Afloat," in which Admiral Semmes gives a history of his cruises in the *Sumter* and *Alabama*.

ports, the war would not only cease, but their course would meet the approval of a vast majority of the people of the United States, for the war is carried on by a party in power, and not by the people.

"Enclosed you have a copy of my instructions to Commander Semmes. Your services in England are so important at this time, that I trust you will cheerfully support any disappointment you may experience in not getting to sea. The experience you have acquired renders your agency absolutely necessary....

> "I am, etc.,
> "(Signed)   S. R. MALLORY,
> "Secretary of the Navy."

Simultaneously with the notification of Captain Semmes's appointment to the *Alabama*, I received a letter from that officer himself, in which he advised me that he would join me in Liverpool by the first vessel leaving Nassau, and requesting me to make such arrangements to get the enterprise complete as I might deem best. This change, coming so late, when the ship was, in fact, ready for sea, and had been delivered to me by the builders, was very embarrassing. We knew that the American Minister was pressing the Government to seize the ship; and the frequent inquiries addressed to the builders by the Customs authorities at London, and the active watchfulness of the local officers of that department at Liverpool, warned me that the situation was critical.

Meanwhile the *Enrica* (*Alabama*) was taken into the Birkenhead Dock, where she was coaled and all her stores were put on board. Everything was kept in readiness for a start at short notice, but a full crew was not shipped, for fear that the men would be restive at the delay, and attract notice by their numbers and indiscreet talking.

In order to preserve due consistency in the order of events, it is now necessary to give an account of the arrangements for "equipping" the *Alabama*—that is to say, the means adopted to supply that portion of her furniture which would complete her outfit as a vessel-of-war. It is not necessary to dwell long upon these arrangements. The battery was ordered very shortly after the contract for the ship was made, and all the ordnance supplies were put in train in good time; but such instructions were given as would ensure their being ready not much before the ship, although the parties contracted with were not informed for what purpose they were wanted, or even how they were to be shipped, until the time arrived for forwarding them. The necessary number of revolvers, short rifles with cutlass bayonets, ammunition, made-up clothing for 150 men, extra stores of all kinds, hammocks, and, in fact, everything required for the complete equipment of a man of-war, were ordered, and instructions were given that the goods when ready should be packed, marked, and held for shipping orders.

About the end of May a suitable agent was instructed to look up a moderate-sized sailing-vessel in London, fit for a West Indian voyage, to carry heavy weights. She was to be staunch and in good condition; but high finish not wanted, and a clipper not required. We got just the craft— a barque of about 400 to 450 tons. Her recommendation was that she had lately brought home ordnance stores—old guns, shot, etc.—from Gibraltar on Government account. She was bought, and in due time was entered out from London to Demerara. The agent was ordered to put 350 tons of coal in her, and the necessary shipping orders were given to the parties holding the *Alabama*'s goods. Our barque was named *Agrippina,* and she attracted no especial notice and no suspicion while loading in the London Docks. It was easy to regulate the forwarding of the cargo and the lading, so as to fit in with the movements of the *Enrica* at Liverpool, without creating the suspicion that there was any connection between the two vessels.

I wished to know something definite as to the time of Captain Semmes's arrival, or at least that he had started from Nassau, before despatching the two ships, because it might be more dangerous to have them waiting at the rendezvous, where a passing United States cruiser might by chance fall upon them, than for the *Enrica* to remain in Liverpool, where no foreign enemy could touch her. But there was a domestic enemy—the Foreign Enlistment Act—upon whom it was necessary to keep a watchful eye.

On Saturday, July 26th, 1862, I received information from a private but most reliable source, that it would not be safe to leave the ship in Liverpool another forty-eight hours. I went immediately to Messrs. Laird's office, and told them that I wished to have a thorough all day trial of the ship outside. Although the testing trial trip had already been made, and the delivery of the ship to me in accordance with the terms of the contract was complete, yet it had been verbally agreed that there should be another trial, when coals and stores were all on board, if I desired it. Captain Butcher was ordered to ship a few more hands, and to have everything ready to come out of dock on Monday's tide. None of the crew were given an inkling of the contemplated movement; but I informed Captain Butcher confidentially that the ship would not return, and directed him to get on board some extra tons of coal, and to complete his stores.

It was important to have as many trusty and intelligent men on board as possible, and I had already detailed Mr. John Low (now a master in the Confederate States Navy), who had rejoined me after going out to Nassau in the *Florida,* to be ready to accompany Captain Butcher.

On Monday the 28th the *Enrica* came out of dock and anchored off Seacombe, and every preparation was made for going out of harbour the next day. A small party of guests were invited to go out for the trial trip, and the next morning—Tuesday, the 29th—the ship was partially dressed with flags, and at about 9 A.M. we got under weigh and steamed down the river with a number of guests on board, and a party of riggers and additional engineers' men to assist if any help was needed. We had also in company the steam-tug *Hercules* as a tender.

The day was fine and the trials were very satisfactory. We ran several times between the Bell Buoy and the north-west lightship. The average speed was 12•8, the sea being quite smooth, and the wind light from north-west. About 3 P.M. I explained to the guests that it was my wish to keep the ship out all night to complete her trials, and that the sea being quite smooth we would run close to the bar, and every one could go up to town in the tug. Shortly after I asked Mr. George Bond, the Liverpool pilot, if he knew Moelfra Bay. He said "yes." I then directed Captain Butcher to take the ship down to that anchorage as soon as the rest of us left, and wait there until I came to him, which, if possible, would be the next afternoon. At 4 P.M. the guests, the extra men, and I, got on board the tug, and parting company from the *Enrica,* she proceeded to her place of anchorage on the Welsh coast, while we went up to town. On the way up the river I engaged the tug to be at the Woodside landing-stage at 6 A.M. on the next morning, telling the master that I wished him to take a few articles to the ship, which would probably remain outside at least for a day. A shipping-master had been previously engaged to have thirty or forty men on the landing-stage at the same time to join a ship at an outport, for a voyage to the Bahamas, and possibly to Havana.

I was on the Woodside landing-stage by 7 A.M. on the 30th. The *Hercules* was already there, and the articles wanted for the *Enrica* were on board. They were a spare anchor-stock, a large piece of scantling, intended for the frame to support the spare spars, and a few brass pieces belonging to the engines. There is reason for some particularity in these small details, as one of the Consular affidavits affirmed that gun-carriages were taken, which is quite untrue. The shipping-master was also on the stage. He had with him about thirty-five or forty men, and nearly as many women, of that class who generally affect a tender solicitude for Jack when he is outward-bound, and is likely to be provided with an advance-note. I told him to get the men on board, but of course the women could not go. He replied that he feared it was a case of all or none. The women, he said, stood in various degrees of tender relationship to the men, and would not part with them unless they could first get a month's pay in advance or its equivalent. There was no time for parley; the mixed group were hurried on board, and we proceeded down the river. As we approached New Brighton I told the master of the tug to take the Rock Channel, which would save distance, and go down to Moelfra Bay. At about 3 P.M. we sighted the *Enrica,* and at four got alongside of her. It had been raining, and the afternoon was dull and cloudy.

There had been nothing to eat on board the tug. Jack and his fair friends were therefore hungry, and not in suitable frame of mind for business. The steward was ordered to prepare a substantial supper as quickly as possible, and when it was ready all hands were refreshed with a fair but safe allowance of grog, to add zest and cheerfulness to the meal. When the men had well eaten, and had finished their pipes, they were called aft, and it was explained to them in few words that the ship had been "cruising in the Channel to get her engines in good working order, and as everything was satisfactory it was proposed to proceed on the voyage without going back to Liverpool, which would be an unnecessary delay and expense. Would they ship for the run, say to Havana, touching at any intermediate port? If the ship did not return to England they would be sent back free of expense, or some other satisfactory settlement would be made with them. They should have one month's pay in advance, paid down on the capstan-head. The ship was a nice comfortable craft, and was well found, and well provisioned." After a short consultation among themselves, all but two or three of the men agreed to go. Articles expressing the terms of the agreement had been prepared, and each man came down to the cabin in turn with his "lady," and signed, the latter receiving the stipulated advance in money, or a note for the equivalent from Captain Butcher.

It was near midnight before everything was arranged, and the tug was lying uneasily alongside; for the wind had shifted to south-west, and was blowing in spiteful squalls, with heavy rain. It seemed inhospitable to turn the ladies out on such a night, but there was no accommodation for them on board, and there were reasons why the *Enrica* should not be found in Moelfra Roads on the next morning. While the *Enrica* was still in Liverpool, it came to my knowledge that the United States ship *Tuscarora,* Captain T. A. Craven, had come up from Gibraltar to Southampton, some time in the early days of July, and that she continued to remain there, or in the near neighbourhood.

The nervous apprehension of the United States Consul in respect to the *Enrica* was well known, and it did not require much acumen to connect the presence of the *Tuscarora* in British waters with the supposed character and probable destination of the former vessel. Arrangements were made with a judicious friend at Southampton to keep me informed of the *Tuscarora*'s movements, and I had received almost daily advices. Just before leaving the Woodside landing-stage in the tug with the men and women, a telegram was handed me, which contained the announcement that the *Tuscarora* had left Southampton, and it was believed that she had gone to Queenstown. Manifestly we were watched, and some one had put Captain Craven on our supposed track. It seemed so clear that he would touch at Queenstown for news, and then lie off Tuskar, or somewhere in the channel to intercept the *Enrica* on her way to sea, or follow her out by the usual route, that I determined to go "north about." I had already consulted with Captain Butcher and our excellent pilot, Mr. George Bond, on that point; both had agreed that it was the best course, and Bond knew that route as well as the other.

After the tug left us the weather grew worse. By 1 A.M. it was blowing hard from south-west, and raining heavily. It was not an opportunity such as a prudent seaman would choose to leave a safe roadstead and venture into the Irish Sea, but the circumstances appeared to justify the move; indeed, I thought them imperative. At 2:30 A.M. (31st), we got under weigh, and stood out of the bay under steam alone. At 8 A.M. the ship was off the Calf of Man, the sky clearing and wind dropping. We set all sail to a middling fresh breeze, and bowled along 13½ knots, good. By 1 P.M. the wind fell light, and we lost the effect of the sails; at noon passed South Rock, and steered along the coast of Ireland. At 8 P.M. entered between Rathlin Island and Fair Head. At 6 P.M. stopped the engines off the Giant's Causeway, hailed a fishing-boat, and Bond and I went ashore in a pelting rain, leaving Captain Butcher to proceed with the *Enrica* in accordance with his instructions.

During the evening it rained incessantly, and the wind skirled and snifted about the gables of the hotel in fitful squalls. Bond and I sat comfortably enough in the snug dining-room after dinner, and sipped our toddy, of the best Coleraine malt; but my heart was with the little ship buffeting her way around that rugged north coast of Ireland. I felt sure that Butcher would keep his weather-eye open, and once clear of Innistrahull, there would be plenty of sea-room; but I could not wholly shake off an occasional sense of uneasiness. Bond gave me the exact distances from point to point, from light to light, and having been taught at school to work up all sums to very close results, I made the average speed of the *Enrica* to have been 12•89 from Moelfra to the Giant's Causeway, and felt well satisfied with the performance. The next morning, August 1st, Bond and I took a boat and pulled along the coast to Port Rush. The weather was beautifully fine, and the effect of the bright sun and the gentle west wind was so exhilarating that I felt no further solicitude about the *Enrica*. From Port Rush we took rail to Belfast, and then steamer and rail *viâ* Fleetwood to Liverpool, where I learned that the *Tuscarora* had come off Point Lynas on the 1st, and then looked into Moelfra Bay, but found nothing there to engage her special attention.

I cannot dismiss Bond without a passing tribute; I came to know him well during the war, and for years afterwards. He was one of those men who perform every office of life with earnestness and zeal; who never complain of too much labour, or too little reward; whose conversation is without covetousness, and who always seem content with the things that are present. His position was not elevated. He began as a river and channel pilot, and ended his career as master of the Clarence Dock in Liverpool; but there was something in the heart and eye and manner of the man which gave an importance and dignity to his employment above its seeming consequence. We meet such men occasionally in what are called the humble walks of life, and they make labour honourable. After his short cruise in the *Enrica,* it would have been useless for me to attempt any special mystery in dealing with him; but he never asked an inquisitive question, and if it was necessary to give him any information, I never doubted that his lips would hold it as a sealed envelope.

When it became manifest that the *Enrica* must be sent away from Liverpool, I telegraphed the agents who were loading the *Agrippina* to despatch her forthwith, and sent up orders which the captain was not to open until all hands were on board and the ship was practically off. On my return to Liverpool, I learned with satisfaction that she was clear of the Channel, and that her cargo was complete. The two vessels were thus safely on their way to the rendezvous—that quiet little bay on the east side of Terceira, whose inviting shelter I would not have known but for the necessity of putting in there with the *Fingal* for water, which has been mentioned in a previous chapter.

I have thought that it will be best, in the further progress of this narrative, to give the actual official reports, explaining each important event, which were written at the time of the occurrence. This course will perhaps interfere with and interrupt the symmetry of the narrative, but I cannot doubt that it will add to its weight as a truthful uncoloured account of the various enterprises, and it will only be necessary to fill in the time between the dates of the reports with brief explanatory remarks. The instructions to the commanders of the two vessels should come first in order.

"London, *July* 28*th*, 1862.

"Captain,—

"You will proceed at once to sea with the barque *Agrippina*, now under your command, and make the best of your way to the bay of Praya, in the island of Terceira, one of the Azores....

"Your experience as a seaman renders it unnecessary to give you special advice as to the care of your ship, and you will of course use all proper precautions in approaching the land; but it is advisable to give you some hints in respect to the anchorage at Praya and its approach. The bay of Praya is open to the east, and is easy and safe of access, there being no sunken rocks or danger of any kind not visible to the eye. With a leading wind, stand boldly in for the middle of the bight until a small islet off the north point is in range with the point of the mainland of the island itself; then haul up for the town, which lies in the northern curve of the bay, and anchor by the lead in eight to ten fathoms water. With the wind from the westward you can beat in by the lead, standing not quite so far on the southern as on the northern tack, and bring up in, say, eight to ten fathoms. You will be visited soon after anchoring by a health officer, to whom you will simply report that you are from London for Demerara, and have put in for supplies. It is hoped that the steamer will not be long behind you; indeed, you may find her there. The name of the commander of the steamer is Butcher. He will have a letter to you with authority to take whatever quantity of coal and other articles of your cargo he may require, and we particularly desire you to give him your best assistance, and afford him every aid in your power to transfer what he needs from the *Agrippina* to his own ship, and you will then proceed to any port he may direct, and land or deliver the remainder of your cargo. In fact, you are to consider all orders from the commander of the steamer as being authorized by us, with or without any other letter of advice.

"If any vessel is at anchor at Praya when you arrive, hoist your number, and should she be your consort she will show a white English ensign from the after shroud of the main rigging. If the steamer arrives after you, she will, after anchoring, make this same signal of the white ensign in the main rigging, which you will answer with your number, after which you can communicate freely. Relying with confidence upon your integrity and willingness to carry out our wishes in the prosecution of the voyage you have undertaken, we do not think it necessary to give you more minute directions in writing, but may find means to communicate with you again before your departure from Praya. Our interests are so deeply involved in the adventure entrusted to your management, that we will fully appreciate your exertions to bring it to a successful termination, and upon your safe return to England, we will be happy to make you a substantial acknowledgment for any extra exertions you may make for the satisfactory accomplishment of the voyage.

"We are, etc.

"Captain Alexander McQueen,
"Barque *Agrippina*."

The above letter was "signed by the registered owners."

"Liverpool, *July* 30*th*, 1862.

"Sir,—

"You will proceed to sea in the steamship *Enrica*, now under your command, and taking the channel by the North of Ireland, will shape a course for the bay of Praya, in the island of Terceira, one of the Azores. At that place you will be joined by the barque *Agrippina*, Captain McQueen, to whom you have a letter, and who will thenceforth be under your orders. As the *Agrippina* is a sailing vessel, and may not be at the place of rendezvous for a fortnight, it will not be necessary for you to arrive ahead of her, and you will therefore economise your fuel as much as possible, making the passage mostly under canvas. You have been informed of the manner of signalling the *Agrippina*, and when she joins you, if the weather permits, you will at once begin to transfer her cargo to your own ship. The paymaster has an invoice of her cargo, showing the contents of every case and bale, so that there can be no confusion or delay. All slops, clothing, and other articles in the purser's department you will please take on board first, and have them placed in the store-rooms, directing the paymaster to issue such of them as may be required by the men.

"Get the gun-carriages out of their cases and place them in their proper places, the carriage for 8-inch gun on the quarter-deck, and the one for the 7-inch rifled-gun immediately forward of the bridge. The carriages for the broadside-guns place opposite the side-ports. The cases containing the guns, being filled with small fixtures and equipments, had better be left as you find them until the Confederate States officer who is to command the ship arrives. The cases containing the shot can be opened, and the shot put in the racks, each rack being so fitted as to receive its proper shot. The shells you will place in the shell-rooms, each in its proper box, the spherical shells in the starboard, and the elongated shells in the port-room. The pistols are in four small cases, made so that two of them will fit into each of the arm-chests intended for the quarter-deck. Put them in the chests as soon as you get them on board. Fill the bunkers from the coals on board the *Agrippina*, and keep both vessels ready for a start at short notice. Captain R. Semmes, of the Confederate States Navy, is the officer who will, I hope, very soon relieve you. He will bring you a letter from me, and thereafter you will consider that all my control or authority over the ship is transferred to him. My private and official intercourse with you has been such as to give me a high estimate of your personal and professional ability, and as we have freely conversed as to the management of the adventure you have undertaken, I do not think it necessary to give you written instructions as to the simple care of the ship.

"You are to consider yourself my confidential agent, and I shall rely upon you as one gentleman may upon another. If you have an opportunity at any time, send me a line, and get out of the reach of the telegraphic stations as soon as possible. I do not anticipate that you will meet with any interruption in making the transfer of cargo, but an easterly gale may force you to get the *Agrippina* out of Praya Bay, in which case you can tow her under the lee of the island and lie by her until the weather permits you to return. In such a contingency leave a letter with her Majesty's Consul, directed to Captain J. W. Clendenin, saying where you have gone, and that you will soon be back.

"It is important that your movements should not be reported, and you will please avoid speaking or signalling any passing ship.

"Wishing you a successful cruise, and hoping to see you soon in good health,

"I am, etc.,

"(Signed)   JAMES D. BULLOCH.

"Captain M. J. Butcher."

"Liverpool, *July* 28*th*, 1862.

"Sir,—

"You will join the Confederate States steamship *Alabama* (*Enrica*) temporarily under the orders of Captain M. J. Butcher, and proceed in her to sea. The *Alabama* may have to cruise several days in the British Channel, and to touch at one or two ports. During this time you are strictly enjoined not to mention that you are in any way connected with the Confederate States Navy, but you will simply act as the purser of a private ship.

"In this capacity you will keep account of all money paid out, and you will assist Captain Butcher in any manner he may desire. You have been provided with an invoice of everything now on board the *Alabama*, as well as the cargo shipped on board the barque *Agrippina*, which vessel you will meet at the port to which the *Alabama* is bound. The invoice of the *Agrippina*'s cargo gives the mark and number of every case and bale, the contents of each, and the part of the vessel in which it is stowed. You will endeavour to make yourself fully acquainted with the invoices, and examine the store-rooms, so that you will be able to give efficient aid in getting everything in its proper place when the transfer of stores is made.

"When the *Alabama* is fairly at sea you will mix freely with the 'warrant and petty officers,' show interest in their comfort and welfare, and endeavour to excite their interest in the approaching cruise of the ship. Talk to them of the Southern States, and how they are fighting against great odds for only what every Englishman enjoys—*liberty!* Tell them at the port of destination a distinguished officer of the Confederate States Navy will take command of the ship for a cruise, in which they will have the most active service, and be well taken care of. I do not mean that you are to make the men set speeches, or be constantly talking to them, but in your position you may frequently throw out to leading men hints of the above tenor, which will be commented upon on the berth-deck. Seamen are very impressionable, and can be easily influenced by a little tact and management.

"When Captain Semmes joins, you will at once report to him, and act thereafter under his instructions. He will be a stranger to the ship and crew, and will be in a position of great responsibility and embarrassment. You have it in your power to smooth away some of his difficulties in advance, especially in having all the stores and cargo of the ship in an orderly state, and the men settled and well-disposed, and I confidently rely upon your exertions to bring about such a state of things. You will consider yourself as temporarily under the orders of Captain Butcher, in whom I place great confidence, and by strict attention to your duties and the display of zeal and judgment in their execution, you will evince a just appreciation of the trust reposed in you, and will prove that your appointment to so important a post has been deserved.

"I am, etc.,

"(Signed)   JAMES D. BULLOCH.

"Acting Assistant-Paymaster C. R. Yonge."

The foregoing letters, together with the statement which immediately precedes, sufficiently describe the despatch of the *Alabama* and her tender. It will be perceived that the *Alabama* left the Mersey without any portion of her armament, and without any stores "contraband of war." The official report of the Surveyor of the Customs to the Collector at Liverpool, dated July 30th, 1862, contains the following paragraph:

"I have only to add that your directions to keep a strict watch on the said vessel have been carried out, and I write in the fullest confidence that she left this port without any part of her armament on board. She had not as much as a signal-gun or musket.

"(Signed)   E. MORGAN,
"Surveyor."

I got back to Liverpool from the Giant's Causeway on August 3rd, and immediately posted the following hasty despatch to the Secretary of the Confederate Navy by the Nassau closed mail:

"Liverpool, *September 3rd,* 1862.

"Sir,—

"For the last fortnight the United States officials in this country have used every possible means of inducing the British authorities to seize, or at least to forbid the sailing of the *Alabama*. Spies were employed to watch the ship while lying in a private dockyard, and affidavits were made that men had actually been enlisted by me to serve in the Confederate States Navy.

"This charge, although perfectly unfounded, for I had been very cautious not to violate any English law, gave me much uneasiness, and learning on Tuesday last from a very reliable source that the Government might not be able to resist much longer the importunities of the American Minister, I determined to get the ship out of British waters, and therefore went to sea in her myself, very unexpectedly, on Wednesday night. The United States ship *Tuscarora* was known to be on the look-out, but favoured by thick weather, which enabled me to get quickly clear of stations from which our movements could be telegraphed, she was dodged, and I have just returned to this place, having left the *Alabama* well clear of the Irish coast, while the *Tuscarora* still remains on the look-out off Queenstown, as the telegraph reports. I have but a moment to mention this fact, as the Nassau closed mail leaves, or rather closes, in an hour. ... I am in receipt of a letter from Captain Semmes, and from its contents hope to see him here in a day or two. The Nassau mail is safe, even though it passes through New York, and letters can be forwarded from Nassau by private hands through the agents of Messrs. John Fraser and Co.

"I am, etc.,

"(Signed)   JAMES D. BULLOCH.

"Hon. S. R. Mallory,
"Secretary of the Navy."

Not long after the above date the Confederate agencies at Nassau, Bermuda, and Havana were so well organized that there was no difficulty in sending reports by the British mails *viâ* Halifax and New York to either of those places, and the agents forwarded them to the Confederate ports by the best class of blockade-runners. It is quite astonishing how few letters from the regular official agents of the Confederate Government in Europe fell into the hands of the enemy. The agents at the islands practised great caution, and put their official mails in the hands of safe messengers, who destroyed them when capture seemed inevitable. There was often, of course, much delay, which caused embarrassment, but I never learned that any letter addressed by me to the Secretary of the Confederate Navy at Richmond ever found its way to Washington instead, although lists of captured correspondence were frequently published in the New York papers.

I began now to look anxiously for the arrival of Captain Semmes, and knowing that he had left Nassau in the steamship *Bahama*, I arranged with the owners of that vessel to charter her for a voyage back to Nassau, and the purpose was that she should take Captain Semmes and his officers to the *Alabama* at Terceira. Some extra stores and two additional 32-pounder guns were got ready to be shipped by the *Bahama*, and Freemantle, who was with me in the *Fingal,* and a few good men were picked up to go also, ostensibly for Nassau. At the last moment about thirty men were induced to take passage in the *Bahama*, the plea being that they were to join a vessel at an outport.

The following extracts from my two next reports to the Secretary of the Navy will suffice to close the account of the outfit of the *Alabama*, and the beginning of her career as a Confederate cruiser.

"Liverpool, *August* 11*th*, 1862.

"Sir,—

"I have already informed you by letter, as well as by private messenger, that the *Alabama* is safely clear of British waters, and that another vessel, with her battery and ordnance stores, had previously sailed for a concerted rendezvous. I have now the satisfaction to report that Commander Semmes, with his officers, has arrived here, and will sail to-morrow in a steamer chartered for the purpose, to join the *Alabama*. It has been deemed advisable that I should go with Commander Semmes as far as the rendezvous, to smooth away as much as possible his embarrassments and difficulties in assuming the command of an entirely new ship with a strange and untried crew. My absence will not be prolonged beyond one month, and I have arranged all other business so that there will be no delay or interruption in the progress of other work. As soon as it would be safe to allude to the movements of the *Alabama* in detail, you shall have full accounts…. Suffice it for the present to say that the United States Consul … has not been able to prove any violation of the Foreign Enlistment Act, or of her Majesty's Neutrality Proclamation….

"It will give me the greatest satisfaction to know that Commander Semmes is fairly afloat in the *Alabama,* and confident of his ability to do good service in her, I will watch with pride her coming success, although I cannot overcome the feeling of disappointment I experienced when first informed that I was not to command her myself. The papers necessary to show all the plans, equipment, etc., of the ship are too bulky to send by the means now offering, but you shall have all these points as soon as possible....

"I am, etc.,
"(Signed)   JAMES D. BULLOCH.

"Hon. S. R. Mallory,
"Secretary of the Navy."

"Liverpool, *September* 10*th*, 1862.

"Sir,—

"I have the honour to report my return to England after a short cruise to the Western Islands, where I had gone with Commander Semmes to see him fairly afloat in the *Alabama*. You have been already informed that I had taken the *Alabama* out of British waters, and leaving her off the north-west coast of Ireland, had returned to Liverpool to prepare a ship for the conveyance of Commander Semmes and his officers as soon as they arrived. The battery and ordnance stores, with a quantity of men's clothing and general supplies for a cruising ship, with 350 tons of coal, were despatched from another port of the kingdom in a sailing vessel bought for the purpose, and the two vessels were ordered to rendezvous at Praya, in the island of Terceira.

"Captain Semmes arrived from Nassau on the 8th of August, and on the 13th I sailed in the steamship *Bahama* with him and all his officers for the previously selected rendezvous.

"In seven days the *Bahama* reached Praya, and we had the satisfaction to find the *Alabama* and her consort at anchor in the bay. It was now Wednesday, August 20th, and no time was lost in commencing the transfer of stores from the tender to the *Alabama*. Favoured by Providence with mild calm weather, we met with no interruption, and the work progressed so briskly that at 10 A.M. on Friday, the 22nd, the last gun of the battery was mounted, the powder and shell all stowed, shot in their racks, and, in fine, the tender was discharged. The remainder of the day until 10 P.M. was occupied in coaling, at which time the 'main-brace was spliced,' and the hammocks piped down, the *Alabama*—so far, at least, as related to her equipment—being ready for action. On Sunday morning (the 24th), the *Alabama* and *Bahama* steamed slowly off the land, and when beyond the marine league which was covered by the jurisdiction of Portugal, our own national colours were hoisted for the first time at the *Alabama*'s peak, welcomed by three cheers from the united crews of both vessels. Now came the business of shipping the men formally for the Confederate States service, making out their allotment tickets, arranging their accounts, etc. This could be done leisurely, for we were on the high seas, beyond the reach of Foreign Enlistment Acts and Neutrality Proclamations, the most annoying foes we have to contend with on this side of the Atlantic.

"By twelve o'clock at night all these matters were arranged; the two steamers stopped their engines, and bidding Captain Semmes a cordial adieu, with heartfelt prayers for his success, I stepped over the *Alabama*'s side.... Commander Semmes has written you enclosing crew-list, etc., and for further information I beg to refer you to his report....

"I am, etc.,

"(Signed)   JAMES D BULLOCH.

"Hon. S. R. Mallory,
"Secretary of the Navy."

There were some minor adventures attending the equipment of the *Alabama* at Terceira which Captain Semmes has narrated in his very full and interesting history of his cruise. To repeat them here would be superfluous. My official reports were usually brief and concise, often written in great haste, and there was neither time to describe incidents of ordinary interest, nor would they have been suited to appear in official documents.

Captain Butcher returned with me in the *Bahama* to Liverpool. We parted company shortly afterwards and did not meet again for many years. I have already given my estimate of Captain Butcher's qualities, and as his name will now disappear from this narrative, I take pleasure in saying that his conduct up to the last moment was confirmatory of my first impressions. He carried out his instructions with zeal and intelligence, and when the *Bahama* arrived at the rendezvous, we had the satisfaction to find that he had already broken bulk on board the *Agrippina,* and had transferred a portion of the stores and some of the heavy weights to the *Alabama,* and had thus lessened the subsequent labour, and shortened the time of our detention at Terceira.

The whole story of the building and equipment of the *Alabama* has now been told, perhaps with unnecessary detail, but that offence may be pardoned, in consideration of the misapprehensions which have heretofore prevailed, the many misstatements which have been made with reference to her origin, and the obligation resting upon me to tell the whole truth, if I ventured to come forward as a witness at all.* Some of the statements respecting the departure of the *Alabama* from Liverpool require to be especially controverted and explained. It has been said that she "escaped by a ruse," and that an offence was committed by taking her away without registration, and without a clearance at the Custom House. The effect of registry in England is to entitle the ship to wear the British flag, and to assume the privileges of British nationality; but the law does not positively require an owner to register his ship.† Disabilities and disadvantages are, however, incurred by the failure to register, and thus the law may be said to practically enforce registration in all cases of British ships employed in trade to and from the United Kingdom. When, however, a vessel is built in England, and is sent abroad for sale or for delivery to a previous purchaser, there is no violation of law, and no penalty is incurred, if she is sent away without a register.

The requirement to take out a clearance at a British port is purely for Customs purposes: (1) to obtain statistics of the quantity and description of merchandise entering and leaving the United Kingdom; and (2) to protect the revenue in the following particular. Ships taking on board, out of bond, such goods as are liable to import duty if consumed in the country, are allowed an exemption if the goods are intended for use during the outward voyage, or for final export, and before a clearance can be effected the Customs authorities require satisfactory proof that the goods of that class stated to be thus shipped are really kept on board and carried away. In the year 1862, and I believe until 1867, when the law was changed, no legal penalty was incurred by a vessel if she left a British for a foreign port without a clearance, provided she was in ballast, and had no stores on board except such as were exempt from duty, or had paid duty. I took legal advice on both the above points, and was fully instructed, besides which, I was furnished with specific examples of ships that had previously gone away direct from the hands of the builders, without registration or clearance. The *Alabama* was in ballast, and had no goods or stores on board that were not either free of import duty or had paid duty. She lay in a public dock for at least a fortnight. She was brought out of that dock in open daylight, and lay a night and part of two days in the river. She then got under weigh in a busy part of the day, when the whole neighbourhood was awake and active, and went to sea with colours flying.

* That the *Alabama* left Liverpool wholly unarmed is proved by the Report of the Surveyor of Customs. See footnote, Chapter II., p. 49.

† The law in respect to clearance and registration was altered in 1867, and the above remarks have reference to the law as it stood in 1861–65.

There could hardly be a movement less like a clandestine "escape," and it has been shown that there was no violation of law. But it may be and has been said, that the party of guests, and the dressing with flags, were intended to convey the impression that the departure was not final, and that the ship would return. If the charge of "escaping by a ruse" is founded upon those lawful and innocent proceedings, there is no occasion for much concern about it. I have never learned that the ethics of war forbid the practice of a ruse to deceive an enemy.

Not a single false statement was made with the purpose to mislead those having authority to make inquiries. No trust was betrayed, no confidence violated. The Foreign Enlistment Act, the Merchant Shipping Act, the Customs Regulations, were carefully examined, and in the opinion of experts none of them were transgressed, and no one has ever been indicted or made to answer in a court of law for his conduct in any matter concerning the building or despatch of the *Alabama*, although the parties implicated were at the time, and continued to be, resident in Great Britain.

Officers of her Majesty's Customs had been closely watching the ship. They were on board the very morning of her departure, and were satisfied that there were no arms or ammunition in the ship, and no goods except such as were free or had paid duty. The "so-called" ruse was not intended to deceive them, but to mislead the United States consular spies, who I knew were ready to make any affidavit that might be considered necessary to effect a seizure of the ship for violation of the Foreign Enlistment Act.

It was furthermore said that the departure of the *Alabama* from the Mersey was "hastened by the illicit receipt of intelligence of the decision of the British Government to stop her." In the "Counter Case" presented on the part of the Government of her Britannic Majesty to the Tribunal of Arbitration at Geneva, this statement is disposed of by pointing out that the report of the law officers was not made until the 29th of July, and therefore no decision had been come to when the *Alabama* left, early on the morning of that day; but the defence is set up that even if "it had been so, the British Government could never be held responsible for the treachery of some unknown subordinate, who may have become informed of their decision or may have anticipated that it would be made."

The statement referred to above is rather in the character of an insinuation than a charge, because it could not have been proved by any direct evidence, unless the alleged informer had been driven by a reproving conscience to confess his treachery. On the other hand, it cannot be proved to be false by any other evidence than a direct and categorical denial. It is not my office to defend, or explain, or to palliate the conduct of the British Government in any particular, but permanent officials, and especially the subordinates in the various departments, are in no way responsible for a policy, but only for the manner in which their specific duties are performed, and I feel it incumbent upon me to declare that no officer, high or low, in any department of the Government, did ever convey to me, or to anyone who afterwards repeated to me, a word or a hint which led me to anticipate what the action of the Government would be, or was likely to be, in any pending case. Although the Confederate Commissioners were not officially recognised, and therefore could have no diplomatic intercourse with the Government, it is well known that outside official circles they were received with very marked and gratifying cordiality, and it is probable that through private friends Mr. Mason could and did have very favourable opportunities of learning the general, and in some instances the specific, purposes of the Government. Whatever he learned that had any bearing upon our naval operations was always repeated to me without delay, and the information thus received often proved to be correct, although it was gathered merely from conversation with those who were accustomed to observe the conduct of Ministers and to draw their own conclusions, and not from the statements of any persons who were in a position to know the actual purposes of the Government.

But in the particular case of the *Alabama* the signs that something serious was about to happen were too visible to escape notice. The numerous statements and affidavits sent to the American Minister by the Consul at Liverpool were necessarily drawn up in legal form, and required the employment of solicitors. I cannot say whether there is, or is not, a species of magnetic sympathy between attorneys, or whether they have any special devices for finding out each other's ways, but I do know that my own solicitor managed to find out the particulars of some of the affidavits, and although they were inaccurate in the affirmations which were at all specific, yet some of them contained allegations which he thought would at least induce the Government to detain the ship for investigation.

Besides this, the Foreign Secretary, pressed by the United States Minister to take some action, referred the affidavits to the Commissioners of Customs, and directed them to inquire and report. For a fortnight before the departure of the *Alabama* inquiries came in showers from the collector, sometimes delivered in person by the surveyor or his subordinates, sometimes in the form of written memoranda. The inquiries were mostly addressed to the builders of the ship, and often referred to matters of which they knew nothing, and so could give no reply. My solicitor got possession of one of the lists of questions, and it lies before me now while I am writing. Almost every inquiry could have been answered by a direct and positive denial of the truth of the allegation; but at the same time it was possible, perhaps probable, that the Government would not be satisfied with denials, however categorical and explicit.

It must be manifest from the foregoing *resumé* that there was good reason for hastening the departure of the *Alabama*, and I trust it will be now admitted that the information which caused the somewhat precipitate movement came to those concerned in it, not by any treachery or breach of trust, but in a very simple, regular, and ordinary way.

The collector of the Port of Liverpool at that time was a Mr. S. Price Edwards. The official documents published in the proceedings before the Tribunal of Arbitration prove, it seems to me, that Mr. Edwards did his duty faithfully—in fact, zealously. On the 21st of July, 1862, eight days before the sailing of the *Alabama*, he appears to have written to his superiors in London informing them that the ship was quite ready for sea, and might sail at any moment, and he asked to be instructed by telegraph if the intention was to detain her.*

When it was known that the *Alabama* was off, and all chance of seizing her had vanished, great annoyance and chagrin was felt at the United States Consulate and among the resident Americans who were in sympathy with the Federal Government. This feeling of disappointment was shown in many ways—among others, in harsh and ungenerous insinuations against the integrity of the local authorities, especially against Mr. Price Edwards himself, who was even accused of having been paid for shutting his eyes.

Many months afterwards I met a gentleman at the house of a friend, and we engaged in conversation for some time, neither knowing who the other was. Later in the evening we were joined by our host, who introduced us. There was a mutual expression of surprise, for the parties were Mr. Price Edwards and the writer. Mr. Edwards asked me if I was aware that he had been accused of taking a bribe from me for letting the *Alabama* go. I replied that I had heard some indefinite insinuations of the kind, but had not given them much heed. He affected to be equally indifferent, but I learned from other sources that he had been deeply pained, and that he

---

* Extract from a letter addressed by the Collector of Customs, Liverpool (Mr. Price Edwards), to the Commissioner of Customs, London, dated July 21, 1862: "I shall feel obliged by the Board being pleased to instruct me by telegraph how I am to act, as the ship appears to be ready for sea, and may leave at any hour she pleases."

never wholly recovered from the feeling of mortification produced by such an unfounded and gratuitous aspersion upon his official integrity.

Subsequently Mr. Edwards fell into some difficulties with the authorities at London in no way connected with Confederate affairs, and was removed from his office. I never knew the cause of his removal, but I met him some time afterwards. He appeared much broken in health and greatly depressed in spirits, and not long after I learned that he had passed beyond the reach of such "ills as flesh is heir to." I am glad to have it in my power to free his memory from the stain which may have clung to it in respect to the "escape" of the *Alabama,* although it is hardly probable that any surviving relative will know that it has been done.

There is just one more disclaimer that I feel in some sort impelled to pronounce in this connection. I have said that no public official, either principal or subordinate, ever gave the faintest hint of the purposes of his superiors in respect to the seizure of Confederate ships. I can also affirm, without the least mental reservation, that no proposition, or suggestion, or promise of reward, was ever made to an *employé* of the Government which could have tempted him to swerve in his loyalty, or to turn one hair's-breadth from the straight line of his duty, and I never saw or heard of anyone who appeared likely to be accessible to such temptations, had they been put in his way.

When I parted from Captain Semmes off the island of Terceira, it was arranged that I should send out the *Agrippina* to him with a cargo of coals and certain other supplies, and the barque was ordered to Cardiff to load. This arrangement was carried out successfully. Semmes met his tender at St. Pierre, in the French island of Martinique, from which place he despatched her to Blanquilla, a small island off the coast of Venezuela, where he took from her a supply of coal, and then sent her to the uninhabited Arcas Cays, off Yucatan. Here he took the remainder of the coal and stores, and sent the barque to Liverpool, proceeding himself to look after General Banks's expedition against Galveston.

Semmes's hope was to catch the troop-ships and transports *en route,* and to make a dash in among them. He wrote me from Arcas Islands, January 4, 1863:—

"I have filled up with coal a second time from the barque, caulked the spar deck, overhauled and set up rigging, and shall sail again to-night on another foray against the enemy. My ship is getting in good order, and I have nearly a full crew, having added twenty-five men to the eighty-five that I brought with me from Terceira, and they are pretty well drilled at the guns. It is not unlikely that before I get out of the Gulf of Mexico I shall 'put up' something, as this is a sort of 'close sea' of the enemy, swarming with his cruisers. After leaving the Gulf I shall carry out the Secretary of the Navy's suggestion as to my cruising ground, and about which we (you and I) have consulted."

In the same letter Semmes asked me to send the *Agrippina* to him again, first to the island of Fernando de Noronha, with instructions to wait there three days, and if he did not arrive to go on to Bahia. The expectation that he would "put up something" before he got out of the Gulf was realized. He did not get among General Banks's transports, but he went off Galveston to look after them, and found there a powerful squadron under Acting Rear-Admiral H. H. Bell, who sent two or three of his ships to meet the approaching stranger and bring her to an account of herself.

Semmes ran slowly off shore, and drew one of his pursuers after him. When he found that the others did not follow, he waited until just at nightfall, when the enemy closed. There was a hail and a reply, then two quickly succeeding broadsides, and a sharp engagement of thirteen minutes, a cessation of the firing on one side, and a hail to report the vessel sinking. The hail was not from the *Alabama*, but it suspended her fire, and her boats were soon busy picking up the crew of the United States ship *Hatteras*.

It was a creditable performance for the first effort of a hastily improvised cruiser with a green crew, to sink an opposing ship in thirteen minutes in a night engagement, and then to pick up every man who had not been killed or mortally wounded in the action. On the other side, I take pleasure in saying that Lieutenant-Commanding H. H. Blake showed commendable spirit and courage in boldly running down upon a ship which he suspected to be the *Alabama*, and therefore knew was his superior in armament and general efficiency, when he had distanced his consorts and could expect no support from them.

The *Hatteras* was an iron paddle-steamer, bought out of the mercantile marine. Her engines were much exposed, and were of the "top-lever," or "walking-beam" type. The armament of the *Hatteras* was four 32-pounders, two Parrot 30-pounder rifles, one 20-pounder rifle, and one 12-pounder howitzer—total, eight guns. The armament of the *Alabama* was six 32-pounders, one 8-inch smooth-bore gun (112 cwt.), and one 100-pounder Blakely rifled gun. The crew of the *Hatteras* was 108 men, that of the *Alabama* 110.

I do not describe the engagement in detail, because the reports of both commanders are on public record, and every incident has been minutely related in "My Adventures Afloat," by Admiral Semmes. There is no doubt that the *Alabama* was the superior ship, and barring an accident, or one of those unexpected chances which sometimes occur in contests between single vessels, and upset all calculations, she ought to have won, and the loss of his ship was no disgrace to the commander of the *Hatteras*.

The *Agrippina* was not a clipper. She made a long passage from the Arcas Islands to England, and sprang her foremast in a gale before getting into the Channel. She was refitted and despatched as quickly as possible, but this time the arrangements failed. Semmes touched at Fernando de Noronha, and then went on to Bahia, but not finding the tender at either place, he coaled from the shore, and proceeded on his cruise to the Cape of Good Hope, *en route* for the China Sea. The *Alabama* left Bahia on the 22nd of May, 1863, and the *Agrippina* arrived there on June 1st. Semmes was a little impatient to get away. He had done much damage to the enemy's commerce on the great ocean highway off the north-east coast of Brazil, and began to think that the neighbourhood could not remain safe much longer. He wrote me from Bahia, May 21st, 1862:

"I have coaled from the shore, and as the authorities are hurrying me off, I have appointed another rendezvous for the *Agrippina*. If you hear anything of my violating the neutrality of Fernando de Noronha, contradict it *in limine*, as being an invention of the enemy. We are having capital success. That 'little bill' which the Yankees threaten to present to our Uncle John Bull, for the depredations of the *Alabama*, is growing apace, and already reaches $3,100,000."

When the *Agrippina* arrived at Bahia, Captain McQueen found there two United States ships, the *Mohican* and the *Onward*. The United States Consul had suspected another British ship then in port of having stores on board for the *Alabama*, and had advised the commanders of the United States ships to capture her if she should leave the port. Captain McQueen soon learned that his vessel had also attracted the notice and suspicions of the United States Consul, and he learned that the *Onward* was especially on the watch for him. In this dilemma he consulted her Majesty's Consul, who told him that he had not a shadow of doubt that if he went outside the *Onward* would capture him, and he would be sent before a United States prize-court.

Captain McQueen waited for some time in great perplexity, being most anxious to comply with Captain Semmes's instructions, but the *Onward* remained also on the look-out for him, and escape from her was impossible. Finally he applied again to her Majesty's Consul, who advised him to sell his cargo and take a freight for England, a proceeding which would protect him from capture, and would be the best possible arrangement for his owners. The Consul did not, of course, know of the *Agrippina*'s connection with the *Alabama*, whatever the general belief at Bahia may have been, and his advice was given in the ordinary course of his duty as the guardian of British interests, the *Agrippina* being a duly registered British ship. Captain McQueen acted upon it, and to satisfy the owner that all was right, he brought home a consular certificate, which alleged that "Bahia had been for some time virtually blockaded by the United States ships *Mohican* and *Onward*."

The *Agrippina*'s homeward freight amounted to £437 15s. 3d. She was too well known to be used for the Confederate service again, and was sold, after some delay, for a purchaser did not readily offer. Her original cost was £1,400, and she fetched at auction £860. The service she had rendered was more than compensation for the loss, but it was evident that the expense of providing a permanent tender for each cruising ship was more than the Confederate Treasury could bear, and besides this, I perceived that the probabilities of bringing the two together at distant and varying points, where they could communicate and make the transfer of stores safely, did not justify the labour and expenditure. The *Alabama* was therefore left to look out for herself, and I felt no great concern, because I was confident of her qualities and fitness for the work she had in hand. I knew that she could supply herself with provisions and various other wants from prizes, and the "cruising fund" was sufficient to meet the requirements of fuel. Her commander writes of her thus:

"I was much gratified to find that my new ship proved to be a fine sailer under canvas. This quality was of inestimable advantage to me, as it enabled me to do most of my work under sail. She carried but an eighteen days' supply of fuel, and if I had been obliged, because of her dull sailing qualities, to chase everything under steam, the reader can see how I should have been hampered in my movements. I should have been half my time running into port for fuel. This would have disclosed my whereabouts so frequently to the enemy, that I should have been constantly in danger of capture, whereas I could now stretch into far-distant seas, and chase, capture, and destroy, perfectly independent of steam. I adopted the plan, therefore, of working under sail in the very beginning of the cruise, and practised it unto the end. With the exception of half-a-dozen prizes, all my captures were made with my screw hoisted and my ship under sail."

The foregoing extract from "My Adventures Afloat," by Admiral Semmes, is confirmatory of what I have said in an early chapter respecting the suitable type for a Confederate cruiser; and the opinion I held at the beginning of the war was maintained to the end, and deterred me from buying any of the ordinary war-ships with non-lifting screws, or any of the wooden ships with insufficient sail power, which private parties desirous to make commissions were constantly pressing upon me.

The *Alabama,* it will be perceived, was commissioned on the high seas, and she never entered a Confederate port. This was always a sore point with Mr. Seward, the United States Secretary of State. He never ceased to call her a pirate, nor to press the British Government to seize her, even after she had been commissioned as a man-of-war under the Confederate flag. The tone of his despatches on the subject was not couched in such language as is commonly used by statesmen accustomed to diplomatic usage. His petulant complaints often gave offence, and brought upon him rebukes and retorts which must have been wounding to the national feeling in the United States if they were ever printed in the Congressional documents.

The European Powers having acknowledged the existence of a *de facto* Government at Richmond, that acknowledgment carried with it the concession of all belligerent rights. By the determination to acknowledge the Confederate States as belligerents, England, among other Powers, bound herself to extend the same privileges to Confederate cruisers as to those of the United States; and it was not only discourteous, but it was highly impolitic in Mr. Seward to taunt foreign Governments with precipitancy in the recognition, and then of harbouring "piratical cruisers."

I suppose there can be no principle of international law plainer than this, namely, when a ship is once commissioned by a recognised *de facto* Government, no other Power can inquire into her origin or antecedents.

The process of commissioning a ship is for the duly appointed captain, with his staff of officers, to take charge of her, read his commission, and hoist his pennant and the national colours. When these formalities have been complied with, no foreign Power can question the character of the ship, or enter upon any inquiry as to the place where she was commissioned. The British authorities could ask the commander of a Confederate cruiser for a sight of his commission, and if that was in order, no further inquiry was admissible.

No European or other neutral Power questioned the foregoing premises during the late Civil War, and it is not therefore necessary to mention any precedents from their history of vessels commissioned abroad or on the high seas.

Cooper, in his "Naval History of the United States," supplies many examples of vessels which were bought, armed, equipped, manned, and almost exclusively officered abroad and by foreigners, and which were then commissioned by the American Government and sent to cruise against English commerce, and to foray upon the British coasts, without previously entering an American port. As one case is sufficient to establish the precedent, I will just mention that of a fine fast English cutter bought at Dover by an agent of the American Commissioners in France. She was taken across the channel to Dunkirk, where her name was changed to the *Surprise*. She was fully equipped, officered, and manned. The Commissioners filled up a blank commission signed by John Hancock, President of Congress, and handed it to one Captain Gustavus Conyngham, who went to sea from Dunkirk on the 1st of May, 1777, and on the 4th captured the English packet *Prince of Orange*. Captain Conyngham took his prize into Dunkirk, the neutral port from which he had sailed only a few days before. The English Minister remonstrated, and the French Government seized the *Surprise*, imprisoned Captain Conyngham, and took away his commission; but the American Commissioners at Paris found means to obtain his release. They bought and fitted out another cutter at Dunkirk, which was called the *Revenge*, and Captain Conyngham was recommissioned to her. The *Revenge* sailed from Dunkirk on July 18, 1777, and captured many British vessels. Some she destroyed; the most valuable she sent into Spanish ports. Fenimore Cooper says that the *Surprise* and *Revenge* were spoken of in the accounts of the day as privateers, but that they were, as a matter of fact, bought and equipped by agents of the Diplomatic Commissioners of the United States.

Commodore Paul Jones fitted out his ship, the *Bonhomme Richard*, in a French port. His crew, picked up chiefly at Nantes, are thus described by Cooper: "A few Americans were found to fill the stations of sea-officers on the quarter-deck and forward, but the remainder of the people were a mixture of Irish, Scotch, Portuguese, Norwegians, Germans, Spaniards, Swedes, Italians, and Malays," etc. The Commissioners stationed in France at that time, and who conducted the naval operations of the American Congress abroad, were Benjamin Franklin, Silas Deane, and John Adams, eminent men, who would have indignantly repudiated the charge of piracy against their improvised cruisers, and yet no agent of the Confederate Government ever took such liberties with neutral rights, or with the laws of nations, as they did.

In regard to the right to commission a ship on the high seas, I will refer to but one case, recorded also in Cooper's "Naval History of the United States." Commodore David Porter made a famous cruise among the English whaling fleet in the Pacific during the war of 1812–15, in command of the United States ship *Essex*. One of his prizes being armed and well suited for cruising, he manned her, partly from his own ship, put his first-lieutenant, John Downes, in command, and commissioned her as a United States ship-of-war, naming her the *Essex Junior*.

In view of these and other well-known examples recorded in the naval histories of England as well as the United States, Mr. Seward's continued harping upon the "foreign origin" of the *Alabama* seemed puerile to the representatives of the various Powers to whom he addressed remonstrances on the subject. However, the *Florida*, although she went into a Confederate port, and was officered, manned, and recommissioned there, was also called by the generic name of "pirate" in all the official correspondence of the United States during the war; and so it appears that, in Mr. Seward's opinion, deeds done by the *de facto* Government of the revolted colonies in 1777, or by the more formally recognised Government at Washington in 1812–15, were just and lawful acts of war, but that similar acts done by authority of the *de facto* Government of the Confederate States in 1862 were "criminal" and "nefarious." The *Surprise*, fitted out, armed, and manned at Dunkirk, might with propriety capture a British vessel four days after she had left the neutral port; the *Essex Junior*, a captured prize, might be lawfully commissioned by a United States officer, at some savage island in the Pacific, and then sent to prey upon British whalers; but the *Alabama*, carrying the commission of a *de facto* Government, recognised as a belligerent Power by every civilized nation, was a "piratical rover" unworthy of shelter or assistance, but fit only to be pursued and destroyed as a common enemy and a common pest.

Let us hope, if we can, that there will be no more wars, foreign or domestic; but Mr. Seward has done much by the pretensions he set up during the great contest of 1861–65 to embarrass the United States whenever they may be again placed in the position of a neutral or belligerent.

The *Alabama* left Liverpool on the 29th of July, 1862. She was commissioned off the island of Terceira on the 24th of August, and she kept the sea almost incessantly for two years. During that period she was rarely in harbour, and never long enough to effect a thorough and satisfactory overhaul of rigging, hull, or engines. She was kept while cruising chiefly under sail, with screw up; but she was purposely taken to the great thoroughfares of American marine traffic, to those well-known points towards which the trade of the world converges, and where it was reasonable to expect United States ships would be sent to keep guard. Hence she was in constant expectation of having to run or to fight. Any morning's light might find her close to an enemy's ship, and prudence required both a sharp look-out and constant readiness. Her engines got rest, but her boilers none. The fires were never allowed to go wholly out, but were banked; and the water was kept in such condition that steam might be quickly got. The chief engineer has told me that he rarely had an opportunity to cool the boilers and clean flues and pipes.

A great portion of her cruising was in the tropics, although she faced every vicissitude of climate. The icy fogs of the Newfoundland Bank, the steaming moisture of the equatorial belt, the burning sun of Malacca and the China Sea—all these in turn, and in quick succession, served to test her endurance. The wear and tear of such a cruise, such a lengthened period of restless activity, with no means to supply deficiencies or to repair injuries, except what might be found in captured vessels, told upon the little craft at last, and early in 1864 Semmes began to think of her requirements, and coming back round the Cape of Good Hope into the Atlantic, he worked leisurely up through the "paths of commerce," capturing a prize now and then, but finding few, for by that time the American mercantile flag had well nigh disappeared.

The effect produced upon the commerce and the shipping interests of the United States by two or three Confederate cruisers was a very striking peculiarity of the late war. While the *Alabama* was in the China Sea many American ships took shelter in the harbour of Singapore and other ports, and were partly dismantled and laid up at a time when trade was good, and there was an active demand for tonnage to all parts of the world. Semmes found on board a prize captured in the Straits of Malacca a copy of the Singapore *Times,* dated 9th December, 1863, containing a list of seventeen American ships, with an aggregate tonnage of about 12,000 tons, which were laid up at that port alone.

The Right Hon. Milner Gibson, President of the Board of Trade, made a speech at Ashton-under-Lyne, January 20th, 1864, in which he commented upon the transference of the carrying trade from American to British ships. He stated that during the year (1863–64) the number of British ships clearing had increased to something like 14,000,000 tons, as against 7,000,000 tons of all foreign tonnage inclusive, and he gave the actual decrease in the employment of American shipping in the trade between England and the United States as something like forty-six or forty-seven per cent.

Mr. Milner Gibson called particular attention to the foregoing results as an example of what could be done by two or three swift steamers, and commented upon the injury inflicted upon the commerce of the United States by the Confederate cruisers, as a warning to other Maritime Powers of what might happen to them. But I have always thought that the

United States Navy Department showed either great apathy or was singularly blind to the real danger to the commerce of the United States, and strangely negligent in using the means to protect it. The points of attack were so apparent that it seems hardly credible that they were never occupied.

The whole traffic between the northern ports of the United States and the Pacific, as well as with Brazil and the states of the La Plata, passes through a belt of no great width, which intersects the equator at about the 30th meridian of west longitude. American outward-bound ships shape their course so as to leave the north-east Trades near the above-named meridian, then work their way through the equatorial "doldrums," and meeting the south-east Trade-winds, they are forced, after crossing the line, generally somewhat further west, thus passing in sight, or very nearly in sight, of the island of Fernando de Noronha. Homeward-bound American ships from the East Indies leave the south-east Trades at very nearly the same point, and those from round the Horn and the La Plata or Brazil pass sometimes rather more to the westward, between Fernando de Noronha and that portion of the South American coast which has its extreme eastern projection between Pernambuco and Cape St. Roque.

If the United States had stationed a few ships to cruise in couplets in the neighbourhood of the above-named "forks of the road," as they have been called by Maury, and a few more, say, in the Straits of Malacca, and on the principal and well-known cruising ground of their whaling-fleet, two or three Confederate cruisers could not have remained for weeks in the track of passing ships, capturing and destroying them without hindrance.

Neither the *Alabama, Florida,* nor *Sumter* was driven from her work in any particular latitude; they shifted their cruising grounds only when it seemed advisable to seek fresh victims elsewhere; and the *Shenandoah* went round the world, sought out the great American whaling-fleet in the North Pacific, and destroyed thirty-eight vessels without so much as seeing a United States ship-of-war.

It is not probable that any other Maritime Power will leave its commerce at the mercy of light cruisers of the *Alabama* type in a future war. In fact, a fair amount of British trade could be carried on in steamers capable of protecting themselves or of escaping by their great speed, because the majority of the modern steamers of the British mercantile marine could carry as heavy guns as the cruisers that would be sent after them, and they have very high speed.

On the 11th of June, 1864, the *Alabama* arrived at Cherbourg. The purpose was to give her a thorough refit, at least so far as the French authorities would permit. Captain Semmes soon learned that the United States ship *Kearsarge,* Captain John A. Winslow, was at Flushing. On the 14th she came round to Cherbourg, and Captain Winslow made a request of the local authorities that a number of prisoners landed from the *Alabama* should be permitted to join his ship. This request was refused, and the *Kearsarge,* without anchoring, went outside and took up a position off the breakwater. It was not probable that she would leave the near neighbourhood until the *Alabama* came out, and it was necessary therefore for Captain Semmes to consider whether he would complete his repairs, and then attempt to avoid an encounter by going out on a dark night, or whether he should go out openly and engage her.

The *Kearsarge* had some advantage in tonnage, and in weight and size of scantling, and she was probably in better condition generally. The effect of the *Alabama*'s long and active cruise has been mentioned above. Captain Semmes, writing about two months before his arrival at Cherbourg, likens her to "the weary foxhound, limping back after a long chase, footsore, and longing for quiet and repose." The *Kearsarge,* on the contrary, was out in pursuit, and there is no reason to doubt that she was fit for any work suited to her class.

The *Alabama* carried six 32-pounder guns in broadside, one 8-inch smooth bore of 112 cwt., and one 7-inch 100-pounder rifled gun (Blakely pattern) on pivots. The *Kearsarge* mounted four 32-pounders in broadside, two 11-inch Dahlgren guns pivoted on deck, and one 28-pounder rifled gun, pivoted on the top-gallant forecastle. She had also a 12-pounder howitzer, which was used near the close of the action. The *Alabama* was pierced for eight 32-pounders, but was two short. However, by shifting one to the fighting side she could, and in fact did, use six guns in the engagement against the five which the *Kearsarge* fought.

In spite of the *Alabama*'s extra 32-pounder in broadside, I think every professional man would say without hesitation that the battery of the *Kearsarge* was the most effective. She not only threw more metal in broadside, but the larger calibre of her two chief pivot-guns gave her a great advantage against a wooden ship. I have not hesitated to point out, fairly as I think, the particulars in which I consider the *Kearsarge* to have been superior in condition and armament to the *Alabama.* The conditions under which the engagement was fought did not admit of any advantage being gained on either side by skilful handling, neither ship having sufficient superiority in speed to enable her to take a raking position. The result of the action was determined by the superior accuracy of the firing from the

Kearsarge. The damage she inflicted upon the Alabama was more than suffi-cient to have destroyed her, and inasmuch as the Kearsarge received no mortal wound, and came out of the engagement with no material injury, it is only a fair admission to say that the result would probably not have been different under the existing circumstances, even if the Alabama had been a larger ship, and more powerfully armed.

The crew of the Alabama were in good discipline, and were well drilled in the manual of the guns, but the impossibility of replenishing the ord-nance stores prevented target practice, and the battery had never been used with shot except in the short engagement with the Hatteras, which was fought at very close quarters, and a few rounds on one occasion fired at a prize, after the crew were removed. The men, therefore, had not been trained to judge of distances, and were wholly without the skill, precision and coolness which come only with practice and the habit of firing at a visible object and noting the effect.

Captain Semmes took a comprehensive view of the relative force and condition of the two ships, and did not think the disparity so great as to render success hopeless. He thought of the cases in which a chance shot reaching a vital spot had disabled ships in previous engagements, or had at least balanced the initial disparity, and felt therefore justified in trying conclusions with his enemy, who it was quite apparent did not intend to grant him a free passage out to sea.

Captain Semmes notified Captain Winslow, through the United States Consul, that he would go out and fight him as soon as he had finished coal-ing, and it will not be doubted that both ships made the best possible preparations for the engagement. On the morning of the 19th of June, 1864, at about 9:30, the Alabama got under weigh, and steamed out of Cherbourg, passing to the westward of the breakwater. The Kearsarge took note of her movement, and knowing that there was no purpose to avoid an engagement, and desirous to prevent any encroachment upon the neutral rights of France, Captain Winslow turned his ship's head off shore, and steamed to a distance of about seven miles, followed by the Alabama. When it was quite certain that both vessels were well beyond the "line of jurisdiction," the Kearsarge turned her head in shore and steered towards the Alabama. The two ships approached rapidly, both were cleared for ac-tion, each with her battery pivoted to starboard.

When they were about one mile apart, the Alabama sheered to port, showed her starboard battery, and almost immediately opened fire, the shot mostly going high. The Kearsarge stood on until she had received three "broadsides" from the *Alabama*,* the shot still going high, and doing no damage except to the rigging. At about a thousand yards' distance, Winslow began to be apprehensive of getting a raking shot, and he then sheered to port, bringing his own starboard broadside to bear, and opened fire.

The action now became active on both sides. Semmes, conscious of the inferiority of his crew in gunnery, had carefully considered the advantage he would gain by fighting at close quarters, and his purpose was to get within short range as soon as possible. Winslow, ignorant of this intention on the part of his adversary, pushed on at full speed to get in-shore of the *Alabama,* hoping thus to prevent any attempt to return into Cherbourg if he should succeed in disabling her. As soon as the two ships passed each other, the *Kearsarge* put her helm to port, with the object to pass under the stern of the *Alabama* and rake her. To counteract this movement and to keep her own broadside bearing, the *Alabama*'s helm was ported also, and the two ships, keeping their helms to port, and steaming at full speed, fell into a circular course, and continued the action heading in opposite directions, in positions generally parallel to each other, while steaming round a common centre.

In about one hour and ten minutes after the *Alabama* fired her first gun, she was found to be in a sinking condition. The 11-inch shells of the *Kearsarge* had made several openings in her sides which it was impossible to stop, and at every roll in the very moderate swell large quantities of water rushed into her.

Semmes made an effort to reach the French coast by assisting the engines with the fore-and-aft sails, but the ship filled so rapidly that the fires were soon put out. Meanwhile the *Kearsarge* steamed ahead, and keeping her helm to port, she passed under the *Alabama*'s stern, and ranging along her port-beam, finally got into a raking position across her bow; but by this time the *Alabama* was so manifestly sinking that the fire of both ships had ceased.

When Semmes discovered that his ship had got her death wound, and that she was hopelessly settling under him, he ordered the colours to be struck. There is some discrepancy in the reports of the two commanders as to the cessation of the firing. Captain Semmes says that the *Kearsarge* fired into him after his flag was down. On the other hand, Captain Winslow states that having ceased firing, he received two shots from the

---

* Captain Winslow's official report.

Alabama's port battery, which drew a return from him. Neither captain, however, charges the other with a wilful default. Semmes states the fact in his report, but in the comments upon the action in his narrative of the cruise, he acquits Captain Winslow of any intentional violation of the rules of humane warfare, and there can be no doubt that the alleged exchange of shots after the surrender arose from a mistake which is not without precedent in previous sea fights.

There was barely time to get the *Alabama*'s wounded men into the boats and despatch them to the *Kearsarge*, when the ship went down, and the officers and crew were swimming for their lives. The *Kearsarge* did not immediately send assistance. It appears from Captain Winslow's report that the boats were disabled, but he managed, after some delay, to get two afloat, and they picked up a few men.

Captain Semmes and the greater portion of his officers and crew were rescued by two French fishing vessels and the English steam-yacht *Deerhound*, owned by Mr. John Lancaster. The French fishermen proceeded into Cherbourg, and the *Deerhound* to Southampton, and the rescued officers and men were landed at those two ports respectively.

The *Alabama* was so badly cut up in her hull that it is doubtful if she could have been again refitted for cruising, even if she could have been kept afloat long enough to reach Cherbourg. An officer told me the day after the engagement that he thought a barrel might have been passed through the hole made by an 11-inch shell at the gangway, and near the water-line. He said one of the men, while sponging his gun, saw the hole, and called his attention to it. He looked out of the port, and when he saw the aperture and the rush of water at every roll, he felt that the *Alabama*'s last moments were close at hand. It is not possible to tell how many times the *Alabama* was hit, but it is quite certain that she received many shot in her hull, more than one of which contributed to her sinking.

The *Kearsarge* fired 173 shot and shell, apportioned as follows: From 11-inch guns, 55 shell; from 32-pounders, 18 shell and 42 solid shot; from 28-pounder rifled gun, 48 shell; from 12-pound howitzer, 9 shrapnel and 1 canister. She was struck twenty-eight times by shot and shell in various places. One shell exploded in her funnel, but except damage to some of her boats, she was but little injured, and strange to say, she had only three men wounded, none killed. The *Alabama* had twenty-one wounded and nine killed, and it is believed that ten were drowned.

I have read with care the reports of the two commanders. They are creditable to the writers, and give a fair, unpretentious account of the action, varying in no essential particular. I have not described the action with minute detail, because the official reports are on record, and Captain Semmes has published a full account of all the incidents appertaining to the engagement, and the events which preceded and followed it. I feel confident that I have given an impartial summary, and I think it may fairly be stated that the *Kearsarge* was in better condition and was more efficiently armed than the *Alabama;* but that she used her superior strength with commensurate skill and effectiveness, and gained the action by the excellence of her gunnery.

In mentioning the points it was proper for Semmes to consider before determining whether he would be justified in engaging the *Kearsarge,* I have said that he took into account the possible occurrence of one of those fortuitous chances which often produce very unexpected results. It appears from the details annexed to Captain Winslow's report that a shell from the *Alabama's* 7-inch rifled gun lodged in the stern-post of the *Kearsarge,* but did not explode. A ship's stern-post receives the "wood-ends" of the planks which form the counter, and a vessel could scarcely receive a shell in a more vital point, if the shell exploded. I have been informed by an officer, who told me that he got the fact from the first-lieutenant of the *Kearsarge,* that this shell struck the stern-post about fifteen minutes after the beginning of the engagement. If, therefore, it had not failed to explode, the stern of the *Kearsarge* would have been shattered, the wood-ends opened, and she would have foundered instead of the *Alabama.* But without reference to time, if the shell had done its work, the result would have been to entirely change the issue of the action.

In all the remarks I have heretofore made with reference to the relative strength and condition of the two ships, I have compared them exclusively as two wooden screw-steamers, but it appears from Captain Winslow's report that, his ship being rather light, he had protected her midship section by stowing the sheet chain-cables outside. The chains were, it appears, arranged perpendicularly from the water's edge, so as to cover the engine space, and they were concealed by a thin plank covering. In fact, the *Kearsarge* over her most vital parts was armour-plated, and this is an important consideration in discussing the principles of naval warfare suggested by this spirited engagement between two single ships propelled by steam.

Captain Semmes, in his report, says that the officers whom he sent to the *Kearsarge* with the wounded, informed him that the covering boards had been ripped off in many directions, and in some places the chains had been broken and forced partly into the ship's side by the *Alabama's* shot and shells. It is manifest that if those projectiles had found their way into that protected section of the *Kearsarge*, the engagement might have had a different result.

Captain Semmes also states, in the history of his cruise, that the *Alabama*'s powder was defective, which he attributed to the long time it had been on board, and the exposure to so many varying climates. It seems to me that there is some reason to accept the opinion that the powder was defective, because the details accompanying Captain Winslow's report mention that the *Kearsarge* was struck twenty-eight times in various places about the hull, but no damage is stated except the shattering of two boats. When the firing became active, the ships were about a thousand yards apart, and the distance was gradually reduced to four hundred yards. At this latter distance I think that the 100-pound elongated shot and shells from the *Alabama*'s Blakely rifled gun would have carried the chain through the side of the *Kearsarge* if they had struck with the velocity due to the power of the weapon. The powder on board the *Alabama* was manufactured and put up into cartridges especially for her by Messrs. Curtiss and Harvey. I do not mind mentioning their names, because they took the order as an ordinary business transaction, and without the slightest knowledge of the purpose for which the ammunition was wanted. The quality at the beginning of the cruise was perfect. Captain Semmes has told me that in the night engagement with the *Hatteras* her sides were all ablaze with the vivid light of the *Alabama*'s exploding shells, and the sharp, quick, vigorous reports gave proof of the purity and strength of the charges.

In reference to the action with the *Kearsarge*, Captain Semmes says: "Perceiving that our shells, though apparently exploding against the enemy's sides, were doing him but little damage, I returned to solid-shot firing"; and several naval experts who witnessed the engagement from the hills near Cherbourg have told me that they were struck with the difference in the appearance of the flame and smoke produced by the explosions of the shells from the two ships. Those from the *Kearsarge* emitted a quick bright flash, and the smoke went quickly away in a fine blue vapour, while those from the *Alabama* exhaled a dull flame and a mass of sluggish grey smoke. It is not unlikely that the effect of climate and the long stowage on board had helped to deteriorate the *Alabama*'s powder, but I think the deterioration was hastened and increased by a local cause, and by a practice the ill effects of which were not suspected at the time.

The internal arrangements of the *Alabama* were designed to secure the largest possible space for essential stores; and as she had means of condensing, it was not thought necessary to provide tanks for more than two to three weeks' supply of water. The magazine was placed so that the top would be two feet and a half below the water-line, and the water-tanks, which were of iron, were fitted on each side and in front of it, and were carried up to the berth deck-beams, thus forming an additional protection. After the loss of the *Alabama*, I learned from the chief engineer that it was often the habit to condense in excess of the quantity which the cooling-tank held; and that the boiling water, almost in the condition of steam, was often passed directly into the two iron tanks on each side of the magazine, and in contact with it. I think this practice contributed largely to the deterioration of the powder, and I have thought it worth mentioning as an element in the case.

Taking a comprehensive and impartial view of all the circumstances, I think it will be admitted that the probabilities of success were in favour of the *Kearsarge*. Captain Winslow was quite right in doing whatever he could to increase the defensive power of his ship, and he was not bound to inform his adversary that he had encased her most vulnerable parts with chain-cables. It has never been considered an unworthy ruse for a commander, whether afloat or ashore, to disguise his strength and to entice a weaker opponent within his reach. The *Kearsarge* was well fought. Captain Winslow reported the result in a clear, plain statement, neither concealing nor exaggerating any circumstance that would tend to enhance his own merit, or to depreciate his adversary, if it were differently told. Anyone who reads his report and the accompanying documents, and who is aware of the effect of her fire upon the *Alabama*, will admit that the *Kearsarge* was in a state of discipline and efficiency creditable to all on board, and to the United States naval service.

On the other hand, it seems to me that the *Alabama* could not have won, except by the occurrence of a fortuitous chance, such as the explosion of the shell which lodged in her enemy's stern-post. Captain Semmes says that every man and officer behaved well, and at the trying moment there was neither panic nor confusion. Captain Winslow says in his report that "the firing of the *Alabama* was at the first rapid and wild; towards the close it became better," which proves that her crew were steady and cool, and that they only lacked practice to make them effective gunners.

The fact that the *Kearsarge* was in some degree "a protected ship," and that the *Alabama* was somewhat inferior in force and general condition, besides having defective powder, are circumstances which sufficiently account for the result of the engagement. Nevertheless, the principle, admitted in theory, that good guns, well handled, are essential to success in naval warfare, found a confirmation in the damage inflicted by the

Kearsarge upon her adversary, and the precision of her fire might have given her the victory even over a much larger ship, less efficient than herself in the above respects.

I hope there is nothing in the foregoing remarks which will appear like a purpose to lessen the credit due to Captain Winslow for the excellent performance of his ship, or to press into undue prominence the defects and inferiority of the *Alabama*.

I have not felt at all impelled to dwell upon Semmes's especial merits, or to take the occasion of this particular incident of his naval career to eulogise him. His defeat did not change the estimate I had formed of his capacity. If he had gained the victory it would not have added to my appreciation of his abilities. As a mere sea-officer under the ordinary requirements of the naval profession, he was not especially distinguished. He had neither the *physique* nor the dashing manner which combine to make a showy brilliant deck officer, and in the gift of handling a ship in fancy evolutions he had no special excellence. But in broad comprehensive knowledge of all the subjects embraced in a thorough naval education, in tact, judgment, acquaintance with diplomatic usage, and the requirements of international law and comity—in the capacity to generalize and to form plans, and in the latent nerve and mental vigour necessary to impress his views upon those under him, and thus to carry them out effectively, he had few if any equals in that service in which he passed the greater portion of his life, and which he left in obedience to a principle which was paramount with him, as it was in the minds of many others of unblemished character and unsullied honour, and who yet were classed together with him under the generic appellations of "pirate," "rebel" and "traitor," in the political phraseology which grew up and was disseminated from the State Department at Washington.

Semmes managed the cruises of the *Sumter* and *Alabama* with admirable skill and judgment. He not only inflicted great injury upon the enemy, but he did much to enlighten the authorities at the neutral ports necessity forced him to visit upon the true nature of the war, and to remove the impression that Confederate cruisers were buccaneers, seeking only plunder, and willing to grasp it regardless of the rights of neutrals or the restraints of international courtesy. He was often compelled to correspond with officials of high position in civil service, as well as in military and naval rank. He had often to act, not only as the commander of a national ship, but as the diplomatic and consular agent of his country as well. In all of these trying positions he acquitted himself admirably. The local authorities perceived that he understood his belligerent rights, but also knew how to advance his claims with firmness and precision, without departing a hair's-breadth from the line of official courtesy and respect. He soon won the confidence of those with whom he came in contact, and his ships were generally received and treated in neutral ports with a kindly consideration which was gratifying to himself and beneficial to the cause he represented. In fact, he was capable of much more than sailing or fighting a single ship. He had the faculties and the acquirements which fit a man for high command, and if circumstances had ever placed him at the head of a fleet, I feel sure that he would have achieved important and notable results.

When the *Alabama* settled down to her final resting place at the bottom of the English Channel, and the *Kearsarge* steamed away with flying colours to announce her victory, it would seem that the pride of the victors might have been satisfied, and their anger appeased, after a little pardonable jubilation. But as the origin of the famous Confederate cruiser gave rise to much controversy, so likewise did the circumstances of her death furnish a topic for discussion, carried on with harsh and bitter petulance by Mr. Seward, and answered with singular forbearance, but with a touch of sarcasm and reproof, by Earl Russell. Captain Semmes and his officers, having landed from the *Deerhound* at Southampton, were free to go where they liked; but Mr. Adams, the United States Minister, soon sent in a complaint to her Majesty's Government and claimed them as prisoners-of-war.

Lord Russell was evidently more surprised than vexed by this preposterous demand. In the official reply he says:—

"It appears to me that the owner of the *Deerhound,* of the Royal Yacht Squadron, performed only a common duty of humanity in saving from the waves the captain and several of the crew of the *Alabama.* They would otherwise, in all probability, have been drowned, and thus would never have been in the situation of prisoners-of-war. It does not appear to me to be any part of the duty of a neutral to assist in making prisoners-of-war for one of the belligerents."

The answer to the above was written by Mr. Seward himself, in a despatch addressed to Mr. Adams—probably he thought Mr. Adams would be too mild. I shall only quote one paragraph, which sufficiently exhibits its general tone.*

"The Earl argues that if those persons had not been so taken from the sea, they would in all probability have been drowned, and they would

* See "United States Appendix," vol. iii., pp. 263, 273, and "British Case," p. 116.

never have been in the situation of prisoners-of-war.... I have to observe upon these remarks of Earl Russell that it was the right of the *Kearsarge* that the pirates should drown, unless saved by humane exertions of the officers and crew of that vessel, or by their own efforts, without the aid of the *Deerhound*."

From Mr. Seward's point of view they were pirates—*hostes humani generis*. If, therefore, they had been saved by the "humane exertions of the *Kearsarge*," it would have been to meet the fate of hanging instead of drowning—an alternative that would not have tempted them to make much effort to get out of the water.

The answer of the British Government to Mr. Seward's demand was "that there is no obligation by international law which can bind the Government of a neutral State to deliver up to a belligerent prisoners-of-war who may have escaped from such belligerent, and may have taken refuge within the territory of such neutral." He adds that they had been guilty of no offence against the laws of England, and had committed no act which would bring them within the provisions of a treaty between Great Britain and the United States for the mutual surrender of offenders, and states the following conclusion:—"Her Majesty's Government are, therefore, entirely without any legal means by which, even if they wished to do so, they could comply with your above-mentioned demand."

The grounds of Lord Russell's refusal were unquestionable, and his reasoning was unanswerable. Mr. Seward must or should have known that the reply to his demand could not have been different from what it proved to be, and his motive in seeking the humiliation of a refusal is inexplicable. But Mr. Seward had fully impressed his views and his spirit upon many of his subordinates who represented the United States abroad at that time, and especially upon Mr. Thomas H. Dudley, the Consul at Liverpool, who manifested a bitterness of temper, and practised a sharpness and asperity in language and correspondence, and a recklessness in his statements, which would have been appalling, but for the conviction that public sentiment in Europe would revolt against such pretentious extravagance.

After the departure of the *Alabama* from Liverpool, many communications were addressed by Mr. Adams to the British Government dwelling upon her so-called escape, and the despatch of her armament from England. In one communication he enclosed a letter from Mr. Thomas H. Dudley, dated January 11, 1864, in which that gentleman with the bitter temper and indiscreet pen enumerated the circumstances affecting the *Alabama*, which, he affirmed, proved her to be a "British ship," and her acts "piratical." The above letter was referred to the law officers of the Crown, who were asked to advise whether any proceedings could be taken with reference to the supposed breaches of neutrality alleged by Mr. Adams and Mr. Dudley. The law officers reported that "no proceedings can at present be taken," but they could not let Mr. Dudley's uncivil assertions pass without comment, and they closed their report with the following remarks:—"So far as relates to Mr. Dudley's argument (not now for the first time advanced) that the *Alabama* is an English piratical craft, it might have been enough to say that Mr. Dudley, while he enumerates everything which is immaterial, omits everything that is material, to constitute that character." The law officers then demonstrate that the *Alabama* is a public ship-of-war of the Confederate States,* "and has been ever since she hoisted the Confederate flag and received her armament at Terceira," and they close their report, or rather their "opinion," in these words:—"It is to be regretted that, in any of the discussions on this subject, so manifest an abuse of language as the application of the term 'English piratical craft' to the *Alabama* should still be permitted to continue."

The law officers who gave the above "opinion" were Sir Roundell Palmer, now Lord Selborne, who was generally supposed to be partial to the Federal cause, and Sir Robert Collier, who had been consulted by the solicitors of the United States Consul in reference to the seizure of the *Alabama* before he received the appointment of Solicitor-General.

Northern men often complained of the sympathy exhibited in some parts of Europe, and especially in England, for the Confederate cause. I have reason to believe that at least five out of every seven in the middle and upper classes in England were favourable to the South, and I confidently believe that the majority were moved to favour that side by the haughty and offensive tone assumed by many of the representatives of the United States.

At the time of the rescue of the *Alabama*'s drowning men by the *Deerhound,* many harsh things were said of her owner, Mr. John Lancaster, in the diplomatic correspondence of the United States, and high officials of that Government recklessly affirmed that the *Deerhound* was in collusion with the *Alabama,* and that Mr. Lancaster had taken his yacht out to watch the engagement under a covert understanding with Captain Semmes.

It is not probable that any American historian will give further currency to those statements. Mr. Lancaster proved to the satisfaction of her Majesty's Government, and to all who read his published letter, that there

---

* For opinion of the law officers quoted above see "British Case," p. 117.

was not the slightest foundation in fact for the assertions of the United States officials in respect to his conduct, and he publicly offered to submit the whole of his proceedings to the yachtsmen of England for their opinion. I would have made no mention of the foregoing incident at all, except for the fact that it remains on record in the printed papers in reference to the Confederate naval operations, and it appeared necessary, therefore, to mention the satisfactory and conclusive proof that the accusations were not true.

CHAPTER VI

A history of the efforts made by the Confederate Government to organize a naval force abroad would be very incomplete if the narrative was limited to a mere statement of the number and names of the vessels which were bought or built in Europe and a description of the arrangements which were made to effect their departure from the neutral ports and to equip them as fighting ships. It is well known that the few Confederate cruisers which may be said to have been of "foreign origin" created much greater disturbance, and excited far more public interest, than their operations would have aroused if they had simply come out of the ports of one belligerent, in the ordinary way, and had inflicted a given amount of damage upon the other. They were the source of very serious complaints and much diplomatic correspondence between Great Britain and the United States, and pages of "Hansard" are filled with the reports of debates in reference to them in both Houses of the British Parliament. They were the means of first drawing serious attention to the Foreign Enlistment Act, and caused the law officers of her Majesty's Government much trouble in expounding the meaning of that somewhat ambiguous statute. They gave occasion for a suit which resulted in a judicial exposition of the Act, and a judgment which has never been reversed, but which was so unsatisfactory to the United States, who were the real plaintiffs, and also to her Majesty's Government, who seemed desirous to satisfy them, that a Royal Commission, composed of learned judges and jurists and distinguished statesmen to the number of thirteen, was appointed to inquire into the character, working, and effect of the laws of Great Britain available for the enforcement of neutrality; and finally, as everyone knows, they gave rise to so much controversy between her Britannic Majesty's Government and that of the United States, in reference to international rights and duties, that an agreement could only be effected by means of a special treaty and a great international arbitration. The diplomatic correspondence has been long since published, and is accessible to all who are interested in the subject.

The United States affirmed that the Confederate Government had established a bureau of their Navy Department in England. They charged the Confederate agents with wilfully and persistently violating the municipal laws of Great Britain, and denounced their acts as being "criminal" and "nefarious." They complained that her Majesty's Government was both lax and slow in putting the law in operation, and that the subordinate officers of the Crown were wilfully passive in executing the orders of their superiors. The answers of the British Government to the complaints of the United States are fully set out in the correspondence and in the proceedings before the Tribunal of Arbitration at Geneva. The merest synopsis of them would require more space than would be admissible in this narrative.

The *gravamen* of the charges was that the British Government did not put the municipal law in operation with sufficient promptness and energy to prevent the acts complained of, and did not enforce the punitive clauses with the rigour which the nature of the alleged offences and friendly consideration for the United States justified the latter Government in expecting. The substance of the answer was that the Government of Great Britain was one of limited and legally defined powers, and that its authority could, therefore, be exercised only in subordination to law; that when there was interference by the Government with the rights of persons or property, redress might be immediately sought and recovered, provided the Government could not maintain its action, in a court of law. The Government could not, therefore, seize vessels alleged to belong to the Confederate States, or arrest persons accused of violating the law, unless there was sufficient *primâ facie* evidence to render a conviction probable; and neither the evidence obtained by the Government through their own officers, or tendered by the United States Minister and Consuls, was considered sufficient by the law officers of the Crown to justify either seizure or prosecution.

One ship was seized, and the United States officials exerted themselves to the utmost to provide evidence, but the prosecution failed, and her Majesty's Government had to pay damages. It was furthermore contended that acts prohibited by municipal law or by the orders and proclamations of the Executive Government were not necessarily prohibited by the law of nations, and there was no obligation to use executive power harshly, or in a manner at variance with the spirit of the national institutions, with no other purpose than to protect one belligerent against the other. In one of Earl Russell's despatches to Lord Lyons, the British Minister at Washington, he says that a phrase used by Mr. Seward in describing the conduct of Great Britain "was rather a figure of rhetoric than a true description of facts"; "that the Cabinet were of opinion that the law was sufficient, but that legal evidence could not always be procured."* ... "That the British Government had done everything in its power to execute the law"; and that, in his belief, "if all the assistance given to the Federals by British subjects and British munitions of war were weighed against similar aid given to the Confederates, the balance would be greatly in favour of the Federals."† Lord Russell added, however, that Mr. Adams, the American Minister, totally denied the foregoing proposition. In this denial of Mr. Adams, we have the clue to the feeling which aroused the temper of the United States, and which caused Mr. Seward to put forward so many unreasonable complaints, and to use such strong and often abusive language in referring to the acts of the Confederate Government and their agents.

One of the most important lessons to be learned in ordinary life in the management of every-day affairs, is that which teaches men to acknowledge and to submit with dignity and patience to the consequences of an

---

* Earl Russell to Lord Lyons, March 27, 1863.
† Parliamentary Document, "North America," (no. 1), 1864, p. 2.

"accomplished fact," even though the result may have disappointed their hopes and baulked their expectations. The statesman whose temper will not suffer him to admit that which is incontrovertible, whose faculties cannot discern the difference between his own will and the inevitable fulfilment of events, who persistently and with ever increasing warmth urges his own opinions and policy against the adverse convictions of those who have already scrutinized the question and pronounced their judgment, can hardly expect to control or direct public sentiment successfully, or to make the cause in which he is engaged acceptable to those not immediately connected with him by some common interest. The Cabinet of Mr. Abraham Lincoln during the period of the Civil War contained a number of able, energetic men, but they never could bring their minds to acknowledge that they were engaged in war with a *de facto* Government, and they never could treat with complaisance the representatives of those foreign Powers who ventured to act upon the principle that the contest between the States was a revolution and not an insurrection.

But the logic of facts proved too strong for them. One of the first acts of the Government at Washington for the suppression of the so-called rebellion was to proclaim a blockade of all the Southern ports. In the Proclamation, dated April 19, 1861, President Lincoln stated that the blockade would be "set on foot" "in pursuance of the laws of the United States, and of the law of nations in such cases provided." The foreign Ministers resident at Washington immediately requested information as to the manner in which the blockade was to be enforced. To the British Envoy Mr. Seward gave the assurance that it would be conducted strictly according to the rules of public law, and with as much liberality towards neutrals as any belligerent could practise. In reply to the Minister of Spain he wrote thus: "The blockade will be strictly enforced upon the principles recognised by the law of nations."*

The proclamation of blockade was limited at first to seven specified States, but by the end of May it was extended to all the principal ports of the Gulf and Atlantic States, including Virginia. The Federal cruisers soon began to make prizes of neutral ships for alleged breach of blockade, and they were condemned with very short shrift by the United States prize-courts. Appeals were taken to the Supreme Court, and Mr. Justice Grier, giving the judgment of the court in a test case, said:

"To legitimatize the capture of a neutral vessel or property on the high seas, a war must exist *de facto,* and the neutral must have a knowledge or

* See "British Case," part ii., p. 5.

notice of the intention of one of the parties belligerent to use this mode of coercion against a port, city, or territory in possession of the other.... The proclamation of the blockade is itself official and conclusive evidence to the court that a state of war existed which demanded and authorized a recourse to such a measure under the circumstances peculiar to the case. The correspondence of Lord Lyons with the Secretary of State admits the fact and concludes the question."

The Great Maritime Powers acted upon the foregoing statements of Mr. Seward and the judgment of the Supreme Court of the United States. They admitted the legality of the blockade, and as a necessary and legitimate consequence they acknowledged the Confederate States as belligerents, and threw open their ports to both parties on the same conditions and under precisely similar restrictions.

Here, then, was an accomplished fact—a *de facto* war. Europe refused to look upon the efforts of eleven great commonwealths, whose entire population, to the number of at least six millions of people, had united in asserting their right to retire from a voluntary union, as a mere insurrectionary opposition to an obnoxious Government. The common-sense, as well as the philanthropy of all nations, rejected the proposition to treat President Davis, Lee, and Stonewall Jackson as common brawlers or rebels, and the people of England especially could not be persuaded to denounce Josiah Tattnall, who towed the British boats into the Peiho, as a pirate, nor could they cast that stigma upon the naval service to which he belonged.

The acknowledgment of the Confederate Government as a belligerent met with such unanimous concurrence among foreign States, that it would have been only an act of common courtesy, and of judicious policy, to accept the judgment. But Mr. Seward could not bring himself to a dignified acquiescence in the common verdict. He indulged in repeated and petulant complaints, and urged with vehement earnestness that all the world should be subservient to his will, and should re-fashion the code of public law to suit his policy. It was a case of one sagacious juror against eleven stubborn men who took a different view of the criminal. What Mr. Seward wanted was that Europe should permit the United States to remain in the enjoyment of every privilege guaranteed by treaties of peace, free and unrestricted access to the ports, the right to buy arms and transport them unmolested across the sea, to engage men and forward them to the battlefields in Virginia without question, and, at the same time, that the whole world should tolerate a total suppression of trade with eleven great provinces, and suffer the United States to seize ships on the high seas and hale them before prize-courts, unless they were protected by the certificate of an American Consul.* He wished to practise all the rights which a state of war confers upon a belligerent, but begged to be excused from performing the duties which attach in equal degree to that condition.

The answer of the Great Maritime Powers was plain and to the point. Substantially it was this: "You may be whatever you like—in a state of peace or in a state of war. If the political agitation which disturbs your country is a mere insurrection which you will suppress in 'ninety days,' the result will be quite agreeable to us; but meanwhile we must claim the right to go into the Southern ports, and get the staples our people want, and give in exchange the products of our industry, which their people want. If, on the other hand, you cannot maintain us in our privileges of trade with the South—if you cannot exercise jurisdiction there, and can only enter the country with great armies, which we perceive are often defeated; if to restore your authority it is necessary to resort to measures which are only admissible when exercised as a belligerent right, then by your own showing there is a state of war, to which there are of necessity two parties, each of whom must, by the common law of nations, have equal rights and duties, and we must protect our status as neutrals by seeing that neither party takes more than he is entitled to receive, or exacts more than he is justified in demanding."

It will thus be seen that the outside world did not originate the event or create the fact. Eighteen or more great States, acknowledging a central Government at Washington, were engaged in war with eleven other great States adhering to a common authority at Richmond. This was the actual condition of affairs. All the special pleading of the politicians at Washington, all the *finesse* of diplomatic reasoning, could not alter the facts. Foreign Powers perceived the actual state of affairs, and the Proclamations of Neutrality, and the regulations specifying the conditions upon which their ports might be used, were framed in accordance with the fact that there was a state of war between two separate Powers, and although one could glory in the full-fledged title of "a Government *de jure*," and the other was shackled with the more restrictive appellation of "a Government *de facto*," yet in regard to belligerent rights and duties they were placed on precisely the same footing by the common consent and common action of the whole civilized world.

In discussing the acts of the Confederate Government, and the efforts made by them to obtain military supplies and a few cruising ships in Eu-

* See Debate: Hansard, vol. clxx., 1863 (2), pp. 581, 582.

rope, it is only fair to call attention to the real position of the two belligerents in reference to the neutral Powers.

It has been often asserted in the diplomatic correspondence of the United States that the agents of the Confederate Government abused the hospitality and infringed the municipal laws of the neutral States, especially of Great Britain. "Criminal evasion," "nefarious transactions," and other cognate expressions, were among the milder forms in which their conduct was denounced by the United States Secretary of State and his consular representatives. Those charges and those epithets have been preserved in the pages of "Blue Books," and remain on record among the proceedings of the Tribunal of Arbitration at Geneva; and there are many people in England even now who think that there must have been some clever evasion of the law, some illicit "tip" from a sub-official, which made the so-called "escape" of the *Alabama* and her consorts possible.

If the charges and the epithets had merely been cast at an individual agent they would be of little importance, and it would hardly be worth while to intrude an explanation or a defence into a narrative of this kind, because an agent must be prepared to bear the consequences of the policy he undertakes to carry out, and if his principals have exacted from him the performance of any acts which may, when stripped of rhetorical flourish, be justly branded as "criminal" or "nefarious," he must be content, if he has consented to retain his office, to assume the responsibility and to endure the ignominy. But I have shown in a previous chapter that it was the principle as well as the policy of the Confederate Government to practise a scrupulous and rigid deference to the rights of neutrals and the municipal laws of those countries from which they hoped to draw supplies. My own instructions were clear and explicit on this point, and I am in the position to know that all orders issued by the Confederate Government to agents and commanders of cruising ships were of the same tenor. If, therefore, the law of England was violated, or evaded in a criminal degree, the fault must be laid to the inadvertence or the negligence or the wilfulness of the agent, and not to the policy of those in whose behalf he was acting.

Seldom is a man competent to take up a complicated Act of the British Parliament, or of any other Legislative Assembly, and define its scope and the limit of its sense and bearing upon his own conduct, especially when the Act contains many clauses combining prohibitory, preventive, and punitive enactments. What he is bound to do, however, is to take due precautions, by consulting experts whose office it is to examine and give opinions on points of law, who are familiar with legal phraseology, and are acquainted with the precedents and the previous judgments of the Courts in cases which may have arisen under the statute, so that he may escape danger of prosecution, and be free from the offence of misusing the hospitality of the country which has offered him shelter and protection. Those precautions were taken before a ship was bought or built in England for the Confederate Government, and the opinion of the learned barristers whose advice was asked has been already given in a previous chapter.* The only doubt that could be felt in regard to the advice was that it was founded solely upon the opinion of the eminent lawyers who gave it, and could not be confirmed by any precedent or previous judgment, because up to the year 1863 no ship had been seized and brought to the test of a trial under the Act.

The Governments at Washington and at Richmond stood at that time on a precise equality before the general laws of nations, and the municipal law of each neutral state. I mean, of course, with reference to their respective rights and duties as belligerents. Whatever was obligatory upon the one was equally binding upon the other. Whatever the agent of one could do without offence, the other could do also. The Foreign Enlistment Act defined the limits to which each could go. It laid down the precepts which each were alike bound to obey, and defined the consequences of disobedience to both without partiality or discrimination. If an agent of the United States could perform any service for his Government in England without infringing the law or laying himself open to the charge of "criminal evasion," an agent of the Confederate States might do the same or an equivalent act with corresponding innocence and propriety.

A member of Parliament—the late Mr. John Laird—stated in the House of Commons that the Navy Department of the United States opened negotiations with the firm from which he retired at the beginning of the Civil War for building a special class of ships. The correspondence, or at least sufficient to establish the fact, was read publicly before the whole House, and the member referred to stated that while he felt bound to suppress the names of the persons through whom the negotiations had been proposed, he would, if it was thought advisable, hand the whole correspondence, "with the original letters," confidentially to the Speaker of the House, or to the Prime Minister, in order that the public should have the assurance that he was not overstating the facts. One of the extracts read to the House was as follows:—"I have this morning a note from the

* See chap. ii., pp. 46–47.

Assistant Secretary of the Navy, in which he says, 'I hope your friends will tender for the two iron-plated steamers.'"

It is proper for me to mention that in a subsequent debate, about four months afterwards, Mr. Richard Cobden stated that he had received a letter from his friend, Mr. Charles Sumner, of the United States Senate, informing him that the Secretary of the United States Navy denied that any order had "been sent from the American Navy Department to any shipbuilder in this country" (England). Mr. Laird did not assert that an order had been sent, but that proposals had been made and negotiations opened on the subject, and that the firm to which he belonged at the time were asked if they would undertake to build as desired, "how soon, and for how much." In reply to Mr. Cobden, he said that "he was quite prepared, if necessary, to prove every word he had said in a former debate was perfectly true; and as the question was one which affected her Majesty's Government, he was ready to put his proofs (namely, the original letters) in the hands of the noble lord at the head of the Government."

The debates referred to may be found in Hansard, vol. clxx., session 1863 (2), and vol. clxxii., session 1863 (4). In the course of the latter debate the Prime Minister (Lord Palmerston) said:—"I cannot, in the abstract, concur with my honourable friend" (Mr. Cobden) "in thinking that there is any distinction in principle between muskets, gunpowder, bullets, and cannon on the one side, and ships on the other." ... "Therefore I hold, that on the mere ground of international law belligerents have no right to complain if merchants—I do not say the Government, for that would be interference—as a mercantile transaction supply one of the belligerents not only with arms and cannon, but also with ships destined for warlike purposes."

The negotiations referred to by Mr. Laird were abandoned for reasons not necessary to mention in detail. The firm could not undertake the work on the conditions as to time of completion, etc., and I do not know whether the United States made overtures to other shipbuilders or not. The naval resources of the United States were so immeasurably superior to those of the Confederate States, both in the supply of materials and the mechanical means for utilizing them, that the Navy Department at Washington did not probably feel any anxiety on the score of ships. The chief supplies which the United States drew from Europe were arms, accoutrements, ammunition, and men. I say men, because it is well known that large numbers of emigrants were induced to go to the United States during the war under implied promises or allegations that they would find remunerative work, and the work supplied them after arrival was that of bearing arms in the United States Army and helping to subjugate the South.

It would be easy for me to name persons of unquestioned respectability in England, especially in Liverpool, who were well aware that bands of so-called emigrants were constantly passing through Liverpool and other English coast towns, *en route* for the United States, often in charge of men who were known to be agents of that Government. The diplomatic correspondence demonstrates incontestably that a system of "evasive enlistment" for the United States army was practised in Europe during the Civil War, and Confederate officers would have no difficulty in proving, if there was any need, that whole battalions of Federal soldiers were captured during the campaigns in Virginia, composed of men who had not been six months in the country, and who could not speak a word of English.

There were two cases in which public inquiry was made as to the character of the passengers by American ships about to leave Liverpool for New York. In one of the cases the *prima facie* evidence of a clandestine enlistment was so strong, that the men were forced to land. I could name the solicitors who were the chief actors in the above mentioned cases. They are one of the leading firms in Liverpool. I am not repeating merely the current belief or suspicion that prevailed at the time, nor am I affirming the existence of a practice the proof of which rests upon such vague evidence as is often tendered in the phrase "it is quite notorious." Perhaps the subject is of sufficient importance to justify, if not to require me to give a particular example.

One day in the very height of the war, a gentleman called at my office and told me that he had reason to feel satisfied that a large number of men would arrive in Liverpool that afternoon, who were really recruits for the United States army; that they were in charge of a person who he thought was a commissioned officer in the United States Service; that they were to embark on board the American ship *Great Western,* then lying in the river, and he thought I ought to take some steps to bring the matter before the proper authorities. I replied that my duties could only be satisfactorily and successfully performed by a prudent reserve, and by maintaining a retiring and unobtrusive attitude. If I ventured into the arena of legal strife with the American Consul, or with persons supposed to be engaged in unlawful proceedings, I should necessarily be forced out of my retirement, which I thought would be more injurious to the interests of the Confederacy than the addition of a few hundred men to the armies of the United States.

My informant, although an Englishman, was a warm partizan of the South. He admitted the soundness of my reasons for not interfering, but was not satisfied to leave the affair to take its course without some opposition. He went to a few others who were known to be "Southern sympathizers," and they placed the evidence in the hands of a local solicitor, who communicated it to the Customs authorities. The alleged facts were forwarded to London, and a junior solicitor of the Customs was sent to investigate the case. I believe the ship was detained one or two days, or at least her clearance was held back. The solicitor of the Customs who made the investigation reported that the evidence of a violation of the Foreign Enlistment Act was not sufficient to justify the arrest of any of the parties, and the ship and her passengers were allowed to proceed. The gentleman who gave me the information went on board with the solicitor he had consulted, and he told me that the men, many of whom were Irishmen, seemed to know that he and those with him were trying to stop them; but feeling safe from interference, they chaffed and indulged in a good deal of rough humour, and he furthermore told me that he saw a person on board who was a cabin passenger, and appeared to have charge of the men, and that he wore a military dress, which some of the men told him was the uniform of a lieutenant in the United States army.

Now, the foregoing incident would prove nothing if there were no sequel to it, but in the winter of 1871 I went to New York on a visit. I was stopping at the house of a gentleman—a New Yorker, of high social position. He had neither a military education nor what may be called the military instincts, and being a man of great practical sense, with a sound perception of the fitness of things, he did not seek a commission in the army, and he was far too valuable a man to be wasted in the office of carrying a rifle in the ranks. But his temperament was too ardent, and his convictions too strong, to admit of his remaining inactive in the struggle, which he perceived was likely to be long and arduous. There could not have been a man more loyal to the United States, more willing to make greater personal sacrifices for the success of the Federal cause. I believe he did as much as any one to keep up the spirit of the men in the field, and to animate the hopes of the desponding who were not in the field; and his services were as important and as conducive to the final success of the Federal Government as those of any man at the North who was not in high command, or in some equally important civil executive office. I could say much of his personal qualities, which made him lovable by those who knew him well, but this is no place for a tribute of that kind.

The gentleman to whom I refer was firmly impressed with the feeling that the neutrality of England was more favourable to the South than to the North, but one of his characteristics was to take fair and reasonable views of other men's motives, and to express his own opinions with moderation and courtesy. One day we were discussing the action of Great Britain, the effect of the Proclamation of Neutrality, and the manner in which the municipal law was applied in restraining the operations of the Confederate agents. He took the ground that they were allowed too great latitude, and that the British Government showed an unfriendly feeling towards the United States in permitting the *Alabama* and other ships to leave England. I, of course, took an opposite position, and we argued the point in a temperate and friendly spirit. I contended that her Majesty's Government could not have stopped the *Alabama* without acting arbitrarily, and going beyond the limits of a fair, impartial neutrality, and to demonstrate that the preventive clauses of the Foreign Enlistment Act were not applied very strictly against the United States, I cited the incident of the ship *Great Western*, which I have mentioned above.

My friend smiled. He could be as reticent as anyone when there was necessity for reserve, but he was too honest to shrink from admitting a fact, or to hedge himself behind a prevarication in a friendly argument. He left me, and went into another room. In a few moments he returned, bringing a small package of papers, filed and backed in voucher form, and then told me that he had been, during a portion of the war, a member of a committee whose office it was to look after men who had been brought over from Europe without any definite purpose on their own part, and who might therefore be available as recruits for the army; that he had nothing whatever to do with engaging the men abroad, and never inquired what inducements were held out to them to come over, but when they were safe across and were of willing minds, the committee paid the expenses, etc. "These papers," he said, "are the documents and vouchers relating to that voyage of the *Great Western* you have just mentioned. And the information upon which your Liverpool friend acted was probably correct."

We were both amused by this accidental discovery of our common connection with a transaction eight years after the event, and I was well satisfied to have such a complete demonstration of the facility with which the United States could and did recruit their armies, without infringing the British Foreign Enlistment Act, because it confirmed me in the opinion I had previously maintained, that the Act was not intended to protect one belligerent from another, but to prevent prejudice to Great Britain herself by acts done within the kingdom which would endanger its peace and welfare. Her Majesty's Government brought the subject of the alleged enlistments to the notice of the American Minister, and appeared to be satisfied with the declaration that there had been none. The Confederate Government had no recognised diplomatic agent to whom inquiries could be addressed, and who could make explanation, and after the departure of two or three ships the complaints and remonstrances of the United States Minister induced her Majesty's Foreign Secretary on more than one occasion to seize and detain vessels in which the Confederate Government had no interest whatever, or, as the Attorney-General expressed it, to "strain the law."

I assert nothing more than the fact that the United States, by means of authorized agents, did induce many men to go from Europe to America during the war, the intent being to enlist them into the army after their arrival. I do not affirm that there was an actual enlistment in any part of Europe, and the disclaimer of the United States Minister was no doubt justified. The process was carried out thus: Able-bodied men were persuaded or stimulated by judicious representations to emigrate to the United States, and they were kindly looked after and cared for on the journey to the ports and on the voyage across the Atlantic by friendly intermediaries. There was nothing illegal in this. Rifles, accoutrements, and ammunition were bought at Birmingham and elsewhere, and were shipped through the great houses of Baring, and Brown, Shipley and Co., to the United States, in the ordinary way of business. There was nothing illegal in that. When the men and the arms arrived in New York, or Boston, or Philadelphia, they were brought together by a happy accident; the emigrants were persuaded that it was a very fine thing to be soldiers, they were dressed in the traditional "blue," the equipment was completed, and they were marched off to Virginia, to be shot down at Seven Pines and Chancellorsville, or to perish by fever in the swamps of the Chickahominy.

The Confederate Government did not require men so much as arms. They were never able to equip the fighting population of the country. They wanted, however, besides arms, ships suitable to cruise and to destroy the enemy's mercantile marine; and the manner of accomplishing their purpose may be briefly described as follows:

A ship suited in structure and general arrangements to carry the weight of a battery on deck, to berth a sufficient crew, and to keep the sea for a long time, was bought or built in England. She was then despatched to an outport without a weapon or an ounce of powder on board, and with a crew just sufficient to navigate her in safety. According to the best advice available, there was nothing illegal in that transaction. Guns, cutlasses, revolvers, ammunition, and stores of all necessary kinds, were bought in London, Birmingham, Sheffield and elsewhere, and were shipped in due form, by a vessel loading in the ordinary way, for the West Indies, or other suitable market for such supplies. There can be no doubt that this part of the transaction was perfectly legal. The two vessels—one fit to bear arms, but having none; the other full of arms, but unable to use them—shaped their respective courses so as to gradually converge until, at some point far removed from British jurisdiction, they found themselves in a fortunate conjunction. The equipment of the ship fit to bear arms was then completed; passengers or seamen from the two vessels, and perhaps from a third, were persuaded that they might have a jolly cruise, and they donned the familiar and jaunty serge frock of the man-of-war's-man, and went to "battle the watch" and to take their chances under the Confederate flag.

I think the foregoing sketches clearly and fairly demonstrate the attitude of the two belligerents in the late Civil War in respect to the British Foreign Enlistment Act, and I should be much surprised to hear anyone not biased by prejudice, or pledged in advance to a particular assertion, say that there is a shade or a shadow of difference between them, whether viewed as a matter of principle or as a question of evading the law.

Now that seventeen years have passed since the end of the war, it is to be hoped that the passions which were then aroused have sufficiently subsided on both sides to make it possible for each to take a fair and equitable retrospect of what the other did. I have met many Northern men who were loyal to their Government, who sacrificed their business and risked their lives in its support, and who never did fall into the frenzied state of bitterness which many of the political party leaders manifested, and who never had any sympathy with the violent and abusive language used by Mr. Seward and some of his consular agents.

In the British counter-case presented to the Tribunal of Arbitration at Geneva (p. 57), I find the following paragraph, which serves as an illustration of the extreme pretensions set up by the United States, and the effect produced by the ill-advised complaints and demands of their representatives. "Pressed by the difficulty of distinguishing between their own operations in Europe and those of the Confederate States in such a manner as to make it appear that the British Government was bound to give free scope to the former and repress the latter, the United States appear to imagine that they found such a distinction in two circumstances. One of these is, that the needs of the Confederacy were, as they allege, more urgent than those of the Union: the former could only obtain their military supplies from abroad; the latter could manufacture some of theirs at home.* The other is, that the United States, having the command of the sea, could transport the goods purchased by them freely and openly, or (as it is expressed) 'in the ordinary course of commerce'; whilst the Confederates were obliged to 'originate a commerce for the purpose'—that is, to get their goods transported by way of Nassau and Bermuda, which are commonly places of no great trade—and further, to make use of those concealments by which the traffic in contraband of war, when not protected by a powerful navy, usually tries to elude the vigilance of the enemy's cruisers. Are we, then, to understand that, according to the views put forward in the case of the United States, the 'strict and impartial neutrality towards both belligerents,' which it is the duty of a neutral Government to maintain, obliges it to find out which of the two stands in the greater need of supplies, and consists in lending aid, by measures of repression, to the belligerent whose force is the greater and his wants the less pressing of the two, and thus assisting him to crush more speedily the resistance of his weaker enemy? Her Majesty's Government is unable to assent to this novel opinion, advantageous as it would doubtless prove to States which, like Great Britain, possess a powerful navy."

The last sentence in the foregoing quotation is pertinent to a comment I have previously made upon the pretensions set up and exacted by the United States during the war. They advanced and were permitted to enforce belligerent rights which were strongly resisted when applied to themselves in former years, and thus established precedents which will occasion much trouble and perplexity to some future Government at Washington, if the United States should be neutral in a war between two countries having powerful navies. It is well known that the great autocratic and monarchical Powers of Europe had shown a willingness for years before the American Civil War to relax the extreme application of the belligerent rights heretofore claimed by them, and relentlessly enforced whenever their interests required. England, once so persistent and arrogant in practising the "right of search," has, during many past years, taken a leading part in the effort to modify the harsh restraints upon neutral commerce, which she herself was formerly so ready to inflict, and to abolish or prohibit the destruction of private property on the high seas. The Great Powers who joined in the Declaration of Paris in the year 1856,

* "Case of the United States," pp. 310–12.

agreed to several very important rules which greatly relaxed the oppressive restraints on neutral commerce in times of war. The most beneficent provisions of that famous Declaration were those which practically affirmed the doctrine that "free ships made free goods," and which furthermore exempted neutral goods from condemnation as prize, if found in an enemy's ship. It is remarkable that the United States, professing the freest and most liberal institutions, and up to 1861 vehemently urging and insisting upon the fullest immunity for their flag, should have so suddenly made a retrograde movement in the liberal policy of their past history, while even the autocratic States of Europe were discarding their dictatorial traditions, and were advancing in the path of greater freedom to commerce, and less interference with the rights and privileges of neutrals.

In the year 1863 Messrs. Pile, Spence and Co., of the City of London, advertised a line of steamers to run regularly between England and Matamoras, in Mexico. The first vessel despatched on the line was the screw steamer *Gipsy Queen,* which performed her voyage and returned in safety. The second vessel was the *Peterhoff,* also a screw steamer. The *Peterhoff* left London with proper clearances from the Custom House, but for greater precaution took a certificate of clearance from the Mexican Consul. In the due progress of her voyage she arrived in the neighbourhood of the island of St. Thomas, where she was stopped by a United States ship-of-war and boarded. Her papers were examined and endorsed with a statement that they were in order, and she was then permitted to proceed on her voyage. In accordance with the original intention of her owners, she went into St. Thomas, replenished her coal, and sailed again for Matamoras. Just as she was leaving the harbour of St. Thomas the United States ship *Vanderbilt* was coming in, and Admiral Wilkes, the senior American naval officer present, ordered the commander of the *Vanderbilt* to pursue her. He did so; he captured her and brought her back to St. Thomas, whence she was afterwards taken to Key West to be adjudicated upon by a prize-court.

The above facts are condensed from a debate on the subject in the British House of Commons, March 27, 1863 (Hansard, vol. clxx., session 1863 (2), p. 71, etc.). In the same volume (p. 575, etc.), will be found another long and spirited debate on the "Conduct of Admiral Wilkes" and "American Cruisers and British Merchantmen." Those debates go further than anything I have written to demonstrate not only the harsh and rigorous manner in which the United States enforced their belligerent rights during the Civil War, but the surprise which was aroused in England by the sudden and complete abandonment and reversal of their previous principles in respect to the "right of search." The purpose of the United States was to hermetically seal up the Southern ports, to deprive the South of every possible means of obtaining supplies from abroad, whether by direct trade or through ports contiguous to it either by sea or by land; and to accomplish that purpose appeared to be of greater importance to the Government at Washington than to maintain a character for consistency in the interpretation of International Law.

At the present day the American shipping trade has fallen to a very low point, but all who are acquainted with the resources of the country, the activity and commercial intelligence of the people, and the mechanical skill they have exhibited in the past, will expect to see their trade revive and American ships again taking their due part in the marine traffic of the world whenever the country can persuade its rulers to remodel the navigation laws. But when the United States resume their due place among the Maritime Powers, they will require a powerful and ubiquitous navy to protect their commerce against the encroachments of some future belligerents, who may, and probably will be, inclined to follow the precedents of 1861–65.

The statements in the foregoing pages having reference to the operations of the United States in England, and the comparison of their conduct with that of the Confederate States in respect to alleged violations or evasions of the municipal law, and of neutral rights, are not made as a reproach to the former, nor are they set forth as grounds upon which to found an argument, or to build up a defence. Whatever was done by a Confederate agent in Europe, can be made to appear neither better nor worse, by proving that some one else has committed or avoided the same errors, and I heartily renounce all faith in, and all tolerance for, the weak and puerile plea of *"Et tu quoque."* But the facts which I have mentioned are parts of the current history of those troublous times when the American Union was suffering its great national convulsion, and the general historian of the future will require information on all such points, in order that he may have the data for a fair impartial judgment.

I have stated that before a keel was laid, or a ship was bought in England for the Confederate Government, advice was taken as to the legality of the proceedings, and that everything was done thereafter in strict conformity with the advice obtained. I can affirm, without the least mental reservation, that no deception whatever was practised upon the Customs authorities in respect to the registry or clearance of the *Alabama,* for as the law then stood, neither registry nor clearance was required, and with reference to the other ships built or bought by me, I can state with equal confidence that every requirement of the law was complied with, whether affecting the registration, clearance, or shipping of the crews.

But to determine whether the agents of the Confederate Government infringed or evaded the municipal law of England, something more will be required by those who are interested in the questions than the mere opinion of lawyers, however eminent, or the assurance of an implicated party, however conscientiously he may affirm his innocence of an evil intent. The course of events has furnished the only authoritative rule which can be applied to the elucidation of any doubtful or ambiguous point of law—that is, a trial before a duly constituted court, and a judicial exposition and decision.

In the well known case, "The Attorney General *v.* Sillem and others," commonly called "The *Alexandra* Case," the Foreign Enlistment Act was discussed at great length by several of the most distinguished lawyers of the English bar, by Sir William Atherton, her Majesty's Attorney-General, Sir Roundell Palmer, her Majesty's Solicitor-General, and Sir Robert Phillimore, the Queen's Advocate, on one side, and Sir Hugh Cairns, J. B. Karslake, Esq., Q.C., George Mellish, Esq., Q.C., and James Kemplay, Esq., on the other. The judgment rendered in the above case has never been reversed, and the interpretation of the Act as laid down by the learned judge on that occasion fixes its meaning and settles the question of the culpability of the Confederate agents. The "*Alexandra* Case" was what lawyers call a prosecution *in rem,* and the Crown contended for a forfeiture of the ship for or upon an alleged violation of the Foreign Enlistment Act, chiefly with reference to the seventh section. It will probably help the reader to understand the case, and to duly estimate the effect of the judgment, if I give a brief history of the circumstances under which the Act was passed, and a short explanation of the principles of neutrality involved in it.

The United States have an Act very similar to that of Great Britain, both as regards the object of the statutes, and the causes which appeared to render them necessary. In the year 1778, the American Colonies, then engaged in their War of Independence with Great Britain, made a treaty (in fact, there were two) with the Government of Louis XVI., by which very large, important and exclusive privileges were granted to the respective parties with reference to the use of each other's ports for the condemnation and sale of prizes, and for the visit, shelter, and equipment of their ships-of-war. Very shortly after the execution of Louis XVI., the French National Convention plunged into a war with England and Holland.

Whatever may be said of the cruelty and arrogance of the men who assumed the control of the French Government in those days of terror, it must be admitted that they did not lack audacity and vigour. They appeared at once to look to the United States as a convenient *point d'appui* for their naval operations, and jumped to the conclusion that under the aforementioned treaties of 1778, they would be permitted to arm and commission privateers in the American ports, to bring into them their prizes, and to have the prizes condemned by the French Consuls. The French Republic declared war against England on February 1st, 1793, and one of the first acts of the Government was to send a Minister to the United States, to inflame the people against Great Britain, and to claim and use the rights and privileges conceded by the treaties of 1778. M. Genet, the person selected for the mission, was certainly not wanting in the qualities of self-assurance, energy and presumption. He arrived at Charleston on the 8th of April, 1793, and began forthwith to organize a system of privateering. He also issued instructions authorizing the French Consuls to hold courts of Vice-Admiralty for condemning the prizes which the cruisers of France might capture and bring into the ports of the United States. Having thus put these naval operations in train, he set out for Philadelphia, and during his journey he resorted to every possible means of inciting the people of the country to acts of enmity against England.

Washington, who was then President, and whose wise judicial mind would have revolted against this presumptuous conduct, even if good faith to England had not influenced him, did not wait for a remonstrance from the British Minister, but issued a proclamation of neutrality on the 22nd of April, 1793. There was some opposition to Washington's prompt and decisive action, for in his Cabinet were several members who were favourable to the French cause, but his strength of character and firmness of will enabled him to put his own views in practice, and to maintain an attitude of strict neutrality. M. Genet appears to have carried matters on with a very high hand, and he tried the temper and the forbearance of the President greatly. He not only persisted in violating the neutral territory, but he entered into various offensive political intrigues, and made himself so obnoxious that his recall was demanded, and the United States Minister in Paris was instructed to say to the French Government that if M. Genet persevered in his proceedings the United States Government would be forced to suspend his functions before a successor could arrive. The result of those troublesome proceedings was to bring the majority of the Cabinet into complete agreement with the President, and they gave rise to the first Act for the Preservation of Neutrality, or what may be called the first American Foreign Enlistment Act, which was passed by Congress early in 1794, re-enacted March 2, 1797, and made final April 24, 1800.

The Act thus made perpetual in 1800 did not, however, prove strong enough for the purpose. The revolt of the Spanish Colonies in South America gave much trouble to the Government of the United States. Agents from those colonies came to New York, Baltimore, and other ports, and bought and equipped vessels to cruise against Spanish commerce, and American citizens fitted out vessels which were officered and manned exclusively by Americans, and after being thus fully equipped for immediate hostilities they were commissioned by the several revolted colonies. Those proceedings involved the United States in constant complaints from Spain, and in diplomatic remonstrance and correspondence with her representatives, and finally, to meet the fresh necessities, a further Foreign Enlistment Act was passed, April, 1818, which was the American Act in force during the late Civil War.

The contests between Spain and her American colonies beginning in 1810, attracted much notice in England, and were from the first regarded with warm interest by the people of Great Britain. The old spirit of maritime adventure, and the passion for enterprises to the Spanish Main and the "El Dorados" on the west coast, which aroused the temper and inspired the actions of Drake, Cavendish, Hawkins, and their contemporaries—those splendid buccaneers, whose deeds have added piquancy and glory to the reign of the Virgin Queen—had not yet been completely superseded by the more peaceful instincts of the nineteenth century, nor wholly and effectively shackled by the growing stringency of a recognised International Code.

It appears that in 1814 Spain was able to persuade England that she ought to do something to check, if not to prevent, the participation of British subjects in the war she was then waging with her recalcitrant subjects in the "Golden South America," and in August, 1814, a supplementary treaty was made between the two Powers, which declared in Article III. that "His Britannic Majesty being anxious that the troubles and disturbances which unfortunately prevail in the dominions of his Catholic Majesty in America should cease, and the subjects of those provinces should return to their obedience to their lawful sovereign, engages to take the most effectual measures for preventing his subjects from furnishing arms, ammunition, or any other article, to the revolted in America."

The treaty did not, however, meet the purposes which inspired it, because we find that in 1818 the interest in the strife had again been greatly aroused throughout Great Britain, partly in consequence of the instinctive attachment of the people to the cause of freedom, and partly in consequence of the extravagant expectations which interested parties had excited by highly coloured statements of the wealth of the Spanish American colonies, and the vast field that their independence would open up to British commerce and enterprise. But in addition to the foregoing causes, much irritation had been produced throughout Great Britain by the reactionary policy of Ferdinand VII., the prohibitory duties he had imposed upon British commerce, and the resentful feelings which were provoked by the alleged ingratitude he had shown to many British officers who had served him in Spain.

There was at the time a strong party even in Parliament who were in favour of supporting the claims of the colonies and giving them help to win their independence. There was an old statute of James I., which specified the conditions upon which British subjects might enter into the service of a foreign prince; and there were further Acts, in the reign of George II., forbidding enlistment or the procuring of others to enlist in a foreign service "without licence under the King's sign-manual." By Statute 29, George II., c. 17, it was enacted "that to serve under the French King as a military officer shall be felony without benefit of clergy; and to enter the Scotch Brigade in the Dutch service without first taking the oaths of allegiance and abjuration, shall be a forfeiture of £500."[*]

The foregoing may be taken as the substance of "British neutrality law" in 1818, when Spain was striving to suppress the revolt of her American colonies.[†] But neither the treaty of 1814 nor the prohibitory Acts of Parliament were sufficient to prevent aid being sent to the insurgents, both in men and materials of war. There does not appear to have been any attempt at disguise. Great numbers of Peninsular veterans, officers and men, went to the revolted provinces, and gave them the benefit of their experience and the prestige of their military fame. An adventurer of some note, who assumed the title of general, and was known as Sir Gregor McGregor, collected an expedition in the ports of Great Britain, with which he sailed in British vessels and under the British flag. He attacked and took Porto Bello, in South America, then in the undisturbed possession of a Spanish force. This violent act of aggression led to strong

---

[*] Phillimore's "International Law," vol. iii., ed. 1857, p. 212.

[†] For the dates and facts in respect to the origin of the British Foreign Enlistment Act, see Appendix to Report of the Neutrality Laws Commissioners, issued for the information of the House of Commons, 1868, from which the account herein is abridged in the leading points.

remonstrances on the part of the Spanish Government, and the British Ministry, on the 10th of June, 1819, introduced a Bill for the Amendment of the Neutrality Laws, which was passed on the 21st by a majority of sixty-one. The Act was strongly opposed, the Opposition being led by Sir James Macintosh, who denounced it as a "left-handed neutrality, aimed at the struggling independence of South America." In the year 1823, Lord Althorp moved for the repeal of the Act, but the motion was defeated, and the statute, as passed on the 21st June, 1819, remained the "Neutrality Law" of Great Britain up to and during the American Civil War. It is known, and was generally alluded to, as the "Foreign Enlistment Act," and it is the Act which is applicable to all cases of alleged violation of the neutrality of Great Britain by either belligerent in the American Civil War.

The passing of the Act of 1819 seems to have put an end to the despatch of expeditions from Great Britain against Spain, for a time, at least; but it was necessary to put it in force on several occasions to prevent or to arrest expeditions fitted out to operate against other countries with which England was at peace. In 1835 an Order in Council was passed exempting British subjects who might engage in the service of Queen Isabella of Spain from the penalties of the Foreign Enlistment Act. Under the terms of this exemption, a British legion was formed, which went to Spain under the command of Sir De Lacy Evans, and served there during the war against the Carlists. In 1862 an Order in Council was again issued suspending the Foreign Enlistment Act so as to allow Captain Sherard Osborne, R.N., to fit out ships and engage British subjects to enter the service of the Emperor of China.

In the Appendix to the Report of the Neutrality Law Commissioners in the year 1867, it is said that "in all, or nearly all, the cases up to the time of the American Civil War, the Foreign Enlistment Act had been invoked to prevent the enlistment and despatch of recruits and soldiers rather than the equipment of vessels." There are only three cases mentioned of interference with, or seizure of vessels, and in each of them the ships were so completely equipped and manned that they might have engaged in hostilities as soon as they were clear of the British port, or else they had emigrants or volunteers on board which it was proved were intended for the service of a belligerent, and no case is mentioned of any vessel being brought to trial.

In order to comprehend the application of the Foreign Enlistment Act to the cases of Confederate ships built or bought in England, it is necessary to bear in mind the circumstances which produced the amendment of the Neutrality Laws in 1819, and the evil it was intended to guard against, and to remedy, by the Act of Parliament.

Mr. Canning, in his speech in support of the Bill, gave a graphic description of an expedition prepared in a British port for hostile attack upon some foreign Power, and he said that if a foreigner visiting England at the time should see the ships with their armament and crews on board, and the transports with the troops, he would naturally ask with what country England was at war. When he was told that the country was not at war, but was in peace and amity with the whole world, he would doubtless be greatly surprised.

The Attorney-General of that day, in introducing the Bill into Parliament, said: "It was extremely important for the preservation of neutrality that the subjects of this country should be prevented from fitting out any equipments, not only in the ports of Great Britain and Ireland, but also in other parts of the British dominions, to be employed in foreign service." He explained that by fitting out "armed vessels, or by supplying the vessels of other countries with warlike stores, as effectual assistance might be rendered to a foreign Power as by enlistment in their own service," and he added "that in the second provision of the Bill, two objects were intended to be embued—to prevent the fitting out of *armed* vessels, and also to prevent the fitting out or supplying other ships with warlike stores in any of his Majesty's ports, not that such vessels might not receive in any port in the British dominions, but the object of the enactment was to prevent them from shipping warlike stores, such as guns and other things—other things obviously and manifestly intended for no other purpose than war."

It is usual for Legislative Acts to be headed or preceded by an explanatory clause, or preamble, as it is called, which states the object of the Act and the evil to be remedied by it. The preamble to the English Foreign Enlistment Act is as follows: "Whereas the enlistment or engagement of his Majesty's subjects to serve in war in foreign service without his Majesty's license, and the fitting-out, equipping, and arming of vessels by his Majesty's subjects for warlike operations in or against the dominions or territories of any foreign Prince, State, Potentate, or persons exercising or assuming to exercise the powers of Government in or over any foreign country, etc., may be prejudicial to and tend to endanger the peace and welfare of this kingdom, etc." It would appear from the foregoing explanations, and the preamble of the Act, that the object was to provide against the fitting out of warlike expeditions in the ports of Great Britain which might be in condition to engage in acts of hostility as soon as they left the neutral port, and to prohibit British subjects from practically engaging in war on their own account, by taking part in the preparation of warlike expeditions in Great Britain, or the arming of ships for war within the United Kingdom. This was the view taken by the learned barristers whose opinions were asked before the contracts for the *Florida* and *Alabama* were made. They advised that it was not illegal for a builder to build, or a purchaser to buy, a ship of any description whatever, provided she was not armed for war and no men were enlisted or engaged to go in her for the service of a foreign State.

The ground is now clear for the report of the test case which has been mentioned above—a case which resulted in a judicial exposition of the law, and an authoritative verdict upon the acts of the Confederate Government in respect to the building or purchase of ships in England.

About the 7th of March, 1863, a small wooden screw-steamer was launched from the building-yard of Messrs. W. C. Miller and Son, at Liverpool. The material of which the ship was built, her general arrangements, and the fact that she was launched from the same yard in which the *Florida* was built, soon attracted the notice of Mr. Dudley's spies, and they began to manufacture affidavits for the information of the American Minister. On the 28th of March, Mr. Dudley made a formal "affirmation" (being, as he stated, averse to taking an oath) that he had reason to believe that the above mentioned vessel, which had been named *Alexandra*, was intended for the Confederate States. The "affirmation" began with the preamble or introductory prelude which was commonly adopted by the American Consuls of the period, namely, that the Government and people of the United States were engaged in a war with "certain persons who have rebelled against such Government, and pretended to set up and assume to exercise the powers of Government, styling themselves the Confederate States of America"; then was added a synopsis of the grounds of Mr. Dudley's faith in that to which he affirmed, and a declaration of his belief in the truth of the affidavits of certain other persons, whose statements were duly sworn to at the same time.

The foregoing "affirmation" and "affidavits" were forwarded to the United States Minister in London, and on the 30th Mr. Adams addressed a letter to Lord Russell on the subject, and an active correspondence appears to have been carried on between that gentleman, the British Foreign Office, the Customs authorities, the Mayor and Head-Constable of Liverpool, the Treasury, and the Home Office. The correspondence fills twenty-four pages of the appendix to the "British Case." A synopsis of it would hardly interest the reader. It is sufficient to say that the upshot of it all was the seizure of the *Alexandra,* and a suit in her Majesty's Court of Exchequer for her forfeiture to the Crown.

The little vessel which had occasioned all this commotion had been launched on the day the Princess of Wales entered London, previous to her marriage, and had been christened *Alexandra,* in commemoration of that interesting event. She was taken into the Toxteth Dock to complete her outfit, and to have her engines placed, and there the work went peacefully on, her builders and owners having some consciousness that the United States Minister was uneasy about her, but not dreaming that they were doing anything illegal, and therefore attempting no concealment or disguise.

On the 5th of April, 1863, the Surveyor of Customs at Liverpool seized her, and all work upon her was suspended. The trial was not begun until the 22nd of June, and as the decision was important, besides furnishing the first and the last judicial exposition of the Foreign Enlistment Act, I feel that a synopsis of the proceedings would not be inappropriate, and I will now give an abridgment of the report which my solicitor got for me at the time.

The "information" in the case was dated May 25th, 1863, and stated that a certain officer of her Majesty's Customs had seized and arrested, to the use of her Majesty, as forfeited, a certain ship or vessel called the *Alexandra,* together with the furniture, tackle, and apparel belonging to and on board the said ship or vessel. Then followed counts to the number of ninety-eight, charging the offences by reason of which the ship had become forfeited to the Crown. The 97th and 98th counts were abandoned by the Crown. The remaining ninety-six counts consisted of the first eight counts repeated twelve times, merely varying the offence charged. Thus, the first eight counts charge that the defendants did *equip* the vessel, the next eight counts that they did *furnish* the vessel, the next eight that they did *fit out,* then they did *attempt or endeavour to equip,* and so on, exhausting the various offences enumerated in the seventh section of the statute, with the exception of *arming* the vessel, which was not charged at all. The first eight counts therefore represented the rest, and were in substance as follows. The first count charged that "certain" persons within the United Kingdom, without having any leave or license of her Majesty for that purpose first had and obtained, *did equip* the said ship or vessel, with intent and in order that such ship or vessel should be employed in the service of certain foreign States, styling themselves the Confederate States of America, with intent to cruise and commit hostilities against a certain foreign State, with which her Majesty was not then at war, to wit, the Republic of the United States of America, contrary to the form of the statute in that case made and provided, whereby and by force of the statute in that case made and provided, the said ship or vessel, together with the said tackle, apparel, and furniture, became and was forfeited. The second count differed from the first only in charging that hostilities were to be committed against the *citizens* of the foreign State. The third count omitted the words "that such ship or vessel should be employed in the service," etc., and merely charged that the defendants *did equip* the vessel with intent to cruise and commit hostilities against a certain foreign State, etc. The fourth count resembled the third, merely varying the description of the belligerent party against whom hostilities were to be committed. The fifth, sixth, seventh and eighth counts resembled the first and second counts, and merely varied the description of the belligerent parties who were affected by the conduct of the defendants. The *intent*, therefore, was stated in two different ways, to meet the ambiguous language of the seventh section, wherein the clause "with the intent or in order that such ship," and the clause "with the intent to cruise," may be regarded either as alternative or cumulative propositions. The defendants pleaded that the vessel was not forfeited for the supposed causes in the information mentioned.

At the trial, which took place on the 22nd June, 1863, and following days, before the Lord Chief Baron of the Exchequer (Sir Frederick Pollock, Kt.), the evidence for the Crown was directed to prove, first, that the vessel was built for the purpose of a warlike equipment; second, that she was intended at some stage or other of her construction for the service of the Confederate States. It may be assumed that the Crown succeeded in proving that the vessel was built for the purpose of a warlike equipment, or at any rate that she was suited to receive a warlike equipment, but on the second point the witnesses were so discredited on cross-examination, that neither judge nor jury appeared to give much, if any, credence to their evidence, and the counsel for the defendants did not call any witnesses. The judge, in charging the jury, after explaining the information, and citing Kent and Storey, proceeded thus:

"These are authorities" (Kent and Storey) "which show that where two belligerents are carrying on war, the subjects of a neutral Power may supply to either, without any breach of international law, and certainly without any breach of the Foreign Enlistment Act, all the munitions of war, gunpowder, every description of firearms, cannon, every kind of weapon—in short, whatever can be used in war for the destruction of human beings. Why should ships be an exception? In my opinion, in point of law they are not." His lordship then, having adverted to the statute and read the seventh section, said: "The question that I shall propose to you" (the jury) "is this—whether you think that this vessel was merely in the course of building for the purpose of being delivered in pursuance of a contract, which I own I think was perfectly lawful, or whether there was any intention that in the port of Liverpool, or any other English port (and there is certainly no evidence of any other), the vessel should be equipped, fitted out, and furnished or armed for the purpose of aggression. Why should ships alone be themselves contraband?... What the statute meant to provide for was, I think, by no means the protection of the belligerent Powers, otherwise they would have said, 'You shall not sell gunpowder, you shall not sell guns.' The object of the statute was this—we will not have our ports in this country subject to possibly hostile movements. You shall not be fitting up at one dock a vessel equipped and ready, not being completely armed, but ready to go to sea, and at another dock close by be fitting up another vessel, and equipping her in the same way, which might come into hostile communication immediately, possibly before they left the port. Now and then this has happened, and that has been the occasion of this statute. The offence against which this information is directed is the 'equipping, furnishing, fitting out, or arming.' From Webster's dictionary it appears that to 'equip' is to 'furnish with arms.' In the case of a ship especially, it is to 'furnish and complete with arms'—that is what is meant by 'equipping.' 'Furnish' is given in every dictionary as the same thing as 'equip.' To 'fit out' is to 'furnish and supply,' as to fit out a privateer, and I own that my opinion is that 'equip,' 'furnish,' 'fit out,' or 'arm,' all mean precisely the same thing.... The question is—Was there any intention that in the port of Liverpool, or in any other port, the vessel should be, in the language of the Act of Parliament, either 'equipped, furnished, fitted out, or armed,' with the intention of taking part in any contest? If you think that the object was to equip, furnish, fit out, or arm that vessel at Liverpool, then that is a sufficient matter. But if you think the object really was to build a ship in obedience to an order, and in compliance with a contract, leaving it to those who bought it to make what use they thought fit of it, then it appears to me that the Foreign Enlistment Act has not been in any degree broken."

The jury found a verdict for the defendants. The counsel for the Crown tendered a Bill of Exceptions to the direction of the judge, in order that all the points of law involved might be argued and decided in the Exchequer Chamber (the Court of Appeal). The Bill of Exceptions was subsequently abandoned, and in November, 1863, the Attorney-General moved a "rule" in the Court of Exchequer to set aside the verdict found, and for a new trial. In the same month cause was shown against and for this "rule" before the Lord Chief Baron and the Barons Bramwell, Channel, and Pigott. The question was very fully argued, and the four judges read very long opinions, two, namely, the Lord Chief Baron and Baron Bramwell, giving judgment for the claimants of the ship, and two, namely, Barons Channel and Pigott, for the Crown. Inasmuch as the four judges were divided, Baron Pigott, according to practice, withdrew his judgment in order that the Crown might appeal. The Crown subsequently appealed to the Court of Exchequer Chamber, but the appeal was dismissed on a preliminary objection of a technical nature. The appeal was then carried to the House of Lords, but was also dismissed on the same grounds. The judgment for the claimants of the ship therefore remained undisturbed, and the questions raised as to the interpretation of the seventh section of the Foreign Enlistment Act have never received any other solution than that which is set out in the charge of the Lord Chief Baron to the jury, which it will be perceived exactly agrees with the opinions given by the learned barristers who were consulted before any effort to build ships in England was made at all.

The United States authorities appear to have been satisfied with the action taken by her Majesty's Government in the matter of the *Alexandra*. On the 6th of April, the day after the seizure, Mr. Adams wrote to Earl Russell: "It is a source of great satisfaction to me to recognise the readiness which her Majesty's Government has thus manifested to make the investigations desired, as well as to receive the assurances of its determination to maintain a close observation of future movements of an unusual character that justifies suspicions of an evil intent."* Mr. Seward, writing to Mr. Adams after the verdict, says: "You are authorised and expected to assure Earl Russell that this Government is entirely satisfied that her Majesty's Government have conducted the proceedings in the case with perfect good faith and honour, and that they are well disposed to prevent the fitting-out of armed vessels in British ports to depredate upon American commerce, and to make war upon the United States. This Government is satisfied that the law officers of the Crown have performed their duties in regard to the case of the *Alexandra* with a sincere conviction of the adequacy of the law of Great Britain, and a sincere desire to give it effect."†

---

* "British Appendix," vol. ii., p. 171, and see also "British Case," p. 40.
† "United States Documents," vol. ii., p. 291, quoted in "British Case," pp. 40, 41.

It must have been refreshing to Earl Russell to receive a commendatory notice from Mr. Seward, for the general tone of the communications from Washington could not have been agreeable reading at the British Foreign Office. The satisfaction of Mr. Seward and of Mr. Adams was confined to the approval of Lord Russell's readiness to seize the ship, and the zeal displayed by the law officers of the Crown in the prosecution of the suit, but they could not have been gratified by the result of the suit, although it was her Majesty's Treasury which had to bear the consequences of the failure to effect a forfeiture. The builders of the *Alexandra*, Messrs. Fawcett, Preston and Co., made a claim for damages, and after much delay and negotiation their solicitors agreed to receive £3,700, "on the understanding that the amount shall be paid without delay," and that amount was paid to them by order of the Treasury.

It is necessary to say something in reference to the witnesses brought forward by Mr. Thomas H. Dudley, the United States Consul, in support of the "information" in the "*Alexandra* Case," in order that the evidence which her Majesty's Government was urged to act upon in this and other cases may be fully understood, and a correct judgment may be formed in respect to the action of that Government in applying the Foreign Enlistment Act to the operations of the Confederate agents during the war.

I have said in a previous chapter that the affidavits upon which the United States Minister based his complaints and accusations were for the most part either wholly false or they contained gross exaggerations. A man may be deeply impressed with the expectation that a certain event is about to happen; the expectation may be fully realized, and yet the information upon which his convictions were formed may have been false in all specific particulars. The *Florida* and *Alabama*, as is now well known, became Confederate cruisers, and Mr. Dudley's predictions in regard to their ultimate purpose have been fulfilled; but the statements made in the affidavits of Da Costa, Passmore, and others, which appear in the proceedings before the Geneva arbitrators, are false; and if either of the ships named had been seized by the Government, their falsehood would have been proved, not only by rebutting testimony, but by cross-examination of the witnesses themselves. This is precisely what happened in the "*Alexandra* Case." The Crown proved by its own witnesses, who were experts, that the ship was so constructed as to be well suited to the purposes of a cruiser, but not for purposes of commerce. When, however, the prosecution attempted to prove specific facts in regard to the intent to equip, etc., the evidence failed, and failed because it was untrue, and therefore entirely broke down in cross-examination. Counsel for the defence were so satisfied that the witnesses had discredited themselves to the jury, that they called no witnesses to deny their statements. Men who are employed as spies, or who are paid to give evidence in regard to matters upon which they can have no personal knowledge except what they may have acquired by dishonest and unworthy means, are easily exposed by skilful cross-examination in the witness-box; and anyone who was present at the trial of the *Alexandra,* or cares to read the report of the proceedings, will feel a contemptuous pity for Mr. Dudley's three witnesses—John Da Costa, George Temple Chapman, and Clarence Randolph Yonge. Sir Hugh Cairns (now Earl Cairns), in his address to the jury, summed up and commented upon the evidence of the above-named "worthies" as follows:

"I cannot help pausing to remind you of the kind of evidence that Da Costa gave. He came forward, and what did he tell us he was? He said he was a shipping-agent and a steamboat-owner; that is his own account, in the first instance, of his character. I am sorry to destroy that illusion; but it turns out, on cross-examination, that he is a crimp and a partner in a tug. He says he is a shipping-agent and a steamboat-owner. How easily great titles may descend to something smaller! He is a crimp and a partner in a tug. He is brought forward by the Crown—I beg pardon, not by the Crown; he is one of the witnesses of Mr. Dudley, the Liverpool Consul.... My learned friend for the Crown could not moderate him. He had one thing to say, and he was always saying it, and whatever he was asked it always came out. 'There is a gunboat'—that is what he came to tell, and he would say nothing else—the *'Phantom'* and 'gunboat'; all I know is 'that was a gunboat.' He would give no answer without mixing up with it that which he thought he came here to prove."

After pointing out the irrelevancy as well as improbability of Da Costa's statements, Sir Hugh Cairns proceeded:—

"I have still to deal with the two illustrious witnesses who remain—the two spies. I will take first Mr. George Temple Chapman.... George Temple Chapman's story is this: He went to the counting-house of Messrs. Fraser, Trenholm and Co., and has an interview with Mr. Prioleau; he represents himself to be a Secessionist, and a warm supporter of the Southern States. He goes with that lie on his lips to have a conversation with Mr. Prioleau. Now, what was the object of telling that lie on the 1st of April (while the seizure is being prepared for)? Mr. George Temple Chapman was sent to the office of Messrs. Fraser, Trenholm and Co., to have an interview with Mr. Prioleau, and to beguile him by a false statement into making admissions to him. I suppose you will see that Mr. George Temple Chapman was sent by the American Consul as a spy, in order to obtain some admission about the *Alexandra*. Well, what came of it? ... Does he say that he was able to extract one single sentence from that firm, or to obtain from Mr. Prioleau, who was confiding in him, believing in him as a compatriot,—does he say that he obtained one single piece of information with respect to the *Alexandra*? ... Nothing of the kind. The whole thing is a failure which recoils on the Crown.... The witness who comes forward and tells this story, cannot put his finger upon a single fact that could bear upon the case of the *Alexandra*."

I was at the office of Messrs. Fraser, Trenholm and Co. when Mr. Chapman called, and after his interview with Mr. Prioleau, he asked to see me. He introduced himself as an ex-officer of the United States Navy, and told me that although a Northern man, his sympathies were, and had been, wholly with the South, and for that reason he had been obliged to leave Boston. I instinctively distrusted him, but he had the external appearance of a gentleman, and I received his visit with as much courtesy as I could command for the occasion. He showed me a letter which he said he had got from the "mulatto wife of Clarence R. Yonge," mentioned elsewhere, and he thought I might like to have it. The letter purported to be a copy of an official letter written by me many months before, and he said Mr. Yonge had kept this copy, and might make improper use of it. The contents of the letter were of no importance, and I handed it back to him, merely saying that it did not concern me. On the trial it came out that his object was to obtain some admission from me, but he failed, and his evidence in respect to our interview was false.

After fully exposing the character of Chapman, and the worthlessness of his evidence, Sir Hugh Cairns proceeded to deal with the third of the trio, thus:—

"Well, but, gentlemen of the jury, I come to the greatest witness of all in this case, the witness who was reserved by the Crown to the last, and was brought forward certainly with some pomp and ceremony. I mean Mr. Clarence Randolph Yonge. How am I to describe this specimen of humanity?—the man who began his career by abandoning his wife and child in his native country ... who became Captain Bulloch's private secretary, had access to his papers, was the companion of those who were engaged in the Confederate cause, persuaded them that he shared in the feeling of patriotism which actuated them; who came over to England, who still assumed the same character—who, received by Messrs. Fraser, Trenholm and Co., became possessed of every secret with regard to the proceedings of those who were engaged in war on the part of the Southern States; who accepted a commission from his native country in her service, became an officer enrolled in her navy, owning allegiance to her, received her pay, distributed her money; who then became a deserter, slipping overboard on leaving the ship of which he was an officer, in order that he might by a lying pretence of a marriage effect the ruin and plunder the property of a widow, who had the misfortune to entertain him in her country and to be possessed of some property of her own; who succeeded in possessing himself of that property; who brought her over to Liverpool, and who then turned her adrift, penniless, on the streets; who then hurried up to London in order to pour into the ear of Mr. Adams, the American Minister, his tale of treachery, betraying every one of his familiar friends, and every one of his brother officers, and the cause of the country to which he had promised allegiance; who stood there in the witness-box before you, who denied no crime and blushed at no villainy, until, indeed, it was suggested that the victim of his villainy had been a mulatto woman, and not his wife, and then all his feeling of self-respect recoiled, and he indignantly denied the charge. This, gentlemen, is the man who is brought forward at the end as the climax of the case on the part of the Crown; but I beg pardon, he is not the witness of the Crown—he is the witness of Mr. Adams, the United States Minister. It is Mr. Adams who forwarded him to the Crown to be put into the witness-box before a jury of English gentlemen, to repeat the tale which that unmitigated villain told in our ears. Gentlemen, I know the honourable and straightforward character of my honourable and learned friend, the Attorney-General, and I felt how he must have loathed and recoiled from his task when, reading from the brief of the American Minister, he put questions to this witness, question after question, which elicited the tale which we heard from Mr. Clarence Randolph Yonge.... But what was it that Mr. Randolph Yonge told us, after all? He gave us a great deal of information about the *Alabama*, he told us how the money was procured to pay the officers on board the *Alabama*, he told us where the *Alabama* went to, etc."

Counsel then pointed out the folly as well as the fatality of bringing forward such a witness, and added, "I do not merely mean to say that this evidence would cover with shame any case that was ever brought before a jury, though that is perfectly true.... But consider this.... We have now got laid before us, by one of the agents, as it was said, of the Confederate Government, everything they contemplated last April at the time when they were engaged in the fitting out and sending away the *Alabama*.... He has disclosed the secrets of the Cabinet Councils in Liverpool, and not one single secret of those Cabinet Councils has reference to the ship you are now trying."*

The trial of the *Alexandra* afforded the opportunity to discover and expose the character of the witnesses which the United States Consul offered to produce in support of his allegations, and looking over the affidavits published among the documents laid before the Tribunal of Arbitration at Geneva, and in the diplomatic correspondence, I find they are nearly all of the same stamp as those of Mr. John Da Costa, namely, utterly inaccurate as regards the specific statements. But although the witnesses in the "*Alexandra* Case" were so thoroughly discredited that the jury could not have believed their testimony, yet the verdict of the jury was really given for the defendants in consequence of the directions of the Lord Chief Baron on the points of law, which may be summed up in the following sentence: "But if you think the object really was to build a ship in obedience to an order and in compliance with a contract, leaving it to those who bought it to make what use they thought fit of it, then it appears to me that the Foreign Enlistment Act has not been in any degree broken."

If it had not been for the trial of the *Alexandra*, the judicial exposition of the law, and the verdict of a jury, there would have been no sufficient and unanswerable reply to the reiterated assertions of the United States Consul and of Mr. Seward, that the acts of the Confederate Government in attempting to procure ships in England were "criminal" and "nefarious." But we have cumulative evidence in almost every form in which independent and authoritative opinion can be pronounced, in regard both to

---

* When I went to Savannah in the *Fingal*, in November, 1862, Mr. Clarence R. Yonge was an assistant, or clerk, in the paymaster's office at that naval station. He had served as acting-paymaster on board of one or two of the vessels of Flag-officer Josiah Tattnall's squadron, and was reported to be fully competent to perform the duties of a naval paymaster. Just before leaving the Confederate States to return to Europe in January, 1862, the Secretary of the Navy directed me to take Mr. Yonge out as my private secretary, and to give him an appointment as acting-assistant-paymaster for the *Alabama* when she was ready for sea. When Captain Semmes joined the *Alabama*, I told him that Yonge was an unsteady and unreliable young man, whose judgment and discretion were not to be trusted, but I had no suspicion in regard to his integrity in money matters, and, of course, could not have dreamed that he was capable of treachery and treason. He was dismissed from the *Alabama* in disgrace, but Captain Semmes did not report the fact to me at the time. He came to Liverpool, but never came near me; he went instead to Mr. Dudley, the United States Consul, to whom he sold himself, with the results specified in the speech of Sir Hugh Cairns, the facts having been drawn from him in the course of his evidence.

the spirit and the letter of the Foreign Enlistment Act, and I will now give a synopsis of that evidence, in order that the reader may have the data upon which to found his own judgment.

First,—there is the legal opinion of the two learned barristers who were consulted before the contract for the *Alabama* was made, and which has already been mentioned.*

Second,—Lord Palmerston, the Prime Minister of England, during the Civil War, when all these "*Alabama* questions" were occupying the public mind, in a speech in the House of Commons, July 23rd, 1863,† said: "I cannot, in the abstract, concur with my honourable friend" (Mr. Richard Cobden) "in thinking that there is any distinction in principle between muskets, gunpowder, bullets and cannon on the one side, and ships on the other. These are things by which war is carried on, and you are equally assisting belligerents by supplying them with muskets, cannon, and ammunition, as you are by supplying them with ships that are to operate in war." After citing cases from United States history, he further said: "Therefore I hold, that on the mere ground of international law belligerents have no right to complain if merchants—I do not say the Government, for that would be interference—as a mercantile transaction, supply one of the belligerents, not only with arms and cannon, but also with ships destined for warlike purposes."

Third,—Earl Russell, the Secretary of State for Foreign Affairs, in a letter to Mr. Adams, argues the question upon the Foreign Enlistment Act, and cites to the American Minister two cases—the *Independencia* and the *Alfred*, which were decided in the United States Supreme Court, and then, appealing to the American Minister upon the authorities of his own country, he says: "It seems clear on the principles enumerated in these authorities that, except on the ground of any proved violation of the Foreign Enlistment Act, which those cases decided had not been violated, in those cases her Majesty's Government cannot interfere with commercial dealings between British subjects and the so-styled Confederate States, whether the object of those dealings be money, or contraband goods, or *even ships* adapted for warlike purposes."‡

Fourth,—her Majesty's Solicitor-General, Sir Roundell Palmer—now Lord Selborne and Lord Chancellor of England—in a speech made in the House of Commons, during a debate on the Foreign Enlistment Act,

---

* See chap. II., pp. 47–48.

† See Hansard, vol. clxxii., session 1863 (4), pp. 1269, 1270.

‡ Quoted or read to the court by Sir Hugh Cairns in the *Alexandra* trial, p. 173.

March 27th, 1863, said: "It would be a great mistake to suppose that the Foreign Enlistment Act was meant to prohibit all commercial dealings in ships-of-war with belligerent countries. It is not intended to do so. Two things must be proved in every case to render the transaction illegal: that there has been what the law regards as the fitting-out, arming, or equipment of a ship-of-war; and with the intent that the ship should be employed in the service of a foreign belligerent."* The Solicitor-General then recites two cases in which decisions have been rendered by the United States Supreme Court upon the corresponding American statute, to demonstrate to the House "what may lawfully be done on the showing of the Americans themselves"; and he then adds: "The circumstances of the case tried before Justice Story were so far exactly the same as those which occurred in the case of the *Alabama,* and, in the absence of any further evidence, the seizure of that ship would have been altogether unwarrantable by law. She might have been legitimately built by a foreign Government, and though a ship-of-war, she might have formed a legitimate article of merchandise, even if meant for the Confederate States."

I might cite many familiar cases from the history of the United States, and from the judgments of the Supreme Court of that country, in opposition to the views put forward by Mr. Seward in respect to the Confederate ships; but the charge was that *English* municipal law was violated and "criminally evaded," and that *British* hospitality was abused in a manner which was "nefarious," and therefore it is not necessary to appeal to any other tribunals than those of the country in which the alleged offences were committed. That appeal has been made, and the verdict rendered is that the Confederates have done no violence either to British law or to British hospitality. We have the judgment of the Prime Minister of England that there is no distinction in *principle* between supplying belligerents with arms and ammunition, or "with ships that are to operate in war," and that a British merchant may sell either guns or ships to a belligerent without infringing either local or international duties. We have the declaration of Earl Russell, the Minister especially charged with the diplomatic relations of the kingdom, that the Confederate States had the right to procure "money or contraband goods, or *even ships* adapted for warlike purposes" in England, provided only they did not violate the express conditions of the Foreign Enlistment Act. We have the Solicitor-General, one of the highest legal advisers of the Crown, stating with all the authority of his office, and with all the prestige of his position as a Member

* Hansard, vol. clxx., session 1863 (2), pp. 47–52.

of Parliament, that it would be a great mistake to suppose that the Foreign Enlistment Act was meant to prohibit commercial dealings in ships-of-war with belligerent countries, and assuming that the *Alabama* was not "equipped" in England, she was a legitimate article of merchandise, even if meant for the Confederate States. Finally, we have had the trial of a test-case, and the verdict of a special jury, under the direction of one of the highest judges in the kingdom, and the decision was that an English shipbuilder may build any kind of ship, to a commercial order, or merely in compliance with a contract, and the purchaser may take her away and do what he likes with her afterwards, without any violation of English law.

It is manifest, therefore, that in the opinion of the highest personages in England, of those who during the whole period of the Civil War were responsible for the Government of the country, who had the exclusive authority to interpret the law and to administer it, who from their exalted position, their experience, and their knowledge of public affairs, were eminently fitted to pronounce judgment upon what was due to her Majesty's Government, both in reference to acts of obedience and acts of courtesy—in the opinion of such men, expressing their views under circumstances of the gravest official responsibility—the Confederate Government, by buying or building ships in England, did nothing contrary to commercial usage, international comity, or municipal law. If the charges of "criminality" and "nefarious evasions of law" had been merely cast at me as an individual, or against any other agent of the Confederate Government, I would not have made the foregoing elaborate explanation, but I have learned the application of the legal phrase, *"qui facit per alium facit per se."* I have always felt that the object was to discredit the Government of the Confederate States, as well as to defeat their purposes, and every feeling of loyalty has impelled me to give all who care to form an impartial judgment the facts and circumstances which should be taken into account. The epithets have already passed into history. They can never be erased from the public documents which they deface. Some future American Secretary of State—perhaps now that the country is reunited it may be an ex-Confederate or his descendant—may look over the files of his Department and wonder at the heat and passion of his predecessor; but I will venture to say that no member of the late Confederate Government, and not one of their representatives abroad, ever has felt a pang of conscience on the subject, or has ever had his peace of mind disquieted by the thought that he was doing, or had done, in respect to the matters at issue, anything of which a loyal man should be ashamed—loyal, I mean, in the broad sense of duty to others as well as to himself.

At some future day, when the actors have passed away, a true and impartial history of the great Civil War and its causes will be written, for it was too notable an event to remain as a mere item in the course of God's providence. Then the truth, and the whole truth, will appear, and the world will be surprised to learn how much the South has been misrepresented, the motives and doctrines of her public men distorted, and even the private life and social habits of her people caricatured for political purposes. Those who were inimical to the South, or were, at least, instigated by motives of political necessity to misstate facts or to suppress a part of the truth, have had the opportunity to publish their statements and to impress them upon the public mind of the present generation, with hardly an effort of retort or correction on behalf of the Southern people.

But the history of the past cannot be wholly forgotten. It must be and is known that in the pure days of the Republic, before the tyrannous "caucus" and the iniquitous "machine" had usurped the control and direction of the public will—when men were judged upon their merits, and political parties were separated by honest diversity of opinion, and not by sectional lines—the South, though greatly inferior in voting power, furnished four out of five consecutive Presidents. She has given such men as Clay, Calhoun, Crittenden, Crawford, and Forsyth to the civil service since the great struggle for independence, and the greatest of the Chief-Justices of the Supreme Court was a Southerner. She has contributed many gallant and able men to the army and navy. The "Father of his Country" was a Virginian planter, and even Farragut, who made his reputation in helping to defeat the South, and has been called the "Nelson of the American Navy," was by birth, by early training, by marriage, by all the domestic and social associations of his life, a Southern man, possessing in a marked degree the peculiarities, and even what may be called the provincialisms, of that part of the United States.

I have mentioned but a small number of the Southerners who helped to elevate the national fame before dissension and distrust had alienated the two sections, and I feel sure that the day will come when justice will be done to the Southern leaders of 1861–65, and that an impartial posterity will by its verdict free their names from the calumnies which have been spoken against them, and will pronounce a retributive censure upon their traducers. After the trial of the *Alexandra,* and the clear, emphatic opinion expressed by the highest authorities of the kingdom in regard to the sale and purchase of ships in England on behalf of a belligerent, it might have been supposed that the Confederate Government would have been permitted to supply its necessities, at least, under restrictions no greater than those imposed upon the United States. But such was not the case. Whether Mr. Seward's warm commendation of the "good faith and honour" of her Majesty's Government, and the zeal of the law officers of the Crown in the prosecution of the *Alexandra*, won Earl Russell to the Federal cause, or whether he yielded to the importunities of Mr. Adams in the spirit of the judge "in a certain city" of whom we read in Scripture, that unfortunate ship was pursued with relentless persecution until the end of the war. She was held under seizure by the Government until April, 1864.* When released, her name was changed to *Mary*, her fittings on deck and below were altered and made suitable to a vessel of commerce, and in July she sailed from Liverpool for Bermuda, and thence to Halifax. Mr. Seward at once addressed a communication to the British Chargé d'Affaires at Washington, and the letter was forwarded to the Lieutenant-Governor of Nova Scotia. That functionary replied that he could not "interfere with any vessel, British owned, in a British harbour, on mere suspicion"; nevertheless, he promised to institute inquiry and to have a strict watch kept on her. The *Mary*, finding no rest for the sole of her foot, or rather for her keel, at Halifax, returned in December to Bermuda, and thence proceeded to Nassau, where, on the 13th of December, 1864, she was seized by order of the Governor, and proceedings were instituted against her in the Vice-Admiralty Court of the colony. The cause was heard on the 22nd and 23rd of May, 1865; and on the 30th of May the Court decided that there was no "reasonably sufficient" evidence of illegal intent to support a sentence of forfeiture, and the vessel was accordingly released. The war had by that time ceased, and the little craft was freed from further persecution.

Before turning to another subject, I will just mention that, in spite of Da Costa's sworn statements to the contrary, I never saw the *Alexandra* until after she was seized, I never had the slightest control over her, and never gave an instruction in reference to her. She was built under a contract with Mr. Charles K. Prioleau, of Liverpool, at his own private cost and risk exclusively. He told me, while she was building, that his purpose was to send her as an unarmed ship to run the blockade into Charleston, if possible, and after her arrival there he meant to present her to the Confederate Government. This transaction would have been perfectly regular and unobjectionable, according to the decision in the trial before the Lord Chief Baron of the Exchequer, and the views of the eminent statesmen whose opinions I have given above; but it was violently interfered with

* See "British Case," p. 41.

and prevented by authorities deriving their power from those Ministers who had declared that there was no difference in principle between selling a gun or a ship to a belligerent, and no violation of neutrality in permitting it to be done; and I assume that if a British merchant may sell a ship, there can be no iniquity in his giving one away. It must be borne in mind, too, that there was no evidence that the *Alexandra*, or *Mary*, was intended to be given to the Confederate States. After her release she was loaded and cleared for Halifax as any other British ship.

Under date of September 1st, 1863, I wrote to the Secretary of the Navy at Richmond on this subject, as follows:—

"The favourable decision in the '*Alexandra* Case' has not made our operations in Europe less difficult. Federal spies have rather increased than otherwise, and I am convinced that nothing more should be attempted in England. While the shipment of arms and every description of warlike implement for the North is freely allowed, while armour plates are being rolled in this country for United States ships, and recruiting is notoriously going on in Ireland for the Federal army, a vessel cannot clear for an island, even though it be a British island, contiguous to the Confederate States, without inquiry, interruption, and delay; and a ship building anywhere in private yards with the external appearance of a man-of-war, is not only watched by Yankee spies, but by British officials, and is made the subject of newspaper discussions, letters and protests from lawyers, and even petitions from the 'Emancipation Society.' The South derives some advantage from her recognised status as a belligerent, but the neutrality of Great Britain discriminates too palpably in favour of the North to deceive anyone as to the fears, if not the sympathies, of the present Ministry."

In the Appendix to the British Case, Geneva Arbitration, vol. ii., there is a list of twelve vessels which were made the subject of correspondence between the United States Minister and her Majesty's Government, and all of them, upon the simple allegations of the United States Consuls at Liverpool and elsewhere, were interrupted in their loading, and interfered with, more or less, by the Customs authorities. Some of them were loading in part with contraband of war, and a portion of the shipments were on behalf of the Confederate Government. In none of those ships did the Confederate States have any interest whatever, except as shippers by them to Bermuda, the Bahamas, and Havana. One of them, the *Phantom*, became a blockade-runner, but she sailed from Liverpool in a perfectly legitimate way.

Some of the cases demonstrate very strongly the recklessness of the United States Consuls in their allegations, and the readiness with which

Earl Russell acted upon them. On March 24th, 1863, Thomas H. Dudley, the United States Consul at Liverpool, wrote Mr. Adams that "this vessel" (the *Southerner*) "came here yesterday either to load or to fit out as a privateer. There is no doubt about this vessel. I suppose it will be impossible for me to obtain legal evidence against these two vessels,* and nothing short of this will satisfy the Government."† Mr. Dudley never permitted himself to doubt, and generally indulged in a sneer at the British Government; but, notwithstanding his positive assertion, Mr. Adams, in forwarding the statement to Earl Russell on the 26th, was obliged to inform his lordship that Mr. Dudley was mistaken, and that the ship referred to had not yet reached Liverpool.‡ The *Southerner* was a large screw-steamer, built at Stockton-on-Tees for a passenger and freight trade. She was provided with all fittings necessary to handle her cargoes, and her saloons were arranged in every respect as a first-class passenger ship. No one fairly inspecting her could have supposed that she would have been fitted up in that style if the intention was to convert her into a "privateer," and her size and draft of water manifestly unsuited her for even blockade-running. Yet the British Foreign Office acted upon Mr. Dudley's allegations, and twenty-four pages of the "Appendix" (pp. 185–209) are occupied with a correspondence in respect to her between Mr. Adams, Earl Russell, the Treasury and Customs officials, the Town Clerk, the Mayor, and Head-Constable of Liverpool. Finally she was surveyed by Mr. T. Hobbs, Admiralty overseer, assisted by Mr. W. Byrne, Assistant Surveyor of Customs at Liverpool, and Mr. Hobbs reported to the Controller of the Navy on June 23rd, 1863, as follows:§

"She is fitted with top-gallant forecastle and poop-deck, with deck-houses continuous fore and aft with the same, in the same manner as the Inman line of screw-boats, now sailing between this port and New York. She is fitted aft under the poop-deck with accommodation for about sixty-six saloon passengers, etc.... I find that her topsides are of iron-plates, three-eighths of an inch thick, and in no way fitted or secured, as I consider, necessary for the working of guns.... I cannot find anything with regard to construction or fittings that would lead me to suppose that she was intended for belligerent purposes."

---

* *Phantom* and *Southerner.*
† "British Case," Appendix, vol. ii., p. 167.
‡ She arrived a few days after.
§ "British Case," Appendix, vol. ii., p. 206.

In consequence of the above report, the Head-Constable of Liverpool advised the Mayor that the officer especially appointed to watch the ship should be relieved, and on the 3rd of July Earl Russell reported the facts to Mr. Adams, and the ship was permitted to go about her business. It appears that she went on a voyage up the Mediterranean, in the course of which she touched at Algiers, from which port another American Consul, by the name of Edward L. Kingsbury, wrote to Mr. Dayton, the United States Minister at Paris, on October 2nd, 1863:

"I have the honour to inform you that, while absent from my post by special permission, I received information that 'the suspected pirate steam-ship *Southerner*' was at Malta, *en route* from Alexandria to Algiers."*

Mr. Kingsbury then gives a full description of the ship, her cargo, passengers, etc., which particulars he got from "a perfectly competent and reliable gentleman of my acquaintance at this place," and adds: "I am also informed that the British and United States flags are painted upon the partitions of the companion way, etc., the ship having been built, it is said, to run between Liverpool and Charleston."

The *Phantom* was detained and watched and written about in the same way. I have said that she became a blockade-runner, but she was wholly private property. The Confederate States never had any interest in her whatever. Mr. Thomas H. Dudley got a man by the name of Robert Thomas to swear that he knew me, and had seen me frequently giving directions about the *Phantom,* and especially on one occasion inspecting and giving orders about the screw, during a trial which occupied twenty minutes.† As a fact, I never was on board the *Phantom,* nor even alongside of her, in my life, and never heard of Mr. Robert Thomas until I saw his name at the bottom of the above affidavit, and I solemnly declare his statements to be false in every particular, so far as they relate to me. Mr. Dudley's affidavits always had a wonderful particularity in the details. He seemed to have been determined, as he had to pay for them, to get his money's worth.

Another one of the suspected craft was an old rickety fifty-gun ship called the *Amphion,* which had been sold out of one of her Majesty's dockyards "as old material," and yet the United States Consul at London succeeded in putting her purchasers to considerable trouble and expense with the Admiralty about her. One vessel—the *Hector*—turned out to be

---

* "British Case," Appendix, vol. ii., p. 209.
† Ibid., pp. 171, 172.

building for the British Admiralty; nevertheless, when she was launched Mr. Adams contrived to get up a correspondence with the Foreign Office and the Admiralty on the subject.*

It would be easy for me to give many more cases of interference with the loading and despatch of vessels from British ports during the war in deference to the suspicions of the United States Minister. Whenever an American Consul thought the Confederate Government had an interest in the cargo, or he felt the desire to show his animosity to a supposed friend or sympathizer with the South, he could always find some one to make the stereotyped affidavit, and the inquiry, interference and delay would almost invariably follow. There is no exaggeration in saying that there was much difficulty and trouble in making shipments by vessels of any description to Halifax, Bermuda, the Bahamas, Havana or Matamoras during the war, and the restrictions and necessary concealments added much to the labour and expense of forwarding supplies to the Confederate States. And yet it must be remembered that the trade, by the repeated declaration of her Majesty's Ministers, was perfectly legitimate, and they professed to enforce their neutrality with impartial fairness, or, rather, indifference to the interests of either belligerent.

I have stated, in the letter to the Secretary of the Confederate Navy quoted above, that the neutrality of England was practised in a way to give great advantages to the United States. While the restrictions placed upon all shipments which were made in vessels not loading for one of the northern ports amounted almost to a prohibition, I never heard of a single interruption to the trade in contraband with the United States, nor do I know of a single instance in which a vessel bound to that country was delayed a moment, or asked what was the destination of her cargo, or made to show whether the purpose was to arm her as a national cruiser, or privateer, after her departure.

The United States Minister at London gave certificates to British vessels loaded with arms and other contraband articles for Mexico during the French invasion of that country, when he had satisfactory proof that the arms were intended for the Mexican Government, but he refused certificates to others who applied to him without such proof. The former were protected from capture by United States ships, but the latter were in several cases captured on the high seas, and carried before the American prize-courts (*vide* the case of the *Peterhoff,* mentioned above).

* "British Case," Appendix, vol. ii., p. 143, etc.

In Hansard, vol. clxx., Session 1863 (2), p. 576, etc., there is a report of a debate in the House of Commons on the above subject (there were several debates). Mr. Roebuck, commenting upon one of the permits given by Mr. Adams says: "That permit is granted. Why? Because that ship carried out arms to the Mexicans, to be used against our ally, France." In another case he says: "The permit was refused; and now I must say that Mr. Adams, the American Minister, is the Minister for Commerce in England."

In the same debate another member, Mr. Peacocke, gave a very graphic and circumstantial account of the manner in which the giving of the permits came about. He said: "The Mexican Government ordered supplies of arms in the United States. The Government of the United States, however, arrested the vessel which was to carry these arms. The Mexican Government, as well it might, remonstrated; whereupon Mr. Seward informed the Mexican Minister that he did not wish to deprive him of a supply of arms to carry on the war against France, but the United States wanted those arms themselves. 'If, however,' added Mr. Seward, 'you will send over to England and get arms, we will give you every facility in our power.' " Mr. Peacocke then explained that the Mexican officer charged with the purchase of the arms came over to England, provided with a letter to Mr. Adams, requesting that Minister to give him every assistance in his power, in order to obtain arms to help the Mexicans in their war with France. "It was under these circumstances," adds Mr. Peacocke, "and not from any individual action taken on his own responsibility, that Mr. Adams furnished the pass." This, it must be admitted, was permitting a very unusual power to the United States Minister, and the exercise of a very comprehensive belligerent right.

But in demonstration of the favour and privileges granted to the United States, as compared with the watchful restrictions imposed upon the Confederate agents, it is not necessary for me to go beyond the unlimited freedom to get and to ship whatever they wanted for their own use which the United States enjoyed during the whole war. I will confine my statement to the official returns, as printed in the British Counter-case, p. 54, etc. It appears that in May, 1862, Mr. Adams, in compliance with instructions from Mr. Seward, pressed on Lord Russell, in conversation, the expediency of revoking the recognition of the belligerent status of the Confederate Government, and mentioned, in connection with this subject, the irritation produced in the United States by the reports of supplies furnished by private persons in England to the Confederates. Lord Russell, in his reply, said "that large supplies of similar materials had been obtained in England on the part of the United States, which had been freely transported and used against the 'insurgents.' "* Mr. Adams admitted that at one time a quantity of arms and military stores had been purchased in England "as a purely commercial transaction," for the use of the Federal army; but said that he had early objected to the practice, for the reason that it prevented him from pressing his remonstrances against a very different class of operations carried on by friends and sympathizers with the "rebels" in England, and it had been discontinued. Mr. Adams added that "we" (the United States) "had, indeed, purchased largely in Austria, but that Government had never given any countenance to the insurgents." Mr. Adams, courteous as he generally was, could not, it appears, refrain from having his fling at Lord Russell on this occasion. He would have no more arms bought in England "as a purely commercial transaction," because so many people sympathized with the "rebels" in that free country; he would go to autocratic Austria, where there was no sympathy with "insurgents."

But Mr. Adams was mistaken in the statement that purchases in England for the United States army had been discontinued. Messrs. Naylor, Vickers and Co., of New York, Liverpool, and London, bought and shipped large quantities of small arms to the United States. They were supplied from Birmingham alone with 156,000 rifles between June, 1862, and July, 1863. They acted very extensively as agents for the United States Government. The Assistant Secretary of War at Washington, in a letter addressed to them on the 20th of October, 1862, sanctioned an arrangement for the supply of 100,000 rifles, and the acceptance of this order was duly notified to the Secretary of War by a letter from Birmingham, dated November 4th, 1862. The arms were sent to Liverpool for shipment. In December, 1863, *fifty 68-pounder guns were proved at the Royal Arsenal at Woolwich,* at the request of Messrs. T. and C. Hood, and after proof they were taken away by Messrs. Naylor, Vickers and Co. and shipped to New York. There were other large purchases on behalf of the United States.

The general results of these operations may be traced in the official returns of exports from Great Britain to the northern ports of the United States, published by the Board of Trade. These show that, whereas the average yearly export of small arms to those ports for the years 1858, 1859, 1860, were 18,329; it rose in 1861 to 44,904, in 1862 to 343,304, and

---

* Mr. Adams to Mr. Seward, reporting the conversation with Lord Russell; the word "insurgents" is Mr. Adams's, not Lord Russell's, who never speaks of the Confederates in that character.

amounted in 1863 to 124,928. These are the recorded shipments of small arms; but there is reason to believe that other shipments, to a considerable extent, were made under the denomination of hardware. Of percussion caps, the average export in the years 1858, 1859, and 1860 was 55,620,000; in 1863 it rose to 171,427,000, and in 1864 was 102,587,000. Of cannon and other ordnance the exports in the year 1862 alone were valued at £82,920, while the aggregate value of the exports for the other nine years, from 1858 to 1861, and from 1863 to 1867, was but £3,336. The exports of salt-petre for the years 1858 to 1861 had averaged 248 tons yearly. The pur-chases for the United States Government raised the amount to 3,189 tons for the year 1862 alone. The amount of lead shipped, which had averaged 2,810 tons yearly, rose in 1862 and 1864 to 13,148 and 11,786 tons respec-tively. I might give further statistics in reference to military clothing and other supplies, but the foregoing is sufficient to show the enormous quan-tity of articles contraband of war which were bought by the United States in England during the war, and then shipped, chiefly from Liverpool, without let or hindrance, interference, vexatious inquiry, or delay, on the part of any local authority, and I wish particularly to call attention to the fifty 68-pounders proved at the Royal Arsenal at Woolwich and then shipped to New York.

The State Department at Washington, and the Consuls who received their inspiration from its chief, indulged often in what Lord Russell called "figures of rhetoric" when addressing her Majesty's Government on sub-jects appertaining to the war. The compilers of the "Case" presented to the Tribunal of Arbitration at Geneva on behalf of the United States, ap-pear to have drunk deeply from the same fountain. It is stated by them, as a complaint, that England was "the arsenal, the navy-yard, and the trea-sury of the insurgents." There is no doubt that the Confederate Gov-ernment bought supplies of all kinds in England, and that money was provided to pay for them, and persons were employed to purchase, for-ward, and ship them; but the quantity of articles bought and money ex-pended must have been, I was almost going to say insignificant—at any rate it was small—in comparison with the operations of the United States.

I have read nearly the whole "Case of the United States," and do not find it asserted that the rifles, cannon, saltpetre, etc., mentioned above, found their way to New York without any purchasing or financial agents to transact the business. It is probable that many agents were employed in such large transactions, and therefore branches of the War, Navy, and Treasury Departments of the United States were to be found in England, in the same sense that those departments of the Confederate Government were represented there. However, we are not left in doubt on this point. From the documents laid before the Tribunal of Arbitration, we learn that the United States engaged large warehouses at Birmingham for the reception of arms when completed, after which they were shipped through the agency of Messrs. Barings and Messrs. Brown, Shipley and Co.,* and we have already seen that they had guns proved at Woolwich. There also appears in the British Appendix, vol. vi., p. 154, a letter from the Secretary of War at Washington to one of his agents—a Mr. Schuyler—in which he says: "You will please express my acknowledgments to Messrs. Baring Brothers and Co. for their prompt and patriotic action in facilitating your operations. The terms offered by Messrs. Baring Brothers and Co., namely one per cent. commission, and five per cent. interest per annum, as agreed upon by them with the Navy Department, are approved."

Messrs. Baring Brothers and Co. are a very eminent banking firm, as all the world knows. Their financial arrangements with the War and Navy Departments of the United States were no doubt in strict conformity with neutral duties—at least, that may be inferred from the statements of Earl Russell, for in a letter to Mr. Adams already quoted above, he said: "Her Majesty's Government cannot interfere with commercial dealings between British subjects and the so-styled Confederate States, whether the object of those dealings be money, or contraband goods, or even ships adapted for warlike purposes." The Confederate agents have advanced this declaration of her Majesty's Secretary of State for Foreign Affairs as a complete justification for all their dealings with British subjects, and they do not deny that it can and should be applied to the agencies of the United States with equal pertinence and comprehensiveness. But there is a special difference between the financial operations of the two belligerents in England in this particular, that while the Confederate Government dealt with private merchants and tradesmen exclusively, who were not bound by any specific undertaking to investigate the spirit and letter of the neutrality laws, but might fairly and conscientiously deal in money, contraband goods, or ships "as purely mercantile transactions," the United States had their Treasury Department in England at the office of bankers whose leading partner was a member of Parliament, who was bound by his oath, as well as by the ordinary precepts of loyalty, to follow with scrupulous nicety the spirit as well as the letter of the law, and to set an example of strict and impartial compliance with her Majesty's Proclamation of Neutrality.

* "British Counter-Case," p. 53.

Mr. T. Baring's name appears in Hansard* as a warm advocate of the North in the debates on the *Alabama* question, and he urged the Government to give the United States some assurance that they would prevent the Confederates obtaining ships in England, which he said might be the cause of a war between Great Britain and the aggrieved Republic across the water. Now, the Government of the United States invariably denounced the shipbuilders, the tradesmen, the financiers, who in the ordinary and legitimate course of their business had commercial dealings with the Confederate Government. They charged them with disloyalty, with violating the neutrality of their country, and endangering its peace, and often added epithets and insinuations which were personal and offensive. Did Mr. Seward and his Secretary of War really think that the house of Baring Brothers, with its Parliamentary member, could lend them money to buy guns, and rifles, and saltpetre—could forward the goods for them and perform such other services in "facilitating the operations" of their agents as to earn the highest commendation they could bestow, and yet be wholly free from a like criminality with those who were only doing the same things in kind, but hardly in degree, for the Confederates? I suppose the use of the word *"patriotic"* in the commendatory letter of the United States Secretary of War in reference to Messrs. Baring must have been a slip of the pen. It is one of those infelicitous and inappropriate expressions which sometimes creep into hastily written documents, or escape from an over-fluent orator. A member of the British House of Commons is quite free to advocate any cause which appeals to his sympathies, and whose principles coincide with his convictions; but when the great commercial firm to which he belongs embarks in a large financial operation with a foreign belligerent, however ably, faithfully, and energetically he may serve the interests of his clients, we must look for some other word to describe his conduct than that expression which can only be fitly used in reference to services rendered from *amor patriæ*.

I most earnestly and emphatically disclaim the slightest wish or purpose to reflect in any way upon the house of Messrs. Baring Brothers, or to intimate that the member of the firm who sat in the House of Commons committed any fault. I have mentioned their name, and commented upon their transactions with the United States, historically. The facts are recorded in the diplomatic correspondence, and in the proceedings in the Geneva Arbitration, and I have used them, together with other statements mentioned above, to illustrate the relative attitudes of the two belligerents

* See especially vol. clxx., 1863 (2), p. 59.

in respect to the neutrality of Great Britain, and to demonstrate that if England was the "arsenal and treasury" of the Confederate Government, as has been alleged, the same may be said in a stricter as well as in a still more comprehensive sense with reference to the United States, whose War Offices were so completely and definitely established that they had warehouses for the storing of arms and the use of public arsenals for proving guns, and whose Treasury may be said to have been represented in the British House of Commons.

In a debate on the Foreign Enlistment Act, March 27th, 1863, Lord Palmerston,[*] commenting upon the allegation that the Government had failed to detain vessels supposed to be intended for the Confederate States upon reasonable suspicion, said, "Is it not fair for us to say that so far as suspicions go, we have been informed—perhaps erroneously—that not only have arms been despatched to the Northern ports of the United States, but that efforts have been made, in Ireland especially, to enlist persons to serve in the Federal army and navy? Unquestionably a great many cases have occurred in North America in which British subjects have been seized and attempts made to compel them to serve against their will in the Civil War."

I have already mentioned two cases in which the suspicions caused interference with two vessels alleged to be taking recruits from Liverpool for the United States army, but I have not been able to discover a single instance of interference with a vessel loading with arms and other war supplies for the United States, and I can find no record of a single ship being detained an hour to give account of her cargo, or her destination, if she was clearing out for a Northern port, and was duly certified by the local United States Consul. It was very different with ships of any description loading for a British colony, for Cuba or for Mexico. The mere allegation of an American Consul that he had reason to believe that she was intended for a Confederate cruiser was sufficient to cause immediate investigation, often complete stoppage of the work during the inquiry, and in many instances a complete prevention of the voyage. Sometimes the complaints of the United States were couched in such exaggerated terms,[†] and they put forward such astounding claims against Great Britain for the depredations of Confederate cruisers, that Lord Russell ventured upon a

---

[*] Hansard, vol. clxx., 1863 (2), p. 93.

[†] See letter of Mr. Adams to Earl Russell, dated October 23rd, 1863, "North America," (no. 1), 1864, Parliamentary Blue Book, p. 26.

retort, as, for example, October 26th, 1863,* he tells Mr. Adams that if her Majesty's Government were to apply the principle of interfering with the trade of shipbuilding as broadly as the United States wished, a source of honest livelihood to great numbers of British subjects would be seriously embarrassed and impeded; and he then remarks: "I may add that it appears strange that, notwithstanding the large and powerful naval force possessed by the Government of the United States, no efficient measures have been taken by that Government to capture the *Alabama*."

I do not propose to discuss the conduct of her Majesty's Government towards the Confederate States during the Civil War with reference either to international law or comity. The result of the war has been to obliterate the political status of those States as a separate and *de facto* Power, and no one is now competent to argue such questions on their behalf with any practical purpose. Nevertheless, it will always remain a subject of interest to the five or six million people of the Southern States and their posterity, and it will always be an embarrassing problem for them to determine the reasons why the British Ministry of 1861–65 acted towards the Confederate States in a manner so inconsistent with their own interpretation of the Foreign Enlistment Act, confirmed as that interpretation was by the unreversed judgment of a court of law. "There is no difference in principle between supplying a belligerent with muskets, cannon, and ammunition, or with ships that are to operate in war." "Her Majesty's Government cannot interfere with commercial dealings between British subjects and the so-styled Confederate States, whether the object of those dealings be money, or contraband goods, or even ships adapted for warlike purposes." "The *Alabama* might have been legitimately built by a foreign Government, and though a ship-of-war, she might have formed a legitimate article of merchandise, even if meant for the Confederate States." "An English shipbuilder may build any kind of ship to a commercial order, or merely in compliance with a contract; and the purchaser may make what use of her afterwards he sees fit." These are the official declarations of the two principal members of the Ministry which governed England during the American Civil War, of the Solicitor-General under the same Government, and the unreversed judgment of the Lord Chief Baron of the Exchequer.

I think anyone who fairly and impartially examines the facts connected with the seizure of ships alleged to have been bought or built for the

* Reply to Mr. Adams's letter above, p. 42, no. 19.

Confederate Government, and the repeated detention of vessels, and interference with their loading, when it was supposed that their cargoes were ultimately intended for a Southern port, will admit that the Foreign Enlistment Act was not administered in accordance with the above declarations and judgment, so far as the Confederate States were concerned; and that the neutrality of Great Britain was practised in such a manner as greatly to embarrass and hinder the efforts of that belligerent who most needed what she could supply, and which the said belligerent was desirous to buy in a fair way of trade.

When the American colonies rebelled against the British Crown, they obtained substantial aid from France, before the Government of Louis XVI. became a party to the war. When the Spanish American provinces revolted from Spain, England and the United States did not preserve a very rigorous neutrality, but permitted the struggling colonists to get much help in men and ships. When Greece was labouring for her freedom, almost the whole Christian world sent her succour of some sort. When Queen Isabella was battling for her crown against Don Carlos, the English Foreign Enlistment Act was suspended to permit a British general, with a British legion, to fight in her behalf. When the conflicting claims of Doña Maria and Don Miguel had kindled the fires of Civil War in Portugal, a British admiral was permitted to command the naval forces of one of the parties and to retain his commission in the British navy. When Pope Pio Nono was fighting for his temporalities, he had his Irish battalion and his foreign legion, recruited without much difficulty among the Catholic States. When the Italian people were expelling King Bomba and the reigning dukes, the chief combatants on the popular side were Garibaldi's volunteers, including many foreigners and "Garibaldi's Englishman" among them. When Servia was striving to free herself from the suzerainty of Turkey, a Russian general commanded her active army in the field, and volunteers from neutral Russia filled her ranks. Even in the Franco-Prussian War of 1870, Garibaldi, the restless Revolutionist, broke up his hermitage at Caprera, and brought a band of men in the traditional red shirt to fight for France.

The list is not exhausted. Memory furnishes me with no record of a struggle for freedom, or between two great contending factions of the same people, or of a weaker state striving to maintain itself against the aggression of a stronger, in which the merits of the contest, the gallantry of the weaker side, or the common human instincts which have impelled men in all past time to help those who appeared to need help, did not bring the required succour in some practical form. The South alone, so far as I know, was left to fight her arduous and prolonged battle with no foreign aid, and with but a grudging allowance of the necessities she was able to pay for. A few gallant, sympathetic men like Prince Polignac and Heros von Borke brought their stout hearts to her aid; but the men who followed Lee and Beauregard, Stonewall Jackson, Longstreet, and other Confederate chiefs, were the sons of the soil, and a few English and Irish, and still fewer Germans, who from long residence had come to love the country and its people and were practically Southerners.

I cannot call to mind—I believe there never has been—a great war, fought against such odds, not in men alone, but in every element of military power, in which the weaker side has persevered so long and endured so patiently, and then after defeat has murmured so little and set so manfully to work to retrieve its losses.

I wish to draw no comparisons between the combatants, and I know too much of both North and South to doubt that there are thousands of brave, earnest, true, and loyal men in each and every section of the Union. Many thousands of gallant men went from every Northern State to the battlefields of the South, and sacrificed their lives, honestly believing that the national life was bound up in the Union of the States, and that they must fight to maintain that Union. There were hundreds of men in the armies of the United States, subalterns and field-officers of regiments, brigade and division commanders, who filled their offices not only with admirable courage, but with all the dash, judgment, and tactical skill that their positions required; but taking a comprehensive view of the war at this distance of time, with temper cool and judgment free from bias, I am of the opinion that the United States did not find the man—he might have been there—I only say that they did not find the man for a chief-commander, who displayed more than average ability as a military strategist.

Sadowa was won, and the Austro-Prussian War was ended in a campaign of about seven weeks, by the superior skill of the Prussian Chief-of-Staff. France was crushed, two of her great armies capitulated, one in the field, one from the shelter of a strongly fortified position. The whole of her eastern and northern provinces were overrun, and her capital was occupied by a German *corps d'armée*, after little more than a year's fighting. No one believes that the Austrians are wanting in courage, or in high military qualities; and French troops have marched as victors over nearly the whole of Continental Europe. Facts now known have proved that Prussia in 1866 was better prepared for active war than Austria, and the German armies were doubtless more efficiently organized in 1870 than those of France. But looking at the relative military strength of these three Powers, their population, wealth, war material in possession, and ability to keep up the supply, it must be admitted that the difference, if any, was not sufficient to account in any way for the quickness and thoroughness of the results, and we must look to the genius of Von Moltke for the explanation.

The South was almost wholly destitute of war material, and could supply herself only by driblets, and at very great cost. Almost from the start she was isolated by blockade from communication with the countries from which she might have drawn supplies. She had no natural lines of defence, but was open to invasion along a frontier of many hundreds of miles. Rivers, sounds, and inlets, which she had no naval force to defend, afforded access to her very heart. Her means of inland communication were hardly more than equal to the requirements of ordinary passenger and goods traffic, and proved wholly insufficient for war transport. The difficulty of arming the troops in the field was so great that they never were supplied with a uniform weapon, and powder was so scarce and difficult to obtain, that it was found necessary to form artificial nitre beds for its manufacture, and some of them were not "ripe" for use at the end of the war. The difficulty of transportation was so great that it was impossible to get supplies to the front, and the troops in the field were often on poor and insufficient rations. The medical staff was so deficient in all kinds of necessaries for the comfort and treatment of the sick and wounded, that many men died from sheer want of them, and thousands were unshod and without greatcoats, even in winter. When all these drawbacks and deficiencies are considered, there still remains the important item of numbers, and I think it is only a fair estimate to say that the actual fighting population of the South, that is to say, the number of males capable of bearing arms, was not more than one-fifth of those of the same class in the States which adhered to the Union. Thus over-matched, the South resisted for four years, and some of the most desperate combats of the war were fought during the advance upon Richmond, and along the lines between the James River and Petersburg, during the last months of the struggle, when she was well-nigh exhausted—when, as General Grant is reported to have said, she had "robbed the cradle and the grave" to supply her armies in the field.

It appears to me that the South could not have held out so long if the opposing power had been wielded with a superior military skill. But I have no wish to pursue this topic further. The military historian of the future will duly consider all these facts, and the generals who figured in the great Civil War will be placed in their relative positions, without reference to the adulations which partial friendship, or partizan bias, may have heaped upon them in the years just passed.

The Southern people know that many persons in England sympathized with them, and that their cause was not without able and eloquent advocates in both Houses of the British Parliament. It was very generally thought that at least two members of the Cabinet were also very favourably inclined towards the South, but that prudential and other reasons, and the belief that the rupture was final, induced the Cabinet, as a whole, to decline committing the Government to an open recognition of the Confederate States.

The action of the Ministers, I think, demonstrated clearly that they were agitated by unsettled views; they vacillated and did not act up to their own declarations; they did and said things which deceived both sides—which excited hopes at the South, and caused irritation at the North; and this wavering policy ended at last in the payment of £3,000,000 to the United States, for alleged offences which Lord Russell had often repudiated, and for not restraining the Confederates from doing in England what he more than once declared he neither could nor would prevent. Perhaps now that the war is over, the States reunited, and the people of the two sections are drawing near to each other in sympathy, and in the bonds of common interests, it is well that the South has no debt of gratitude to pay, and that the North is finding out that she has no real grudge to nurse against England. These great political convulsions follow the inscrutable laws of Providence, and when the main issues and the grand results are controlled by a Power we cannot resist, and dare not question, it is hardly worth while to perplex our minds, and to vex our souls by snarling at each other over the paltry details.

It is necessary, perhaps, to state that the Foreign Enlistment Act referred to in this narrative is the Act of 1818, and all the remarks upon the neutrality laws of Great Britain, and the registry and clearance of vessels, have reference to the condition of the law during the years 1861–65, when the alleged offences of the Confederates were committed. Since then (1867) the law in respect to the clearance of vessels has been changed, and in consequence of the report of the Neutrality Commission, a new and very stringent "Foreign Enlistment Act" was passed in 1870. The statute as it now stands will prove very vexatious to the shipbuilding trade whenever England is again a neutral during a great war. It seems to me that the ship-building trade will then be at the mercy of the Consuls of the contending parties.

CHAPTER VII

—

An explanation of the Foreign Enlistment Act, and the manner in which it was made applicable to the operations of the Confederate agents in England appeared to be a necessary part of the history of those operations; and the account of the "*Alexandra* Case," which furnished a practical exposition of the statute, has again carried the narrative far in advance of the due course of events.

The chief purpose of the Confederate Government in sending me to Europe was at first to get ships afloat capable of keeping the sea as long as possible, and otherwise fitted to cruise and destroy the enemy's commerce; and my original instructions were to put six suitable vessels in commission with all reasonable despatch. Insufficiency of money, and the pressing wants of the Navy Department in other respects, compelled me to limit the number to the two whose despatch from England has already been described; and it soon became manifest that they were enough to drive the American commercial flag away from the principal routes of trade. But the designs of the Government assumed a broader range after my departure from Montgomery, and the reality and magnitude of the war in which the country was involved had become apparent.

By the time of my return to the Confederacy in the *Fingal* (November, 1861), the battles of Bull Run and Leesburgh had been fought; there had been some active campaigning in Western Virginia; Port Royal and the chief inlets of the great North Carolina Sounds had been occupied by the United States forces; and a blockade of the southern coast from the Chesapeake to the Mississippi, and even beyond as far west on the gulf-shore as Sabine Pass, had been proclaimed. The coast was too long for the number of ships then on the United States navy-list to guard effectively; but Europe, and indeed all the neutral states, were satisfied with the assurance that a sufficient force would soon be placed off the ports and chief inlets to justify the distinction between a genuine and a paper blockade, and they had acknowledged the state of war and the legitimate consequences appertaining to that condition.

The Confederate Government had also removed to Richmond, the several Executive Departments had been more completely organized, and there was a general conviction among the higher and more experienced officials that the contest would be fierce, and probably long. Winter weather had set in. Active campaigning had ceased along the northern frontier of Virginia. The two combatants were warily watching each other, and each was preparing to renew hostilities on a large scale. The United States were organizing a great army on the Potomac, for an effective, and they hoped a crushing, advance upon Richmond in the early spring of 1862. The Confederate Government was straining every nerve to equip the forces necessary to repel the threatened invasion, and to occupy the many weak points along the extended line of land frontier and sea coast.

Although the enemy's naval strength had enabled him to occupy with but little resistance a number of important points, such as Port Royal, Roanoke Inlet, etc., and to place there, under cover of his ships, military forces which proved to be a constant and embarrassing menace, yet on the whole the balance of success up to that time was in favour of the Confederates. The advance upon Richmond by way of Bull Run had certainly been the largest and most important operation of the war at the close of 1861, and the invading army had been so thoroughly beaten at that now historic creek, that the remnant fled into Washington without organization or cohesiveness, a mere flying rabble. General McDowell's army at Bull Run was a larger and more efficient force in every respect than the hastily gathered and ill-armed volunteers under Beauregard and Johnston, and I believe it is generally admitted that his dispositions were judicious, and that his plan of advance and attack was skilfully and energetically executed, so far as his own efforts and those of his staff were concerned. According to all sound rules of calculation, he ought to have won the battle in spite of the unquestioned gallantry and stubborn hardihood of the Southern troops. The sudden panic which seized the Federal army, and which drove whole brigades into confusion, and then precipitated them into a headlong rout of unparalleled confusion and dismay, is simply a fact in the history of the war which I shall not attempt to explain. I saw the effect in the feeling of hopeful confidence which the event had inspired among the Southern people, and yet it was manifest that the higher authorities at Richmond were not possessed by any vain expectation that another Federal army would run away, or that the Confederate States would win their independence, except by hard fighting and patient endurance.

The War Department was steadily and systematically collecting material, and massing troops. The Navy Department was striving to build and equip vessels at several coast places, and on some inland waters, for harbour and river defence, and had begun to entertain hopes of doing something more abroad than to commission ships to cruise against the enemy's commerce. The Treasury Department was hard at work upon the finances, devising means of converting the great staples which remained in the country into money, or discussing how they might be used as the basis of credit in Europe to meet the wants of the two fighting departments of the Government.

I have already (Chapter III.) given some account of the views and purposes of the Navy Department at the time above referred to, and of the especial duties assigned me. In the subsequent course of the narrative the change in respect to my own services and employment has been necessarily mentioned, and now I must further relate a still more important advance in the purposes of the Confederate Government with respect to naval operations against the enemy.

It will be remembered that on my arrival at Savannah with the *Fingal* in November, 1861, I was immediately ordered to Richmond for consultation with the Navy Department. Among the many matters discussed was the subject of ironclad vessels, and the Secretary of the Navy (Hon. S. R. Mallory) was much impressed with the importance of getting vessels of that description to match the enemy's "Monitors," and to open and protect the blockaded ports. He told me that he had sent Lieutenant James A. North to England to inquire into the construction of such vessels, but had not yet heard from him.

Mr. Mallory's earnest desire was to find the money to build, and to decide upon the best type of armoured vessels for operations on the coast. It was impossible to build them in the Confederate States—neither the materials nor the mechanics were there; and besides, even if iron and skilled artizans had been within reach, there was not a mill in the country to roll the plates, nor furnaces and machinery to forge them, nor shops to make the engines.

I gave all the information I then had on the subject, and Mr. Mallory directed me to make further and more especial inquiries as soon as I got back to England, but nothing definite was decided when I left Richmond. Just before leaving Savannah *en route* for Wilmington, to run the blockade of that port, I received specific instructions on the subject in a letter from the Navy Department, of which the following is a copy:—

> "Navy Department,
> "Richmond, *January* 14*th*, 1862.
>
> "Sir,—
>
> "I desire more particularly to direct your attention to the subject of constructing iron or steel clad ships in France or England than was done in my letter of the 11th inst. Lieutenant North has had this matter in charge, but has not yet been able to do anything with it. I earnestly desire to have an armoured steam-sloop of moderate size, say of about 2,000 tons, and to carry eight or ten heavy guns, built in England upon the most approved plan and in the shortest time, and the evident change of feeling and opinion in England in relation to our country induces me to believe that we may now contract for the construction and delivery of such a vessel."

Then follow some general comments upon the *Gloire, Warrior,* and *Black Prince:*

> "Many plans of such a vessel have been submitted, and herewith I send you the drawings, without specifications of the one devised by Naval-Constructor Porter and Chief-Engineer Williamson.... I submit this plan for your information only; but so anxious am I to have an ironclad ship built, that should you and Lieutenant North, with whom I associate you in this matter, be able to contract, or to make the preparatory arrangements to contract, for an armoured, either steel or iron clad, ship, you will proceed with despatch to

prescribe the character of the vessel, and I will place the funds in England at once....

"I am, etc.,
"S. R. MALLORY.
"Secretary of the Navy.

"Captain James D. Bulloch,
"Savannah, Georgia."

Anyone who cares to refer to the leading newspaper articles, and who remembers the general tone of public sentiment in England at about the date of the above letter, will, I think, admit that there was a very apparent tendency of opinion towards a feeling of sympathy with the Confederate cause, and that the Government at Richmond had reason at that time to expect, if not formal recognition, at least that degree of passive encouragement which would enable their agents to obtain all necessary supplies without further restraint than was sufficient to maintain a fair impartial neutrality.

I arrived in Liverpool on the 10th of March, and began at once to examine into the question of ironclads, which the Secretary of the Navy had so much at heart. On the 21st of March I advised him that I was in full treaty with competent builders, and hoped to be able to send a detailed report, with plans, etc., in a very short time. I soon perceived, however, by the strict watch upon the *Florida,* which I was then trying to despatch from Liverpool, and from the espionage upon the *Alabama,* and other signs, that the Foreign Enlistment Act would be most rigorously enforced in respect to all undertakings on behalf of the Confederate Government, and in a despatch dated April 11th, 1862, I reported my fears on the subject, and ventured to ask whether it would not be well to concentrate all the resources of the Navy Department for the defence of the home ports, and I then added:—

"I find that several parties would contract for any description of ship, but, as I have before remarked, an ironclad sea-going ship must be large, and would require at least a year to complete after the order was received on this side. I would therefore respectfully suggest that wooden vessels be laid down at once at the various ports in the Confederacy, where timber is abundant, then, by sending over scale drawings, or working plans, of their decks and sides, the iron plates, rivets, bolts, etc., could be made here, marked, and shipped to arrive as soon as the vessels would be ready to receive them."

Later in the war, vessels were built in the Confederate States—at least they were begun—and engines were sent from England for them; but my suggestion did not promptly reach the Navy Department, and at the beginning the Government was impressed with the feeling that the arrogant tone of Mr. Seward's despatches to the United States Ministers abroad, and the excessive harshness with which the right of search and of capture was practised by the United States cruisers upon neutral vessels, would either create active opposition, and perhaps interference with the blockade, or would so irritate the Maritime Powers that they would not be over-strict in pressing their neutrality laws. Hence it was thought advisable to begin a few ironclad vessels at once.

At any rate, it was my duty to carry out the views of the Executive Government, and I pushed on with all possible arrangements, so as to be ready to act promptly as soon as definite instructions were received. Communication by letter with the Confederate States was generally slow, as our mails had to go to Bermuda and Nassau, and thence wait the departure of a blockade-runner which the Government agent would be willing to trust. Sometimes, however, we sent cypher despatches through Baltimore, and got very quick replies; but this could only be done under great reserve, and for very special purposes. On the 10th of June, 1862, I received a long despatch from the Navy Department, treating of general matters. It was dated April 30th, and so had been forty-one days coming. That letter contained specific instructions to begin at least two ironclad vessels, and I replied by the first returning mail for Bermuda, *viâ* Halifax.

The following extract from my despatch relates to the above-mentioned instructions:

"Finding, on my arrival in England in March, 1862, that Lieutenant North had, as he informed me, specific orders to buy or build a frigate, and that he had already made arrangements to contract for such a vessel as soon as the necessary funds arrived, I devoted myself primarily to the especial duties assigned me; but as vessels (ironclad) capable of acting efficiently either in the attack or defence of our coast must necessarily be of light draught, I put myself in communication with eminent iron-shipbuilders, whose position enabled them to obtain the official reports of all experiments, with the view of determining the minimum draft compatible with seaworthiness. It resulted, from a close calculation of weights and form of model, that by using turrets instead of broadside batteries, whereby the sides would be relieved from much strain and the heavy weights be thrown over the centre, a vessel might be built of about the following dimensions: length, 230 feet; beam, extreme, 42 feet; draft, with crew and stores for three months, 15 feet; engines, 350-horse-power nominal; speed, 10½ knots; tonnage, 1,850.

"I immediately directed the plans and scale-drawings of such a ship to be made, and reported to you by letter that I would forward them as soon as they were ready and an opportunity offered. While this was going on— I think about the middle of May—Lieutenant North received a remittance of $150,000, unaccompanied by any letter of advice, as I was informed; and supposing it to be for the uses mentioned in his original instructions, he prepared at once to close up a contract for an armoured frigate, and notified me of the fact.

"I advised him that a ship of less size, cost, and draft could be built; but he deemed his orders specific and peremptory as to class of ship, and contracted for a frigate of 3,200 tons accordingly. About the 10th of June I received your letter of April 30th, in which you say: 'I write to Commander Semmes to take command of the largest of the two vessels built by you, and I write also to Lieutenant North to take command of the other vessel'; and you direct me to furnish those officers with funds for cruising expenses. As to myself you say: 'I hasten to urge upon you the necessity of having at least two armoured vessels built and equipped at the earliest possible moment.' 'Act upon your own judgment, to save time. British inquiry and experiments, and your own knowledge of the bars and waters of our country, will enable you to act advisedly.'

"To render these instructions possible of fulfilment, you inform me that one million of dollars has already been placed to my credit with Messrs. Fraser, Trenholm and Co., and that you hope to increase the amount to two millions very soon.

"Fortunately, I was in a position to act promptly upon those instructions. The drawings and plans ordered were nearly finished, and on the day after the receipt of your letter I requested the parties who had been assisting me all along to make a tender for the contract, having previously provided myself with estimates from other builders who competed for Admiralty contracts. In a few days the price was agreed upon, and I gave a verbal order for two vessels, so that no time should be lost in contracting for the large quantity of armour plates required. By giving the order for both vessels to the same builders I got a reduction of £1,250 on the cost of each, and by adopting the same size and model of ship, and a like form of engines, they can both be completed in very nearly the same time. Besides this, experience has taught me that it is far safer to keep our business as little extended as possible, as otherwise the chance of our transactions being ferreted out by the Federal spies, who abound even in this country, is greatly increased.

"For full description of these vessels, I beg to refer you to the drawings.... A clause in the contract gives me the right to modify or alter them in certain particulars, as experience, during the progress of the work, may suggest."

Here follows a minute description of the peculiar construction and rig of the ships.

"The first of these ships will be ready for sea in March, 1863, and the second in May. Cost of each, fully equipped, except magazines and battery, £93,750."

I added that the contracting parties had shown great confidence in me by taking this large contract upon my assurance that the money would be forthcoming, and I hoped that the remittances would be forwarded so as to ensure prompt payment of the several instalments as they fell due. The builders with whom I contracted for the above ships were Messrs. Laird Brothers, of Birkenhead, and the whole of the arrangements were made in the same way as those for the building of the *Alabama*. They treated with me as a private individual, and the contract was a purely "commercial transaction," the agreement being that they should build and deliver the two vessels to me in the port of Liverpool, finished according to the stipulated specifications, but furnished only with such fittings and outfit as were required for an ordinary sea-voyage. In order to avoid every possible appearance of an intent to arm them within British jurisdiction, it was arranged that no magazines were to be placed in either ship, nor any special places for stowing shells and ordnance stores.

I have stated very confidently that at the time of contracting for the *Alabama* the Messrs. Laird knew nothing of my connection with the Confederate Government, but at the date when the contracts for the two armoured vessels were concluded, the *Florida* had already left Liverpool and the *Alabama* was nearly ready to start. My name had been often mentioned in the United States Consul's affidavits as an agent of the Confederate Navy Department, and they (the Messrs. Laird) had no doubt been informed of those affidavits, and knew therefore as much, but no more, than anyone else whose attention had been attracted to the two handsome-looking and handy vessels which were alleged to be the property of one of the belligerents across the sea.

I wish to make no mystery of these proceedings, nor to set up a pretence that the Messrs. Laird did not believe that the two formidable vessels they were about to build would ultimately find their way to a Confederate port; all that I affirm is that they never heard from me that I was not building the vessels for my own personal account, and throughout the whole of the transactions nothing was said by them as to the intent. They undertook "to build the two ships in obedience to an order, and in compliance with a contract, leaving it to those who bought them to make what use they thought fit of them," a transaction which, it must be remembered, was subsequently pronounced by the Lord Chief Baron of the Exchequer to be perfectly legitimate.

Before closing the contracts with the Messrs. Laird, I had of course considered and discussed with my solicitor whether armour-plating a ship could be considered "equipment" within the meaning of the Foreign Enlistment Act. He went carefully over the opinions given by counsel with reference to the *Alabama,* and said that the statute did not forbid the building of any description of ship, that the prohibitory clauses referred to the arming or furnishing a vessel with ammunition and ordnance stores for warlike purposes. I afterwards learned that Messrs. Laird took counsel's opinion also before undertaking to build the ships, and they were informed that there was nothing illegal in the proposed transaction. It will be perceived that every possible effort was made to get at the meaning and application of the Foreign Enlistment Act, so that there might be no intentional or heedless violation of the municipal law, and no reckless indifference to the Queen's neutrality.

The judgment of the court in the case of the *Alexandra* was not rendered until April, 1863, and the explicit declarations of Lord Palmerston, Earl Russell, and the Solicitor-General (Sir Roundell Palmer) were not made until March, 1863; but it was shown in the preceding chapter that those declarations and that judgment confirmed the opinion previously given by counsel, namely, that it was perfectly legal for a British subject to build a ship of any description as a purely mercantile transaction, and deliver her unarmed to a purchaser, even though the ship was "destined for warlike purposes"; or "even if meant for the Confederate States" as the Solicitor-General expressed it.

By the middle of July, 1862, the work on both ships had fairly begun, and there were reasonable grounds for hope that they would be permitted to leave Liverpool, when completed, in an unarmed state. They were known in the yard while building as "294" and "295," but those numbers did not attract the notice, nor suggest the mystery attributed to the figures "290," by which the *Alabama* was at first known. The circumstances connected with the building of these two vessels, and the very peculiar arrangement by which they were taken into the Royal Navy as her Majesty's ships *Scorpion* and *Wivern*, are important and interesting as historical reminiscences, and to avoid the possibility of overdrawing them or of giving a fresh colouring to a single incident, I shall, at the cost of sacrificing some regularity and smoothness in the narrative, merely give extracts from my official reports to the Confederate Navy Department on the subject, in the precise order of date, with such other correspondence as may appear necessary to a full and clear illustration of the whole matter.

In a despatch dated "Liverpool, August 11th, 1862," I reported as follows:—

"The armour-clad ships are getting on finely, and I have great hopes that I shall be allowed to use the revolving turrets.... If the war continues until spring, these vessels may yet have important and conclusive work in the question of the blockade. The difficulty of getting them fairly to sea will be very great, however, and I confess that thus far I do not see the means to be adopted."

September 10*th*, 1862, I wrote to the Secretary of the Navy thus:—

"I trust you have learned by this time what I am doing in iron, and have received my plans, etc. The work is going on to my entire satisfaction, and if funds do not fail, you shall have two formidable ships ready in the early spring.... At the proper time I will suggest the means of getting officers out for these ships. For the present I think they had better not be sent here. The presence of a number of naval officers in England could not fail to excite comment, and their movements would be closely watched. I do not hesitate to say that embarrassment has already been occasioned by the number of persons from the South who represent themselves to be agents of the Confederate States Government. There are men so constituted as not to be able to conceal their connection with any affairs which may by chance add to their importance, and such persons are soon found out and drawn into confessions and statements by gossiping acquaintances, to the serious detriment of the service upon which they are engaged.

"The proper armament for the turret-ships is engaging my serious thoughts. Experiments are in progress at Shoeburyness to determine this very point, and I will watch the results until the time requisite for the construction of the guns compels me to make a choice.... I have resolved to construct the turrets to revolve, and run the risk of being interfered with, and there will be two guns of the heaviest calibre practicable for actual service in each turret, mounted parallel to each other, and four and a half feet from centre to centre. The ports will be oval, large enough vertically to give twelve degrees of elevation and five degrees of depression, with just width enough to clear the chase of the guns, so that an object can be seen over the side sights.

"I have the working drawings of Captain Cowper Coles' turret, and will send them by first safe opportunity. You are aware of the difficulty of sending letters, and the consequent necessity of being as brief as possible. I cannot, therefore, reason upon points of interest, but must request you to be satisfied with simple statements. I am making a collection of all the official reports of expriments upon matters connected with ships and their armaments, and have the evidence given before the 'Defence Committee' and the 'Plate Committee' of the House of Commons. These are in pamphlets, are too valuable to be lost, and could not be replaced, so I must await a safe opportunity to send them."

"*Liverpool, September 24th.*— ... I have nothing to add except that the ships are progressing as rapidly as could be expected, and that I am more pleased with them every day. The ships being of entirely new design, I see reasons to modify the plans from time to time, but only in immaterial points not involving important alterations.... I confidently expect to afford you great satisfaction in the character of these ships. I think they will be as near an approach to cruising ships as can be devised, when the powers of defence and offence are considered in conjunction with their light draft of water, fifteen feet extreme."

"*Liverpool, November 7th*, 1862.— ... *Armour-clad Ships.*—An unusual amount of bad weather has somewhat interfered with a certain portion of the work upon the ships of this description; but the builders are as anxious as I am to have them ready in the stipulated time, and have covered them with comfortable sheds, and have even introduced gas, so as to insure additional hours for work during the short foggy days of this climate. I have decided upon the means of getting the first of these ships clear of British jurisdiction in a manner not to infringe her Majesty's proclamation; but the attempt will be attended with difficulty, and will require to be conducted with such caution and secrecy that I fear to mention the plan even in this way.... In each attempt to get a ship out a different plan must be pursued. As the first of these ships will be ready in April, it is time to arrange for getting the officers detailed and in a position to join her.

"I am still firmly of the opinion that to send a staff of officers to this country would excite comment and suspicion, and would probably end in failure to accomplish the end in view. I have reason to be sure that if I had not sent the *Alabama* and her armament away before the arrival of Captain Semmes and his officers, she would have been stopped. I beg leave, therefore, to throw out the following suggestion for your consideration. Select the officers for each ship, also a few leading men and marines—non-commissioned officers who are natives of the South, or *bonâ-fide* citizens of the Confederacy—to give nationality to the crew and to ensure the actual possession of the ship until the men shipped at large are got into a good state of discipline.

"Send the first detachment out in a steamer especially provided for the purpose, so as to be under the control of the senior officer, and direct them to proceed at once to the island of Madeira. Upon arrival at Madeira, the senior officer should be instructed to notify me by the English, as well as by the Portuguese, mail, to coal his ship, have everything ready to sail at short notice, and if he finds his presence excites comment, to go out on a short cruise, leaving a letter with her Majesty's Consul, addressed to Captain W. Arkwright, British ship *Carnatic*.... The steamer employed for this service should be sailed under the British flag, or, better still, the French flag, if a French owner can be found for her, and she should be managed in every way as a merchant vessel, the officers and their staff being simply passengers. The *Julia Usher*, a small steamer belonging to Messrs. Fraser, Trenholm and Co., will very shortly sail for a Southern port. If she gets in you might employ her for the service—or the *Giraffe*, if she can be supplied with coal, would be a still better ship, from her great speed. It would be well to combine movements, so that the officers should not arrive much ahead of the ship they are to join, and with the state of the blockade under your own eye, you can arrange their departure from the Confederate port, so as to reach Madeira about the 10th of April.... As Captain Semmes will soon have a thoroughly organized crew, I respectfully suggest that one of these ships be put at his disposal. The officers sent out could be transferred to the *Alabama*. I am sure Captain Semmes would be pleased with such an arrangement, and I have written him that it was my intention to bring the matter to your consideration. There may be difficulty in communicating with Captain Semmes, but I shall soon know, as he will probably be at the first rendezvous agreed upon in a fortnight. I have already sent out a cargo of coal to meet him at Port Royal, Martinique....

"I will not add anything on the subject of my being detailed for the command of one of the ships, but beg to refer to a previous letter in which I have set forth my feelings and hopes. My ambition is to get afloat, but after what you say in your letter of July 12th, I feel bound to submit with becoming grace to any assignment of duty for myself you may think the interests of the public service may require. You will pardon, I trust, the personal character of these remarks. They are induced by that professional pride you are well aware an officer should always possess."

"*Liverpool, November 21st,* 1862.—.... The work upon the armoured ships progresses favourably."

"*Liverpool, December 18th,* 1862.—I am gratified to learn that you approve of the designs for the two armour-clad ships.... As their life must necessarily begin with a sea-voyage of over three thousand miles, it was absolutely necessary to secure good sea-going qualities and fair speed, which I think could not have been accomplished on less draft and dimensions. I designed these ships for something more than harbour or even coast defence, and I confidently believe, if ready for sea now, they could sweep away the entire blockading fleet of the enemy."

"*Liverpool, January 23rd,* 1863.—.... I was prepared for all ordinary opposition, and no mere physical obstruction could have prevented our ships getting out, partially equipped at least. There has arisen a political question which is very embarrassing. The Ministry have ordered the Collectors of Customs to examine and report frequently upon all vessels building in their districts, and armoured ships cannot escape notice. Our transactions have become well known—Southern papers received lately publish them, and a letter in the *Times* from the South clearly indicates that armoured ships are expected from this side to break the blockade. I have been aware that indiscreet persons who should have known better have written to private persons at the South on such matters, and I am not surprised at the result. Lord Russell says in effect that the '290' evaded the law, and rather intimates that it shall not be done again. I am convinced that the present British Ministry will do almost anything the United States Government asks, and you are well aware that an 'Order in Council' will override the ordinary rules of law. Parliament meets February 5th, and I am reliably informed that the question of furnishing supplies to the belligerents will come up. I am consulting the best legal authority, but confess that the hope of getting the ships out seems more than doubtful—indeed, hopeless, unless there should be a change in the political character of the Ministry. I will of course go on as if no obstacle existed, so as to be ready to avail myself of chance circumstances."

"*February 3rd,* 1863 (cypher despatch, *viâ* Baltimore).— ... I have been delayed in giving orders for ordnance stores, etc., for iron ships, by want of money; but financial agent authorizes me to order them, and says in any event he can and will manage to supply the necessary funds when the payments are required. Unforeseen causes have kept back work on iron ships. Have tried very hard to hasten the completion, but insurmountable difficulties have occurred. No armoured ships for Admiralty have ever been completed in time specified; whole character of work new, and builders cannot make close calculations; great labour and unexpected time required to bend armour-plates; and the most important part of the work, the riveting, is far more tedious than anticipated.... Think British Government will prevent iron ships leaving, and am much perplexed; object of armoured ships too evident for disguise."

On the 9th of March, 1863, I received a despatch from the Secretary of the Navy, dated "Richmond, January, 1863." In reference to sending out officers for the armoured vessels, the Secretary wrote thus:—

"I concur with the views you express upon the inexpediency of sending naval officers to England. The plan suggested in your despatch of November 7th, 1862" (see p. 270) "is so difficult of accomplishment that I will at once submit to your judgment another, and request you to give me your views as promptly as practicable. It would be difficult, if not impossible, for us to obtain the services of a suitable steamer; and failing in this, we should be compelled to charter an English sailing vessel at Nassau for the purpose. I suggest to you, therefore, that you at once put yourself confidentially in communication with Mr. Slidell, and learn from him whether you cannot fit out the vessels at a French port, in which event the officers could go to France, *incog., viâ* England, in the ordinary way, and escape observation. I do not suppose that the French Government would give any formal assent to this proposition, but I do suppose that not only no obstacle would be offered, but that facilities would be extended.... I am not at liberty to state the reasons of this opinion, but they are sufficiently strong to induce me to press the subject upon your attention. If you could run over to Paris and see Mr. Slidell it would be the best, perhaps the only course to pursue. I do not desire, by any suggestion here made, to change any plan that you may deem best for getting the ships to sea. I do not know your entire plan, and offer my suggestions for your consideration, content to leave the matter to your uncontrolled discretion. I trust you will be able to advise me of your determination in time to avoid any delay in my co-operation."

On the very day of the receipt of the above despatch I was able to send, *viâ* Baltimore, a reply in cypher, dated "Liverpool, March 9."— "Completion of armoured ships having been delayed, change of plan can be made. You can send officers to France as soon as possible. Will go to consult with our commissioner in France (Mr. Slidell) in a few days," etc.

I must call particular attention to the cautious intimation of the Secretary of the Navy that the Government at Richmond had good reasons to suppose that facilities would be extended to us in France. The grounds upon which such expectations were based will appear very clearly in the subsequent arrangements with reference to the two English ironclads, and in the account of the efforts to build and fit out ships in France. On the 11th of May, 1863, I received two despatches from the Secretary of the Navy in cypher. The first, dated "Richmond, March 19th, 1863," contained the following:—

"Your despatch of February 3rd, 1863" (see p. 272), "reached me yesterday. I share your apprehensions as to our ships. The importance to our cause of getting them to sea at an early day renders the subject one of great anxiety. I am in possession of information which prompts me to suggest to you the following proposition, should you find that the [British] Government designs to prevent their departure. Do not risk correspondence, but proceed to Paris and consult Mr. Slidell, after conferring fully with Mr. Mason, and arrange, in the manner which your judgment shall approve after such consultation, for the transfer of the vessels to French owner, and their equipment in a French port. M.——*, a Member of the Corps Législatif, and who is said to have the confidence of the Emperor, is indicated as a party willing to receive the transfer and complete the outfit," etc.

The second despatch was dated "Richmond, March 27th, 1863," and merely enclosed a copy of a letter from the Secretary of the Navy in cypher to Mr. Slidell, our commissioner to France. The letter to Mr. Slidell was in the Navy Department cypher, and I was directed to translate its contents and then to act upon them in conjunction with Mr. Slidell. The following is a copy of the letter, which I transcribe in full, as it bears upon other operations in France which will be narrated in a subsequent chapter:—

"Richmond, *March 27th*, 1863.

"The Secretary of State having laid before me certain portions of your despatch of January 11th, No. 23, I am induced to invoke your aid in such manner as you may deem most advisable in the attainment of two objects of the first importance to the interest of our country. You have doubtless noticed certain indications in England of a disposition to prevent the departure of the ships built there for our service. The officer in England in charge of this duty, a close observer of public sentiment there, expresses much anxiety upon

---

* The name is suppressed because the person was not the one with whom the arrangement was subsequently made.

this subject, in which I fully share. Under these circumstances, Commander Bulloch is instructed to confer fully with Mr. Mason and yourself as to the practicability of transferring those ships to M.——, or other French citizen, with the view of removing them from England as early as possible, and fitting them out in France. If this can be accomplished, they might be probably loaded with supplies for the French army in Mexico, cleared for Vera Cruz, and sold to us at Terceira or elsewhere. Our early possession of those ships in a condition for service is an object of such paramount importance to our country, that no effort, no sacrifice, must be spared to accomplish it. Whatever may be the terms which M.——may prescribe as the conditions of thus placing them at our command will be promptly met, and apart from all pecuniary consideration involved in the enterprise, its success would entitle him to the gratitude of the country.

"To the good judgment of Commander Bulloch I must necessarily leave all details, earnestly asking your assistance to open and conduct this measure to a favourable conclusion.

"The second subject referred to is the construction of new ships for our country in France. The size and general character of the ships would be best determined by Commander Bulloch, after consultation with the builders, and due consideration of the means of construction, the time involved, etc. The character of our rivers and harbours, however, necessarily demands light draught. Payment for contracts would be made in interest-bearing bonds, or in cotton delivered here upon demand at prices controlled by its current value in this market.

"I am, etc.,
"(Signed)   S. R. MALLORY.

"Hon. John Slidell,
"Paris."

Before the receipt of the foregoing despatch, Mr. Slidell had communicated to me his belief that we should be allowed much more latitude in our naval operations in France than in England, and I had already been in conference with him on the subject. My next despatch to the Navy Department of importance in reference to the ironclads was under date of "Liverpool, June 30th, 1863":—

"First in importance as well as interest are the ironclads already under construction. These should have been ready for sea between March and

June, according to the original terms of contract. I have already reported that mechanical difficulties of construction, not within the reach of foresight, had delayed the progress of these vessels, but the action of the British Government in reference to our operations in Great Britain, culminating in the seizure of the *Alexandra* and her trial in the Court of Exchequer, has still further delayed their completion. As long ago as the latter part of March, I went to Paris to consult with Hon. John Slidell with reference to a possible sale of these ships to a French subject. Through M. Arman, a distinguished naval architect of Bordeaux, Mr. Slidell and I were introduced to the Messrs. Bravay and Co., of Paris, with whom a satisfactory arrangement has been made. Messrs. Bravay and Co. have bought the ships from me for a nominal sum,* and the contract with the builders has been transferred to them, or rather, the builders have made a new contract agreeing to complete the ships for the Messrs. Bravay and Co. precisely as they were to have been finished for me.

"This exchange of property required to be managed with great caution, because it was well known that the true ownership of the vessels was suspected, and that any attempt to equip them for sea, or even to launch them, would result in their seizure and indefinite detention by means of the interminable proceedings of the Court of Exchequer. In order that the transaction might bear the scrutiny of an English court, I thought it advisable to take the advice of counsel on the points of English law. His opinion was that the mere building of a ship in England, for whatever purpose, was not contrary to the Foreign Enlistment Act; that the seizure of the *Alexandra* and the stoppage of several other ships for inquiry in consequence of affidavits lodged by the United States Consuls were illegal and arbitrary acts, but that the ironclads were liable to the same proceedings, and if they should be seized we could not expect to release them from the Court of Exchequer during the war, if at all.

"It was known that ... Clarence R. Yonge had already stated to the United States Minister in London his belief that the ironclads referred to were intended for the Confederate Government; that the United States Consular spies were already watching their daily progress, and that the British Foreign Office would act promptly whenever it suited Mr. Adams' purpose to demand their seizure. It was therefore necessary to disconnect myself with the ships as quickly as possible. I was advised by counsel that

---

* The precise facts are, that Messrs. Bravay bought the ships for a specified amount, and they engaged to re-sell them beyond British jurisdiction for an amount which should include a commission to them.

under any circumstances there would doubtless be a legal inquiry into the title to the property, and that all the papers and letters relating to the sale must be such as would bear judicial scrutiny and tend to prove the *bonâ fide* character of the transfer. As the builders would naturally be the principal witnesses, it was absolutely necessary to prevent them from suspecting that there was any collusion between the nominal purchasers and myself. With this view I first wrote a formal letter to the Messrs. Laird, stating that the interference of the British Government in all attempts to build ships suspected of being for the Confederate States was such as to make it certain that they would not be allowed to complete the ironclads for me; that I was not willing to run the risk of their seizure, which would either result in entire confiscation or my being kept out of the use of the large sum of money already expended for an indefinite time, and requesting them to sell the ships for such sum as would ensure me a reasonable profit, and to release me from all further obligations under the contract.

"Fortunately, just at this time the Russian Government made an offer for the ships, and I hastened to Paris to regulate the correspondence on the part of the French purchasers, to suit the advice of my English solicitor. As you will readily perceive, the affair required a good deal of management, and occupied far more time than if the transaction had been a real one. It is not necessary to go into further details. Suffice it to say that our two ironclads are now the property of Messrs. Bravay and Co., of Paris, agents for the Pasha of Egypt. The papers are all in proper legal form, the Messrs. Laird are convinced that the sale is *bonâ fide,* and I have expressed the most cordial regrets that there should have been a necessity for such a proceeding.

"To keep up this illusion I can no longer appear on board the ships, or even in the yard of Messrs. Laird, but can only direct their further completion from behind the desk of the Messrs. Bravay and Co. These necessary proceedings have created additional delay in finishing the ships, but the work shall now be pushed on as rapidly as possible."

Then follows a specific report of the condition of the ships.

"The engines of both ships have been ready for several months. One ship is entirely plated, and could have been in the water six weeks ago if it had not been for the political necessity of keeping her back.... I cannot hope that these two ships will be ready to take the sea before October. I can only assure you that every effort will be made to hasten their completion. I will keep the Messrs. Bravay under a constant pressure."

In an historical narrative of this kind it is the duty of the writer to take care that no persons who were connected with the transactions, and whose names and credit as men of business are in any way implicated, shall be left in a doubtful position, by reason of a looseness in the general statements, or a want of particularity in the details. I have stated in the letter to the Secretary of the Navy, quoted above (June 30th, 1863), that it was necessary to manage the arrangements with Messrs. Bravay so that the Messrs. Laird should not suspect that the sale of the ships was not *bonâ fide* and final. Every step in the business was taken, in conjunction with my solicitor, in the ordinary somewhat circumlocutory way, which appears to be unavoidable in the legal transfer of property, and I believe that if the Messrs. Laird ever read this book, they will receive the first intimation of the true character of the transaction from the disclosures on the subject here made. The Messrs. Laird acted as agents for the sale of the ships, and I simply arranged with Messrs. Bravay that they should apply for tenders for two ships in the ordinary way of business. The Lairds would naturally have preferred building new ships in response to this proposition, but they acted with their accustomed good faith, and promptly reported to me the offer they had received as a probable opportunity to sell the two ironclads.

When in the course of the arrangements they applied to me for definite and specific authority to sell the ships which they could produce to Messrs. Bravay, they wrote thus: "It will be necessary that we should have clear instructions, either direct to Birkenhead or through your solicitor, of the price at which we are to negotiate the sale." After giving their own views of the price which might be fairly asked, they add: "As the inquiry came to us in the ordinary course of our business for building vessels, and not with any special reference to vessels we might have in course of construction, we hope that you will agree with us that these prices should include a commission of two and a half per cent. on the transaction to us, as we not only lose the opportunity of tendering to our correspondent for new vessels, but shall have considerable trouble in making the transfer and arranging money matters and other details."

In reply to the foregoing I wrote to the Messrs. Laird that, having made inquiry through my bankers, I was satisfied in regard to the financial position of Messrs. Bravay, and had learned that they had executed large commissions for the Egyptian Government, and had at the time an open order for two ironclad vessels from the Pasha. I therefore felt assured that they were able to carry out the proposed transaction, and it might therefore be closed on the terms proposed; and I added:

"Your claim for a commission upon the amount of the sale is, under the circumstances, quite usual and justifiable, and if two and a half per cent. is the established commission in such cases, I readily agree to it.... Hoping that in better times we may be able to renew our business associations, which have been as satisfactory to me as our social intercourse has been agreeable, and assuring you of my personal esteem and regard,

"I am, etc.,

"(Signed)   JAMES D. BULLOCH."

During the negotiations an offer was made for the purchase of the ships on behalf of the Russian Government, and Messrs. Laird, looking to the official and therefore reliable source from which the inquiry came, and the financial security of such a transaction, were inclined to entertain it. To refuse the offer upon grounds which would seem reasonable to them was at first a little embarrassing, but I wrote my solicitor, who of course knew of the arrangement with Messrs. Bravay, that the excessively friendly relations which appeared to exist between Russia and the United States made me suspicious of any proposition coming from St. Petersburg. It was possible, I said, that the Russian Admiral might be acting on behalf of the United States Navy Department, and the ships might get under the wrong flag, and I suggested that this was a sufficient reason for declining the proposition.

It is useless to give further details. The sale to Messrs. Bravay, and the transfer of the property, was effected by my solicitor and the Messrs. Laird in conformity with strict commercial and legal usage and requirement. The chief object was to keep the Messrs. Laird free from any knowledge of the secret understanding with Messrs. Bravay, so that they might be able to answer all inquiries, either from the Foreign Office or the Customs authorities, without embarrassment or hesitation. This purpose was effected, as will appear to anyone who cares to read the official correspondence on the subject, which fills one hundred and forty-five pages of the Appendix to the "British Case," vol. II.

The arrangement with Messrs. Bravay, regarded as a mere business transaction, was based upon a letter from M. François Bravay, the senior partner, dated "Alexandria, Egypt, 28th December, 1862," to his brother, M. Adrien Bravay, who was the resident managing partner of the firm in Paris, and the reply to that letter, dated "Paris, 15th January, 1863." In the above-mentioned letter from M. François Bravay, he writes generally about his business relations with the Viceroy, but the first paragraph of the letter is the only one which need be quoted here.

"I write you a few lines" (he says) "to inform you that the Viceroy positively wishes me to complete some commissions for him, in spite of the resolve I have manifested to him not to execute them. He has ordered me to have built for him in France two armoured frigates, after the best and most perfect designs. He stipulates above everything that it shall not be made known that they are for the Egyptian Government, for he has political reasons for that. Make arrangements to get designs and the contracts in the best form."

The reply acknowledges the receipt of the above letter, and in reference to the particular subject says:—"Your letter transmits to us the commission which his Highness the Viceroy has given, to have built in France two armoured frigates, after the latest models. We will at once take the necessary steps for the execution of that order, in obtaining from the French Government the same facilities for its execution that have been already granted us in reference to the guns that we have had constructed for his Highness," etc.

These and other letters, which were shown to Mr. Slidell and to me, sufficiently demonstrated that the Messrs. Bravay had extensive business relations with the Viceroy of Egypt, and that they were therefore in a position to justify the purchase of such vessels as the two at Birkenhead. It was necessary to have the *status* of the Messrs. Bravay fully established in the above respects, for manifest reasons of a purely business character, because the Messrs. Laird would not have paid attention to an offer coming from irresponsible parties. But Mr. Slidell had received private and confidential information that the Imperial Government would not interfere with any subsequent arrangement Messrs. Bravay might make for the delivery of the ships to the Confederate Government, after they had been despatched from England, and, moreover, it was intimated to him that if her Majesty's Government objected to a private firm taking the ships away without a guarantee that they were not intended for a belligerent, the Imperial Government would state on behalf of Messrs. Bravay that they were satisfied with the explanations of that firm, and would request permission for the departure of the ships as the property of French subjects. This hint, conveyed to Mr. Slidell through a very direct and satisfactory source, was the foundation of the whole agreement with the Messrs. Bravay.

The order of the Viceroy for the two armoured vessels was dated before we had met either of the Messrs. Bravay, or had thought of an arrangement of the kind for getting the ships out of British jurisdiction. It was made use of only as a plausible reason why a private firm should want vessels of such formidable structure and armament, and was not manufactured for the occasion. Subsequently it will appear that the Grand Vizier of Egypt denied that an order for ironclad vessels had been given to Messrs. Bravay. Perhaps there were political reasons for the denial, just as there were for keeping the order secret. Or perhaps the order, being rather in the character of a request, or what may be called a "permissive commission," the Grand Vizier might have found it convenient, at the particular time when the inquiries were made, to deny any knowledge of it.

The arrangement by which it was hoped that the departure of the two ships from Liverpool would be assured having now been fully explained, it only remains to describe the progress and result of the undertaking, which can best be done by a transcript of such portions of my official despatches to the Secretary of the Navy as relate to the subject.

"*Paris, July 8th*, 1863.—I have the honour to send you with this letter a complete set of drawings of our two ironclad vessels, which in future reports I will allude to as Nos. 294 and 295. I also send the detailed specifications upon which the ships are being completed." After a full and most specific explanation of the drawings, the despatch continues: "I reserve my remarks upon the special service upon which it would be advisable to employ these ships for a separate despatch."

The Secretary of the Navy had previously alluded to the desirability of using the ironclads for re-opening the Mississippi and regaining possession of New Orleans, and had invited me to comment upon that proposition. The work on the vessels had up to this time progressed without interference, although we had been well aware that they were closely watched. After the arrangement with the Messrs. Bravay, which was completed on the 17th of June, 1863, it was of course my duty to proceed with all contingent plans as if expecting that the ships would be permitted to sail, and I reported on the subject of their employment as follows:—

"Paris, July 9th, 1863.

"Sir,—

"The several despatches I will now have the honour to send you are of such a nature, and treat upon subjects a knowledge of which by the enemy would be so ruinous to our interests, that I have thought it advisable to send them by a special messenger, and have selected Lieutenant W. C. Whittle, Confederate States Navy, for this important service. It is possible that Lieutenant Whittle may be forced to destroy the despatches, and yet may be able to reach you in person; I have therefore fully instructed him as to their contents, and have given him full verbal explanations of the drawings of the ships and turrets....

"No very great difficulty was experienced in getting crews for the *Florida* and *Alabama,* and I think any vessels fitted out to cruise against commerce, thereby holding out to the men not only the captivating excitement of adventure, but the possible expectation of prize-money, might almost at any time pick up a goodly number of passable seamen. But the ironclads are too manifestly for other purposes to deceive any mere adventurer. Their grim aspect and formidable equipment clearly show that they are intended for the real danger and shock of battle, and I do not think reliable crews could be obtained from among the floating population of European seaports. The ships are so rigged as to require but few able seamen. The actual force of the crews need be only artillerists, but these must be men willing to fight for the sake of their country alone, and must be actuated by the same spirit which has converted our farmers and backwoodsmen into the veterans who are now sweeping irresistibly through Maryland and Southern Pennsylvania under the leadership of our great General Lee. Engineers and firemen can be got here, and men enough to work the ships and perhaps one gun on each. They would thus be able to overcome any wooden ship, or fleet of them. I respectfully propose, then, that the ships, when ready for sea, should be ordered to proceed as quickly as possible to Wilmington, North Carolina. One could fall in with the land at New Inlet, and the other at the main 'ship bar' at the mouth of Cape Fear river.

"By steaming quietly in at early daylight, they might entirely destroy the blockading vessels—not one should be left to steal away and make known the fact that the ironclads were on the coast. Crews might be ready at Smithville or Fort Caswell, to be put on board the ships as soon as they had destroyed or dispersed the blockaders, and in a very few hours afterwards the two vessels would be ready to strike a decisive blow in any direction, north or south. I am earnest and anxious on the subject of crews, because the ships are too formidable and too valuable to be trusted in the hands of a mere set of adventurers, who, actuated by no feeling of patriotism, and controlled only by force, might fail at a critical moment, either from indifference or disaffection, thus disconcerting the best devised plans, or perhaps even occasioning fatal disaster. When the departure of the ironclads from Europe can be definitely determined, say within two weeks, a special messenger can be sent to report specifically to you, so that all necessary steps may be taken and arrangements made to carry out the further views of the Department.

"In view of the intimate knowledge I necessarily possess of the construction and capabilities of the ironclads 294 and 295, I feel called upon to throw out a few suggestions as to the service for which they would be most available, and I trust you will not think me presumptuous for doing so. I feel confident that they will be as good sea-boats and as easily handled as armoured vessels can be, but as you will perceive from the drawings and descriptions, they are large ships, both in length and breadth, and in the rapid current and short turnings of the Mississippi, they would be at great disadvantage, and their full force and power as rams could not be made use of. If they could be accompanied by smaller and shorter vessels to assist them in turning, or to occupy the enemy's ironclads while they were thus engaged, the difficulty might be somewhat removed, but in such narrow waters they would be very much in the condition of a boxer with one arm tied behind his back. I am supposing now that they would have to fight their way up the river in face of the enemy's fleet of ironclads. If these latter can be held above Vicksburg or Port Hudson, and '294' and '295' were simply expected to force their way past the forts and steam up to the city, that object could easily be accomplished. Of course, in such an event, there would be a movement of troops by land, and also of the Mobile flotilla, through Lake Pontchartrain; otherwise, on the approach of the ships by the river, the garrison of New Orleans would burn the city, retire upon the lake, and escape by means of their transports through Ship Island Pass.

"The Atlantic coast offers enticing and decisive work in more than one direction. Without a moment's delay, after getting their crews on board off Wilmington, our vessels might sail southward, sweep the blockading fleet from the sea-front of every harbour from the Capes of Virginia to Sabine Pass, and cruising up and down the coast, could prevent anything like permanent systematic interruption of our foreign trade for the future. Again, should Washington still be held by the enemy, our ironclads could ascend the Potomac, and after destroying all transports and gun-boats falling within their reach, could render Washington itself untenable, and could thus create a powerful diversion in favour of any operations General Lee might have on foot. Third, Portsmouth, New Hampshire,... is a wealthy city in itself, and opposite the town is an important national dock and building-yard. The whole lies invitingly open to attack and destruction. Suppose our two ironclads should steam, unannounced, into that harbour on some fine October morning, and while one proceeded to demolish the navy-yard and all it contained, the other should send a flag of truce to the mayor, to say that if $1,000,000 in gold or $5,000,000 in greenbacks were not sent on board in four hours the city would be destroyed after the manner of Jacksonville and Blufton.* Portsmouth could afford to pay for its existence. Philadelphia is another point open to such an attack. The river is navigable, the banks comparatively low, so that no plunging fire could be brought to bear upon the ships, and once in front of the city they could dictate their own terms. Such operations as are thus hastily sketched would inflict great damage upon the enemy, besides creating a striking effect in Europe, and the ships would thus be employed in a manner which would bring into use their full power, so that no strength would be wasted....

"I am, etc.,

"(Signed)   JAMES D. BULLOCH.

"Hon. S. R. Mallory,
"Secretary of the Navy, Richmond."

To the Secretary of the Navy I wrote:—

"Liverpool, *July* 20*th*, 1863.

"You will remember that Lieutenant R. R. Carter was ordered to report to me for duty in the ironclad you originally intended me to command. Although you have changed the sphere of my duties, I continue to employ him as an assistant in the inspection of work actually in progress, as well as to advise with on all matters of importance. I propose in a few days to put him in communication (through the purchasers of '294' and '295') with Captain Blakely, to arrange for the arming of those ships, as it is important that I should keep entirely out of sight in the matter. I take pleasure in saying that Lieutenant Carter yields me the most cheerful and intelligent assistance, and I esteem myself fortunate in having him with me at this time....

---

* Two Southern towns which had been just then reported to have been burned by the United States forces.

"The opportunity to send this has unexpectedly occurred, and I am forced to be brief and hurried, only adding that matters still progress favourably with '294' and '295.' ... Application will very shortly be made for permission to arm them in England, and the French owners anticipate no difficulty. If, however, their application is refused, we will have to transport the armament to a Continental port, which will involve some delay....

"As I can only shape plans to suit possible changes of circumstances, it is quite impossible to go further into detail on this subject."

Not long after the date of the above despatch we began to feel the effects of Mr. Adams's representations to Earl Russell, especially on the subject of the ironclads. Under date "Liverpool, October 1st, 1863," I reported to the Secretary of the Navy thus:—

"The newspapers, which seem to pass very regularly through the lines of the armies, will doubtless have prepared you for disappointment in all our English undertakings. Of course, I shall continue to act as if certain of success, but am forced to acknowledge that I have but little hope....

"The articles alluded to in my despatch of June 30th, 1863,* would have been ready for departure now if it had not been for interference, such as you can readily imagine. They cannot, however, be wholly lost, for reasons you will understand by referring to the letter alluded to above."

The difficulty and delay in communicating with Richmond was always a cause of great embarrassment in arranging for co-operative movements and in exchanging views. Opportunities were often lost, from the miscarriage of despatches, and suggestions which were approved in purpose were only known when it was too late to act upon them. About October 15th, 1863, I received a despatch from the Secretary of the Navy, advising me of the safe arrival of Lieutenant Whittle with a large batch of despatches from me, including that of July 9th, 1863, on the subject of the proper service for the ironclads. Lieutenant Whittle left Paris on July 10th, and reached Richmond on August 20th. The despatch of the Secretary of the Navy just above mentioned was dated "Richmond, August 29th, 1863." He said:

"I have very carefully examined the drawings (of '294' and '295'), and so far as I can form an opinion of structures so novel in all their details, I think they will be very efficient ships; and that they will probably excel all

---

* Nos. 294 and 295.

other ironclads of which I have any knowledge in sea-going qualities.... My regret and disappointment at their delay in England is very great, but I understand the difficulties in your path, and cannot well see how you could have done better than you have. Their presence at this time upon our coast would be of incalculable value, relieving, as they would be able to do, the blockade of Charleston and Wilmington, and nothing must be suffered to interfere with their completion at the earliest practicable moment.... It is deemed expedient to send an officer of rank out to bring over '294' and '295,' and Captain Barron has been selected. To him I have communicated your views as to appropriate employment for them, and I will thank you to confer with him freely about them. He will receive them from you, as did Captain Semmes the *Alabama,* for I deem it important that you shall carry out the plans you have devised for placing them in our possession.... The arrangements made by you for the completion of '294' and '295' and their final transfer, seem the very best that could have been effected, and I doubt not your judgment and discretion will conduct the negotiation to a successful conclusion. Your suggestions as to the enterprises to be undertaken by them command much consideration, and Captain Barron will receive upon this subject especial instructions."

In respect to manning the vessels, the Secretary of the Navy said: "The method suggested by you would meet the case if Wilmington should at the time be in its present condition with reference to the enemy.... You will regard this plan, however, namely, manning the vessels from Wilmington as suggested by you, as the one to be carried out unless otherwise changed." A great portion of the above despatch was devoted to the subject of supplying funds, which was always weighing upon the minds of the heads of Departments at Richmond.

Captain Barron arrived in due course, and there came with or followed him a sufficient number of other officers to supply the staff for the two ironclads. By the time of his arrival it was already manifest that our expectations with reference to those vessels could not be realized, and he retired to Paris and there waited, hoping against hope that some fortunate turn of events, or some change of policy in the two chief Maritime Powers, would enable him to get afloat. Captain Samuel Barron was well known in the United States service before the war as a gallant dashing officer, and he had some fine young officers with him. Sometimes a sense of companionship in misfortune serves as a consolation, but it was rather an aggravation than a relief to my own disappointment, to contemplate those ardent men yearning for employment and chafing at their compulsory inactivity. It was a hard case to be so near to a great opportunity and yet to miss it. The final annihilation of all hope of getting our ironclads and so ending the blockade and securing supplies to the famishing armies in the field, was reported in the following despatches to the Navy Department:—

"Liverpool, *October* 20*th*, 1863.

"Sir,—

"In my despatch of October 1st, 1863, I called your attention to the newspaper accounts of the seizure of the ironclads '294' and '295,' which had doubtless reached Richmond, but feared to trust particulars to the ordinary mails. Now, by the hands of Lieutenant R. R. Carter, I will report in detail all that has transpired in reference to those ships. When the proceedings in the case of the *Alexandra* had exposed the extent and unscrupulous character of the system of espionage the United States officials had established in this country, and had developed to the full the great treason of Mr. Clarence R. Yonge, it became evident that no ships partaking of the character of war-vessels would be safe from seizure unless they were known to be the property of some foreign Government not a belligerent. It was of pressing importance to destroy any trace of Confederate ownership in '294' and '295' at once, and the arrangements with Messrs. Bravay, of Paris, previously discussed as a probable and very plausible means of security, were speedily consummated in the manner already reported to you in my despatch of June 30th, 1863. The transfer papers, and indeed all the correspondence involved in the negotiation, were so carefully drawn in accordance with British law, that the solicitor employed to conduct the sale remarked on its completion, 'The ships are now irretrievably the property of Messrs. Bravay and Co., and could not be recovered by any process they might think proper to resist.' It certainly seemed that the British Government, when informed of the ownership, could and would reply to the further demands of the United States Minister that, the ships being the property of French citizens, their completion and final departure, at least to a French port, could not be forbidden. Under these circumstances I was naturally hopeful of success in getting them both to sea, and once more in our own possession; for even though the British Government might refuse Messrs. Bravay permission to arm them in England, it was difficult to see how that Government could be compromised as towards the United States by permitting a French subject to take his property, even though in the shape of ships, to his own country.

"Under any circumstances, it would have been prudent for me to absent myself from this neighbourhood; but at the time of the Bravay operation I was just beginning some new contracts on account of the Navy Department in France, and thus my absence from England involved neither loss of time nor waste of opportunity. During the month of July everything seemed to progress favourably; the ships steadily advanced towards completion, and there did not appear any reason to doubt that they would be ready to take the sea during the month of October.

"In August it became evident that the United States officials were getting uneasy, a fact made manifest by increased activity and boldness on the part of their spies, and undisguised efforts to tamper with the *employés* of the Messrs. Laird. Towards the end of that month these causes began to operate in such a manner as to seriously interfere with and retard the progress of the work. At the same time the Custom House officials began to make visits of inspection to the ships, and to press inquiries as to their destination and ownership, indicating that the Government was listening to the affidavits and persistent protests of the American Minister. Finally, the Messrs. Laird, hoping that if the Government were furnished with proof that the ships did not belong to the Confederate States, they would be relieved from further annoyance and inconvenience, asked and obtained the permission of the Messrs. Bravay to avow their ownership of the vessels. The result of this was a call upon M. A. Bravay at his house in Paris, by Captain Hore, R.N., who, on the part of his Government, made minute inquiries as to the intent of the purchase by Messrs. Bravay of such formidable ships.* Receiving apparently satisfactory answers to all of his questions, Captain Hore then made a direct offer to purchase them for the British Admiralty, which proposition M. Bravay declined to entertain, at least until the vessels were fully completed according to their designs, and had been delivered to him in a French port. This ended the interview with Captain Hore, and the circumstances were minutely detailed to me by M. A. Bravay on the day of their occurrence.†

"In the meantime, matters continued to grow worse at Liverpool. The nature of some of the affidavits sent up to the Foreign Office by

* See "British Appendix," vol. ii., p. 372.

† The statement of M. Bravay is confirmed in all essential points by Captain Hore's letter, "British Case," Appendix, vol. ii., p. 372.

the United States Consul leaked out, and although most of them were glaringly false, still they seemed to be whispered into willing ears, and had such effect that the Lairds were directed not to attempt a trial trip with either ship without giving notice to the Customs officials, and were finally forbidden to do so at all, except with a guard of marines, or other force from one of her Majesty's ships, on board.

"During most of this time I was in France, coming to Liverpool only for a day or two at a time to receive and write letters by the Bermuda mail, yet the United States Consul, through his spies, was swearing to my constant presence here, and superintendence of the ships. The local authorities are well aware that this latter statement is untrue. It has also been discovered that most, if not all, the affidavits upon which the Government is acting have been furnished by Chapman, Yonge and others, whose utter want of character was so clearly proved in the proceedings against the *Alexandra.* The course pursued by the Foreign Office can only be accounted for upon the supposition that the head of that Department is a partizan of the North, and is acting for its interest, instead of simply and consistently following the strictly neutral course he professes to have adopted. No one would expect this Government to permit the equipment of a ship-of-war for one belligerent, any more than it would be expected to permit the open enlisting of troops for the other belligerent. Yet interference with either of these should, it would seem, be conducted according to the law of the land, and not in accordance with the whim or partiality of a Minister of State.

"The fact that men are constantly enlisted in Ireland for the Federal army, and have been shipped by hundreds from this port, is so notorious as to be generally discussed, yet I have not heard up to this date, that the rights of a single British shipowner have been violated, nor his ship detained for a single hour in order that the destination or character of the passengers might be inquired into, while in the case of a ship building in a private yard, this Government furnishes detectives to watch her progress, listens to and acts upon the statements of perjurers and avowed traitors, and finally interferes and prevents her completion in a most unusual and illegal manner, as I am informed, for fear that she may at some future time fall into the hands of the Confederate States.

"The inference is so clear that I shall not suggest it, but will simply particularize by repeating that the two rams building by Messrs.

Laird have been virtually seized by orders from the Foreign Office, and are now in the possession of the Customs officers of this port, assisted by one of her Majesty's gunboats, and a guard of marines from her Majesty's ship *Majestic*. The actual seizure took place only about a fortnight ago (October 9th), although the public has been prepared for such an event by intimations in the so-called Government organs, and discussions upon the matter in all the newspapers of the kingdom.

"I have inquired into the causes of this act, and learn, from the best possible sources, as follows:—It has been made known to the authorities that a large number of Confederate naval officers have during the past three months arrived in England. The *Florida* came off the Irish coast some six weeks since, and proceeding to Brest, there discharged the greater portion of her crew, who were sent to Liverpool. These circumstances were eagerly seized upon by the United States representatives here, and they have so worked upon Lord Russell as to make him believe that the presence of those officers and men has direct reference to the destination of the rams. At any rate, the declaration of the United States Consular spies to that effect has been the cause of their seizure at this time, because the reason assigned is that the ships may be captured on their trial trips, or even forcibly carried out of Liverpool, without the consent of the Messrs. Laird, by these very officers and men.

"The precautions taken to prevent such an attempt are, under the circumstances, ludicrous. One of the rams is in the Great Birkenhead Float. To be got out she must pass through a kind of lock; a large *caisson* must be lifted, which can only be done at a certain stage of the tide; and finally, a gate requiring machinery to move it must be opened to give her egress. I learn upon inquiry that if it were desired to remove her from the dock, the keeper would require five hours' notice. Yet this Government have thought it necessary to place a gunboat with extra marines alongside of her, the fasts of the gunboat being actually placed over those of the ram, and until within the last few days have kept a sixty-gun frigate at anchor opposite the dock-gate, for fear that this formidable ship might jump over all the obstructions and proceed to sea in charge of the aforementioned officers and discharged seamen, without bending a sail or lighting a fire.

"Now, sir, the final issue of this affair is no longer a practical question. No amount of discretion or management on my part can effect the release of the ships. Mr. Slidell has always given me to understand that the Emperor of the French was aware of the nature of the transaction with the Messrs. Bravay, and that at the proper time the French Government would come forward in support of the claims or assumed rights of its subjects. I have already intimated to Mr. Slidell, in a cautiously worded letter, what has happened here, and asked what steps the French Government will take.... It is my opinion that the British Government will not let the ships be removed from their present position unless the French Government comes forward and relieves it from all responsibility or presumed obligation to the United States, by requesting that the ships may be allowed to leave Liverpool as the property of a French subject. Whether the Emperor is prepared to change places with her Majesty's Government or not can only be determined when M. Bravay asks the protection or countenance of his own Government; and I will do all in my power to press a decision in the matter, and will report to you the result at the earliest possible moment.

"I have always been under the impression that it would have been better for the Messrs. Bravay to have avowed their ownership of the ships at the time of the assumed sale, and to have asked permission to complete them. Thus would our minds have been at least set at ease. If the answer had been 'No,' we should have saved the money since expended, and could have sold the ships in reality, as they were, and have put the proceeds to other pressing uses. I waived those views in deference to those of Mr. Mason and Mr. Slidell, who thought that I should not interfere with or dictate too much to Messrs. Bravay in the management of details, and who thought that we should await some direct act of interference on the part of the British Government before calling upon the French owners to act. My hands are now tied until those French subjects succeed in effecting the release of the ships, which can only be done through the medium of their own Government. Under all the circumstances, you will perceive how impossible it is for me to predict the future of these ships. I can only say that if they are released from seizure, no time will be lost in getting them clear of such a casualty again. I feel bound to say that the presence of the *Florida* in these waters, and the discharge of her crew, have very materially added to our complications here; but I need not go into detail upon matters which have already taken place, and can only be felt in their effects without the possibility of prevention.

"I have conversed freely with Lieutenant Carter (bearer of this) upon all our affairs in Europe, with the view of his mentioning the substance to you, and I respectfully request that you will give him an opportunity to explain some things to you which would unnecessarily swell the dimensions of this despatch, and which I do not wish to put formally upon paper.

"I have the honour, etc.,

"(Signed)   JAMES D. BULLOCH.

"Hon. S. R. Mallory,
"Richmond."

I reported in the above despatch that the "actual seizure" of the rams was effected about one fortnight before the date upon which it was written, namely, about October 9th, 1863. This was sufficiently correct for the information of the Navy Department at that time; but for a clear and complete exposition of the case in all its bearings, a more precise statement of dates is necessary. It appears from the official correspondence that Mr. Layard, the Under-Secretary of State for Foreign Affairs, wrote to her Majesty's Minister at Washington on the 5th of September thus:— "We have given orders to-day to the Commissioner of Customs at Liverpool to prevent the two ironclads leaving the Mersey.... Mr. Adams is not yet aware that orders have been given to stop the vessels. You may inform Mr. Seward confidentially of the fact."

In pursuance of the above intimation, the Messrs. Laird were notified on the 9th or 10th of September that the ships would not be permitted to sail or even to make a trial trip, without special notice and permission; but the actual or formal seizure was not effected until October 9th, 1863. On the 27th of October a body of marines was put in charge of the ships, and two gunboats stationed to watch them, the workmen being sent on shore.

The facts, then, are briefly as follows. The ships were "detained" September 9th, and "seized" October 9th, after which they were closely watched and guarded, and the work of completing them virtually stopped, to the great inconvenience and injury of the Messrs. Laird, who were simply executing an ordinary commercial order. Finally, after much correspondence and remonstrance, they were permitted to go on with work, but always under vexatious inspection and restraint.

This state of affairs continued for four months, during which long period no steps were taken to test the legality of the seizure, or to bring any of the parties alleged to have been implicated in the equipment of the ships to an account. The particulars of the proceedings against the ships were reported by me to the Confederate Navy Department in the following despatch:

"Liverpool, *February* 17*th*, 1864.

"You have doubtless learned by means of newspapers, which seem to pass very regularly through the lines of the opposing armies in Virginia, as well as from the published correspondence between Mr. Seward and the United States Minister at the Court of St. James, that every attempt to build a ship for the service of the Confederate States is opposed not only by the active exertions of the American Minister and his numerous subordinates, the Consuls of that nation, but that through Lord Russell the entire machinery of the British Government which can in any way be used for such a purpose has been set in motion and put at Mr. Adams's disposal, not to be worked in accordance with English custom and English law, but in such a manner as may be dictated by the Cabinet at Washington.

"The spies of the United States are numerous, active, and unscrupulous. They invade the privacy of families, tamper with the confidential clerks of merchants, and have succeeded in converting a portion of the police of this country into secret agents of the United States, who have practised a prying watchfulness over the movements and business of individuals intolerably vexatious, which has excited the disgust and openly expressed indignation of many prominent Englishmen, and the frequent criticism of that portion of the British press which is really neutral. These practices, though wholly inconsistent with the spirit of justice and the fundamental principles of constitutional government, are not only permitted, but to all appearance are directly countenanced and encouraged by the present Ministry, and the rights of British subjects are violated, and their pecuniary interests damaged, by the seizure of property in their hands upon the affidavits of persons who have already perjured themselves before her Majesty's Courts.* A nation is undoubtedly justified in the enforcement of its neutrality by all legal processes, but where the customary forms of law are departed from, where a large latitude is permitted to one belligerent and the other is watched with a jealous and even vindictive scrutiny, the obligations of neutrality are violated. That these obligations are violated

* *Vide* Yonge and Chapman *in re Alexandra*.

in the action of Great Britain to the Confederate States must be apparent to the world at large. The point is conceded by many Englishmen, at any rate.

"The conjoint efforts of Lord Russell and Mr. Adams have proved irresistible, and it is now settled beyond a doubt that no vessel constructed with a view to offensive warfare can be built and got out of England for the service of the Confederate States. The arrangement by which I hoped to get the two ironclads, '294' and '295' beyond the jurisdiction of England, depended, as you have already been informed, mainly, if not exclusively, upon the intervention of the Emperor of the French. It was hoped, and there was good reason for the hope, that such intervention would come to our aid at the proper time.

"It was confidently believed that if the British Government, fearing that the Messrs. Bravay would resell the rams to the Confederate States, should cause them to be seized, and should demand of those gentlemen any guarantee that the vessels should actually be delivered to the Pasha of Egypt, the Emperor of the French would express to her Majesty's Government his knowledge of the connection, in a business way, of Messrs. Bravay with the Egyptian Government, and would request the release of the ships as the property of French subjects. In this expectation, based upon intimations purporting to have come directly from the Emperor, we have been grievously disappointed. It has been intimated to Mr. Slidell, through no less a personage than the Duke de Morny, that the Emperor cannot make such a request at this time, although his desire is that somehow or other the release of the rams should be effected, and their possession by the Confederate States be again secured.

"Thus reduced to a struggle with the British Government, who, in case of a decision favourable to us in the Court of Exchequer, will exhaust us by continual delays and appeals even up to the House of Lords, it has been determined to make a *bonâ fide* sale of the ships, if possible, and I have given Messrs. Bravay instructions to that effect, in a letter, a copy of which I enclose, marked *A*. It is possible that the Government may not allow the sale of the ships, and we may be forced to defend the suit, but the lawyers are so confident that the title of the Messrs. Bravay will be sustained, that I hope with some degree of confidence that Lord Russell may abandon the case and permit Messrs. Bravay to sell the ships, although I am satisfied he would never suffer them to leave England, except as the property of

some responsible Government other than that of the Confederate States.

"Under date of October 20th, 1863, I had the honour to report very fully to you on the subject of the seizure of the rams, and I will now briefly trace their fortunes to the present time.

"It was naturally supposed that as British subjects of position and wealth were interested pecuniarily in the case, and as it was one of great public interest, the Government would take steps to bring it at the earliest possible time before the Exchequer Court. My solicitor was of opinion that it would be brought up during the January term; and I patiently awaited the turn of the year. There seems to be something peculiar in the construction of the Court of Exchequer and in the mode of procedure therein. The defendants in a suit have no power to hasten proceedings, but must await the action of the prosecution. The solicitors for the Messrs. Laird and for the Messrs. Bravay were at first of the opinion that the Government was only desirous of affording the United States Minister a hearing in support of his suspicions, and that in justice to their clients a hearing would be granted at the earliest possible time. Weeks passed, however, and no "information" was lodged in the Exchequer Court, nor could the solicitors for the defendants obtain from the Government any assurance as to when the case would be tried, or what would be the precise nature of the indictment, or "information," as it is technically called, in the Court of Exchequer.

"About the end of December (1863) I took legal advice on the following points: (1) Is there any way of forcing the Government to take action? (2) Can any damages be recovered from the Government if the verdict is favourable to the defendants? (3) Will the Government permit the ships to be sold to a foreign Power? On the two first points counsel gave technical opinions not necessary to insert here. In reference to the third, the opinion was "The Government would not probably allow the ships to be sold to a foreign State, but might be willing to settle the whole matter in full by making the purchase themselves, provided Messrs. Bravay would sign a quit claim." My own solicitor, who from his professional as well as political associations was favourably situated for coming to a correct conclusion, expressed to me very decidedly his opinion that Lord Russell would not act in accordance with law; that he was in feeling a thorough partizan of the United States, and, acting in that spirit, he would create all the delay possible in bringing the case to

trial, and would further embarrass the defendants by successive appeals from each consecutive verdict. He also felt convinced that Lord Russell would never permit the rams to leave England, unless the Emperor of the French would claim them as French property, and thus relieve her Majesty's Government of all responsibility to the United States.

"My own observation of the progress of the case had brought me to like conclusions, and on the 27th of January I went to France to bring the matter to a close without further delay, and by direct appeal to the Emperor, through Messrs. Bravay. Although in the beginning there was good reason to hope that the Emperor would intervene at this stage of our proceedings, I had for some time begun to doubt it, and on my arrival in Paris the doubt was confirmed. The Emperor caused the Messrs. Bravay, as well as the Hon. John Slidell, to be informed that he could not make the request to the British Government to release the rams. There was a good deal said about the personal sympathy of the Emperor for the South, and his earnest desire that by some means or other we might get our ships out, but he could not help us, so the sympathy and the hope were sheer mockery, when we had been buoyed up with the expectation of something more.

"I now laid the whole case before Hon. John Slidell, Hon. James M. Mason, and Captain Barron, all of whom were in Paris.... They expressed the unanimous opinion that there was no hope of getting the ships out, and that there was nothing left for me to do but to recover, if possible, the money expended. I lost no time in settling preliminaries with Messrs. Bravay, and to put the transaction in a formal business shape handed them the enclosed letter, marked *A,* already alluded to above—an act which, I assure you, sir, gave me greater pain and regret than I ever thought it possible to feel. The British Government have within the last two or three weeks filed the "information," which includes 130 counts. The case is set for trial, I believe, in April or May. Messrs. Bravay will not receive an answer to their application to sell in time for me to report the result by Commander Wm. L. Maury, who will take this despatch, but you will probably see the result in the newspapers before I shall have an opportunity of writing again."

On the 3rd of April, 1864, I received a short cypher despatch from the Secretary of the Navy, dated "Richmond, February 24th, 1864," express-

ing the greatest reluctance to part with the rams, and saying that nothing short of the impending loss of them would justify their sale. He had not then received the above explanatory report upon the whole case, and I replied, under date of "Liverpool, April 14th":—

"You may rest assured that nothing has been done in the matter alluded to by you except from necessity. I have freely consulted with Mr. Mason and Mr. Slidell, and their opinions were identical with my own. Commander Wm. L. Maury is, I trust, ere this in Richmond, with despatches fully explaining the causes which compelled the course adopted. I send you by to-morrow's mail, *viâ* Halifax, a number of Parliamentary papers relating to the rams. The affidavit of Chapman, with reference to a pretended conversation with me, is wholly untrue. Not one single sentence which he has sworn to ever passed between us. As this man perjured himself in the case of the *Alexandra*, his testimony would not probably be received if the case of the rams is ever brought to trial; yet it is upon such testimony as this that Lord Russell orders the forcible seizure of the ships. The letter from Commander Maffitt to me, which you will perceive was used by Mr. Adams to induce the seizure of the rams, did not reach me through the men of the *Florida*, by whom it was sent. When those men arrived in Liverpool I was absent on the Continent. They got into the hands of a solicitor, and gave him the letter, which he seems to have sent to the United States Consul, and the immediate cause of the seizure of the ships was due to this circumstance."

On the 2nd of May, 1864, I received another despatch from the Navy Department on the engrossing subject of the rams. It was dated "Richmond, March 21st, 1864." The Secretary of the Navy was still ignorant of the critical state of affairs, not having received my despatches forwarded by Commander Maury, and he directed me not to sell the rams "until that measure shall have been submitted to the President, with the reasons for it."

I got an opportunity to reply on the 13th of May, as follows:—

"I should never think of departing from your instructions nor the implied wishes of the President, except in a case wherein such a course alone would prevent positive disaster, the danger of which you could not have foreseen, nor even then without the advice and support of my natural and proper counsellors, the Commissioners of the Confederate States. I may say, however, that in this particular instance I am no longer a free agent, but am in the condition of a disabled ship taken possession of by a current she has no power to stem. The rams are in the possession of the law officers of the British Crown, and they are acting under the instructions of a Minister who has on every occasion shown in practice personal animosity to the Southern cause, and who seems regardless of the forms of law in his efforts to prevent our getting any material aid from Great Britain. Hoping to regain possession of these much-needed ships, or, failing in this hope, at least desiring to recover the large sum of money expended upon them, I have placed the case in the hands of able solicitors, who are acting in accord with eminent counsel.

"Now, sir, unless it is desired to establish a great grievance against the British Government, and it is thought that the money already expended upon the ships may be advantageously sacrificed to gain that end, I respectfully submit that my duty is to manage the case in a practical business way, and to be governed by the advice of the counsel employed. The only chance of gaining the pending suit rests upon the ability of Messrs. Bravay to prove their contract with the Pasha of Egypt, and upon the consistency of their own testimony. If the case goes to trial and the Bravays fail in the above points, the verdict will undoubtedly be in favour of the Crown, and our ships and money will both be lost.

"This is the opinion of counsel, and I am advised to let Messrs. Bravay sell the vessels to the British Government if they do not feel quite prepared to go into court with a clear case. On the very day of the receipt of your despatch of March 21st, I notified Messrs. Bravay to suspend all pending negotiations for the sale of the rams. The elder M. Bravay is now in Egypt. If on his return he expresses confidence in himself and in his case, we will stand to the issue of the trial. If, on the contrary, he professes doubt, or unwillingness to submit to a personal examination, it is Mr. Slidell's opinion that I should permit the actual sale of the ships, he being satisfied, as well as myself, that such would be the decision of the President, and of yourself also, if you were aware of the actual state of affairs. The solicitors and counsel employed are of opinion that if the first verdict is for the defendants the Crown will appeal to the Exchequer Chamber, and from thence to the House of Lords, and that the case will not reach this latter Court of Appeal during this entire year.

"I trust you have not thought that I have been needlessly fearful of the result, and have yielded too readily to the advice of my solicitors.... I held out as long as was justifiable, and clung to hope as long as there was a ray of it. No one could have had stronger inducements to get the rams to sea than I had. Suppressing all allusion to patriotic impulses, and setting aside the loyal duty and allegiance I owe to the country, there are personal reasons which could not fail to have spurred me to great exertions. Although I was not to have had the honour of commanding either of the ironclads, I felt satisfied that their qualities and performances would redound to my professional credit, and if they fail to do service for the country in this great war for its independence, I frankly confess that with a feeling of deep regret for the public loss will be mingled one of purely selfish personal disappointment."

On the 30th of May, 1864, I again received a despatch from the Navy Department, written this time with a full knowledge of the state of affairs affecting the rams. The above mentioned despatch was dated "Richmond, April 7th, 1864," and began thus:—

"Commander Maury reached Richmond on the 3rd inst., and delivered your several despatches. The hopes in which I have long and confidently indulged of certain important results to our country from your efforts abroad, and which hopes were shared by thousands around me, are prostrated by the intelligence he brings. One reflection alone can alleviate the bitterness of this disappointment, and this is the reflection that it results not from any cause within our control, and that your whole course, as the immediate and principal agent in the enterprise, has been marked by equal energy, sagacity, and tact. Knowing from my own what must be your depression under this great national misfortune, I deem it proper to say this in reference to your action."

The Secretary of the Navy confirmed the decision to sell the rams, and the remainder of the despatch was devoted to other matters of business. During the whole of the time, from the first "detention" of the rams, on September 9th, 1863, until the "information" was filed in the Exchequer, namely, February 8th, 1864, a period of five months, not a single step was taken by her Majesty's Government to justify the seizure, or to show cause for the detention. It now appears, from the official correspondence published in the "Appendix to the British Case,"* that those five months were diligently occupied in looking up evidence and in digesting the numerous affidavits of the United States Consul at Liverpool.

That gentleman manifested his usual fecundity of resource in supplying "statements." Those in this case were of the stereotyped form, the persons swearing to them being generally of the well-known type of "affidavit monger." They "believed this," and had "heard that," but were always wide of the mark when they came to deal with specific facts.

---

* "*Alabama* Claims, British Case," vol. ii.

After the formal seizure on the 9th of October, the ships were kept literally in a state of siege—Captain Inglefield, of her Majesty's ship *Majestic*, was the officer charged with their special custody. The Government had been persuaded by Mr. Adams that the discharged crew of the *Florida* had been sent to Liverpool for the purpose of forcibly seizing the rams and taking them to sea, and if there had been a hostile fleet off the harbour, Captain Inglefield could not have been more perplexed and anxious, more nervously active and watchful in his precautions and preparations to discover and defeat a cutting-out expedition, than he appears to have been with respect to the alleged hostile seamen from the *Florida*, who were probably smoking their pipes at the "Sailors' Home," or were already dispersed in other ships, in happy or careless unconsciousness of the agitation they were creating.

On the 6th of October, 1863, Captain Inglefield wrote, in reply to "confidential instructions" from the Admiralty: "I conceive the possibility that an attempt might be made to carry the vessel in question out of British waters by force." ... "The Custom-house authorities having placed their means entirely at my disposal, I have organized a system of espionage which cannot fail to give me the earliest possible information of any movement on the part of the ironclad vessel in question."* On the 8th of October he received orders by telegraph "to give every assistance to officers of the Customs in effecting and maintaining the seizure of both iron ships," etc.; and on the 9th he wrote in reply:† ".... In obedience to the above, I consider it most expedient that the *Liverpool*‡ should be moved down the river to a berth immediately abreast of the entrance to the Great Float, so that she may perfectly command the basin, and be nearer her guard-boat. The gunboat will remain within the entrance to the Great Float, and during the night an armed pinnace will row guard." On the 11th of October he reports further: "The gunboat will take up a position beside the ironclad vessel, and during the daytime the marines will remain on board of her. After the workmen have left, a sentry will be placed on the forecastle, and another on the poop of the ram; Messrs. Laird's ship-keepers remaining in charge of stores.... I shall then direct a lieutenant of marines to remain on board the iron ship during the night, only withdrawing his party when the workpeople return in the morning."§ On the

---

* "Appendix to British Case," p. 384.
† Ibid., p. 393.
‡ The *Liverpool* was a large screw frigate of sixty guns.
§ "Appendix to British Case," p. 400.

25th of October he wrote again: "If an effort is made to carry off the rams, I think it will either be at night, or in such thick weather as we constantly experience at this time of year. Unless the gunboat arrives to-day, I must employ the ferry-boat to-morrow morning; for though the *El Mounassir* is not masted, nor are her turrets on board, she is, nevertheless, an available ironcased ram, which would be of considerable service (even in her present condition) for breaking a blockade."*... "The arrival of the *Heron* and *Britomart*, which I am looking for anxiously, will obviate the necessity of seeking the assistance of the ferry-boat, etc."

In consequence of the above letter, the Secretary to the Admiralty wrote to the Under-Secretary for Foreign Affairs on October 26th:—"My lords are quite prepared, if Earl Russell thinks it desirable, to send the *Prince Consort†* to anchor at the mouth of the Mersey."‡

There are more documents of similar purport in the official correspondence, but the above quotations will sufficiently demonstrate the great naval force that was employed in guarding these mastless and turretless rams from being carried off, the items being: her Majesty's ship *Majestic*, say sixty guns; her Majesty's ship *Liverpool*, sixty guns; three gunboats—say one pivot-gun each—and the proffered reinforcement of her Majesty's armour-cased ship *Prince Consort*.

Captain Inglefield is a gallant officer, I have no doubt on that point, and he would probably make skilful and suitable arrangements to repel a sea attack upon the Mersey, if he should be appointed to the naval command at Liverpool in a time of war; but I cannot help thinking that, as he sipped his wine at dinner in the *Majestic*'s cabin, after writing one of the above reports to the Admiralty, there must have floated athwart his mind a suspicion that there was a comical side to the whole transaction. I cannot bring myself to believe that an experienced naval officer would give credence to such a preposterous allegation as that an attempt would be made to carry off the rams by force, or that any effort would be made to move them from their positions, which could not have been prevented by the remonstrance of a single Custom House officer, with a pen behind his ear and a memorandum-book in his hand.

The Confederate Government was impelled by every motive of policy, if not of principle, to conciliate foreign Powers, and especially Great Britain, and it is inconceivable that any Minister of State, nay, I may say

---

* "Appendix to British Case," p. 418.
† The *Prince Consort* is an ironclad.
‡ "Appendix to British Case," p. 417.

that any reasoning being, could have supposed that the President of the Confederate States would have countenanced, or that any responsible agent of that Government would have made, such an attempt.

It was said, I believe, that as the *Alabama* was taken out of the Mersey without permission, the same thing might be done with the ironclads, but the cases are not comparable with each other. There is a great difference between taking up your hat and quietly walking out of a man's house without asking his leave when he has not forbidden your departure, and the act of knocking him down and stepping over his prostrate body to get out when he has prohibited your going. It has been shown, and I think it will be admitted by all fair-minded people, that the taking away of the *Alabama* infringed no law, and it has never been alleged that she was restrained in any way, or that a single false statement was made in reference to her movements. I mean that her Majesty's Government have never alleged it. But in the case of the rams, they were restrained by the orders of the duly authorized civil authorities from making even a trial-trip without especial permission, and the Messrs. Laird would not have connived at their being removed from their works; and no one acting on behalf of the Confederate Government would have dreamed of attempting a forcible removal. Besides, as a mere practical question, the condition of the vessels was such that they could not have been carried off without so much open preparation, and so much assistance from local people, that there could have been no disguise and no *coup-de-main*. The "scare" originated at the United States Consulate. The arrival of the *Florida's* men was seized upon as a fortuitous circumstance. Mr. Adams appears to have convinced Earl Russell of "the desperate character of the chief persons engaged in the insurrection in the United States," of whom he says, in one of the letters to his lordship:—"I shall be little surprised at learning of their resort to any expedient, however audacious or dishonest, which may have for its object the possession of these formidable ships."*

It is well known among business men that a ship remains exclusively in the custody of the builder, and is in fact his property, until the last instalment of her price is paid and the builder's certificate is handed over to the contractor or purchaser. The latter has, of course, a contingent interest in her, equivalent to the portion of the stipulated price he has paid, but he cannot take possession or remove her until she is completed and paid for. If there is delay in the completion beyond the time specified for delivery,

---

* Published in Liverpool *Daily Mercury*, with other official correspondence, March 10th, 1864.

or injury to the ship in course of building, the loss falls upon the builder, and not upon the purchaser.

The inconvenience and injury to the Messrs. Laird by the seizure of the rams, and the lashing of gun-boats alongside, and the mounting of guards on board, must have been serious. They protested, and pointed out the improbability—in fact, the impossibility—of any party of men being found who would attempt to take the ships away from them by force. On the 17th of October, 1863, they wrote to the Under-Secretary of the Treasury:—"Both vessels are incomplete, and unfit for sea-going. The second vessel has not even got her masts or funnel in, and both are in the sole charge of our own people. We believe, further, that if any such project as the forcible abduction of these vessels had ever been thought of, it could not successfully have been carried out in the port of Liverpool."

At one time it was proposed to stop the work upon the ships entirely, but this would have compelled Messrs. Laird to discharge a large number of men, which Captain Inglefield thought would increase the ill-feeling already exhibited by the operatives in Messrs. Laird's yard towards the naval officers and men employed in maintaining the seizure, and the builders were permitted to go on with their work, although under such restrictions and "espionage" the progress was necessarily slow and unsatisfactory.

Meanwhile, the Government was diligently employed looking up evidence. They even went to the expense of sending a commission to Egypt to examine the Viceroy and his Grand Vizier as to their business relations with Messrs. Bravay. Finally, after coquetting for some time about the purchase of the ships, they sent down experts from the Admiralty, who carefully examined and valued them, and then, with the law-suit in one hand and the valuation in the other, they made a direct offer to Messrs. Bravay, which was accepted, and the preliminary terms upon which the two rams should pass into the Royal Navy were settled on about the 20th of May, 1864.

Formal notice of suit for the forfeiture of the rams had been given on the 8th of February, and in the "information," both the Messrs. Laird and Messrs. Bravay were made parties to the suit. It is ordinarily supposed, when a defendant in a case of this kind abandons his defence and accepts the terms offered by the Government, that he admits the weakness of his position, and the legality of the proceedings which have been taken against him. But after the withdrawal of the case by the Crown it was thought advisable to prevent any such conclusion with reference to Messrs. Laird and Messrs. Bravay. On the day after the formal notice of withdrawal of the suit, namely, May 27th, 1864, the Attorney-General, with Sir Hugh Cairns, appeared in the Court of Exchequer at Westminster, and the former said:—

"The Crown had asserted that there was a valid seizure for a valid cause of forfeiture. The claimants had to the last asserted that there was no such valid cause of forfeiture, but the matter had been by arrangement withdrawn from the cognizance of the court, so that no determination of it would be necessary, and that had been done upon the footing that the Crown had agreed to pay to the claimants the value which the Crown themselves had placed upon the property, and that, too, entirely without prejudice to the position of the Crown or the claimants with regard to the question that would have required to be tried if the arrangement had not been made. The mode of doing it and giving effect to that arrangement had not been finally arrived at; but no mode would be adopted that would in any degree authorize me to say that there was any admission by the claimants that it was a valid forfeiture."

The Messrs. Bravay made no concession which could be taken as a surrender of their right as French subjects to buy or to have built for them a vessel of any description in England. They did only what other private parties have often done, namely, consent to an arrangement rather than to continue an expensive and tedious litigation with the State, and it is hardly probable that the law officers of the Crown would have advised a settlement which resulted in a pecuniary profit to the claimants, if they really thought that Messrs. Bravay had infringed the terms of the Foreign Enlistment Act. It is fair and reasonable to assume that, having in remembrance the judgment of the Court of Exchequer in the "*Alexandra* Case," and also that of the Vice-Admiralty Court of Nassau in respect to the *Oreto,* they had no hopes of obtaining a favourable verdict, and no expectation of proving that there had been "a valid seizure for a valid cause of forfeiture."

I am bound to say that as soon as it was decided to get out of the difficulty by buying the ships, the Admiralty conducted the operation in a perfectly fair and straightforward way. The ships were valued with scrupulous regard to their intrinsic worth, and with due reference to the state of the shipbuilding trade at the time, and as a mere commercial transaction the sale was satisfactory, the aggregate amount agreed to be paid by the Government being about £30,000 in excess of the original contract price of the two ships, which proves that they were good vessels of their kind, and that the work upon them had been faithfully executed.

The whole of the purchase money did not of course revert to the Confederate Treasury, but only a part proportioned to the amount that had been paid on account; and although the circumstances which brought this pecuniary reinforcement to the funds of the Navy Department were most distressing, yet the relief came at a time when much work would have been necessarily abandoned, and some important contracts cancelled, if it had not been obtained. In the month of September, 1863, I had reported that the prospective wants of the Department were £705,300 in excess of the visible supply. Mr. Secretary Mallory had made every possible effort to meet the deficiency, but it had not been made good, the demands always increasing in a larger ratio than the means for meeting them. These matters of finance have, however, been dealt with and explained in another chapter.

The gratitude of the United States to Earl Russell for the seizure of the rams was even greater than the gratification Mr. Seward expressed for the prosecution of the *Alexandra*. As soon as the purpose of her Majesty's Government was known in Washington, Mr. Adams was instructed to thank Lord Russell, and to say that the President was gratified in being able to regard his conduct in the light of a sincere desire, on just principles, to maintain friendly relations with the United States. Mr. Adams concluded his letter of thanks in these words:—"I am therefore instructed to inform your lordship that the Government will hereafter hold itself obliged, with even more care than heretofore, to endeavour so to conduct its intercourse with Great Britain as that the war in which it is now unhappily involved may, whenever it may terminate, leave to neither nation any permanent cause of discontent."*

The Government of Great Britain zealously fulfilled its share in accomplishing the purpose which Mr. Adams so ardently hoped would follow the seizure of the rams. Earl Russell applied the Foreign Enlistment Act so stringently with reference to the Confederate States, that it was very difficult to forward the most essential supplies, and while the drain of battle, and the lack of necessary comforts were thinning the ranks and wasting the strength of the armies in the field, and the difficulty of placing funds in Europe was daily increasing, the cheapest and most favourable market, that of England, was well nigh closed to the Confederacy, while the United States were permitted to buy and ship what they liked, without hindrance, and at the ordinary current prices.

* Appendix to "British Case," vol. ii., p. 400.

I do not wish to overstate the case, but I say without hesitation, and without fear of contradiction, that the practice of stopping ordinary merchant steamers and detaining them for examination and inquiry, unless they were loading for a Northern port, drove the Confederate agents to such shifts in order to get their purchases out of England, that the cost of every rifle and every ounce of powder was greatly increased, irrespective of the high blockade rates for freight. A notable and distressing feature of this unequal treatment of the two belligerents was that the restrictive watchfulness practised over the weaker side became more cold and rigid as the disparity of strength became more and more manifest.

But while Earl Russell thus did all in his power to conciliate the United States, and to conduct his intercourse with them so that the termination of the war should "leave to neither nation any permanent cause of discontent," the Government at Washington did not act in the spirit of Mr. Adams's promise. No sooner was the war over than Mr. Seward began to collect complaints against Great Britain. He originated what are known as the "*Alabama* Claims." He began and continued for several years an active, harassing, and sometimes angry correspondence with the British Foreign Office, and finally his successor haled her Majesty's Government before an International Court, with a result which all the world knows.

Anyone who cares to read "The Case of the United States" in the Geneva Arbitration, will be struck with the harsh epithets and disparaging insinuations which are cast upon the Ministry which governed England during the war, and indeed upon British officials generally, and will think that the assurance given by Mr. Adams was forgotten as soon as the occasion which inspired it had served its purpose.

The Government of the United States did not exaggerate the importance of preventing the departure of the rams from Liverpool, and the passionate appeals, and strong asseverations of Mr. Adams are not surprising. He knew the formidable character of the ships, and foresaw the havoc they would work if they ever got into the hands of a competent Confederate officer. The defensive powers of the rams were quite up to the standard of the years 1861–63. They were cased over the vital parts with 4½-inch armour upon twelve inches of teak backing, and an inner skin of ⅝-inch iron plates. Each had two revolving turrets with 5½-inch armour over twelve inches of teak. In each turret there would have been two guns of the best possible manufacture, mounted parallel to each other, and five feet from centre to centre. Calibre of gun, 9-inch rifled; weight of projectile, about 220 pounds; weight of gun, about twelve tons. If one of the rams had gone into smooth water, and had suffered a "Monitor" to make deliberate practice at her with 15-inch shot at short range, as in the engagement between the *Weehawken* and the *Atlanta* in Warsaw Sound, no doubt in time her plates would have been loosened and the backing splintered; but their power and speed was such that in open water, with room to manœuvre, I think they would have had no difficulty in running down any "Monitor" then afloat, and I confidently believe that they would have broken up the blockade completely, and then perhaps they would have paid New York or Boston an unpleasant visit.

I have now given a full and accurate account of the formidable vessels "294" and "295," from the first discussion of their plans to the time when they became part of the naval force of Great Britain. Those persons who permit their judgment to be swayed by political bias, who were unfriendly to the South during the war, and who have pledged themselves to the opinion that the Confederate Government should not have been allowed to get ships in England under any circumstances, may say that the foregoing confession of the ultimate ownership and purpose of the rams fully justified their seizure. But I think that those, on the other hand, who only wish to come to a right judgment after a dispassionate examination of the facts, will be brought to the conclusion that there was no valid reason for the interference of her Majesty's Government, and that the proceedings against the vessels prescribed by Earl Russell, and so rigidly enforced by the Customs authorities and by the naval commander at Liverpool, were not in accordance with the principles of international duty laid down for its practice by the Government itself, and that they went far beyond the purpose of the prohibitory clauses, and were in excess of the powers granted in the preventive clauses of the Neutrality Laws of Great Britain, as expounded by the Solicitor-General in Parliament, and defined by the judgment of the Court of Exchequer in the *Alexandra* case.

In forming an opinion with reference to Earl Russell's proceedings against the rams, it is clearly essential to consider, not what is known now, but what were the actual circumstances and the precise position of affairs at the time of the seizure; and it is equally important to bear in mind the statements made by leading members of the Government in the House of Commons in explanation of the Foreign Enlistment Act, and defining what each belligerent might do towards supplying its wants without infringing the statute. Without quoting again in full the principles of action laid down by the Government, I may for the present purpose merely remind the reader that the Prime Minister, Lord Palmerston, said that there was no difference in principle between supplying a belligerent with rifles or with ships that are to operate in war, and that on the mere ground of international law it was quite admissible to supply either of two belligerents not only with arms and cannon, but also with ships destined for warlike purposes; that the Solicitor-General said it was a great mistake to suppose that the Foreign Enlistment Act was meant to prohibit all commercial dealings in ships-of-war with belligerent countries, and that even the *Alabama,* though a ship-of-war, might have formed a legitimate article of merchandise, even if meant for the Confederate States; and that Earl Russell himself, in a letter to Mr. Adams, said that her Majesty's Government "cannot interfere with commercial dealings between British subjects and the so-styled Confederate States, whether the object of those dealings be money or contraband goods, or even ships adapted for warlike purposes."

The letter from Earl Russell containing the above statement was read in Court by Sir Hugh Cairns, the leading counsel for the defendants in the trial of the *Alexandra,* and was commented upon by him as the opinion of a Minister of the Crown, and it probably had a good deal of weight, not in determining the "direction" of the Lord Chief Baron, but in affecting the minds of the jury.

When the Messrs. Laird engaged as a purely commercial transaction to build the rams, the views of the Government were not fully and specifically known, and neither those gentlemen nor the Confederate agent had any other guide to the scope of the Foreign Enlistment Act than the opinions of their legal advisers. But the statements above referred to were made in the House of Commons, and the letter of Earl Russell was written, several months before the seizure of the rams. They were not merely the opinions of three eminent men upon an abstract question of international or municipal law, but they were the declarations of two responsible Ministers of the Crown, and of a chief law officer of the Government, in reference to a specific Act of Parliament, and must have been intended to lay down the principle upon which the act would be administered in the practice of their neutrality. When those statements of Ministers and of the Solicitor-General were followed by a judgment of the Court of Exchequer which fully confirmed their view of the municipal law, it can hardly be doubted that the Confederate Government was justified in thinking that their agents might supply all their wants in the ordinary commercial way, and that they might buy in the British markets and from British subjects, not only "contraband goods," but "even ships adapted for warlike purposes," provided there was no intention that in the port of Liverpool or in any other port (of the British dominions) the vessels should be, in the language of the Act of Parliament, "either equipped, furnished, fitted out, or armed," which the Lord Chief Baron in his summing up declared all meant the same thing, and referred exclusively to the warlike armament.

It has been alleged that while any ordinary ships, even though well suited in structure and general arrangements for warlike purposes, might be legitimate objects of sale by British subjects to a belligerent, yet armourcased vessels were fitted for hostile operations, and could attack and destroy an enemy immediately after leaving port, without being armed at all in the sense of being provided with guns, and therefore the privilege which might be permitted to trade in the former, would not be permissible with reference to the latter class. In reply to this I will call attention to the fact that the official statements previously quoted were made by Ministers, and the judgment of the court was rendered, when not only other armoured vessels had been built, and were building, but when the particular vessels in question, namely, those bought by Messrs. Bravay, were well-advanced in their construction, and that neither in the Ministerial statements nor in the judgment of the court was there any limitation to the broad and inclusive declaration, that "even ships adapted for warlike purposes" were on a parity with gunpowder and saltpetre as articles of commercial traffic.

But there is something more than mere negative testimony to offer on this point. On the 5th of September, 1863, Mr. Adams wrote a very strong letter to Earl Russell, which certainly contained an ill-concealed threat of serious consequences if the rams were permitted to leave England.* Earl Russell sent a brief memorandum to Mr. Adams on the 8th of September:—"Lord Russell presents his compliments to Mr. Adams, and has the honour to inform him that instructions have been issued which will prevent the departure of the two ironclad vessels from Liverpool."† Now it must be borne in mind that the letter of Mr. Adams, of September 5th, referred exclusively and specifically to the two rams, "294" and "295," and Lord Russell's memorandum of the 8th had reference to them also. On the 11th of September, three days after, Earl Russell replied in full to Mr. Adams's letter of the 5th. There was no question now of a duplicate *Alabama,* or of any ordinary ship merely capable of being subsequently adapted to warlike purposes. Earl Russell was replying to a remonstrance against the departure of the two iron-cased rams alleged to be building for the Confederate Government, and he wrote thus:—

* "British Case," Appendix, vol. ii., pp. 352, 353.
† Ibid., p. 355.

"With regard to the general duties of a neutral according to international law, the true doctrine has been laid down repeatedly by Presidents and judges of eminence of the United States, and that doctrine is, that a neutral may sell to either or both of two belligerent parties any implements or munitions of war which such belligerent may wish to purchase from the subjects of the neutral, *and it is difficult to find a reason why a ship that is to be used for warlike purposes is more an instrument or implement of war than cannon, muskets, swords, bayonets, gunpowder, and projectiles to be fired from cannon and muskets. A ship or a musket may be sold to one belligerent or the other, and only ceases to be neutral when the ship is owned, manned, and employed in war, and the musket is held by a soldier and used for the purpose of killing his enemy. In fact, the ship can never be expected to decide a war or a campaign, whereas the other things above mentioned may, by equipping a large army, enable the belligerent which acquires them to obtain decisive advantages in war."* Earl Russell, in continuation, points out very forcibly that if the Confederates had been able to obtain some vessels and "a limited supply of arms from the United Kingdom," the Federal Government had obtained a far greater supply of warlike stores; and then he adds that her Majesty's Government had reasons to believe, although they could not prove, that agents of the Federal Government had been employed to engage emigrants to go to the United States for the purpose of entering into the military service of the Federal Government.

The linking together of a ship and so great a variety of contraband goods, as being equally articles of legitimate trade between neutrals and either of two belligerents, and the illustration of the inefficiency of a ship in comparison with arms to decide a campaign, which Earl Russell so forcibly employs in the above letter, are quite in harmony with the declarations previously made by himself, by Lord Palmerston, by the Solicitor-General, and with the judgment of the Court of Exchequer, on the right of a British subject to build and sell, and a belligerent to buy, an unarmed ship in England.

I think anyone reading the paragraphs of the letter I have quoted above, knowing that they were parts of a long argumentative reply to a demand for the seizure of the rams, would naturally expect that they were intended to lead up to and to justify a refusal; but in the last paragraph of the letter Earl Russell confirms the promise contained in his memorandum of September 8th, and says that the vessels will be detained "until satisfactory evidence can be given as to their destination."

---

* See "British Case," Appendix, vol. ii., pp. 358–360.

For several months previous to the seizure of the rams the Foreign Office had been inundated with affidavits by Mr. Dudley, the Liverpool Consul. The law officers of the Crown had looked with distrust upon these Consular statements. They recognised probably the stereotyped form with which they had become unpleasantly familiar in the *Alexandra* case. They saw the names of Clarence R. Yonge and George Temple Chapman attached to some of them, and doubtless shrank from again bringing two such witnesses before a jury. At any rate, they reported several times that the "depositions were insufficient," that there was "no evidence capable of being presented to a court of justice," etc.

The last time the law officers were consulted before the seizure of the vessels appears to have been on the 19th–20th of August. The opinion is signed by Sir Roundell Palmer, who was then the Solicitor-General, now Lord Selborne and the Lord Chancellor of England. He alludes to the fresh affidavits that had been forwarded by Mr. Dudley, and concludes with the following final opinion:—"There is in fact no additional evidence, and we therefore continue to think that the interference of the Government, by seizure of these vessels or otherwise, would not be warranted by any of the depositions which have been brought to our notice."*

I suppose it will be admitted that every Government has the right to determine the standard of its own neutrality, subject only to the requirements of international law. I mean, that if the municipal law does not confer the power necessary to comply with neutral duties as prescribed by international law, the statutes should be amended; but if the municipal law is stronger than the law of nations requires, the neutral is not bound to enforce it with full rigour.

It is well known that the United States complained bitterly because her Majesty's Government, so they alleged, were precipitate in acknowledging the Confederate States as belligerents. The reply was in effect that the United States had themselves both created and acknowledged the state of war, and that the British Government had only recognised a condition of affairs which already existed. The South could have urged a valid plea to belligerent rights, and the claim could hardly have been denied, but the chief Powers took the initiative, and acknowledged the existence of a *de facto* Government at Richmond, as soon as the President of the United States proclaimed a blockade of the Southern ports. This recognition did not, however, carry with it a diplomatic equality with foreign States, and

* See "British Case," Appendix, vol. ii., pp. 337, 338.

the Confederate Government could not therefore communicate its views nor urge remonstrances in a direct official manner.

Great Britain laid down at a very early date the rules of neutrality by which she would be guided. It was manifest from the very beginning that those rules, even if administered with scrupulous impartiality, would give the United States an advantage, because of their open ports and their command of the sea. But the Confederate Government, perceiving the improbability of getting a modification of the rules, refrained from wrangling over them, and was content to use the opportunities of supplying the wants of the country to the best possible advantage. One of the chief requirements of the South was ships, not only for the purpose of cruising against the enemy, but to run the blockade.

If there had been anything in the municipal law of Great Britain which prohibited the purchase of an unarmed ship for any subsequent purpose whatever, or if the responsible Ministers of the Crown had stated specifically that there was a difference in principle between trading with a belligerent in arms and in ships, and that they would permit the one and forbid the other, the justice of the distinction would have been doubted, and the policy questioned, but both belligerents would at least have known what to expect. The odds against the Confederacy, great enough in all conscience at best, would have been somewhat increased, but the Southern people would have fought their battle with none the less spirit, even though with less chance of success. But the Foreign Enlistment Act (as it stood in 1861–65) did not forbid a British subject to build or sell a ship of any kind to any mortal man who could pay for her. This has been settled by the decision of a court of law, which has never been reversed, and there is not in the original definition of their neutral policy, nor in the subsequent statements of Ministers, any notice or hint that it was their purpose to draw the line at ships, and to set a ban upon that branch of trade alone. On the contrary, whether we examine the speeches of the Prime Minister and the Solicitor-General in Parliament, or the despatches of the Foreign Secretary, we find one uniform maxim, one fundamental rule of action, namely, that there is no difference in principle between selling a belligerent rifles and gunpowder or ships, and that her Majesty's Government cannot interfere with or forbid either.

The feeling of the Government on the above subject was never more plainly expressed than in Earl Russell's letter of September 11th, 1863, to Mr. Adams, in which his lordship not only reiterates the general proposition that muskets and ships may be dealt in alike, but with striking particularity he proceeds to specify a condition of affairs in which rifles and cannon, swords, bayonets and gunpowder, may be more useful to one belligerent than a ship to the other, and says that neither a ship nor a musket ceases to be neutral until it is in the possession of a belligerent and is about to be used by him against his enemy, and yet in that very letter he announces the purpose to seize the alleged Confederate vessels.

It appears from the printed documents that the vessels were seized by the order of her Majesty's Secretary of State for Foreign Affairs on his own authority as a Minister of the Crown. There was at that time "no evidence capable of being presented to a court of justice"; the seizure was therefore an act of the State, an exercise of prerogative, and not a process of law. Earl Russell stated that the object of the seizure was to detain the ships until the Government could obtain satisfactory evidence of their destination. To get the evidence the Government took a great deal of trouble, and must have incurred no little expense. A special Commission was sent to Egypt to inquire whether the Viceroy, Ismail Pasha, had really ordered Messrs. Bravay to build two armour-cased vessels for him in Europe; and I may state at once that the Viceroy said he had not. This was all the evidence the Government ever did get, and no legal proceedings were ever taken against either the Messrs. Bravay or Messrs. Laird, except the filing of the "information." But was her Majesty's Government under any obligation to go to all this trouble and expense to inquire into the business relations of a French mercantile house and a foreign Government? Was it not perfectly legal for Messrs. Bravay, being French subjects, and their country at peace with both belligerents and with Great Britain, to contract for any ships they liked in England? and did it matter at all, as a question of law, what they intended to do with them after taking them away from Liverpool? Is it to be understood that the precedent is now established that whenever Great Britain is a neutral in all future wars, the Government will undertake to compel every shipbuilder in the kingdom to report who he is working for, and will then require the person, even though a neutral foreigner, to prove what he is going to do with the ship? If this is so, the Consuls of the belligerents will give her Majesty's Foreign Office more work than any ordinary staff can accomplish.

When the arrangements were made to sell the two rams to Messrs. Bravay, there was no necessity for manufacturing any plea of a pretended contract with the Viceroy of Egypt. It was well known both in Paris and in Alexandria, and it was known to the French Government, that the firm had been for years in business relations with the Egyptian Government, and that they had executed large contracts for the Viceroy in France. The letters from M. François Bravay respecting the commissions he had undertaken on account of the Viceroy, and the reply of the Paris house, quoted in a previous part of this chapter, were written months before any arrangement in respect to the rams at Liverpool was contemplated, and therefore could not have been prepared as a cover for that transaction. Indeed, at the date of those letters neither Mr. Slidell nor I knew anything whatever of Messrs. Bravay, and had never met any member of the firm. It is well known in Europe that his Highness Ismail Pasha, and his predecessor, Said Pasha, had very large and peculiar dealings with private persons in England and France, and that they both made efforts to add to their military and naval strength secretly, wishing for political reasons to avoid the interference or inquisitive supervision of the Sublime Porte.

When the Messrs. Laird were requested to sell the ships, they were open, of course, to all practicable offers, and they looked about for a purchaser, just as any other business men would have done under the same circumstances. They knew that the sale of the ships would involve the release of one contractor, with whose financial position they were satisfied, and the substitution of another, as to whose commercial credit they must be assured. Any ship-builder in England would have treated the matter in this way, and no other. When the Messrs. Bravay came forward to buy the ships, it is not probable that Messrs. Laird inquired particularly into the precise nature of their dealings with the Viceroy. It did not concern them to know whether the "order" from the Egyptian Government was a specific contract in writing or not; I do not even know whether they asked anything about it. As prudent business men, they inquired into the financial position of the Messrs. Bravay, and, being satisfied with the security they could give for the payment of the two ships, they reported the offer and effected the sale. The whole transaction was carried out in a perfectly legal way, and the ships became the absolute property of the Messrs. Bravay. No process of law could have destroyed their title. Of this we were assured by eminent counsel. They made all subsequent payments, and when Her Majesty's Government called upon Messrs. Laird to say for whom they were building the ships, they replied "For Messrs. A. Bravay and Co., No. 6, Rue de Londres, Paris."

The Viceroy had refrained from making a specific contract in writing for any ships "for political reasons." When brought to the ordeal of a formal diplomatic inquiry, he repudiated the transaction for the same reasons; but even though he thus denied the validity of the alleged commission to M. Bravay, how could that destroy the right of the Paris firm to the property which they held by a clear, indisputable title in England? If a neutral has the right to sell a rifle or a ship to a belligerent, and her Majesty's Ministers and the Court of Exchequer have both declared that he has, why may not a neutral buy from another neutral a rifle or a ship and sell either or both of them afterwards to a belligerent for a profit?

I think anyone who examines this case fairly upon the facts will be driven to acknowledge, even if he does not willingly admit, that in seizing the two rams at Birkenhead, and in bringing about a forced sale to the British Admiralty, Earl Russell departed from the rules of neutrality laid down by her Majesty's Government, from the principles often affirmed by himself, and from the judgment of a competent court, and that he applied the Foreign Enlistment Act, not merely to prevent the danger of hostile collision, or an infringement of law within the kingdom, which the Lord Chief Baron said was its intent, but so as to afford protection to a belligerent, which he distinctly said was not the intent.

I have not pretended to discuss this question with reference to international law as commonly understood, and I do not bring it forward as a matter of complaint on behalf of the late Confederate States. Arguments upon dead issues cannot change results or moderate past disappointments. My whole and only purpose in this narrative is to demonstrate that the Confederate Government, in the effort to supply its wants in England during the Civil War, acted with due circumspection, and endeavoured to conform to the laws of the realm and to the principles of neutrality as they were expounded by the highest constituted authorities in the kingdom.

My acquaintance with the Messrs. Bravay began and ended with the transaction described in this chapter. I have never seen a member of the firm since. Mr. Adams, in one of his strongly worded letters on the subject, speaks of M. Bravay as "a French commercial adventurer, proved to have been capable of prevarication, if not of absolute falsehood." As a matter of fact, M. Bravay was not placed in a position requiring him to prevaricate, and was certainly not tested to the extreme point insinuated by Mr. Adams. He exhibited proof of his large dealings with the Viceroy, and showed the correspondence with reference to the building of two ships, merely as evidence that he could undertake a large transaction. I think no one who was conversant with the circumstances would have doubted that he was telling the truth in the statement then made, and I have never heard of his making any other. The firm performed their agreement with Mr. Slidell and me with perfect good faith as regards all monetary transactions, and unhesitatingly waived the stipulated commission when the enterprise failed. The only way in which it could possibly be said that they misled us was in this respect, that they were very sanguine that the Viceroy would not deny the verbal order for the ships, and that even if he did, then, as French subjects, they could get the vessels out of England and take them to a French port. In these respects they failed both in their expectations and in their promises; but there was a political element in the transaction which helped to give them confidence and to mislead us; and there was another disappointment in store for the Confederate Government emanating from the same political source, which will be fully explained in another chapter.

CHAPTER VIII

English Political Parties and the Civil War.—Pertinacity of Mr. Secretary Seward.—Vacillation of the Liberal Government.—Present Position of the Liberal Party.—The French Proclamation of Neutrality.—Arrangements for building cruisers at Bordeaux.—Appropriation of £2,000,000 for Ironclads by Congress.— Financial difficulties.—Propositions to purchase vessels from the French Navy.— Correspondence concerning the vessels building in France.—Deceptive attitude of the French Government.—The vessels sold by their imperative orders.—Panic at Boston and New York regarding the Confederate cruisers.

The compilers of the "Case" which was laid before the Tribunal of Arbitration at Geneva on behalf of the United States, asserted that England was the "arsenal and treasury" of the Confederate States. The Board of Trade returns demonstrate that both belligerents drew upon Great Britain for the "sinews of war," but that the United States obtained them in far greater quantities and with incomparably less difficulty than their adversary. However, the statement was in itself true, although the inference which it was the purpose of the "Case" to suggest was not true.

It is hardly an exaggeration—it certainly is not a mere "figure of speech"—to say that Great Britain is the arsenal, treasury, and dockyard of the greater part of the world. There is scarcely a civilized country which is not a debtor to England, either for a direct loan, or for help to develop her resources by the construction of what are called "internal improvements." British guns and British powder do duty in every war.

British-built ironclads form a part of nearly every foreign navy, and the commercial flags of many countries cover hulls of the well-known British type. No one whose faculties are not dwarfed by prejudice, or whose powers of observation are not contracted by national conceit, can or will deny that in the great mechanic arts, in building ships and manufacturing the heavy engines to propel them especially, Great Britain has outstripped all competitors. She actually owns about sixty per cent. of the world's shipping, and has supplied to others a portion of the remaining forty per cent.

France, in regard to ships, at least, has been exceptionally independent, and both Germany and Italy are diligently extending their dockyard capacities; but I think a practical man who wanted a first-class ship and engines, or a large quantity of well-made arms for quick delivery, or a batch of great guns in which he could feel confidence, or any heavy iron or steel work, would almost instinctively come to England to supply his want; and if a foreign company wished money for some great engineering enterprise, they would be more likely to carry the scheme to London than to any other capital, and would look for the money in Lombard Street before going anywhere else.

This was certainly the view taken by the Confederate Government at the beginning of the Civil War. It was to England that their agents were first sent, and it was to England that they looked for a quick supply of all necessities. Her Britannic Majesty's Proclamation of Neutrality was issued on May 13th, 1861. That document began with the usual preamble, then cited the clauses of the Foreign Enlistment Act (second, seventh, and eighth) which were most likely to be infringed, then expressed a kindly intimation that the primary object was to save British subjects from the danger of breaking the law through inadvertence, and finally warned all persons that they would incur the penal consequences of the statute and of the law of nations if they offended them in any particular.

The proclamation was eminently British, and therefore eminently constitutional. There was, first, the royal acknowledgment of the supremacy of the law, then the loving solicitude for the subject, then the warning to all parties not to infringe the statute, then a plain straightforward statement that those who did offend would be left to take the consequences, whether by due process of law within the kingdom, or by such penalties as a belligerent might inflict if the offender was caught without the kingdom. There was no voluntary exposition of the law in the proclamation, no dogmatic prohibition against specified acts; everyone was commanded not to infringe the statute, but he was left to discover precisely what was forbidden and what was permissible through his own instincts, or, if he was wise and prudent, by the help of those who were learned in the law.

To the representative of a belligerent the document at first blush seemed very plain and very satisfactory. He had only to consult two or more eminent gentlemen of the "wig and gown," and to walk within the lines prescribed by them, in order to obtain all that it was admissible for him to buy with money, and to be sure of what he could do, without fear of penalty, or the feeling that he was oppressed by a load of obligation. It has been shown in a previous chapter that the Confederate agents took every practicable precaution, and made every possible effort to discover the intent, the scope, and the technical meaning of the law. They seem to have been correctly advised, because the opinion given them by counsel at the very beginning of the war was confirmed by the official statements of Ministers of the Crown, and afterwards settled beyond further dispute by the decision of a court of law. However, the Confederate Government soon found that even in constitutional England the declarations of Ministers do not always establish a policy with the rigid constancy of the Medes and Persians, and that a Secretary of State can enforce restraints upon trade, and can practically hinder a traffic which is not only guiltless in principle, according to his own previous showing, but which the duly constituted courts have declared to be legal.

It is neither my wish nor my purpose to impute unworthy motives or fears to any British Minister, and nothing would induce me to write a single sentence that could influence the people of the South to harbour an unkind thought against Great Britain. I have already expressed the opinion that a great majority of the people of England sympathized with the South, and I could name many eminent men in both Houses of Parliament who took the trouble to examine the questions at issue between the two sections of the Union, and who were satisfied that the South was right in principle and justified in law. Some of the leading literary journals of the kingdom warmly espoused and ably defended the Southern cause during the whole of the contest, and have not been moved from their political opinions, or persuaded to shrink from expressing them on all suitable occasions, by the glamour which success has cast over the opposite and victorious side.

The commissioners and the principal agents of the Confederate States in England had opportunities for learning the feelings of different members of the Government, and of prominent men in both of the great parties, with a very near approach to certainty. I shall not be guilty of the indiscretion of classifying the Cabinet by name, but I may say that it was a common belief among the representatives of the Confederate States that two members of the Ministry, at least, were very favourable to the South, and that still another would have been disposed to give some support to certain members of the House of Commons who wished to bring in a motion for the recognition of the Government at Richmond, if he had not been impressed with the belief that the separation of the States was final, and that it would be both unnecessary and impolitic for the Government to give undue offence or encouragement to either of the combatants.

The Liberal Party was in power during the whole of the war, and the same Party, and a Cabinet composed of very nearly the same Ministers, were again in power at the time when the Treaty of Washington was negotiated in 1871—a treaty whose object it was to settle the "*Alabama* claims," and which resulted in the Geneva Arbitration, and the £3,000,000 damages. I have never thought that the leaning towards either side in the American Civil War was due to any well-defined Party tendencies in Great Britain. I have the strongest possible reasons for believing that if the Conservative Party had been in power, their policy would have been strictly neutral, and the Confederate Government would not have been recognised. But at the same time I believe that the Advanced Liberals, or Radicals, as they are sometimes called, and who are generally supposed to have Republican tendencies, were favourable to the North. The politicians and statesmen of that class are in general harmony with the Liberal Party, and most independent observers think they are gradually getting the control of it. Those Advanced Liberals had persuaded themselves to regard the Government of the United States as "a Government for the people by the people," and they feared that a final dissolution of the Union would be considered a failure of the Republican form of Government, and would check, if not destroy, the progress towards a more Democratic system in Europe.

The temperament and type of mind which inclines a man to Radical and thorough changes, makes him also ardent, active, and aggressive. He rarely if ever convinces his open and avowed political adversary, who is altogether a person of different mould, but he as rarely fails to persuade, or to overcome by his restless untiring energy, the scruples of those who are bound to him by hereditary loyalty to a Party name, which has come to be associated in their minds with ideas of benevolent legislation and philanthropic progress, but who are nevertheless often startled by the suddenness and rapidity of the forward movement.

There were some strong men of the above type in the counsels of the Liberal Party, if not in the Cabinet, at the time of the Civil War, and the ardour with which they supported the Federal Government, and the vehemence with which they denounced the Southern leaders and the Southern people, are still fresh in the memory of those representatives of the Confederacy who survive. Even at this late date, when the best men at the North and at the South are trying to forget the injuries inflicted upon each other during the strife, when there seems to be a growing desire on both sides of the Potomac to shun all references to the causes of the war, and to fix the memory and the hearts of the people upon subjects of past history which they can dwell upon with feelings of common sympathy, the English Radical, true to his unfailing instincts, and heedless of the fact that the lately dissevered States are again both in amity and in union, continues to arouse the bitter memories of one side, and to inflame the jealous suspicion of the other, with no other visible or imaginable purpose than to illustrate some favourite political crotchet.

As recently as last year (May, 1882) a leader of the Radical wing of the Liberal Party, and a member of the Cabinet, used the opportunity, while delivering a literary address, to taunt the South with reference to that "institution" which expired seventeen years ago, and chose for his illustration a poem which is none the less unfair in spirit because its statements may be borne out by exceptional facts. Is it possible that men filling high and responsible positions can think it prudent and politic (I do not say friendly and Christian-like) thus to remind the six million Anglo-Americans of the Southern States that there are still among the leaders of that Party which now governs England probable future Ministers who can thus ignore the duties of international comity, and who wilfully transgress those rules of courtesy and respect for the feelings of others which are commonly thought to be essential marks of a well-bred man in private life?

Everyone even moderately acquainted with American political history, and who knows anything of the exigencies of Parties in the United States, must be aware that it is possible for a comparatively small minority of the electors in that country, when impelled to act and vote together by some common feeling, to hold the balance between the two principal Parties, and when such a contingency arises at the time of a Presidential election, they may have it in their power to determine the foreign policy of the Government. This may be seen now in the tampering of both Parties with the question of Chinese immigration, each wishing to conciliate the trans-Rocky-Mountain States.

Thoughtful and observant men perceive a danger to England in the Irish American vote. If any considerable portion of the Southern people should be impelled by a feeling of irritation against England to cast their votes with that already embittered faction at the North, the complications of the Irish question might be increased so as to become a permanent menace and real danger to Great Britain. Men at the South who read and reflect would regret such a course of events, and the alliance which would tend to produce such consequences; but where universal suffrage prevails, it is the floating masses who turn the scale; and they, as all experience has shown, act from impulse, and not from conviction.

I would like, so far as it is in my power, to convince the people of the South that a vast majority of both of the great English Parties, and of the people of Great Britain generally, have the most kindly feelings for the United States, without reference to geographical divisions, or the partialities which were manifested during the Civil War. I confidently believe that the best men among Conservatives and Liberals alike have no other wish than for the happiness, prosperity, and perpetuity of the American Union. I believe that sympathy for the South was more general among Conservatives than among Liberals; but probably this difference was only apparent because the Radicals, who are a section of the Liberal Party, were to a man, so far as I know, for the North. The Conservative and the Moderate, or genuine Liberals, whatever were their opinions or sympathies during the war, have ceased to foster any ill-will towards either side, and they have the good sense and the good feeling to avoid all reference to irritating reminiscences when they have occasion to speak of the United States. The unadulterated Radical is, however, too thorough to be fettered by the dictates of prudence or the restraints of a politic reserve. To refrain from expressing an opinion because it might wound his neighbour's feelings, or unnecessarily irritate his opponent, seems to him very like the suppression of the truth. He confounds bluntness with honesty, and in the eagerness to enforce his views he adds denunciation to argument. His Liberalism consists in an unlimited license to all others to think and to act as he dictates. He is full of flattery, and practises even an appearance of subserviency, to those who will take the lead in measures that he approves, but becomes restive and even dictatorial if there is any hesitation or sign of halting. The labouring man is his hobby, the peer and the landowner are his aversion; but it is noticeable that his fondness for and interest in the artizan and the workman are not so much for the individual as the class, and are manifested rather in exciting their jealousy and ill-will against those who are above them than in stimulating their pride and arousing their energies with the laudable purpose to elevate themselves. It seems hardly possible for a "Radical" to defend a principle or to support a policy wholly upon the merits of the questions involved, and then to accept the result with patience if defeated, and with moderation if success-ful.

During the American Civil War the English Radical took sides with the North. He defended the action of the Federal Government with ardour, and praised the patriotism of the Northern people with enthusiasm. He condemned the leaders of the South with harshness, and traduced the whole population south of the Potomac with heat and passion, embrac-ing them in one general, sweeping, all-inclusive denunciation. He seized upon slavery as an effective "cry" by which to prejudice the public mind, and persisted in asserting that the North was fighting to free the slave, in spite of the declaration of President Lincoln and a joint resolution of both Houses of Congress that the war was undertaken for the restora-tion of the Union, and not for the abolition of slavery. So long as the world lasts there will be found in it men of hot temper and dogmatic will, and therefore an exhibition of vituperative passion and intolerance must be expected from them whenever the course of public events is contrary to their wishes or theories. But the "Advanced Liberal" had an undoubted right to his opinion, whether founded upon prejudice or calm convic-tion; and the Southern people will, I am sure, be glad to forget the op-probrious epithets which were cast upon them during the heat of the struggle, now that "grim-visaged war" has given place to cheerful, smiling peace with its bounteous blessings, if they are not constantly reminded of them by indiscreet references to the irritating subjects which disquieted their minds and aroused their resentment in the trying times between the attack upon Fort Sumter and the surrender of Lee at Appomattox Court-house.

It is not impossible—indeed, if the Liberal Party remains in power it is not improbable—that a Radical Minister of Foreign Affairs may have to treat upon some delicate and important question of international policy with an American Secretary of State, or a President of the United States, who followed Lee through the Virginian campaigns, or who was born and bred in the same part of the country as Jefferson Davis and Stonewall Jackson; and it would clear the negotiation of some embarrassment if the English representative could feel conscious that he had done nothing to perpetuate a family feud after the opposing parties had composed their differences and were again living in union and harmony. No public man could now win the favour of any respectable body of electors in New York or Massachusetts by speaking ill of the South or of the Southern people, and no man would be tolerated in Northern society who at-tempted to keep up the animosities of the war, and certainly no foreigner can hope to gratify either North or South by words or acts whose manifest tendency would be to irritate or offend either side.

If I mention Earl Russell's name in this connection, it is not with the purpose to class him among the Radicals, or to intimate that he ever did use language in respect to either North or South which could be construed into ridicule or reproach. Whatever may have been his lordship's private opinions as to the merits of the contest, or whatever may have been his sympathies, I have never seen in one of his numerous despatches, or in the published reports of his speeches, a single sentence or utterance which could arouse the personal hostility of any reasonable Southern man. Earl Russell, as the Foreign Secretary, was necessarily the active member of the Cabinet in carrying out its neutral policy, and is not to be held individually responsible for what either Federal or Confederate may have thought objectionable in that policy. In saying that his sympathies were with the North, I merely give currency to the impression commonly held by the representatives of the Confederate States in England during the war, and I can give no other grounds for the impression than the opinion to the same effect which was often, and I may say unanimously, expressed by those politicians and other frequenters of the London clubs and London Society with whom we were brought in contact. But I do not now affirm that Earl Russell carried out the neutral policy of the Government with a deliberate purpose to favour one belligerent; all that I say is, that the course pursued by him was not in accordance with the principles laid down by himself and his colleagues, and by the judgment of the Lord Chief Baron of the Exchequer.

It must be admitted that his lordship had a very trying and difficult office to fulfil. The United States Minister gave him no peace and but little rest. The duty of replying to the long argumentative despatches of Mr. Adams, and the perusal of the numerous consular affidavits which accompanied them, must have been a very serious labour, and it is only fair to remember that there was no recognised Confederate agent who could address him officially and freely, and thus modify the effect of the statements on the other side, or set before him reasons for non-interference. The Radical element within the Liberal Party, if not actually within the Cabinet, was also a strong and active force, always exercised to check the Government in any apparent concession to the South, and ever striving to nullify the benefit which the Confederate States might obtain from their recognised position as belligerents.

The speeches of individual Ministers, and the official despatches of Earl Russell, laid down certain rules of action, and clearly set out the principles of neutrality it was their purpose to enforce. They would have no enlistment of her Majesty's subjects to serve either belligerent, nor any arming of ships within any portion of the British dominions. Vessels-of-war should not lie in British ports to watch each other's movements, and they should not use British harbours as places of outfit and supply from which they might issue to cruise against their enemy. But the British tradesman was to be as little hampered as possible, and was to be left free to sell and deliver arms and ammunition, and even ships suitable for war-like purposes, to either belligerent. There was no difference in principle, and no distinction in law, between the traffic in one or the other of the above articles, and her Majesty's Government could not strain the principles of neutrality to suit a particular case, or apply them especially and with discriminating rigour to the trade of shipbuilding alone, because that would tend to impede and embarrass a business in which great numbers of her Majesty's subjects found a source of honest livelihood.*

These were the principles to which the British Government clearly committed itself, and anyone who will take the trouble to read the Parliamentary debates on questions affecting the action of Great Britain as a neutral, or the despatches of Earl Russell, will perceive how strongly and repeatedly those principles were asserted, and their justice and fairness defended, by members of the Cabinet. There is no doubt that the plainness with which members of the Government spoke in reference to the equality of both belligerents before the law, and the repeated declarations that a British merchant might sell an unarmed ship to either North or South as lawfully as he might sell a rifle or a sabre, gave dissatisfaction and offence to Mr. Seward, who, as was said in the "British Case," wanted her Majesty's Government to discover what articles the Confederates most needed, and then to strike them off the list of goods which might be legally dealt in.

The statements of Ministers in regard to neutral duties and the freedom of trade with belligerents were never withdrawn nor even modified by any counter-declaration in Parliament, but the practice of the Government became, under the joint pressure of Mr. Seward's remonstrances and the influence of the extreme Radicals, more and more restrictive with reference to the especial wants of the Confederates, until at last they did practically enforce the very policy which it is alleged in the "British Case" that the United States wished them to agree to at the beginning. Her

---

* See Earl Russell's letter to Mr. Adams, Oct. 26th, 1863, "North America," (no. 1), 1864, "The *Alabama*," continuation of correspondence presented to Parliament, March, 1863.

Majesty's Government have realized the truth of a saying which has almost obtained the force and currency of a proverb, namely, that a concession of principle, or the yielding of a point to strong and persistent pressure and persuasion, is never received in the spirit of a spontaneous offering, and is never remembered with gratitude.

The Southern people believed that a policy once clearly enunciated by a British Ministry would be consistently followed, and they thought that it was only necessary to keep within the lines of that policy, in order to obtain all that their necessities required. They watched with interest, but at first without misgiving, the vigorous efforts by appeal, by argument, and even by threats, which were made by the United States to procure a change in that policy. They knew that those efforts were strongly supported by the extreme politicians who belonged to the Party then in power, but still the rules of action laid down were plain and emphatic. They had been stated by the Ministers chiefly responsible for the foreign relations of the country, and had been defended by the law officers of the Crown. They were afterwards confirmed in principle by judicial sentence.

When the Government at Richmond contemplated the situation of affairs, there did not appear to be any cause to fear that the declarations of Ministers would prove to be mere figures of speech, or that a judicial decision would be made inoperative by the action of a Secretary of State. However, it is now a matter of history that the hopes of the Confederate Government and of the Southern people were ill-founded. Her Majesty's Government yielded to the joint pressure from within and from without, and they did at last precisely what the United States demanded in the beginning, and what several members of the Government had declared they could not do without showing favour to one belligerent, and interfering unjustly and unduly with one particular branch of trade, which they had often affirmed was quite as proper in principle and in law as any other. The Southern people were naturally disappointed at the unexpected wavering of the British Government, and if at the time they felt irritated and resentful, it can hardly be thought surprising. But they found no opportunity to express their resentment by effective remonstrance, and they have practically condoned the injury, and I believe would soon forget it altogether if the Radicals will only let by-gones be by-gones.

Mr. Seward, however, was in a different position. Having carried his point by a combination of persuasion and bravado, greatly helped by the efforts of his Radical allies, he never did forget, and never did forgive, the impartial utterances of Ministers and the original intent expressed by them to give a fair field and no favour to either side. He appears to have kept a record of every indiscreet admission by a member of the Government, of every speech which could be distorted into an encouragement to the South, while the words of comfort and support to the United States, and the great final concession, were forgotten, or at least cast aside. His fixed and unalterable purpose was to extort from her Majesty's Government, not only an acknowledgment of their original error, but retribution for it, and he bequeathed his purpose and his policy to his successor in office.

The diplomatic correspondence and the records of the Geneva Arbitration demonstrate the vigour and relentless zeal with which that purpose and policy were prosecuted. It is now known that six years after the war the United States wrung from Mr. Gladstone's Government (the same Party, and in part the same Ministers, who were in power in 1861–65) an expression of "the regret felt by them for the escape of the *Alabama* and other vessels from British ports, and for the depredations committed by those vessels,"* and finally induced them to submit the questions at issue to a Tribunal of Arbitration, not, however, to be decided according to the principles and rules of international law in force and binding upon all nations at the time when the alleged causes of complaint were said to have arisen, but upon certain new rules, especially agreed upon by the contracting parties—rules which are binding upon no other Powers, and which, together with the expressions of regret, and the Ministerial admissions, which were most adroitly used by the advocates of the United States, placed Great Britain in a very weak position before the Arbitrators.

The vacillation of her Majesty's Government in dealing with the questions which grew out of the American Civil War, and the very apparent contradiction between the polemical theory of neutral duties expounded by a portion of the Ministry and the practice of those duties by the Secretary of State who directed the foreign policy, can only be understood and explained by taking into account the peculiar condition of that Party to which the Ministry belonged.

It is manifest to independent observers of English politics that the Liberal Party embraces within its ample fold two principal sections, whose policy would lead to very different results if carried out in its entirety. Those two great divisions of the Party are held together by a traditionary

* See Article I., Treaty of May 8th, 1871.

link, and by agreement upon certain general principles of reform in regard to domestic affairs and some not very clearly defined doctrines with reference to colonial and foreign policy; but they seem to differ very widely both as regards the extent of the required reforms and the mode in which they should be accomplished. That division of the Party whose wish it is to proceed most swiftly and thoroughly in the direction of reform, and who also manifest the purpose to withdraw more and more from international politics and from imperial control over the colonies, has been for the last quarter of a century increasing its power and influence. It has not yet achieved complete control of affairs, and cannot strictly and specifically direct the policy of the Government; but it has for some years held a position of so much authority and influence, by reason of its increasing numbers and the vigorous energy of its members, that no Liberal Ministry is possible without its support, or without one or more representatives from its ranks in the Cabinet. Now, it would be wholly out of place, in a narrative of this kind, to discuss English Party politics, or to pronounce an opinion whether the principles of the Advanced Liberals would conduce more to the happiness and wealth of Great Britain and to the maintenance of the Empire than a more Conservative policy; but it is not improper to state, what it seems to me must be manifest to all disinterested students of current English history, that so long as the Liberal Party is not impelled by a common motive, and is not controlled by statesmen who agree upon the method as well as in respect to the general principles upon which the home and foreign policy of the country shall be conducted, there must continue to be confusion, apparent contradictions, weakness, vacillation, and more or less sacrifice of prestige, accompanied sometimes with loss of money.

The lack of consistency, and the inability to follow in practice the line of policy laid down in theory by the Ministry during the American Civil War, cost Great Britain £3,000,000, and placed the country in a very weak and undignified position before the Tribunal of Arbitration at Geneva. England was made to stand before that international court in the character of a defendant—I was almost going to say a criminal. She was represented by the plaintiffs to have acknowledged her sin and to have apologized for it; she was charged through her officials with all sorts of complicity with fraud against her own municipal laws, and with connivance at the violation of her neutrality; and really, the reply to all this seems to have been rather a plea for mitigation of damages than a bold, confident, unflinching repudiation of the charges and insinuations.

If the independent critic looks at the condition of English affairs now, in the year 1882,* he will perceive lamentable confusion and danger to the Empire both at home and abroad—Ireland disturbed, discontented, mutinous; the Eastern Question, with its necessary appendages, in a chronic state of fermentation; the House of Commons wrangling over measures declared to be of vital importance, and yet often wasting days in discussing side issues and abstract questions, which, when they have been determined, settle nothing.

The difficulty is the same as that which caused the vacillation during the American Civil War—the impossibility of making the theory and practice of the Government tally, the inability to confirm by official act and by legislation the policy and the promises sketched out in Ministerial speeches and other forms of declaration.

The Southern people may, I think, feel assured that the course pursued by her Majesty's Government towards the Confederate States was not the outcome of an unfriendly and unsympathetic feeling on the part of the majority of British subjects to them or to the cause for which they were fighting; but it arose from the necessity of a sort of compromise between the Ministers, who wished to conduct the foreign policy of the country at that time upon what they had pronounced to be the proper line of neutral duty and due consideration for every branch of home trade, and those extreme men in their Party who, after the policy was declared and published, urged and enforced a modification to suit their special leanings.

Until the great Liberal Party can decide which section of its leaders shall assume the control of its policy, and is prepared to give to that section undivided support, the people of Great Britain must make up their minds to submit to some confusion in public affairs, some apparent vacillation and inconsistencies in the action of "Liberal Cabinets." It is manifest that the Liberal Party is undergoing the process of readjusting its constituent forces, and the future policy of that Party will depend upon which class of politicians may gain the ultimate ascendency, and whether their control of affairs proves to be thorough and undisputed. It appears to be practically impossible for two sections of the same Party, who differ materially concerning the methods of government, to agree upon a middle course which shall fulfil the conditions of a "happy mean." Experience has shown that the action of a political organization in that condition is intermittent, and is active or passive, vigorous or feeble, according as the opinions of one or the other section prevail at a given time, or on the

---

* This chapter was written in June, 1882, as explained in the preface, and the Egyptian War was in prospect.

occasion of a particular emergency. Sometimes the influence of the two factions is so nearly in equilibrium that nothing can be done, and then public affairs drift until there is a crisis, when the ship of State has to beat up to the lost position, like a vessel working to windward against a leeward tide.

The Commissioners of the Confederate States perceived, as the war progressed, the tendency of her Majesty's Government to drift from the position assumed by the leading Ministers of the Crown in their interpretation of neutral duties and the freedom of trade. Mr. John Slidell, the Commissioner to France, occupied in many respects a more favourable position for discovering the purposes and feelings of the Government to which he was accredited than his colleague in England. Although not officially recognised as the diplomatic agent of the Confederate Government, he was permitted to communicate with the Ministers of State, and even with the Emperor himself, freely, and it may almost be said confidentially. He was thus able to discover from the highest sources whether it was the purpose of the Imperial Government to enforce with rigour the restrictions set out in the declaration of neutrality, or whether the strict and explicit terms of that declaration would be made pliable in the common interests of every branch of French trade.

The Proclamation of Neutrality issued by the Emperor Napoleon III. was published nearly a month after that of her Britannic Majesty, namely, June 10th, 1861, but the prohibitions were much more emphatically stated. Instead of a general enumeration of what was contrary to law, and a warning to all persons not to transgress, it set out under five heads or clauses the precise and specific acts that would not be permitted, or which were forbidden.

The third clause was in these words:—*"Il est interdit tout Français de prendre commission de l'une des eux parties pour armer des vaisseaux en guerre, ou 'accepter des lettres de marque pour faire le course maritime, ou de concourir d'une manière quelconque à équipement ou l'armament d'une navire de guerre ou orsaire de l'une des deux parties."*

The above clause, it will be perceived, forbad any French subject to co-operate in *any manner whatever* in the equipment or armament of a vessel-of-war or a privateer for either belligerent, and French lawyers afterwards consulted were unanimous in the opinion that the Government would be bound to prevent any ship leaving France for the service of the Confederate States.

There was no question here of the probable interpretation of a somewhat ambiguous statute, no dependence upon a Government pledged by constitutional requirement, as well as by habitual usage, to submit questions involving the rights of individuals to the legal tribunals. The Executive Government of France was at that time well-nigh autocratic, and it was fully understood that whatever might be the declared policy, it might and could be modified in practice without any public notice or any formal appeal to the law courts to determine the meaning of specified statutes.

It was generally believed at the time, and so far as I know it has never been doubted, that the British and French Governments came to an early agreement that they would act in general concert during the American Civil War. It is, I believe, equally well known that the French Emperor was more favourable to the recognition of the South than the Government of her Britannic Majesty, and that at one period of the war he was prepared to take decisive action in that direction, but was deterred by the disinclination of the British Ministry to follow.

The reasons why the Confederate Government sent their agents to England in the first place have already been stated. The dogmatic prohibitions of the French declaration of neutrality confirmed the prudence of that course from a business point of view. In England it was reasonable to expect more liberty of action, a freer as well as a cheaper market, and surer means of discovering what might be safely attempted. In France, everything might and probably would depend upon the secret purposes of the Chief of the State, and the effect which the chances of success or defeat to the South might have upon him.

It is no part of the object of this narrative to discuss the general policy of the French Government during the Civil War, or to suggest how far the desire to acquire a predominating influence in Mexico may have inclined the late Emperor to favour the South. Manifestly, an Imperial Government would stand a better chance of sustaining itself in Mexico against two rival Republics, than against one undivided Democratic Union pledged to resist European interference with the balance of power in America.

A French army on the left flank of the Confederacy, and free transportation of contraband goods through Mexico, might have been a very encouraging support to the Government at Richmond, and the privilege of getting ships fit to break the blockade, and to cover the import of indispensable supplies into Wilmington and Charleston, might have been a judicious concession to that Government. Some such reflections have doubtless occurred to many who watched the course of events at the time. Confining myself in these respects to a simple record of historical facts, I will only state that during the year 1862 Mr. Slidell received intimation that if the Confederate Government would make arrangements to build ships-of-war in France, the builders would not be interfered with, and that the vessels when completed would be permitted to leave the French ports upon any plausible plea the builders might state. The suggestions were made to Mr. Slidell by persons who were in positions of close relationship with the Emperor, and when he became satisfied that they were made with authority, their purport was reported by him to the Secretary of State at Richmond, and in the autumn of 1862 he wrote and advised me to come to him in Paris for consultation on the subject.

When Mr. Slidell first made the suggestion, I was unable to take any decisive action. The contracts on behalf of the Navy Department in England were so large, that there appeared to be a startling deficiency in the financial arrangements to meet them, and although Messrs. Fraser, Trenholm and Co. had already made advances to the Navy Department, and did afterwards pledge their own commercial credit at critical periods, yet at the particular time in question they were under such heavy advances for the War Department that I could not ask them to take further liability. I explained the situation of affairs to Mr. Slidell, but he was much impressed with the importance of the assurances he had privately received, and urged me to come to Paris and try the French dockyards as soon as the finances would admit of fresh operations, instead of depending upon the wavering policy of the British Ministry, and the probable delay, expense, and publicity of a law-suit.

The Secretary of the Navy was especially desirous to keep a sufficient number of cruisers afloat to thoroughly alarm the enemy for the safety of his commercial shipping, and thus to draw off his best ships from the blockade in order to protect it. He had no sooner learned the havoc the *Alabama* and *Florida* were committing than he instructed me to send out at least four ships of similar type, to provide against their loss or capture. He made every possible effort to supply the necessary funds, and finally arranged with the Secretary of the Treasury that a part of the £3,000,000 European loan then in contemplation should be devoted to that purpose. He informed me that a special fiscal agent of the Treasury Department would be sent to Europe to manage the distribution of the loan, and to assume a general control of the finances, and that he would be fully instructed as to the requirements for the navy.

In March, 1863, the success of the loan seemed to be assured, and both Mr. Mason and Mr. Slidell thought that in view of the official advices I had received, that a portion of it would be appropriated for the specific purpose of building additional cruisers, I might venture at least to make all the preliminary arrangements.

I had previously reported to the Navy Department the manifest signs of a purpose in the British Ministry to enforce the Foreign Enlistment Act more rigidly with reference to ships than any other articles of trade, and had reported my purpose to act upon the information Mr. Slidell had received and upon his advice. About the middle of March, 1863, Mr. Slidell sent the business agent of a large shipbuilder to inform me what his principal could undertake, and I went immediately to Paris to put affairs in such train that the work could be begun as soon as the financial arrangements were satisfactorily settled. Mr. Slidell made an appointment for a joint consultation between himself, the builder with whom he had already conferred, and me. The class of vessel and the armament did not require much consideration, the chief, and indeed the only important points for serious deliberation, were the terms of the neutrality proclamation, and the probable chance of getting the ships to sea when completed.

The shipbuilder who thus came forward to supply our wants was M. L. Arman. His establishment was at Bordeaux; he had done much work for the French navy, was then building two iron-cased floating batteries and a very large troop-ship for the Government, and there could be no doubt that he had the plant and all the necessary staff and commercial credit to justify his undertaking large contracts for any description of ships. M. Arman was also a deputy in the Corps Législatif for the Gironde; he had been personally decorated in his own shipyard at Bordeaux by the Emperor, and during the whole period of the transactions which followed, he appeared to have no difficulty in obtaining personal interviews with the Minister of State, M. Rouher, and even with his Imperial Majesty himself.

M. Arman stated that he had been confidentially informed by the Minister of State that the Emperor was willing for him to undertake the construction of ships for the Confederate Government, and that when the vessels were ready to be delivered, he would be permitted to send them to sea under the French flag to any point which might be agreed upon between him and the representative of the Confederate States.

I mentioned to M. Arman that building the ships with such an assurance from the Government, it would not be necessary to practise any concealment as to their mere character and equipment, and it would soon be apparent that they were vessels intended not for commerce, but for war. There was no reason, I said, to suppose that the United States would be less desirous to prevent ships leaving French than English ports for the service of the Confederate Government, nor was it likely that their representatives would be less watchful in France than they were in England,

and I suggested that as soon as it became apparent that he was building vessels suitable for war, the United States Minister would learn the fact through his spies, and he would lay his suspicions before the Minister for Foreign Affairs, and I asked how he thought the matter would then be dealt with?

He replied that the probability of such an inquiry had been fully considered, and he had been informed that if he would apply to the proper public department for authorization to complete, arm, and despatch the ships for a specified purpose, which was in itself lawful, the Government would not force him to make any further or more specific explanations, but that he would be permitted to despatch them to the destination set out in the original application, on the plea that the Government could not impede a legitimate branch of French trade. He furthermore said that he had informed the Emperor that he purposed building the ships for trading between San Francisco, China and Japan, that they would be clippers, having great speed both under canvas and steam, and would be armed for defence against pirates in the Eastern Seas, and with the view to possible sale to either the Chinese or Japanese Government. M. Arman assured us that the Emperor fully understood the matter, and so did M. Rouher, and that there would be no difficulty in arranging all details with the several Executive Departments under whose supervision it would be necessary for him to act. He should simply state, without the slightest hesitation, the purpose for which he was building the ships, and ask for the necessary authorization in the usual formal matter-of-course way.

I had no means of testing the statements of M. Arman in regard to his personal communications with the Emperor and M. Rouher, but they confirmed the intimations that had been conveyed to Mr. Slidell through persons of position who were in close relations with the Imperial Court, and who had inspired him with confidence by having communicated other information of approaching events which proved to be correct, and could not have been foreseen or obtained by clandestine means. Mr. Slidell was very confident that the policy of the Imperial Government, and the purposes the Emperor then had in view, were such as to render it very desirable that the Confederate States should be able to maintain their position, and he had reason to believe that the hesitation of England alone prevented their recognition by France.

My course under the circumstances was clear. My instructions were to keep as many cruisers at sea as possible, and I could only exercise my own judgment to the extent of determining the best class of vessel, the places where they could be built with the least fear of seizure or detention, and the mode of putting them in commission as Confederate ships-of-war afterwards. The result of the consultation with Mr. Slidell was that I proceeded to Bordeaux, inspected M. Arman's premises, and finally arranged with him all the particulars for four clipper corvettes of about 1,500 tons and 400-horse-power, to be armed with twelve or fourteen 6-inch rifled guns—the *"canon rayé de trente"* of the French navy, that gun being adopted because of the facility of having the batteries constructed in France from the official patterns.

There was some delay in beginning the work, by reason of the incompleteness of the financial arrangements; but General Colin J. McRae, the fiscal agent of the Treasury, arrived about the 1st of May, and he was able to make such arrangements that not much time was lost. The designs and specifications of the ships were settled on the 15th of April, and by the middle of June good progress had been made, and the engines were fully up to the vessels in condition. Time was, of course, an essential element, and M. Arman was so full of other work that he could not undertake the four ships for the prompt delivery required—ten months from date of contract; he therefore arranged with M. J. Voruz, of Nantes, for the construction of two of them.

M. Voruz was an eminent ironfounder and engineer, and a member of the Corps Législatif for the Loire Inférieure. He employed a local shipbuilder to put up the hulls, but he assumed the entire responsibility for the ships, and subsequently undertook the construction of the guns and their gear for all the ships. I am glad of this opportunity to bear witness to the business capacity, the commercial and personal integrity, and the kindly social qualities and intelligence of M. Voruz; and I do so now because it will obviate the necessity of frequent allusions to him in the further account of our operations in France. M. Arman was the principal actor in those transactions. He it was who invariably went to see the Minister of State in reference to them, and it was he who was permitted to see the Emperor on the subject. M. Voruz never alleged that he had received any personal communication from a member of the Government with reference to building the ships for the Confederate States, but he received due authorization to make the guns for them, and he did not doubt that their ultimate destination was perfectly well known, and he did not anticipate that there would be any difficulty in despatching them from France when they were completed.

When, as will afterwards appear, the Imperial Government changed its policy, and not only forbad M. Arman to send the ships to sea, but peremptorily ordered him to sell them to a neutral State or permanently lay them up, M. Voruz closed his part of the transaction promptly and in a business-like and equitable manner. He sold the two vessels in his charge to a foreign Government, completed them for account of that Government, rendered a prompt statement of the transaction, and refunded the amount he had received from the Confederate agent, with due proportion of the profit at which he had been able to sell the ships. M. Voruz effected this satisfactory settlement without employing any expensive intermediaries, and proved himself to be a thorough man of business in this as well as in other enterprises which he conducted for me during the war, fulfilling his engagements always with promptness and scrupulous fidelity. Having made the foregoing statement, I shall hereafter mention M. Arman alone in connection with the ships, as he conducted all the efforts which were made to avoid the necessity of selling them.

On the 30th of June, 1863, I received a despatch from the Secretary of the Navy, which he considered to be of such importance that it was sent by a special messenger, Lieutenant G. S. Shryock, of the Confederate Navy. The following is a copy of the despatch:—

> "Confederate States of America,
> "Navy Department,
> "Richmond, *May 6th,* 1863.

"Sir,—

"Herewith you will receive copy of a Secret Act of Congress appropriating £2,000,000 for the construction of ironclad ships-of-war in Southern Europe, which Act was induced by the belief that we can have such vessels constructed and equipped in France and delivered to us upon the high seas or elsewhere. The President has selected you as the agent of the Government to accomplish the important object thus provided for by Congress. In view of the great improvements which theory and experiment have produced in the construction and equipment of armoured ships in France and England, as well as of your thorough knowledge of the subject and your means of observation, it is deemed expedient to leave to your judgment, untrammelled by instructions, the size and details of the vessels, subject to the consideration that in draft of water, speed and power, they must be able to enter and navigate the Mississippi river; that their first trial must be a long ocean voyage; that their antagonists carry 11-inch and 15-inch guns; and that they must be completed and delivered at the earliest day practicable.... You will regard the £2,000,000 as the only fund for building, equipping, manning, providing, and furnishing the vessels for one year's service. Your immediate attention to this subject is important, and every effort must be made to have the ships completed at the earliest day practicable. To this end I suggest to you a conference with Mr. Slidell.

"I am, etc.,

"(Signed)   S. R. MALLORY."

At the date upon which the above letter was received, I had already been in conference with Mr. Slidell, with the result, as has already been explained, of an engagement with M. Arman for four wooden screw corvettes of great speed. On many accounts I should have preferred building the ironclads provided for by the Act of Congress in England, but it had ere then become manifest that her Majesty's Government would not permit any vessel "suitable for war" to leave a British port unless the ownership was clearly and explicitly accounted for, and that ownership was satisfactory. Moreover, it was now equally manifest that the Government at Richmond were satisfied with the friendly hints and suggestions that had been thrown out from the Tuilleries, and felt assured that it was only necessary to act with due prudence and in a strict mercantile way, and ships might be had in France as well as rifles and cannon. It was only necessary, according to the intimations voluntarily vouchsafed, to refrain from violating the neutrality of France by enlisting French subjects, or by engaging in hostilities too quickly after leaving French jurisdiction, and no branch of trade would be interfered with. This was the purport of the confidential statements made to Mr. Slidell, and reported by him to the Secretary of State at Richmond, and it was in reliance upon them that the appropriation was made by the Confederate Congress to enable the Navy Department to build warships in France.

At the time of my visit of inspection to M. Arman's works at Bordeaux on the business of the corvettes, I had examined the two armour-cased batteries he was building for the Imperial Navy, and we had discussed, and he had made drawings of, an armour-cased vessel of dimensions and draught suited for service on the Southern coast. Mr. Mallory had directed me to get, if possible, less draught of water than that of the rams building in England; but upon receipt of the specific instructions of May 6th, founded upon the Secret Act of Congress, it was necessary still further to modify the plans to some extent.

An expert will perceive at a glance that the problem proposed by the Secretary of the Navy was not easy of solution. Vessels-of-war, suited for

service in the Mississippi river, must be of light draught and comparatively short; they must have great steam-power, to contend with the rapid
current, and they must also be handy, with capability to turn in short
space. To oppose other vessels armed with 11-inch and 15-inch guns they
must be well protected with armour, and then to get to their fighting
ground they must make a sea-voyage of 5,000 miles. The design finally selected was for a vessel of the following dimensions and steam-power—the
measurements reduced to English standards. Length between perpendicu-
lars, 171 feet 10 inches; breadth to outside of armour, 32 feet 8 inches;
mean draught, with 220 tons of coal, battery, and all stores on board,
14 feet 4 inches. Engines, 300 horse-power nominal, twin screws, working
separately, so as to be capable of a counter motion at the same time. The
armour-plating was 4¾ inches amidships, tapering gradually to 3½ inches
at the extremities, in single plates, manufactured by Messrs. Petin Gaudet
and Co. at Rive de Gier. The details of specifications for ship and engines
provided for everything to be of the very best quality, conforming in dimensions and material to the types of the Imperial Navy, and the guaranteed speed was not less than twelve knots in smooth sea, with 220 tons of
coal and all other weights on board. The bunkers were, however, planned
to contain 290 tons of coal. In calculating the displacement, 100 tons was
allowed for guns and ordnance stores, and the arrangement was to have
one heavy gun forward, to be mounted in a fixed armoured turret, so as to
be fired in the line of the keel or on either bow, and two 6-inch rifled guns
in an after turret or casemate. The bow guns were to be 300-pounders
of the Armstrong pattern, and they were made to M. Arman's order by
Sir William Armstrong at Elswick; the lighter guns were to be made in
France.*

The question of "ways and means" confronted us here again, as in all
our undertakings. The Secretary of the Navy informed me that every
possible effort would be made to place the amount appropriated by Congress in Europe as quickly as possible, but to start the work there was no
other immediate resource than the loan. General McRae, the financial
agent of the Treasury, was fresh from Richmond. He had been advised of
the contemplated Act of Congress, and knew the earnest wish of the Government to have the ironclads built; but he found himself overwhelmed
with drafts in favour of the purchasing agents of the War Department, and
there were many contracts rapidly maturing, which demanded cash payments, and for which the credit of the Government was pledged. The

---

* Two 70-pounder Armstrong guns were afterwards substituted.

bankers of the Treasury, Messrs. Fraser, Trenholm and Co., were also hard pressed. The only way of remitting to them was by produce shipped through the blockade, and as the system of blockade-running exclusively on Government account had not yet been fully adopted and organized, the only means of shipping was by private vessels, which wanted most of their space for account of their owners. After consultation with the Commissioners, Messrs. Mason and Slidell, and General McRae, it was not deemed prudent to begin more than two of the ironclads until I had heard more definitely from the Navy Department how the amount appropriated by Congress was to be made available in Europe.

I may just state, *en passant,* that the Secretary of the Navy was never able to place the amount in Europe—at least, for the exclusive purposes contemplated in the Act. Other pressing needs of his own and the other branches of the Government more than absorbed all the proceeds of produce that could be got through the blockade, and only two ironclads were ever begun in France. In fact, there was a time when the fiscal agent could not have supplied the funds to meet the instalments, if relief had not come from the compulsory sale of other ships. In view of the subsequent acts of the French Government, which will be narrated in due course, it was fortunate that we did not embark more largely in shipbuilding enterprises in France.

I have always understood that when the proposition to raise a loan in Europe was first broached, the Confederate Government was not greatly impressed with the scheme, and was somewhat reluctant to accept the offer of the bankers who proposed to undertake the negotiation. After some discussion it was, however, determined to make the experiment with the moderate amount of £3,000,000. The financial enterprise was undertaken by Messrs. Erlanger, of Frankfort and Paris, and they managed the transaction with great skill and ability. When the prospectus was issued there was a prompt and gratifying response. In a very short time the amount subscribed was £15,000,000, or five times the amount wanted, and it was thought that a much larger sum still would have been offered if it had been applied for. The financial agents of the Confederate Government lamented their inability to issue bonds for the whole amount offered, but, looking back upon the transaction now, all must feel gratified that the loss to the European public was limited to the smaller figures.

The necessities of the financial situation defined the extent of our naval operations in France, and on the 16th of July, 1863, I closed a contract with M. L. Arman for two ironclad vessels of the dimensions and power aforementioned. About a fortnight after the completion of the arrangements in respect to the above contract, I received a cypher despatch from the Secretary of the Navy, on the subject of getting ships in France, and as it affords conclusive proof of the hopes that were held out and the expectations which were aroused at Richmond in consequence, I think a portion of its contents may properly be given here, as a part of the facts necessary to a full understanding of that strange episode in the war which forms the chief subject of this chapter. The following is an extract from the above-mentioned despatch, dated "Richmond, May 26th, 1863":—

"My letter of the 6th instant enclosed you a copy of a Secret Act of Congress, relative to building ships abroad. Since that letter was written I have received additional assurances, which I regard as satisfactory, that iron-plated ships-of-war can be constructed in France by French builders and delivered to us ready for service upon the high seas or elsewhere.

"Heretofore I have brought to your attention an intimation which I deem not unworthy of notice, from the quarter whence it reached me, that one or more of the ironclads of the French Navy might be so transferred as to come into our possession; and as I have heard only incidentally from you on the point, and know that you have recently, by your visit to France, had an opportunity of learning the value of this suggestion, I again ask your attention to it.

"The immediate possession of two or three good armoured ships, capable of entering the Mississippi, would be of incalculable value to us, and though the hope of thus obtaining them is not sanguine, I still deem it proper to attempt it. You will therefore, if you have not already acted, take such measures for this purpose as you may deem best."

In reply to the portion of the foregoing despatch which referred to the possible purchase of one or more ironclads from the French Navy, I informed Mr. Mallory that "inquiries have been and continue to be made. Most of the ironclads already built or now under construction for the European Powers, are either too large, and of too heavy draft for our especial purposes, or they are mere floating batteries, too small and heavily armed to cross the Atlantic."

The subject was fully discussed with Mr. Slidell, and he did not see how the negotiation could be opened in such a way as to get the proposition before the Emperor, unless it should appear that he had determined to recognise the Confederate Government independently of England, and there was no evidence that he intended to take any such decisive step alone. Mr. Slidell thought that we should be content with the covert intimation that no ship-builder we might employ would be prevented from despatching the vessels to sea when they were completed. Personally, I fully agreed with Mr. Slidell, and on the general question I subsequently wrote to the Secretary of the Navy as follows:—

"You may rely upon it that the purchase of men-of-war from any of the European navies is not practicable under existing circumstances. The transaction would necessarily be managed through intermediaries, who, from the very nature of the negotiations, would be forced to sacrifice principle by prevaricating, and then all sorts of objectionable means would have to be used, even bribery, and after all we would only get cast-off vessels. I make these remarks as the result of experience, for I have had propositions from many persons, and I know wherein they are all wanting."

The construction of the corvettes at Bordeaux and Nantes and the two ironclad vessels progressed rapidly, and for some months there did not arise any question which suggested a doubt in regard to the purposes of the Imperial Government in respect to their departure when completed. On the 23rd of November, 1863, I reported that the armoured vessels were quite three-fifths finished, and that the corvettes would probably be ready for sea within the contract time; but by that date affairs began to change in their aspect. The American papers began to discuss the probable destination of the ships, and it was stated that Mr. Dayton, the United States Minister, had addressed a protest to the French Government against their completion, and it was even affirmed that he had been assured by the Minister of Marine that none of the ships would be allowed to leave France. Commenting upon these uncomfortable rumours in a subsequent despatch (November 26th, 1863) to the Secretary of the Navy, I wrote as follows:—

"The extent to which the system of bribery and spying has been and continues to be practised by the agents of the United States in Europe is scarcely credible. The servants of gentlemen supposed to have Southern sympathies are tampered with, confidential clerks, and even the messengers from telegraph offices, are bribed to betray their trust, and I have lately been informed that the English and French Post Offices, hitherto considered immaculate, are now scarcely safe modes of communication....

"Mere suspicion is not, I regret to say, the basis of Mr. Dayton's protest. He has furnished the French Government with copies of certain letters alleged to have passed between the builders, which go to show that the ships are for us. The confidential clerk who has had charge of the correspondence of M. Voruz, one of the parties to the contracts, has disappeared, and has unfortunately carried off some letters and papers relating to the business. M. Voruz has not yet discovered the full extent to which he has been robbed, but is using every effort to trace the theft to its source, and to discover how far he can prove complicity on the part of the United States officials. We know that the stolen papers contain evidence that the ships are for us, for the fact has been so stated by the Minister of Marine to one of the builders; but the French Government has only thus become aware of a transaction it was perfectly well informed of before. Indeed, I may say that the attempt to build ships in France was undertaken at the instigation of the Imperial Government itself. When the construction of the corvettes was in progress of negotiation, a draft of the proposed contract was shown to the highest person in the Empire, and it received his sanction—at least, I was so informed at the time. At any rate, I have a copy of the letter addressed to the builders by the Minister of Marine, giving authority to arm the corvettes in France, and specifying the number of guns, and I have the original document signed by M. Chasseloup Laubat himself, granting like authority for the rams. It can never, therefore, be charged that the Confederate States Government, through its agent, has violated the neutrality of France by attempting the construction of ships in her ports, and if Mr. Dayton has received the assurances we see printed in the American papers, the time is rapidly approaching when the policy of the Imperial Government in reference to American affairs must be positively and definitely expressed....

"The builders are still sanguine that they will be allowed to send the ships to sea, but I confess that I do not see any such assurance in what they say, and the manner in which the protest of the American Minister has been received is well calculated to confirm my doubts. When Mr. Dayton went to the Minister of Foreign Affairs with a complaint and with copies of certain letters to substantiate it, the Minister might have said, 'These are alleged copies of the private correspondence of two prominent and highly respected French citizens; they could only have come into your possession by means of bribery or treachery. I cannot, therefore, receive them as evidence, and must insist that you produce the originals and explain how you came to be possessed of them.' It strikes me that such a course would have effectually silenced Mr. Dayton, and we could have felt some assurance of getting our ships to sea. Instead of this, the stolen letters have been received without hesitation, and the United States officials profess to be satisfied with the action, or promised action, of the French Government. The builders are sent for, and warned by the Minister of Marine, and although those gentlemen come from their interviews still possessed by the belief that the ships will be allowed to depart, and thus, as I said before, excite hopes, I cannot be blind to the significancy of the above circumstances.

"My belief is, that the construction of the ships will not be interfered with, but whether they will be allowed to leave France or not will depend upon the position of affairs in America at the time of their completion. If at that time our cause is in the ascendant, the local authorities will be instructed not to be too inquisitive, and the departure of our ships will be connived at. If, on the contrary, the Federal cause prospers, the affair of the 'Confederate ships' will be turned over to the responsible Ministers of the Empire, who will justify their claim to American gratitude by a strict enforcement of the neutrality of France. Hoping always for the best, I shall not permit any fears to create delay in the progress of work. The ships shall be ready as soon as possible, and every effort shall be made to get them to sea in the manner least calculated to compromise the French authorities, if they choose only to be judiciously blind."

On the 18th of February, 1864, I reported further to the Secretary of the Navy as follows:—

"I have the honour to enclose herewith duplicate of my despatch of November 26th, 1863, on the subject of the ironclads and corvettes building for us in France, wherein I ventured to express some apprehension as to the policy the Imperial Government would pursue when the ships approached completion. That policy has been pronounced sooner than I anticipated, and the Emperor, through his Ministers of Foreign Affairs and of Marine, has formally notified the builders that the ironclads cannot be permitted to sail, and that the corvettes must not be armed in France, but must be nominally sold to some foreign merchant and despatched as ordinary trading vessels. I believe that M. Arman has acted in a perfectly loyal manner thus far in these transactions, and he sincerely regrets the present turn of events. He has proposed that a nominal sale of the vessels should be made to a Danish banker, and that there should be a private agreement providing for a re-delivery to us at some point beyond the jurisdiction of France. This would simply be substituting France for England, and then Denmark for France, and the Danish banker for Messrs. Bravay, and if the two most powerful maritime nations in the world have not been able to resist the importunities of the United States, it would be simply absurd to hope for success through the medium of Denmark, a weak Power at best, and just now struggling almost hopelessly for her very existence.* The proposition was therefore declined, as it only involved an increased and useless expenditure of money without a hope of profit.... This case may be summed up in a very few words. It is one of simple deception. I never should have entered into such large undertakings except with the assurance of success. I was, not as a private individual, but as an agent of the Confederate States, invited to build ships-of-war in France, and, so far at least as the corvettes are concerned, received every possible assurance that they might be actually armed in the ports of construction. During three or four months after the contracts were made, the work advanced very rapidly, but latterly there has been a gradual falling off, which caused me to fear that the builders had received some discouraging intimations from the Government. I am not fully convinced on this point, but the result would seem to indicate that my suspicions were not unfounded. By affording refuge to our ships at Calais, Brest, and Cherbourg, the Imperial Government has shown us more favour than that of her Britannic Majesty, and I presume that the Emperor, trusting to the chances of war and diplomacy, hoped that, before the completion of the ships, affairs both in America and Europe would be in such a condition as would enable him to let them go without apprehension. He now favours us so far as to tell us frankly to sell out and save our money, but this can scarcely ameliorate the disappointment....

"The two Bordeaux ironclads and the four corvettes would have been a formidable attacking squadron, and would have enabled its commander to strike severe and telling blows upon the Northern seaboard. The loss of the ironclads changes the whole character of the force, and deprives it of its real power of offence. It is difficult to predict what may be the state of Europe even a month hence, and how the progress of events may affect the chances of getting the wooden ships to sea. I shall, however, make every effort to get at least two of them out, to supply the places of our present cruisers should the casualties of the sea reduce their number. There really seems but little for our ships to do now upon the open sea. Lieutenant-Commanding Low, of the *Tuscaloosa*,† reports that in a cruise of several months, during which he spoke over one hundred vessels, only one proved to be an American; and she being loaded entirely on neu-

---

* Then engaged in war with Prussia and Austria in respect to the Holstein-Schleswig Provinces.

† Prize of the *Alabama*, commissioned by Captain Semmes.

tral account, he felt forced to release her after taking a bond. The *Alabama* also only picks up a vessel at intervals, although she is in the East Indies, heretofore rich in American traffic. Nevertheless, if all our ships should be withdrawn, the United States flag would again make its appearance; and it is therefore essential to provide the necessary relay of vessels. There is, however, no resisting the logic of accomplished facts. I am now convinced that we cannot get ironclads to sea, and unless otherwise instructed, I will make no more contracts for such vessels, except with such a pecuniary guarantee for actual delivery upon the ocean as will secure us against loss."

M. Arman having received positive instructions not to attempt to send the ironclad vessels to sea, but being still permitted to suppose that the corvettes would not be stopped if sent to sea without their guns, it was arranged with him to push the completion of the latter vessels to the utmost, and to go on with the armoured ships more leisurely, while we were considering what might be done with them. The course of events and the *dénouement* is more clearly and fairly explained in the following despatch, written to the Secretary of the Navy at the time, than by any version I could give of the transaction now. The despatch referred to was written June 10th, 1864, and was as follows:—

"It is now my painful duty to report upon the most remarkable and astounding circumstance that has yet occurred in reference to our operations in Europe. Previous despatches have informed you under what influences, impressions, and expectations I undertook the construction of ships of war in the building-yards of France, and how smoothly and satisfactorily the work progressed for several months after it was begun. I reported to you when it became evident that the Government was interfering and checking the progress of the work, and finally informed you when the authorities forbade the completion of the rams, and directed the builders of the corvettes to sell them.

"When the consultation between Messrs. Mason, Slidell, and myself was held in Paris, the result of which has already been reported to you, it was unanimously agreed that the ironclads must of necessity be sold, but it was thought that the corvettes should be completed, as the builders were confident that the Government would not interfere with their departure, if despatched as commercial vessels, and under the assumed ownership of private individuals. Thus fortified by the opinions and advice of Messrs. Mason and Slidell, I gave M. Arman, the principal builder, written instructions to sell the ships, upon his representation that such a course was necessary in order that he might be able to show to the

Minister of Marine that his business connection with me had ceased. There was at the same time an express understanding between M. Arman and me that the sale of the corvettes should be purely fictitious, and that the negotiations in respect to the rams should be kept in such a state that we might get possession of them again if there should be any change in the policy of the Emperor's Government before their completion. Scarcely a month since, I had a long consultation with M. Arman regarding all of these matters, Mr. Eustis being present. M. Arman showed me a contract of sale of one of the ironclads to the Danish Government, and told me he was then negotiating for the sale of the other to the same Government. As Denmark was then at war, it had been arranged that the nominal owner-ship of the rams should vest in Sweden,* and that Government, I was informed, having consented to do this piece of good service for Denmark, M. Arman said that a Swedish naval officer was then at Bordeaux super-intending the completion of the rams, as if for his own Government. In the contract of sale M. Arman had agreed to deliver the ships at Gotten-berg, in Sweden, and he told me that he had made this unusual stipulation in order that he might be able to send the ships to sea under the French flag and in charge of men of his own choice. 'Now,' said he, 'if you are willing to sacrifice one of the rams, and will consent to the *bonâ-fide* delivery of the first one, I am sure that the second can be saved to you. When the first ram is ready to sail,' continued M. Arman, 'the American Minister will no doubt ask the Swedish Minister if the vessel belongs to his Government. The reply will be "Yes"; she will sail unmolested, and will arrive at her destination according to contract. This will avert all suspicion from the second ram, and when she sails under like circumstances with the first, my people, having a previous understanding with you, will take her to any rendezvous that may have been agreed upon, or will deliver her to you or your agent at sea.'

"The above is almost a verbatim report of the proposition made by M. Arman, which, after some discussion upon matters of detail, was accepted, and I have since felt a reasonable assurance of seeing one of our rams at work upon the enemy. A day or two after I called on M. Arman again, taking with me Captain Tessier, my agent in France, a man of in-

---

* I reported this fact, just as I understood M. Arman to state it, at the time of the consultation referred to; but upon subsequent inquiry, I learned that he did not mean me to infer that any public official of the Swedish Government took part in the transaction, but that a Swedish banker had undertaken to carry out the arrangement. However, the whole plan fell through; the ship was actually sold to Denmark, and was sent to Copenhagen without any disguise, and under the French flag, with a French commander and crew.

telligence, a capital seaman, and of course master of the French language. The object of the visit was to discuss the arrangements necessary to get the corvettes to sea, and to send to them their armament and crews. I told M. Arman that it would not take a long time to set everything afloat when the proper moment arrived, but that the undertaking was one which not only involved a large expenditure of money, but which required to be managed with great caution and secrecy. When the expedition was ready I said it would be absolutely necessary for it to sail promptly, because delay would cause exposure, and certain interruption and failure would follow, and having due regard to such a contingency, it was very important and indeed essential that I should, if possible, get some assurance that when we were all ready to move, the Government would permit the vessels to leave Bordeaux. M. Arman replied that he thought there was no doubt about the corvettes being allowed to sail unarmed, but he was to have a personal interview with the Emperor in ten days or a fortnight, and would then bring the matter to a close, by direct appeal to his Imperial Majesty.

"Many details relating to the best mode of shipping the guns, the engagement of reliable captains, and the possibility of getting seamen from the ports of Brittany were discussed, all in a most satisfactory manner. Before separating, M. Arman expressed great regret at the delay and interference we had met with, and said that as he had made the contracts for building all the ships in perfect good faith, and with the assurance that his Government understood the whole transaction, and would permit him to carry it out, he felt doubly bound to assist in every possible way, and to assume any responsibility that might be necessary.

"In face of the foregoing statements, you will readily imagine my astonishment when Captain Tessier arrived here (Liverpool) yesterday afternoon, bringing me a letter from M. Arman, informing me that he had sold both the rams and both the corvettes to 'Governments of the North of Europe,' in obedience to the imperative orders of his Government. He (M. Arman) could not write particulars.... Captain Tessier was charged to deliver further verbal explanations as follows:—

"M. Arman obtained his promised interview with the Emperor, who rated him severely, threatened imprisonment, ordered him to sell the ships at once, *bonâ fide*, and said if this was not done he would have them seized and taken to Rochefort. Captain Tessier also brought me word that the two corvettes at Nantes were ordered to be sold, and the builders of those ships sent me, by him, a copy of the letter of the Minister of Marine conveying the order to them. The order is of the most peremptory kind, not only directing the sale, but requiring the builders to furnish proof to the Minister of Foreign Affairs that the sale is a real one. The Minister of Marine writes the order in a style of virtuous indignation; specifies the large scantling, the power of the engines, the space allotted to fuel, and the general arrangements of the ships as proving their warlike character, and dogmatically pronounces the one to which he especially refers *'une véritable corvette de guerre.'* When you call to mind the fact that this same Minister of Marine, on the 6th day of June, 1863, wrote over his own official signature a formal authorization to arm those very ships with fourteen heavy guns each (*canons rayé de trente*), the affectation of having just discovered them to be suitable for purposes of war is really astonishing.*

"I certainly thought this kind of crooked diplomacy had died out since the last century, and would not be ventured upon in these common-sense days. Fortunately, I have a certified copy of the permit to arm the ships, and I will get the copy of the indignant order to sell them certified also. Captain Tessier saw Mr. Slidell in Paris, who told him that he had been informed of the sale, and was both astonished and indignant."

My first impulse was to resist and to take legal proceedings to prevent the transfer of the ships to the purchasers. But a moment's reflection satisfied me that such a course could not restore the ships to us—at least, it was manifest that they could not be reclaimed for use during the war. The proclamation of neutrality issued by the Emperor of the French on the 10th of June, 1861, contained a specific prohibition against any aid whatever being given by a French subject to either belligerent, and if the Government had determined to enforce that prohibition strictly and literally, no effective resistance could be offered, and no plausible evasion could be attempted.

In England, where in theory the law is paramount, and members of the Government had often declared that they neither could nor would exceed the restrictions as prescribed by statute, we found that pressure could and did overcome Ministerial scruples, and that the law might be and was not only "strained," but that the judgment of a court could be made inoperative by the interference of a Secretary of State. In France, the neutrality laws were in themselves more specific than the corresponding English Act, but the power of the Executive Government to modify or to enlarge the legal prohibitions was far greater than in England, and while the permission or the connivance of a Minister of State would condone any apparent contravention of the law, his official prohibition would render an appeal to it worse than useless.

---

* See copy of official authorization, p. 360.

When Captain Tessier brought me the unwelcome and discouraging report of the forced sale of our French ships, I was so fully occupied with pressing affairs in England, that it was impossible for me to go to France at once, but I sent him immediately back with a letter to Mr. Slidell, and with instructions to arrange with M. Arman to meet me in Paris, and followed in a few days. A consultation with Mr. Slidell resulted in nothing but the conviction that the Imperial Government had changed the views which had been previously expressed, and that it would be impossible to retain possession of the ships, or to prevent their delivery to the purchasers by any process of law. It was manifest that the builders of the ships were as much surprised and disappointed by the action of the Government as we were. They would not have undertaken the transaction unless they had been impressed with the belief that the supreme Government fully understood and approved what they were doing, and they were ready and willing to comply with their engagements, and to assume any reasonable responsibility in the effort to fulfil them.

The course of the Civil War about this time took an unfavourable turn for the Confederate States, and the South began to show signs of exhaustion, which were painfully manifest to those of us who were conscious of the strain, and the inadequacy of the means to resist it.

The apparent change in the probable result of the Civil War, the manifest evidence that the Mexican enterprise was bitterly resented by the people of Mexico and was also sorely vexatious to the majority in France, and the loss of prestige which failure in that expedition would doubtless inflict upon the Imperial *régime,* must have been very disquieting to the Emperor and to those immediately attached to his person and his Government. At the same time, Great Britain persistently declined to join with him in any act which might tend to strengthen the South, or to bring pressure upon the United States in respect to the recognition of the Confederate Government, and he did not therefore feel equal to the effort of maintaining his position at home and abroad, with the United States for an additional and open enemy, and the South unable to assist.

I can think of no other causes why there should have been any change in the policy of the Imperial Government towards the South; and as those causes are sufficient to account for a departure from a course which was adopted for "reasons of State," we may assume that "reasons of State" required the change. Nevertheless, it was our duty to act up to the very end of the struggle as if final success was assured, and to relax no effort that could in any way contribute to that end, or which might strengthen the position of the Confederate Government in seeking the reparation which could have been justly claimed from that of France for the injury inflicted upon the South by the sudden and total change of policy.

There was no reason why the Government at Richmond should have refrained from making those transactions public at the time, except that to have done so would have borne the appearance of malice, and the effect would have been to alienate the sympathies of the Imperial Government, which Mr. Slidell was assured were still with the South; but it cannot be doubted that if the Confederate Government had been able to maintain itself, and to achieve the independence of the Southern States, some explanation of those arbitrary and contradictory proceedings would have been required—at least, they would have been taken into account in settling the conditions of a treaty of amity and commerce between France and the new American Republic.

Ex-President Davis, in his history of the "Rise and Fall of the Confederate Government," has not mentioned either the invitation to build ships in France or the sudden and peremptory withdrawal of the permission. He has dealt very fully and almost exclusively with the grand military events which marked the progress and failure of the greatest effort ever made by any people to obtain the right of self-government. Perhaps it might have appeared to him scarcely worth while to swell the contents of a necessarily voluminous history with a vain lament over disappointed hopes which, had they been realized, would have been too late to change the result; and he may have thought that the circumstances were in themselves trivial and unimportant when compared with the magnitude of the struggle at home, the brilliant promise of success which at one time animated the Southern people and encouraged them to persevere, and the distressing consequences of the final catastrophe.

At the time when Ex-President Davis was preparing his account of the origin, progress, and results of the great Civil War, the Imperial *régime* had itself passed away, under circumstances of distress and affliction to its author, and of much humiliation and trouble to France. The contrast between the brilliant meridian of the life of Napoleon III., when he ruled the French people with autocratic will, and when his mere manner of greeting a foreign ambassador on the occasion of a State ceremony was thought to have a political meaning which disquieted all Europe, and the sudden and total extinction of his power and his influence, might have aroused the irony of a personal enemy, and have furnished the occasion for the sarcasms of a hostile critic. But the final course from the Imperial throne in Paris to the death-bed at Chiselhurst was so swift, and the intervening way was so rough and painful, that sympathy displaced all bitter memories, and compassion left no room for malignity.

It is not improbable that Ex-President Davis perceived what is now known, that failing health and corporal suffering had greatly impaired the mind and weakened the will of the late Emperor of the French, and that even in 1864 he had neither the energy nor the sagacity which enabled him to re-impose the Napoleonic *régime* upon France, or which brought him out of the Austro-Italian War with the bulk of the military honours, and two provinces of his ally in addition. The foregoing would seem to be sufficient reasons why the conduct of the Imperial Government of France towards the Confederate States was passed over in silence by an author who was himself the chief figure and the chief sufferer in the history he was writing. Mr. Davis was not desirous to cast any reproach upon the fallen Emperor, and it would have been impossible for him to mention the encouragement the Confederate Government had received, and the subsequent denial of all practical help, without expressing some condemnation of both the policy and its author.

But in a narrative whose especial object it is to give a true and exhaustive account of the effort made by the Confederate Government to create a navy, the transactions in France, and the conditions under which they were attempted, cannot be omitted. Many persons who are still living at the South know that the Confederate Congress authorized the building of ships-of-war in France, and they have a legitimate right to be informed why the purpose failed, if anyone employed in carrying it out publishes a narrative of the events at all. If I thought that the mention of these transactions now would excite the ill-will of the Southern people against France, or that a statement of the facts would be the origin of a grievance against the present French Government on the part of the United States, I would omit them altogether; but I feel assured that the South is better and more wisely employed than in nursing its disappointment and treasuring up wrath, and that even the North is settling down to a condition of mind in which contentment with the present, and hopefulness as regards the future, are uniting to obliterate all that was irritating and vexatious in the past.

Captain Tessier brought me the report of the peremptory commands of the Imperial Government on the 9th of June, 1864, and I went to Paris in about a fortnight to consult with Mr. Slidell, and to get full explanations from M. Arman, who came up from Bordeaux by especial appointment to meet me. The mystery of the transaction appeared so profound, the disappointment and injury to the Confederate States was so grievous, that Mr. Slidell desired to be fully and minutely informed, and I requested him to permit his chief-secretary, Mr. George Eustis, to go with me to see M. Arman and to assist in the investigation.

The official reports to the Navy Department were full and explicit. They mentioned every circumstance which could help to illustrate the management of the enterprise and the conduct of the Imperial authorities, and the replies from Richmond demonstrated with clearness and force, both the disappointment of the Confederate Government and the consciousness of the deceptive hopes that had been held out to Mr. Slidell, and which were also aroused by suggestions to the Secretary of the Navy through other sources having every appearance of genuine authority.

The despatches referred to were of a confidential character—they were written under the influence of a disappointment which naturally aroused feelings of resentment. Suspicion was excited against persons, and they were mentioned in terms of censure which subsequent inquiry proved in some cases to be unmerited. To publish the official correspondence with the Confederate Navy Department in full would not add weight to the evidence, and would furnish no additional fact at all essential to a complete explanation of the transactions.

M. Arman produced official documents to prove his authority to undertake the construction and armament of the ships, and the official order to sell them. He gave Mr. Eustis and myself a full and particular account of his last interview with the Emperor, in which, as he informed us, his Majesty reproved him for the delay in disposing of the ships, and peremptorily ordered him to get rid of them at once, and to produce proof of the sale, so that M. Drouyn de l'Huys might be able to satisfy the United States Minister in respect to them. Under this irresistible pressure the corvettes and one of the rams built at Bordeaux were sold to Prussia, the second ram was sold to Denmark, and the two Nantes corvettes to Peru. To add to the mystery of these proceedings, and as an aggravation of the apparent treachery to the Confederate States, we were compelled to submit to the despatch of the vessels to Prussia at a time when that country was at war with Denmark. M. Arman explained to us that to meet this difficulty the sale to Prussia had been effected through a banker of Amsterdam, who had acted as the intermediary, but he informed us that the French Government were fully conscious of the arrangement.

I have already stated that M. Voruz closed up the sale of the two ships built by him, and settled the entire transaction in full. The financial negotiations with M. Arman were more complicated. At a later date, an arrangement was made with him by which we got possession of the ram which had been sold to Denmark, and this caused so much delay in the final settlement, that at the termination of the war the accounts with M. Arman were still open. The transactions had involved large payments and expenditures, and although M. Arman had refunded a considerable amount at the time when the first corvette was sold to Prussia, yet there was still a large balance in question at the end of the war, which has never been settled.

In the year 1867 the United States instituted a suit against M. Arman in respect to his transactions with the Confederate Government, and for the payment to them of the money he had received on account of the Confederate Navy Department, but the French Court gave judgment for the defendant. Subsequently M. Arman failed, whether in consequence of the above prosecution or too great an extension of his business I have never been informed, but the sudden termination of the war, and the total extinction of the Confederate Government, left him in the position of freedom from any legal liability to a former representative of that Government; and as the French Courts decided against the claim set up by the United States, he became, as it were, the residuary legatee of the defunct Confederacy, and the total of the remaining assets was left in his hands, and was sacrificed in his misfortunes.

M. Arman died a few years after the above-mentioned events. It is at least due to his memory that I should say that he offered to settle his accounts with me after the close of the war; but when he did so, we did not agree as to the balance due, and I was not willing to assume any further responsibility with reference to Confederate affairs. Subsequently he proposed to pay over to the United States, by way of compromise, a considerable amount, if I would certify the statement of accounts and the United States would accept a compromise and refrain from taking legal proceedings against him. I declined to give the certificate because the statement did not exhibit the balance which I would have claimed on behalf of my principals, and I had no authority to make an arrangement or compromise for their successors.* When M. Arman discovered that the United States purposed to sue him, he determined to repudiate their claim *in toto,* and the result proved that from a pecuniary point of view he was well advised.

---

* The disagreement between M. Arman and myself was not in respect to the amounts received and disbursed by him, but I objected to the large commissions charged for effecting the forced sale of the ships by order of the Government.

Although the statements made by M. Arman to Mr. George Eustis and to me in respect to his interviews with the Emperor and M. Rouher could not be verified by direct inquiry, nevertheless their substantial accuracy was proved by the course of events, and by the official documents which he produced, and which he subsequently gave me. Moreover, if he had undertaken to build and arm those formidable ships for the Confederate Government without a clear and distinct understanding that the administrative and executive officials would be restrained from interference, he would have been acting in direct violation of law, and in open and flagrant contempt of the specific and very peremptory prohibitions of the Emperor's Proclamation of Neutrality, and it can hardly be supposed that the French Government would have taken no legal proceedings against him. As a matter of fact, he was rebuked for not selling the ships promptly when ordered to do so, but he was never reproved for the original undertaking. He continued to occupy his seat in the Assembly, and to receive marks of personal consideration from the highest personages in the Government, and although the counsel employed by the United States did their best to excite prejudice against him, and charged him with breaking the municipal law, and endangering the peace of France by taking part in an attempt to cause a violation of her neutral duties, the court gave judgment in his favour, and even compelled the United States to give security for the costs of the suit.

Mr. Slidell also had a personal interview with the Minister of Marine, about the 25th of June, 1864, and was informed by that functionary that the affair of our ships no longer appertained to his department, but had been referred to the Minister of Foreign Affairs, a proceeding which fulfilled the prediction I had ventured to make in regard to the action of the Imperial Government, should the Confederate cause appear to be losing ground at the time when the ships were near completion, an intimation which I made to the Navy Department in a despatch dated November 30th, 1863, which has been given already in this chapter.

My last report to the Secretary of the Navy on the subject of the attempt to build ships in France was dated August 25th, 1864, and concludes as follows:—

"It would be superfluous for me to comment further upon the unfortunate termination of our French operations. I have laid all the circumstances connected with them fully before you. There was never any pretence of concealing them from the Emperor's Government, because they were undertaken at its instigation, and they have failed solely because the policy or intentions of the Emperor have been changed."

The fortunes of war, it is well known, exercise a strong influence over the policy of neutrals, and there can be no doubt that the relative position of the two belligerents in America had greatly changed when the Emperor of the French caused Mr. Slidell to be informed that it was no longer possible for him to remain quiescent, and that the Confederate ships in France must be sold to some other nation, as he could not permit them to go to sea, either armed or unarmed, unless the United States were satisfied in regard to their destination. There is no denying the fact that up to about midsummer of 1863, the Confederates were able to keep the Federal armies well at bay, and on several occasions Washington was in more danger of capture than Richmond, to wit, after the battle of Bull Run, the defeat of General McClellan on the Chickahominy, and of General Hooker at Chancellorsville. This is manifest from the panic created at the North by the fear of invasion at those times, and the alarm and uneasiness were forcibly exhibited in the telegraphic calls made by the authorities at Washington upon the Governors of the various Northern States, to hurry forward the militia for the defence of the capital, and the excited, urgent, well-nigh agonizing appeals of some of the Governors, notably Mr. Curtin, of Pennsylvania, and Andrews, of Massachusetts, to the courage and patriotism of the citizens in order to arouse their zeal.

In a volume entitled "Report of the Secretary of the Navy in Relation to Armoured Vessels" (Washington, Government Printing Office, 1864), there appear a number of letters from official persons at Boston and New York, urgently beseeching the Secretary of the United States Navy, Mr. Gideon Welles, to place and maintain Monitors in those harbours for their protection. Under date of November 12th, 1862 (p. 596 of volume referred to), the Committee of the Boston Board of Trade called Mr. Welles's attention to "the comparatively defenceless state of the harbour of Boston," and added: "In view of the recent reckless depredations of the piratical steamer *Alabama,* and her reported near proximity to our bay, and also the apparently well authenticated fact recently made public that powerful rams are now partially constructed in England to be used by the rebels in an attack upon our principal cities on the northern coast ... it cannot be regarded strange that this community should be pervaded by deep solicitude as to the absence of immediate means to make any adequate defence," etc. The Committee express their unwillingness to embarrass the Government, or to "make the claims of Boston harbour for protection unduly prominent," but they nevertheless affirm that "the harbour of the third commercial city in the Union ought no longer to be allowed by its weakness to invite the aggression of a desperate enemy." The situation at Boston must have been alarming, and the Committee seem to have been determined to spur Mr. Gideon Welles's energies to the utmost. They were not content with stating the facts of the case, but they supplied him with the opinion of experts. "It is believed by practical men" (they wrote) "that through Broad Sound" (one of the principal entrances to this harbour) "a reckless and daring piratical ironclad steamer might enter without serious injury and lay our city under contribution."

Governor Morgan, in November, 1862 (p. 597), informed Mr. Welles that the municipal authorities of New York "have already taken some measures for raising a fund to protect the harbour by private subscription."

On November 18th, 1862, the Boston Marine Society took alarm (p. 598), and they backed the appeal of the Board of Trade by a still more urgent petition for protection. Their Committee wrote in the following terms:—"Our citizens are deeply concerned on the subject, and look to the Government ... to make such arrangements as will afford that protection which shall allay their fears and anxieties." In the same letter they made a statement which looks very like a confession that Boston had earned a special claim to a little retributive vengeance from the South. The statement is as follows:—"There are obvious reasons in the history and condition of the city of Boston which might tempt an audacious and ambitious foe to lay it under contribution or to waste the property of its people.... The applause with which such an act would be hailed by the enemies of the Union in the Southern States would nerve the invader to run the risk, while the moral effect abroad, should it be unfortunately successful, might be disastrous to the cause in which our country is engaged."

When General Lee advanced into Maryland after defeating General Hooker at Chancellorsville, the panic at the North revived, and in June, 1863, General John E. Wool and Mr. George Opdyke, the Mayor of New York, again wrote most urgently to the Navy Department on the subject of the inadequate defences of that city. General Wool was at that time the Military Commander at New York, and on the 28th of June, 1863, he wrote a letter to the Secretary of the Navy (p. 604), which contains the following startling statements:—"The volunteers and militia of this city are being sent to Pennsylvania to aid in the defence of that State. We shall be at the mercy of any privateer that may think proper to assail this city. The temptation is indeed great, for the want of men to man the guns in the forts of the harbour."

It appears manifest from the official appeals, reports, and statements of high civil and military functionaries who were charged with the care and protection of the chief cities of the North, that for more than two years after the beginning of hostilities, those cities were harassed by an oppressive consciousness of danger, and that extreme efforts were necessary not wholly to capture Richmond, but to keep the so-called "rebels" out of Pennsylvania. Although the full extent of the fears entertained by the Governors of some of the Northern States and the people of New York and Boston was not generally known abroad, yet all who read the accounts of the war perceived that the Federal Government had no mere rebellion to deal with; and during the year 1862, and even up to the middle of 1863, it was very generally believed in Europe that if the Southern ports could be kept open so as to admit a sufficient quantity of arms and other military supplies, the Confederate Government would be able to maintain a successful defence, and finally to win a separate and independent position.

If the rams built at Birkenhead had not been interfered with and then stopped by her Britannic Majesty's Government, they would have got to sea a month or two before the time when General Wool was impressing upon the United States Navy Department the defenceless condition of New York, and while Governor Curtin was appealing for help from all quarters to repel General Lee's threatened advance into Pennsylvania. The weak and accessible points along the Northern coast were well known to the Confederate naval authorities, and the Liverpool rams would have been sent to them, and there can scarcely be a shadow of doubt that they would have fulfilled in great part the predictions of General Wool and the Committee of the Boston Board of Trade.

The invitation to build ships in France was given during the period of successful resistance at the South, and of apparent doubt and trepidation at the North. It was withdrawn when force of numbers and immeasurable superiority in war material began to prevail, and when aid and encouragement was most needed by the weaker side. It suited the Imperial policy, and appeared to be consistent with the designs upon Mexico, to extend a clandestine support to the South when the Confederate armies were still strong and exultant. It was neither prudent nor wise to maintain a doubtful or hesitating attitude towards the winning side when it became apparent that the prospect had changed, and that neither the Emperor Maximilian nor Mr. President Davis could probably maintain his position. *"Voila tout"* is a brief and terse French phrase, which expresses the explanation of the diplomatic summersault better than any English equivalent, and its use may be pardoned on the occasion of describing an occurrence which has special reference to the Government of France.

There does not appear, in the correspondence between the United

States Minister at Paris and the Minister of Foreign Affairs, any evidence that either Mr. Dayton or Mr. Seward suspected that the Confederate agents had been acting in France with the secret encouragement and consent of the Imperial Government. It is not probable, however, that the American Minister would have mentioned his knowledge of such a fact unless his application for the detention of the ships had been refused. The prompt compliance with their demands satisfied the United States, and they were content to know that no hostile vessels from a French port would ever be permitted to arouse the apprehension of General Wool and the "Boston Marine Society," and they did not care to pry into the secret history of their origin.

In the "Case of the United States," presented to the Tribunal of Arbitration, it is stated that the authorization obtained by M. Arman to arm the four corvettes, and his conduct with reference to the rams, were unknown to the Minister of Foreign Affairs, and that when the Minister of the United States at Paris brought the subject to the attention of M. Drouyn de l'Huys, he took immediate steps to prevent a violation of the neutrality of France.

When M. Arman applied to the Ministry of Marine and the Colonies for the authorization to arm the ships, he stated precisely what it was previously understood by the Imperial Government that he should state, namely, that the ships were intended for a line of packets between San Francisco, Japan, China, etc.; and that the armament was required for their protection against pirates in the Eastern seas, and, moreover, to fit the vessels for a possible sale to the Japanese or Chinese Government. M. Arman had been told that he must give a plausible reason for building such formidable ships, and that the Government would not interfere with their despatch from France, or permit an inquisitive inquiry into their ultimate destination and purpose.

The foregoing was in precise accordance with the hints given to Mr. Slidell by persons in high positions who were in close and constant intercourse with the Emperor. I have no means of knowing whether M. Drouyn de l'Huys had been informed of the arrangement with M. Arman, or the intimations conveyed to Mr. Slidell, but I have the original document, signed by M. Chasseloup Laubat, Minister of Marine and of the Colonies, authorizing M. Arman to arm the ships (see p. 360). It will be perceived that the battery of each corvette was to have been twelve or fourteen *"canons de trente,"* and it will hardly be thought credible that the experts at the Ministry of Marine, or the officials who inspected the guns, were deceived as to the character of the ships, or that they ever thought such powerful armaments could have been intended for defence against Chinese pirates in the year 1863.

It will now, I think, be admitted that the fall of Vicksburgh, by which the Mississippi was opened throughout its whole course to the United States gunboats, and the Confederate States severed in twain, and the nearly simultaneous repulse of General Lee at Gettysburgh, were the turning-points of the war. Up to the date of those events the South was able in the main to beat back invasion, and sometimes, by a supreme effort, to assume the offensive. But by that time the drain of battle and disease had greatly diminished her fighting population, and the stringency of the blockade had become so great, that it was impossible to supply the reduced numbers in the field with effective arms and ammunition, and all other necessary supplies could only be obtained at uncertain intervals and in insufficient quantities.

During the last advance upon Richmond the Confederate troops fought with their accustomed intrepidity, and by unflinching courage in resistance, and patient endurance in the lines around Petersburgh, they prolonged the last fatal campaign for a whole year—say from "the battle of the Wilderness" to the surrender at Appomattox Court House. But it was manifest that the power of the country was overstrained; and while the struggle and the resistance of the Confederate forces at all points after the disaster at Gettysburgh was an effort which in future history will place the Southern people among those nations who are most notable for military aptitude and prowess, it was nevertheless a contest that gave but little promise of final success. As the South grew weaker, the chief European States became more and more rigid and discriminating in their neutrality, until finally they practically prohibited that branch of trade which was most likely to afford sufficient succour to the overmatched Confederacy, and left untrammelled the traffic in those articles which were most needed and most easily obtained by the United States.

It is not my wish or purpose to revive the memory of past disappointments, or to arouse a feeling of enmity against those countries whose deceptive neutrality contributed to the defeat of the South. The history of the naval enterprises of the Confederate States which were organized abroad would, however, be very incomplete, and the disparity between the hopes entertained by the people of the South and the results accomplished would not be capable of explanation, unless the whole of the facts and circumstances are fully stated. The South has accepted the result of the war, business and social relations are again intermingling the people of the two sections on terms of friendship and intimacy, and the great majority on both sides can now recur to the events of the war and discuss them as historical incidents, and not as subjects for strife and recrimination. One of the chief purposes of this narrative is to acquaint the Southern people and others who may be interested in the great Civil War with some of the transactions which appear to be but little known; and I wish to deal with the occurrences purely as historical facts, and to point out the natural and reasonable inferences without bias or exaggeration.

COPY OF FRENCH MINISTER OF MARINE'S LETTER GRANTING
AUTHORITY TO ARM THE FOUR CORVETTES.

A Monsieur Arman, Deputé au Corps Législatif,
Rue Godot de Mauroy 1.
Ministère de la Marine et des Colonies, 2me Directoire Personnel,
2me Bureau, 1re Section, Inscription Maritime,
Paris, le 6 *Juin,* 1863.

Monsieur,—

Je m'empresse de vous faire connaitre, en réponse à votre lettre au 1re de ce mois, que je vous autorise volontiers à pouvoir d'un armement de douze à quatorze canons de trente les quatre batiments à vapeur en bois et en fer qui se construisent en ce moment à Bordeaux et à Nantes.

Je vous prie de vouloir bien m'informer en temps utile de l'époque à laquelle ces navires seront prêts à prendre la mer afin que je donne les instructions necessaires à MM. les chefs du service de la Marine dans ces deux ports.

Recevez, monsieur, l'assurance de ma haute consideration,
Le Ministre Secrétaire d'Etat de la Marine et des Colonies,
(Signé)   CHASSELOUP LAUBAT.
Pour copie conforme,
(Signé)   J. VORUZ, aîné.

It will hardly be thought by anyone that if the purpose had been to conceal from the French Government the true destination of ships so wholly fit for war, and so manifestly unfitted for commerce, the attempt to deceive would have been made through the transparent pretence that they were designed for a line of packets between San Francisco and China.

CHAPTER IX

Misconception by the United States of the attitude of the English and French Governments.—Repurchase of the Sphinx *from Denmark.—Precarious condition of the Confederate Cause at that period.—Correspondence concerning the despatch of the* Stonewall (Sphinx) *from Copenhagen in conjunction with the* City of Richmond *from London.—The* Stonewall's *challenge to the United States ships* Niagara *and* Sacramento.—*Surrender of the* Stonewall *to the Cuban Government at the end of the War.—Her subsequent delivery to the United States.*

———

From the contents of the preceding chapter, it will be perceived that the French Imperial Government wholly changed its attitude of tacit encouragement to the Confederate States just at the time when the secret pledges were ripe for effective fulfilment, and when the possession of the ships built under cover of official connivance might have supplied a great and pressing need, and would have measurably increased the power of the Southern States to continue the unequal contest.

One of the strangest features in the retrospect of these Confederate operations in Europe is the evidence we have of the misapprehension of the United States in regard to the feeling of the two great maritime Powers—England and France—towards the American belligerents. In the diplomatic correspondence of the United States during the war there often appear commendatory acknowledgments of the friendly neutrality of France and other Continental Powers, and in the "Case of the United

States" presented to the Tribunal of Arbitration at Geneva, "the proceedings against M. Arman's vessels" are cited "as a proof of the fidelity with which the Imperial Government maintained the neutrality which it imposed upon its subjects." Her Britannic Majesty's Government, on the contrary, is denounced by Mr. Seward for its partiality to the Confederate States, and is charged in both the official despatches and in "the Case" with the gravest offences against international law and neutral duties, and the complaints and insinuations were often expressed in such offensive language, and were sometimes so personal, that in reading them now it is impossible to suppress a feeling of surprise that they were borne so meekly, and answered with so much forbearance.

Whether the Government of the United States ever suspected the secret encouragement which the Emperor of the French gave to the South, does not appear in the printed correspondence, and cannot be now known. What Mr. Seward and the compiler of "the Case" commended, was the prompt, energetic action of the Imperial Government at the critical moment, and they probably cared very little about the original promises or intimations to Mr. Slidell, even if those promises were known to them. The indignation, one might even say the contempt, with which they speak of the British Government of that date, appears to have been the outcome, not of animosity against Great Britain, but of irritation produced by the vacillation of her Majesty's Ministers.

If General Lee had won the battle of Gettysburgh and had been able to hold the line of the Potomac through the winter of 1863–64, and if, meanwhile, affairs had gone on smoothly with Bazaine and the Emperor Maximilian in Mexico, the answer to Mr. Dayton in reference to the Arman ships would have been very different to the reply which was actually given, and Mr. Seward was no doubt conscious of that probability. He knew that there would be a decided answer to a categorical demand one way or the other, and that official action would be prompt and effective, and he was impressed with the respect which energy and promptness in action always inspire, whatever the motive.

The Confederate Government had greater cause to complain of the uncertain and hesitating policy of the British Ministry than that of the United States, because the injury to the former was far greater than to the latter; but I can find nothing in the despatches of Mr. Secretary Mallory, or in any other official document from Richmond, approaching to the acrimony of Mr. Seward's angry expostulations.

It has been impossible to give a clear and comprehensive account of the Confederate operations in England without pointing out and demonstrating the deceptive character of British neutrality during the American Civil War; but I have not confounded the disappointment which resulted from vacillation with the chagrin and vexation which was provoked by a broken pledge. It has been necessary to comment upon the difference between the neutral duties of Great Britain, as expounded by several Cabinet Ministers, and the manner in which they were practised by the Secretary of State for Foreign Affairs, but no responsible Confederate authority has ever intimated that her Majesty's Government held out the least hope that anything would be permitted which was not in accordance with law, and with the conditions of the Queen's Proclamation of Neutrality.

If the Confederate States had gained their independence, the only complaint they could have urged against Great Britain would have been somewhat in this form:—"You called attention to your municipal law, and announced the purpose to maintain a strict and impartial neutrality. You warned us not to infringe the specified statute, nor to expect any favour which would imply a departure from your neutral duties; but in point of fact you 'strained the law'* against our agents, and as regards your declaration of neutrality, you practically helped our enemy by restricting our means of getting supplies, which were freely furnished to him." The case against France would have been very different, say in this form:—"We had not the least purpose to come to you for the supply of our special wants. We preferred to use the dockyards of England, and to rely upon the manifest meaning of British law and the constitutional mode of applying it, than upon the personal feeling of the highest persons in the State; but you invited us to come to you, gave us pledges, and even suggested the pretence upon which the apparent purpose of your neutral declarations might be evaded. Then at the critical moment you withdrew the promises, and acted just as if you were repelling an infringement of your neutral rights, giving us a diplomatic repulse, whose sting was not softened by the pleasant and sympathetic phrases in which it was communicated to us."

The Confederate Government fully comprehended this difference between the conduct of England and France, and Mr. Mallory's despatches on the subject comment upon the hostility of the United States to the Mexican policy of the Imperial Government, and the improbability of that hostility being in the least degree modified by the suppression of M. Arman's efforts to supply the Confederate Navy Department with a fleet of ships.

---

* *Vide* speech of Solicitor-General quoted in another chapter.

The desire to retain a hold upon the French ships was so great that every possible plan was suggested and discussed. Mr. Slidell even had private unofficial interviews with one or two of the Ministers, with the purpose to obtain leave to complete the vessels leisurely, on the condition that no attempt should be made to remove them from the ports of construction without special permission, or until the end of the war. The object was to maintain such a lien upon the vessels that we could regain possession of them if circumstances should at any time induce the Imperial Government to return to its original policy of encouragement to the South. Some concessions were offered to Mr. Slidell which had at first a hopeful appearance, but the ultimate conditions attached to them were found upon reflection to be impracticable; and meanwhile the builders had gone so far in fulfilling the peremptory orders to sell, that the vessels were no longer within their unlimited control.

About the 1st of August, 1864, all efforts to come to any arrangement with the Government were abandoned, and we had the mortification to know that officers and agents of those who had bought the ships were superintending their completion. When the corvettes and the rams built at Bordeaux were sold to Prussia and Denmark, those Powers were at war about the Schleswig-Holstein Provinces, and during an armistice the Prussian ships were, I believe, hurried off to their destination. M. Arman reported this to me at the time. I continued to keep up communication with M. Arman, because he had promised that if any change in the progress of the Prusso-Danish War should induce either of the purchasers to dispose of one or more of the ships, I might again get possession.

With the view to be reliably informed of the events at Bordeaux, I frequently sent Captain E. Tessier there, who acted as my agent in that and several other transactions requiring tact, prudence, and a familiar knowledge of Continental languages and customs. My appearance in Bordeaux for a single day would have excited suspicion, and Captain Tessier was warned to guard against exhibiting any greater curiosity about the vessels than a professional man visiting a maritime city and its dockyards would be likely to show.

Captain Tessier was familiar with the designs of the rams and the peculiar service for which they were intended, namely, on a shoal coast and in the Mississippi river. He soon informed me that the engineer who was superintending the ram bought by Denmark was making alterations which materially changed the original plan, and that the method of securing the armour-plates, and some other portions of the work, was being done in a manner he felt sure I would not approve. It is probable that the chief object of the Danish agent was to get the vessel completed for immediate service, and that time was more important in his estimation than extreme care and nicety in construction. Captain Tessier could only communicate secretly or confidentially with M. Arman, and it was impossible to interfere in any way with the acts and purposes of the actual owner.

There appears to have been much delay in the completion of the Danish ram. Whether the difficulty of getting her out of France during the continuance of the war with Prussia was the cause or not, I have never been informed, but when she was at last finished, hostilities had ceased, and questions arose between M. Arman and the Danish Government about the acceptance of the ship. M. Arman informed me that the Danish Ministry of Marine wished to annul the purchase, because, as he stated, the vessel was not ready in time to take part in the war, and was not wanted for the peace establishment. The ship was, however, taken to Copenhagen in November, and while she was there M. Arman sent an agent whom he often employed in his transactions with foreign Governments, and who represented him in the business with Denmark, to communicate the state of affairs to me, and to arrange for a re-delivery of the ram to the Confederate States. The representative of M. Arman in the negotiations for the sale of the ships was of course familiar with all the arrangements by which those already delivered had been despatched from France, either during actual hostilities between Prussia and Denmark, or during a short armistice. M. Arman had offered in October to manage the transactions with the Danish Government in such a way as to effect a re-delivery of the ship to me; but the vessel was then incomplete. I had every reason to suppose that the sale to Denmark was believed to be *bonâ fide*, both by the French Foreign Office and the United States Minister, and I thought it would be imprudent to enter into an engagement which could by any possibility arouse suspicion, and again draw attention to a Confederate agent. When, however, M. Arman sent his representative the second time with a proposition for the delivery of the ship, the circumstances had wholly changed. The vessel was clear of French interference. She was in Copenhagen, or at least she was *en route* for that port, and the purchasers were desirous to annul their bargain. M. Arman proposed to instruct his agent to manage the negotiations at Copenhagen so as to give me time to collect a staff of officers, prepare the necessary supply of stores and a tender, and to select a suitable rendezvous. He said that when I was ready his agent would get leave to engage a Danish crew to navigate the ship back to Bordeaux, but instead of returning to that port he would take her to the appointed rendezvous, and deliver her to the Confederate officer appointed to command her.

The business arrangements relating to the management of affairs at Copenhagen involved some complications, and they were not finally settled until December 16th, 1864. All the details of this transaction are as fresh in my memory as if they had occurred within the current year. The ship was reported to be suitably provided with everything necessary for her navigation, and she had on board her battery, say one 300-pounder and two 70-pounder Armstrong guns, with a quantity of shot, shells, fuzes, etc., but no ammunition or small arms.

In spite of the great value which even one iron-cased vessel thus armed would have been to the Confederate Government if she could be promptly placed at a given point on the Southern coast, I foresaw the intricacy and complexity of the arrangements necessary to accomplish such a purpose, and the merely physical difficulties at that season of the year were not to be overlooked.

When the rams were begun at Bordeaux with the full knowledge and approval of the Imperial Government, it was purposed, and was so stipulated, that they should be ready for sea in May, or, at the latest, in June, 1864. The vessels were of small size, and were designed for operations in the Mississippi river and the shoal harbours of the Gulf coast of the Confederate States. Their draught in their best fighting trim was to have been fourteen feet. To load them deeper would of course be admissible for the purpose of making a passage, but under such conditions their qualities would be unfavourably affected, both as regards speed and buoyancy, and yet to get them across the Atlantic it would be necessary to weight them heavily with fuel and other stores. If there had been no interference with the work, and no prohibition of their delivery to the Confederate States, both rams would have been in our possession, outside of the river Gironde, in the early part of June, 1864, and we would have had mild summer weather to drop them safely over to their working ground, with the Azores, Nassau and Havana for coaling stations.

At the date of the proposition for the delivery of the *Sphinx*, it was approaching mid-winter, and the vessel was at Copenhagen, with all the intricacies of the Sound, the narrow waters between Denmark and Sweden, the tempestuous gales of the German Ocean, the dangers of the English Channel, and the fierce Biscay gales to encounter and overcome before she could reach a safe place of rendezvous to receive her ordnance stores and her fighting crew.

Besides this, the condition of affairs had meanwhile greatly changed in America. The weak fortifications at Mobile, and the mere pretence of a naval flotilla which the Confederate Government had been able to provide for the defence of that city, had proved wholly insufficient to resist the vigorous attack of Admiral Farragut's powerful fleet, and the bay of Mobile, with the adjacent inland waters communicating with New Orleans, were in complete possession of the Federal military and naval forces. The United States had also obtained control of the Mississippi from the northern boundary of the Confederacy to its delta, and they had got such a firm grip of the passes of the river, and of every approach to New Orleans, that an attempt to displace them, or even to make such a naval demonstration in that quarter as would cause them serious apprehension, would have required a far greater force than one small ironclad ram.

Galveston was believed to be still in possession of the Confederate troops, but the Trans-Mississippi States had been completely dissevered from the remainder of the Confederacy, and an effort to accomplish anything for their defence by the despatch of so small a naval expedition to the only point accessible from the sea, and affording at the same time means of communication with the interior, appeared well-nigh Quixotic. If any effective aid could be rendered to the hard-pressed armies still gallantly holding General Grant at bay from behind the fieldworks of Richmond and Petersburgh, and striving to check Sherman's march through Georgia, that support must be sent to the Atlantic coast.

It was known in Europe that a combined naval and military attack was about to be made upon Wilmington. The Confederate forces in the southwest were so greatly reduced in numbers that it was quite manifest they could not protect the open country from devastating "raids" and keep a sufficient force in General Sherman's front to check his march towards Savannah. In fact, he had already passed the last effective barrier at Atlanta, and there were only a few weak battalions between the head of his advancing columns and his objective point. The force available for the defence of Wilmington was too small to justify much expectation of a successful resistance, and General Lee's supremest efforts were barely sufficient to keep General Grant from breaking his lines, or turning the right of his entrenchments and so cutting him off from communication with the interior or from retreat. The enemy held the fortifications at the mouth of the Savannah river, and access to that port had long been closed. Charleston was almost beleaguered by land, and a powerful co-operating naval squadron made access to the harbour impossible. The collection of a large fleet off Wilmington, preparatory to the combined attack upon its defences, effectually barred the Cape Fear river from the approach of a blockade-runner. The Confederacy was thus almost hermetically closed against communication from without, and the Government was practically shut up in Richmond, with scarcely a single line of communication open with the country lying beyond the boundary of General Lee's earthworks.

The foregoing may seem to be a sensational synopsis of the condition of affairs, but there is not a single statement that is not confirmed by the facts, and they have not been consciously exaggerated in any particular.

Neither the Confederate Commissioners nor the practical agents of the War and Navy Departments were, however, willing to admit that all hope was lost, nor were they willing to cease active exertions so long as the Executive Government was intact, and was able to hold possession of a port or to maintain an army in the field. Commodore Barron and the staff of naval officers who came to Europe with him to take charge of the English ironclads were still in France, concealing themselves as much as possible from public notice, but fretting under their forced inactivity, and ready, I knew full well, to undertake any service, even though it might appear a "forlorn hope."

The Commissioners, with Commodore Barron and Major Huse, carefully considered and discussed with me the proposed enterprise. We took account of all the circumstances, the strained and well-nigh depleted condition of the finances being a prominent difficulty, and it was unanimously determined that the effort should be made. No time was lost in consultation. As soon as it was known that the ram had been permitted to leave Bordeaux, and was thus free from suspicion, I had despatched Captain Tessier to Copenhagen to learn what he could of her condition and performances during the voyage. He got to Copenhagen soon after the arrival of the vessel, before she had been painted or otherwise set in special good order, and found means to go on board and make a personal but necessarily casual inspection. He made a written report, in which he said that he had been able to satisfy himself that the vessel exhibited no visible signs of straining. "The sheer of the ship was true, and the putty or cement filling between the edges of the plates was not even cracked. On deck I tried the butts of the deck-planks, the water-way seams, the butts and scarfs of the watery-ways, covering boards and rails, and found them all in perfect order. The *Sphinx* certainly did then show no sign of weakness." Captain Tessier remarked upon the alterations and insufficient fittings to which he had previously called my attention soon after the sale of the ship to Denmark, but it was now too late to restore them, even if he could have suggested anything of the kind to the people in charge without exciting suspicion.

Although compelled to be content with a hasty examination of the ship, Captain Tessier was able to get a copy of the *"Rapport de Mer,"* or official report of the voyage from Bordeaux to Copenhagen, made by the French captain who took her round to the French Consul. The report was a mere amplification of the ship's log for the information of the Consul, and gave the performance of the ship and her speed without other remarks than that she behaved and steered well in all weather, and that the twin screws worked satisfactorily. It appeared from the log that from Bordeaux to Cherbourg she averaged ten and a half knots per hour, from Cherbourg to Beachy Head, bearing north, ten knots, the weather being moderate and wind generally E.N.E., which was a head wind. After passing the South Foreland, the wind and sea increased, and the speed was eased to five knots, and afterwards it was regulated in accordance with the weather. The "report" concluded with the statement that the ship had behaved well under all circumstances, "especially during heavy squalls on the 5th and 6th of November, when sailing vessels were scudding under very short canvas."

I mention the foregoing particulars because the performances of the ship were not so satisfactory when the Confederate naval officers got possession of her, her average speed then proving to be only eight and a half knots in good weather, and dropping to five and even four with moderate head sea. During the voyage to Copenhagen the engines were in charge of an inspecting engineer from the works of Messrs. Mazelin, where they were constructed, and the ship was probably also in the trim best suited to her size and peculiar design, although it appears from the *"Rapport de Mer"* that she was loaded to fifteen feet, which was one foot more than her calculated fighting trim. When she began her voyage as a Confederate ship, the engineers in charge were strangers to both the vessel and her engines. The only really trustworthy and loyal engineer was a young man of hardly sufficient experience for the position. They were, however, the best men who could be got at the time, and it is not surprising that a better class of artizans could not be induced to undertake a service in which the discomfort, exposure and danger were manifestly greatly in excess of the remuneration it was possible to offer. Besides this, the ordnance stores, fuel, and other supplies necessary for the adequate equipment of the ship for the long Atlantic voyage in the depth of winter over-weighted her, and reduced her to a condition in which she was not intended to be placed, except, perhaps, for a short run from one coast port to another, and then only under favourable conditions of weather.

The inspection made by Captain Tessier and the *"Rapport de Mer"* were independent accounts of the condition and performances of the ship, and although it was manifest that the alterations made after the forced sale had somewhat affected her character and efficiency, yet it was thought advisable to go on with the arrangements for getting her to sea as a Confederate ship. It was hoped that the mere knowledge of the fact that the Confederate Government had been able to get an ironclad vessel in Europe, and that she was actually *en route* for the American coast, would animate the spirits of the Southern people in the struggle, which was becoming more hopeless day by day, and there was also some expectation that exaggerated rumours of her power and efficiency would reach the United States, and that the arrangements it might be thought necessary to make in order to meet and defeat her attack, would cause some delay or confusion in the proposed operations against Wilmington and other ports on the coast of Georgia and the Carolinas.

Captain Thomas J. Page, an old and experienced officer, bred in the United States navy, who had been sent out from Richmond to command one of the so-called Birkenhead rams, was selected for the first place in the enterprise. He had kept himself so completely out of sight since his arrival in Europe, that it was felt to be almost certain that he would not be known to any spy whom the United States officials might possibly employ to watch the ship; besides which, he was a man particularly well suited for secret service by reason of a marked constitutional tendency to silence and reserve when among strangers or newly made acquaintances. Captain Page was sent to Copenhagen to pick up such personal acquaintance with the ship as was possible, to supervise the local expenditure, and to take passage in her for the rendezvous.

Lieutenant R. R. Carter had returned to Europe after his successful voyages with the *Coquette,* mentioned in another chapter, and was on special service with me. This officer is justly entitled to some special notice. I was obliged to impose upon him many and various duties, often of a kind to give him hard work and much anxiety, with but little chance of gaining personal distinction. He was thoroughly well informed in every branch of naval education, and had, besides, an ingenious mind, with quick perceptions, and an admirable aptitude for applying with intelligence and vigour the means at hand to the end in view. These qualities fitted him to design as well as to execute, but he had a keen perception of the duty as well as sound policy of sticking close to the plan he was appointed to carry out, and was never drawn away from the course sketched out for him by the hope of making his own position more prominent, or the expectation of creating some striking effect.

Every naval enterprise undertaken by the Confederate Government in Europe depended for its success upon the fidelity of each of the several agents employed to the instructions and plans laid down by the director of the expedition. It was absolutely necessary for everyone to whom a part in the effort was allotted to conform strictly to the time and method of performing each detail, and in these respects Carter was the most scrupulously loyal man I ever knew. He seemed to merge his individuality for the time being into that of his immediate chief, to think with his mind, and to act with his impulse. Many well laid schemes in war have been frustrated, or their effects neutralized by forgetfulness on the part of subordinates, implicit obedience being as necessary in those who execute, as strategic skill is required by those who direct movements of any importance.

Failure in execution could never befall Carter's share in an enterprise except through what the French call *force majeure*, and when he set about his allotted part of an undertaking, the directing authority could turn his thoughts to other matters without harassing fear or doubt in regard to details. I detached Carter from special service with me, and he was sent to Niewe Diep to arrange for coaling the ram at that place, to look after other matters in connection with her, and finally to join her as first-lieutenant.

A very necessary initiatory arrangement with reference to the despatch of the ironclad from Copenhagen was to select a merchant of respectability at that place to transact the local business, and to engage a Danish crew for the proposed voyage to Bordeaux, so that all might be done in accordance with the laws of the country and the customs of the port. This was a matter of some delicacy, as it was absolutely necessary to acquaint the agent to some extent, at least, with the ultimate movements of the ship, and to arrange with him a secret telegraphic code, in order that the preparation and departure of the supply tender from England might be regulated with due reference to the requirements of the vessel at Copenhagen. We were happy in finding a very suitable agent, who managed his part of the transaction with prudence and fidelity. I supplied him with a cypher code by which he was able to keep me well informed of the condition and movements of the ram, and I could send instructions and advice in regard to the tender.

At the time when this expedition was taken in hand, the financial condition of the Confederate Treasury in Europe was at a very low point, and there was great difficulty in providing the necessary cash for any unexpected purposes. Indeed, there appeared to be a startling deficiency of funds to meet actually existing contracts. The greater portion of the money which had accrued from the compulsory sale of some of our ships had been transferred to the general Treasury account, partly to pay interest on bonds, and partly to pay bills drawn by the War Office at Richmond in favour of the purchasing agents in Europe. In fact, the wants of the army had then become of paramount importance, and it was manifest that they would absorb the whole financial resources of the Government. To follow the usual practice of buying a tender, even though there might be promise of profitable employment for her afterwards, was out of the question. Happily there was in London a handy steamer built for blockade-running, and the owners had employed Lieutenant Hunter Davidson, of the Confederate navy, to take charge of her for a proposed voyage to Bermuda, *en route* for Wilmington.

Mr. W. G. Crenshaw, of Richmond, Virginia, had served in the Confederate army up to the close of the campaign which ended with the battle of Sharpsburg and the retreat of General Lee from Pennsylvania. He was a merchant of approved skill and experience, and upon his return to Richmond after the above-mentioned military operation, the War Department made an arrangement with him to go to England, and to organize a company for the especial purpose of running supplies through the blockade, and to personally superintend the purchase of commissary stores, and such other articles as might be within the range of his mercantile experience. Mr. Crenshaw was therefore in some degree a Government agent, but the essence of the arrangement with him was that he should act purely in a private character, and that he should draw foreign capital, as well as his own commercial credit, into the enterprise. Mr. Crenshaw succeeded in adding some impulse to the trade of blockade-running, and he built or purchased a number of good steamers, which helped to provide the Confederate armies with the means of keeping the field. The vessel above alluded to was one of his fleet, and the happy circumstance of her active movements being in charge of an officer whom I knew, and whose discretion I could trust, at once suggested her employment as the tender for our Danish ram.

I applied to Mr. Crenshaw for the loan of her, merely informing him that I required her to take some passengers and freight to a port intermediate to Bermuda, after which she could proceed on her proposed voyage, and stating that such temporary use of his ship would be of great service to the cause in whose behalf we were both interested. Mr. Crenshaw replied by letter, and stated that the steamer referred to was about to sail with the purpose to take into Wilmington "commissary stores, and from fifty to a hundred tons of railway supplies, much needed in the Confederacy; the railway companies having been admitted into the line (*i.e.*, his company) to enable them to get supplies for the repair of their rolling-stock." He added:—"This boat can only expect to get in on January (1865) moon by leaving England by 26th or 28th instant, and going with as little delay as possible to Bermuda," and he closed his letter thus:—"With these facts we place the steamer at your service, if you require her, and enclose a letter to that effect to Captain Davidson. We shall be well content with any use you make of her, being perfectly willing to forego the pecuniary profit that we might make, if the service will be better promoted, and with all the lights before you, you are quite competent to form a correct opinion."

It is sufficient to say that I accepted Mr. Crenshaw's generous offer, hoping and believing at the time that the deviation from his proposed voyage and the delay would not defeat the expectation of saving the January moon for running the blockade. Unhappily, the delay was greater than appeared likely to occur—the ship met with a mishap after performing her service for me, and never got into Wilmington at all. In the general crash which soon followed, I made efforts to pay full compensation for the loss Mr. Crenshaw and his associates experienced from the failure of their contemplated voyage, and he made no complaint of the only settlement it was possible to arrange; but I felt that he must have sustained a considerable loss, and I am happy to say that he bore it with the equanimity admirably manifested by the majority of the Southern people in contemplating their ruin at the close of the war.

Affairs were now in train for getting the ram away from Copenhagen. Page and Carter were looking after the principal ship; the ordnance and other necessary supplies for her complete equipment were ordered, and forwarded to London for shipment in the tender, which may be known as the *City of Richmond*, and Davidson, as the responsible commander of that vessel, managed the receipt and stowage of everything on board.

Commodore Barron with his company of officers were still in Paris, or that neighbourhood, and he detailed some of the latter, whom he directed to report by letter, and to take their further instructions from me. Two of the officers—Lieutenants W. F. Carter and Samuel Barron—were brought over to London to assist in necessary details; the remainder, with a few men (seventeen in all) who had served the cruise in the *Florida*, were collected on board the *Rappahannock* at Calais, and ten or eleven men already on board that vessel were told off for the ram. These movements and arrangements were full of exciting interest at the time, and all performed their parts with zeal and animation. The memories connected with them, however, are not inspiriting, and there must always be a lack of buoyancy and ardour in the narrative of an effort which has belied the hopes and expectations which inspired it.

There is a lustre inseparable from a successful enterprise, and a splendour inherent to victory, which no power of language and no play of fancy can impart to defeat. The accounts of the great Civil War written by Northern men are more or less gilded by the glamour of success, and may well be recorded in an exultant flow of phrases, even when kept within the limits of strict historical accuracy. Those who venture to tell what was done on the Southern side can only hope to gain a hearing through the interest which belongs to the facts themselves. They need not, and should not, affect the dying notes of the swan; but they are restrained from attempting to counterfeit the soaring melody of the skylark.

Preparations were pushed forward as rapidly as possible, both at London and Copenhagen; but at the latter place there were a good many difficulties and complications which arose without warning, and had to be met and removed as best they could. Both ships were not ready to start until January 4th, 1865, and on that day I telegraphed our Danish agent by cypher code, "Sail as soon as you can," to which I received a reply on the 5th, to the effect that the ram would sail next day. Then followed telegrams on the 7th, "Ship is off"; 8th, "Ship has been gone one day, and I have heard of no interruption"; and again later on the same day, "Ship stopped; heavy gale and snowstorm at Elsinore." There was then an awkward silence of two or three days. But the *City of Richmond* was ready for sea, and had been dropped down the river as far as Greenhithe; to detain her would excite suspicion, and it was necessary to get the officers and men over from Calais and away from England without further delay.

The most satisfactory way in which the subsequent movements of the enterprise can be told will be to give the actual instructions written at the time, and extracts from the official correspondence.

"London, *January 9th*, 1865.

"Sir,—

"Lieutenant Samuel Barron leaves for Calais tonight, and will report to you in person on board the *Rappahannock* at an early hour to-morrow morning. You will despatch him in charge of all the

Florida's men now on board the *Rappahannock* to London, by the steamer leaving Calais to-morrow night; and you will also send over by the same steamer Lieutenant Bochert, in charge of the men now attached to the *Rappahannock* who have been especially selected for the service for which you have been detailed. Send in the same steamer with the men all the officers detailed for the service (a list of whom you have), except Lieutenant Read. Come over to London yourself, together with Lieutenant Read, by the night mail-boat to-morrow, and report to me in person as soon as possible after your arrival on Wednesday morning. I wish to have a short conversation with you, and to give you final instructions and despatches; and as you will have to proceed at an early hour to Greenhithe, and may have to go on board the steamer in a small boat, you should not be encumbered with luggage, all of which should be sent by the steamer which conveys the principal part of the officers and men. Lieutenant Barron will repeat to you my verbal instructions and explanations, and I need not point out to you how necessary it is to follow without deviation the prescribed arrangement.

"I am, etc.,

"(Signed)   J. D. BULLOCH.

"Lieutenant G. S. Shryock,
"Confederate States Navy,
"Calais."

Lieutenant Shryock reported to me in London at half-past six A.M. on the 11th January, and after an hour's conversation started to join the *City of Richmond,* with the following letter of instructions prepared for him in advance:—

"London, *January* 10th, 1865.
"Sir,—
"Immediately upon receipt of this you will proceed to Greenhithe, and from thence find your way on board the steam-ship *City of Richmond,* upon reaching which vessel you will report yourself, together with all the officers and men sent from Calais last night, to Lieutenant Hunter Davidson for a passage to join the Confederate States ship *Stonewall.** There will be put on board the *City of*

---

* *Stonewall* was the name given to the ram when she was commissioned as a Confederate ship.

Richmond an additional number of men, who formed part of the crew of the late Confederate States ship *Florida,* a list of whom will be handed you by Paymaster Curtis. You will assume direct command of all the officers and men, but for manifest reasons of policy and convenience you will berth and govern your command generally under the directions of Lieutenant Davidson.

"When you reach the appointed rendezvous and meet the *Stonewall,* you will report with your command to Captain T. J. Page, and take all further instructions from him. You have a list of the officers of the expedition and the men sent from the *Rappahannock.* Paymaster Curtis will muster all the other men and hand you a list of them. I have a list of all who should be on board, but some may be left behind, and I wish you to instruct the paymaster to make out a correct list of the entire command, officers and men, and send it to me by the pilot, or by Mr. Early, under cover to M. P. Robertson, Esq., Rumford Court, Liverpool. Lieutenant Read will accompany you to join the *Stonewall,* and Passed-Assistant-Surgeons Green and Herty, each of whom will be attached to your command for the purpose of joining the *Stonewall.*... The *City of Richmond* only awaits your arrival on board to sail, and you will join her at the earliest moment possible on the morning of the 11th January, 1865.

"I am, etc.,

"(Signed) J. D. Bulloch.

"Lieutenant George S. Shryock,
"Confederate States Navy."

The following is all that is essential of the letter of instructions to Lieutenant Davidson, and which was dated London, January 10th, 1865:—

"There is unfortunately a possibility that the British authorities may stop the men who are to come from Calais, when they arrive at Gravesend to-morrow morning, in which event Lieutenant W. F. Carter will communicate the fact to both of us at the earliest possible moment, when we must speedily decide what course to pursue. This cannot be finally determined in advance, but the probability is that it would be absolutely necessary for you to sail with the stores and the few seamen who may have joined the ship from London, as your own ship might be compromised by further detention, and the entire expedition be thus broken up.

"The *Stonewall,* as you are aware, sailed from Copenhagen on the 6th instant, but a telegram of the 8th informed me that she was then at Elsinore, detained by a heavy snow-storm. Since that date I have had no communication from her, and am doubtful whether she has sailed again or not. In the absence of any news, we must suppose that she did not get away from Elsinore before to-day, that she will require three days to get to Niewe Diep, two days for coaling at the latter place, and two days in addition to reach a position in the Channel opposite the mouth of the Thames. If these surmises are correct, the *Stonewall* will be opposite the mouth of the Thames on the 17th instant, and if not detained here beyond to-morrow, you will have a start of six days. It has been arranged that the *Stonewall* shall make an average speed not to exceed eight knots per hour, and this low speed has been determined upon to allow for adverse weather. By setting off her days' runs on the chart, you will be able to determine the dates upon which she is likely to reach a position off Ushant, and when you may expect her to reach the rendezvous at Belle Isle; but inasmuch as the time of her sailing cannot be absolutely determined, I hope and desire that you will prolong your stay at Belle Isle as much as possible, making it not less than an entire week, if you can do so with safety and hear nothing of your consort. As it is barely possible that the *Stonewall* may get off sooner than we anticipate, and may arrive at Quiberon Bay, Belle Isle, at an earlier date than we have supposed, I think it best for you not to cruise many hours off Ushant. Perhaps you might just lose a night there. When you have remained at, or off, Belle Isle for a week, it has been arranged for you to proceed to the bay of Angra in the island of Terceira, where you will please remain on some reasonable pretence a few days, and then, should you hear nothing of the *Stonewall*, proceed to Bermuda, where I will have letters awaiting you with further advice, and notice of her movements.... You know that the United States ship *Niagara* is now at Dover, waiting, I fear, to intercept your ship. I offer no suggestion on this point, because you will know how to give her the slip when you get to sea, far better than I can point out the method to you from the land.... I am aware that you are actuated by the same desire for the success of this expedition as I am, or as any other Southerner can be, and when you have sailed I shall await the result with hopeful confidence."

The officers and men from the *Rappahannock,* after arrival at Gravesend on the morning of January 11th, were taken on board the *City of Richmond* by Lieutenant W. F. Carter, who was sent to meet them on landing, and Lieutenants Shryock and Read also found their way safely on board, and Davidson put to sea that afternoon, but was forced to seek shelter under Cherbourg breakwater from a heavy gale, which he prudently declined to face in the Bay of Biscay with his small and heavily weighted paddle-steamer. He wrote me from Cherbourg on the 13th:—

"It was indeed most lucky that I determined to come down Channel on the French coast, for the steamer would have suffered on the English side from the heavy sea, besides which, I might have been forced into one of the harbours on that side. Your officers and men are all very manageable, and we get on very well. The chances are now that this part of the expedition is all right."

The gale which drove Davidson into Cherbourg proved to be one of those prolonged winter tempests which often vex the British Channel at that season, and he did not get away until the 18th. He wrote just at starting to report progress, and said: "The crew are a splendid-looking set of fellows. We are rather crowded, 125 on board all told, and the men must be somewhat uncomfortable, but we manage very well." Meanwhile Page was doing his best to get the ram through the Kattegat, in spite of much bad weather and frequent snowstorms.

Carter wrote from Belle Isle on the 25th January, thus:—"We left Niewe Diep at noon on the 20th instant, discharged Dutch pilot into a fishing boat off Dungeness on the 21st at 10 A.M., and steamed down Channel with light wind and smooth sea. After passing Ushant on the 23rd and hauling up south-east for the rendezvous, the wind freshened to a gale, and quite a sea right ahead. Strange to say, we shipped only spray, which must be owing to her having lightened forward, with having used coal from forward." Coming through the North Sea the little ship was well-nigh smothered, and it was natural that the improved buoyancy should be comforting and satisfactory. It appears from Carter's letter that with the good weather in the English Channel they were able to make for three days an average speed of nine knots instead of the stipulated eight, and thus recovered some of the loss from detention and head wind.

The meeting of the two vessels at the rendezvous and their departure are thus described by Davidson, in a letter from Funchal, Madeira, dated "February 6th, 1865":—

"I left Cherbourg 18th January, and carried out instructions on the way to Quiberon, where we found a snug anchorage on the 20th, and laid quietly, permitting no communication with the shore until the morning of the 24th at 10 o'clock, when the *Stonewall* hove in sight, to the rapturous delight of all who were in the secret."

After explaining the reasons why the *Stonewall* did not receive the quantity of coal intended for her, and which should have been sent out from St. Nazaire, he proceeds thus:—

"She" (the *Stonewall*) "was in a filthy condition, and required more labour to clean her than to get the stores on board and stowed afterwards. The weather was very bad and wet, too, and prevented us from lying alongside. It was therefore hard to work satisfactorily. However, on the 28th January, early, the barometer rising and the weather promising well, the *Stonewall* and this vessel left the bay and soon ran out of sight of land, going nine and ten knots, for San Miguel. It blew a gale at times, with as heavy a sea as I have ever seen. The *Stonewall* would often ship immense seas, they seeming at times to cover her from knight-heads to taffrail, but yet she never seemed to be injuriously affected by them, but would keep her course very steadily. On the morning of the 30th January, after a most uneasy night, we became separated about five miles, this ship having forged ahead, and being afraid to run off in such a heavy sea. About noon, however, it moderated for a while, and the barometer rising steadily, we kept away and ran down to her, signalling, 'How do you do?' Answer, 'All right.' This was so satisfactory that I signalled 'Shall I go on?' Answer, 'Am very short of coals, and must make a port, Ferrol.' Signalled, 'Shall I follow you?' Answer, 'Suit your convenience about following.' "

Davidson then added that the detention of his ship had already caused the loss of one moon for running the blockade, and considering the necessity there was of his getting to Bermuda quickly in order to save the next moon, and considering also that it did not appear necessary to the safety of the enterprise that he should remain any longer in company with the *Stonewall*, he determined to part company, and signalled "Adieu," which was answered with "Many thanks," and then he says:—"At 1:30 we parted company, and at 3:30 lost sight of her, she still heading the sea to the northward and westward, facing the gale under easy steam, no doubt waiting for the weather to moderate before running down on the coast of Spain."

Captain Page also wrote from Isle d'Houat, near Quiberon, giving a full account of his tedious delays and the disappointment he felt at not getting a full supply of coal, but he did not like to wait for the return of the coal-tender from St. Nazaire. He advised me that he had taken charge of the ram on behalf of the Confederate Government, and that M. Arman's agent, who was with him, had complied with all engagements satisfactorily, and was therefore entitled to receive the stipulated commission for his services. The Danish crew were discharged and sent to St. Nazaire, and the ram was chartered and commissioned in due form as the Confederate ship *Stonewall*.

In the heavy weather after leaving Quiberon Bay, the *Stonewall* made a good deal of water, and it was thought that she must have sprung a leak somewhere, but owing to the crowded state of the ship a satisfactory examination could not be made. This apparent defect was an additional reason for making a harbour, and when the gale moderated, Page bore up and ran into Corunna, and the day after arrival there he took the *Stonewall* across the bay to Ferrol, "where all facilities were politely tendered by the officers of the Naval Arsenal."

The first advice of the *Stonewall* from Ferrol was without date, but she arrived there about February 2nd, and Page soon began to lighten the ship by discharging some of the heavy weights into "a good dry hulk," which the naval authorities had kindly put at his disposal, with the purpose of finding the leak. It appears, however, from his correspondence, that the facilities granted him upon his first application were quickly withdrawn. Writing to me under date of February 7th, he says:— "To-day there came off an officer to inform me that in consequence of the protest of the American Minister the permission to repair damages had been suspended, and I must restore the things in the hulk to the ship." Page added, however, that the commanding officer told him that his case was under consideration at Madrid, and that he thought all would be right in a few days. In the end permission was given to make all necessary repairs, but many difficulties were met with, the authorities appearing to be very desirous to hurry the ship off, yet not willing to turn her out of port in an incomplete state.

On the 10th February Page wrote that the United States frigate *Niagara*, Captain Thomas Craven, had arrived; and a few days after the United States ship *Sacramento* joined the *Niagara,* and both vessels anchored at Corunna, about nine miles distance, from whence they could watch the *Stonewall.* Their presence, Page said, gave the Spanish authorities much uneasiness. It was now manifest that the *Stonewall*'s movements were known. The two United States ships at Corunna would either attack her when she attempted to leave Ferrol, or they would follow her across the Atlantic. Besides this, advice of her being at sea would be sent to New York, and preparations would be made by the United States naval authorities to give her a warm reception. The leak was discovered to be in consequence of defective construction in the rudder casing, and this, together with other injuries caused by the rough handling the ship had encountered during the tempestuous voyage from Copenhagen, satisfied Page that the repairs would detain her several weeks at Ferrol. He took also into consideration the latest news from America, which appeared to indicate that the South could not resist much longer. Finally, he determined to go to Paris for consultation, and he directed Carter meanwhile to push on with the repairs. While Page was absent, the *Niagara* and the *Sacramento* ran across the bay from Corunna and anchored at Ferrol. In a letter reporting the incident, Carter said:—

"We of course got ready for accidents, and in lighting fires sparks flew from the funnel. In a few minutes a barge from the navy-yard, with an officer of rank, came alongside, asking if we meant to attack the *Niagara*. I replied that we had no such intention, but purposed to defend ourselves from an attempt to repeat the affair at Bahia.* He said, 'This is not Brazil. The Admiral requests that you will let your fires go out, and warns you against any attempt to break the peace.' Two guard-boats were also stationed near us, and remained there every night while the *Niagara* was in port. However, we kept steam all night, and the chain unshackled, so as to get the ram pointed fair, in case the *Niagara* moved our way."

It was decided, after consultation with the Confederate Commissioners, that, in spite of the gloomy prospects across the Atlantic, no possible effort that could be made from Europe should be abandoned. Page therefore returned to Ferrol, with the purpose to pursue his enterprise, which, I may just say in brief phrase, was to go to Bermuda, get some additional ordnance stores and a few picked men from the *Florida* waiting there for him, and then attempt to strike a blow at Port Royal, which was then supposed to be the base of General Sherman's advance through South Carolina.

Vexatious delays detained the *Stonewall* at Ferrol until March 24th, when Page got to sea. The United States ships *Niagara* and *Sacramento* had manifested every purpose to follow and attack the *Stonewall* when she left Ferrol. The *Niagara* was a large, powerful frigate, mounting ten 150-pounder Parrot rifled guns; and the *Sacramento* was a corvette, very heavily armed for her class, the principal pieces being two 11-inch and two 9-inch guns. The *Niagara* was also a ship of great speed, and could easily have kept clear of the *Stonewall*'s dangerous beak. The *Stonewall* was protected by 4¾-inch armour, and mounted one 300-pounder and two 70-pounder Armstrong guns; but she was a small ship and low in the water, and the *Niagara*'s battery could have commanded her decks. Page, being quite sure that he would be followed out and attacked as soon as he had passed the line of Spanish jurisdiction, cleared for action before getting under weigh,

* This was an allusion to the capture of the *Florida* at Bahia by the United States ship *Wachusett*.

in full sight of the two United States ships. The upper spars, to the lower masts, were struck and stowed on deck, and the boats were detached from the davits.

In this trim the *Stonewall* steamed out of Ferrol on the morning of March 24th, 1865, accompanied by a large Spanish steam-frigate. At about three miles from the shore the frigate fired a gun, and returned to Ferrol. The *Stonewall* then stood off and on all the remainder of the day, with her colours flying, in plain view of the two United States vessels, which remained at anchor. Carter, in a letter, says:—"We could see the officers standing in the *Niagara's* tops using spyglasses."

At dark the *Stonewall* stood close in to the entrance of the harbour, and then, being satisfied that the enemy did not intend to come out and fight, Page bore away and steamed down the coast to Lisbon, where he arrived in due course, the *Niagara* arriving about thirty-six hours after him.

Commenting upon the failure of the *Niagara* and *Sacramento* to follow the *Stonewall* and attack her, Page wrote me from Lisbon as follows:—"This will doubtless seem as inexplicable to you as it is to me, and to all of us. To suppose that those two heavily armed men-of-war were *afraid* of the *Stonewall* is to me incredible, yet the fact of their conduct was such as I have stated to you. Finding that they declined coming out, there was no course for me but to pursue my voyage."

Captain Thomas Craven, who commanded the *Niagara,* was not the officer who is mentioned in another chapter as the commander of the United States ship *Tuscarora,* and who had a correspondence with the Governor of Gibraltar in respect to the Confederate ship *Sumter.* Captain Thomas Craven was an elder brother of the latter-named officer. His conduct in making so much parade of a purpose to stop the *Stonewall,* and the subsequent failure to accept her invitation to come out and engage her, was a good deal criticized at the time. I have no means of knowing what explanation of his conduct he made to his own Government, and I should be sorry to repeat any of the gossip of the period which might suggest a slur upon his courage. His reputation in the United States navy, while I held a commission in that service, was such as to place him above any suspicion. He was certainly an able and efficient officer, and I mention the incident with the *Stonewall* as an historical fact, and without the slightest purpose to cast an imputation upon his memory.

At Lisbon Page was made to feel that he was the representative of a losing cause. He was permitted to get a supply of coal, but it was manifest that the authorities wished him clear of the port. He got away as soon as possible, proceeded to Santa Cruz, in the island of Teneriffe, replenished his fuel there, and thence stood down into the north-east Trades. On April 25th he hauled up for Bermuda, but encountered north-west winds and heavy head swell immediately after leaving the Trade winds, and being in rather short supply of coal, he shaped his course for Nassau, arriving there May 6th. From Nassau he proceeded to Havana.

At the time of Page's arrival at Havana the war was practically at an end. In a few days he learned of General Lee's surrender, and soon after of the capture of Mr. Davis. Manifestly he could now venture upon no offensive operation. The small amount of funds he took from Ferrol was exhausted. Major Helm, the Confederate agent, could do nothing for him in that way. The position was perplexing, and quite exceptional. As a last resource, negotiations were opened with the Cuban authorities for the surrender of the ship to them, if they would advance the money necessary to pay off the crew.

When it was known through a resident merchant that the Captain-General was willing to make the necessary advance and take the ship, Carter was sent to state the requirements and get the money, and his brief report of the interview was as follows:—

"After five minutes' conversation, the Captain-General asked what sum we required. I said '$16,000.' He said, 'Say $100,000.' I replied that my orders were to ask for $16,000. He then turned to an official at a desk and bid him write, continued asking questions, and when the document was handed to him for perusal, he looked at me again and said, 'Shall we make it $50,000?' But I obeyed orders, and $16,000 was ordered to be paid."

Upon the receipt of the money, Page "paid off the crew to May 19th, 1865, and delivered the *Stonewall* into the hands of the Captain-General of Cuba." In July, 1865, she was delivered to the Government of the United States, and the conditions of the surrender are set out in the annexed correspondence between the Spanish Minister at Washington and Mr. Seward, the United States Secretary of State. She was subsequently sold by the United States to the Government of Japan.

It may be thought by those who are inclined to be severely critical that, in the arrangements for despatching the *City of Richmond,* some liberty was taken with the municipal law of England, and that there was some violation of her neutral territory. Scarcely anyone, however, will maintain that the shipment of arms by the steamer was illegal; and the officers and men from Calais were unarmed, in plain clothes, were not above an hour upon English soil, and merely passed across a minute portion of English territory as ordinary travellers. If it is possible to construe those movements as an offence, it cannot be said that her Majesty's Government was in any degree chargeable with neglect, because neither the Customs nor police authorities could have known of the purpose in advance, and could not therefore have made any arrangements to stop it, even if the state of the law would have justified interference.

At Calais, however, the conditions were wholly different. A Confederate man-of-war was lying at that port. She was in a dock near the railway-station, and could be seen by every passenger *en route* from London to Paris in the daily mail trains. Officers in the Confederate uniform walked her quarter-deck, the Confederate flag was hoisted and struck morning and evening, and all the routine and etiquette was preserved on board of her that is commonly practised in national ships lying in the dockyards of their own countries. Her presence was permitted by the French authorities, and she was *openly* used as a *depôt* ship, because no disguise was possible. Men were collected on board of her and afterwards distributed to the *Florida* and other vessels on previous occasions, and she was used in the same manner to supply the wants of the *Stonewall*. If there was any violation of French neutrality, it was done with the tacit consent of the Imperial authorities, and without greater concealment than is practised in all well regulated business transactions. No information was asked, and none was offered.

The United States urgently pressed at Geneva the charge that Great Britain had been both lax in her neutral duties and partial towards the Confederate States, and commended the rigid exactness of France. The foregoing are some of the facts which may serve to illustrate the true attitude of those two neutral Powers, and may help those who are still interested in the subject to determine the foundation upon which the "*Alabama* Claims*" were based.

THE SURRENDER OF THE *STONEWALL*.

The following is the text of the correspondence between the United States Government and the Spanish Minister at Washington, in reference to the *Stonewall:*

MR. TASSARA TO MR. SEWARD.

Washington, *July* 14*th*, 1865.

The undersigned, Minister Plenipotentiary of her Catholic Majesty, has the honour to bring to the knowledge of the honourable the Secretary of State, that, agreeably to official communications which he has received from Madrid, the order has been given to the Captain-General of Cuba to deliver the war-vessel *Stonewall* to the person whom the

Government of the United States may commission, the due formalities intervening. In thus acting, the Government of her Majesty judges that the reasons adduced in the note of the 30th of May last are not sufficient to found the right of revindication which that of the United States believes it has over the forementioned vessel. Animated, nevertheless, by the same noble and loyal sentiments which it has shown during the four years of the war happily terminated in this country, it omits entering into a discussion without object, and the *Stonewall* is placed at the disposal of the Government of the United States. With reference to the security for the expenses to the commander of the *Stonewall* of $16,000, which sum, having been considered as the sole and special cause of the surrender of the vessel, it is to be believed that the Government of the United States will not refuse to reimburse; it being understood, nevertheless, that this is not a condition for the delivery of the *Stonewall*, which delivery is and must be considered absolutely unconditional. The undersigned avails himself of this occasion to reiterate to the honourable Secretary of State the assurance of his highest consideration.

GABRIEL G. TASSARA.

To the Hon. the Secretary of State
of the United States.

MR. SEWARD TO MR. TASSARA.

Department of State, Washington, *July 17th,* 1865.
The undersigned Secretary of State of the United States has the honour to acknowledge the receipt of a note which was addressed to him on the 14th instant by Mr. Tassara, Minister Plenipotentiary to the Queen of Spain. In that note Mr. Tassara informs the undersigned that her Catholic Majesty has ordered that the armed steamer *Stonewall,* which has been the subject of previous correspondence between the two countries, shall be delivered up to the Government of the United States, and that this decision has been made with a waiver of discussion upon the question whether the demand of the United States for the surrender could be maintained upon strict principles of international law. Mr. Tassara has been pleased also to assure the undersigned that the surrender has been ordered on the ground of the mutual good-will which has happily prevailed between the two countries during the period of the insurrection which has heretofore greatly disturbed the relations of the United States with many of the foreign Powers. The undersigned is still further informed that while Spain will receive from the United

States, as they heretofore offered to pay, an indemnity of $16,000, the amount of the expenses which the Captain-General of Cuba incurred in obtaining possession of the *Stonewall,* yet the surrender is tendered without making it dependent on such reimbursement as a condition. Mr. Tassara's communication has been submitted to the President of the United States, and the undersigned has now the pleasure to inform Mr. Tassara that orders will be promptly given for the bringing away of the *Stonewall* from Havana, and the reimbursement of the sum of $16,000 to the Spanish Government. It only remains to be added that this Government appreciates equally the promptness, the liberality, and the courtesy which have marked the proceedings of her Catholic Majesty's Government on this interesting subject, and that the proceedings will have a strong tendency to confirm and perpetuate the ancient and traditional friendship of the two nations.

The undersigned avails himself of this occasion to offer Mr. Tassara renewed assurance of his highest consideration.

WILLIAM H. SEWARD.

To Senor Don Gabriel Garcia y Tassara,
Minister Plenipotentiary, etc.

CHAPTER X

Jubilation in the United States at the loss of the Alabama.—*Admiral Farragut's criticism on the action.*—*The moral law inoperative in time of war.*—*The United States and privateering.*—*United States precedents favourable to the Confederates.*—*Difficulty of settling the affairs of the* Alabama *and supplying her place.*—*The* Sea King, *afterwards the* Shenandoah.—*Correspondence respecting the* Shenandoah *and the* Laurel, *with the instructions to the officers concerned.*—*Smallness of the crew of the* Shenandoah.—*Volunteers from her prizes.*—*Her cruise amongst the whalers.*—*Means taken to stop her proceedings at the end of the Civil War.*—*Her return to Liverpool and delivery to the United States representatives.*—*Loyalty of the crews of the Confederate cruisers.*—*Inactivity of the United States Navy.*—*Summary of the injury done to American commerce by the cruisers.*

———

When the *Alabama*'s graceful bends and the supporting timbers were torn and shattered by the great 11-inch shells of the *Kearsarge,* and the famous little craft settled down to the bottom of the English Channel with much gurgling of water through her riven sides, and a great sigh as the wind escaped from her open hatchways, there was much jubilation among "loyal" Americans. The despatches of Mr. Seward, the reports of Mr. Adams, the exultant congratulations exchanged by members of the United States Consular corps, the comments of the Northern press which immediately followed that sea-fight off Cherbourg when its result was known, appear to have been out of all proportion to the magnitude of the struggle and the national glory which can be claimed for the victory.

That the merchants of New York and Boston should have proved unable to suppress their exuberant delight, is not perhaps surprising, because a Confederate cruiser roving at will upon the high seas meant loss of trade and high premiums, and her destruction held out a faint promise of relief from loss, and a restoration of commercial profits and prestige. But the excitement was not confined to the mercantile classes, nor was the stimulus to Mr. Seward's acrid temper and pungent pen the only effect. Captain Winslow's achievement aroused the ardour and animated the patriotism of the United States Navy in an extraordinary degree. Even Admiral Farragut, calm as he generally was, and capable of daring and skilful effort, lost for a brief time at least the accurate poise of his judgment, and was so completely aroused by the general enthusiasm as to be entrapped into that popular style of expressing delight at a triumph, which was commonly practised by the majority of the "Union commanders," and the "loyal press." Writing to his son* on July 20th, 1864, the gallant Admiral says:—

"The victory of the *Kearsarge* over the *Alabama* raised me up. I would sooner have fought that fight than any ever fought on the ocean. Only think! it was fought like a tournament, in full view of thousands of French and English, with a perfect confidence on the part of all but the Union people that we would be whipped. People came from Paris to witness the fight. Why, my poor little good-for-nothing *Hatteras* would have whipped her (the *Alabama*) in fifteen minutes, but for an unlucky shot in her boiler. She struck the *Alabama* two shots for one while she floated. Winslow had my first-lieutenant of the *Hartford,* Thornton, in the *Kearsarge*. He is as brave as a lion, and as cool as a parson. I go for Winslow's promotion."

At the date of the above letter the Admiral was lying off Mobile in command of a powerful fleet, composed of fourteen wooden ships and four Monitors, which formed his line of battle in the attack upon the Confederate defences a few days afterwards, and six or eight gunboats besides. He was naturally in a martial and combative humour; but the criticism upon the action off Cherbourg breakwater appears to be rather overdrawn and unprofessional.

As a matter of fact, not a score of people knew from a Confederate source that the engagement would take place, or when, and the "thousands of French and English" who are said to have witnessed it, must have been either the floating and idle population of a seaport, the majority of whom probably did not know one ship from the other, or they were persons who got their information from the United States Consul, and who were there-

* See "Life and Letters of Admiral D. G. Farragut," by his son, Loyall Farragut, p. 403.

fore hopeful, if not confident, that the *Kearsarge* would win. There were a few naval officers who went to the best points of observation with the expectation that there would be an opportunity to take some interesting and useful notes; but as the ships steamed away from the land some seven miles* to get well beyond the "line of jurisdiction" before the action began, but little of the effect could have been seen. The allusion to the *Hatteras*, and the hypothetical prediction that she "would have whipped the *Alabama* in fifteen minutes, but for an unlucky shot in her boiler," can hardly be considered as a fair—it certainly is not a judicious—professional criticism, the simple facts being that the fire of the Confederate ship reduced her adversary to a sinking state in *less* than *fifteen* minutes, while she herself received so little injury from "the two shots for one" fired at, but apparently not into her by the *Hatteras*, that she would not have gone into port except for the necessity of landing the prisoners which she picked up out of the water, without leaving a man of them to drown.

Semmes made no pretence of having performed a great naval exploit in sinking the *Hatteras*, and Lieutenant-Commander Blake was in no way disgraced by his defeat; but any fair and competent naval critic will admit that when one ship sinks another in thirteen minutes in a night engagement, and handles her boats so well as to pick up all hands, the feat is creditable to the victor. The *Kearsarge* practised upon the *Alabama* for about one hour and ten minutes, with two 11-inch pivot-guns, two 32-pounders, and a 28-pounder rifled gun, in broad daylight and smooth water, before placing her *hors de combat*; and when the latter ship foundered, so slowly that there was time to get all of her own wounded into a boat, the remainder of her crew would have drowned if it had not been for the fortunate proximity of an English yacht and two French fishing-smacks.

If there was either rhyme or reason in suggesting an hypothesis, I might say that it is far more likely that the *Alabama* would have "whipped" the *Kearsarge* in fifteen minutes if the 100-pounder shell had exploded in the latter's stern-post,† than that the *Hatteras* would have inflicted that punishment upon the *Alabama* if she had not received the "unlucky shot in her boiler."

The wreck of the *Alabama* lies at the bottom of the "silver streak" which separates England and France. The remains of the *Hatteras* are

* Captain Winslow says seven miles. The estimate of Semmes and his officers was that the action was fought nine miles from Cherbourg.

† See account of the engagement, p. 197.

rusting many fathoms down in the briny waters of the Gulf of Mexico. These are the facts which impartial history has already recorded, and no suggestions of what might, could, or should have been can bring those two vessels again to the surface.

It does not appear to have occurred to Admiral Farragut that by depreciating the *Alabama* he was casting ridicule upon the excessive jubilation over the performance of the *Kearsarge*. If his "poor little good-for-nothing *Hatteras*" could have "whipped the *Alabama* in fifteen minutes," it is difficult to perceive the ground for setting so high an estimate upon Winslow's exploit with the *Kearsarge*, seeing that he took about four and a half times as long to effect the same purpose. There are many men whose temperaments are so ardent and whose imaginations are so active, that neither their tongues nor pens can be kept within the limits of a plain story, or a reasonable, impartial and judicious criticism; but when a man has had a half-century's experience of naval life, and can say, in the words of an old sea-song—

> "For forty long years
> I've ploughed the salt ocean,
> And served my full time
> In a man-of-war ship,"

it is disappointing to find a chance and inconsiderate burst of feeling, which he has accidentally let slip in an unguarded moment, formally set out in print as his estimate of a sea-fight.

In fact, Captain Winslow appears from the records to have been the only person in the United States who was content to look upon his victory in a moderate and modest temper. It was a spirited and creditable exploit, for which he was justly entitled to commendation, and even to a step in rank, but that it was in any way remarkable, when compared with many other engagements between single ships which are doubtless fresh in the memories of naval men, and others who are familiar with naval history, will hardly be seriously contended.

The exultation produced throughout the United States by the destruction of the *Alabama*, and the vituperative language in which all who were thought to have contributed to her origin and career, either by active effort or by failure to restrain her movements, were denounced, must be regarded as the measure of the menace she was to the safety of American commerce, and the ruin she inflicted upon it, according to the estimate of the interested parties, namely, those who suffered by her so-called depredations. The manifest effect which the appearance upon the sea of a few Confederate cruisers created upon the enemy, and the large additional increase of the war expenditure of the United States which they made necessary, was a justification for the policy of putting them afloat, and was an unintentional, although a very practical, panegyric upon the perseverance, energy, and judgment of their commanders.

The news of the sea-fight off Cherbourg and its unhappy result reached Richmond through the lines of the opposing armies in Virginia before the official report found access through a blockaded port, and Mr. Secretary Mallory, in a despatch dated Richmond, July 18th, 1864, wrote me as follows:—"The loss of the *Alabama* was announced in the Federal papers with all the manifestations of joy which usually usher the news of great national victories, showing that the calculating enemy fully understood and appreciated the importance of her destruction. You must supply her place if possible, a measure which, important in itself, the information conveyed by your letter above referred to renders of paramount importance."* In a subsequent despatch on the subject, Mr. Mallory wrote as follows:—"The blows of our cruisers have destroyed the foreign trade of the enemy, and given great discouragement to his whale fisheries, the tonnage of which has declined to its limit of 1840, while our naval operations here, including the construction of a few ironclads, have constrained him to add at least a hundred millions to his expenditure to meet them."

There can be no doubt that the destruction of unarmed and peaceful merchant ships, while quietly pursuing their voyages on the high seas, is a practice not defensible upon the principles of the moral law; and it does not in these modern times harmonize with the general sentiments of commercial nations. At an early period of the war I found occasion to call the attention of the Secretary of the Navy to the subject, in a despatch treating especially of the anticipated cruises of the *Florida* and *Alabama;* and in that despatch I reported as follows:—"The feeling everywhere in Europe is strongly against the destruction of private property at sea, which cannot always be identified as that of your enemy. The *Harvey Birch* turns out to have been owned (in part at least) by a warm sympathizer with our cause, and the cruise of the *Sumter,* although evincing great energy, skill, and tact

---

* The letter referred to was a report from me in reference to the action of the French Imperial Government withdrawing the permit to build ships in France.

on the part of Captain Semmes, has resulted in no profit, but, on the contrary, has tended to excite some feeling against us among the commercial classes in Europe."

The individual members of the Government at Richmond no doubt held opinions on the above subject which were in harmony with the common sentiment of Europe; and if in matters of State policy, and under pressure of great political convulsions, the application of the moral law could be regulated upon the principles which should be paramount in the personal relations among men, they would have been happy to spare the commerce of the United States, and the peaceful trader would have been left to pursue his commercial voyages without fear or molestation. But no one will pretend that Cabinets and Ministers in their collective capacities can act under the same restraints of conscience or of law as control the conduct of individuals in their personal intercourse with each other; and when two nations unhappily fall out and go to war, the Government of each does its best to inflict the greatest possible amount of injury upon the other, on the principle that the more burdensome and afflicting the state of war can be made to the opposing party, the more quickly will he consent to terms of peace.

The proposition that Governments cannot, or at least do not, apply the moral law under the restraints which check and control private action, needs only to be stated. No practical man who has read history, or observed the conduct of Governments, will require any demonstration. It was true in Pagan times, when the Romans carried the war into Carthage, and in Christian times, when the Government at Washington permitted General Sheridan to burn every corn-mill and destroy every blade of corn in the Shenandoah valley because it was supposed to be the granary of the Confederate army, notwithstanding hundreds of women and children were thus left to suffer and well-nigh to starve. It was equally true when the German armies swept up every article of food and every bottle of wine in their victorious march through the "pleasant land of France." It had its last exposition in the bombardment of Alexandria by the British fleet; and the distinction between the private interpretation of the moral law and its application by a responsible Government has been expounded by the Right Honourable W. E. Gladstone, the Prime Minister of England, with special reference to the demolition of the Alexandrian forts and the invasion of Egypt by the orders of that Cabinet of which he is the chief, at a time when, according to his own statement, there was no war between the respective countries.

The diplomatic correspondence of the United States during the Civil

War teems with denunciatory assaults upon the Confederate Government for attacking their commerce. The *Alabama, Florida,* etc., are invariably called "piratical cruisers," and their commanders "pirates." The destruction of American ships at sea was described by Mr. Seward, Mr. Adams, and the Consuls, as being opposed to the sentiments of "civilized and commercial nations," as "unauthorized acts of violence upon the ocean," as the indulgence "of a purely partisan malice," as "barbarous acts," "malicious and piratical," etc.

When these fierce denunciations were made current through the Parliamentary Papers which were issued from time to time, the British public began to refresh their historical reminiscences, and they soon learned that the Confederate States were only conforming to a mode of aggressive warfare invariably practised by the United States themselves in their former wars, and from the discussions and comments which frequently appeared in the daily press, they learned that the Great Powers who took part in what is called "The Declaration of Paris of 1856," proposed to abandon the belligerent right of search at sea, and to abolish privateering, but the United States declined to join in the declaration.

In point of fact, the Great Powers in the Declaration of Paris agreed to four propositions, which were in effect as follows:—Free ships should make free goods; neutral property, except contraband of war, should be free from confiscation when found on board of an enemy's ship; privateering should be abolished, and efficiency should be necessary in order to legalize a blockade. The United States were invited to assent to the foregoing propositions, but declined to accept the abolition of privateering unless the Powers would agree to a further stipulation excepting all private property from capture on the high seas. The counter-proposal of the United States was not acted upon.

At a very early date after the beginning of the Civil War, the Government at Washington reopened negotiations with her Majesty's Government with reference to the foregoing propositions, and proposed to accept them unconditionally. The United States would not agree to the abolition of privateering when it was first proposed, unless they could secure all private property from the liability to capture on the high seas by national men-of-war as well by private cruisers. This was an intelligible course at the time, because the United States had a very small navy, but had facilities for covering the sea with privateers, and if the right to employ them was surrendered, they would be at a great disadvantage in a war with one of the great naval Powers, and it was reasonable that they should claim the exemption of private property from capture as a counterpoise. When, however, the Civil War began, the United States perceived the danger to their own commerce from possible Confederate privateers, and knowing that their own regular naval force was greater than any the Confederacy would be able to oppose to it, they were willing to join in the Declaration of Paris, pure and simple; but the negotiations did not come to any definite result.

The British public learned the foregoing facts, and they learned also that during the American War of Independence, and to a much greater extent during the war of 1812–15, the cruisers of the United States were repeatedly and specifically ordered to destroy British merchant ships at sea, and not attempt to bring them into port. In face of these facts, which the over-astute diplomacy of Mr. Seward either suppressed or at least ignored, the European sentiment in respect to the action of the Confederate Government was gradually modified, until at last public opinion settled down to the very general belief that the United States had no sort of justification for their complaints and denunciations, and that, as between the two belligerents, the Confederates were practising a perfectly lawful and justifiable mode of harassing their enemy, and adding to the cost and burden of the war which was being waged against them, and the violent interference with their claim to self-government.

It is generally known that some months after the end of the war, the late Admiral Semmes, although a paroled prisoner, was arrested at his house in Mobile, and carried to Washington, under military guard. He was held in confinement there for some time, and the purpose was to institute criminal proceedings against him with reference to his acts while in command of the *Sumter* and *Alabama*. The civil authorities at Washington seemed very desirous to discover a plea by which they might sustain the charge of piracy so often hurled at him during his cruises, but they happily perceived in time the wickedness of such a proceeding, and they caught a glimpse of the ridicule and contempt it would have aroused in Europe, and the purpose was abandoned.

About that time, Mr. John A. Bolles, the Solicitor to the Navy Department of the United States, published an article in the *Atlantic Monthly*, under the title of "Why Semmes of the *Alabama* was not tried." Mr. Bolles cites Cooper's "Naval History" to prove that during the "Revolutionary War" many British vessels were captured by Colonial cruisers and destroyed at sea. Referring to the history and policy of the United States during the war with England, commonly called the "War of 1812," he says:—"Not less than seventy-four British merchantmen were captured, and destroyed as soon as captured, under express instructions from the

Navy Department, and in pursuance of a deliberate purpose and plan, without any attempt or intent to send or bring them in as prizes for adjudication. The orders of the Department upon this subject are numerous, emphatic, and carefully prepared. They deserve to be studied and remembered, and they effectually silence all American right or disposition to complain of Semmes for having imitated our example in obedience to similar orders from the Secretary of the Confederate Navy."

Mr. Bolles gives copious extracts from the orders issued to Captains Charles Stewart of the *Constitution* and Charles Morris of the *Congress*, to Commandants Blakely, Warrington, Parker, Creighton, and other officers in command of United States ships. A few will answer the present purpose.

"The great object," says one of the orders, "is the destruction of the commerce of the enemy, and the bringing into port the prisoners, in order to exchange against our unfortunate countrymen who may fall into his hands. You will therefore man no prize unless the value, place of capture, and other favourable circumstances shall render safe arrival morally certain. You will not agree to the ransoming of any prize," etc. Another says:—"You will, therefore, unless in some extraordinary cases that shall clearly warrant an exception, destroy all you capture; and by thus retaining your crew and continuing your cruise, your services may be enhanced ten-fold." Again:—"Your own sound judgment and observation will sufficiently demonstrate to you how extremely precarious and injurious is the attempt to send in a prize, unless taken very near a friendly port and under the most favourable circumstances.... Policy, interest, and duty combine to dictate the destruction of all captures, with the above exceptions."

One of the extracts contained in Mr. Bolles's article is strikingly pertinent. It is as follows:—"A single cruiser, if ever so successful, can man but a few prizes, and every prize is a diminution of her force; but a single cruiser destroying every captured vessel has the capacity of continuing, in full vigour, her destructive power so long as her provisions and stores can be replenished, either from friendly ports or from the vessels captured.... Thus has a single cruiser, upon the *destructive plan*, the power perhaps of twenty acting upon pecuniary views alone ... and thus may the employment of our small force in some degree compensate for the great inequality (of our force) compared with that of the enemy."

Mr. Bolles comments upon the policy of the United States, and the orders issued to their men-of-war, in the following words:—"Such were the policy and the orders of President Madison and of the Secretary of the Navy in 1812, 1813, 1814; and such, beyond question, would be the plan and the instructions of any Administration under the circum-stances."

The foregoing extracts, taken from among those cited by Mr. Bolles, clearly indicate the policy of the United States when they were at war with Great Britain.* That policy was most deliberate and determined, and the orders were explicit to destroy—destroy—destroy. In comparing the practice of the United States in 1812–15 with that of the Confederate States in 1862–64, it is important to consider the difference between the two Governments in respect to the possession of open ports. Great Britain was never able to keep a blockading force at all points of the American coast, and there were a good many ports to which there was easy access at all times.

With the Confederacy the position was very different. There are, to begin with, very few deep-water ports along the coast-line of the South-ern States, into which large prizes could have been taken, and those soon fell into possession of the United States forces, or were effectively sealed against entry except by swift steamers especially designed for blockade-running. The United States therefore adopted as a deliberate policy the practice of destroying their prizes, whereas the Confederate States were compelled to permit the destruction of captures by their cruisers because there were no home ports to which they could have been taken. I can state without hesitation or reserve that the destruction of prizes by the *Alabama* and other Confederate cruisers was not "in pursuance of a deliberate pur-pose or plan." Captain Semmes sent nearly all of the prizes made at the beginning of his cruise in the *Sumter* into neutral ports—for example, into Cienfugos, on the south side of Cuba—and he addressed several clear and ably written appeals to the authorities at that and other places for permis-sion to leave the captured vessels, as it were, in safe deposit, and in the interest of whoever it might concern, until they could be properly adjudi-cated. His object, and that of the Confederate Government, was to give neutrals who might have property on board the prizes the opportunity to prove their title, and thus to escape from the consequences of their own indiscretion in shipping their goods under a belligerent flag. The neutral Powers were unanimous in excluding prizes from their ports on any plea, and thus every expedient by which the immediate destruction of captured vessels might have been avoided was prohibited to the commanders of the

---

* Copious extracts from Mr. Bolles's article appear in Sir A. Cockburn's review of the Geneva Arbitration, and the above extracts are taken from that source.

Confederate cruisers, and they were compelled to burn or scuttle the enemy's ships on the high seas, often much to their regret.

Copies of the orders issued to the captains of the United States ships during the war with Great Britain were accessible to Mr. Seward, and the "deliberate purpose and plan" pursued by the Government of the United States in reference to the destruction of British ships must have been known to him; but he manifested his characteristic hardihood in wilfully discarding or ignoring every precedent which could be alleged against his own claims and pretensions, or which could be urged in justification of his opponents. The brusque disingenuous diplomacy of Mr. Seward often did more to arouse sympathy for the South, and toleration for the acts of the Confederate Government, than any amount of argument in their favour could have effected, and when the British public saw the commotion which the *Alabama* and her consorts created, and were reminded that those vessels were precisely, though reluctantly, following the example of the United States in their wars with Great Britain, there was a perceptible change in the tone of feeling, and John Bull, that is to say, the ordinary unofficial Britisher, rather enjoyed the idea of Brother Jonathan being metaphorically "hoist with his own petard."

With the foregoing facts patent to all who have cared to search the records, no apology for the determination of the Confederate Government to strike at the commerce of the United States is necessary, and when the specific orders to replace the *Alabama,* quoted above, reached England, I was already looking up a suitable vessel and arranging the "ways and means," under the general discretionary powers conferred upon me in the original instructions.

The despatch of a vessel from England suitable in size, structure, and sailing qualities to keep the sea as a cruiser involved a twofold expense, and two entirely separate sets of arrangements. The proposed cruiser must of necessity dispense with every vestige or similitude of warlike equipment, and it was equally indispensable to keep the crew and the general outfit within the reasonable requirements of the alleged voyage. It was therefore necessary to provide a second ship, to carry the armament, extra stores, officers, and as many additional men as could be safely embarked, to a place of rendezvous. The supply-ship must be loaded in a different port from the cruiser, and there must be a reasonable and rational consistency in the business arrangements for her outward voyage, so that the type of vessel and cargo might be conformable to the requirements of her alleged port of destination.

After the despatch of the *Alabama* and *Florida*, it became manifest that no vessel especially constructed for war could be got out of a British port. It has been shown in a previous chapter that her Majesty's Foreign Secretary had so far yielded to the pressure put upon him by the United States Minister that he would, and often did, order the detention of even merchant steamers manifestly unsuited to war-like purposes, if the United States Consul at the port of loading lodged a complaint against her, or sent in to the Collector of Customs an affidavit that "he had reason to believe the vessel in question was intended to be converted into a Confederate cruiser."

The closeness with which the building-yards were watched, and the secret system of inspecting ships loading at the ports for foreign voyages which the United States Consuls had established, was well known; and long before the loss of the *Alabama* I had reported to the Navy Department my conviction that a further expenditure in building or buying vessels especially constructed for war would be a useless waste of money, as it was manifest to me that no such craft would be permitted to leave a British port unless her Majesty's Government was satisfied that she was the property of a neutral State, whose Government would assume the responsibility of her movements. The Navy Department had adopted the above view, and the Government at Richmond, reluctantly abandoning the hope of obtaining in Europe vessels fit to act offensively against the harbours on the Northern coast and in opening the blockade, had determined at or about the time of the *Alabama*'s loss to apply the whole of the resources of the Treasury in purchasing military and other necessary supplies, and in building streamers suitable in speed and structure to run the blockade, and for making short maritime raids along the Northern coast. Such vessels were then in course of building, under the arrangements General Colin McRae, the fiscal agent of the Treasury, was able to make, as stated in another chapter; but the arrangements were made at such a late period of the war, that the best class of ships, those best suited for dashing out of the blockaded ports and practising a "guerilla warfare" on the enemy's coast-line, were not completed in time to take an active part in the war. The Secretary of the Navy did not, however, at any time wholly abandon the purpose of keeping a few cruisers at sea. He had specifically instructed me to supply, whenever the state of the funds would admit, any vacancy in the number, and had directed my especial attention to the American whaling fleet in the North Pacific.

The first effect of the *Alabama*'s destruction was rather to add to the immediate drain upon the resources of the Navy Department, because her officers and crew lost everything, and it was necessary to re-supply them. Besides which, the men had been a long time at sea, and, happily for them, had a good deal of pay due. Then, also, there were rescued and wounded men at Cherbourg and elsewhere who had to be looked after, and even the poor fellows who had given their lives for the defence of the Confederate flag had relatives, and their claims were legacies which could not be suffered to remain unsettled.

The winding-up of the *Alabama*'s affairs involved some complications, and the expense was far greater than if she had been the property of a recognised Government, with diplomatic and consular agents to come forward with their official authority and prestige, and to make open provision for all necessities. It was not possible to collect the *Alabama*'s crew in one place, or to bring them together at one time, lest it should be charged that we were making preparations for a warlike expedition; and even in such works of mercy as relieving the shipwrecked and distressed, it was necessary to practise a certain amount of mystery and concealment, and to use intermediaries, which added both to the cost and delay of the settlement.

In the ordinary course of events, and from the regular prearranged appropriation of funds, there would not have been sufficient money in hand to fit out a fresh expedition. The "depositaries" of the Confederate Treasury were then, as at most times, overweighted with liabilities on behalf of the Government; and although there was a moderate balance in their hands on account of the Navy Department, yet in the aggregate they were under great advances, and the remittances in cotton and other produce came forward with less and less rapidity and regularity, in consequence of the increasing stringency of the blockade. There was, however, an unexpected contribution to the available assets of the Navy Department about two months after the loss of the *Alabama,* by reason of the forced sale of the English rams by Messrs. Bravay; and after consulting the special fiscal agent of the Treasury as to his ability to furnish the funds for the large contracts which were then open, and for which he had been directed to supply the means, it was determined to use as much of the proceeds of the above-mentioned sale as might be required for the despatch of another naval adventure, and I took active steps without further delay to select and equip the necessary ships.

The ordinary iron screw-steamers of commerce, as far back as 1864, were in almost every essential particular unfit for our purposes. They were constructed almost exclusively for steaming, had no arrangement for lifting their screws, and were masted only with the purpose to furnish auxiliary sailing-power as a partial relief to the engines, and for economy of fuel in fair winds.

The reasons why a Confederate cruiser should have full sailing- as well as steaming-power have been already explained; and those combined requirements were especially necessary in a vessel it was the purpose to send after the American whaling fleet in the distant North Pacific and Sea of Okhotsk. The necessities of our position greatly narrowed the field for selection, and it was only through a fortunate chance that a suitable vessel was found. In the autumn of 1863 I went to the Clyde to look up a steamer (the *Coquette*) for a special purpose, mentioned in another chapter. Lieutenant Robert R. Carter was with me, and in the course of our search we caught sight of a fine, composite, full-rigged ship, with something more than auxiliary steam-power, and all the necessary arrangements for disconnecting and lifting her screw. We were charmed with the ship, but could only make a very hasty and imperfect inspection of her, as she was in all the bustle of loading for her first foreign voyage. I took, however, a careful note of her, and learned that she was then bound for Bombay, and would return to England in due course, probably in eight to ten months.

As soon as the "ways and means" to fit out the contemplated expedition were provided, I sent an experienced broker to scour the Clyde and the principal shipping ports, and he was so fortunate as to fall upon the very screw-steamer I had seen at Glasgow ten months before. He reported at once by telegraph, and posted a letter the same day, advising me that the ship had just been discharged, was then entirely empty, and could thus be thoroughly inspected, but that she was already under partial engagement for another voyage, and if I wanted to secure her no time was to be lost. Having perfect confidence in my broker, I telegraphed him to buy after careful inspection. The despatch of the Secretary of the Navy (dated July 18th, 1864) quoted above, which contained the urgent precept to replace the *Alabama* if possible, reached me on the 30th of August, and replying from Liverpool under date of September 16th, 1864, I wrote on that subject as follows:—

"I have the satisfaction to inform you of the purchase of a fine composite ship, built for the Bombay trade, and just returned to London from her first voyage. She is 1,160 tons builder's measurement, classed A 1 for 14 years at Lloyd's, frames, beams, etc., of iron, but planked from keel to gunwale with East India teak. She is full-rigged as a ship, with rolling topsails, has plenty of accommodation for officers of all grades, and her ''tween decks' are 7 feet 6 inches high, with large air-ports, having been fitted under Government inspection for the transport of troops. Her engines are direct acting, with two cylinders 47 inches in diameter and 2 feet 9 inches stroke, with ample grate and heating surface, nominal horse-power 220, but indicating 850 horse-power, and she has a lifting screw. My broker has had her carefully examined by one of Lloyd's inspectors, who pronounces her a capital ship in every respect, and from whose report I have extracted the above items. Yesterday she went into a graving-dock to have her bottom examined and the screw-shaft carefully inspected, and the report on both these points is favourable. The log of the ship shows her to be a fast sailer under canvas, for with screw up she has made 330 miles in twenty-four hours by observation. You will be gratified to learn of this good fortune in finding a ship so admirably suited to our purpose, and I will only now assure you that no effort will be spared, and no precaution neglected, which may help to get her under our flag. You may rely upon it that the purchase of men-of-war from any of the European navies is not practicable under existing circumstances."

The vessel referred to in the foregoing extract was perhaps the only ship of her type and class in Great Britain, and her comely proportions and peculiarities of structure could not fail to make her an object of interest and attraction in the London Docks. Her fitness for conversion into a cruiser would be manifest at a glance, and I felt confident that the spies of the United States Consul would soon draw his attention to her, and that she would be keenly and suspiciously watched.

I knew that to set my foot upon her deck, or to be reported at any time within visual range of her, would be the immediate occasion of a consular report to Mr. Adams, which would be promptly forwarded to Earl Russell, with the customary affirmation, and the hope of getting the ship to sea as a Confederate cruiser would be nipped in the bud. I felt equally certain that any alteration of her internal arrangements or the addition of any fittings or furniture to her cabins, not in harmony with her mercantile character, and not required for her return voyage to Bombay, would cause inquiry; it would be discovered that she had not been taken up by the Government for the transport of troops, and the inference would be that she was preparing for "piratical depredations upon the commerce of a friendly Power." It was absolutely necessary to permit no one having the faintest odour of "rebellion" about him to go near her. She must be provided with an owner who would be willing to sell her again at an out-port, and who could be trusted to see that the essentials for her alleged voyage would be provided, and that all requirements of the law would be complied with.

In matters of business, and in the preparation of an important enterprise especially, it is more satisfactory to superintend the arrangements in person, and to inspect their progress with one's own vision, than to behold them through the eye of faith; but the necessities of our position compelled all Confederate agents to trust often to the fidelity and judgment of intermediaries, and I can say in my own case that although I sometimes suffered by the mistakes, and once or twice through the over-zealous effort of a deputy, I was never deceived nor betrayed. Every man in England who undertook to perform a service for the Confederate States under engagement with me did his work with scrupulous honesty. The gentleman who acted for me in the purchase of the above-mentioned ship bought her in his own name, ballasted her with coal, and had her cleared out for Bombay, giving the captain a power-of-attorney to sell her at any time after leaving London. For this service he declined to receive any remuneration whatever, and I promised that when she received her Confederate crew and armament, no prize should be captured until the captain who took her out had been allowed sufficient time to return to England and cancel the register.

The ship for the contemplated cruise being thus secured, it was necessary to get a tender, or supply vessel, for her as quickly as possible. I was advised by my broker to examine a new iron screw-steamer built for, and then employed in, the packet service between Liverpool and Ireland. With that purpose I made a short passage in her. She was strong, roomy, a good sea-boat, and steamed thirteen knots per hour during the run. Her draft of water was moderate, and as all those qualities in combination suited her for blockade-running, I perceived a probability of making her earn her own expenses, or perhaps even recoup the cost of her purchase.

The steamer referred to was called the *Laurel*. She was bought, and put in the hands of a shipping agent in Liverpool, who advertised her for a voyage to Havana, to take freight and a limited number of passengers. The shipping agent was informed in advance what amount of freight and how many passengers would be forthcoming, and being a clever business man, he had no difficulty in declining proposals from other sources without exciting suspicion. The freight, of course, consisted of the stores and armament for the cruiser, and the passengers were the officers and a few choice men for her. To allay all suspicion, bills of lading were issued in the ordinary way, passage-money was paid, and tickets were issued for the passengers under assumed names, so that the clerks in the office of the ship's agent would perceive that everything was going on in the ordinary course of their business. The passengers were, however, kept out of sight, and only appeared on the night when a tug was ready at the Prince's Landing-stage to take them on board the *Laurel*.

On the 28th of September, 1864, Lieutenant R. R. Carter arrived in Liverpool direct from Richmond. I had requested the Secretary of the Navy to send him out for special service with me as soon as he could be spared from the *Coquette,* and his arrival was a gratifying response to my application. Carter had mentioned to the Secretary of the Navy the handsome and handy ship we had seen at Glasgow in the autumn of 1863, and among the instructions and suggestions he brought me from the Navy Department was a proposition to get, if possible, the ship, and send her after the American whaling-fleet.

Carter and Commander John M. Brooke had served together as lieutenants in a scientific expedition, which had been sent out by the United States Navy Department some years before the war, and the course of the cruise had taken them over the routes and localities frequented by the whalers. Those officers had discussed the subject with the Secretary of the Navy before Carter left Richmond, and he had been instructed to furnish me with all necessary information verbally. I had obtained from Commander M. F. Maury a set of the "Whale Charts" published in connection with his "Physical Geography of the Sea," and it was my purpose to compile from them a memorandum for the information and guidance of the commander of the proposed expedition; but Carter's personal experiences, refreshed by his consultations with Brooke, were a better source of information than my theoretical researches could have supplied, and while I was occupied with the details of the outfit, he took the cruising directions in hand and prepared a clear and able paper on the periodical localities of the whaling fleet, which was included in the general instructions to Lieutenant-Commanding Waddell, and which he followed to such good purpose that, in the terms of a letter from himself, he "succeeded in destroying or dispersing the New England whaling fleet."

On the 5th of October, 1864, both vessels were ready for sea. The London ship was directed to sail as early as possible on the morning of the 8th, and as soon as her departure was reported by telegraph, the *Laurel* was taken into the Mersey, and at about eight o'clock in the evening of that same day the passengers to go in her quietly assembled on the Prince's Landing-stage, and a tug in waiting took them to her, and she proceeded at once to sea.

The account of the purchase and despatch of the two vessels having now been given in general terms, the most important and the most interesting details cannot be explained in a more brief and satisfactory manner than in the subjoined extracts from the official reports forwarded to Richmond at the time, and from the subsequent correspondence.

Under date of October 20th, 1864, I reported to the Secretary of the Navy as follows:—

"I have the great satisfaction of reporting the safe departure on the 8th instant of the ship described in my despatch of September 16th, and now that the entire expedition is far away at sea, beyond the reach of interference on the part of any United States authority in Europe, I may venture to furnish detailed information. The cruising ship was formerly the *Sea King*, the very vessel, it appears, that Lieutenant Carter suggested to you in Richmond, and it is an interesting coincidence, that while you were discussing her merits and fitness for conversion into a cruiser, I was negotiating for her purchase at this distance from you. The tender, or supply-vessel, is the screw-steamer *Laurel*, which I was compelled to purchase for the special purpose. She is, however, a fine fast vessel, and if Lieutenant Ramsay gets her into Wilmington or Charleston, you will find her very useful. I enclose herewith my letters of instructions to Lieutenant-Commanding Waddell, and to Lieutenants Whittle and Ramsay, and also a list of the officers. The letters above referred to will inform you how the two vessels were despatched, and I need only say that the arrangements combined most satisfactorily, and that the two vessels sailed, the *Sea King* from London, and the *Laurel* from Liverpool, within a few hours of each other.

"I heard from the *Sea King* off Deal. Everything was in fine condition, and she was making twelve and a half knots, under steam and fore-and-aft sails. Lieutenant Ramsay sent me a line or two from the pilot-station off Holyhead to say that not a single package had been left behind, and that the *Laurel*, though deep, had averaged over eleven knots since leaving the Mersey. The battery for the *Sea King* consists of four 55 cwt. 8-inch smooth-bore guns, and two Whitworth 32-pounders, besides which, she has two small 12-pounders, which originally belonged to her.... In spite of every precaution, the Federal spies appear to have discovered that something was in progress, and Mr. Adams had the United States ships *Niagara* and *Sacramento* off the mouth of the Thames, but they failed to identify our ship. However, a few days after the departure of the *Sea King* they were reported to have overhauled and detained for some time a peaceful Spanish steamer that had just left the Thames.

"The British Government will scarcely give our public ships common shelter, and we cannot send an unarmed vessel in the direction of North America without embarrassing and annoying inquiries from the Customs and Board of Trade officials. But United States ships-of-war are permitted to lie in English ports and watch British ships, as in the case of the *Georgia*, previously reported, and are allowed to cruise and overhaul neutral ships off the largest port of the kingdom, and in waters which were once considered exclusively British."

The letters of instructions enclosed in the foregoing were as follows:—

No. 1, to Lieutenant Whittle, dated October 6th, 1864:—"You will proceed to London by the 5 P.M. train to-day, and go to Wood's Hotel, Furnival's Inn, High Holborn. Take a room there, and give your name as Mr. W. C. Brown, if asked. It has been arranged for you to be in the coffee-room of the hotel at 11 A.M. precisely to-morrow, and that you will sit in a prominent position, with a white pocket-handkerchief rove through a button-hole of your coat, and a newspaper in your hand. In that attitude you will be recognised by Mr.——, who will call at the appointed time, and ask you if your name is Brown. You will say 'Yes,' and ask his name. He will give it, and you will then retire with him to your own room, hand him the enclosed letter of introduction, and throwing off all disguise, discuss with him freely the business in hand. Mr.—— will introduce you to Captain Corbett, with whom you are to take passage to Madeira, and you will arrange with him how to get on board without attracting notice. Say to Captain Corbett that I regret not seeing him, but it has been thought best for me not to go to London, as I am so well known there, and tell him that I have full confidence in his desire to serve us, and will be happy to make the warmest acknowledgments when he returns. Say that I desire him to carry you to Madeira, and explain how he is to communicate with the *Laurel*. . . . It is important that the *Sea King* should not be reported, and you will request Captain Corbett not to exchange signals with passing ships, or at any rate not to show his number. The object of your going out in the *Sea King* is to acquaint yourself with her sailing and other qualities, and to observe the crew. You can also inspect the internal arrangements, and discuss with Captain Corbett the necessary alterations; and you can learn the stowage of the provisions and other stores, and pick out the positions for magazine and shell-room. Perhaps the construction of these might be actually begun under the superintendence of Captain Corbett. You will bear in mind that until she is regularly transferred, Captain Corbett is the legal commander of the *Sea King,* and for obvious reasons of policy, as well as from courtesy, you will express all your wishes in the form of requests. When you reach Madeira and the *Laurel* joins company, you will report to Lieutenant-Commanding Waddell, and thereafter act under his instructions."

No. 2, to Lieutenant J. F. Ramsay, dated October 8th, 1864:—"You will proceed to sea to-night in command of the steamship *Laurel,* and carry Lieutenant-Commanding James I. Waddell, his staff of officers, and the other passengers of whom you have been advised, to Funchal, in the island of Madeira, with quick despatch. At Funchal you will hasten to take on board as large a supply of coal as you may consider safe, bearing in mind that you may have to steam for twenty days. The *Sea King*, Captain Corbett, has sailed from London this morning, and her commander has been instructed to time his passage so as not to arrive off Funchal until the 17th instant, by which time it is hoped you will have coaled up, and will be ready to weigh at a moment's notice. The *Sea King* will not anchor at Funchal, but will merely appear off the roadstead, and by way of designation will hoist the official number of the *Laurel*, which you will answer with the same number, and then weigh and join her as quickly as possible. In communicating afterwards with the *Sea King* you will be governed by the directions of Lieutenant-Commanding Waddell, and you will render him all the assistance in your power in transferring the supplies from the *Laurel* to the *Sea King*, and if the transfer cannot be accomplished near Madeira, by reason of stress of weather, or from any other cause, you will proceed with him to the second rendezvous. Your experience as a seaman and your acquaintance with business* will enable you to assist very materially in making the transfer and in treating with the men for their entry into the service of the Confederate States, and your zeal and interest in the success of the expedition are confidently relied upon. When the transfer is completed, and Lieutenant-Commanding Waddell can dispense with your further services, you will proceed to Nassau, New Providence, observing great precaution in approaching Eleuthera from the north-east. You might sight the island from your mast-head during the day, but it would be safer to lie off to the eastward, and time your movements so to get in with the land after dark, and run down close to the bank, arriving off Nassau by daylight.†... As soon as you arrive at Nassau you will communicate with Mr. L. Heyleger, and show him this letter, which will serve as an introduction. Mr. Heyleger will be able to give you the latest news from the Confederate States, and you will consult freely with him in reference to the propriety of taking your ship in. If you are satisfied with the speed of the ship, take her in by all means, as a voyage through the blockade would establish a new character for her, and would obliterate the traces of her past history, inasmuch as her name and nationality could both be

---

* Although Lieutenant Ramsay held a commission in the Confederate navy, he had been several years in the merchant service, and he had a Board of Trade certificate of competency as master, and was, therefore, eligible for the command of a British merchant ship.

†The precaution was thought necessary on account of the *quasi* blockade of the Bahama Channels and of Nassau by United States ships.

changed. This matter, however, I must of necessity leave to your discretion, after consultation with Mr. Heyleger. Should you reach a Confederate port, report yourself at once by letter to the Secretary of the Navy, and as my report of the expedition may not have reached the Department, send him a copy of this letter. Say to the Hon. Secretary of the Navy that I respectfully request him to send you out as soon as possible, to take command of one of the Government blockade-runners now approaching completion. If after consultation with Mr. Heyleger it is thought best not to attempt the voyage inward, load with Government cotton and return to Liverpool or Havre, as you may be hereafter advised.... Do not let yourself be known as a Confederate officer, except to Mr. Heyleger, and while at Madeira allow no communication with the shore, except through yourself, and do not show your number to any passing ship. I wish all the men who join the Confederate service to sign a 'quit claim' for both the *Sea King* and *Laurel* for an expressed consideration, and you will advise Lieutenant-Commanding Waddell how this is to be done. Write me fully from Nassau under cover to M. P. Robertson, Esq."

The instructions to Lieutenant-Commanding Waddell were rather in the form of an advisory letter than specific orders, except in respect to the purpose and direction of his cruise. My experience with the *Alabama* and other expeditions which were necessarily organized at out-of-the-way places, where there was no dockyard accommodation or facilities, had satisfied me that it was useless to lay down a rigid rule of action. Conditions of weather and other causes might render it impossible to equip the cruising ship at the first rendezvous selected, and it would therefore be necessary to seek another, and many other contingencies might arise which could only be met by the ready wit of the officer in charge, or that happy inspiration which rarely fails the right-minded man who is earnestly intent upon doing his duty, whatever difficulties he may encounter.

The transfer of the armament and stores of the *Sea King* was happily and successfully effected in the near neighbourhood of the first rendezvous selected, and neither the interest nor the clearness of the narrative will be lessened by omitting those portions of the letter to Lieutenant-Commanding Waddell which were merely descriptive and advisory, or merely confidential as between ourselves. The essential portions of the above-mentioned letter of advice and instruction, which was dated October 5th, 1864, were as follows:—

"You will sail from this port (Liverpool) on Saturday, the 8th instant, in the screw-steamer *Laurel,* under the command of First-Lieutenant J. F. Ramsay, taking with you all the officers detailed for your command except First-Lieutenant Whittle, who will take passage in the ship with Captain Corbett, with the view of learning her qualities and devising the best and speediest manner of making such alterations and additions in her internal arrangements as may be necessary, and to observe the character and disposition of the crew. A few picked men selected from the crew of the late Confederate States ship *Alabama*, who have been especially retained for the purpose, will accompany you in the *Laurel*, and will constitute the *nucleus* of the new force you will have to organize at the place of rendezvous. Among those men is the chief boatswain's-mate of the *Alabama*, a fine seaman and an experienced man-of-war's man. I advise you to give him an appointment as acting-boatswain as soon as you get out of the Channel, and to explain to him the intent of your leaving England. He will assist you materially in persuading the men of Captain Corbett's ship to enlist. I would not, however, mention the *direction* of your intended cruise to him.

"Lieutenant Ramsay will be directed to proceed with quick despatch to Funchal, and to coal up the *Laurel* as speedily as the facilities of that anchorage will admit. For obvious reasons, there should be as little communication with the shore as possible, and none of the officers or men should be allowed to land. Indeed, I may say here that every precaution should be practised to prevent the direction or intent of your voyage being known. When the *Laurel* returns, or even reaches Nassau, everything will be exposed; but then you will be far on your cruise, and beyond the reach of interference. The main object of the *Laurel's* voyage being to place you and your officers, with the men above mentioned and the naval stores, on board the cruising ship, and to attend upon you until you are fairly in possession, Lieutenant Ramsay will be ordered to govern the movements of that ship in accordance with your wishes, and he will only proceed to carry out his special instructions when you no longer need his assistance.

"When Captain Corbett appears off Funchal and his signal is recognised, you will join him with the *Laurel*, communicate with him and Lieutenant Whittle, and discuss the further steps necessary to transfer the supplies from the tender to your own ship, which you will christen *Shenandoah*. The quantity of stores is not large, and the heaviest weight, in a single piece, will be less than three tons.... It is possible that the weather may be fine and calm, in which case you could lash the two vessels alongside of each other; and by steaming slowly ahead with one, so as to tow the other, and keeping well under the lee of the island, the transfer may be effected without the delay and risk of seeking another anchorage.... Some tact will be necessary in dealing with the men and persuading them to ship;

but you will be greatly assisted by the influence of the *Alabama's* men, who are ready and willing to serve. Immediately upon leaving Funchal, I would move them all on board the *Shenandoah*.... It is necessary to bear in mind that Captain Corbett is the legal commander of the *Shenandoah* (*Sea King*) until he formally transfers her to you, and all action in regard to the ship and her crew should be conducted through him or with his co-operation.

"In regard to pay, it is quite impossible for you to conform precisely to the law regulating the pay of the navy.... Seamen, so far as our service is concerned, are merchantable articles, with a market value, and you must either pay the price demanded or dispense with their services. I am satis-fied, therefore, that if in the exercise of your discretion you deem it nec-essary to go beyond the established pay allowance, the Navy Department will take the steps necessary to legalize your act....

"When the *Shenandoah* is formally handed over to you, Captain Corbett will give you a bill of sale of the ship, and you will permit him to take the register, and such other papers relating to the previous status of the ship as he may desire to carry with him, and I have stipulated with the ostensi-ble owner that you will make no prizes until Captain Corbett has had time to reach England and cancel the register, for which purpose you should allow thirty days. It will therefore be important for you to despatch the *Laurel* as soon as possible.... All the work you have to do on board the *Shenandoah,* such as mounting the battery, building the magazine, and putting up such additional store-rooms as may be required, can be done while under weigh; and you should therefore leave the anchorage at which your supplies are received simultaneously with the *Laurel,* with the view of insuring your arrival upon the cruising ground at the appointed time....

"If there should be any objection on the part of the Colonial authori-ties (at Sydney) to your taking a large supply of coal, claim your right under the Queen's Order in Council to get a supply sufficient to carry you to the nearest port of your own country, which is the precise limitation of the order, and that will afford you an ample supply. After leaving Mel-bourne or Sydney, proceed to the New Zealand whaling-ground, and thence northerly between the New Hebrides Islands to the Caroline Group, Ladrones, Bonins, etc., as specified in the enclosed memorandum."

I omit the minute sailing directions for the cruise, references to charts, etc. The memorandum supplied a very general summary of the proposed route, and was as follows:—"A fast vessel with auxiliary steam-power leav-ing the meridian of the Cape of Good Hope (say on the 45th parallel of south latitude) on the 1st day of January, would reach Sydney in Australia in forty days. Adding twenty days for incidental interruptions, and leaving the coast of Australia on the 1st of March, passing through the whaling-ground between New Zealand and New Holland and the Caroline Group, touching at Ascension, and allowing thirty days for incidental delays, would reach the Ladrone Islands by the 1st of June. She would then, visiting the Bonin Islands, Sea of Japan, Okhotsk, and North Pacific, be in a position, about the 15th of September, north of the island of Oahu, distant sixty to a hundred miles, to intercept the North Pacific whaling-fleet, bound to Oahu with the products of the summer cruise."

The letter of advisory instructions to Lieutenant-Commanding Waddell ended as follows:—"Enclosed herewith you will find a form of bond to be signed by captains of prizes you may ransom, and also short forms of depositions to be taken from captains and mates of prizes, and which you can extend to any degree of minuteness you may think advisable in particular cases. I can think of nothing else worthy of special remark. You have a fine spirited body of young officers under your command, and may reasonably expect to perform good and efficient service."

All the initiatory arrangements for the *Shenandoah*'s cruise were satisfactorily accomplished, with reference both to the meeting of the ship and tender at Funchal, and the prompt transfer of the stores off Madeira, and thus the delay and risk of seeking a second place of rendezvous was avoided. The *modus operandi* is sufficiently explained in the following extracts from a despatch which I addressed to the Secretary of the Navy, dated Liverpool, November 17th, 1864:—

"I have the satisfaction to report that the *Shenandoah* has received her officers and armament, and is now an actual cruiser under the Confederate flag. Captain Corbett, who was employed to take the *Sea King,* now the Confederate States ship *Shenandoah,* to the rendezvous, has returned to England, and from his verbal statement, as well as from an official report of Lieutenant Ramsay, dated Santa Cruz, Teneriffe, October 21st, 1864, I have learned that the two vessels met at Madeira without accident, and at the appointed time. The *Laurel* proved so fast that she arrived sooner than I expected, and lying in Funchal Roads for two or three days after coaling to await the arrival of her consort, the circumstance excited some suspicion, and the United States Consul endeavoured to induce the Portuguese authorities to detain her, but he failed to suggest a justifiable plea.

"On the morning of the 18th ultimo the *Sea King* appeared off the bay of Funchal, and having signalled as directed, was at once recognised and quickly joined by the *Laurel.* Fortunately the weather was fine, and the two ships were able to anchor under 'Las Desertas,' an uninhabited island near the main island of Madeira, and beginning work with spirit and energy, all the armament and stores were transferred by an early hour on the 20th of October. On that day the two ships separated, and Lieutenant Ramsay proceeded to Teneriffe to land Captain Corbett and the seamen who declined to enter the Confederate service. I regretted to learn that only a small minority of the men sent out in the *Sea King* could be induced to enter for the *Shenandoah* when the object of her cruise was made known to them.... Lieutenant Ramsay reports that although the ship started on her cruise very short-handed, the officers were all in fine spirits. I feel sure that the crew can be steadily reinforced from prizes....

"The announcement that another Confederate cruiser is at sea cannot fail to have a depressing effect upon the foreign commerce of the United States, by increasing the rate of insurance in and upon American bottoms; and her appearance is at this time especially opportune, in consideration of the loss of the *Florida*. I can readily imagine with what indignation you will learn of the cowardly and murderous assault of the United States ship *Wachusett* upon the *Florida*. It has excited very severe comment in Europe, and the Brazilian Government seems to have acted with promptness and spirit. There is a rumour that France and England will join Brazil in her demand upon the United States for satisfaction, but both of the former Powers have shown so much forbearance, and Great Britain has of late been so partial and submissive in her intercourse with the United States, that it is difficult to imagine a change of conduct.

"I find it difficult to account for the unwillingness of the men to ship for the *Shenandoah*. Captain Corbett was instructed to engage for the *Sea King* only young, and as far as possible unmarried men, whose spirit of adventure and lack of home cares would, it was thought, incline them to a roving cruise. In this expectation I have been disappointed, for the majority of the men declined to enter the service on any terms, and Lieutenant Ramsay, yielding to a feeling of disappointment, writes that he 'never saw such a set of curs in all his (my) experience at sea.' In a hurried private note Lieutenant-Commanding Waddell informs me that an engineer in whom great reliance was placed to influence the firemen to ship, and who professed to have such a strong desire to serve the Confederate States that he was willing to run the blockade, belied all his promises, and actually did his best to persuade the men in his department from remaining. You are of course aware that no overtures can be made to men in Great Britain, except in a few exceptional cases, and when a body of seamen are sent abroad it must be under some legitimate pretence, and their subsequent entry into the Confederate service depends upon their humour, the solid inducements held out to them, and the tact with which the prospects of the cruise may be represented. An officer would find his hands greatly strengthened in every way by the presence of a reliable force of sufficient strength to give him physical possession of his ship, and which would render him independent of the caprices of the men to whom he is forced to appeal.

"It is not likely that a ship so suitable in every way for conversion into a cruiser as the *Sea King* will be found very soon, and it would not be safe to attempt another adventure of the kind until the excitement growing out of this one has subsided. If another proper ship can be found, and arrangements can be made for arming her with reasonable prospects of success, I will not shrink from the undertaking; but I am impressed with the conviction that if the war continues until next summer, a formidable naval expedition can be fitted out at a rendezvous where there will be no danger of interruption, and to which mechanics to assist in converting the ships can be sent without fear of discovery. I shall have the honour to report in detail on this subject by Lieutenant R. R. Carter, when he returns, and I will ask you to allow him to bring out a body of men and officers, the former to constitute a nucleus for the crews of the vessels, and to ensure safe possession of the property at the rendezvous."

Eighty men were sent out in the *Sea King,* and out of that number, including a few by the *Laurel,* it was hoped that at least sixty, or even seventy, would volunteer for the *Shenandoah,* but, in point of fact, only twenty-three consented to remain. The staff of officers of all grades, including three petty-officers who went out in the *Laurel,* was fortunately large, numbering nineteen, but the force to handle the *Shenandoah* at the start was only forty-two, all told.

Waddell, like most naval officers, had probably never joined a ship for service before, except when she was fully manned and in apple-pie order for a cruise, or at a Government dockyard, with ample force of men and abundant supplies to fit her out. On this occasion he found himself on the high seas in a ship 220 feet long and 35 feet beam, with standing royal-yards, and fitted to carry royal-studding-sails—everything dirty and in confusion, the decks lumbered with the armament and stores, and a crew of forty-two men and officers to navigate the ship and equip her at the same time.

The master, Irvine S. Bulloch, the paymaster, W. B. Smith, and the chief-engineer, Matthew O'Brien,* had made the cruise in the *Alabama,*

---

*O'Brien was first-assistant-engineer of the *Alabama.*

and had seen some rough-and-tumble work in discharging her tender and equipping the ship for her cruise at the island of Terceira, but the remainder of the wardroom sea-officers had been trained by no such experiences. They were mostly young men fresh from the United States Naval Academy at the breaking out of the war, and had seen little or no sea-service, except in the smart school-ship, which is sent out yearly for a summer cruise from Annapolis. Waddell was an officer of twenty-three years' experience in the United States Navy, and Whittle, the first-lieutenant, a smart, intelligent young officer, had seen some service. Lieutenant S. S. Lee had picked up some rough experiences in the merchant service, and was therefore more at home than most of the others. Fortunately, the *Shenandoah* had the advantage of good steam-engines and an ample supply of coal—enough, if need be, to steam to Sydney; but all will admit that the first impressions of those who had to put her in condition for her work could not have been exhilarating.

But although the staff of officers was chiefly composed of very young men, who were about to make their first effort in a responsible position, they were full of pluck and that ingrained *verve* and aptitude for the sea which is characteristic of the Anglo-Saxon race, whether born and bred in Great Britain, or in any part of what Sir Charles Dilke has called "Greater Britain," meaning by that broad and inclusive designation the English-speaking countries which have been colonized by Britons. They went to work with a will. In twenty-four hours they had two of the 8-inch guns and one Whitworth 32-pounder mounted. The next day two more 8-inch and the second Whitworth were on their carriages, and on the 29th of October, eight days after leaving the anchorage at Las Desertas, the ports were all cut and the whole battery of six guns was completely equipped and in place.

Waddell wrote me a short hurried note on the day he took command of the *Shenandoah*, while affected by the disappointment occasioned by the scant response to his appeals for volunteers and the apparently hopeless task of reducing the chaos around him to ship-shape trim. Under the circumstances, I was not surprised that the tone of his report was somewhat desponding; but there was no evidence of a wish to be out of the work—only a fear that he might not be able to accomplish all that was expected of him. If the letter had come promptly to hand, I would have doubtless felt some misgivings, from a mere feeling of sympathy; but it did not reach me until the middle of November, and then I knew that his mind would be at ease, for he would have settled fairly down to his work; and I had assured him that, whatever deficiency there might be in the number of his crew at the start, he would be able to recruit from his prizes, as the *Alabama* and *Florida* had done. This prediction was fully verified, as, out of four prizes captured before crossing the Line, fourteen men volunteered for the *Shenandoah*, which reassured everyone on board, and gave them confidence in the final success of the cruise.

The ease with which the Confederate cruisers were generally able to get volunteers from captured vessels was a striking peculiarity of the Civil War. The *Alabama* left Terceira in August, 1862, with eighty-five men. In January, 1863, she fought and sunk the United States ship *Hatteras*, and had then a crew of one hundred and ten, the twenty-five additional men being volunteers from captured vessels. The *Shenandoah* was especially fortunate in this respect. From one of the whalers captured by her every man volunteered except the captain and chief officer. The *Florida* was obliged to leave Brest in February, 1864, very short-handed; but when she reached Bahia, in the following October, she had completed her crew to a full complement, almost exclusively by volunteers from prizes. It may be said that the men were induced to volunteer by the wish to escape the discomforts and confinement they had to submit to as prisoners; but this will hardly account for the promptness with which they volunteered and the spirit with which they joined in the work of the ships, often proving the handiest and most contented men on board.

The treatment of the captured seamen was always kindly, and every possible effort was made to lessen their hardships. Besides this, the rapid accumulation of prisoners soon rendered it necessary either to "bond" a prize, or to bargain with a passing neutral to take them off, and thus it could never have been a severe strain upon the patriotism of a "loyal American" seaman to spend a few days under moderate restraint, at the very worst in single irons, but with the same food and drink as his jailors, and surely he might have borne it with patience if his "loyalty" had been of a genuine type, or if its seat had been in the place where the highest and strongest and purest emotions are commonly thought to have their origin.

As a matter of fact, the captured crews of American ships expressed but little if any veneration for the "old flag," and did not appear to look upon the new arrangement of bunting at the peaks of the Confederate ships as a foreign invention. Many of the more intelligent of the officers, and not a few captains, expressed no animosity against the South, or surprise at the secession of the Southern States, but, on the contrary, often declared their conviction that the war was the natural and unavoidable consequence of the violent, unconstitutional, and exasperating agitation of extreme politicians at the North.

I am not at all disposed to follow the line of argument suggested by the foregoing statement, or to trace the cause why seamen sailing under the flag of the United States were so ready and willing to transfer their allegiance to a "so-called" Rebel Government. I merely state an historical fact which came to my knowledge through official reports from the commanders of the Confederate cruisers, and the accuracy of which I have tested by personal inquiry, and by conversations with officers of various grades and with seamen who served afloat in Confederate ships during the Civil War.

It is not within the scope or purpose of this narrative to relate the adventures of any Confederate ship after she was duly commissioned, excepting in so far as may be necessary to fairly and truly set forth the manner in which the naval policy of the Confederate Government was carried out, and to illustrate the conduct of the neutral Powers towards the two belligerents.

After leaving Las Desertas, October 20th, 1864, the *Shenandoah* shaped her course for the usual position for crossing the Line, and all hands were actively employed in making the necessary alterations and stowing away stores. On the 15th of November she crossed the Line. By this time she had captured several prizes, and the additions thus made to her crew relieved the pressure upon the originally small force on board, and relieved also the expenditure of fuel, for in the Trade winds the sails could be used with good effect. Waddell's object was to reach Melbourne or Sydney in time to begin his cruise against the whalers, in accordance with the programme, and thus to carry out the plan sketched in his instructions. He did not therefore linger at the "two forks" of the marine roads north and south of the Line, as Semmes did with the *Alabama*, in order to intercept passing traders, but made the best of his way to the Australian port from which the real practical work of his cruise was to have its beginning. Nevertheless, his look-outs did not keep their eyes shut. Every passing sail was reported, closely inspected, and if the cut of her jib suggested her nationality, the *Shenandoah*'s head was laid for her, and she was made to show her colours and her right to wear them. On the 25th of January, 1865, the *Shenandoah* arrived at Melbourne, and up to that date she had destroyed eight American ships, six of which she fell in with at or near the great converging points of trade in the equatorial belt of the Atlantic.

The *Shenandoah* entered the port of Melbourne as a regularly commissioned ship-of-war of a recognised belligerent Government. Her flag and the commission of her commander were her credentials, and Lieutenant-Commanding Waddell was justified in claiming, and the Colonial authorities could not deny him, such facilities for repairing and provisioning his ship as the necessities of the case required, without violating the conditions of her Majesty's Proclamation of Neutrality and the stipulations of international law as commonly understood. If the *Shenandoah* had only required to supply ordinary defects and to re-provision, she would no doubt have been made to comply strictly with the "Admiralty Regulations," and she would have been compelled to quit Melbourne at the expiration of forty-eight hours, but the examination of the ship by the local engineers who were employed to effect the repairs, proved that an injury to the screw-bearings could not be got at and properly restored without taking the ship out of the water. Application was made to the Governor to put the *Shenandoah* on the "slip," which belonged to a private firm, and the request was granted; but the Colonial authorities were so rigid in enforcing the "Orders for the Proper Preservation of Neutrality" which had been issued by her Majesty's Government, that the use of all appliances belonging to the Government, and all official assistance in repairing or provisioning the ship, was refused. Before placing the ship on the slip it was necessary to take some of the weights out of her, and after the repairs were completed a few days were necessarily occupied in the re-shipment and re-stowing of the discharged stores. In consequence of the above-mentioned causes, the *Shenandoah* did not get away from Melbourne until February 18th, 1865, but notwithstanding the delay, she was rather ahead of the time for leaving the coast of Australia set out in the memorandum for her cruise.

The ship was now in good condition, with men enough to handle her safely, and there was an assurance that every prize would, if desired, supply a reinforcement. All on board were in good health and spirits; the shade of despondency which had somewhat overshadowed Waddell when he left the barren Desertas had wholly vanished, and he placed his ship upon the course necessary to fall into the prescribed route with a light heart and in hopeful spirits. There does not appear to have been an accident or a single misadventure which prevented Waddell from carrying out his programme, and he followed it faithfully and with success.

On the 21st of May, 1865, the *Shenandoah* entered the Okhotsk Sea under steam, with the purpose to proceed as far as Jonas Island, about two hundred miles from the entrance, which was reported to be a favourite rendezvous for "right whalers," but the ship got jammed in the ice several times; moreover, there was much fog, and the temperature was several degrees below zero. Altogether the danger was imminent, the ship was not fitted for forcing her way through ice-fields, and there was no one on board who had any experience in Arctic navigation. After making a fair and reasonable effort to get well into the Sea of Okhotsk, and fearing to do the ship some irretrievable injury if he persisted, Waddell came out through the Amphitrite Straits, the same by which he had entered.

The *Shenandoah*'s course was now shaped for Behring's Straits, the second officer of a whaler captured just inside the Okhotsk Sea, and who had volunteered into the Confederate service, acting as a pilot to the whaling grounds. The cruise in the Behring's Sea was short, but effective. The whalers were caught in couplets, triplets, and quartets, and no less than four were ransomed and released in order to get rid of the numerous prisoners. It was June 13th when the *Shenandoah* left the Sea of Okhotsk, and turned her head to the northward and eastward to enter the great Arctic Sea. She made the first catch on the 22nd, and her last prize on June 28th. During those eventful six days she captured, and either destroyed or ransomed, twenty-four ships.

The *Shenandoah* was commissioned as a Confederate cruiser on the 19th of October, 1864, and sailed from Las Desertas on the next day. Her cruise as a ship-of-war may be said to have ended on the 28th of June, 1865, because she neither captured nor attempted to capture a single vessel after that date. Three months may be fairly deducted for the detention at Melbourne and the time occupied in making the passage from the Equator in the Atlantic to Melbourne, and thence to the localities of the whalers, she being then out of the track of American traders. It appears from an extract from her log now before me, that she fell in with and captured only two vessels between the 13th of November, 1864, and April 1st, 1865. We may say, then, that she was only cruising actively in the ordinary "fair way" of American commerce five months. During that time she captured thirty-eight ships, thirty-four of which were destroyed, and four were ransomed, the latter being converted into cartels to transport the prisoners to the United States, or to the nearest port where they could be suitably cared for. The thirty-eight captured vessels had crews which numbered in the aggregate 1,053 men, and their value, according to the depositions of the masters taken at the time of the captures, was $1,361,983. The object of the *Shenandoah*'s cruise was to thoroughly disperse, and in great part destroy, the American whaling fleet, and for the complete fulfilment of that object her route and the time of her operations at each particular locality were carefully considered, and set out in the instructions and memorandum given to Lieutenant-Commanding Waddell.

I have already mentioned that the programme was followed with unusual precision and effect up to the 28th of June, 1865. The original design was that the *Shenandoah* should leave the Arctic Sea in time to reach a position sixty to one hundred miles north of the island of Oahu, in the Sandwich Group, about September 15th, the expectation being that she would then be in time to intercept the North Pacific whaling fleet *en route* to the usual place of resort after the summer's cruise. After entering Behring's Straits, Waddell stood to the northward and westward, intending to run along the coast until abreast of Cape North, and then to work as far into the Arctic Sea as the state of the ice would admit. He soon, however, found his progress completely blocked, and he prudently and very properly determined not to risk the danger of disabling his screw, if not losing his vessel, in a struggle against obstructions she was not fitted to encounter. Within a week he had destroyed every whaler in sight from his mastheads, or of whose locality he could get any satisfactory information.

On the 28th of June, 1865, while coming out of Behring's Straits and very near the entrance, the *Shenandoah* fell in with a fleet of ten whalers in a lump; and as it was flat calm, she had no difficulty in capturing them all. At an early hour in the morning she had captured the barque *Waverly*, of New Bedford, and had burned her. Of the ten last taken, two were ransomed to receive the prisoners, and the remaining eight were burned. This was the last day's work of the *Shenandoah*, and on the 29th of June she left Behring's Straits, and after clearing the Aleutian Group stood to the southeast, with the purpose to get into the track of vessels engaged in the Californian trade, and to learn something positive in regard to the progress of the war.

After leaving Melbourne on the 18th of February, the *Shenandoah* soon passed beyond the reach of communication with those who could give her any information—in fact, she was wholly and completely severed from all communication with Europe and America—and the whalers she captured in the Okhotsk Sea, and the first captures in the neighbourhood of Behring's Straits, were all equally ignorant of what had happened during the preceding three or four months. Lieutenant-Commanding Waddell has stated that on the 23rd of June he captured the ship *William Thompson* and the brig *Susan Abigail*. Both of those vessels had left San Francisco in April, and he got from them a number of San Francisco papers, which contained the correspondence between Generals Grant and Lee relative to the surrender of Lee's army. The same papers, however, contained a statement that Mr. Davis and his Cabinet were at Danville, and that "Mr. Davis had issued a proclamation informing the Southern people that the war would be carried on with renewed vigour." None of the whalers had later news than the above, and none of them thought that the war was over.

As evidence of this, Waddell mentions that eight men from the ships captured on the 28th volunteered for the *Shenandoah*, and were actually shipped for her on the 29th. He says they were "men of intelligence, all trained soldiers," and that "it is not to be believed that these men would have taken service in the *Shenandoah* if they believed the war was over."

Even in Europe it was not universally thought that the surrender of General Lee would immediately end the war. Many were of the opinion that the scattered forces in the south-west would be able to unite with the troops under General Johnston, and that resistance might be continued in the mountainous parts of North Carolina and Southern Virginia, and that it might even be possible for Mr. Davis and the Executive Departments of the Government to reach the Trans-Mississippi States and to maintain a defensive warfare in Arkansas and Texas, if not with the prospect of ultimately recovering the lost ground, with at least the expectation of securing favourable terms of peace. It was, however, soon apparent to those of us abroad who knew the condition of the country, and who perceived the impossibility of keeping even a moderate force supplied with the most indispensable necessaries, that the mortal blow had been struck, and that there could be no recovery.

Personally, I felt under a very grave responsibility with reference to the *Shenandoah*, which I knew to be far beyond the reach of all the ordinary channels by which news is disseminated, and with which it was impossible to communicate by any means at my command. When Mr. Davis was taken prisoner, and there was no longer a Civil Government to control the remnant of the military forces, or to conduct the negotiations for peace, I felt satisfied that the time had arrived when it was no longer possible to continue hostilities either with safety or with credit. It was manifest that there was no longer a *raison d'etre* for a Confederate cruiser, and I felt impelled to make any effort that could be attempted in order to stop the *Shenandoah* in her operations, which might at any moment cease to be legitimate acts of war, and become, by the common law of nations, that which Mr. Seward had always affirmed them to be, although he had never acted upon the allegation.

As soon as the arrest of Mr. Davis was known in England, I communicated my views to Mr. James M. Mason, the diplomatic representative of the Confederate States, and ventured to suggest that he should request her Majesty's Secretary of State for Foreign Affairs to forward through the British Consuls, at several points which I named, letters to the commander of the *Shenandoah*, containing instructions which should be in accordance with the state of affairs. When I first mentioned the subject to Mr. Mason, he thought the proposal hardly practicable, but on the 13th of July, 1865, he addressed me the following note:—

> "28, Grove Street, Leamington,
> "*June* 13*th,* 1865.
>
> "Dear Sir,—
>
> "Recalling our late conversation about taking measures to arrest the cruise of the *Shenandoah,* I think the time has come when it should be attempted, and I know of no other mode than that you suggested, of proposing to the Foreign Office here that the order might be sent through that Department. If you concur, let me hear by note the several points to which the orders should be sent, and send me the form of the order, which, after examining, I will return to you.
>
> "The order must of course be sent open to Earl Russell, and therefore worded accordingly. I think it should state that in the present posture of events in the Confederate States, and the difficulty of communicating with any authority there, it had been determined here, and with my full sanction as the representative of the Government, that the war should be discontinued on the ocean. You will know best what order to give as to the disposition of the ship and her materials. On hearing from you I will write to Earl Russell, enclose the orders, and inquire whether his Government will transmit them through their Consuls abroad.
>
> "I am, etc.,
> "(Signed)   J. M. MASON.
>
> "Captain James D. Bulloch,
> "Liverpool."

In my reply to Mr. Mason I forwarded to him the order as suggested, and the following is a verbatim copy.

> "Liverpool, *June* 19*th,* 1865.
>
> "Sir,—
>
> "On the 9th day of April last, General Lee was forced to evacuate the lines of Petersburgh and Richmond, after three days of continuous and sanguinary battle, and on the 14th of the same month, being surrounded by overwhelming numbers, he surrendered the remnant of his army to General Grant, only, however, when its last

ration had been consumed and its military supplies were entirely exhausted. This event has been followed consecutively by the surrender of Generals Johnston and Taylor, commanding the Confederate States troops east of the Mississippi, and of General Kirby Smith, the Commander-in-Chief of the Trans-Mississippi Department.

"President Davis, Vice-President Stephens, and several members of the Confederate Cabinet, have been arrested, and are now held as close prisoners by the United States Government. President Johnson has formally declared the war to be at an end, and has removed all restrictions upon foreign commerce by reopening the Southern ports to general trade. Furthermore, the principal European Powers have withdrawn the recognition of belligerent rights accorded to the Confederate States in 1861, and have forbidden the entry of vessels bearing the Confederate flag into their ports for any purpose of repair or supply.

"I have discussed the above circumstances with the Honourable James M. Mason, the diplomatic representative of the Confederate States in England, and in accordance with his opinion and advice I hereby direct you to desist from any further destruction of United States property upon the high seas, and from all offensive operations against the citizens of that country.

"Ignorance of the present condition of the *Shenandoah,* and of the point at which this letter may reach you, renders it impossible to give specific instructions in regard to the disposal of the ship, but you can refer to a letter in your possession dated October, 1864, for advice on that point. Your first duty will be to take care of the *personnel* of your command, and to pay off and discharge the crew, with due regard to their safety and the facilities for returning to their respective homes.

"The orders issued by the Maritime Powers with regard to the treatment of Confederate ships hereafter indicate that you would be allowed to enter any port for the *bonâ fide* purpose of disarming and dismantling the *Shenandoah,* and that under such circumstances you would enjoy the protection of the laws, so far at least as the individual safety of yourself and the officers and men of your command is concerned. If you have sufficient money to pay off your crew in full, direct the paymaster to take receipts from each man, which shall expressly waive all further claim against yourself or any representative of the Confederate States on account of pay or other

422 · James D. Bulloch

emolument. If you have not money enough to pay off in full, and cannot negotiate a bill on England, pay to the extent of your funds, and give each man an order on yourself, payable in Liverpool, for the balance due to him, and come here to settle your account.

"The terms of a proclamation lately issued by the President of the United States are such as to exclude most of the officers of your command from the privilege of returning at once to their original homes, and I would advise all of you to come to Europe, or to await elsewhere the further development of events in the United States before venturing to go to any part of that country, or to the Confederate States. Circumstances you will readily understand, and the force of which you will appreciate, compel me to be brief and general in these instructions, and you will therefore exercise your discretion in arranging all details. I will remain in Liverpool for an indefinite time, and you can communicate with me at my usual address.

"I am, etc.,
"(Signed)   JAMES D. BULLOCH.

"Lieutenant Commanding James I. Waddell,
"Confederate States Ship *Shenandoah*."

Mr. Mason forwarded the foregoing letter to the Foreign Office, with an application for its transmission through her Majesty's Consuls, and received a prompt reply from the permanent Under-Secretary of State. The subjoined are copies of the letter of Mr. Mason to Earl Russell and the reply:—

"28, Grove Street, Leamington,
"*June* 20*th*, 1865.

"My Lord,—

"It being considered important and right, in the present condition of the Confederate States of America, to arrest further hostile proceedings at sea in the war against the United States, those having authority to do so in Europe desire as speedily as practicable to communicate with the *Shenandoah*, the only remaining Confederate ship, in order to terminate her cruise. Having no means of doing this in the distant seas where that ship is presumed now to be, I venture to inquire of your lordship whether it will be agreeable to the Government of her Majesty to allow this to be done through the British Consuls at ports where the ship may be expected. I have the honour to enclose herewith a copy of the order it is proposed to transmit, and will be obliged if your lordship will cause me to be informed whether, upon sending such orders unsealed to the Foreign Office, they can be sent through the proper channels to the Consuls, or other representatives of her Majesty, at the points indicated, to be by them transmitted, when opportunity admits, to the officer in command of the *Shenandoah*. These points are Nagasaki in Japan, Shanghai, and the Sandwich Islands. I trust that your lordship will, from the exigency of the occasion, pardon the liberty I have ventured to take, and will oblige me by having the enclosed copy returned to me.

"I have, etc.,
"(Signed)   J. M. MASON."

"Foreign Office, *June 22nd*, 1865.

"Sir,—

"I am directed by Earl Russell to acknowledge the receipt of your letter of the 20th instant, enclosing a copy of a letter which you are desirous of having forwarded to the commander of the *Shenandoah* through her Majesty's representatives and Consuls at the Sandwich Islands, Nagasaki, and Shanghai, and I am to state in reply that his lordship has no objection to sending this letter to the places named and to her Majesty's colonial and naval authorities, it being always distinctly understood that the *Shenandoah* will be dealt with in the courts, if claimed, according to law. The enclosure in your letter is returned herewith, as requested.

"I am, sir, etc.,
"(Signed)   E. HAMMOND."

In conformity with the terms of the foregoing letter, several copies of the instructions to Lieutenant-Commanding Waddell were sent by Mr. Mason to the Foreign Office, and he was informed that they would be forwarded in due course. I feel justified in saying, and it is proper that I should say, that the afore-mentioned instructions were not sent to Lieutenant-Commanding Waddell because of the belief that he needed an order, or even a suggestion, to induce him to cease committing hostilities upon the ocean the moment he received information that they had ceased upon the land. But if he conformed rigidly to the memorandum for the progress of his cruise, it was not probable that he would receive any reliable information until September, as he would only have come down from the

North Pacific to a position one hundred miles north of Oahu on the 15th of that month, and the vessels he was there expected to meet would themselves have been ever since the early spring in high latitudes, and would have known as little as he did of the course of events in the United States. There was also but a very faint expectation that the letters forwarded through her Majesty's Foreign Office would reach him; still it was thought to be right, not only as a matter of policy, but of principle, to manifest a just appreciation of the true condition of affairs, and to put upon record the fact that those who had heretofore been trusted with the power to organize naval expeditions against the United States perceived when they ceased to be either lawful or honest, and had done what was possible to stop their depredations.

The *Shenandoah* left the Arctic Sea, and was clear of Behring's Straits on the 29th of June, 1865. She passed through the Aleutian chain of islands under steam, and the course was shaped for the Californian coast, but it was many days before she sighted a sail. On the 2nd of August a vessel was seen in the distance, and as the wind was light, and Waddell was very desirous to speak her, steam was ordered, and the *Shenandoah* stood towards her. The vessel proved to be the British barque *Barracouta*, fourteen days from San Francisco. She hove to, received a boat from the *Shenandoah*, and startled those on board with the report, or rather with the definite information, that all the Confederate armies had surrendered, that Mr. Davis and several of his Cabinet were prisoners—that, in fact, the Confederate Government had ceased to exist as a *de facto* Power, and that the authority of the United States had become paramount from the Potomac to the Gulf of Mexico, from the Atlantic to the Rio Grande.

It will be admitted, even after the calm reflection of seventeen years, that the commander of the *Shenandoah* was in a critical and perplexing position. There never had been so sudden and so total a subversion of one national sovereignty and the substitution of another. On the morning of that 2nd of August, Waddell justly thought that his commission conferred the right to defend his ship against all comers on the high seas, to take her to any neutral port, and to claim every privilege that could be asked by any belligerent. Before the sun set on that day, the document had become a worthless piece of paper: he could not fire a shot, even to save his crew from capture, and he could enter no port for shelter, except as a political refugee or a voluntary captive.

In the temper then prevailing in the United States, it would have been a wilful and blind submission to harsh and vindictive imprisonment, if nothing worse, to take the *Shenandoah* to an American port. There can be no doubt that immediately upon the final cessation of hostilities the great majority of the people of the Northern States settled themselves down to their ordinary pursuits without giving much thought to the manner in which the Government would adjust matters at the South; and the treatment of the Southern leaders, as well as the "reconstruction" of the several State Governments, was left in the hands of those politicians who had obtained the control of the Republican Party, and whose animosity against the South, and especially against the most prominent men of the South, was manifestly vindictive and of a personal character. No one can read the speeches of several members of the Senate and House of Representatives at that time (there would be no difficulty in mentioning more than one name), or can recur to the indignities and iniquities committed by the "carpet-bag" Governors and Federal civil officers who were thrust upon the Southern States, without admitting the truth of the foregoing proposition.

The arrest and long confinement of Mr. Jefferson Davis in a casemate at Fortress Monroe was a palpable manifestation of vindictive personal malice and revenge. The Government of the United States had treated with him for four years on terms of absolute political equality, they had over and over again acknowledged him as the head of a *de facto* Government, and the President of the United States, with the Secretary of State, had both gone personally to Fortress Monroe, and had there negotiated with the agents and representatives of Mr. Davis in reference to a plan of reunion. To treat him as a malefactor was contrary to every principle of honourable warfare; to have arraigned him for treason would have shocked the sense of justice, and would have aroused the indignant remonstrance, of all civilized peoples, whatever might have been the seeming acquiescence which diplomatic restraint imposes upon Foreign Governments. It would have been, and it was, indeed, equally impossible to sustain any criminal charge against him, because the preposterous and wicked insinuation that he had permitted cruelty to prisoners-of-war, and that he had the faintest possible complicity with the assassination of President Lincoln, was scouted by every honourable man in Europe, and was probably never believed by any honest man in the United States.

Mr. Davis had been too long and too prominently before the world to have escaped close observation and criticism. His intellectual qualities and his moral attributes were not unknown in Europe. His speeches in the Senate of the United States, especially those delivered shortly before the time of secession, and his State papers as the President of the Confederacy, were familiar to the educated classes in England, and even to many in Continental Europe, and every sentiment expressed in them would have served as a witness against the charges of treason and guilt which were insinuated, but never boldly alleged, against him. At the end of a long and tedious imprisonment, which permanently impaired his health, he was unconditionally released, without any official explanation of the causes for his confinement or an honourable public withdrawal of the insinuations which had been advertised in the Party press. No other judgment can therefore be pronounced upon the proceedings against him than that they were suggested by personal malice and enforced by vindictive malevolence.

I should be very sorry to think that the majority of the people of the North approved of the treatment of Mr. Davis or the "Reconstruction Policy" of the dominant Party leaders; but they made a grave mistake in permitting the professional politicians to have their way without a check or remonstrance. The course pursued by them inflicted more and deeper wounds upon the Southern heart than all the ravages of the actual struggle, and has delayed by many years the restoration of mutual confidence, even if it has not wholly and for ever destroyed the belief in the advantages, security, and happiness to be obtained by a Federal Union and a written Constitution.

There were thousands of persons at the South who had no personal acquaintance with Mr. Davis, and were not drawn to him by any ties of common friendship, or early associations. I had never even seen him, except during one short official interview in May, 1861. But every man with a scintilla of chivalry in his heart rebels against the shame of expiating his own alleged faults through the sufferings of a fellow-creature, whoever he may be. Every Southerner worthy of the least consideration looked upon Mr. Davis as a victim through whom the whole South was being punished, and every indignity inflicted upon him was felt to be an affront and an indignity to all.

When the people of any country are content to give their thoughts and energies wholly to private occupations, whether those occupations are for the accumulation of wealth or the pursuit of pleasure, and are willing to leave the Government in the hands of those who make politics a trade and the privileges and emoluments of office their aim, that country will and does cease to enjoy the true and honourable fruits of freedom. The masses who possess the much-vaunted right of franchise neither select their representatives nor watch their conduct afterwards. The "Caucus" dictates who shall fill the public offices, and the so-called "Machine" directs the policy of the Government. Hence it is that a small clique of unscrupulous but clever, energetic men, acting as the legally chosen representatives of a majority, but often wholly out of accord with the best men of their Party, may and do bring shame and disgrace upon the institutions of their country, and have given grounds for the opinion, often expressed in these latter years, that there is no tyranny so unreasonable, so unprincipled, so intolerable, as that of a mere majority. Any careful reader of current political history will be impressed with the conviction that the chief danger to the perpetuity of the American Union in its present form lies in the tendency of the educated and wealthy to be content with the personal luxuries which appear to be easily obtained in that favoured land, and who find their patriotic hopes exalted, if not wholly satisfied, by the rapid progress in material wealth which they behold on every side.

The foregoing reflections did not probably pass through Waddell's mind in their entirety when he got the *Barracouta's* news of the downfall of the Confederate Government, but he knew that he and all with him, and like him, had been denounced in State documents and Consular reports as "pirates." He knew that Mr. Seward had only been restrained from treating Confederate prisoners to the doom of traitors and buccaneers by the plain and resolute threat of retaliation, and now that so wholesome a deterrent had been removed, he thought it more than likely that the favourite maxim might be converted into a practical deed, and that if the *Shenandoah* was surrendered to the United States, he might be made a victim to illustrate the soundness of a theory which had not been abandoned, but only held in abeyance. After some deliberation he determined to take the ship to Liverpool, confident that whatever responsibilities he had incurred, or whatever faults he might have inadvertently committed, he would at the hands of a British Ministry and before an English Court receive impartial consideration and a fair, equitable hearing.

The "British Constitution" is the freest system of restraints and privileges that has ever been devised by man for his own political control. Perhaps its great merit is to be found in the fact that it is not a mere compilation of hard-and-fast rules and precepts. It is not a formal arrangement of clauses dogmatically defining the privileges of the people and limiting the power of the Crown. It is often appealed to with pride and satisfaction by Britons of all classes at home, and it is equally the object of admiration and desire by oppressed nationalities the whole world over, and yet neither statesman nor jurist can precisely define its limits or prescribe the boundary of its action.

The phrase "British Constitution" appears to be as broad as the British Empire and as elastic as the air of the British Isles. It never has been compressed into a distinct code, and has never been ratified by any Convention of the Estates of the Realm, or by appeal to a popular vote. Consecutive Acts of Parliament, decisions of the highest Courts of Appeal, and precedents founded by Cabinets and confirmed by their successors, ever since the days of Magna Charta, all taken together, constitute, I suppose, what is meant by the "British Constitution," and the power to change or modify it by the same processes, without any violent wrench, or any special appeal to the masses, whether in corporate organizations or as a huge democracy, probably accounts for the satisfactory manner in which it has hitherto worked.

The freedom of the British Constitution has some practical drawbacks. It permits, indeed it appears to have originated and confirmed, a system of circumlocution and "red tape" in the management of public business which is often inconvenient, and it certainly cannot be said to have obliterated the tendency to individual crime which is unhappily common to the whole human race. But no fair critic of national institutions can, I think, refuse to admit that there is no country in which questions involving the privileges or rights of private persons, the liberty and property of the subject, or his punishment if need be, the freedom and protection of the alien, or his extradition and surrender if demanded, are so fairly and justly considered upon their merits, and without a thought of expediency or any fear of consequences, as in Great Britain. British Ministers are not immaculate—they are sometimes weak and vacillating, as the late Confederate Government found to its cost; but there is throughout all Britain a general and instinctive antipathy to political "jobs," and a Minister or anyone in public office who attempted to practise them would soon find the British public on the scent, and he would be run to earth, dug out, and ignominiously cast among the rubbish of damaged reputations. The confidence of the British public in the personal integrity of those who administer the Government, not only in the high offices of State and on the Bench, but who manage the executive departments and are the permanent officials, is a fact that cannot escape the notice of all who habitually take note of national characteristics, and that fact serves to demonstrate that the political institutions of Great Britain are sound in theory, and that they are still in unison with the best instincts of the age.

In order to manifest his full understanding of the change in his own position and in the character of his ship in consequence of the *Barracouta*'s report, Waddell at once disarmed the *Shenandoah* by dismounting the guns and lowering them, with all their gear and appurtenances, below. The ports were closed, the funnel whitewashed, and the ship was again, to all external appearance, an ordinary mercantile screw-steamer. Having determined to bring the ship to England, no time was lost by detours or stoppages for any purpose. Vessels were occasionally passed, but no heed was paid to them except on one occasion, when a change of course at night and the use of both sail and steam was resorted to for the purpose of parting company.

On the morning of November 5th, 1865, Tuskar was made, being the first land sighted since taking a departure from the Aleutian Islands, at the entrance to Behring's Sea, and the next day, November 6th, the *Shenandoah* let go her anchor in the Mersey about half a cable's length astern of her Majesty's ship *Donegal*.

The officers had left Liverpool just thirteen months before, inspirited by the prospects of an adventurous cruise and the hope of performing some useful service for their country. They were now again at their starting-point, but with very different hopes, and not without some misgivings. As soon as possible after anchoring, Waddell communicated with Captain Paynter, the commander of the *Donegal*, informed him that the object in bringing the *Shenandoah* to Liverpool was to place her in the possession of her Majesty's Government for such disposition as might be proper and legal, and handed him an official letter, addressed to Earl Russell, setting forth all the facts and circumstances of the case, which he requested Captain Paynter to forward.

The *Shenandoah* was immediately placed under detention by the officers of Customs, a party of men from the *Donegal* was put on board of her, and the gunboat *Goshawk* was lashed alongside. Mr. Adams, the United States Minister, was promptly informed by the Consul at Liverpool of the *Shenandoah*'s arrival at that port, and on the 7th of November, 1865, he wrote a letter to the Earl of Clarendon, who was then the Secretary of State for Foreign Affairs, on the subject. Mr. Adams did not make a formal demand for the surrender of the *Shenandoah* to the United States, because, as it appears from his letter, he was "without special instructions respecting this case," nor did he suggest that Lieutenant-Commanding Waddell and the officers and crew should be treated as pirates, although he alludes to the ship as "this corsair." He was content to ask Lord Clarendon to take such measures as might be necessary to secure the property on board, and to take possession of the vessel with the view to deliver her to the United States in due course. Mr. Adams's letter, with that of Lieutenant-Commanding Waddell, and other documents relating to the *Shenandoah*, were referred to the law officers of the Crown on the same day (November 7th, 1865). The law officers "advised" in substance as follows:*—"We think it will be proper for her Majesty's Government, in compliance with Mr. Adams's request, to deliver up to him, on behalf of the Government of the United States, the ship in question, with her tackle, apparel, etc., and all captured chronometers or other property capable of being identified as prize-of-war, which may be found on board her.... With respect to the officers and crew ... if the facts stated by Captain Waddell are true, there is clearly no case for any prosecution on the ground of piracy in the courts of this country, and we presume that her Majesty's Government are not in possession of any evidence which could be produced before any court or magistrate for the purpose of contravening the statement or of showing that the crime of piracy has, in fact, been committed.... With respect to any of the persons on board the *Shenandoah* who cannot be immediately proceeded against and detained under legal warrant upon any criminal charge, we are not aware of any ground upon which they can properly be prevented from going on shore and disposing of themselves as they think fit, and we cannot advise her Majesty's Government to assume or exercise the power of keeping them under any kind of restraint."

On a subsequent reference of the case, the law officers advised again as follows:—"With respect to the question whether the officers and crew of the *Shenandoah* may now be permitted to leave the ship and go on shore, we have only to repeat the opinion expressed in our report of yesterday's date, namely, that these persons, being now in this country and entitled to the benefit of our laws, cannot be detained except under legal warrant upon some criminal charge duly preferred against them in the ordinary course of the law. If her Majesty's Government are now in possession, or consider it probable that, if an information were laid before a magistrate, they would shortly be in possession of evidence against any of these persons sufficient to justify their committal for trial, either upon any charge of misdemeanour under the Foreign Enlistment Act or upon the graver charge of piracy, we think it would be right and proper to take the necessary proceedings without delay, in order to have such charge duly investigated; but at the present time we are not informed of any such evidence in the possession or power of her Majesty's Government by which such a charge would be likely to be established."

---

* For the letter of Mr. Adams and the opinion of the law officers, see "British Case," pp. 157, 158.

The "law officers" who gave the foregoing advice and opinions, and whose names are attached to the documents,* were Sir Roundell Palmer, Sir R. P. Collier, and Sir Robert Phillimore. The first is now Lord Selborne, Lord Chancellor of England, the second is now a member of the Judicial Committee of the Privy Council, and the third is Judge of the Probate, Divorce, and Admiralty Division of the Supreme Court of Judicature. These eminent lawyers and judges having declared that they were not aware of any ground upon which the officers and crew of the *Shenandoah* could be indicted either for a misdemeanour under the Foreign Enlistment Act or for piracy, it may be assumed that those who bought and despatched the *Sea King* from England were equally free from liability for violation of any English municipal law, and the charge of fitting out "piratical expeditions" from Great Britain must also fall to the ground in this case, as in all others in reference to which that preposterous allegation has been made. All the parties having anything to do with the purchase, building, or despatch of the *Alabama, Florida,* and *Shenandoah* were, and continued to be, residents of England, and were both amenable to the law and within its reach. It is manifest from the opinions of the law officers of the Crown that the numerous affidavits supplied by the American Consuls contained no valid evidence, and that the Government instituted no proceedings because there was no proof upon which to base an indictment.

It should be mentioned, as part of the history of the *Shenandoah,* that when Captain Corbett, who took her out as the *Sea King* and delivered her to Lieutenant Waddell off Madeira, returned to England, he was arrested, taken before a magistrate, and committed for trial, upon the affidavits of some of the seamen, who alleged that he had attempted to enlist them, or to induce them to enlist, for the Confederate service. He was tried for this alleged violation of the Foreign Enlistment Act before the Lord Chief Justice and a special jury. The evidence produced at the trial was very conflicting. Several witnesses who had sailed in the ship were examined for the defence, and they contradicted on many material points the verbal testimony and the depositions which were offered in support of the prosecution. They stated on oath that Captain Corbett took no part in the endeavours to induce the men to enlist, and their statements were fully confirmed by the report sent me at the time by Lieutenant Waddell; in fact, he complained of the lukewarmness of Captain Corbett, and explicitly affirmed that he did nothing to help in providing a crew for the

* See "British Case," p. 158.

Shenandoah. The jury acquitted Captain Corbett, and no other legal proceedings were ever taken in England in respect to the *Sea King* (*Shenandoah*) or her consort, the *Laurel*.

In consequence of the opinion of the law officers of the Crown which has been quoted above, instructions were sent to Captain Paynter, commanding her Majesty's ship *Donegal*, who was in charge of the *Shenandoah*, to release all the officers and men who were not ascertained to be British subjects. Captain Paynter reported, on the 8th November, that, on receiving instructions to the above effect, he went on board the *Shenandoah*, and, being satisfied that there were no British subjects among the crew, or at least none whom it could be proved were British subjects, he permitted all hands to land with their private effects. On the 9th of November Captain Paynter had an interview with the American Consul in a tug alongside of the *Shenandoah*, and arranged with him for the delivery of the ship to anyone he might appoint to take charge. On the 10th of November, 1865, a Captain Freeman went on board, under orders from Mr. Dudley, the United States Consul, and the *Shenandoah* was delivered over to him by the commander of her Majesty's gunboat *Goshawk*, who was then in charge; and thus ended the career of the last of the Confederate cruisers, which during the three previous years had wrought such ruin to American commerce, and had incidentally helped so much to increase the supremacy of the British mercantile marine.*

Mr. Seward, Mr. Adams, and the Consuls, in their reports and complaints in respect to Confederate cruisers, dwelt strongly, persistently, and tauntingly upon the allegation that the crews of those vessels were British subjects illegally engaged to wage war upon a friendly Power; and more than a month after the surrender of the *Shenandoah* to the United States and the dispersion of her crew, Mr. Adams sent to the Earl of Clarendon a deposition made by one Temple, who alleged that he had served in her throughout the cruise. The object of Mr. Adams appears to have been to prove from this man's affidavit that the crew of the *Shenandoah* were chiefly British subjects, and that therefore they should not have been released, but should have been tried for violation of the Foreign Enlistment Act. Why he should have urged a reopening of such a question so long after the particular event, and so many months after the end of the war, it is difficult at first to perceive; but as the matter was brought up again before the Tribunal of Arbitration, the purpose of Mr. Adams was probably

---

* For details of the surrender of the ship to the United States, see Lieutenant Alfred Cheek's letter and Captain Paynter's statement, "British Case," p. 159, etc.

to put on official record a point which the representatives of the United States could refer to at any future time.

In the "Case" presented on behalf of the Government of her Britannic Majesty to the Tribunal of Arbitration, the above-mentioned deposition of Temple, which was sent by Mr. Adams to the Earl of Clarendon, was referred to in these words:—"It was clearly shown, however, that Temple was a person unworthy of credit, and some of his statements in his depositions were ascertained to be gross falsehoods. The crew of the *Shenandoah*, if Temple's evidence were to be believed, included Americans, Prussians, Spaniards, Portuguese, Danes, Malays, and Sandwich Islanders. About fifty men were stated by him to have joined her from United States ships." The affidavit of Temple was a fair example of the evidence and the witnesses generally tendered by the United States Consuls to her Majesty's Government, and it is not surprising that the law officers looked upon all such Consular documents with distrust. They accepted and acted upon them for the purposes of the "*Alexandra* Case," and the result was an ignominious exposure on the part of the witnesses, a verdict for the defendants which stands to this day as a complete contradiction of the allegations against the Confederate agents, and a bill of costs and damages amounting to nearly £4,000, which her Majesty's Government had to pay, and which the United States ought to have recouped out of the £3,000,000 awarded them at Geneva, seeing that the suit against the *Alexandra* was instituted at their request and in their interest, and with the expectation that they could make good their depositions.

It has been already stated that there is no purpose in this narrative to defend or to explain the conduct of her Majesty's Government with any reference to the claims set up by the United States, or the allegations of neglect to enforce the conditions of the Foreign Enlistment Act and the Neutrality Proclamation against Confederate agents and Confederate ships, which the representatives of the United States brought against the British authorities both at home and in the Colonies. But it so happens that the charges of "nefarious," "illegal," and "criminal" conduct on the part of the Confederate agents, with which the American State Papers are so highly seasoned, are also used with the purpose to convict her Majesty's Government of unfriendliness to the United States and of partiality to the Confederacy, and thus the counter-statements and arguments necessary to refute the charges of illegality and crime alleged against one party, serve undesignedly as an explanation and defence of the neglect and partiality imputed to the other.

It is necessary that a few of the charges and complaints alluded to above should be specifically mentioned, in order that the conditions under which Confederate cruisers were equipped and kept at sea may be clearly understood. One of the allegations of the United States was that Confederate ships were permitted to enlist men in British ports, and even so late as June, 1882, an article appeared in the American *Army and Navy Register*, a paper purporting to be the organ of the United States army and navy, in which it is stated that the crew of the *Alabama* were men from her Majesty's ship *Excellent*, the gunnery-school ship of the Royal Navy.

As a matter of fact, not a single man was ever enlisted in a British port for a Confederate ship. The nucleus of the *Alabama*'s crew was composed of the men who sailed in the *Enrica* and the *Bahama* to Terceira. They were the ordinary sea-faring men who can be got together at any time in a large port like Liverpool, and were engaged to navigate a private ship on a specified voyage which was perfectly legal in itself. Four or five men who had been to the Confederate States in the *Fingal* were taken out to join the *Alabama*, and those few probably suspected that they would somehow or other find their way into the Confederate service; but in no case was any man informed that he would be asked to do anything or to go anywhere not specified in the shipping articles signed by him until he was far beyond British jurisdiction, or any responsibility which could be attached to her Majesty's Government in respect to his enlistment. No threat or unpleasant alternative was ever held out to a single man to induce him to enlist, and in every case the engagement was purely and wholly voluntary.

The difficulty of obtaining a sufficient number of men by ordinary and legal shipment of the crews was so great, that in every instance the cruisers were compelled to leave their rendezvous short-handed, and they filled up their number to the necessary fighting complement by means of voluntary enlistments from the American crews found on board the captured ships. That the enlistments were voluntary, and that the men were kindly treated, is abundantly proved by the good discipline on board the Confederate vessels-of-war, and the remarkable fidelity of the men to the officers who commanded them and to the flag under which they had agreed to serve. No set of men could have behaved better than the crew of the *Alabama*. They showed steadiness and pluck in the engagement with the *Kearsarge*, and conducted themselves with admirable sobriety and obedience when brought on shore from the sunken ship. One of them, named Michael Mars (he deserves this mention), volunteered to take charge of some important papers for Captain Semmes. He put them inside of the breast of his "frock," and jumped overboard from the sinking ship. When picked up and carried to the *Deerhound*, he handed the parcel to his commander, just as he would have delivered a package in the ordinary course of duty.

When the *Florida* went into Bahia in October, 1864, one watch was permitted to go on shore on liberty. The men came on board at the appointed time without any desertion. At the time of her capture by the *Wachusett*, the port-watch—some sixty odd men—were on shore. They came to England with their commander, and after arrival a large number of them wrote me a letter requesting to be sent to some other Confederate ship, or if not, to the Confederacy, and expressing a readiness to serve "their country" whenever it might be thought necessary. I have the above document in my possession now. It is signed by every petty officer in the port-watch, with his rating annexed to his name, and by twenty-eight A.B.'s and ordinary seamen as well. The behaviour of the *Shenandoah*'s crew in preserving their discipline and bringing the ship to Liverpool without questioning the authority of Waddell, when they were informed of the collapse of the Government they had enlisted to serve, may also be mentioned.

It has never been alleged, so far as I know, that a single prize was ever plundered, or that the men showed any disposition to plunder which required special and severe restraint. If there ever has been such an insinuation, the allegation is wholly untrue, and could be easily disproved. In the one single case of the *Shenandoah* it has been admitted that some men were added to her crew at Melbourne, but they stowed themselves away, and were not discovered until the ship was at sea, and so even in that instance they were not enlisted within British jurisdiction.

Pressed crews, or men enlisted under false pretences, or through "criminal" and "nefarious" concealments, would not have remained faithful under all the trying circumstances in which the Confederate cruisers were placed. For six or seven years after the war I often met a man just in from a voyage, who would remind me with evident satisfaction that he was one of the "old *Alabama*'s," or some other Confederate cruiser. Often one or more would call especially as if to report, and they seemed to think it quite natural to advise me of their whereabouts and doings.

Such incidents are among the agreeable and comforting reflections in respect to a war which has left but few gratifying reminiscences. They suggest that there must have been some inherent right and justice in the cause which could arouse so much fidelity among its voluntary partizans abroad, as well as so much self-sacrificing courage and endurance at home, or else they must be taken as a tribute to the tact and judgment, the suavity and kindly severity of the Confederate naval officers, who were able to keep their ships in discipline, and yet to inspire the men with confidence and devotion to their adopted flag.

Another complaint of the United States was that the British and Colonial authorities permitted "excessive hospitalities" to Confederate cruisers, and practised in some instances "discourtesies to vessels-of-war of the United States." The above complaint was placed in the "Case of the United States" presented to the Tribunal of Arbitration in the form of a specific charge against her Majesty's Government, and it was alleged that the rules adopted for the treatment of belligerent vessels "were utterly disregarded" in the case of Confederate ships-of-war, and were "rigidly enforced against the United States." The specifications in support of the complaint were chiefly in reference to the permission given to Confederate ships to obtain coal in British ports, whereby they were able to continue their cruises.

It does not concern me to reply generally to the complaints of "excessive hospitalities" to one side, and "discourtesies" to the other. Those who are anxious on the subject will find the groundlessness of the charges fully demonstrated in the British "Counter-Case." I will confine myself exclusively to the complaints which refer to the visits of Confederate ships to British ports, and the supply of coal they were permitted to receive. During the course of the war the total number of visits paid by Confederate ships to British home or Colonial ports was twenty-five, eleven of which were made for the purpose of effecting necessary repairs to engines. Coal was obtained on sixteen of the twenty-five visits, and on sixteen occasions the limit of stay fixed by the regulations was exceeded by special permission or by order. In one of the cases, however, the excess was only two hours, and in one it was enforced in order to give an American merchant vessel the advantage of twenty-four hours' start. The total amount of coal obtained by Confederate cruisers in British ports was in round numbers 2,800 tons.

Let us now refer to the other side. The official returns—which, however, are said to have been necessarily incomplete—show an aggregate total of 228 visits of United States ships to British ports. On thirteen of these repairs were permitted, on forty-five coal was obtained, and the limit of stay prescribed by the regulations was exceeded forty-four times. The returns of the quantity of coal received by each United States ship are so imperfect that it is impossible to arrive at the precise aggregate amount obtained by all of them, but it is specifically stated in the British "Counter-Case" that the United States ship *Vanderbilt* alone took on board "2,000 *tons within the space of less than two months*," which is more than two-thirds of the whole amount obtained by all the Confederate ships put together. When it is remembered that the United States ships had free access to their own ports, often within a few hundred miles of the places where they were permitted to obtain coal, while the Confederate ships were wholly dependent upon the foreign supply, it will be manifest that the complaints are easily shown to have been groundless.

In the "Case of the United States" it is specifically charged that in *three* instances Confederate ships were allowed to coal in British ports in contravention of the regulations of January 31st, 1862, but in the British "Counter-Case" it is proved that the coaling of the *Florida* at Barbadoes was the only instance which could be considered a departure from those rules. In the above-named instance, the Governor permitted the *Florida* to obtain a supply of coal within the limits of the regulations upon the report of her commander that he had run short from stress of weather.

It will be perceived that the United States were only able to specify three instances in which the regulations were relaxed in favour of Confederate ships, and those cases have been reduced in point of fact to one, and that of doubtful application. But how stands the case with reference to United States ships? Let it be borne in mind that, according to the regulations referred to, no vessel of either belligerent could obtain coal from a British or colonial port until the expiration of three months from the date of her last supply at the same or any other British port. In the British "Counter-Case," pp. 117, 118, it is stated that the United States ship *Vanderbilt* obtained at St. Helena, 18th of August, 1863, 400 tons of coal; at Simon's Bay, 3rd of September, 1,000 tons; at Mauritius, 24th of September, 618 tons. Thus, within a period of but little more than one month, this United States ship obtained coal at three British colonial ports, in direct contravention of the regulations.

But this is not all—the United States ships *Tuscarora, Kearsarge, Sacramento, Wyoming, Narraganset, Wachusett, Mohican,* and *Dacotah* are mentioned as having been permitted to obtain coal within the prescribed period. The *Sacramento* is stated to have practised a ruse to evade the regulations. After coaling at Cork between July 28th and August 1st, 1864, she was allowed to receive 25 tons more at Plymouth on the 16th of August, and 30 tons more were sent to her from Dover by the United States Consul, in a vessel which left without clearance for the purpose. There are other cases of evasion of the regulations by United States ships mentioned in the British case, but the foregoing are sufficient, when contrasted with the privileges granted to Confederate ships, to utterly quash the charges, and discredit the complaints of "excessive hospitalities" to Confederate cruisers and "discourtesies to vessels-of-war of the United States," which were so often and so petulantly made by Mr. Seward and his Consuls, and appear to have been recklessly repeated in the formal legal argument presented to the Tribunal of Arbitration.

It does not appear from the published documents attached to the proceedings at Geneva that the United States sent any ships in pursuit or in search of the *Shenandoah*. She was permitted to sail round the world, and destroy many American ships in a deliberate manner, and according to a fixed programme, and never saw a United States vessel-of-war. During the two years' cruise of the *Alabama* she was met by only two United States ships until she voluntarily went out of Cherbourg to engage the *Kearsarge*. One of the two was the *Hatteras*, which she sunk, and the other was the *San Jacinto*, too powerful a ship to engage, and from which she escaped by a ruse.

The *Florida* was compelled to remain at Brest from August, 1863, until February, 1864; and her presence there was so well known that the United States ship *Kearsarge* was sent to watch her. The *Kearsarge* appeared off, or came into, Brest Roads, September 17th, October 30th, November 27th, December 11th and 27th, 1863, and January 3rd, 1864. At the last-named date the *Florida* was at anchor in the roadstead, to all appearance ready for sea; but for some reason the *Kearsarge* disappeared, and when she returned the *Florida* had sailed. The *Florida*'s cruise after leaving Brest, her "raid" to within thirty miles of the Capes of the Delaware, her subsequent run through the equatorial "forks" of the great maritime roadway, and her arrival at Bahia, have been narrated in a previous chapter; but during all of this period of eight months she never saw a United States ship-of-war until she found the *Wachusett* lying idly at anchor in the last-named port. If the *Wachusett* had been in the right place, she would probably have met the *Florida* in the open sea, there would have been a fair fight, and the discreditable occurrence at Bahia would have been avoided.

It does appear extraordinary that, with the large naval force which the United States controlled during the war, a few Confederate ships should have been permitted to cruise through the two great oceans at will, and to destroy so many vessels just where any intelligent naval officer would know where to find them, and where it should have been known that the hostile cruisers would be sent. I have not been able to obtain all the returns of captured ships. The *Florida*'s papers were nearly all lost, and some of the other ships did not send regular reports, and at the sudden termination of the war there were many other things to think of, and a precise record was not made. From the documents now in my possession, or which have been submitted to my inspection in past years, it appears that the regular Confederate cruisers destroyed one hundred and seventy-five vessels; and this number does not include the vessels captured and destroyed by Lieutenants-Commanding J. T. Wood and John Wilkinson in their short dashes out of Wilmington with the *Tallahassee* and *Chickamauga.*

But this was not the whole of the injury inflicted upon American commerce by the few Confederate cruisers. In the "Case of the United States" presented to the Tribunal of Arbitration, some startling figures are given to illustrate the indirect damage. On p. 130 of the above-mentioned document it is stated "that while in 1860 two-thirds of the commerce of New York were carried on in American bottoms, in 1863 three-fourths were carried on in foreign bottoms." On the same page there is an account of the number and tonnage of American vessels which were registered in the United Kingdom and in British North America (namely, transferred to the British flag) to avoid capture, from which I extract the following:—"In 1861, vessels 126, tonnage 71,673; in 1862, vessels 135, tonnage 64,578; in 1863, vessels 348, tonnage 252,579; in 1864, vessels 106, tonnage 92,052."

I can conscientiously affirm that this destruction of private property, and diversion of legitimate commerce, was painful to those whose duty it was to direct and to inflict it. But the United States have always practised that mode of harassing an enemy; and Mr. Bolles says, in his article in reference to the proposed trial of Admiral Semmes, that they would do so again under like circumstances. It is greatly to be regretted that when the United States wrung the Treaty of Washington from Great Britain in 1871, and brought her Majesty's Government before a great International Court of Arbitration, the proposition to exempt private property from destruction at sea in future wars was not discussed and definitely determined. Unfortunately, that treaty and the important conclave of eminent statesmen and jurists at Geneva have settled nothing in respect to international law that has any binding force upon any Power except Great Britain and the United States, and upon them only for the specific purposes of the treaty, because her Majesty's Government not only agreed to be judged by rules manufactured for the occasion, and not applicable to neutral duties as commonly understood, but her Majesty's Ministers weakened, if they did not wholly destroy, their case in advance by imprudent speeches in public, and by indiscreet admissions, as well as by a strange and unstatesmanlike vacillation that gave their adversary in the case an advantage which was manifest to all who were interested in the proceedings and followed them with attention.

The career and fate of the *Shenandoah* after her surrender to the United States may be of some interest, although the former was not lustrous, and the latter was merely the lot common to many stately craft, whether historic or commonplace. Shortly after the surrender, Captain Freeman was ordered to take the ship to New York. It was winter, and the fierce westerly gales seemed unwilling to permit the transfer of the ex-Confederate craft to her late enemies without a rough protest. Captain Freeman appears to have made an earnest effort to fulfil his instructions. He fought against head winds and seas for some time, but finally returned with the ship to Liverpool, having lost some of the upper spars and the greater portion of the sails.

The *Shenandoah* was then put up for sale, and was finally bought for the Sultan of Zanzibar. She was fitted out with some show of luxury as to cabin fittings, and it was rumoured that she was to be used as a yacht, but, whether she proved to be too large and too expensive for the convenience of the Sultan and the resources of the Zanzibar exchequer or not, she was soon set again to the peaceful occupation for which she was originally built, and carried many a cargo of "ivory, gum, coral, and coal" for his sable majesty, and weathered the blasts of many monsoons, until at last, in 1879, fourteen years after she struck the Confederate flag, the teak planks were torn from her bottom by a rough scrape on a coral reef, and her iron ribs were left to rust and crumble on a melancholy island in the Indian Ocean.*

One of the difficulties attending the enterprise for which the *Shenandoah* (or *Sea King*) was bought, arose from the necessity of providing a tender for her, which of course involved a large additional outlay, at a time when other necessities were pressing, and the financial agents were not over-well provided with funds. When it was determined to undertake the enterprise, prompt action was absolutely necessary to insure success, and all that could be done to secure an economical expenditure was to buy a good vessel for a tender that could be used as a blockade-runner, or would be likely to fetch something approximate to the cost afterwards.

These expectations were happily fulfilled by the *Laurel*. Lieutenant Ramsay carried out his instructions with intelligence and energy. After parting company with the *Shenandoah* off Madeira, he proceeded to Teneriffe, and landed there Captain Corbett and the crew of the *Sea King*. From Teneriffe, Ramsay proceeded to Nassau, and took the *Laurel* from that

---

* An interesting leader appeared in the *Daily Telegraph* (London) on her career and final shipwreck at the time of her loss.

port into Charleston with a most valuable cargo of supplies, shipped by Mr. Heyleger, the Confederate agent at Nassau. Immediately after the arrival of the *Laurel* at Charleston, early in December, 1864, the Secretary of the Navy directed me to sell her when she came out; but upon further consultation with Lieutenant Ramsay, she was transferred to the Treasury Department at cost price. She was then loaded with cotton on account of the Treasury, and got safely through the blockade. While in Charleston the name of the *Laurel* was changed to the *Confederate States*. She was the subject of some correspondence between the United States Minister to England and her Majesty's Government, which appears to have ended with the following statement contained in a letter from Earl Russell to Mr. Adams, in March, 1865:—"Her Majesty's Government are advised that although the proceedings of the steamer *Confederate States*, formerly *Laurel*, may have rendered her liable to capture on the high seas by the cruisers of the United States, she has not, so far as is known, committed any offence punishable by British law."*

As the *Laurel* was transferred from one Department of the Government to the other, there arose no question of profit or loss; but, looking to the service she rendered to the *Shenandoah*, the freight she would have earned on the inward cargo to Charleston if it had been carried on private account, and her transfer at cost price, the transaction as regards the Navy Department resulted in a very substantial profit.† I cannot state whether the *Laurel* (*Confederate States*) made more than one voyage through the blockade. She belonged to another Department. I had no further control over her, and have never learned what became of her at the close of the war, which came to an end in a few months after her first departure from Charleston.

* See "United States Case," p. 123.
† The blockade rates of freight were then about £50 per ton.

CHAPTER XI

———

When Mr. Stephen R. Mallory was placed at the head of the Navy Department in the Provisional Government which was hastily organized at Montgomery in February, 1861, there was but little to gratify his ambition in the high office assigned him. The entire want of the commonest, as well as the most essential, materials and resources for building and equipping a navy was painfully apparent, and he must have felt how impossible it would prove for him to satisfy the public expectations, or to accomplish anything that would be accepted as evidence of due forethought and energy on his part. In war, people hope for brilliant operations, if not always for complete success, and as it is impossible for a Department of State to explain either its purposes or the means of fulfilling them to the general public, the absence of striking results is often attributed to the want of genius to plan or of energy and skill in administration.

It is difficult to imagine a more troublesome and trying position than that which was thrust upon Mr. Mallory. His colleague at the War Office was compelled to assume grave responsibilities, and to undertake a burdensome task. The lack of military resources was quite as manifest as the want of naval materials, but there was plenty of bone and sinew in the country, and hosts of ardent, gallant spirits, and these required no urging to rally them to the flag. They were as good material for soldiers as could be found, and the Secretary of War was able to collect and organize a force which met with a notable success at a very early period of the contest, and the army and its administrative staff were launched into public notice, and introduced to national favour, with a prestige that the sister Department could not imitate and the sister service could not rival.

Nothing could induce me to disparage the professional ability, the sense of honour, or the gallantry of those officers of the United States navy who remained, if I may use the phraseology of the period, "faithful to the old flag," an expression which in plain language simply means that the officers from the North retained their commissions in the navy of a Federal Union composed of their own native States. But I feel bound to say that I am not restrained from criticism or reproach by the vigilant and resolute exertion of any moral force opposing and overcoming a severe and acrimonious spirit. I neither feel now, nor have I ever been moved to, the slightest sentiment of ill-will against the *personnel* of the United States navy, and I have no grudge to gratify, and no personal injury to retaliate. There is therefore no temptation for me to depreciate the exertions of that corps during the Civil War, or to intimate that the victories achieved by United States ships over the very inadequate resistance the Confederates were able to oppose to them have given the full measure of the skill and daring of the American navy.

Any fair critic will admit that Farragut showed that he had the qualities in kind which make a great naval commander. To what degree he possessed them can hardly be said to have been fully tested. There was undoubtedly energy in preparation, and an admirable exhibition of personal resource and courage in his operations on the Mississippi and at Mobile, but then the inefficient armament of the forts, the insufficiency of the artificial obstructions, and the feebleness of the opposing Confederate vessels, are so strikingly manifest to those who have been able to obtain trustworthy reports, that the success achieved cannot be regarded with much surprise, while on the other hand defeat could only have been the result of signal failure in the execution. From the performances of the United States navy during the Civil War, it may be fairly inferred that there is more ability in the service than the opportunities revealed; and I have no doubt that if the occasion had required greater exertion and higher professional qualities, the necessary fortitude and skill would have been forthcoming.

Lord Napier of Magdala was greatly commended, and was raised to the peerage, because he organized and carried out the expedition to Abyssinia with much judgment, prudence, and skill, and the final movements were so rapid that he effected a complete success with very slight loss to his own forces. He was justly thought to have exhibited a rare union of military qualities, to wit, the faculty of duly proportioning the means to the end, combined with a comprehensive knowledge of strategy in design and tactical skill in execution. The British Government and the military critics perceived that the occasion did not exhaust his powers, but that there remained behind a reserve of latent strength which might be relied upon in case of a future and greater demand. The honours conferred upon him were intended, therefore, to mark the estimate which had been formed of his capacity; but no one thought of comparing the march to Magdala with Bonaparte's swoop upon the plains of Piedmont and Lombardy in 1796, and neither English poet nor prose writer has ever linked the names of Napier and Napoleon in the same military chaplet.

Farragut's honours were equally well earned, and no one can say that he might not have rivalled the historic admirals of by-gone years if he had experienced the same training, and had been put to the same tests; but the run past the forts on the Mississippi, and the entry into Mobile Bay, are no more comparable to Nelson's exploits at Copenhagen and Aboukir than the march through Abyssinia and the storming of Magdala are deserving of comparison with the rapid advance of the French into Northern Italy and the "terrible passage of the bridge of Lodi." There should be a fitness in similitudes, otherwise what is meant for praise degenerates into adulation.

It has been written that an indiscreet friend is more dangerous than a prudent enemy. Admiral Farragut commanded the largest and most powerful force that had ever been controlled by any American naval officer, and I have always thought that the consequences which resulted from the operations of that force in the waters of the Mississippi were more fatal to the Confederacy than any of the military campaigns. The achievements of Admiral Farragut's fleet enabled General Grant to cross the Mississippi with safety, and to get into the rear of Vicksburgh. The fall of that essential position was thus assured. David Porter's flotilla, which had been working down from the Ohio, was able to unite with Farragut's fleet, which had forced its way up from the Gulf of Mexico, and the Confederacy was thus finally cut in twain. Besides the large number of admirable fighting-men Texas could and did contribute to the Confederate army, that great State had become the chief source of supply for cattle, horses, and other essentials. The entire control of the Mississippi by the United States naval forces, which resulted from the fall of Vicksburgh and Port Hudson, was a fatal blow to the Confederacy, and reduced the war from the position of a contest having many probabilities of success, to a purely defensive struggle for safety.

So far as can be learned from the current histories of the period, the above-mentioned decisive results were chiefly due to the exertions of Farragut, supplemented and assisted by the untiring exertions of David D. Porter (now Admiral Porter). Those two naval commanders used the forces under their respective commands with daring and persistent energy, and a nearer approach to intuitive genius than was exhibited by any of the military leaders on the Federal side, and they have won for the navy the chief credit for the ultimate success of the United States. There can be no doubt that Generals Grant and Banks dawdled about Vicksburgh and Port Hudson for a considerable time to very little purpose, and there is nothing in the published records to show that they would ever have got possession of those strongholds of the Confederacy if Farragut and Porter had not opened the great river for them, and it is not impossible that General Grant owes his great reputation to the opportunity afforded him by Farragut's exploits on the Mississippi, and obtained the advantages which enabled him to overwhelm Lee through the consequences which inevitably followed the naval operations in the south-west.

Admiral Farragut had at least these marks of genius, a quick and intuitive perception of the practicability of an enterprise and a perception of the force necessary to justify an effort. When satisfied on those points, he never hesitated, but delivered his blow promptly and with all the strength he could wield. He deserved success and won it. If a single one of the higher officers of the United States army had possessed corresponding inspiration and vigour, the Confederacy could not have resisted and beaten back the vastly superior power of the Federal Government for four years.

When the results which follow a military or naval enterprise are notably important and decisive, the world is not inclined to be critical as to the relative means of attack and defence, but when biographers or admiring fellow-countrymen seize upon the most brilliant of foreign worthies and appropriate him as the type of their own national hero, calm spectators are irresistibly impelled to inquire into details and to investigate the title upon which the comparison is founded. Admiral Farragut is justly entitled to a monument of his own, but to insist upon putting him upon the same pedestal with Nelson, as some indiscreet Americans have done, is to invite a comparison which is unfair to his well-earned reputation.

Nelson won his great victories over opponents who were superior in force, and had, besides, great advantages both in position and formation. Running past stationary batteries has never been considered a very great achievement by any authority on naval tactics, and the Confederate flotillas opposed to the United States ships on the Mississippi and at Mobile, were manifestly too weak in numbers, armament, and manœuvring power to offer an effective resistance.

The Confederate States cannot be said to have had a navy at all. The few cruisers it was possible to put afloat formed an irregular marine force, which was too weak to act with any effective aggressive power, and was therefore never collected for a united attack upon any given point. The commanders of those few vessels were compelled to be content with the injury they could inflict by the destruction of commercial ships. Semmes, in the *Alabama*, gave the United States ship *San Jacinto* the slip at Martinique because the disparity of force would have exposed him to the imputation of folly rather than courage if he had engaged her, but he never shunned a meeting with any other United States ship, and cruised where, according to all reasonable calculations, he was likely to encounter them. Apart from Maffitt's desperate enterprise off Mobile, both he and Morris took the *Florida* to localities where it has always appeared strange none of the enemy's ships were seen. Maffitt was chased among the Bahamas, and he practised the merest prudence in declining a combat at that time, because the pursuing ships were not only greatly superior in size and armament, but his vessel was shorthanded and the crew scarcely trained to the manual of the guns. Morris had no purpose to resort to any ruse in order to escape from the *Wachusett* at Bahia. His intention, officially reported, was to go to sea in open daylight as soon as his repairs were completed, and to fight if pursued, as he fully expected to be. It is a pity that Captain Collins surrendered his own judgment and his own better instincts to the guidance of Mr. Consul Wilson, and was thus led to perpetrate a great wrong. If he had only waited a few days he could have followed the *Florida*, or gone in company with her to sea, and he would have had the opportunity to place his name on a level with Winslow's. The *Sumter, Georgia,* and *Shenandoah* were clearly unfit for offensive warfare. They were ordinary merchant vessels, armed sufficiently to overawe, and if need be to overcome any threat of resistance from commercial ships, and perhaps to beat off the attack of one of the converted vessels of the United States navy, but manifestly unequal to cope with the weakest of the gunboats of the regular United States marine. The commanders of all the above-named ships, to use a sporting phrase, were "heavily handicapped" in the race for purely naval honours, and yet I may venture to say that they shrank from no exposure and no risk, which they would have been justified in seeking, and as they manifested on all occasions a degree of fortitude, sagacity, and professional skill proportionate to the trial, it may fairly be inferred that they had in reserve sufficient stored-up strength and ability to have made a creditable use of better means and broader opportunities.

The object in getting as many cruisers at sea as possible, and at the earliest time after the beginning of hostilities, was, as has been previously stated, twofold. Primarily the purpose was to destroy the enemy's commerce, and thus to increase the burden of the war upon a large and influential class at the North, and the collateral purposes were to compel the United States Navy Department to send many of their best ships abroad for the pursuit of the Confederate cruisers, and to increase their naval expenditure, which it was thought would tend to weaken the blockade, retard the preparation for attack upon exposed portions of the Southern coast, and also to add largely to the aggregate cost of carrying on the war.

The foregoing expectations were not wholly realized. The United States Navy Department did not send many nor the most suitable vessels in pursuit of the Confederate cruisers, and, strange to say, instead of consulting Maury's charts and the Chambers of Commerce of the large shipping ports, from whom the precise localities where American trade would most require protection, and where the attacking cruisers would be sure to go, would best have been gathered, the protecting ships were left to make passages from port to port in a purposeless sort of way, often arriving a day too late or departing a day too soon to meet the objects of their search.

It appears from the proceedings before the Tribunal of Arbitration at Geneva that the United States set up a claim against Great Britain for the cost of maintaining at sea the vessels that it was found necessary to send in pursuit of the Confederate cruisers. Among the vessels alleged to have been employed for the above purpose, were "the *Onward,* of 874 tons, the *Ino,* of 895 tons, converted merchant vessels without steam-power, also the *Gemsbok, National Guard,* and *Sheppard Knapp,* and finally the *George Mangham,* a mortar (sailing) schooner of 274 tons."* It is hardly necessary to say that no Confederate cruiser that was sent to sea during the war would have been driven from her work by any such vessels; indeed, even the converted ships, such as the *Georgia* and *Shenandoah,* would have liked no better fun than to have encountered them in couplets or even triplets. Even the *Vanderbilt,* wholly dependent on her engines, and requiring, as it appears from the record, 2,000 tons of coal in little more than six weeks, was a most unsuitable ship to send upon such service, besides which, her extreme vulnerability was palpably against her. The crowns of her huge boilers, the cylinders, condensers, and almost all the working parts of her engines, were far above the water-line, and her two great "walking beams," with their ponderous connecting rods, stood many feet above her upper deck. All of the foregoing were exposed to shot, and the space they occupied was so large that she could only have escaped being disabled by a mere chance, before she could have closed with either the *Alabama* or *Florida.* I feel bound, however, to mention that the Secretary of the United States Navy, in a report dated December 7th, 1863, announces in effect that the protection of the foreign commerce of the country was not thought to be of such paramount importance as the sealing up of the Southern ports, for he says that even if the probabilities of encountering the Confederate cruisers "were greater than they are ... it would not promote the interests of commerce nor the welfare of the country to relax the blockade for that object."†

It was of course open to the United States to adopt whatever war policy they thought best, but it must have required some boldness, or some obliquity of vision in regard to the fitness of things, to claim compensation for maintaining such wretchedly inappropriate craft as are mentioned above for the purpose of pursuing the *Alabama* and her consorts.

When the determination to attack the commerce of the United States was settled by the Confederate Government as a leading purpose of its policy, efforts were promptly made to carry it out. The only suitable ship remaining in the Confederate ports was secured, fitted out, and despatched from New Orleans, and an agent was sent to Europe to obtain proper

---

* See "British Counter-Case," pp. 139, 140; also "Appendix to British Case," vol. vii., pp. 58, 63, 111.

† Quoted in "British Counter-Case," p. 140.

vessels for the same purpose. The particulars of the necessary proceedings to carry out the above-mentioned policy have already been narrated, but the *Sumter* was hardly at sea, and the agent had scarcely reached the field of his operations in England, before it became manifest that there was pressing need of a naval force to defend the numerous inlets which penetrate the Southern coast, and to protect those harbours which could be used for blockade-running. To provide the vessels for those necessary purposes the Navy Department was compelled to rely upon such means as were close at hand, and the poverty of the country was at once revealed. The United States possessed all the resources, machine-shops, and skilled labour necessary to quickly prepare vessels suitable for operating on the Southern coast. There were four national dockyards, and large supplies of materials at each, and at certainly three of the principal Northern seaports there were private shipbuilders, quite capable of undertaking almost any description of Government work. It is hardly necessary to add that there were many machine-shops, cannon-foundries, and powder-mills in the Northern States, and there was also an ample supply of coal and iron. These are patent facts, and need no proof. The Navy Department of the United States had then at its command everything that could be desired, or at any rate, all that was really indispensable for the construction and equipment of any description of vessels which ingenuity and experience suggested as best suited for blockade, for attacks upon the Southern coast defences, or for operations in the shallow sounds and inlets which penetrate the shores of nearly every State from Virginia to Texas. The utter destitution of the South, both as regards materials and the means to make use of them, has already been explained in a previous chapter. There was but one public dockyard, which, however, the Federal forces had greatly injured before abandoning it, and there was not a single private yard fit to undertake work of any importance. There was but one foundry, the Tredegar Works, at Richmond, capable of casting a large gun, and that was the only establishment where forgings of any importance could be effected. Everyone knows that the South was destitute of iron, and the supply of coal was limited in quantity and poor in quality.

The Confederate Government appears to have had no difficulty in learning the general purposes of the enemy, and it was soon known that Monitors and other descriptions of iron-cased vessels were building at the North, and that the foundries were turning out 11-inch and 15-inch guns for their armament. It was impossible to build any vessels wholly of iron at the South, because, in the first place, the necessary material was wanting, and secondly, there was no machinery or appliances for manufacturing angle iron, or bending frames, etc. All the Confederate Navy Department could do was to select the points least accessible to the enemy or which could be most surely defended, and then lay down wooden vessels, which could be cased with iron afterwards. It was necessary to use green timber, because there were no stored-up supplies, but that would not have been of much consequence if the vessels could have been quickly built and otherwise prepared for service. The necessities of the situation demanded quick completion, and not durability of structure. But while the materials were faulty, and the suitable places for laying down the ships were few, there was no compensation in the ability to make speed with the work, because of the scarcity of skilled labour.

I have not the documentary records necessary to give a systematic account of all that was attempted, but the very best vessels which it was possible to complete were mere make-shifts. They were plated either with layers of thin iron, insufficiently bolted, or with ordinary railway metals; and the difficulty of bending the plates and rails and fashioning the timber backing compelled a resort to the weakest forms of structure, both as regards the power to resist shot and to secure small openings for ports. But the inefficiency of the vessels in respect to strength and suitability of design was still further increased by the want of sufficient motive-power to admit of their being properly manœuvred.

Two or three examples will suffice to demonstrate the unhandiness of the miserable make-shift vessels which were provided for the defence of the most important points. The *Tennessee* was built at Mobile,* and was the mainstay of the defences at that harbour. She was an unwieldy structure, the armoured portion being a citadel 79 feet by 29 feet inside of the backing, which was composed of timber and plank 25 inches thick. The citadel was constructed with a sloping roof, having an inclination of thirty degrees; and the iron casing was composed of 2-inch and 1-inch plates laid on to the thickness of 6 inches, decreasing in some places to 5 inches. The vessel herself was 209 feet by 48 feet beam, and her draft of water was 14 feet. The armament was composed of six 6- and 7-inch cast-iron guns, which had been rifled and strengthened by shrinking wrought-iron bands upon the breech sections. This vessel, unshapely in design, and not over-strong either for defence or attack, might nevertheless have made a formidable, perhaps even a successful, resistance to the entrance of Admiral Farragut's fleet into Mobile if she had been provided with a pair of pow-

---

* The wooden hull was built at Selma, 150 miles up the Alabama river, and she was towed to Mobile to receive her plating, engines, and equipment.

erful engines working twin screws; but her power of locomotion consisted of the paddle-engine of an ordinary river steamer, which by an ingenious contrivance was made to work the screw-shaft, but it was quite inadequate to manœuvre the ship efficiently, and she had therefore neither the speed nor the ability to reverse quickly which are so essential in an armoured vessel with a fixed battery and designed to be used also as a ram.

Two vessels of formidable dimensions and design were laid down at New Orleans, but, in spite of the greatest exertions, only one was so far finished as to be able to take part in the defence of the river. The name of the one nearly completed was the *Louisiana*. She was hurried down to the neighbourhood of Forts Jackson and St. Philip three days before Admiral Farragut's successful attempt to force the passage, but she was in very poor condition to offer any effective resistance. She had a central "casemate," or citadel, for the protection of the battery, and was cased with a covering of double T-rails, as a substitute for plates, which could not be obtained. The iron-casing was not completed when she left New Orleans. Her engines being still unconnected, two tugs were employed to tow her down, and gangs of mechanics were still at work upon engines and hull while she was thus in tow. The crew were chiefly raw hands, reinforced by a company of artillerymen who had volunteered for the occasion; and they were actually mounting the battery while *en route* for the scene of battle. Up to an hour before the Federal fleet advanced to the attack she had not motive-power to stem the current; indeed, it was found impossible to shift her berth or to wind her under steam, and as a last necessity she was lashed to the shore under Fort St. Philip, in which position she could only use a part of her guns.*

Two armour-cased vessels were built at Charleston. After many months of hard work they were got ready for service; but in their case, as in most of the others, the engines were the chief defect, and proved upon actual trial too weak, and otherwise unfit to manœuvre the vessels efficiently. They were, nevertheless, taken out of the harbour one night, and dispersed the blockading ships; but, owing to insufficient steam-power, they were unable to pursue, and one of them was barely able to get back to a safe anchorage in the harbour.

The *Arkansas,* another Confederate iron-cased ram, deserves a passing notice. She was built at Memphis, and when nearly finished was taken up

---

* The consort of the *Louisiana* was in such an incomplete state that she could not be used for the defence of the river at all, and she was destroyed after the Federal fleet passed the forts.

the Yazoo River for greater safety, and was there completed. On the 15th of July, 1862, she dashed out of the Yazoo into the Mississippi, dispersed three Federal "ironclads" who tried to block the way, and passing through Admiral Farragut's fleet, which lay directly in her route, receiving the broadside of nearly every ship at point-blank range, she escaped unharmed, and let go her anchor under the batteries of Vicksburgh. On the 5th of August following, she attempted to go down the river to co-operate with General Breckenridge in an attack upon Baton Rouge; but the engines, always the weakest point in these unhappy vessels, gave way, and not only caused the failure of the expedition, but the loss of the *Arkansas* herself. A short distance above Baton Rouge her port engine broke down, but was got in fair working order. She was compelled to lay at anchor all night to effect the repairs, and the next morning she got under weigh, and soon met the Federal "ironclad" *Essex,* which, with other gunboats, was approaching to attack her. At this critical moment the starboard engine gave way, and the patched-up port engine proved wholly powerless to control her movements. The unfortunate craft was thus rendered helpless and unmanageable, and the officer in command, Lieutenant Henry K. Stevens, found himself face to face with one of two alternatives, the destruction of his vessel by himself, or her capture by the enemy. He chose the former, and he succeeded by great efforts and clever expedients in landing her upon the river bank, where he set her on fire, and she burned to the water's edge and blew up, although every effort was made by the enemy to secure her.* The enemy's gunboats perceived that something was wrong with the *Arkansas,* and had opened fire upon her before Stevens succeeded in placing her against the bank, but he effected his purpose and escaped with his officers and crew.

I have selected for examples the very best of the iron-cased vessels the Navy Department was able to construct within the Confederate States, and it will be admitted that they were a very inefficient means of defence against the well-equipped, well-manned, well-armed, and powerfully engined vessels of the United States navy.

Admiral Farragut appears to have had a deep-rooted and ineradicable dislike, and even contempt, for "ironclads," and his feelings in regard to them are often expressed in language which is both vigorous and comical. Writing from Pensacola, August 21st, 1862, he says:—"We have no dread of 'rams' or 'he-goats,' and if our editors had less, the country would be better off. Now they scare everybody to death." Again, September 3rd,

---

* "Life of Admiral D. G. Farragut," p. 289.

commenting upon an order he had received from Washington to destroy the *Arkansas* "at all hazards," he says:—"I would have given my Admiral's commission to have gotten up to the *Arkansas*. I wanted a wooden ship to do it. The ironclads are cowardly things, and I don't want them to succeed in the world." But notwithstanding the above opinions, her destruction drew from him the following remark in a report to the Secretary of the Navy:—"It is the happiest moment of my life that I am enabled to inform the Department of the destruction of the ram *Arkansas*, not because I held the ironclad in such terror, but because the community did."* The fact is, that with the gallant Admiral ignorance, or perhaps I should say inexperience, in regard to the power of a really efficient armoured vessel, was at the bottom of his blissful indifference.

It is certainly no vainglorious boast, but the mere expression of a professional opinion founded upon some knowledge of the structure of such vessels, which impels me to say that if the two Liverpool rams which Earl Russell detained at the request of Mr. Adams had been off Sand Island Light in August, 1864, the United States fleet would not have got into Mobile Bay, or if two similar vessels had been at the head of the passes of the Mississippi in April, 1862, no naval force then at the disposal of the United States could have passed up to the Crescent City. Admiral Farragut never encountered an ironclad fit for the proper work of her class. The *Tennessee* was so deficient in steam-power that she could neither be used efficiently as a ram nor avoid being rammed by the attacking ship. The diagram annexed to the plan of the naval engagement in Mobile Bay represents the *Tennessee* with a Monitor and three wooden ships, one bearing the Admiral's flag, ramming her on the port side, and a Monitor in a raking position under her stern. Admiral Farragut says "she was sore beset," and "we butted and shot at him until he surrendered."† No professional man will doubt that if the *Tennessee* had been a properly constructed ironclad, with engine-power suited to her size and weight, she would have made short work of her wooden adversaries. But she was well-nigh helpless as regards ability to manœuvre, and her consorts were three insignificant little wooden craft, not fit to be classed as fighting ships for line-of-battle at all.

When the Secretary of the Confederate Navy and his professional advisers perceived the necessity of providing vessels for harbour and coast defences, their first perplexity was the selection of suitable sites for building

* "Life of Admiral D. G. Farragut," pp. 289, 293, 294.
† "Life and Letters," pp. 423, 433.

them. Even such ports as Savannah, Charleston, Mobile, and New Orleans, which offered the greatest facilities, were so poorly protected by fortifications that for at least six months after President Lincoln's proclamation of blockade they were at the mercy of the United States navy. I have not the least hesitation in saying that up to January and February, 1862, both Savannah and Wilmington could have been entered by the Federal vessels then blockading them. The foregoing opinion is based upon a personal inspection of the defensive works, and close daily examination of the ships off the ports, with good glasses, which enabled me to clearly determine their class and effective strength, and in some instances to identify particular vessels. The great sounds and estuaries which abound along the Southern coast were wholly indefensible by any means in the power of the Confederate Government, and several large rivers, upon which building-yards might have been and in fact were established, afforded access to Federal vessels ascending from the sea, and others, taking their rise within the territory held by the United States, afforded equal facilities for the descent of the enemy's gunboats, which his command of labour and material enabled him quickly to complete.

Blockaded and threatened by the way of the sea, liable to attack through numerous inlets and navigable watercourses, and open to invasion along many hundreds of miles of defenceless frontier, it was manifestly a difficult and perplexing problem to determine how the enemy could be held aloof from the very heart of the country, and from the localities where vessels could be built so as to be safe from hostile attacks before completion, or to be within possible reach of the coast when finished. By midsummer, 1861, some twelve or fifteen wooden gunboats were laid down on York river and the Pamunky in Virginia, and others were contracted for at New Orleans, on the St. John's river in Florida, at Richmond, Norfolk, Charleston, Savannah, and the Chatahoochee. Afterwards additional vessels were started at Memphis and Nashville. The foregoing were not intended to be armoured, but after the achievements of the *Merrimac* in Hampton Roads, every possible exertion was made to build ironcased vessels at Charleston, Savannah, Wilmington, Richmond, and on the inland waters of Alabama, Georgia, and the Carolinas.

Many of the vessels, while in course of construction, were destroyed to prevent their capture by the enemy, and in other cases they were hurried off in very incomplete condition to safer retreats. Thus all of those building on the York and Pamunky rivers were burned when General Johnston was forced back upon Richmond by the advancing columns of General McClellan, whose flanks were covered by naval flotillas on the James river and on the York. Two were lost by the capture of Nashville; others, being still on the ways, were necessarily destroyed when Norfolk was evacuated, and one (the *Arkansas*) was hurried up the Yazoo river in an incomplete state, as already mentioned above.

It will thus be perceived that the effort to build a naval force within the Confederacy was attended with many difficulties. The progress of the work was often checked, and often wholly interrupted by the imminent danger of attack, and the labour and expenditure of months was sacrificed, sometimes, as in the case of the two formidable vessels at New Orleans, when they were nearly ready for effective use. For the equipment of the home-built ships it was necessary to construct and to organize ordnance works, laboratories, and machine-shops, and establishments of the kind were improvised under great difficulties at Richmond, Charlotte in North Carolina, Atlanta in Georgia, and Selma in Alabama. Those points were selected because they were well in the interior, and were thus as safe as possible from the danger of sudden attack and destruction; but that essential advantage was not free from a counterbalancing inconvenience, in the circumstance that they were far removed from the building sites, and every piece of machinery, and every gun, however heavy and difficult to handle, had to be transported many miles along railways already overworked by the necessary transportation of supplies for the army, or, in some cases, even by ordinary country roads.

The officers of the Confederate navy had so few opportunities to manifest their professional acquirements and personal qualities—indeed, so few of them were employed in strictly naval operations at all—that scarcely more than some half-dozen will find their names recorded in any future history, and the Confederate navy as a corps will hardly appear as a factor in the Civil War. And yet I may venture to say that among those who held the naval commissions of President Davis, were men who would have dared anything, and who would have won a place in history, and made their short-lived service famous, if they had only possessed the materials to work with, and the opportunity to use them. I would not fear to put that proposition to the surviving officers of the United States navy who are old enough to have known and who still remember their former colleagues, and I would deposit a large stake on the result of the ballot. It would be neither generous nor judicious—I feel that it would not be even just in me—to thrust too prominently forward the names of those officers who came under my personal observation under trying conditions, and in whom I had the opportunity to discover distinguished fitness for naval enterprises. My purpose is to manifest a just appreciation of the merits and services of every officer whom it is necessary to mention by name, but to avoid every expression of praise that may approach to personal panegyric.

The Confederate navy had great disappointments to bear, and speaking of the corps collectively, it may be fairly said that they bore the trial patiently. At first there was some little strife about the adjustment of rank, but it soon ended, and every man submitted uncomplainingly to the necessities of the situation, and officers who were fit to direct squadrons, and to conduct important operations, were content to command paltry flotillas of converted river-craft, or hastily and imperfectly constructed gunboats, poorly armed, and with manifestly insufficient motive-power. With such wretchedly inadequate means they had to meet powerful ships of modern construction, armed with guns of the newest and best type, conscious alike of the hopelessness of the struggle and the impossibility of achieving the least personal renown.

It requires a high degree of moral courage for a military or naval officer to undertake an absolutely necessary service, when his professional knowledge and experience assure him that the enterprise contains no element of success, and when he is conscious that the inevitable failure will bring upon him the disparaging criticisms, and often the hostile censure, of an expectant but unreasoning public. Such were the conditions under which Hollins attempted to block the river-route to island No. 10, and Mitchell the passes of the lower Mississippi; and Tattnall, Lynch, Buchanan, and Richard L. Page undertook to defend the great North Carolina Sounds, and the water approaches to Charleston, Savannah, and Mobile, under equally depressing circumstances. Those men and their brother officers generally submitted to the personal mortification of defeat with dignified composure, and at the end of the war they retired to private life, and in many cases to a hard and precarious struggle for maintenance, with a degree of patient acquiescence which was creditable to their manhood.

I have never heard a single ex-Confederate officer speak disparagingly of the achievements of his former colleagues who remained in the United States navy and who rose to rank and fortune in consequence of the war, and I have never met one who appeared to be ashamed of his own position, whether, like gallant old Tattnall, he was employed as inspector of the port of Savannah on the modest stipend of $1,200 a year, or serving out tea and sugar from behind the counter of a general grocer, as some I know have done. It is probable that there are still many persons who deny both the expediency and equity of "secession." There may be some cantankerous spirits who still maintain that "traitor" and "rebel" are appropriate epithets to apply to those officers whose hearts and consciences impelled them to surrender place and fortune for the sake of a principle; but I will hazard the opinion, that all who are capable of justly estimating the difference between honour and shame will admit that if the Confederate naval service has no brilliant victories to record, and gained no purely naval honours, it has manifested in its reverses qualities which are essential ingredients of genuine heroism. Success was not within its grasp, but the failure was not ignominious. The allotted duty was perilous, and the effort was unavailing. The defeat was decisive, and the immediate consequences were crushing, but the courage which sustained the shock of battle has been supplemented by the patient fortitude necessary to endure the calamity, and thus the effect of the sting has been greatly soothed.

The selection of suitable building sites for vessels, and safe positions for laboratories and machine-shops, was only the initiatory work of preparing a local marine force. The materials had to be brought to the manufacturing points, chiefly in the raw state, and to a great extent absolutely in the condition of their primitive elements. At the Norfolk Navy Yard there was fortunately a considerable number of naval guns of varying calibres, and there was also a moderate quantity of shot and shell; and the powder-magazine, with its contents, was saved through the exertions of a few Virginian naval officers who had resigned their commissions in the United States service, but had not yet been commissioned in that of the Confederacy. Those officers organized a party which removed a great portion of the powder, and showed such a determination to resist any attempt to damage the remainder or to injure the building, that when the dockyard was partially destroyed and evacuated by the United States naval forces at the time of the secession of Virginia, they left the magazine intact.

But the guns thus saved were almost exclusively of the old smoothbore type and pattern, and were not therefore fit to be pitted against the modern Dahlgren, Parrot, and other ordnance with which the wooden ships and the newly constructed Monitors and ironclad gun-vessels of the United States navy were armed.

The Confederate Navy Department was happy in the selection of the officers to organize and administer its ordnance branch. At first the only possible resource was to utilize the old guns found in stock. The material of those guns was fortunately good, and generally they were heavy in proportion to their calibre. Some of them were rifled without enlargement of bore, others were reamed up to larger calibres and then rifled, and all, when thus prepared, were strengthened with wrought-iron bands shrunk on between the breech and trunnions. It was then necessary to provide elongated shot, shell, fuzes, sights, and other delicate equipments, all of which had to be designed and manufactured quickly, with indifferent means, and without the possibility of submitting them to the tests of careful experiment and comparison. I feel sure that the naval officers employed in the Ordnance Bureau will not object to my selecting Commander John M. Brooke for special mention in connection with that department of the service. The fact that his name was given to the improvised ordnance of the Confederate navy is at once a testimony to the value of his efforts, and a justification for the very imperfect tribute to his zeal and intelligence I have it in my power to put on record. Whatever serious injury the Confederate gunboats or iron-cased vessels were able to inflict upon the enemy's ships was effected with the "Brooke gun," and the large orders for ordnance stores which were sent to Europe, and which passed in due course of business through my hands, bore the stamp of his sagacious judgment and discreet supervision.

But notwithstanding the utmost efforts of those on the spot, and the most ingenious devices, the home resources proved insufficient for the equipment of the vessels built within the Confederacy. It soon became manifest that the most essential articles could only be obtained in the necessary quantity abroad, and the finances of the Navy Department were never able to wholly, or even at times promptly, supply the demands of the service within the Confederacy, and the drain of the ocean cruisers and the general European undertakings as well. The shifts to which the Confederate Government were compelled to resort in the effort to equip their military and naval forces were exceptional and peculiar, but the consequences of putting off the preparation for war until hostilities are imminent were so clearly demonstrated by the events of 1861–65, that no statesmen who have given due attention to the progress and result of the American Civil War will be inclined to run the risk of a great future peril for the sake of a present show of economy.

Geographical position, climatic and other physical causes, made the Southern States almost exclusively agricultural in their habits and industries, and although the people were martial in their instincts, and furnished a due quota of officers for the military and naval services of the Federal Union, yet it is well known that the principal Government factories for arms of all kinds, and the principal arsenals for the storage and preservation of the war material of the country, were in the Northern States. Some years before the war, the small arms had been removed from the arsenals at the South to Springfield and other national gun-factories at the North, for the purpose of being converted into a more modern type, and at the date of the outbreak of hostilities a large portion of them had not been returned. The great cannon foundries and powder-mills were also at the North, and hence the accumulation of war material of every kind had always been far greater in that section of the country than in the other.

So long as the States were in friendly harmony and in close national union, the foregoing arrangement did not appear to be dangerous or especially inconvenient, because in case of a foreign war and the probability of invasion, both arms and munitions could be rapidly distributed. The Southern States retired from the Union singly and at intervals. None of them applied for their quota of arms at the time of their secession, and probably would not have received them if they had done so, and hostilities began so soon after the formation of a Southern Confederacy and a general Government (which at first was only provisional), that there was no time to make ready. The foregoing is, in brief, the only explanation which can be given of the seeming fatuity of the South in venturing upon a great war without due, or indeed without any, preparation.

The destitution was not the result of unwise parsimony in the past administration of public affairs, nor wilful apathy on the part of those who were suddenly summoned to manage them. The position was simply this: a close and confidential partnership was suddenly and violently dissolved, and the assets of the firm remained chiefly in the possession of one of the partners.

When I was first sent to England in May, 1861, the Secretary of the Navy directed me to buy, and forward with prompt despatch, a very considerable quantity of naval supplies, but the most pressing and immediate want at that time appeared to be arms and ammunition, and the original orders were almost exclusively limited to those articles. As soon as the determination to build gunboats at the home ports and on the inland waters was put into active operation, it became necessary to take a more comprehensive view of the wants of the service, and it was at once perceived that the vessels could not be suitably equipped without largely supplementing the home supply of every article essential to the outfit and maintenance of a fighting ship. Orders were at once sent to me in England for every description of naval stores, including such articles as submarine batteries and wire, accoutrements for marines, clothing, blankets, iron in every form required for ship-building, tools, and skilled mechanics to use them, small marine engines for torpedo-boats, powerful marine engines for ironclad gunboats, and, in addition, large requisitions for special ordnance stores, according to lists and specifications especially drawn up by Commander Brooke. The last-mentioned included many articles of delicate, or at least nice mechanical design, and careful supervision and inspection was necessary to ensure exact and satisfactory perfection of finish, both in workmanship and material.

Among the officers sent to Europe for service in the ironclad vessels it was hoped might be got to sea was Lieutenant William H. Murdaugh. Besides having the special experience and general professional knowledge which fitted him for ordnance work, he possessed admirable tact and judgment, and also the reticence and faculty of self-control which are essential for the satisfactory performance of duties requiring secrecy. The special ordnance stores were nearly all overlooked and certified by him. The whole of the work was performed creditably, and the goods passed out of the manufacturer's hands, and went through the shipping-ports without attracting notice or causing any embarrassing scrutiny. The execution of the foregoing special orders brought Lieutenant Murdaugh into constant and confidential communication with me, and I was most desirous to appoint him to another and still more important service, but the war came to an abrupt end just before the maturity of the enterprise in which he was to have had a leading part.

The orders for general naval supplies arrived in England at a time when the contracts for the cruising ships were in full operation, and they alone would have absorbed more than all the visible financial resources of the Navy Department. But the excessive demand for war material occasioned by the wants of both belligerents, coming unexpectedly even upon so ample a market as that of Great Britain, rendered it impossible to execute the orders *en bloc*—in fact, the requisitions followed each other and were cumulative, hence it was both admissible and prudent, as a matter of economy, to make forward contracts providing for a steady periodical delivery of the goods.

The earliest remittances from the Navy Department were made in the form of bank credits and sterling bills, and they were not accompanied with any explanation of the means by which they would be continued. It was manifest that the supply of sterling and the accumulation of private funds in the hands of British bankers would soon be exhausted, and the Confederate Treasury would be compelled to devise some other means of making the Appropriation Bills passed by Congress available in Europe. The shoe soon began to pinch. Under date of April 30th, 1862, the Secretary of the Navy, discussing the contracts on account of his Department, wrote thus:—"I have placed about $1,000,000 to your credit with Messrs. Fraser, Trenholm and Co., for these objects, and hope to increase the amount to $2,000,000 soon." The above was in addition to the remittances in sterling previously mentioned. In reply to the financial portion of the foregoing letter, I reported under date of July 4th, 1862, as follows:—"The credit of your Department is thus far very sound, as I have been able to pay all liabilities very promptly. There is a double advantage in basing all transactions upon cash payments—work is more quickly done, and you have the benefit of a liberal discount. In some of my contracts the discount for cash has been as high as ten per cent. The contracts alluded to in the cypher are for a very large amount, but not so large as the sum mentioned in your letter of April 30th, which you inform me will be put to my credit with Messrs. Fraser, Trenholm and Co. for the specific purposes referred to in that letter. With the various incidental expenses attending such contracts, and the cost of what you are well aware must be the necessary adjuncts, the entire amount mentioned in your letter would be absorbed, and I sincerely hope the remittances will be regular and ample. I feel called upon to say, however, that money appropriated in Richmond is very much reduced in amount when converted into pounds, shillings, and pence, by the high rate of exchange, and that to complete the outstanding contracts will require £390,000 (three hundred and ninety thousand pounds)."

Before the above letter reached Richmond the Secretary of the Navy had been fully aroused to the importance of keeping up the supply of funds, and the correspondence manifests that he laboured earnestly to that end. The Confederate Congress was liberal in voting money grants, as was manifested in the appropriation of $10,000,000 to the Navy Department "for building ironclad vessels in Southern Europe." I have never heard that the votes asked for by either of the fighting Departments were ever cut down or refused. But it was one thing to have a vote of credit, and quite another to make that credit available for use in Europe. The manner of proceeding at the beginning of the war, and until the latter part of 1863, was as follows:—Congress appropriated certain sums in gross for the building of ships and the purchase of naval supplies, which could only be procured abroad. The Secretary of the Navy made requisitions upon the Treasury for the amount of the appropriations, and received in payment Treasury notes, which were available for all local purposes, but could not be used in their original form for purchases abroad. He was therefore compelled to devise some means for converting the Treasury notes into foreign funds, and the only course open to him after the supply of sterling was exhausted was to buy cotton and other produce, and ship them through the blockade to the Government bankers, Messrs. Fraser, Trenholm and Co., whose instructions were to place the net proceeds to the credit of the representative of the Navy Department in Europe.

The War Office at Richmond included several distinct Bureaux, designated by the titles of "Ordnance," "Provision and Clothing," "Medical," "Nitre," etc.; and the funds of that Department were apportioned between those several Bureaux, and credited to each specifically in the books of Messrs. Fraser, Trenholm and Co. There was a corresponding division of offices in the Navy Department also; but the Secretary of the Navy at a very early date adopted the view that it would be more convenient to keep the whole of the financial resources appropriated for naval uses abroad in the form of a general credit on behalf of the representative of that Department, and Messrs. Fraser, Trenholm and Co. were instructed to open an account with me, and to place the proceeds of the cotton shipped for account of the navy to my credit. In advising me of the foregoing arrangement, Mr. Mallory instructed me to keep the accounts of the several Bureaux separate, and to charge each with the specific expenditure on its behalf; but he explained that his object was to relieve me from the very possible embarrassment of receiving an order for supplies at a time when there might be no funds to the credit of the special Bureaux to which the order referred, and I would have to wait for authority to make the necessary transfer. This arrangement was a bold departure from the customary "red-tape" of departmental routine; but as the Secretary of the Navy had been a participator in revolutionizing the Government of the United States, he did not shrink from originating a minor revolution in the mere matter of official book-keeping.

At any rate, the arrangement worked satisfactorily. I never had the least trouble with the accounts, while my colleague of the War Department was often forced to make complicated arrangements with the bankers, and sometimes to assume grave responsibilities in pledging the credit of the Government, while waiting for instructions to use the surplus funds of one Bureau to meet the deficit of another. The anxiety of Mr. Mallory on the subject of providing and maintaining the "ways and means" was clearly and strongly manifested in his correspondence. Under date of September 20th, 1862, he wrote thus:—

"Since then (namely, the date of my last report), I have endeavoured to place in your hands the balance of the funds required for your operations, but the exchange of the country is nearly exhausted, and can only be procured in very small amounts.... Cotton goes out in but very small lots, and this, our only source for obtaining exchange, cannot meet a tenth part of our wants. It is evident to me, therefore, that we cannot rely upon exchange for placing you in funds, and that other means must be resorted to. If the agent of the Treasury Department can dispose of Confederate Bonds, even at fifty cents, he will do so; and he is instructed in this event to pay your requisitions upon him, to enable you to complete your contracts. Another suggestion occurs to me which you may act upon. You may possibly be able to obtain advances upon our agreement to repay the amount with eight per cent. interest in cotton, the question of the price of the cotton to be determined when the advances are made; and this price may be stated, or you may agree to deliver the cotton at the current rates here when called for. You might offer another proposition, viz., that the amount of all advances made to you will be expended here by the Treasury Department in the purchase of cotton on account of the creditor, he being allowed the difference of exchange between Richmond and London. Cotton thus purchased would be stored by the Treasury, and kept with all the care and diligence which the legal consequences of such a contract would involve, and transportation to the sea-ports and all facilities of shipment would be extended, none but the necessary expenses incident to such storage and shipment being required. Cotton thus purchased would be regarded and treated as the property of the British creditor.... Do not permit our credit in Great Britain to suffer, if by any legal act, or the exercise of all your energy, you can avert it."

In addition to the foregoing, the Navy Department sent out large amounts in Confederate Bonds, with the necessary authority to negotiate them, or to use them in any possible way. It was found, however, that sending bonds to different parties did not work satisfactorily. Even the *bonâ fide* agents of the Government, each desirous to use them to the best possible advantage for his own special purposes, became practically competitors one with the other.

The agents abroad perceived and reported the consequences of this unavoidable competition. The authorities at Richmond recognised the unsatisfactory character of the practice, even before the reports from abroad were received, and in September, 1863, the Hon. J. P. Benjamin, being then the Secretary of State, drew up a scheme which provided for a special fiscal agent, who should be empowered to deal exclusively with all bonds. The various heads of departments agreed to the arrangement; each agent was directed to surrender all bonds in his possession to the fiscal agent, General C. J. McRae, who was instructed to negotiate them, and to distribute the proceeds *pro rata* among the special agents.

The first efforts to ship cotton to Europe on Government account were attended with great difficulty and delay. The ships engaged in the blockade trade were owned exclusively by private firms who wanted the whole of the freight space for their own account. The few steamers bought by the Navy Department within the Confederacy would have been fit for voyages to Bermuda and the Bahamas, but they were absolutely required for the defence of the home ports and rivers, and had already been armed and assigned to that service. Nevertheless, the Navy Department managed to export the staples in quantities which would have been thought large if they had been made on private account. On the 29th of December, 1863, the Secretary wrote me as follows:—"Up to this date thirty-one hundred bales of cotton have been shipped from Charleston and Wilmington *via* Bermuda and Nassau, to go thence to Messrs. Fraser, Trenholm, and Co., to your credit, and shipments are now being made nearly every week. I have not sufficient information from our agents at the other ports to enable me to advise you of the whole number of bales they have shipped, but I have reason to know that the losses by capture have been inconsiderable." At a subsequent date he wrote me thus:—"Twelve thousand bales have been purchased by this Department ... and will go forward as rapidly as the limited means of transportation will admit."

The Secretary of the Navy wrote so often and so strongly in reference to the difficulty of placing funds in Europe, that I ventured to suggest, as early as January, 1863, that the Government should "have its own fleet of packets to ply direct, and thus escape the killing freights on private steamers." Invited by the Secretary of the Navy to communicate freely and to make suggestions on that important subject without hesitation, I wrote him in October, 1863, as follows:—

"I learn from Mr. Charles K. Prioleau that since the beginning of the war 100,000 bales of cotton have been run through the blockade on account of various mercantile houses, and this lucrative trade not only continues, but arrangements are now in progress to enlarge it. At present prices, 100,000 bales of cotton would yield nearly double the net amount of the proceeds of the Erlanger Loan, and it would seem not only advisable, but absolutely necessary, for the Government to take the trade into its own hands. Southern merchants would be deterred by patriotic feelings from complaining of such an interference with their customary traffic, and those foreigners who have already made abundant profits would have neither right nor reason to murmur. An agent of your Department in the regular receipt of cotton, even though in moderate quantities, would have an established credit, and could extend his operations with a feeling of confidence.... If we could accumulate a considerable supply here, the Government through its mercantile agent would not only rule the market, but important political influences might be brought to bear."

Replying again to the inquiries of the Department in reference to financial matters, I wrote on November 25th, 1863:—

· "Undoubtedly the most tangible and most readily available source of money supply is the cotton itself, and although the risk of capture is great, and the cost of transportation heavy, the profit is so large that this mode of remittance offers the surest and speediest return, besides being eventually the least burdensome to the country. I feel justified, therefore, in urging the expediency of sending out cotton as rapidly as possible, and, if you think proper, I can build two or three fast light-draught paddle-steamers to do the work between the Confederate States and the islands, so that you might control all the shipments for your own Department, both ways.

"This would be a good operation in any event. A successful voyage or two would pay for the ships, and if built to order and properly constructed, they would be well suited to the coasting trade, and in the event of peace would meet a ready sale.... The vessels now under construction by builders, and those lately finished for blockade-running, are hurriedly put together, and are too light for long wear and tear, but in five months staunch and really serviceable ships could be built, and if your view of the probable duration of the war would justify looking that much ahead, I respectfully recommend the above proposition to your consideration."

Again I wrote:—

"If the Navy Department would take the blockade-running business into its own hands, it might soon have a fleet of formidable swift light-draught steamers at work, so constructed as to have their engines and boilers well protected either by coal when the bunkers were full, or cotton when they were empty. The beams and decks of the steamers could be made of sufficient strength to bear heavy deck loads without exciting suspicion, and then, if registered in the name of private individuals, and sailed purely as commercial ships, they could trade without interruption or violation of neutrality between our coast and the Bermudas, Bahamas, and West Indies. When two or three of the vessels happened to be in harbour at the same time, a few hours would suffice to mount a couple of heavy guns on each, and at night, or at early dawn, a successful 'raid' might be made upon the unsuspecting blockaders. From time to time two or three of them might be filled with coal, and sent out for short cruises off Hatteras and in the Gulf of Mexico, from Mobile, to pick up transports, etc. After a raid or cruise, the vessels could be divested of every appliance of war, and resuming their private ownership and commercial names, could bring out cargoes of cotton to pay the expenses of the cruise, or to increase the funds of the Government abroad. Such operations are not impracticable, and if vigorously carried on without notice, and at irregular periods, would greatly increase the difficulty of blockading the harbours, and would render hazardous the transportation of troops along the line of the coast and through the Gulf of Mexico."

In addition to the remittances by sterling bills, by Confederate bonds, and the shipment of cotton, the Secretary of the Navy secured the appropriation of a very full proportion of the loan commonly called the Erlanger Loan to the use of his Department.

The foregoing statements in respect to the supply of funds for naval purposes are perhaps of no great historical importance now, but the Southern people made unparalleled, or at least unsurpassed sacrifices to effect their separation from the Federal Union, and I cannot divest myself of the feeling that this narrative is somehow in the nature of a report to them of the use that was made of the resources which were drawn from their very blood.

Thousands of persons at the South knew (the knowledge, unhappily, was only too current) that the Government were making efforts to obtain ships-of-war in Europe. That which was only a hope with those in authority became a settled conviction and a fixed expectation in the minds of the people generally. The appearance of an ironclad fleet to open the blockade and to cover the import of the much-needed and longed-for supplies was not to them a mere vision of fancy: it had become to many a reality which they thought might be accomplished any day. They looked for the expected succour with confident desire, and the disappointment was great in proportion to the height to which their hopes had risen.

The Southern people in the aggregate exhibited so many admirable qualities during their struggle, and the consequences of their defeat were so overwhelming, that the failure of any particular enterprise, or the efforts of any one individual, however important may have been his office, is hardly worthy of mention now. But people who are brave in the presence of danger, and patient under the infliction of suffering, are not likely to be wanting in generosity, and the survivors of those who made the sacrifices and suffered the disappointment will be glad to learn that the men who were placed in charge of the great Administrative Departments of the Government were conscious of the responsibilities of their position, and devoted their faculties with zeal and singleness of purpose to the service of the country.

As one who was appointed to execute the general purposes of the Administration, I can testify to the earnest solicitude of the Departmental chiefs to provide the means, and to the encouraging support by words and deeds they always extended to their agents abroad. To say that no mistakes were made would be to affirm that those high officials were possessed of supernatural gifts; but while the wise and prudent learn perhaps from the failure of great schemes some surer road to success, it is only the weak and foolish who affect a profound sagacity after the event, and become noisy and malicious in their criticism.

The glamour of success imparts a brilliancy to the fortunate enterprise which it is not in the nature of things to expect for the effort which has failed; but there are always a certain number of discriminating minds who are able to perceive the inherent advantages which have contributed to the success and the insurmountable difficulties which have made the failure inevitable. Mr. Davis and his Cabinet, and the great chieftains like Sidney Johnston, Lee, and Jackson, most of whom have already passed away, may trust their reputations to the impartial historian who will some day write the history of the greatest Civil War which has ever convulsed a nation or astonished the world.

The Secretary of the Navy not only laboured with great earnestness to provide funds, but he certainly wrote always with great frankness, and not only encouraged but directed me to correspond without reserve, and to give him suggestions without hesitation. I never, therefore, felt the least embarrassment in recommending a change of procedure or a fresh departure whenever experience or the outlook from abroad seemed to render a particular course advisable. Difficulty and delay in communicating sometimes prevented the suggestions from reaching Richmond until the most advantageous time for action had passed. Sometimes the experts at the Navy Department anticipated the suggestions, and orders to execute would cross the recommendations *en route*. In compliance with the general precept to communicate fully and freely, I wrote to the Department on November 7th, 1862, as follows:—

"It appears from Northern accounts that you are building quite a number of rams in the home ports. It strikes me there must be a lack of engines and the means of making them in the Confederacy. It would take but a short time to run up a number of engines, say from sixty to one hundred horse-power nominal, as would be suitable for any vessels intended for harbour defence. Up to one hundred horse-power good double engines, extra strong and low for small vessels or rams, with large cylinders and boilers in convenient parts, can be built here for forty pounds per horse-power. Larger engines for rather less. I think there would be great economy in ordering a number of engines in England for such vessels as you may contemplate building hereafter.... They can be packed very compactly for shipment."

In reply to the despatch containing the foregoing extract, the Secretary of the Navy wrote as follows:—"Your suggestion as to engines is impor-tant.... If the conditions of your finances will permit it, build four marine engines to drive twelve feet screws with the greatest power, and send them, if possible, in a vessel belonging to the Government."

Orders were subsequently sent for two more large engines, and for twelve pairs of engines for torpedo boats. All of the foregoing were in-tended for vessels either building or which it was the purpose to build in the Confederate ports, and sketches of the engine spaces were sent at the same time, but these were incomplete as to measurement and in some other particulars, which created delay in the execution of the orders. One very especial order was received in January, 1863, for a pair of engines with fourteen feet screw, "the engines to be extra powerful, boiler surface to be amply sufficient for working the engines to their extreme power, and all important pieces to be duplicated." The last mentioned engines were intended for an ironclad, said to be building at Richmond.

I have already stated that the want of skilled labour was a great source of embarrassment to both the War and Navy Departments, and great ef-forts were made to obtain artizans from abroad. The Secretary of the Navy wrote me urgently on the subject, under date of April 11th, 1863, and directed me to send out mechanics, and if possible a leading man capable of superintending the manufacture of Bessemer steel. There was of course much difficulty in finding men of good character and suitable skill, who would be willing to take the risks of a voyage to the Confed-eracy, with the very possible chance of capture by a Federal cruiser, and with the assurance of much hardship even after safe arrival at a Southern port. Only trusty and competent men would be of any real service, and it would have been both unjust and impolitic to conceal from them the posi-tive dangers and discomforts of the proposed undertaking. To counter-balance the more moderate but sure and regular remuneration easily earned in England, and the comforts and security of domestic life at home, it was necessary to offer very substantial emolument, and the arrangements required some time to complete.

The result was reported in a despatch treating generally of the subject, and the following extract will sufficiently explain what it was found possible to effect:—

"Owing to the high rate of pay they (skilled artizans) receive at home, I have met with unexpected difficulties and delays in the execution of the above project. I have found it wholly impossible to get a man capable of manufacturing Bessemer steel to go at all; indeed, I am assured by the principal manager of the Cyclops Steel and Iron Works that the practical obstacles in the way of starting a Bessemer steel factory in the Confederate States under existing circumstances would be insurmountable. I will report more fully on this point hereafter.... I have engaged a Mr. Thomas Ludlam, who has been foreman of the Low Moor Iron Works, to organize a party of skilled mechanics, and to take them out under his own immediate charge in such a vessel as I may provide. Mr. Ludlam is capable of taking charge of a foundry for any kind of work, and, indeed, can select the site, lay out the plan, and superintend the erection of the building and machinery. He can also make the ordinary tools used in such establishments, and understands the use of the steam-hammer. He will take with him three principal under-foremen, three men especially skilled in heavy casting for great guns, three pattern makers, and by his advice I have authorized him to engage what he calls a 'jobber,' a most useful man in any iron workshop, a practical man of every trade, who, Mr. Ludlam says, can make a horseshoe or repair an engine. I am told that all the large establishments employ such a person."

Mr. Ludlam was despatched with his party from England in due course, but unfortunately they got separated at Bermuda, as accommodation could not be found for them all on board the same blockade-runner. However, the greater part of them got in and fulfilled their engagements faithfully; but owing to the pressure of the war and insurmountable local difficulties, it was found impossible to construct new works, or even to enlarge those already in operation, and the highest skill and qualities of the imported men could not be fully utilized.

The Confederate Government was represented at Bermuda, Nassau, and Havana by three gentlemen of great energy, industry, and business capacity. Major N. S. Walker, after serving in the field during the campaign which resulted in the repulse of General McClellan from the advance upon Richmond in 1862, was sent to act as the representative of the War Department at Bermuda, but the labour of receiving and forwarding supplies for every branch of the Government was soon heaped upon him. Mr. L. Heyleger held a corresponding office at Nassau, and Major Charles J. Helm at Havana. The services rendered by the above-named gentlemen were of inestimable value, but were of that nature which could only be known to a few, namely, to the chiefs of Departments at Richmond, and the purchasing and forwarding agents in Europe. They had the control and management of all the public business at their respective stations. Their office was to receive the supplies shipped from Europe, and then to forward them to a blockaded port, and that included the supervision of the blockade-runners, the distribution of pilots, the arrangements for keeping up the large quantity of coals required for the service; and there was much correspondence and much financing to meet the necessary expenditure.

In all great wars there are men who contribute to the general objects of the contest, and yet must be content with such reward as comes from the consciousness of duty faithfully performed. The Confederate agents at Nassau, Bermuda, and Havana were of that class. Their services were well known and appreciated by those who had official correspondence with them during the war, but a brilliant dash at the head of a troop of cavalry, or participation in a successful sortie from beleagured Richmond, would have made their names current where they are not likely to be mentioned now. Active service at the front wins the "bauble reputation." The men who work in the rear are not despised or even undervalued, but they must have the nerve to stifle their ambition. They may expect fair and just commendation, but then they must not aspire to stand side by side with those who wear the "myrtle crown."

The goods for the Navy Department were shipped almost exclusively to Nassau, Havana, and Bermuda; and the prompt, zealous, and intelligent co-operation I received from the agents at those places justifies the foregoing short digression, which is but a small tribute to their memory.

The danger of losing or leaving behind some essential parts of the marine engines in the necessary transhipment at an intermediate port was always a cause of uneasiness, and when the most important of those especially ordered by the Navy Department was completed, I thought its delivery at a Confederate port safe and whole was a matter of sufficient importance to justify the purchase of a steamer fit for the purpose of taking them direct from Liverpool to Wilmington. Lieutenant Robert R. Carter had been sent to Europe in April, 1863, for service in a cruising ship or in one of the ironclads, but his qualifications made him peculiarly and especially useful in assisting me in the various occupations of equipping ships, purchasing and forwarding goods, etc.; and, as he was with me when the engines were completed, I detached him for the command of the ship. The ordinary blockade-runner would not suffice. A larger and more substantial vessel than the usual type of steamer built for that purpose was required, and Carter and I went to the Clyde in search of a suitable one. We were so fortunate as to find a twin-screw steamer of about 700 tons almost complete, and were told that she would be ready for a trial trip in a fortnight. A close inspection satisfied us that she had all the requisites for the immediate purpose, and by indirect inquiry I learned that she could be bought for a moderate advance upon the builder's contract price. If the calculated speed could be guaranteed, I felt sure that the vessel would be a good purchase, because she could not only, in all probability, take in the engines and other valuable ordnance stores, but she would recoup her cost to us by bringing out cotton.

Ships of a certain class were dear at that time, and the price asked was high, but if the enterprise was advisable at all, the difference of £1,000 more or less was not worth considering. I therefore made a full bid for her at once, on the conditions that dead weight sufficient to immerse her to her calculated load draught should be put in her, and that in that trim she should make not less than thirteen knots over the measured trial course. The offer was accepted, the ship was weighted to the required draught, and was taken down the Clyde for trial, Robert Carter and I being on board. There was a fresh breeze blowing directly up the Frith and the tide was flood; thus, by running over the course each way a number of times, and taking the average, we could arrive at a very accurate estimate of her speed.

The ship was far more rigidly tried than steamers usually are on such occasions. We steamed to and fro between the Cloch Light and the Cumbrae for about two hours, and the average of all the runs gave a mean speed of thirteen and a half knots. We then tried the steering capacity by putting the helm hard over, and noted both the time of completing the circle and its diameter. The engines were also tested, by reversing from full speed and noting the time required to effect a full stop. Indeed, the ship was tested in every possible way in which it occurred to us that she might be tried in an attempt to run the blockade, and as she fulfilled the promises of the builder, the conditional offer was confirmed, the ship was bought, christened *Coquette*, and on the 11th of October, 1863, she got round to Liverpool, where she took the engines on board.

The *Coquette* was of course registered as an English ship, and to avoid the possibility of seizure or detention no contraband goods were put on board at Liverpool. About the 25th of October she was safely cleared out for Bermuda, and in the official report of the transaction I advised the Secretary of the Navy as follows:—

"I have already reported that Lieutenant R. R. Carter would go in charge of this vessel. For obvious reasons she leaves here under the British flag, but Lieutenant Carter will have a bill of sale in his possession, and can change the flag whenever it may be expedient.... By this steamer I send forward a pair of marine screw engines of 200 horse-power nominal, with all the tools necessary for erecting them, and also spare indiarubber valves, and, indeed, everything necessary to keep them in working order. The boilers are riveted up in as large pieces as can be handled, and hammers and spare rivets are sent for completing them.... If Lieutenant Carter gets in with the ship you will be able to carry out the design of sending out cotton to meet the engagements of the Navy Department in Europe, and should you desire to establish regular operations of this kind, I could purchase two or three light draught paddle-steamers of high speed, several of which class are now coming to completion, and they could do the work between the islands and the coast, while the larger vessel commanded by Lieutenant Carter might be employed to ply between the islands and Europe."

The *Coquette* arrived at Bermuda in due course, took in there a very large and valuable addition to her Liverpool freight, and proceeded towards Wilmington. After getting inside of the Gulf Stream the culpable carelessness of an engineer caused an accident to one of the cylinders, which compelled Carter to return to Bermuda, but the next effort was successful, and he got safely into Wilmington.

In a despatch dated July 8th, 1864, the Secretary of the Navy wrote me as follows:—"The *Coquette* has been remarkably successful under Lieutenant Carter's able command, but her speed has so steadily declined in consequence of deposits on her tubes, which cannot be cleansed, that under constant apprehension of capture he recommends her sale, which I have authorized for £16,000, which will be placed to your credit."

The freight earned, or perhaps I should say saved for the Government by the *Coquette* on her inward voyages, and the profit on the several cargoes of cotton she brought out, paid for the ship many times over. It seemed at first sight an extravagant expenditure to buy a ship merely to transport a pair of marine engines across the Atlantic, but the position of affairs was exceptional, and Confederate agents were often compelled to act in apparent violation of ordinary business principles, and they were happy when the result was such as to fulfil the primary and essential purpose.

Robert Carter was capable of higher class professional work than running the blockade, and in compliance with my request the Secretary of the Navy sent him back to England as soon as the *Coquette* was handed over to her purchasers.

The successful voyages of the *Coquette* and the urgent representations of General McRae (the general fiscal agent of the Treasury), confirmed the Government at Richmond in the conviction that it was of prime importance to adopt a systematic arrangement for exporting cotton on account of the Treasury Department, and that it was advisable to have steamers specially designed for the purpose, and to sail them under special Government regulations. It was determined that the financial arrangements should be made by the Treasury Department, and that when the steamers were regularly at work the details of their management should be assigned to the Secretary of the Navy.

About April–May, 1864, General McRae was instructed to get the scheme in operation, and he made the contracts for raising the necessary funds, already explained in a previous chapter.* By an understanding between the Treasury and Navy Departments, it was arranged that the steamers should be built under my supervision, and I was directed to place myself in communication with General McRae, and assist him in every possible way. This division of duties was in order to relieve the fiscal agent of the responsibilities attaching to the selection of type and the construction of the steamers, which it was thought should have, in the interests of the Government, the supervision of an expert. General McRae was very energetic in the effort to effect a prompt and equitable financial arrangement, but the transaction involved large cash advances, and it must be admitted that the security he had to offer, namely, a pledge to recoup them by the somewhat uncertain shipment of cotton through the blockade, could hardly be considered "first-class." On the 9th of June, 1864, General McRae informed me by official letter that his financial arrangements were so far complete that he had obtained the consent of the contractors to begin the ships. He requested me, therefore, to proceed without further delay, and was so impressed with the importance of starting the enterprise with the quickest possible despatch, that he suggested the purchase of four steamers to begin with, and that I should build the remainder of an improved class.

What was accomplished under the foregoing arrangement cannot be explained in briefer phrases than in the following report made by me to the Secretary of the Navy, under date of September 15th, 1864:—

"In a previous despatch I have had the honour to inform you that the

---

* See chap. iii., p. 75.

duty of building and arranging for the outward voyages of the steamers especially intended for Government service had been assigned to me, and General McRae has since then shown me the regulations adopted by the several heads of Departments, by which it appears that the management and navigation of the ships to and from the Confederate ports will be under the control of the Navy Department. Under these circumstances it is proper for me to report from time to time the progress made in the construction of the steamers, and to inform you what vessels have been bought and when despatched from England.... Below you will find a complete list of the steamers bought as well as building under the foregoing arrangement.

"*Bought.*—Steamers (paddle), *Owl, Bat, Stag, Deer,* all of the same dimensions and power, as follows:—length 230 feet, beam 26 feet, depth of hold 10 feet 9 inches, tonnage 771. Engines, vertical oscillating, of 180 horse-power nominal. These vessels were bought on the stocks too far advanced to be modified in any material way, but are good ships, with capacity for 800 bales of cotton, besides coal to run out from Wilmington to Bermuda, on rather less than 7 feet 6 inches draught. The *Owl* is, I hope, by this time in Wilmington, and the *Bat* is on her voyage to Halifax, from whence she will sail to Wilmington. The *Stag* will probably sail from this port in ten days, and the *Deer* three weeks afterwards.

"*Building.*—Under this head there are ten steamers, as follows:—Two paddle-steamers of steel, sister ships.... These two steamers have been designed and modeled with great care. They will carry, I think, three days' fuel and 1,500 bales of cotton, on but little over 9 feet draught, and are expected to make fourteen knots thus loaded. Two paddle-steamers, also of steel; length 210 feet, beam 23 feet, depth 10 feet.... These two are specially designed for the shoal waters of Texas and Florida, and will carry 350 bales of cotton and three days' fuel on a draft of 5 feet, or 650 to 700 bales and the same quantity of fuel on a draught of 6 feet. Two paddle-steamers, length 240 feet, beam 30 feet, depth 13 feet, horse-power 260 nominal, framed, and plated from light load-line up with steel, bottoms plated with iron. Will carry 1,000 bales of cotton under hatches and three days fuel on draught of 9 feet, and can carry 150 tons weight in addition on a draught of 10 feet. Two paddle-steamers, all of steel; length 225 feet, beam 24 feet, depth 11 feet, horse-power 160 nominal. Will carry 800 bales on 6 feet. Two twin-screw steamers; length 250 feet, beam 28 feet, depth 15 feet 6 inches, engines, two pair, 130 horse-power nominal each....

"You will thus perceive that there are fourteen fine steamers either already completed or in course of construction for the Government.... The ten steamers especially built are very fine vessels in every respect, and can be readily duplicated, so that I hope you will be relieved from the necessity of buying any more of the ships which may be sent out on speculation. The agreement with the two firms advancing the money to General McRae stipulates that these steamers must be commanded by British captains until they have been paid for.... Until otherwise instructed I will engage captains for the first voyages of the steamers only, at the same rate of pay as private owners offer, and when the ships reach Wilmington you can make such permanent arrangements with their captains as may be possible. I would suggest that as fast as the ships are paid for, navy officers be put in command, as a general rule, although it would be advisable to retain some of the merchant captains in the service, because among them are a number of very clever seamen, with great experience in blockade-running. The naval officers to command the steamers should be selected with reference to special qualifications for the work, and should have leave of absence for that particular employment, and the ships ought to be kept registered in the names of private persons, otherwise serious embarrassment may arise, as Lord Russell has stated in Parliament that if it could be shown that the steamers trading between the Confederate States and the British Islands were owned by the Confederate States Government, they would be considered as transports, and would be forbidden to enter English port except under the restrictions imposed upon all men-of-war of the belligerent Powers....

"It has often been said that the Government cannot compete with private enterprise in supplying its own wants. This I am convinced from experience is a great mistake, and it is, besides, equivalent to the declaration that even in these trying times energy and zeal can only be obtained by money. The Government will soon have a number of the finest steamers that can be built for the special purpose of blockade-running, and I venture to assert that if proper agents are selected to manage them, and the agents are granted the facilities and powers that are given by merchants to their agents, the entire wants of the public services can be supplied regularly and efficiently, and with far greater convenience and less cost than at any previous period, or by any arrangement with mercantile companies."

Under cover and by means of the arrangements for a fleet of blockade-runners made by General McRae, the opportunity was offered to build four steamers especially for the Navy Department. Two of the four were intended for service at the mouth of the Cape Fear river, to cover the approach of steamers attempting to run into Wilmington, and to make night attacks upon the blockading squadron. A short extract from the report to the Secretary of the Navy in reference to those vessels will explain both their type and purpose:—

"They have been designed as tow boats, to deceive the Federal spies, but will require insignificant alterations to convert them into serviceable gunboats for local work. It will only be necessary to fill up the space between the beams, and add a few stanchions under the permanent position of the guns. The deck plans are now in the hands of the gunmakers, to have the carriages adapted. The armament of each will be one 8-inch rifled gun, to penetrate the enemy's Monitors, and one 9-inch gun, somewhat of howitzer shape, but built on the Armstrong principle and rifled. Experiments at Portsmouth have shown that with the present style of traverse carriage and slide, guns of any weight within the capacity of the deck to bear can be worked upon the smallest-sized gunboats in her Majesty's service, even in a considerable sea; and I was readily persuaded to rifle the 9-inch gun, in view of the formidable character of the shell which can thus be used, containing a bursting charge of 15 lb. of powder, which, it strikes me, would demoralize the crew of any wooden ship, if it did not destroy her. By reducing the charge, and using the Armstrong pillar fuze, a shell can be made to burst in an opposing ship at any distance within the extreme range of the gun."

The dimensions of the two boats were as follows: length 170 feet, breadth 23 feet, depth 12 feet 6 inches, draught 7 feet 6 inches. They were to be propelled by twin screw engines of 120 horse-power collective for each boat, and their calculated speed was twelve knots. The two larger vessels were designed for the purpose of making more extensive cruises, from Wilmington along the enemy's coast. The engines and boilers were kept below the water-line, and compartments were placed above them to be filled with cotton for additional protection. Every device for strengthening the ships and protecting their vital parts was resorted to, that could be adopted without running the risk of exciting suspicion, and with the power and speed allotted to them, and the armament they would have been able to carry, they would have been very formidable ships indeed. There was another vessel building at the same time under special arrangement with a private firm, who had undertaken to deliver her at an appointed rendezvous. It was the purpose to use the three last-mentioned vessels for an expedition against one or more of the sea-ports along the Northern coast, that of Portsmouth, New Hampshire, especially. Besides their regular armament, the vessels were to have been provided with a large supply of Hall's rockets.

Lieutenants W. H. Murdaugh and Robert R. Carter had been selected to command two of the ships, and I had applied to the Secretary of the Navy to send out Lieutenant J. Pembroke Jones to command the third. The rendezvous for the ships had been carefully selected, and such precautions had been taken as seemed to promise perfect success, but the rapidity with which the closing disasters followed each other after the fall of Wilmington, and the impression that an aggressive enterprise of that kind would hardly be justifiable as a mere expiring effort, caused its abandonment. Before the ships could have been ready to leave England, General Lee had surrendered, and it was impossible to communicate with the civil authorities of the Confederate States.

Six of the steamers bought or built under the McRae arrangement reached the coast in time to make one or more voyages through the blockade, two or three more were *en route,* but five or six were not completed at the close of the war. Only one of the four built especially for the Navy Department was finished (namely, one of the small vessels for harbour service), and she was sent out in command of Lieutenant John Low; but she did not arrive in time to perform any service.

As an historical fact, I must state that I had always favoured the construction of vessels especially for harbour defence and for coastwise enterprises, and had also recommended that the Government should take in hand the entire export of cotton by vessels especially designed for the purpose; but it is also true that the pressure of affairs was very great upon the Departments, and it did not appear to them advisable, or even possible, to divert funds from the purchase of supplies for the armies in the field, and from naval undertakings which appeared to be of greater importance, for any other objects.

There can be no doubt that the Confederate Government, and the leading men at the South also, were deceived by the official statements of her Majesty's Ministers, and by the tone of their unofficial speeches at various places and on various occasions. The official expositions of the Foreign Enlistment Act, and the often-repeated assertion in Parliament, and in the official correspondence of her Majesty's Secretary of State for Foreign Affairs, that unarmed ships were no more contraband than rifles and powder, produced the belief at Richmond that even ironclad vessels without guns or special naval equipment would not be prevented from leaving England as the property of private individuals. And then, also, the assurances received from the French Imperial Government were such as to make the obtaining of war-vessels in France almost a matter of certainty.

If the foregoing expectations had been realized, and the Liverpool rams, with those built at Bordeaux, had been permitted to go to sea, the Confederate Government would have been able to open some of the Southern ports to private enterprise, and could have made far more formidable and effective attacks upon the Northern sea-coast than by means of the lighter vessels which were designed to combine the offices of running the blockade and making hostile marine raids. When the hopes of getting regularly constructed armour-clad vessels were crushed, the alternative course was adopted, and great efforts were made to put it in operation, but many obstacles stood in the way. Money was more scarce, the blockade was more efficient, and shipbuilders were more fully employed, and thus precious time was lost and opportunity was missed, and the whole that could be then accomplished was not sufficient to turn the scale or to greatly delay the final result of the war.

Very soon after the beginning of the war the various Departments of the Government at Richmond were beset by speculators, who applied for contracts to furnish not only the ordnance supplies which would be needed to provide the armies in the field, but artillery, heavy ordnance, steam-engines, and other machinery, steamers for running the blockade, and even ironclad vessels. Pressed for ready cash, and greatly embarrassed in contriving the means for turning the produce of the country into funds available abroad, the heads of the War and Navy Departments were induced to grant a favourable hearing to the speculators, and many contracts were made, the terms being generally payment in cotton at a Confederate port, and at a fixed price, varying from eight to ten cents per pound. In some instances cotton scrip was issued to the contractors in advance, and in a few cases it was agreed that the agent of the Government in Europe should receive and forward the goods, and pay one-half the contract price on delivery, the remainder to be paid after the arrival of the goods at a Confederate port.

The Navy Department, with the avowed purpose of protecting the Government, and to guard against extravagance in price and carelessness in manufacture, stipulated in respect to the most important contracts for the navy that they should be executed under my supervision, and that I should certify to the reasonableness of the cost, the fitness of material, and the perfection of finish.

This was doubtless, under the circumstances, a prudent requirement, and does not appear to have been objected to by the contractors, who, so far as I know, were satisfied with the conditions of payment, and had no wish either to supply a bad article or to tamper with the market value. Cotton delivered to them in payment at eight cents per pound, when it was worth two shillings or more in Liverpool, left so large a margin for profit that there was no temptation to act unfairly in matters of detail, and it is probable that most of the contractors were very willing to shift all responsibility in regard to cost and quality from themselves to an official representative of the Government.

But while the requirement was prudent as a preliminary business arrangement, it gave occasion to much trouble and embarrassment which the Navy Department did not foresee. When the peculiar financial position of the country is considered, and the difficulty of communicating with the agents in Europe is taken into account, it cannot now be thought strange that the home authorities were inclined to favour the proposals of private parties, who offered to supply the necessities of the Government on conditions which would greatly relieve the demands upon the Treasury, and would substitute as the medium of payment that staple which could be readily controlled, in place of cash or sterling, which it was most difficult to supply.

The embarrassment and inconvenience referred to above arose from two causes. In the first place, the contractors, who had been provided with a Government officer to refer to, were inclined to throw all the labour as well as the responsibility upon him. By a not unnatural process of reasoning, each thought his own special business was the most important enterprise in which the Government was engaged, and that the prompt and satisfactory completion of that business should be the prime object of the supervising officer. Secondly, some of the private individuals who had contracted to supply ships-of-war had no technical knowledge of their structure, cost, or the time necessary to build them, nor had they even thought of the bearings of the Foreign Enlistment Act, and the obstacles to be overcome in getting the ships out of Great Britain.

Besides the two above-mentioned causes of trouble, there was another which did not at first appear likely to occur, at least to the authorities at Richmond. Several of the contractors found when they came to calculate the cost of the undertaking they had assumed, and perceived the necessity of making periodical payments in cash, that they could not command the necessary funds, and they at once began to clamour for help, and to propose modifications in the conditions of the contracts, or cash advances which I was not authorized to grant, even if they met my approval.

Looking back upon the office it was my fortune to occupy during the war, I can say that nothing gave me so much harassing perplexity, or tried my patience and forbearance to so great a degree, as the supervision of the private contracts, and one at least of them is indelibly stamped upon my mind as having greatly contributed to the failure of those enterprises from which the Confederate Government and the Southern people anticipated the most important results. In a general despatch to the Secretary of the Navy on the foregoing subjects, dated September 24th, 1862, I reported as follows:—

"... I feel it, however, my duty to remark generally upon the various contracts which private individuals have made with the Navy Department, and which I am directed by you to supervise on the part of the Government, because I know that you cannot be aware of the state of affairs in Europe, and are liable to be misled by the statements of interested parties at home, who may profess their ability to fulfil any and every agreement. I disclaim any special application of my remark to the gentlemen who have thus far brought over contracts to be supervised by me, because they are all strangers to me, and I have no wish to interfere in the slightest degree with their private concerns, but as a public officer, and the recognised agent of your Department, it is my bounden duty to inform you upon all matters which from the peculiar circumstances of the country are necessarily beyond the reach of your personal knowledge.

"If these contracts were taken by persons who could raise the money necessary to carry them out upon their own credit, there would be an advantage in giving them out, but such does not appear to be the case, and the result therefore has been only embarrassment to me, and a degree of publicity to the affairs of the Department which I fear may be still more embarrassing. The best mode of explaining the manner in which contracts of the kind mentioned are put in train of execution here, will be to sketch briefly a supposed case. A person arrives in England with a contract to build and deliver a ship to the Confederate Government. Being destitute of money himself, his first step is to look up some one who can furnish the necessary capital. Bankers of established position will not engage in such irregular transactions; he is therefore forced to seek for some keen sharp financier who is ready for any transaction wherein there appears a chance of profit. Such a person being found, the original contractor either sells him the contract outright for a certain named sum, or they agree to divide the profit. The capitalist, not wishing to take the entire risk upon himself, casts about among his friends for aid, each of whom must be assured of a certain gain.... To give character to the transaction, all these persons are informed that the ship is for the Confederate Government, and that the Confederate Government is responsible for the payments. The matter is discussed, and soon comes to the ears of those who are dealing directly with the legitimate agents and officers of the Government; the irregularity of the whole transaction is commented upon, and the credit of the Government is measurably injured.

"I assure you, sir, that in this hasty sketch I have not at all exaggerated the process by which these contracts are set in train, and it is very doubtful whether a single one of them will ever be brought to a conclusion. Thus far there has not been a beginning. I attribute the success which has heretofore attended the operations on account of the Government in a great measure to the caution and secrecy which have been preserved, and to the absolute good faith with which all liabilities have been met. Secrecy is, however, out of the question when so many indiscreet persons are employed, and future difficulties will be greatly increased.

"An officer of the Government, with a commission in his pocket, and orders to purchase any amount or description of material, and with authority clearly expressed to borrow any amount of money on the credit of the Government, would be able to negotiate on better terms than any private individual whose own personal credit could not guarantee the transaction. My experience in Europe has taught me that it is always best and cheapest to deal with principals, and with those who stand at the head of their respective trades or employments; and when contracts are given out to intermediaries who are neither experts nor men of capital, there is invariably delay, disappointment, and loss. You will, I am sure, understand and appreciate the motive which induced me to write thus; I will therefore make no further apology. If you were in a position to know, or rather to learn, these things from your own observation, I would not venture to advise you."

The contract which occasioned the gravest anxiety and embarrassment was one for the building of six ironclad vessels, to be delivered at sea; and the financial conditions were that the ships should be paid for in cotton at the market value of cotton in a Confederate port, and at the time when the payments were due. The general type of the ships was expressed in the contract, but all details were to be worked out in England; and the Secretary of the Navy had attached the proviso that the builders, the specifications, the armaments, and the prime cost of the ships were to be approved by me, and that the payments were to be made upon my certificate that all specified conditions had been fulfilled. I accepted without hesitation the eminent builders selected by the contractor, and there was neither difficulty nor delay in settling all details as to structure, cost, and time of completion; but the contractor had no personal means, and the capitalist with whom he opened negotiations in London required something more tangible than the engagement to deliver a certain amount of cotton at a Confederate port, and at an indefinite price. They soon came to me with a proposal that I should give bonds pledging the Confederate Government to deliver a quantity of cotton which, at eight cents per pound, should be equivalent to the cost of the ships. I pointed out to them that the whole tenor of the contract was that the ships should be paid for only after delivery beyond British jurisdiction, whereas by signing the proposed bonds I should be paying for them in advance. Moreover, I said that the financial conditions had been settled in Richmond, and were specified in the contract, and I had no authority to change them in any way. Mr. Mason, the Confederate Commissioner, was then applied to, and he was asked to issue bonds, or to cause some of those already in Europe to be handed over for the purposes of the contract, but he declined to take any responsibility in the matter. The original contractor was not able to find the money from any other source, and not a keel of the proposed vessels was ever laid down.

The contracts made by the Confederate Government with private parties are of no historical importance, and I would gladly have avoided any allusion to them, but they found their way into the diplomatic correspondence, and the particular one just above mentioned was introduced into the "Case of the United States" before the Tribunal of Arbitration at Geneva,* and therefore they could not be ignored in a narrative purporting to give a true and complete account of the Confederate naval operations in Europe.

The contractor for the six ironclads was so unfortunate as to have some of his papers captured in a blockade-runner, which untoward circumstance, added to his financial negotiations in London, gave great publicity to the whole transaction. He was spoken of in the newspapers as a Confederate agent. The effect was to draw attention to those armour-cased vessels which were building at the time, and there can be no doubt that the unhappy exposure which befell that so-called private transaction contributed to strengthen the complaints and demands of the United States Minister, and served to influence the course adopted by her Majesty's

* "Case of the United States," pp. 66, 67.

Government in respect to the Liverpool rams, and other vessels alleged to be building for the Confederate States.

It is necessary to state that very few of the contracts made by the Navy Department and referred to me were ever completed. Some were abandoned because the parties could not find the money, some proved to be impossible of execution, and in other cases the articles offered were so inferior that they were rejected.

There is another subject which is of no consequence in itself, but which was often spoken of by people at the South during the war, and has been mentioned since, in one or two publications, somewhat in the form of a complaint against the Confederate Navy Department. It was alleged that vessels suitable for war were offered to the Secretary of the Navy, or he was advised where they could be found, and that he was either indifferent to the proposals, or neglected to instruct the agent abroad to buy them. I am able to state that the Navy Department received many such proposals and intimations, and that they were often referred to me with instructions to make due inquiry and investigations, and to miss no opportunity of securing a good and suitable ship, whenever one was offered and the condition of the finances permitted the purchase. In explanation, it is proper for me to say that the proposals came generally from two classes of persons, namely, speculators, who were merely in search of a commission, and did not shrink from offering any patched-up hulk they could lay hold of, or honest men, really desirous to do the South a service, but having no technical knowledge of ships, and no faculty for estimating the essential requirements of a Confederate cruiser. The former class were soon got rid of, but it was not always so easy to decline the kindly meant proposals of the latter, without leaving sometimes the impression that there was lack of zeal, or some failure to appreciate a good offer.

Two or three typical cases will illustrate the character of those well-meant offers, and will demonstrate their impracticability. On one occasion the Secretary of the Navy directed me to examine "two vessels which he was advised could be bought and got to sea without difficulty." They were described in very general terms as "two fine steam frigates." Upon looking into the proposal, the vessels proved to be two very large paddle-steamers, formerly belonging to the Indian navy.

The "two fine steam frigates" were manifestly out of date, or they would have been retained in the Indian navy. Their paddles had been taken off and the coal-bunkers removed. In that condition they were brought to England from Bombay, and in that condition they were offered for sale. The engines were 800 horse-power nominal, and the estimated consumption of fuel was sixty tons per day. They were full-masted for vessels of their class, but with paddles shipped they were practically and essentially steamers, and the price asked for them was £65,000 each, which was £17,500 more than the cost of the *Alabama.*

The reasons for not buying them were reported to the Secretary of the Navy in the following words:—"I rejected them because of their great draught of water, large consumption of fuel, and number of men required to man them, to say nothing of prime cost, which was beyond my means. In fine, they would not make efficient cruisers unless we were in possession of regular and numerous coaling *depôts.*"

At another time a large number of steamers, said to belong to Messrs. Overend, Gurney and Co., were thrown out of employment, and were laid up in the London docks for many months inviting the notice of speculators. These ships were iron screw-vessels of large size, and with barely auxiliary sail-power. They had no arrangements for lifting their screws, or for otherwise rendering them inoperative as drags upon the ships when the engines were stopped. They might have been serviceable to the United States as transports; and any maritime Power having command of its own ports, or with colonial ports where the supply of coal could be replenished, and to whom the expense of a large and continuous consumption of fuel was a matter of little moment, might have found useful employment for them. But they would have been a dear bargain to the Confederate navy at any price, and any professional man would have seen at a glance their unfitness for cruising under conditions which would render them helpless without steam, and would limit their active operations to the process of running from one port to another in search of fuel.

On several occasions vessels of foreign navies were offered, or the attention of the Navy Department was invited to them, but in every such case the ships proved to be either defective in condition or unsuited in size and type for the very special and peculiar requirements of a Confederate cruiser; and besides this, the parties offering them had not given the least thought to the manner of getting possession of the ships, and effecting their departure from the neutral port. It had never entered their minds to doubt that the ships could be bought and despatched without any difficulty, and when one offer or proposition was declined, they soon cast about and provided another under corresponding or equally unfavourable conditions.

During the whole period of the war only one offer to supply a vessel for the Confederate navy, of a character suited to the required service, and to be delivered at sea, was made by persons whose experience and business position justified a serious consideration of the proposal. Early in the year 1863, when the operations of the *Alabama* had created some stir in Europe, an English ship-building firm made me an offer to build a vessel of similar type, and deliver her beyond British jurisdiction. The conditions were that there was to be no pay unless the vessel was actually delivered at sea, but if she was thus delivered I was to pay a stipulated sum in excess of the cost price. The builders were quite able to wait for their money, and were in a position to fully comprehend the nature of the transaction and the responsibility they were assuming. I therefore accepted the offer, and reported it to the Navy Department as an enterprise having some promise of success. The vessel was to have been generally of the *Alabama* type, but larger, and every possible improvement experience suggested was adopted. The builders at first appeared to be sanguine of getting a ship to sea which they said would eclipse the *Alabama,* and they showed no signs of faltering until the deck-beams were all in place and some progress had been made with the outside planking. In this condition of the ship the senior partner of the firm came to me and said that the course pursued by her Majesty's Government in reference to ships alleged to be intended for the Confederate Government, notwithstanding the favourable decision in the *Alexandra* case, had caused him to carefully consider his position, and having discussed the matter with his solicitors, he had come to the conclusion that the enterprise he had undertaken was impracticable. He said he was satisfied that when the time arrived for despatching the ship the Customs authorities would either exact such pledges as would prevent his delivering her to a Confederate agent abroad, or if he declined to give the required guarantee the vessel would be seized, and therefore he was reluctantly compelled to withdraw his proposal.

There was one other proposition for the delivery of a ship at sea which was accepted, but only because it came through a most respectable source, and not because there was any assurance of success. An American gentleman, of good position, a Northern man who had held office under the United States, was residing in London or on the Continent during the greater part of the war. He had taken the Southern side in the issues which had dissolved the Union, and had come abroad to avoid the consequences of his avowed sympathy with the South. The gentleman referred to was well known to the Confederate Commissioners, and was recognised and received by them as a person in full and friendly agreement with themselves on the political questions of the day. He often appeared to be desirous of manifesting his good will by some personal service, and more than once called my attention to vessels which he had been informed could be bought under conditions providing for delivery at sea before payment, but in every case the representations made to him proved to be exaggerated as regards the fitness of the vessels, or the practicability of effecting the delivery.

The proposals and suggestions of the gentleman referred to were always received with respect and consideration, because they were made without the least purpose to secure any personal profit out of the transaction. One of the propositions was for the delivery of an ironclad frigate, and the proposal came from a foreign banker, who alleged that his relations with his own Government were of such a nature that he could buy the ship (which was then in England) on its behalf, and would undertake to deliver her at sea to anyone appointed by me to receive her. The banker said that very considerable amounts would have to be paid to certain important intermediaries, and those amounts would be included in the price of the ship, and he stated the conditions of the transactions thus: 1st, perfect secrecy; 2nd, satisfactory security in London for the payment after delivery; 3rd, a price which should not exceed £300,000.

At the time this offer was made there was nothing like the amount named at the credit of the Navy Department unpledged to running contracts, but Mr. Charles K. Prioleau told me that if I determined to act upon the proposal, his firm would provide the required security, and I authorized the gentleman who brought the offer to say to the banker that the stipulated amount would be lodged in a London bank, so as to be secured to him upon the delivery of the ship, as soon as he would propose a practicable scheme for effecting the delivery. It would have been manifestly imprudent to lock up so large a sum of money unless some plan of proceeding was suggested which common-sense could approve as being likely to succeed. The practical obstacles to the undertaking must have been thought insurmountable when they were critically examined, because the banker did not repeat his proposal, after the conditions upon which the money would be deposited were named to him.

I never had any faith in the practicability of undertakings which involved the employment of expensive intermediaries who held fiduciary positions, and whose help to effect the desired purpose required them to act unfaithfully to their trust, and I never encountered the least difficulty in accomplishing any enterprise that was feasible in itself by means of men who were willing to give their services loyally and honestly for a compensation fairly proportioned to the service rendered. There was a very large correspondence with persons who offered their aid in getting ships, and looking over the letters and propositions after this lapse of time, I congratulate myself that the zeal which those stirring times inspired never so far overmastered discretion as to lead me into enterprises which would have in some measure justified the epithets of Mr. Seward and his Consuls. If any of those who have charged the head of the Navy Department with lack of foresight or judgment in not buying the vessels offered directly to him through private parties should be induced to read this narrative, I hope the foregoing explanations will satisfy their minds; at any rate, they will perceive that the complaints have been heretofore directed against the wrong person, and the alleged neglect must be placed to the account of the subordinate agent, and not to the departmental chief.

There were two vessels which are not mentioned in any preceding portion of this narrative, but which were despatched from England, and afterwards passed under the Confederate flag. They were not bought or equipped under my directions, and I am not in possession of the minute details respecting their origin which have enabled me to give a full and complete account of every particular incident in respect to the other Confederate vessels.

If this was a mere historical sketch of personal adventures, or a record of personal services, I would omit all mention of enterprises which did not originate with me, but it has been found necessary to explain the general naval policy of the Confederate States, and to supply all the facts which bear upon the complaints of the United States against Great Britain, and which gave occasion for the Geneva Arbitration. In the diplomatic correspondence the names of the Confederate ships *Georgia* and *Rappahannock* frequently appear, and they have also a prominent place in the "Case" presented by the United States to the Tribunal of Arbitration. The *Rappahannock* was cited by the representatives of the United States for the purpose of contrasting the conduct of the French Government with that of her Britannic Majesty in reference to the treatment of Confederate ships, although no claim for damages was urged in respect to her. The *Georgia* was, however, put by the United States in the same category with the *Alabama, Florida,* and *Shenandoah,* and pecuniary compensation was claimed for the vessels destroyed by her, on the plea that her Majesty's Government might and should have prevented her leaving England, or should have caused her to be pursued and captured afterwards, before she had assumed the Confederate flag and had been commissioned by a Confederate officer. Those two ships, therefore, cannot be omitted from an historical sketch of the naval operations of the Confederate States in foreign parts.

In a despatch dated September 20th, 1862, the Secretary of the Navy informed me that Commander M. F. Maury would shortly leave Richmond "for England on special service," and that officer arrived in Liverpool about the end of November.

Commander M. F. Maury, though bred to the naval profession, is known chiefly as a man of science, whose researches have conferred great benefits upon commerce. Wherever ocean winds blow, or the great marine currents pursue their majestic flow, they have borne his name. By careful and patient inquiry, and the application of a remarkable faculty for tracing general physical laws, he brought the circulation of the marine winds and currents so completely within the practical knowledge of the ordinary ship-master, that he could determine his route to the most distant ports with confidence, and could calculate precisely how to shape a course so as to secure the advantage of a favouring trade, or to avoid delay in beating against a foul wind. By thus marking out the great sea-routes, Commander Maury conferred a great pecuniary benefit upon merchants, especially when trade was chiefly dependent upon sailing vessels, and his happy gift of explaining philosophical subjects in graceful flowing phrases, and combining scientific precision of demonstration with easy and eloquent diction, has brought the "Physical Geography of the Sea" quite within the comprehension of the ordinary reader, and has placed his great work on that subject among those books which are styled popular literature.

The Confederate Government very probably had a political purpose in sending Commander Maury to Europe. It may have been thought that his literary reputation and his wide acquaintance with scientific men would afford the means of spreading the Southern version of the causes which produced the war among a large and influential class who generally give but little heed to politics, whether foreign or domestic.

The duty chiefly assigned to Commander Maury was to investigate the subject of submarine defences, and he gave much time to researches into electricity, the manufacture and use of gun-cotton, torpedoes, magnetic exploders, and insulated wire. He had also general authority to buy and despatch a vessel to cruise against the commerce of the United States whenever he thought the attempt practicable. Under the foregoing authority, he bought, in March, 1863, a new iron screw-steamer which had just been completed at Dumbarton, on the Clyde. The ship was named *Japan*. She was fitted out as an ordinary merchant steamer, and on the 1st of April, 1863, she was cleared out from Greenock in ballast for a port or ports in the East Indies. Her crew, numbering forty-eight or fifty men, were shipped at the Sailors' Home in Liverpool, signing articles for a voyage to Singapore and any intermediate ports, and for a period of two years. There is no doubt that she left Greenock in the condition of an ordinary ship of commerce. The Customs authorities certified, upon subsequent inquiry, that "they saw nothing on board which could lead them to suspect that she was intended for war purposes." About the time when the *Japan* left the Clyde, a small steamer called the *Alar* cleared from New Haven for St. Malo with the guns, ordnance stores, and other necessary supplies intended for the *Japan*. The two vessels met off Ushant, and running into smooth water between that island and Brest, the armament and stores were duly transferred. Commander Wm. L. Maury, a cousin of Commander M. F. Maury, and an officer of experience and ability, with a staff of officers, was put on board, the name of the vessel was changed from *Japan* to *Georgia*, and she was duly commissioned as a Confederate man-of-war.

Some of the men who had shipped at Liverpool for the alleged voyage to Singapore, etc., refused to enter the Confederate service, and were brought back to England in the *Alar*. In consequence of the information obtained from those men by the United States Minister, representations were made to her Majesty's Government, and two persons named Jones and Highatt were indicted for violation of the Foreign Enlistment Act, the allegation being that they had induced British subjects to enter the Confederate service. The case was tried at the Liverpool Assizes, before Lord Chief Justice Cockburn. "The jury found both defendants 'Guilty,' and they were required to enter into recognizances of £500 each, with two sureties of £100 each, to appear and answer judgment. The points of law which had been raised in the case were, however, not argued, and no penalty was inflicted on the defendants except the payment of a fine of £50 each."*

As soon as the guns, stores, and some additional men were received on board the *Georgia*, Commander Maury proceeded on his cruise. Passing through the Azores, *en route*, he crossed the equatorial belt at the points which have been called the "forks of the road," and arrived at Bahia in May, 1863. At Bahia he replenished stores, took in coal, and continued his cruise towards the Cape of Good Hope, arriving at Simon's Bay August 16th, 1863. On the passage from Bahia to the Cape of Good Hope he captured the American ship *Constitution,* loaded with coal, and replenished his stock from her. He left Simon's Bay August 29th, and returned to the North Atlantic, touched at Teneriffe about the middle of October, and ar-

---

* Taken from the report of the trial.

rived at Cherbourg on October 28th. It was a little more than six months since the *Georgia* had left the neighbourhood of Ushant on her projected cruise, and during that time she had captured and destroyed six or seven American vessels, but Commander Maury found that he could not remain and cruise in the track of commerce for any length of time, because the *Georgia*'s sail-power was insufficient to make her independent of the engines, and he was compelled to seek a port at comparatively short intervals for a supply of coal.

Commodore Barron was still in Paris with a greater portion of the officers who had come to Europe with him for service in the "ironclads," and being the senior naval officer, Commander Maury reported to him. The *Georgia* required some repairs, and the French Admiralty permitted her to make use of the Government dock, and the repairs were effected by the dockyard mechanics. She remained at Cherbourg nearly four months. Commander Maury was detached on account of ill-health, and Lieutenant Evans, who had been in the ship ever since she was put in commission, and who had also made the cruise in the *Sumter*, was placed in command.

Commodore Barron was in hopes of employing the *Georgia* on a special service, and with that purpose she was sent to cruise for a short time, but the design was not carried out, and on the 25th of March, 1864, she arrived at Pauillac, and proceeded to Bordeaux, where she remained until April 28th, the French Government at first consenting to her remaining a fortnight for repairs, and then tacitly permitting a further delay. Under date of April 14th, 1864, Commodore Barron informed me by letter that he should send the *Georgia* to cruise off the coast of Morocco until short of fuel, then return to a European port and report to me. He added that as soon as she was off from Bordeaux he would turn her over formally to me for sale. I requested him in reply to order the ship direct to Liverpool, and on the 29th of April, 1864, he notified me of the abandonment of the Morocco cruise, and advised me as follows:—"Evans sailed from Bordeaux yesterday, and hopes to be in Liverpool on Tuesday morning."

The *Georgia* reached Liverpool on May 2nd, 1864. On the first tide after arrival she was taken into the Birkenhead Dock, where she was dismantled, her guns and military stores were landed, and the crew paid off and discharged. All of the foregoing was done as quickly as possible, in order to satisfy the authorities that there was no intention to send the ship to sea again as a Confederate cruiser, and in reply to inquiries from the Customs authorities it was stated that the purpose was to sell her.

Shortly after the arrival of the *Georgia* at Liverpool, orders were sent from London that if not *bonâ-fide* sold, she should be required to leave the port as soon as she had received necessary repairs. But as the statement of the purpose to sell was borne out by the dismantling and by an advertisement in the Liverpool papers, no further official inquiry was made in respect to her. On the 1st of June, 1864, the ship was sold to a wealthy and influential merchant carrying on a very extensive business in Liverpool. The purchaser removed every vestige of war fittings, effected a charter of the ship to the Portuguese Government, and on the 8th of August, 1864, with a British register and under the British flag, she sailed from Liverpool for Lisbon.

The United States ship *Niagara* had been dodging about the coast and looking into English ports for some time, and was manifestly informed in respect to the sale of the ex-Confederate cruiser and her subsequent destination. She disappeared only a few days before the *Georgia* left Liverpool, and when the last-named ship, confidently relying upon the double security of her British register and her Portuguese charter, made Las Rocas, off the mouth of the Tagus, the *Niagara* was there to meet her. The result of this unhappy encounter was that a prize crew was put on board the *Georgia*, and she was sent to give an account of her proceedings before a United States prize court. The English purchaser told me afterwards that the ship was sold by order of the United States Government before any legal forfeiture was pronounced against her.

The United States often made short shrift with their neutral prizes, and dispensed with the formalities of judicial investigation and condemnation, which often followed long after the appropriation of the captured vessel to the public service. Such prompt and informal proceedings were no doubt convenient at the time; but they will serve as precedents which may some day be awkward for American merchants, whose ships may be disposed of in like manner by a future belligerent.

During the latter part of 1863 a number of "despatch-boats" belonging to the Royal Navy were offered for sale at Sheerness, and on the 14th of November of that year one of them, called the *Victor*, was sold to a mercantile firm who acted for an agent appointed by Commander M. F. Maury to effect the purchase. The *Victor* had neither masts nor rigging on board, and her Majesty's Government followed the customary practice under such circumstances, and permitted the purchasers to equip the ship at Sheerness Dockyard, under the supervision of a Mr. Rumble, who was the inspector of machinery. No attempt was made to put any warlike equipment on board, but only the fittings necessary to her safe navigation, and a party of men were engaged to take her out for a trial trip. Before all the arrangements were complete, Commander Maury had reason to fear that some suspicions had been aroused, and on the night of November 24th, 1863, the ship was hurried off from Sheerness, and was taken across the Channel to Calais. During the transit a small party of Confederate naval officers were put on board, the ship was commissioned as a vessel-of-war, and she entered Calais the next day as the Confederate ship *Rappahannock*.

The ship was partially in distress, having had a slight accident to her machinery, and being otherwise incomplete in her equipment. The United States Minister at Paris made strong remonstrances on the subject, but the French Government replied that the *Rappahannock* had sought the shelter of a French port under an apparent necessity, and she could not therefore be refused an asylum. The further objections of the United States Minister were overruled, or at least they were disregarded, and the necessary equipment of the ship to render her seaworthy was continued and completed at Calais, although the Government ordered the local authorities to take such precautions as to prevent any preparation for an armament, or the putting of any warlike stores on board.

After the arrival of the *Rappahannock* at Calais, Commander Maury resigned the control of her to Commodore Barron, who was for several months in hopes that he might be able to send her to sea, and he consulted me with reference to the despatch of an armament and other necessary stores from England to a rendezvous, but it was found impossible to fix upon any time when the *Rappahannock* could be despatched from Calais, and that purpose was abandoned. There were some questions with the French Government as to the departure of the ship from Calais, but they are of no historical importance, because the final decision was that she might leave without any warlike equipment, and with no greater number of men on board than she brought into that port.

The detention of the *Georgia* at Cherbourg, her cruise to the southward, and appearance at Bordeaux, mentioned above, had reference to the anticipated movements of the *Rappahannock,* Commodore Barron having for some time a hope that a meeting of the two ships might be arranged, when the armament and crew of the former might be transferred to the latter. When, however, he determined to turn over the *Georgia* to me, and directed her to proceed to Liverpool for that purpose, the design was of course abandoned, and no further effort was made to remove the *Rappahannock* from Calais as a vessel-of-war, but the French Government permitted her to remain there as a Confederate ship, and she was used as a sort of *depôt,* and in preparing for the despatch of the *Stonewall* she served as a convenient rendezvous for the officers and men required for that enterprise.

On the 8th of February, 1865, I received a despatch from the Secretary of the Navy, dated December 16th, 1864, from which the following is an extract:—"Orders by this steamer go to Commodore Barron to return to the Confederate States and to direct all officers whom you may designate to report to you for orders, and to send the others home. He is further instructed to turn over to you the control and direction of the *Rappahannock*.... Conference with Commodore Barron will enable you to judge correctly of the situation of the *Rappahannock*, and to reach a definite conclusion as to the course which the interest of the country requires in her case." The Secretary suggested that it was not advisable to continue the expense of maintaining her as a ship-of-war at Calais, unless there was some reasonable hope of getting her to sea.

On the 28th of February, 1865, Commodore Barron notified me of the purport of his instructions, desired me to designate the officers I wished to remain, and added:—"I have instructed Lieutenant-Commanding C. M. Fauntleroy, Confederate States steamship *Rappahannock*, to carry out any instructions that you may give in reference to the disposition of the ship, and to render you every facility for examining into her condition, and also to give you all the information he possesses which may aid you in determining what should be done with her."

The ultimate fate of the *Rappahannock* is beyond my ken. All that I know of her may be stated thus. On March 31st, 1865, in a general despatch to the Secretary of the Navy, I reported as follows in reference to her:—"On the 28th ultimo Commodore Barron resigned command as senior naval officer on the Continent, and, by official letter, turned over all unfinished business heretofore under his charge. Subsequently, under date of March 4th, he informed me that there was no business under his control except such as related to the *Rappahannock*. March 2nd I ordered careful survey of that ship by a board of officers, Lieutenant William H. Murdaugh president, directing minute examination into condition of hull and outfit, and general statement as to capacity for keeping the sea. Report of survey, dated March 9th: 'Outfit good, but incomplete; frame timbers sound, but requires some new deck-planks and recaulking—can carry but four and a half days' fuel at full speed, and eleven at a reduced rate; has tanks for 2,340 gallons of water and no condenser; and, in fine, with a crew of 100 men, her bunkers full of coal, and the stores and outfit necessary for cruising on board, she could only carry provisions for six weeks, and even then some of the wet provisions would have to be carried on deck.' "

I informed the Secretary of the Navy that in consequence of the above report "I have directed Lieutenant-Commanding Fauntleroy to pay off and discharge the crew, detach the officers, and strip and lay up the ship. This has been done, and she now lies in dock at Calais in charge of a master's mate."

Even if the *Rappahannock* had been in perfect condition for cruising, the state of affairs in March, 1865, would not have justified me in sending her on a cruise. The Confederate finances in Europe could not have supplied the necessary funds, and, moreover, it was manifest that the Confederate armies could not hold out much longer. The mere cost of keeping the ship at Calais, with a few ship-keepers, was an embarrassing expense, and yet the vessel was unsaleable. At last I got a ship-broker to assume charge under a nominal sale, and he brought her over to England as an English ship, but by the time this was accomplished the end had come—the Confederate Government had expired—I could give no legal title to her, and I was only too glad to be disembarrassed of all connection or concern with her. She was, I believe, claimed by the United States, and no one appearing to resist the claim, she fell into their possession. At any rate, I never called upon the purchaser for payment of the nominal amount for which the ship was sold to him, nor has he made any claim for the expenses of removing her from Calais. How he got rid of her, or whether he was reimbursed for his outlay, I have never inquired, but it is not likely that I would have remained in ignorance on those points if the final disposal of the vessel had left a deficit.

Commodore Barron was well known in the United States navy as a gallant officer. He came to Europe buoyant with the hope of commanding the Liverpool rams; he bore the disappointment and the many months of forced idleness in Paris with patience, and retired to privacy and partial poverty after the war, having been denied the opportunity which would have at least afforded him the chance of winning naval honours.

After the fall of Fort Fisher, which closed the Cape Fear river and Wilmington to foreign trade, there was no port left open to the ordinary blockade-runner east of the Mississippi, and it became a question of very serious consideration how to get further supplies into the Confederacy. Commander M. F. Maury thought that he might make his investigations into the subject of submarine defences useful in keeping open Galveston or some other inlet on the coast of Texas, and offered to go out for that purpose if I would ship the necessary material to Havana. This proposal was carried out. I forwarded to the Confederate agent at Havana, by steamer from Southampton, the quantity of insulated wire, copper tanks, magnetic exploders, etc., suggested by Commander Maury, and he took passage in the same steamer. On his arrival at Havana, the news of General Lee's surrender had already reached that place; and that event was so soon followed by the surrender of the forces under General Johnston that it appeared to Commander Maury useless to make any effort to get into a Texan port. He therefore abandoned the project.

It has been mentioned in a previous chapter that Lieutenant James H. North was sent to England at an early period of the war to examine into the construction of ironclad vessels, and that he was authorized to contract for a ship of that class, which, if completed and got to sea, he was to have commanded. Lieutenant (afterwards Commander) North contracted on the Clyde for an armour-clad ship of the broadside type. She was a large vessel, fully up in all respects to the ships of her class at that date; but when she was almost complete it became so manifest that her Majesty's Government would not permit her to go to sea, that Commander North consulted the Confederate Commissioners, Messrs. Mason and Slidell; and acting under their advice, he permitted the builders to sell the ship to the Danish Government. The sale was *bonâ fide*, and the ship was delivered to the purchasers in due course, and was paid for.

Commander North was instructed by the Navy Department to turn over the proceeds of the sale to me for general naval uses. Before those orders were received, £105,000 of the amount had been loaned to the fiscal agent of the Treasury Department to complete the sum necessary to meet the interest on the seven per cent. Bonds of the "Erlanger Loan," due September, 1864. At a later date, October, 1864, Commander North transferred to me a further sum of £67,000. Upon the receipt of the transfer order from the Navy Department, I confirmed the loan to the Treasury, and upon the requisition of General McRae and his urgent representation I advanced £40,000 in addition out of the Naval Exchequer to meet drafts drawn by agents of the War Department.

These loans were necessary by reason of the great wants of the War Department and other heavy drains upon the financial agents. They were immediately reported to the Secretary of the Navy, and at a later period the Confederate Congress confirmed them as a permanent transfer, and by an arrangement between the heads of Departments a still further appropriation of the funds originally assigned to the navy was made for the use of the army, and for the general demands upon the Treasury.

In point of fact, no fresh naval enterprises were set in train, nor were any fresh contracts made for that Department after February 1st, 1865. By that time it had become manifest that all available resources should be appropriated to such efforts as might keep up the supplies to the armies in the field, or to meet the contracts which were still open, and the numerous Treasury drafts which were rapidly accumulating in the hands of the fiscal agents.

Among the printed correspondence on the subject of Confederate affairs in Europe are several letters relating to the "ironclad frigate built on the Clyde" and sold to Denmark. It appears to have been the impression of some of the United States Consuls that she was still the property of the Confederate States at the end of the war, and that the sale to Denmark was a sham. The action of the Danish Government at the time of the sale, and the delivery of the ship by the builders, should have satisfied them that their suspicions were unfounded, but the statement made above is a true and precise account of the disposition that was made of her.

The published report of a case in the Scotch Courts, called "The *Pampero* Case," makes it necessary for me to give some account of that vessel. In June or July, 1862, Lieutenant George T. Sinclair arrived in England on special service, his orders being to build, if possible, a vessel suited for a cruiser, and to go to sea in command of her himself. In pursuance of those instructions, he made an arrangement with an eminent firm of builders on the Clyde for a composite screw-steamer. The vessel was nearly ready for sea, but was still in possession of the builders, and was, in fact, their property, when she was seized by the Government. The following extract from the published account of the proceedings in the Scotch Courts will afford all the information in my possession, and, indeed, all that is of any public interest in respect to the above vessel, inasmuch as she never really became a Confederate vessel at all:—

"In November, 1863, the *Pampero* ... was lying at Lancefield Quay (Glasgow), and was detained by the Government. This case did not go to trial. The condition of the ship at the time of seizure was similar to that of the *Alexandra*, and had the case proceeded there would have been in the Scotch courts the prolonged litigation, expense, and uncertainty which had characterized the *Alexandra* case in England. Under these circumstances, the owners of the vessel came to a compromise with the Government. It was agreed that a verdict should be entered for the Crown on one count of the "information," that the owners should retain and trade with the vessel, but that they should not sell her for two years without the consent of the Crown. Therefore the judgment delivered by Lord Armidale allowed the owners to withdraw from the cause ... without any liability being incurred by any parties to the suit, and found for the Crown on the 37th count," etc.

No other attempts were made to obtain in Europe vessels for the Confederate naval service than those which are described in this and the preceding chapters, and the facts relating to those efforts have been told without reservation.

Besides the numerous opprobrious epithets applied to the Confederate Government and its agents by Mr. Seward and the Consuls, for attempting to carry on a naval war against the United States, it appears to have been their impression that British shipbuilders, conscious that they were acting illegally, charged extravagant prices for the vessels supplied to the Confederacy, and that the "nefarious practices" of the Confederate agents required a lavish expenditure of money. In refutation of that opinion, which frequently appears in the correspondence—rather, however, as an insinuation than a positive assertion—I will merely state that every transaction conducted by me on behalf of the Navy Department was based upon cash payment, and no more than actual value at the time was paid for any articles, whether ships or general supplies.

The peculiar position of affairs imposed upon a Confederate agent expenses of an exceptional character, which would not have been necessary under different circumstances. Often contraband goods had to be shipped under disguises and concealments, in order to escape the liability of having the vessel seized on suspicion of being intended for a cruiser, and whenever a vessel was really despatched with the purpose to convert her into a man-of-war, it was necessary to provide a tender, and to incur other incidental expenses. But nothing more than actual value was ever paid for any ship, and no risk or responsibility was assumed by any one who built a vessel for me, or sold one to me on behalf of the Confederate Government, except what is ordinarily embraced in such transactions, and I venture to say the same in reference to any other naval agent of that Government.

A few specifications may help to confirm the above statement, and may possibly be of some historical interest.

The *Alabama* cost £47,500 as delivered by the builders; her naval equipments and other incidental expenses required an additional sum of £13,437 8s. 7d., and she was supplied with £20,000 as a cruising fund, and for pay of officers and men. No remittances were made to her while cruising, and Captain Semmes drew no bills, so that the entire expenditure on account of the *Alabama*, from the time her keel was laid until she sunk off Cherbourg, was £80,937 8s. 7d., and I do not believe any vessel of her class was ever built and kept two years in commission for less.

The expenditure on the *Florida*, up to her arrival in Brest, September,

1863, had been in cost, £35,950, other expenses, £9,678 4s. 9d., or total expenditure to that date, £45,628 4s. 9d. The foregoing figures do not include the amount which may have been expended while she was in Mobile, and does not include her cruising fund, which was supplied by arrangements with the Treasury when she left Mobile.

The gross expenditure in the purchase and all the expenses of the *Shenandoah*'s cruise was £53,715 10s. 9d.

The foregoing accounts are of course exclusive of the cost and expenses of the tenders, but they include the cost of everything supplied to the vessels named. In regard to the tenders, it may be stated that if taken in the aggregate, they much more than recouped their cost by the successful voyages made through the blockade, and by their subsequent sale after they had completed the original service for which they were bought.

It is true that the *Agrippina* did not sell at her cost price, and the freight she earned on her last homeward voyage from Bahia did not make up the deficit; but the *Laurel* must be credited with a large sum on account of inward freight to Charleston. She then brought out between 600 and 700 bales of cotton, and was sold at cost. The other naval tender made several successful voyages through the blockade, and was then sold for more than two-thirds of her cost. Looking at those transactions, therefore, from a commercial point of view, it may be affirmed that the Confederate cruisers were not set afloat or maintained in an extravagant manner.

CHAPTER XII

Official dispositions of Holland, Brazil, Spain, Portugal, France, and Great Britain to the Confederate States.—The position assumed by Mr. Seward at the beginning of the Civil War.—The policy of the British Government.—English feeling in favour of the North.—Facts about slavery in America.—English sympathy transferred to the South.—Lack of courtesy and dignity in United States representatives.—The Alabama Claims.—Synopsis of the negotiations respecting those claims.—Position of the British Government in regard to them.—The three rules of the Treaty of Washington.—A possible application of them to the United States.

———

There was one result of the Confederate naval operations in Europe which Mr. Davis and his Cabinet could not have foreseen, and to which they had no purpose to contribute when it was determined to attack the enemy's commerce from across the sea. It doubtless often occurred to them, as it did to many others, that questions of belligerent rights and neutral duties would arise, and that the United States would become involved in complicated discussions with foreign Powers, which might in some way or other be helpful to the cause of the South. As the war progressed, and they beheld the arrogant pretensions of Mr. Seward, and the haughty offensive and dictatorial tone in which he urged them, it was thought that he would very probably draw upon himself and upon his country something more than diplomatic reproofs. Perhaps some even thought that Europe would tire of the long contest, and the harassing interruption of trade with the Southern States, and would intervene, either by force or persuasion, to stop the war and restore the normal conditions of commerce.

But among all the various hopes or surmises which may have been discussed at Richmond, or which stirred the minds of the Southern people, no one ever dreamed that Great Britain would be selected as the chief object of Mr. Seward's malice, and that she—ever more yielding to the United States than any other Power with which there was a controversy, and always more restrictive than France, especially in the treatment of Confederate cruisers—would have been selected to pay the penalty of recognising the Confederate States as belligerents, and to recoup to the United States a portion of the losses inflicted by the war. No country whose ports were visited by Confederate cruisers was so restrictive and exacting as Great Britain, and no Government was more cautious and reserved in granting privileges or permitting official courtesies to Confederate commanding officers or diplomatic agents which could be construed into an admission of anything beyond the merest belligerent rights.

Perhaps it would be well to give a few examples of the action of some other Powers and the privileges granted to Confederate cruisers in their ports.

Holland.—The *Sumter* was the first Confederate vessel that got to sea. She was down among the windward West India Islands in July–August, 1861, and visited during those months two ports of the Dutch possessions, namely, St. Anne's, Curaçoa, and Paramaribo. She was permitted to remain at the first port eight days, and at the second eleven days. At both places she was allowed to obtain coal and other supplies, and she was received and treated by the authorities in every respect as a national ship-of-war. Mr. Seward remonstrated, and in one of his despatches in February, 1862, he directed the United States Minister at the Hague to call attention to the "subject of the intrusion of piratical American vessels seeking shelter in the ports of the Netherlands and their colonies"; but the Dutch Government was never induced to withdraw the recognition of belligerent rights conceded to the South, or to treat Confederate ships-of-war otherwise than those of the United States.

Mr. Pike, the Minister of the United States at the Hague, insisted that the vessels of the Confederate States were "piratical craft," or, at best, he said, they could only be looked upon as "privateers," and therefore should be excluded from ports of the Netherlands. In reply, Baron van Zuylen, the Netherlands Minister of Foreign Affairs, stated the views of his Government, as follows:—"The vessel armed for war by private persons is called a 'privateer.' The character of such vessel is settled precisely, and, like her English name (privateer) indicates sufficiently under this circumstance that she is a private armed vessel—name which Mr. Wheaton gives them ('Elements of International Law,' ii., p. 19). Privateering is the maritime warfare which privateers are authorized to make for their own account, against merchant-vessels of the enemy by virtue of letters of marque, which are issued to them by the State. The *Sumter* is not a private vessel; is not the property of unconnected individuals—of private ship-owners. She therefore cannot be a privateer; she can only be a ship-of-war, or ship of the State, armed for cruising.... It cannot be held, as you propose in your despatch of the 9th of this month, that all vessels carrying the Confederate flag are, without distinction, to be considered as privateers, because the principles of the law of nations, as well as the examples of history, require that the rights of war be accorded to those States."*

Brazil.—The *Sumter* went from Paramaribo to Maranham in the Empire of Brazil. She was allowed to remain ten days, and to take in as much coal as she wanted. The United States Consul made a protest to the President of the province, but the reply was that the *Sumter* was a belligerent vessel, and, as such, must be allowed to receive all necessary supplies. The United States Minister at Rio de Janeiro carried on a long correspondence with the Minister of Foreign Affairs on the subject, and denounced the conduct of the President of Maranham as "an unfriendly act towards the United States, and a gross breach of neutrality"; but the Imperial Government approved the conduct of their officer in recognising the *Sumter* as a national ship-of-war.† At a later period of the war the *Florida, Georgia,* and *Alabama* were admitted to Brazilian ports on precisely the same footing as vessels of the United States. It was alleged that the *Alabama* had violated the neutrality of Brazil by making captures within the territorial waters of the Empire off the island of Fernando de Noronha. The President of the province of Pernambuco, within whose jurisdiction the alleged offence was said to have been committed, sent instructions to the Governor of the island to order the *Alabama* away, but meanwhile she had left the neighbourhood, and on May 11th, 1863, she entered the harbour of Bahia, and was permitted to remain there fourteen days.

The United States Minister remonstrated, and even went so far as to maintain that the *Alabama* should have been seized and detained at Bahia; but the Brazilian Government replied that the President of Bahia had

---

* See "British Case," Appendix, vol. vi., pp. 70, 76, 77, and Sir A. Cockburn, pp. 83, 84, for correspondence between Mr. Pike and Baron van Zuylen.

† See "British Counter-Case," p. 120, and Appendix to "British Case," vol. vi., pp. 17, 42.

done right in receiving the *Alabama,* and that he would not have been justified in refusing her the hospitalities of the port without positive evidence of her having infringed the neutrality of the Empire. Subsequently, instructions were issued to exclude the *Alabama* from Brazilian ports on the ground that she had burned captured vessels within the territorial limits of the Empire, but there never arose an occasion to enforce the order, as the ship proceeded from Bahia to the East Indies, and did not again appear on the South American coast. Captain Semmes wrote me a categorical denial of the report upon which the above-mentioned instructions were issued, and he would have been able to prove its falsehood if it had been necessary or convenient for him to bring the *Alabama* again into a Brazilian port.

Spain.—In January, 1862, the *Sumter* entered the port of Cadiz, and was not only permitted to obtain supplies, but she was allowed the use of a Government dock to make her repairs. In February, 1865, the *Stonewall* was compelled to put into Ferrol in consequence of a serious leak in her rudder-casing, and she was allowed to remain more than a month refitting. In reply to the protest of the United States Minister, the Spanish Minister of Foreign Affairs said:—"The Government of her Majesty could not disregard the voice of humanity, in perfect harmony with the laws of neutrality, and does not think they are violated by allowing a vessel only the repairs strictly necessary to navigate without endangering the lives of the crew."* Subsequently, in May, 1865, the *Stonewall* entered the Spanish Colonial port of Havana. The Captain-General not only recognised her as a vessel-of-war, although the Confederate Government had to all appearance ceased to exist, but he advanced to her commander the amount necessary to pay off the crew.

Portugal.—From Ferrol the *Stonewall* proceeded to Lisbon, where she was permitted to remain the full time to which the stay of vessels belonging to both belligerents was restricted, and was also permitted to take in a supply of coal. The Minister of the United States made the usual protest, but in reply to his representations the Portuguese Foreign Minister wrote thus:—"Regarding the supply of coal, against which you insist, allow me to observe that the vessel being a steamer, his Majesty's Government could not avoid with good foundation that she should be provided with that article, with the same reason that it could not deny to any sailing-vessel in a dismantled state to provide itself with sails."†

* Quoted in "British Counter-Case," p. 123.
† Ibid.

France.—The *Sumter, Alabama, Florida, Georgia,* and *Rappahannock,* were on every occasion of visiting French ports received with marked consideration, and were allowed to take supplies of coal and to repair damages with a degree of freedom and latitude in excess of the privileges granted them by any other Power.

The *Sumter* called at Martinique in November, 1861. She was permitted to remain fourteen days, and to take in a full supply of coal, enough, in fact, to carry her across the Atlantic. The *Alabama* touched at Martinique in November, 1862, to meet her tender, the *Agrippina.* Her Britannic Majesty's Consul at St. Pierre reported to the Governor that he had reason to believe that the *Agrippina* was a supply ship for the *Alabama,* and that the meeting of the two ships at the island was probably for the purpose of furnishing the *Alabama* with coal. The above information was given to the Governor before the *Alabama*'s arrival, but it had been elicited from the captain of the *Agrippina* by the Consul, and he deemed it his duty to acquaint the French authorities with the fact. In a report of the circumstances to his Government, dated November 26th, 1862,* the British Consul says:—"I next deemed it proper to acquaint the Governor with what I had just learned. He did not seem much surprised, and observed that if the *Alabama* came into port he would act exactly as he had done on a former occasion in the case of the *Sumter,* when the French Government had altogether approved of the measures he had taken in regard to that vessel." When the *Alabama* arrived a few days after, she received permission to remain as long as necessary and to land her prisoners.

The *Florida* was allowed to remain several months at Brest, to repair damages in a Government dock, to land her small arms and have them repaired by a local gunsmith, and finally, to discharge a large portion of her crew, and to take on board other men to make good the original number. The United States Minister at Paris protested against the privileges extended to the *Florida,* and especially with reference to the repairs to her machinery. M. Drouyn de l'Huys replied that "if she were deprived of her machinery she would be *pro tanto* disabled, crippled, and liable, like a duck with its wings cut, to be at once caught by the United States steamers. He said it would be no fair answer to say the duck had legs and could swim… and finally he said that they (the Imperial Government) must deal with this vessel (the *Florida*) as they would with the United States ships; or the ships of any other nation," etc.† The presence of the *Florida*

---

* "British Case," p. 107.

† See report of United States Minister, quoted in "British Case," pp. 71, 72.

at Brest gave rise to an official conversation between M. Drouyn de l'Huys and the American Minister, which manifests very strongly the determination of the French Government to recognise the Confederate States as a belligerent Power, and to repudiate the preposterous demand of Mr. Seward that their cruisers should be treated as pirates. Mr. Dayton, the American Minister, in a despatch to Mr. Seward, reported the conversation referred to in the following words:—

"On the 19th instant" (October, 1863) "I received a note from M. Drouyn de l'Huys, requesting to see me on the next day in reference to certain matters of business. I, of course, attended at the Foreign Office at the time named. He then informed me that it had been reported to him that the United States steamship *Kearsarge*, Captain Winslow, now in the port of Brest, kept her steam constantly up, with the view, as supposed, of instantly following and catching the *Florida* upon her leaving that port; and that France, having resolved to treat this vessel as a regularly commissioned ship-of-war, could not, and would not, permit this to be done. He said that the rule which requires that the vessel first leaving shall have twenty-four hours' start must be applied. To avoid the difficulty which, he said, must inevitably follow a disregard of this rule by Captain Winslow, he requested me to communicate to him the determination of this Government, and apprise him of the necessity of complying with the rule. Inasmuch as nothing was to be gained by inviting the application of force, and increased difficulties might follow that course, I have communicated to Captain Winslow the letter, of which I herewith send you a copy."*

In reference to the permission granted to the *Florida* to fill up the vacancies in her crew, Mr. Dayton reported in the same despatch as follows:—

"The determination which has been reached by the French authorities to allow the shipment of a crew, or so large a portion of one, on board the *Florida* while lying in their port, is, I think, wrong, even supposing that vessel a regularly commissioned ship-of-war. I told M. Drouyn de l'Huys that, looking at it as a mere lawyer, and clear of prejudices which my official position might create, I thought this determination an error. He said, however, that in the conference they had reached that conclusion unanimously, although a majority of the Ministry considering the question were lawyers."

The *Georgia* was permitted to remain nearly four months at Cherbourg,

---

* Quoted in "British Case," p. 72.

where she was repaired in the Government dock, and was then again allowed after a very short cruise to enter the port of Bordeaux, and to remain there a month, or a full fortnight after her repairs were completed.

The *Rappahannock,* only a few hours after leaving a British dockyard, entered the .port of Calais, having been transformed from an English despatch-boat to a Confederate vessel-of-war during the run across the Channel. Nevertheless, she was received by the French authorities as a regularly commissioned ship-of-war, and was permitted to lie in the dock at Calais to receive workmen from England to complete her engines, and to remain in that harbour from November, 1863, until March, 1865, flying the Confederate flag and pennant, and actually performing the office of a *depôt,* or receiving vessel, for officers and men destined for employment in other ships.

Most of the foregoing specifications of the privileges granted to Confederate vessels-of-war in the ports of the Maritime Powers have been incidentally mentioned in the course of the preceding narrative; but they are recapitulated with more particularity, and are brought together, in order to demonstrate with what unanimity the Governments of foreign States recognised the right of the Confederacy to commission ships-of-war, and the uniformity with which they all repudiated the assumption of the United States that those ships were either "piratical vessels" or "privateers."

An examination of the diplomatic correspondence, and of the proceedings before the Tribunal of Arbitration, will supply the most abundant evidence, not only of the greater facilities for obtaining supplies and repairs, and the greater privileges generally which were allowed to Confederate vessels in the ports of all the other Maritime Powers than were permitted to them in British ports, but will also demonstrate that those Powers were almost invariably more decided in their manner of setting aside the protests of the United States, and more resolutely determined to make no distinction whatever in the treatment of vessels of both parties in the Civil War than Great Britain; and yet the United States, in the "Case" presented to the Tribunal of Arbitration, contrasts the strict observance of neutrality of some of the other Powers, and of France particularly, with the partiality which they allege was shown to the vessels of the Confederate States by her Britannic Majesty's Government.

Great stress is of course laid by the United States upon the action of the French Government in respect to the vessels built by MM. Arman and Voruz for the Confederate States. The secret understanding which induced the Confederate Government to attempt to build ships in France has been fully explained in a previous chapter. The character of that understanding may not have been known to the Minister of the United States, and he may not even have suspected that Mr. Slidell had received covert encouragement from the Imperial Government. But when he obtained copies of private papers belonging to the builders through the treachery of a clerk, and was thus able to approach the French Minister of Foreign Affairs with very plausible reasons for official inquiry into the character and destination of the ships, the Imperial Government was only brought face to face with a contingency which must have been foreseen when Mr. Slidell was advised to make use of French dockyards. Mr. Dayton could give the Foreign Minister no information with which he was not already acquainted, and the Government could not hesitate between one of two courses.

It was possible for M. Drouyn de l'Huys to reply that M. Arman was building the ships in the ordinary course of his business, as a purely commercial transaction, and that he purposed to despatch them for delivery abroad, which was not contrary to French law, and therefore the Government could not interfere with the legitimate trade of the country. This is precisely what Mr. Slidell had been told would be the answer to any remonstrance from the United States. The alternative course was to affect ignorance of M. Arman's original intentions, to assume an appearance of surprise and vexation at his attempt to infringe the Proclamation of Neutrality, and to compel him to break his engagements with the Confederate agent. The Imperial Government, for political reasons, did not feel willing to encounter the possible danger of adopting the first course, and there was no other choice but to follow the latter.

The vessels were not only built manifestly for war, but there had been no attempt at disguise, and no omission of any of the equipments necessary to make them efficient as fighting ships. Magazines and shell-rooms were placed in each, and all the bolts, traverses, and gear required for mounting and manœuvring the guns were provided. In fact, the guns themselves had been manufactured under the authority of the Minister of Marine, and the open, undisguised purpose was to despatch the ships from France, ready to go into action, except in respect to their fighting crews. If there had been no covert understanding, the usual, at least the natural and equitable course, would have been to have seized the ships and to have taken legal proceedings against the builders for their forfeiture, and against M. Arman for infringement of the Neutrality Laws. That course would have involved awkward exposures, because M. Arman, not finding it possible to deny the equipment of the ships, would have been forced to give a true history of the whole transaction in order to save the property from forfeiture, and as an act of self-defence.

The compilers of the "Case of the United States" presented to the Tribunal of Arbitration make the following remark in reference to the forced sale of the Arman ships:—"The course pursued by France towards these vessels is in striking contrast with Great Britain's conduct in the cases of the *Florida* and the *Alabama*."* To those who may read this narrative, or who care to search the records of the Geneva Arbitration, the cases will not appear to be at all parallel. Setting aside the secret permission of the Imperial Government, and looking only to the actual condition of the Arman ships at the date of Mr. Dayton's complaint, it must be admitted that any neutral Power would have had no hesitation how to act—the obligation to intervene and to require explanation was manifest. The ships, as the French Minister of Marine said, were *"véritable corvettes de guerre,"* and were "equipped," "fitted out," and "furnished" in every respect as fighting ships, prepared to begin hostilities at the moment of passing the line of French jurisdiction. The *Alabama* and *Florida,* on the contrary, were vessels wholly unprovided with arms or munitions of war, and without any equipment or appliances which would have enabled them either to mount or use a battery of guns. They left England as helpless as all ordinary merchant ships, and could have been captured by the smallest and most weakly armed gunboat, without the possibility of making any resistance.

It in no way concerns me to defend the action of her Majesty's Government against the charge of practising a lax rule of neutrality, and of having pursued a course which was unfriendly to the United States and encouraging to the South. Those who are curious to know what has been said on both sides must refer to the "Cases" presented by the two Governments to the Tribunal of Arbitration. My office and my purpose is to state only such facts as will serve to place the action of the Confederate Government in a perfectly true and clear light, and then to demonstrate that the "criminal proceedings" and the "nefarious transactions" attributed to the representatives of that Government have no solid foundation, and rest upon no genuine or specific occurrences, but that all such expressions are mere "figures of rhetoric," which the State Department at Washington adopted as the means of manifesting its chagrin and disappointment because the civilized world would not pronounce Mr. Davis, Lee and Jackson rebels, and refused to treat Semmes, Maffitt, Waddell and Morris as pirates.

* See "United States Case," p. 73.

The correspondence between Mr. Seward and the United States Ministers at the Hague, Paris, and Rio de Janeiro manifests that he was angry with all alike, and complained with equal petulance against all who extended the favour of belligerent rights to the Confederacy, but he was never able to fix upon any other Power a specific act which in his judgment demanded a formal claim for damages. He found the occasion for such a pretension against Great Britain in the fact that ships were obtained in England which were afterwards used to make war upon the United States, and having found the pretext, he seems never to have abandoned for a moment the purpose to exact retribution, but prosecuted his aim with persistent and implacable consistency and vigour. The "Secretary of State" is the member of the American Cabinet who has the management of the Foreign Affairs of the country, and he is the exponent of the national will and the expounder of the public feelings in regard to all that affects international relations. Mr. Seward held that office during, and for some time after, the Civil War, and he was therefore the medium of communication with foreign Powers, and he had the opportunity to impress his own views upon the foreign policy of the United States, and to explain that policy in the spirit and language suited to his own temper and taste.

I know nothing of Mr. Seward personally, and have no purpose to criticise his special attributes, or his management of public affairs in the high office he held under President Lincoln. It is far less my wish to invade the domain of his private feelings, or to impugn the motives which gave life and energy to his acts. It has been necessary to comment upon the petulant, haughty, and dictatorial style of the official correspondence between the State Department at Washington and the representatives of foreign Powers during the Civil War, and it will furthermore be necessary to demonstrate that the grievances of the United States were urged by the Consuls, and even some of the higher agents who got their inspiration from Washington, in a manner not only out of harmony with the rules of diplomatic courtesy as commonly practised, but often in a style which was offensive.

In the statement of facts pertaining to the claims of the United States against Great Britain, and in commenting upon the mode of pressing them, a frequent mention of the high functionary who both formulated the demands and gave the key-note to the tone in which they should be urged is unavoidable, but no fact has been or will be mentioned, and no document will be quoted, that has not already been published among the diplomatic records, or which does not appear among the proceedings of the Geneva Arbitration; and in the comments upon the facts and documents Mr. Seward's name cannot be separated from the statements, complaints, and demands which were set forth by himself, or by his authority. The author or expounder of a national policy which becomes historic, sacrifices his individuality so far as the public judgment is concerned. His name ceases to be an appellation suggestive of purely personal traits and attributes, but takes a generic form, and may be, and generally is, used as an historical synonym for the political events with which it is inseparably linked.

Mr. Seward is mentioned throughout this narrative in the impersonal sense suggested in the foregoing paragraph, a practice which is necessary for a clear and concise explanation of the subject, and which is justified by historic precedent and example.

The *Alabama* was the first foreign-built ship which took the sea under the Confederate flag, and her career presented more that was generally interesting to the public than the performances of either of her consorts, hence her origin, captures, and the treatment accorded to her by the home and colonial authorities of Great Britain attracted more than their due share of notice, and were the chief corner-stone upon which the United States based their complaints against her Majesty's Government. Indeed, her name was thrust so prominently and at such an early date into the diplomatic controversies which arose from the Civil War, that it came in time to be used as the specific title by which the murmurs, the pretensions, and finally the demands of the United States were designated, and they are all classed and scheduled in State Papers and in historical reminiscences under the generic title of the "*Alabama* Claims." But although the famous Confederate craft was a prominent factor in the diplomatic war, which was waged for a longer time than the actual struggle, yet the grievances of the United States took a much wider range than the limits of her cruise, or the injury inflicted upon American commerce by her depredations.

In order that the general reader may be able to understand the comprehensive character of those claims, and may also understand how it came about that England and the United States appeared before an International Tribunal, it will be necessary to give not only a sketch of the general as well as the specific complaints which were urged against the Government and people of Great Britain, but to describe to some extent the manner in which her Majesty's Government received and treated the complaints during the progress of the war.

The surrender of Fort Sumter on the 13th of April, 1861, was the initial act of the Civil War. The President of the United States issued a proclamation on the 15th of April calling out troops to the number of 75,000 men.* On the 19th of April he issued another proclamation, declaring a blockade of the ports within the States of South Carolina, Georgia, Alabama, Florida, Mississippi, Louisiana, and Texas; and on the 27th of April still another, extending the blockade so as to include the Southern ports as far north as Virginia. On the 3rd of May, 1861, the proclamation of the blockade was published in the London newspapers; on the 10th of May copies of the proclamation of blockade, and of the counter-proclamation of President Davis, were received by Lord Russell from the British Minister at Washington, and finally the blockade was officially communicated to Lord Russell by the United States Minister on the 11th of May.

On the 6th of May Lord Russell stated in the House of Commons that after consultation with the law officers the Government had come to the conclusion that the Southern Confederacy must be treated as belligerents, and on the 14th of May her Majesty's Proclamation of Neutrality was issued, which acknowledged the existence of a Civil War, and thereby recognised the Confederate States as belligerents. The example of Great Britain was soon followed by the chief Maritime Powers in the following order:—France, June 10th; Netherlands, June 16th; Spain, June 17th; Brazil, August 1st. The remaining European Powers issued "notifications" at various dates, prohibiting the entry of privateers or prizes into their ports, and defining the conditions under which the public vessels of both parties should be permitted to enter and receive supplies, and drawing no distinction between them as belligerents.

Mr. Seward took prompt notice of the foregoing recognitions of the Confederate States, and vehemently denied the right of other nations to acknowledge their *de facto* status as that of a belligerent Power. He affirmed that the so-called Government at Richmond merely represented "a discontented domestic faction." Writing to Mr. Dayton on the 30th of May, 1861, he says:—"The United States cannot for a moment allow the French Government to rest under the delusive belief that they will be content to have the Confederate States recognised as a belligerent Power by States with which this nation is at amity. No concert of action among

---

* The dates and order of the Proclamations are taken from the "British Case," pp. 4, 5, etc., which gives the United States source from which they were obtained.

foreign States so recognising the insurgents can reconcile the United States to such a proceeding, whatever may be the consequences of resistance."*

In a subsequent despatch to Mr. Dayton (June 17, 1861), Mr. Seward says:—"It is erroneous, so far as foreign nations are concerned, to suppose that any war exists in the United States. Certainly there cannot be two belligerent Powers where there is no war. There is here, as there has always been, one political Power, namely, the United States of America, competent to make war and peace, and conduct commerce and alliances with all foreign nations. There is none other, either in fact or recognised by foreign nations.... The French Government says, in the instruction which has been tendered to us, that certain facts which it assumes confer upon the insurgents of this country, in the eyes of foreign Powers, all the appearances of a Government *de facto*, wherefore, whatever may be its regrets, the French Government must consider the two contending parties as employing the forces at their disposal in conformity with the laws of war. This statement assumes not only that the law of nations entitles any insurrectionary faction, when it establishes a *de facto* Government, to be treated as a belligerent, but also that the fact of the attainment of this status is to be determined by the appearance of it in the eyes of foreign nations. If we should concede both of these positions, we should still insist that the existence of a *de facto* Government entitled to belligerent rights is not established in the present case."†

On the 21st of July, 1861, he wrote on the same subject to Mr. Adams as follows:—"The United States and Great Britain have assumed incompatible, and thus far irreconcilable positions on the subject of the existing insurrection. The United States claim and insist that the integrity of the Republic is unbroken, and that their Government is supreme, so far as foreign nations are concerned, as well for war as for peace, over all the States, all sections, and all citizens, the loyal not more than the disloyal, the patriots and the insurgents alike," etc.‡

The foregoing quotations will sufficiently demonstrate the position assumed by Mr. Seward on the part of the United States, a position which foreign Powers unanimously declared to be untenable, and at variance with the recognised principles of international law.

* "United States Appendix," vol. i., p. 192, quoted by Sir A. Cockburn, p. 82.
† Ibid., vol. i., p. 202, quoted by Sir A. Cockburn, p. 82.
‡ Ibid., vol. i., p. 214, quoted by Sir A. Cockburn, p. 82.

The views of the British Government were expressed in a despatch to Lord Lyons, her Majesty's Minister at Washington, dated June 21st, 1861. Lord Russell, in the despatch referred to, mentions that Mr. Adams had complained of the Queen's Proclamation of Neutrality as having been hasty and premature, and then adds:—"I said (to Mr. Adams), in the first place, that our position was of necessity neutral; that we could not take part either for the North against the South, or for the South against the North. To this he willingly assented, and said that the United States expected no assistance from us to enable their Government to finish the war. I rejoined that if such was the case, as I supposed, it would not have been right either towards our admirals and naval commanders, nor towards our merchants and mercantile marine, to leave them without positive and public orders; that the exercise of belligerent rights of search and capture by a band of adventurers clustered in some small island in the Greek Archipelago or in the Atlantic would subject them to the penalty of piracy; but we could not treat 5,000,000 of men, who had declared their independence, like a band of marauders or filibusters. If we had done so we should have done more than the United States themselves. Their troops had taken prisoners many of the adherents of the Confederacy; but I could not perceive from the newspapers that in any case they had brought these prisoners to trial for high treason, or shot them as rebels."*

The policy of the British Government was more fully explained and justified in a letter from Lord Russell to Mr. Adams, dated May 4th, 1865. His lordship is writing on the subject of the blockade, and the action of Great Britain in recognising the Confederate States as a belligerent Power, and he says to Mr. Adams:—

"Let me remind you that when the Civil War in America broke out so suddenly, so violently, and so extensively, that event, in the preparation of which Great Britain had no share, caused nothing but detriment and injury to her Majesty's subjects; Great Britain had previously carried on a large commerce with the Southern States of the Union, and had procured there the staple which furnished materials for the industry of millions of her people. Had there been no war, the existing treaties with the United States would have secured the continuance of a commerce mutually advantageous and desirable. But what was the first act of the President of the United States? He proclaimed on the 19th of April, 1861, the blockade of the ports of seven States of the Union. But he could lawfully interrupt the

* Quoted by Sir A. Cockburn, pp. 82, 83.

trade of neutrals to the Southern States upon one ground only, namely, that the Southern States were carrying on war against the Government of the United States; in other words, that they were belligerents. Her Majesty's Government, on hearing of these events, had only two courses to pursue, namely, that of acknowledging the blockade and proclaiming the neutrality of her Majesty, or that of refusing to acknowledge the blockade, and insisting upon the rights of her Majesty's subjects to trade with the ports of the South. Her Majesty's Government pursued the former course as at once the most just and the most friendly to the United States.... So much as to the step which you say your Government can never regard 'as otherwise than precipitate,' of acknowledging the Southern States as belligerents. It was, on the contrary, your own Government which, in assuming the belligerent right of blockade, recognised the Southern States as belligerents. Had they not been belligerents, the armed ships of the United States would have had no right to stop a single British ship upon the high seas."[*]

It would be a useless waste of time and space to make further quotations from the diplomatic correspondence on the foregoing subject. No one who has taken any interest in the questions of public law which arose out of the Civil War, and has made the least effort to acquaint himself with the views of those Powers whose maritime position and commercial privileges required them to assume a decisive attitude, can doubt that the United States stood quite alone in the assumption that "the Southern States were still in the Union," that their civil leaders "represented merely a discontented faction," and that the people were only "insurgents" whom the Government at Washington should be permitted to chastise and reduce to obedience in its own fashion.

Every foreign Power with whom the United States found it necessary to remonstrate dissented from the foregoing pretensions, and affirmed the dissent with so much determination, that it would have been politic in Mr. Seward to have refrained from pressing them after he had once attempted to satisfy his conscience by a firm and formal protest; but he never ceased to rail and wrangle, until Europe became tired, if not nauseated, by his ceaseless complaints and his bitter vituperations.

When the *Alabama* was commissioned as a Confederate ship-of-war off Terceira, and her visits to the ports of several of the Maritime Powers made it manifest that all were alike determined to grant her the status of

---

[*] "United States Documents," vol. i., p. 295, quoted by Sir A. Cockburn, p. 80.

a national cruiser, and to put her upon the same footing as the public vessels of the United States, the question of belligerent rights assumed a more practical form. Mr. Seward then found a tangible cause of complaint against Great Britain, and it must be admitted that, having once formed the purpose to seek redress from her Majesty's Government for the alleged offence of recognising the South as a belligerent State, and for granting the privilege of supplying her wants in the United Kingdom, he pursued his aim with great energy and steadiness, until he wrung from Mr. Gladstone's Government in 1871 a confession of regret, and from the British Exchequer the sum of $15,500,000, half of which still lies in the United States Treasury for want of a recognised claimant to whom it can be justly paid.

All that is necessary to a clear understanding of the origin of the various Confederate cruisers has already been fully explained in previous chapters; all that relates to the alleged default of her Majesty's Government in respect to those vessels, which has not been made manifest in the course of this narrative, will be found in the proceedings of the Geneva Arbitration. A recapitulation of the circumstances connected with their building and despatch from England is therefore unnecessary; a lengthy review of the "Cases" presented by the two Governments to the Tribunal, or even a synopsis of the arguments of both sides, would require a volume, and would not be interesting, even if it were necessary to a satisfactory knowledge of the so-called "*Alabama* Claims," and how they were made up and maintained. A few specifications of the various complaints and the replies, and a brief *resumé* of the principal claims set out by the United States in the "Case" presented to the Tribunal of Arbitration, are, however, essential to a full illustration of the whole subject.

It has been already stated that the grievances of the United States covered a much wider field than the charges founded upon the depredations of the *Alabama* and her consorts. They were not all, or even the most warmly asserted of them, based upon tangible acts of omission or negligence in the performance of neutral duties, but were in the form of lamentations for the alleged unfriendliness of her Britannic Majesty's Government, and of chagrin in consequence of the alleged want of sympathy of the British public with the aims and objects of the war as expounded by Mr. Seward.

The mere statement of the "Case of the United States" occupies a large Parliamentary Blue Book of a hundred and thirty-one pages. There is a short introductory chapter of seven pages, in which it is stated that a Joint High Commission appointed by Great Britain and the United States met at Washington "in the spring of 1871," and that statement is followed by a protocol of the conferences of the Joint Commission as to the "*Alabama* Claims," and a copy of the "Treaty of Washington," or so much of it as relates to the settlement of those claims. The second chapter, or Part II. of the "Case," has the following heading in very large print: "Unfriendly course pursued by Great Britain towards the United States from the outbreak to the close of the insurrection."

The foregoing somewhat sensational opening of the "United States Case" manifests the spirit in which the "*Alabama* Claims" were prosecuted. Alleged "unfriendliness" on the part of her Majesty's Ministers, and a want of sympathy on the part of the British public, formed the text of the legal exposition of those "Claims" before the Tribunal of Arbitration, just as they had been the underlying stimulant which gave force and tartness to the diplomatic remonstrances from Washington, and had inspired the inflammatory manifestoes of the United States Consuls during the war.

No one can read the "Case of the United States," and the arguments in support of it, without perceiving that the chief object was to prejudice the arbitrators by disparaging the institutions and laws of Great Britain, and by impugning the motives of the British Government, and seeking to cast reproach upon the particular Cabinet Minister whose office it was to administer the foreign affairs of the country. The "Case" is full of such statements, insinuations, and allegations as follow:—"Her Majesty's Government was actuated by a conscious unfriendly purpose towards the United States"—"the feeling of personal unfriendliness towards the United States continued during a long portion or the whole of the time of the commission or omission of the acts complained of"—"the facts established show an unfriendly feeling which might naturally lead to, and would account for, a want of diligence bordering upon wilful negligence"—"Great Britain framed its rules, construed its laws and its instructions, and governed its conduct, in the interest of the insurgents." The colonial authorities are said to have shown "a persistent absence of real neutrality which should throw suspicion upon the acts of the British officials as to the vessels, and should incline the Tribunal to closely scrutinize their acts." Earl Russell is arraigned before the Court of Arbitration as a Minister who "evinced a consistent course of partiality towards the insurgents," and he is charged with specific acts of delay in acting upon the information furnished him by the United States Minister, which it is insinuated arose from a friendly feeling towards the Confederate States.

Those who wish to fully appreciate the spirit which inspired the representatives of the United States at Geneva, and which actuated the compilers of the "Case," must refer to the printed statements and arguments of the two principals in the controversy. My purpose is only to furnish such facts and to make such extracts as may be necessary to justify the course pursued by the Confederate Government, and to demonstrate that if, as alleged, the sympathies of the British Government and the British public were with the Southern people, that sympathy was given to them partly because they won it by their own merit and the intrinsic justice of their cause, and partly because the United States repelled and turned it from themselves by the extravagance of their pretensions, and the arrogance with which their claims to it were asserted. The allegation that the British people were generally friendly and sympathetic towards the South is not confined to the statements to that effect in the "United States Case," but it appears throughout the diplomatic correspondence between Mr. Seward and the American Minister and Consuls in Great Britain during the war. The fact was constantly affirmed and bitterly resented by the newspapers in the Northern States; it was denounced by members of both Houses of Congress, and the Northern people were manifestly offended, and were often led to express their disappointment and surprise in terms of bitter reproach against the British public.

Those who have read the proceedings before the Geneva Tribunal, and have cared to examine and to compare the statements in this narrative with the explanations and arguments of the British representatives, have all the data necessary to form independent opinions in regard to the alleged partiality of her Majesty's Government towards the Confederate States, and I will say nothing on that score. But my own personal observation, confirmed by the testimony of every other agent of the Confederate Government whose duties compelled him to reside in England during the Civil War, convinced me that the great majority of the people in Great Britain—at least among the classes a traveller, or a man of business, or a frequenter of the clubs, would be likely to meet—were on the Southern side. Circumstances threw me a good deal with army and navy men, and I can affirm that I never met one of either service who did not warmly sympathize with the South.

The assertion so frequently made by the representatives of the United States to the foregoing effect was, therefore, in all probability true; but whether it was either good taste or sound policy to make the admitted fact a subject of official complaint, and to thrust it prominently forward in a legal process against her Majesty's Government, is questionable, to say the least of it. No Minister of State can be held responsible for the private opinions of those immediately under his control; far less can the alleged

sympathies of a whole people, or any portion of them, be justly charged
as an offence for which the responsible Government of the country can be
called to account.

There can be no doubt that the tendency of public feeling in England
during the few months immediately preceding the Civil War, and for a
short time after the beginning of hostilities, was decidedly favourable to
the North. The majority of the people in Great Britain knew little or
nothing of American political history, and were wholly unable to trace the
approach to a sectional division of Parties which had been gradually maturing, and which had at last been fully accomplished through the Presidential election of 1860. They had been induced to believe that "the
peculiar institution" of the South was the sole cause of the trouble; and
their well-known sentiments on the subject of slavery in the abstract impelled them instinctively to give their sympathies to the North, whose
cause was pictured to them, in highly coloured phrases, as that of the
oppressed negro against the hard, exacting, and cruel taskmaster, who
fattened upon the fruit of his muscles, and yet denied him even the con-
solations of religion.

The reasons why this feeling changed and was converted into sympathy with the South will, I think, become manifest to all who care to read
the "Blue Books," the proceedings before the Geneva arbitrators, and
other public documents which record what may be called the "war correspondence" of the United States.

First, then, at the very beginning of the contest the slavery question
was thrust into the foreground, and the freedom of the slave was placed
before Europe as the motive which had aroused the philanthropic North
to action. If the political leaders and the public press in the Northern
States had been content to state their case in moderate language, or had
merely represented slavery as a national evil from which they wished to
purge themselves, while the South insisted not only upon the right to
maintain, but to extend it, but little curiosity to test the accuracy of the assertion would probably have been aroused, and the sympathy of the English people might have been retained. But from the beginning those who
spoke and wrote on behalf of the North assumed a style of invective, and
mingled so much vituperative denunciation of the Southern people with
assertions of their own patriotic impulses and purity of purpose, that public interest abroad was excited in a manner which they did not expect.

Every possible effort was made by the Northern press and by the public men of the North to prejudice the people of Great Britain against the
South. The antislavery poems of Whittier and Longfellow, the lectures of

Emerson, the letters and speeches of Motley and Everett, were reprinted by hundreds and sown broadcast over the British Isles. To these were added the violent political harangues of Sumner, Thaddeus Stevens, and others in the Federal Congress, and the bitter, intemperate, and vituperative denunciations of Wendell Philips, Lloyd Garrison, and many others of like spirit who were not in Congress.

The British public was startled by this deluge of depreciation and invective. The desire to make inquiry was aroused, and those papers which had from the first taken the Southern side began to enlighten the people in reference to the true causes of the war.

Benevolence in Great Britain assumes a practical form: it partakes as little as possible of the nature of an emotion. A man who pronounces a blessing upon the hungry and the naked, and says to them, "Go in peace; I pray that God may feed and clothe you," is not called in England a philanthropist, but a hypocrite. The poor, the needy, and the oppressed require something more than tears and prayers to relieve their present distress, and a contribution of money, or a practical plan for the permanent redress of their grievances, is worth more than all the sighs that pity ever evoked, or the deepest and strongest denunciations that were ever launched against the tyrant oppressor from political platforms, or were ever uttered in the sedate atmosphere of a lecture-room.

The information in regard to the slavery question, which soon began to find its way to the people of Great Britain, was not supplied from the South nor by Southern men. Those persons from the South who might have enlightened the public mind of Europe upon the causes of the war, and who could have exposed the exaggerated statements and pretensions put forth on behalf of the North, had more urgent affairs to occupy them. But whenever knowledge is sought and inquiry is keenly aroused, there are always to be found men who are willing to collect the facts and disseminate them.

Two or three leading English papers sent correspondents to the United States, and one—the *Times*—sent a representative who wielded a ready and eloquent pen to Richmond. Several daily papers and one or two of the monthlies began and continued to write from the Southern standpoint, and as the subject grew in interest and importance, investigation was stimulated, and the true bearing of the slavery question, and the conduct of the North in respect to it, was widely discussed and explained by numerous letters to the press, by pamphlets, and by speeches in and out of Parliament. The information thus laid before the British public was to the following effect:—

Slavery, as it existed in America, was an inheritance from the mother country. It was forced upon the colonies against the protest of some of them, notably of Virginia. At the close of the War of Independence, it existed in all the colonies, and was recognised as a legal institution by the constitution of the United States when the Federal Union was formed. From climatic and other causes, slave labour was more profitable throughout one section than the other, and the slave population gravitated by a natural law towards the States lying south of the Potomac. No Northern State emancipated its slaves, but the greater portion of them were transferred to the South by sale, and the remnant gradually disappeared. When the North was thus freed from slavery, not through any self-sacrifice, but chiefly by trade and barter, helped by natural causes, the agitation for its abolition elsewhere, and the abuse of the South for maintaining it, began.

When Wilberforce, Brougham and Clarkson aroused the British Government and the British people to a sense of the injustice of slavery, their fervid eloquence was directed against the institution itself, and not against those who had inherited it, and were in no sense responsible for its origin, and the whole country, conscious of its complicity in founding a system which had come to be regarded as an offence, contributed £20,000,000, to remove the shackles from the slave, so as to make a great act of national atonement, not a measure of confiscation, but of true benevolence.

The agitation in the Northern States was carried on in a very different spirit. The original Abolitionists and the political Party leaders with whom they in course of time became amalgamated, adopted only one method, and that was abuse and invective. Neither Puritan nor poet, neither statesman nor public writer, neither State Legislature nor other corporate association at the North, ever proposed a practical plan for the abolition of slavery, or suggested that the wrong over which they professed to be grieving was a national sin, and should be redressed by a common sacrifice. Speeches in and out of Congress, novels, pamphlets, poems, sermons, were filled with invective denouncing the wickedness of the slave-holder, but never contained a hint or suggestion how the sin should be purged, or a generous offer to share in the process.

Meanwhile, emigration was yearly giving to the Northern States increasing political power. They soon began to use that power in passing protective laws which well-nigh prohibited the import of Manchester goods and Birmingham wares, and thus permitted the great mill-owners of New England to grow rich from the manufacture of slave-grown cotton, and the iron-masters of Pennsylvania to supply the implements for its production at large profits to themselves.

Every article worn by the Southern slave, every tool used by him, yielded a profit to the Northern commission merchant, and almost every acre of slave-tilled soil paid a tax in the form of interest upon advances to a Northern banker or money-lender. This constant, steady drain had gradually impoverished one section and enriched the other, and it had become manifest to all who examined the subject thoughtfully that the burden and the "odium of slavery" rested upon the South, while the profits accrued to the North.

Notwithstanding the continued tirades against slavery and the slave-holder, the leaders of the Republican Party at the North continued even up to the election of Mr. Lincoln to bid for votes at the South, and from those at the North who were still desirous to give the South fair play in the Union, by professing a respect for State rights. The fourth article of the Republican platform adopted at Chicago in 1860 is in these words:— "The maintenance inviolate of the rights of the States, and especially the right of each State to order and control its own domestic institutions according to its own judgment exclusively, is essential to that balance of power on which the perfection and endurance of our political fabric depends." Mr. Lincoln, in his inaugural address, thus expounded the policy of his administration:—"I have no purpose, directly or indirectly, to interfere with the institution of slavery in the States where it exists; I believe I have no lawful right to do so, and I have no inclination to do so. Those who nominated and elected me did so with a full knowledge that I had made this and many similar declarations, and had never recanted them."

In spite of the prohibition of the slave-trade, it continued to be carried on in American vessels trading to Cuba and Brazil, down to the very outbreak of the war, and the vessels employed in it were almost exclusively fitted out at Northern ports. "Lord Lyons (the British Minister at Washington) stated in September, 1860, that in the previous eighteen months eighty-five vessels had sailed from American ports to be employed in the slave-trade; of ten vessels captured in one year by the American Squadron on the coast of Africa, seven were from New York."*

The foregoing statements in regard to the slavery question, and the position of the Northern States in respect to it, are not made as an exposition of the subject on behalf of the South with any partizan purpose. I confidently affirm that they are only a fair, though very short, summary of the numerous articles on the subject which appeared in the English news-

* See "The American Union," by Mr. James Spence, p. 151.

papers, or which were otherwise set before the British public during the Civil War. I have carefully eliminated every extravagant expression, every strained or far-fetched inference, which appeared in the articles and letters referred to, and I have equally omitted to mention or to paraphrase all statements which bear the likeness of angry retort or recrimination.

Some of the newspaper articles and pamphlets published in England during the early months of the war gave copious extracts from the speeches of the Northern Abolitionists and prominent men in the Republican Party, and called attention to their violent, abusive, and exasperating tone. Mr. James Spence, in his work "The American Union," furnished such extracts from speeches of William Lloyd Garrison, as follows:—"So long as this blood-stained Union existed, there was but little hope for the slave"—"this Union is a lie; the American Union is a sham, an imposture, a covenant with death, an agreement with hell." To inform the British public how the North proposed to deal with the question of slavery, Mr. Spence quoted from a book written by a leading Abolitionist named Helper, as follows:—"Compensation to slave-owners for negroes. Preposterous idea!—the suggestion is criminal, the demand unjust, wicked, monstrous, damnable! Shall we pat the blood-hounds for the sake of doing them a favour? Shall we fee the curs of slavery to make them rich at our expense? Pay these whelps for the privilege of converting them into decent, honest, upright men?" And he adds:—"In other passages they (the slave-holders) are compared to 'mad dogs'—with 'small-pox, as nuisances to be abated'; they are classed with gangs of 'licensed robbers,' 'thieves,' and 'murderers,' and addressed in terms and insulted with epithets such as none, however disinterested, can read without strong feelings of indignation." Lest it should be thought that the "wretched ribaldry," the coarse invectives, and the exasperating insolence of this man Helper were only the ravings of a maniac, or the wild incoherent utterances of an irresponsible fanatic, Mr. Spence informed his readers that the book was addressed to the American people, and was recommended for circulation by the signature of sixty-eight members of Congress from Northern States, including Mr. William H. Seward and Mr. John Sherman.

The majority of those who read the information thus for the first time submitted to their judgment, came to the conclusion that the North, in the aggregate, had as much moral complicity with slavery as the sugar-planters of the Mississippi bottoms, or the cotton-growers of the Gulf States, and they perceived that the Southern people had just cause to be dissatisfied with a Union whose protective tariff was impoverishing them, and in which they were exposed to continuous invective and abuse in respect to a domestic institution whose pecuniary profit accrued in the greater part to that portion of the country in which the abuse was coined, and from which it passed into foreign circulation.

When the people of Great Britain learned the whole truth, and contrasted the conduct of the North in reference to slavery before the war with the appeals for sympathy after the beginning of hostilities, they perceived the weakness of the claim and the insincerity of the pretext, and this discovery aroused a feeling first of indifference to the North, and then, by a natural process of reaction, they transferred their sympathies to the maligned Southerner. The popular verdict in England was that "the struggle between the North and South was a contest for political power and ascendancy, and that in reference to slavery the North discarded or ignored all practical measures for emancipation, and confined their operations to oratory, preaching, sentimental poems, fiction, and invective."*

The opinions of the responsible statesmen of Great Britain may be stated in the following extract from a speech delivered by Earl Russell at Newcastle on the 14th of October, 1861:—"We now see the two parties (in the United States) contending together, not upon the slavery question, though that I believe was probably the original cause of the quarrel, not contending with respect to free-trade and protection, but contending, as so many States in the Old World have contended, the one side for empire, and the other for independence."†

It does not concern any Southern man to defend the foregoing opinion of the people and of the governing class in Great Britain. I am simply recording facts to illustrate the process by which the United States lost the sympathy which they doubtless had at the beginning of the secession movement, but which they never ceased to allege was transferred to the South immediately after the outbreak of hostilities. The attitude of both North and South towards the institution of slavery is now well understood. The impartial historian of the future will hardly represent such men as Henry Clay, John C. Calhoun, Jefferson Davis, and Alexander H. Stephens, in the light of hard taskmasters whose object was to extend the area of slavery and to oppress their fellow-men, while Wendell Philips, W. H. Seward, Charles Sumner, and Abraham Lincoln, were fired by a

---

* Quoted in substance from "The American Union," and from "Life and Liberty in America," by Dr. Mackay.

† Quoted in "United States Case," p. 23.

philanthropic zeal to circumscribe its limits, and to abolish its practice from love for the victims. No future pen, writing with truth and fairness, and guided by a sense of just impartiality, will exhibit Sydney Johnstone, Robert Lee, and "Stonewall" Jackson as men who fought to rivet shackles upon the slave, and will at the same time describe Ulysses Grant, Wm. T. Sherman, Philip Sheridan, and Benjamin F. Butler as drawing their swords to sever the bonds. Such a record would be a greater travesty of history than was ever imposed upon a credulous posterity.

Another reason why the sympathy of Europe, but especially of Great Britain, was alienated from the North, arose from the offensive manner in which Mr. Seward continued to use the terms "insurgents" and "pirates" in communicating with foreign Powers in respect to their neutral duties, and their attitude towards the Confederacy. The popular feeling in England on that subject may be clearly demonstrated by the following quotations from a lengthy paper written by Sir Alexander Cockburn, giving the reasons why he dissented from some portions of the award of the Geneva Arbitration. "Men" (he said) "refused to see in the leaders of the South the 'rebels' and the 'pirates' held up by the United States to public reprobation, and thus the effect which a more generous appreciation of the position and qualities of their adversaries might have had in neutralizing the feeling in their favour, tended only to increase it" (p. 114). "Whatever the cause in which they are exhibited, devotion and courage will ever find respect, and they did so in this instance. Men could not see in the united people of these vast provinces, thus risking all in the cause of nationality and independence, the common case of rebels disturbing peace and order on account of imaginary grievances, or actuated by the desire to overthrow a Government in order to rise upon its ruins. They gave credit to the statesmen and warriors of the South—their cause might be right or wrong—for the higher motives which ennoble political action, and all the opprobrious terms which might be heaped upon the cause in which he fell could not persuade the world that the earth beneath which Stonewall Jackson rests does not cover the remains of a patriot and a hero" (p. 72).

The official view was expressed in the course of a speech by Earl Russell in the House of Lords, 9th of June, 1864. He said:—"It is dreadful to think that hundreds of thousands of men are being slaughtered for the purpose of preventing the Southern States from acting on those very principles of independence which, in 1776, were asserted by the whole of America against this country. Only a few years ago the Americans were in the habit of celebrating the promulgation of the Declaration of Independence, and some eminent friends of mine never failed to make eloquent and stirring orations on those occasions. I wish, while they kept up a useless ceremony (for the present generation of Englishmen are not responsible for the War of Independence), they had inculcated upon their own minds that they should not go to war with four millions, five millions, or six millions of their fellow-countrymen who want to put the principles of 1776 into operation as regards themselves."*

Again, the English official sense of decorum was offended by the uncivil and often sarcastic manner in which the United States Consuls communicated their complaints both to the home and colonial authorities. I might give many extracts from the letters and protests of Mr. Dudley at Liverpool, Mr. Graham at Cape Town, and the Consul at Nassau; but it is hardly necessary. Those gentlemen adopted all the opprobrious epithets of their departmental chief, and hurled them at the British officials with a reckless disregard of official courtesy, or of the inevitable contempt which they were likely to excite. Sir Alexander Cockburn says:—"The offensive tone which the United States Consuls allowed themselves to assume towards British authorities is not a little remarkable."†

Many Americans of refinement and education, who have travelled abroad and have learned to understand and appreciate the requirements as well as the advantages of diplomatic courtesy and restraint, have no doubt felt both regret and shame because the style adopted by some of the national representatives in their official papers during the Civil War was not a little more in harmony with the standard types of public manifestoes; but, unhappily, the exigencies of American home politics are such that the highest and most important offices must often of necessity be given, not to the men who are fittest for them through training, culture, and a comprehensive acquaintance with affairs, but to men who have made themselves most useful and most indispensable to the success of a particular Party, and to the maintenance of its power. Such offices as that of Consul and others are, as it were, farmed out to the great "wire-pullers" and "machine" operators; and thus it often happens that a village politician, who knows nothing of international commerce or international law, whose vocabulary of political phrases is limited to the Party slang of the

---

* Quoted in "United States Case," p. 26.

† If any American cares to read the public correspondence of the consular, and some even of the higher representatives of the United States during the Civil War, he will understand how much offence may be given through the neglect of diplomatic courtesy, and how sympathy may be alienated from a national cause by brusqueness and want of tact on the part of its official exponents.

day, who never wrote a public letter in his life, except to the chairman of the committee for manipulating the county vote, is suddenly transformed into a consular agent, and is sent to an important commercial port across the sea, where he is often required to deal with intricate questions of maritime law and usage, to correspond with official persons of dignity and importance, and to attend public meetings and receptions, all of which require some previous training, a good deal of technical knowledge, and familiarity with the rules of etiquette.

If some of the United States Consuls during the period of the war were more zealous than discreet, and injured the cause they were burning to serve by thrusting into their official correspondence the warmth and effrontery which they knew from experience was effective in a political campaign at home, it is only fair to remember that they acted according to their lights, and that the sin lies not in the individual, but in the system which renders such scandals possible.

As the name of Mr. Dudley, the United States Consul at Liverpool, is of necessity frequently mentioned in connection with the "*Alabama* Claims," it is an imperative act of justice for me to mention that he was appointed to the consular office at Liverpool at the beginning of the war, and was retained in that office during the whole of its continuance, and for several years after its close. He must therefore have won and maintained the entire confidence of his Government. All who examine the records will admit that he manifested both zeal and ability, although he sometimes permitted the former to outrun his discretion. His own personal statements were doubtless made in good faith, but he often accepted the evidence of talebearers without duly testing the probability of the story or the character of the informer, and thus the evidence tendered by him failed when brought to the test of judicial inquiry, and appears to have been frequently discredited, or at least looked upon with suspicion, by the law officers of the Crown.

Liverpool, London, and Paris have often been fortunate in escaping the evil consequences of the haphazard manner of selecting consular representatives so often practised by the United States. It will be remembered that Nathaniel Hawthorne was once the American Consul at Liverpool; and the successor of Mr. Dudley, General Lucius Fairchild, was a gentleman whose social qualities endeared him to many persons in England beyond the circle of Liverpool society, and who was, besides, a man of cultivation and knowledge of affairs, fit in every respect to represent his country creditably in any office.

There was one branch of the public service, and one corps of public officials, upon whom the United States might have justly relied, not only to sustain the national prestige abroad by skill and gallantry in battle, but to maintain its influence through the uniform practice of tact, judgment, and good temper.

Naval officers of all nations acquire a sort of generic type in respect to the outward manifestations of official decorum. The advantage of frequently appearing at foreign Courts and mixing with high personages, the frequent necessity of conducting important correspondence with Ministers of State, of attending conferences, and taking part in public ceremonies, all of which fall within the general professional experiences of most naval officers, prepare and fit them by habit and training to act with dignity, self-possession, tact, and judgment under circumstances which would embarrass, if not confound, the ordinary civilian, even though he might be well versed in the conventional usages of polite society.

It may be very fairly claimed that the naval officers of the United States, taken as a class, have never heretofore shown a deficiency in that special training and in those especial accomplishments which appear to be the natural effects of a sea life, supplemented by naval education and discipline, under whatever flag. Unhappily, it must be admitted that some commanding-officers of United States ships during the war lost their true and genuine professional poise, and by an unaccountable inadvertence, or, as it may be hoped, a temporary aberration, they fell into the consular vein of correspondence, and acted on some occasions in the spirit of their political chiefs at home, and thus contributed to increase that British sympathy for the South of which Mr. Seward so bitterly complained.

In February, 1863, the *Florida* touched at the British island of Barbadoes, and was permitted to take on board some lumber for necessary repairs, and to receive ninety tons of coal. Admiral Wilkes, who commanded the United States squadron in the West Indies, and had been on the lookout for the *Florida* off Martinique, soon heard of her visit to Barbadoes and the privileges granted her there. He proceeded at once to that island, and sought a personal interview with the Governor. Governor Walker explained the principle upon which he had acted, but the irate Admiral was not satisfied. He went on board of his ship and addressed the Governor a letter of mingled remonstrance and reproach, which also contained a demand for an explanation. Governor Walker declined to give any explanation in reply to such a letter, but forwarded it to the Duke of Newcastle, who was then Secretary of State for the Colonies, with a statement of the facts.

The report of the Governor and the letter of Admiral Wilkes were referred to the law officers of the Crown, to report whether there had been any breach of neutrality on the part of Governor Walker, or any departure from the conditions of her Majesty's Regulations. The law officers in their report comment upon the incident as follows:—"We are of opinion that his Excellency the Governor of the Windward Islands does not appear to have been guilty of showing any undue partiality to the *Oreto* (*Florida*), or to have committed any literal breach of her Majesty's Regulations. We would take the liberty of observing, further, that his Excellency owes no account to Admiral Wilkes of his conduct in the matter of his discharge of his duties towards her Majesty, and that the very offensive tone and language of that officer's letter ought to apprise his Excellency of the inexpediency of long personal interviews and explanations with him. It is manifest that upon this, as upon other occasions, these interviews and explanations are made the pretext for writing subsequent letters of this description, intended to be used hereafter very disingenuously, as proof of charges made at the time of the favour shown by her Majesty's officers to the Confederate States."

The law officers who signed the report of which the foregoing is an extract were Sir William Atherton, Attorney General, Sir Roundell Palmer (now Lord Selborne), Solicitor-General, and Sir Robert Phillimore, Queen's Advocate; and if three such eminent jurists felt impelled to go rather out of their official line of duty to pass such a stricture upon Admiral Wilkes's conduct, it is manifest that he must have trampled rather roughly upon British susceptibilities.

The Duke of Newcastle, instructing Governor Walker in respect to the whole occurrence, under date of July 16th, 1863, writes him as follows:— "You were quite right in refusing to enter into correspondence with that officer (Admiral Wilkes) upon the matter adverted to in his despatch of the 5th March. On this, as on other occasions, it has become evident that interviews and explanations such as you accorded to Admiral Wilkes were made the pretext for placing on record charges more or less direct against officers of her Majesty. And I think that, as the Governor of one of her Majesty's Colonies owes no explanation of his conduct to an officer of the United States navy, it will be prudent hereafter to avoid such explanations as far as the rules of courtesy will allow. It is the wish of her Majesty's Government that matters of complaint should in general be discussed between the two Governments concerned, rather than between any subordinate officers."*

* This correspondence and the report of the law officers is quoted by Sir A. Cockburn, pp. 166–68.

It will thus appear that the executive and the legal branches of her Majesty's Government both regarded Admiral Wilkes's bearing towards the Governor of Barbadoes in the same light, and the incident must have had some effect in prejudicing the cause of the United States.

In February, 1862, the Confederate ship *Sumter,* Captain Raphael Semmes, was lying in Gibraltar. The United States ship *Tuscarora,* Captain G. Augt. Craven, came there to watch her, but wishing to avoid the restrictions upon her movements to which it would have been necessary to submit if she also continued to occupy the anchorage at Gibraltar, she crossed the bay, and took up a berth at the Spanish port of Algeciras, from which she could command a view of the *Sumter,* and either note her departure or get daily advice of her probable movements. It appears from the published correspondence in the Appendix to the British Case, vol. ii. (pp. 27–29, etc.), that Captain Craven was in the habit of sending a boat across the bay, ostensibly to communicate with the United States Consul, but the visits manifestly assumed the character of a system of espionage upon the *Sumter.* At last Captain Semmes reported the circumstances to the Governor and to the senior British naval officer, and complained of being thus watched by an enemy in neutral waters. In consequence of Captain Semmes's report, a letter was sent to Captain Craven, signed jointly by the Governor and the senior naval officer, and the communication was as follows:—*

"Gibraltar, *February* 20*th,* 1862.

"Sir,—

"A boat from the *Tuscarora,* now at anchor at Algeciras, came across the bay yesterday morning. Captain Semmes complains that she pulled round the *Sumter,* as if watching her. It is necessary for the maintenance of the neutrality of this port that advantage should not be taken of the close proximity of a foreign anchorage (in some places only two and a half miles distant) in aid of any warlike purpose. Considering as we do that the presence of the boat represents the ship herself, we are of opinion that its presence, under such circumstances, is an infringement of the rules of which you were given a copy on the 12th instant. We have, therefore, to request you will be good enough, during the stay of the *Tuscarora* in the Spanish

---

* For the following correspondence see "British Case," Appendix, vol. ii., pp. 27–41.

waters of this bay, to abstain from sending your boats at all into these waters.

"I have, etc.,

"(Signed)   W. J. Codrington.

"F. Warden."

On the same day Captain Craven replied to the foregoing letter as follows, but addressed his reply to the Governor alone:—

"United States' Steamer *Tuscarora,*

"Off Algeciras, *February* 20*th,* 1862.

"Sir,—

"I have the honour to acknowledge the receipt of your communication of this day. The complaint of the captain of the pirate *Sumter* is without a shadow of truth. I summoned before me the coxswain of the boat, and, in the presence of the officer who brought me your letter, asked him as to the course he steered in returning from Gibraltar yesterday. He replied that he came straight across, passing somewhat to the southward of the *Warrior.* The boat was sent over on business for the ship, and from the course taken by the officer of the boat I know, from my own observation, that he made a great circuit to the southward. The officer who went in the boat has not returned. I am mortified, sir, in thus being compelled to make explanations against the accusations of a man regardless of truth and honourable sentiment. Your request that I will not send boats to Gibraltar deprives me of sending for mails or communicating with the United States Consul; and I must in good faith inquire whether it is right that, on the loose accusation of a notorious corsair, you desire to prohibit me from intercourse with the town under your command.

"(Signed)   G. Aug. Craven."

The Governor of Gibraltar replied to Captain Craven as follows:—

"Gibraltar, *February* 21*st,* 1862.

"Sir,—

"I have to acknowledge the receipt of your letter of yesterday, and to express my regret that you should think it necessary to use such terms in your correspondence with me as 'the captain of the pirate *Sumter,*' 'notorious corsair,' and 'a man regardless of truth and honourable sentiment.' I do not wish unnecessarily to be made the recipient of terms of abuse levelled against any one, still less against an officer who, in his written and personal communications with me, under circumstances of annoyance and difficulty to himself, has not forgotten what is due to his own position, and to the position of those with whom he was in correspondence. The Government of England has recognised the United States and the so-called Confederate States of America to be belligerents with belligerent rights. You are aware of this fact, and it renders your terms of 'pirate' and 'notorious corsair,' applied to a Confederate vessel in this anchorage, incorrect, and offensive to the authority thus granting and maintaining the rights of neutrality. You have not touched upon the main ground of the decision of Captain Warden and myself as to your boats coming into Gibraltar from Algeciras, viz., that they are, in law, part of the ship itself, and that their presence here, coming from Spanish waters close to Gibraltar, is an infringement of rules which must be observed. With regard to your being deprived of sending for mails or communicating with the United States Consul of Gibraltar whilst you are at Algeciras, I can only say that the decision of Captain Warden and myself, in our joint letter of yesterday, refers only to the points mentioned in that letter; the use of this anchorage will be given and limited to both belligerents equally, but it is not right for one belligerent to obtain for his ship the advantage of absence in a neighbouring foreign port, and of presence at the same time in this port by means of his boats.

"It would have been better to have made strict inquiry into the facts as to the course taken by your boat, before you declared the complaint to be 'without a shadow of truth.' I have to inform you that your boat did not pass 'straight across' from the water-port to you, and that it did not pass 'somewhat to the southward of the *Warrior*.' Your boat went out of the straight course materially; it passed to the east, to the north, to the west, and pretty close to the *Sumter;* it passed north and west of the *Samarang* port-vessel; afterwards between the Peninsular and Oriental hulk and her Majesty's ship *Warrior*. These facts are established by English officers who saw your boat.

"I regret the necessity of having thus to remark upon the expressions and statements in your letter. Difficult questions arise, and official differences may take place under the painful circumstances of the war between the Northern and Southern States of America;

but it has ever been, and still will be, a pleasure to me to show to the navy of the United States the consideration and hospitality which the English Government wishes to afford to all those who make use of the harbours under its control.

"I have, etc.,

"(Signed)   W. J. CODRINGTON."

On the day after the foregoing letter was forwarded to Captain Craven, he wrote the following letter* to the Governor:—

"United States' Steamer *Tuscarora,*
"Off Algeciras, *February* 22*nd,* 1862.

"Sir,—

"I have the honour to submit to you that on my arrival in the waters of Gibraltar, on the 12th instant, I received from the Colonial Secretary, under your instructions, an official copy of 'Rules laid down with regard to belligerent vessels entering the port.'

"In accordance with those rules, I, with the vessel under my command, promptly departed from British waters. I observe, however, that the corsair *Sumter* remains in undisturbed possession of her anchorage at Gibraltar. May I ask, sir, under what section of the rules that vessel is permitted to remain in British waters while a vessel belonging to the United States is excluded? In behalf of the Government of the United States, and under the well-defined principles of international law, I have to protest against what appears to be a departure from those rules, which require that neutrals shall be impartial and honest.

"I have, etc.,

"(Signed)   G. A. CRAVEN."

The repetition of the epithet "corsair," and the general tone of the foregoing letter, manifestly offended the Governor, and brought from him a reply dated on the same day (February 22nd), from which the following is an extract:—

"The Confederate steamer *Sumter* remains here under proper authority, and I decline to discuss with you the rules to which you refer, your particular interpretation of them, or to account to you for my proceedings under them. In reference to the last sentence in your letter—I quote your

---

* "British Case," Appendix, vol. ii., p. 41.

words—that 'you protest against what appears to be a departure from those rules, which require neutrals' (meaning, I presume, the English Government and myself, as Governor of Gibraltar), 'should be impartial and honest.' If you are aware of the effect of this latter epithet, you have communicated to me for the English Government a direct and insulting insinuation, as indecorous for you to have written as it is improper for me to receive. If you are not aware of it, it is right for me to show you the effect of language which, I trust, a regard for your own position will prevent you from repeating in your correspondence with me."*

The foregoing correspondence needs no comment to add to its point and pungency. Captain Semmes was amply revenged for the epithets of "pirate" and "corsair," and for the reflection which Captain Craven ventured to cast upon his veracity, and probably no naval officer has ever received a more dignified and yet cutting rebuke from a high foreign functionary.

The Governor of Gibraltar at that time was Lieutenant-General Sir W. J. Codrington, an officer of the highest consideration in the British army. The senior naval officer was Captain F. Warden, C.B., also distinguished in his branch of the service. Notwithstanding the prohibitions of the Governor and his explanation of the "rules," Captain Craven appears to have persisted in sending his boats to Gibraltar, which gave occasion for the following order from Captain Warden to Captain Chads, of her Majesty's ship *London,* dated Gibraltar, February 22nd, 1862:†—"With reference to the orders dated 21st instant, under which you are acting, I have to acquaint you that the *Tuscarora* having sent a boat to the water-port this morning, and taken off supplies without permission, it is my direction that the boats of the *London* are held in a state of constant preparation for the purpose of preventing any boat belonging to the *Tuscarora* from passing the *London* into this bay at all so long as that ship remains in Spanish waters. It is undesirable that force should be used unless absolutely necessary; but force is to be used rather than permit any violation of the rules laid down. Similar orders have been issued to the *Scylla* and *Amphion.*"

The United States Consuls put themselves in the way to receive some rebukes, and Mr. Seward and one or two of his diplomatic staff invited an occasional thrust, but the "retort courteous," when administered by a civil functionary, is often so concealed in the phrase which envelops it, as to be scarcely discernible at first sight. When, however, the "counter-thrust"

---

* "British Case," Appendix, vol. ii., p. 31.
† Ibid., p. 30.

comes from a military or naval man who knows how to wield his pen, it goes straight to the core with the keenness of the sabre or the sharp point of a marlin-spike. The *esprit de corps* of military and naval officers renders them sensitive to slights or impertinences offered to their immediate commanders while performing the duties of their office, and they are also inclined to resent all acts of rudeness to the representatives of their Government. The alleged partiality of the sister British services for the Confederacy during the late Civil War, may very likely be traced, in part at least, to the feeling of resentment against the United States aroused by the brusque and inconsiderate manner in which some American naval officers claimed their assumed rights, or remonstrated against the "rules," which only placed them on the same footing with their adversaries while lying in British ports.

I have no wish to make too much of the foregoing point, and therefore refrain from mentioning other manifestations of jealousy and ill-temper which are alluded to in the "British Counter Case," or which appear in the published correspondence. But the alleged leaning of the British Government and people towards the South is so prominently set out in the diplomatic manifestoes of the United States, and in their "Case" before the Tribunal of Arbitration, that it appeared to be absolutely necessary to demonstrate that if the allegation is true, there were some reasons for the preference.

It is manifest from the published correspondence that the purpose to seek redress from Great Britain for the depredations of the Confederate cruisers was formed not long after they had begun their operations, and it appears that Mr. Adams intimated the willingness of the United States to submit the questions at issue to some form of arbitration as early as October, 1863.

On the 20th of May, 1865, Mr. Adams wrote a very long letter* on the subject of the claims and complaints of the United States to Earl Russell, and began by recapitulating the points he wished to maintain, which he specifies under nine different heads. Mr. Adams was not only a man of ability and of large official experience, but he was a gentleman by birth and education. He was held in high personal esteem by Earl Russell, and his courtesy, tact, and conciliatory manners are often acknowledged. But even he sometimes yielded to the influences from home, and was entrapped into giving currency to the exaggerated statements which unhappily characterized the State Papers of that period which received their

---

* "British Case," Appendix, vols. iii., iv. Correspondence respecting the *Shenandoah*, p. 10.

inspiration from the Department of Foreign Affairs at Washington. The fourth point which Mr. Adams mentions his purpose to maintain is thus specified:—"That during the whole course of the struggle in America, of nearly four years in duration, there has been no appearance of the insurgents as a belligerent on the ocean, excepting in the shape of British vessels, constructed, equipped, supplied, manned, and armed in British ports."

The simple truth is that the Confederate ship *Sumter* was built in Philadelphia. She was bought by the Confederate Navy Department in New Orleans, in April, 1861. She was fitted out at that port, sailed out of the Mississippi in broad daylight, was chased by the United States ship *Brooklyn,* but escaped, and took several prizes into the Spanish Colonial port of Cienfugos, where she was received and recognised as a duly commissioned ship-of-war, before Mr. Adams had penned his first protest in respect to the *Florida* or *Alabama,* before, in fact, either of those ships were launched, and long before any Confederate ship of alleged British origin had put to sea.

Besides the *Sumter,* the following named vessels were fitted out and sent to cruise from Southern ports during the year 1861. *Calhoun* from New Orleans, *Jeff Davis* from Savannah, *St. Nicholas, Winslow, Sallie, York* and *Nashville* from other ports. During the year 1862, the *Echo* was despatched on a cruise from a Confederate port. In 1863 the captured American ships *Retribution* and *Boston* were commissioned, and in 1864 the *Chickamauga* and *Tallahassee* were despatched from Wilmington. In the "British Case" (p. 7) it is stated that the above-named vessels were reported to have captured, in the aggregate, from sixty to seventy vessels.

The foregoing facts were so notorious at the date of Mr. Adams's statement, that it is surprising they should have escaped his memory. Moreover, in the United States "Case," claims are made against Great Britain for the depredations of nine vessels in addition to those which it was admitted were either bought or built in England, although neither equipped nor armed there.

The claims in respect to the foregoing nine vessels were thrown out by the Tribunal of Arbitration. Seven of the nine were American built ships, or at least they were bought by the Confederate States in Confederate ports, were armed, equipped and manned within the Confederacy, and never entered a British port, if at all, except as commissioned ships-of-war. The remaining two were ordinary blockade-runners, built, it is true, in England, but taken to Wilmington by private parties on their own account exclusively, where they were sold to the Confederate Navy Department. The whole number of vessels in respect to whose alleged depredations the United States claimed compensation was thirteen,* of which only four could by any possible straining of the facts be said to have been fitted out in England, and yet Mr. Adams ventured to affirm, at so late a date as May 20th, 1865, "that there was no appearance of the insurgents as a belligerent on the ocean, excepting in the shape of British vessels, constructed, equipped, supplied, manned, and armed in British ports."

Many of the statements made in the voluminous despatches of Mr. Seward and the United States "Case" could be as easily disposed of as the foregoing, by a simple mention of the facts. The looseness of the allegations, and the fallacy of the conclusions founded on them, are frequently adverted to in the replies of her Majesty's Government, and in the British "Counter-Case." Under date of August 30th, 1865, Earl Russell wrote to Mr. Adams at great length in justification of the conduct of her Majesty's Government during the Civil War, and in respect to a "Claims Commission." In the above-mentioned letter Earl Russell said to Mr. Adams as follows:—

"In your letter of 23rd October, 1863, you were pleased to say that the Government of the United States is ready to agree to any form of arbitration. Her Majesty's Government have thus been led to consider what question could be put to any Sovereign or State to whom this very great power should be assigned. It appears to her Majesty's Government that there are but two questions by which the claim of compensation could be tested. The one is: Have the British Government acted with due diligence, or, in other words, with good faith and honesty, in the maintenance of the neutrality they proclaimed? The other is: Have the law officers of the Crown properly understood the Foreign Enlistment Act when they declined, in June, 1862, to advise the detention and seizure of the *Alabama*, and on other occasions when they were asked to detain other ships building or fitting in British ports? It appears to her Majesty's Government that neither of these questions could be put to a foreign Government with any regard to the dignity and character of the British Crown and the British nation. Her Majesty's Government are the sole guardians of their own honour. They cannot admit that they may have acted with bad faith in maintaining the neutrality they professed. The law officers of the Crown must be held to be better interpreters of a British statute than any foreign Gov-

---

* In addition to the thirteen above-mentioned, claims were made in respect to four vessels alleged to be tenders of the *Florida* and *Alabama*.

ernment can be presumed to be. Her Majesty's Government must, therefore, decline either to make reparation and compensation for the captures made by the *Alabama,* or to refer the question to any foreign State. Her Majesty's Government conceive that if they were to act otherwise they would endanger the position of neutrals in all future wars. Her Majesty's Government are, however, ready to consent to the appointment of a Commission to which shall be referred all claims arising during the late Civil War which the two Powers shall agree to refer to the Commissioners."*

There could scarcely be a more positive declaration of the views and purposes of her Majesty's Government in respect to the "*Alabama* Claims" than is pronounced in the foregoing extract from an official letter of the Minister of Foreign Affairs, written, not with haste, during a heated controversy, but after peace was fully restored between the late belligerents, and when there had been ample time to advise calmly with his colleagues and with the law officers of the Crown, and to determine whether there had been any illegality in the equipment of Confederate cruisers within British jurisdiction, or any failure to fulfil neutral duties which could make a claim for damages on the part of the United States tenable.

The reader will remember the verbal statements of Ministers and of the Solicitor-General mentioned in a previous chapter, which were to the effect that a builder might legally contract to deliver an unarmed ship of any description to a belligerent as a mercantile transaction; and those statements, taken in conjunction with the declaration contained in the extract from Earl Russell's letter just above quoted, can be interpreted in no other sense than that her Majesty's Government, in August, 1865, declined to admit that there was any violation of British law in the manner of obtaining ships for the Confederate service in England, or that there had been any default in the performance of their neutral duties which could render them liable to a claim for compensation on behalf of the United States.

The correspondence in respect to the claims was continued until November, 1865, when Earl Russell became Prime Minister, and was succeeded at the Foreign Office by the Earl of Clarendon. On the 21st of November, 1865, Mr. Adams informed Lord Clarendon by official letter that the United States adhered to the opinion that the claims which Earl Russell had thought fit to exclude from consideration were just and reasonable, and therefore saw no occasion for further delay in giving a full

---

* "British Case," Appendix, vol. iv., "North America (1), 1866," p. 31.

answer to the proposition for a *Joint Commission* contained in his lordship's letter of August 30th, 1865, which proposition he was instructed to say "is respectfully declined."*

On the 2nd of December, 1865, Lord Clarendon wrote a short letter to Mr. Adams, in which he briefly alludes to a long and controversial communication which Mr. Adams had addressed to him on the 18th of November.† Lord Clarendon wrote as follows:—"I have the honour to acknowledge the receipt of your letter of the 18th ultimo.... There are many statements in your letter which I should be prepared to controvert if it were not that her Majesty's Government consider that no advantage can result from prolonging the controversy, of which the topics are generally exhausted, but which might possibly, if continued, introduce acrimony into the relations between this country and the United States; two nations who from kindred origin and mutual interest should desire to be knit together by bonds of the closest friendship.... While abstaining therefore from any discussion of the passages in your letter to the correctness of which I am unable to subscribe, it is nevertheless my duty in closing this correspondence to observe that no armed vessel departed during the war from a British port to cruise against the commerce of the United States, and to maintain that throughout all the difficulties of the Civil War by which the United States have lately been distracted, but in the termination of which no nation rejoices more cordially than Great Britain, the British Government have steadily and honestly discharged all the duties incumbent on them as a neutral Power, and have never deviated from the obligations imposed upon them by international law."

During the months of December, 1865, and January, 1866, an active correspondence was kept up between Mr. Adams and the British Foreign Office, upon subjects relating to the Civil War, and in reference to a concurrent revision of the Foreign Enlistment Acts of the two countries, but the letter from Lord Clarendon, quoted above, appears to have put a stop to the especial discussion of the "*Alabama* Claims" for some time.

In May, 1866, there was a change of Government in Great Britain. The Ministry was defeated in the House of Commons in a division on a measure relating to the extension of the franchise and a redistribution of seats. The Cabinet took the adverse judgment of the House as a vote of "want

---

* "British Case," Appendix, vol. iv., p. 161.

† For Mr. Adams's letter see "British Case," Appendix, vol. iv., Parliamentary Paper, no. 1, 1866, p. 154, etc. Lord Clarendon's letter, p. 162.

of confidence," and resigned. The late Earl of Derby was requested by her Majesty to form a new Government, and thus the Conservative Party came into power, with the Earl of Derby as Prime Minister, Mr. Disraeli as Chancellor of the Exchequer, and Lord Stanley as Foreign Secretary. The chief offices in the retiring Cabinet had been held by Lord Palmerston, Earl Russell, the Earl of Clarendon, and the Right Honourable W. E. Gladstone. Lord Russell and Lord Clarendon, as the Secretaries of State for Foreign Affairs, appear most prominently in the official correspondence, but Lord Palmerston by speeches in Parliament, and Mr. Gladstone by speeches both in and out of the House, associated their names especially and emphatically with the questions which the Civil War originated, and thus made themselves joint exponents of the policy of the Ministry and of the Liberal Party in respect to the neutral duties of Great Britain and the claims set up by the United States.

The retiring Ministry had held office during the whole period of the Civil War, so that there had been no room for divergence of views or reversal of policy. The same Cabinet which advised her Majesty to recognise the Confederate States as a belligerent Power, continued to direct and control the relations of Great Britain with the two contending States while the contest lasted, and enunciated the position assumed by the British Government in respect to the claims of the United States after the termination of the war, and after a careful consideration of all the demands of Mr. Seward and the statements and arguments advanced in support of them.

It is important to consider at this point what was the precise position thus occupied by the outgoing Ministry, and which their successors were compelled to step into. It may be briefly described thus:—"Her Majesty's Government, being the sole guardians of their own honour, cannot submit their conduct to the judgment of any other Sovereign or State without sacrificing the dignity and character of the British Crown and the British nation. They cannot admit that they have acted with bad faith in maintaining their neutrality, and they must therefore decline to make reparation and compensation for the captures made by the *Alabama,* or even to refer the question to any foreign State. Finally, they see no advantage in prolonging the controversy, but while abstaining from any further discussion, they must observe that no armed vessel departed during the war from a British port to cruise against the commerce of the United States, and they must maintain that the British Government steadily and honestly discharged all the duties incumbent on them as a neutral Power, and have never deviated from the obligations imposed upon them by international law."*

In the foregoing brief summary I have employed very nearly the precise words used by her Majesty's two Secretaries of State for Foreign Affairs in their final communications to the United States Minister in respect to the "*Alabama* Claims," and it certainly must appear to the ordinary reader that the retiring Ministers were not only at ease in their consciences, but that their minds also were settled in the conviction that they had done no wrong to the United States, and would pay no claims founded on the assumption that they had been guilty of any breach of neutrality or default in observing the obligations of international law.

Mr. Seward appears to have given her Majesty's new advisers some months of rest, but Lord Russell's refusal to admit liability for the depredations of the Confederate cruisers, and Lord Clarendon's wish that the controversy on the subject should end, was not accepted as a final and irreversible decision by the Government at Washington. On the 27th of August, 1866, Mr. Seward reopened the subject in a long despatch to Mr. Adams enclosing a "summary of claims of citizens of the United States against Great Britain," all of which were founded upon the alleged "depredations committed by the *Alabama*" and her consorts upon American commerce.† The despatch and the formidable list of claims were transmitted to Lord Stanley in a note dated September 17th, 1866.

Mr. Seward knew perfectly well the origin of the *Sumter*, and he knew that the former British Minister with whom he had corresponded on the subject of the "*Alabama* Claims" had asserted, and had proved beyond the power of controversy, that none of the ships named by him had been either armed or manned in England, and yet, in a despatch purporting to be written in a friendly spirit, he reopens the discussion as follows:—"You" (that is, Mr. Adams) "will herewith receive a summary of claims of citizens of the United States against Great Britain for damages which were suffered by them during the period of our late Civil War, and some months thereafter, by means of depredations upon our commercial marine, committed upon the high seas by the *Sumter*, the *Alabama*, the *Florida*, the *Shenandoah*, and other ships-of-war which were built, manned, armed, equipped, and fitted out in British ports, and despatched therefrom by or through the agency of British subjects, and which were harboured, shel-

---

* See letters of Lord Russell and Lord Clarendon to Mr. Adams quoted above.
† See "Appendix to British Case," vol. iv. (no. 1), 1867, p. 1.

tered, provided, and furnished as occasion required during their devastating career, in ports of the realm, or in ports of the British Colonies in nearly all parts of the globe."

The foregoing statement, so far as relates to the *Sumter*, was wholly and notoriously incorrect, and the manner of stating the case, even with reference to the other vessels, was so grossly exaggerated and overdrawn as to appear more like passionate and reckless assertion than a dignified, well-considered synopsis of facts. Mr. Seward then dwells upon the considerations which have inclined the United States "to suspend for a time the pressure of the claims upon the attention of Great Britain," reviews at some length the points discussed in previous correspondence, and which had all been beaten threadbare, directs Mr. Adams to represent the most important features, which he thinks "may not hitherto have sufficiently engaged the attention of the British Government," and finally tells him that the harmony heretofore existing between the two countries "has been, as we (the United States) think, unnecessarily broken through the fault of Great Britain," and can probably never be restored unless the serious complaints then again brought to the notice of the British Government shall be amicably and satisfactorily adjusted.

There is one paragraph in Mr. Seward's letter of August 27th, 1866, which strikingly illustrates the tendency to exaggerate facts which characterized his official correspondence, and demonstrates the persistency with which he repeated broad and sweeping assertions which could not be sustained by specific particulars. He says:—"Upon a candid review of the history of the rebellion, it is believed that Great Britain will not deny that a very large number of the Queen's subjects combined themselves and operated as active allies with the insurgents, aided them with supplies, arms, munitions, men, and many ships of war."

Did Mr. Seward mean that her Majesty's subjects entered into a philanthropic combination, and showered the favours enumerated above upon the Southern people out of love for them, or with any political purpose to assist in breaking up the American Union, or did he merely mean that British tradesmen sold to the Confederate agents whatever supplies they wanted, and could pay for, and honestly delivered the goods at the times and places agreed upon? If he intended to convey the former meaning, people of common-sense will think that he was practising a hyperbolic flourish of phrases which tended rather to dilute than to strengthen the semblance of facts contained in them. But if his purpose was only to affirm the latter proposition, then practical men will say that no law, statute or moral, municipal or international, requires a tradesman to close his shop against one of two belligerents lest he should be considered an ally of the other, and that such legitimate trading by any people could not be alleged as a matter of complaint against the Government to whom they owed allegiance.

Mr. Adams forwarded a copy of Mr. Seward's despatch with a list of the claims to Lord Stanley on the 17th of September, 1866. Lord Stanley informed him verbally that it would be impossible for him to reply without first consulting his colleagues. Some delay was reasonable; in fact, it was unavoidable under the circumstances, because the members of the new Cabinet could not have known the details of the claims, the grounds upon which they were based, or the precise position which had been assumed by their predecessors in office, and it was therefore necessary to examine the previous official correspondence before deciding upon the terms of their reply.

On the 30th of November, 1866, Lord Stanley forwarded a long despatch to Sir F. Bruce, her Majesty's Minister at Washington, in which he reviewed *seriatim* the points contained in Mr. Seward's letter above mentioned. It would be useless to repeat or even to summarize the arguments and counter statements of the British Foreign Secretary. He certainly did not admit those broad assertions which Mr. Seward ventured to believe that Great Britain would not deny. In fact, he said that "Her Majesty's Government feel bound to notice expressions and statements* in Mr. Seward's despatch which they consider unsupported by evidence, and which, in justice to their predecessors in power and to the honour of the country, they cannot allow to pass unexamined."†

The only parts of Lord Stanley's answer which are of any practical importance now, are the few sentences in which he states the decision to which her Majesty's Government had come, after a critical examination of Mr. Seward's allegations and arguments, and the replies which had already been made to them by the previous Ministry. He said:—"Having dealt so far with Mr. Seward's argument, and pointed out the wide discrepancies that exist between his views of the question and those entertained by her Majesty's Government, I now proceed to consider the practical proposition with which he concludes" (namely, that the British Government should acknowledge the claims, and agree to a plan for their amicable adjustment). "It is impossible for her Majesty's present advisers to abandon

---

* Expressions and statements in reference to arming, equipping, and manning ships, etc.
  † See Lord Stanley to Sir F. Bruce, "British Appendix," vol. iv., "North America (no. 1), 1867," p. 26, etc.

the ground which has been taken by former Governments, so far as to admit the liability for the claims then and now put forward. They do not think that such liability has been established according to international law or usage; and though sincerely and earnestly desiring a good understanding with the United States, they cannot consent to purchase even the advantage of that good understanding by concessions which would at once involve a censure upon their predecessors in power, and be an acknowledgment, in their view uncalled-for and unfounded, of wrong-doing on the part of the British Executive and Legislature."

The ground taken by the former Government was that they declined to make reparation and compensation for the captures, etc., or to refer the question to a foreign State; although they would agree to the appointment of a Commission to which all claims arising out of the Civil War should be referred which the two Powers would agree to refer; but it will be remembered that the United States had declined the proposition for a Commission under the limitations required by her Majesty's Government, and that Lord Clarendon had closed the correspondence on the subject.* The declaration of Lord Stanley in the above quotation from his despatch to Sir F. Bruce, if taken by itself, could only be received as a final decision to maintain the precise ground taken by Earl Russell, and if that had been his purpose, the "*Alabama* Claims" would have ceased to be an international question, unless the United States had thought it worth while to make them a *casus belli*.

But her Majesty's Government were manifestly unwilling to leave the questions at issue in a condition that would tend to keep alive feelings of irritation between the two countries; a sense of injury unredressed on one side, and of claims unjustly pressed, and therefore necessarily refused, on the other. In concluding his despatch, therefore, Lord Stanley said in effect that her Majesty's Government were fully alive to the inconvenience which would arise from the continued existence of unsettled claims between two powerful and friendly nations, and that they would be willing to adopt the principle of arbitration, provided a fitting arbitrator could be found, and the two Governments could agree upon the precise questions to which arbitration should apply; and he instructed Sir F. Bruce to ascertain from Mr. Seward whether the United States would accept the principle of arbitration as proposed above, and if so, whether he would state the precise points which, in his opinion, should be so dealt with. Finally, Lord Stanley said that any such proposal would require very deliberate consid-

---

* See Lord Russell's letter of August 20th, 1865, previously quoted.

eration on the part of her Majesty's Government, but that it would be entertained in a friendly spirit, and with a sincere desire that its adoption might serve to renew the good understanding formerly existing, and, as he hoped, hereafter to exist, between Great Britain and the United States.*

The correspondence between the two Governments continued throughout the year 1867 and up to October, 1868, without approaching to anything like a definite agreement. The discussions gradually extended so as to include other claims besides those relating to the Confederate cruisers, and to embrace questions of naturalization, boundary, etc. At the above-mentioned date Mr. Reverdy Johnson had relieved Mr. Adams as the United States Minister at London, and he appears to have had general instructions and specific powers with reference to the mode of settling all claims and other questions which were at issue; and the negotiations between him and Lord Stanley now began to take such a practical form, that protocols were framed from time to time to set out and record the points agreed to. I shall confine my notices of the protocols and the subsequent Convention exclusively to the Articles which have reference to the "*Alabama* Claims."

On the 10th of November, 1868, a "Convention between Great Britain and the United States of America, for the settlement of all Outstanding Claims," was signed in London by Lord Stanley and Mr. Reverdy Johnson.† Under the terms of the above Convention the contracting parties agreed generally to refer all claims on the part of their respective subjects, which had been or might be presented from the 26th of July, 1853, to a date specified in Article III., to four Commissioners, two to be named by her Britannic Majesty, and two by the President of the United States, the Commissioners to meet in London, and to appoint an arbitrator or umpire before proceeding to any other business, etc. Article VI. of the Convention referred to the "*Alabama* Claims" and the conditions upon which they were to be considered by the Commissioners were thus specified:—"With regard to the before-mentioned *Alabama* class of claims, neither Government shall make out a case in support of its position, nor shall any person be heard for or against any such claim. The official correspondence which has already taken place between the two Governments respecting the questions at issue shall alone be laid before the Commissioners; and (in the event of their not coming to a unanimous decision as provided in Article IV.), then before the arbitrator, without argument, written or verbal, and without the production of any further evidence. The Commissioners

---

* See "British Appendix," vol. iv., "North America (no. 1), 1867," pp. 30, 31.

† Ibid., "North America (no. 1), 1869," pp. 11–14.

unanimously, or the arbitrator, shall, however, be at liberty to call for argument or further evidence, if they or he shall deem it necessary."

On the 23rd of November the two Plenipotentiaries who signed the above Convention agreed to substitute Washington for London as the place for the meeting and sitting of the Commission.* The Convention in its original form reached Mr. Seward on the 24th of November, 1868,† and under date of November 27th he wrote Mr. Reverdy Johnson, pointing out the President's objections to it, and specifying the modifications which he desired should be made in a number of the Articles, in order to recommend the Convention to acceptance by the Senate and approval by the Congress of the United States.‡ Mr. Seward thought it not improbable that her Majesty's Government would be disappointed in finding that objections were made to the ratification of an agreement duly signed by the Plenipotentiaries of the two countries, and that they might possibly be reluctant to continue the negotiations. To meet this difficulty he directed Mr. Johnson to inform Lord Stanley that the communications between the United States Government and their Plenipotentiary had been conducted by a large use of the "cable," and that there had been an unavoidable misconstruction of the instructions, and a misapprehension of the explanations, which they greatly regretted.

The British Minister at Washington informed Lord Stanley by cable telegrams, on the 27th and 30th of November, that Mr. Seward and the Cabinet at Washington disapproved of the Convention, and had insisted upon certain very important modifications. Lord Stanley replied on the 8th of December by letter, expressing his surprise, and stating that it had never been intimated to him that Mr. Johnson was not acting under sufficient instructions from his Government; indeed, he had been informed by him, subsequently to the signing of the Convention, that Mr. Seward had stated in a telegraphic despatch that if the place of meeting was Washington, and not London, "all will be right." Lord Stanley closed his despatch with the statement that until the receipt of the telegrams above-mentioned, both he and Mr. Johnson were under the impression that the Convention which had been signed was in accordance with the instructions of Mr. Seward, as interpreted by Mr. Johnson himself, and would therefore meet the approval of the United States Government.§

* See "British Appendix," vol. iv., (no. 1), 1869, p. 15.

† Mr. Thornton to Lord Stanley, ibid., p. 22.

‡ Ibid., pp. 25–29.

§ See Lord Stanley's letter to Mr. Thornton, "British Case," Appendix, vol. iv., "North America (no. 1), 1869," pp. 16, 19.

Before the foregoing despatch of Mr. Seward (November 27th, 1868) reached London there had been another change of Ministry. The General Election which took place in the autumn of 1868 brought the Liberal Party again into power, with Mr. W. E. Gladstone as Prime Minister, and the Earl of Clarendon as Secretary of State for Foreign Affairs.* Mr. Johnson had therefore to continue his negotiations with the Ministers who were in office during the Civil War, and who were her Majesty's advisers when the questions at issue in respect to the *Alabama* and her consorts arose.

It is impossible to tell with any degree of certainty what would have been the course of her Majesty's Government at this juncture if the Conservative Party had remained in power, and in a mere synopsis of the actual occurrences which led up to the final Treaty of Washington and the Geneva Arbitration, surmises and hypothetical conjectures would be wholly out of place. Mr. Reverdy Johnson communicated Mr. Seward's despatch to Lord Clarendon on the 22nd of December, 1868, and it appears that her Majesty's Government were satisfied with the reasons given for declining to confirm the Stanley-Johnson Convention; at any rate, they made no formal protest. On the 24th of December Lord Clarendon wrote to the British Minister at Washington stating that her Majesty's Government were prepared to meet the wishes of the United States in the manner which he would then explain. His lordship then discussed the principles involved in the proposed modifications, demonstrated wherein he thought they were insufficient or otherwise defective, and finally he enclosed "a fresh draft of Convention," which he directed Mr. Thornton to submit to Mr. Seward; and if approved by him, "Mr. Johnson" (he suggested) "might be authorized by telegraph to sign it, in which case it might be returned to Washington so as to admit of its being laid before the Senate by the middle of January, and pronounced upon by that body before the rising of the Congress on the 4th of March."† Mr. Seward suggested some alterations in the draft forwarded by Lord Clarendon, which were accepted; and the amended Convention was signed by the two Plenipotentiaries in London on the 14th of January, 1869.‡

By the conditions of the Stanley-Johnson Convention the *Alabama* class of claims were to be adjudicated upon the official correspondence which

---

* Mr. Gladstone had been Chancellor of the Exchequer in the former Liberal Ministry, and Lord Clarendon had succeeded Earl Russell at the Foreign Office in the same Ministry.

† "British Case," Appendix, (no. 1), 1869, pp. 30–32.

‡ See Lord Clarendon's letter, and copy of Convention, ibid., pp. 35–38.

had already taken place exclusively, without argument, written or verbal. Under the new or Clarendon-Johnson Convention, the Commissioners were "bound to receive and peruse all other written documents or statements which may be presented to them by or on behalf of the respective Governments in support of or in answer to any claim, and to hear, if required, one person on each side on behalf of each Government as counsel or agent for such Government, on each and every separate claim."*

It very soon became manifest that the new Convention would not fare better than the first, although Mr. Seward's objections to the former had been received in a spirit of concession, and his proposed alteration had been accepted without any apparent reluctance.† On the 1st of February, 1869, Mr. Thornton, her Majesty's Minister at Washington, reported to Lord Clarendon that Mr. Charles Sumner had presented a petition to the Senate against the ratification of the Convention, and on the 22nd of the same month he further reported that the Convention had been sent by the President to the Senate for its approval, but that the Senate Committee on Foreign Relations, of which Mr. Charles Sumner was chairman, had reported adversely to its ratification. Mr. Thornton inclosed in the last-mentioned despatch to Lord Clarendon a "copy of a resolution adopted by the Legislature of Massachusetts."‡ The resolution was as follows:—"Resolved—That the Massachusetts Legislature, in general court assembled, firmly believe that any treaty between England and America touching the premises aforesaid, which may be submitted now or at any future time for ratification, which does not, by its terms, concede the liability of the English Government for acts of her *protégés,* the *Alabama* and her consorts, will be spurned with contempt by the American people, and that a ratification thereof would be dishonourable to our nation and unjust to our citizens."

On the 19th of April, 1869, Mr. Thornton informed Lord Clarendon by letter that the Claims Convention signed on January 14th (the Clarendon-Johnson Convention) "was submitted to the Senate in Executive Session on the 13th instant, with the adverse report which had previously been decided upon by the Committee of Foreign Relations," and that it had been rejected on the same day by the adverse vote of fifty-four senators against only one in its favour.§

---

* Ibid., Article II.
† Lord Clarendon's letter above, January 16th, 1869.
‡ "See "British Appendix," vol. iv., (no. 1), 1869, pp. 43, 44.
§ Ibid., pp. 51–53.

Mr. Thornton further reported that Mr. Charles Sumner availed himself of the occasion to make a long speech, which the Senate subsequently ordered to be made public, and it had been inserted in all the newspapers of the country. Mr. Thornton, in giving a synopsis of Mr. Sumner's speech, said that the sum of his assertions was "that England had insulted the United States by the premature, unfriendly, and unnecessary proclamation of the Queen, enjoining neutrality on her Majesty's subjects; that she owes them an apology for this step; that she is responsible for the property destroyed by the *Alabama* and other Confederate cruisers, and even for the remote damage to American shipping interests, including the increase of insurance; that the Confederates were so much assisted by being able to get arms and ammunition from England, and so much encouraged by the Queen's Proclamation, that the war lasted much longer than it would otherwise have done, and that we (England) ought therefore to pay imaginary additional expenses imposed upon the United States by the prolongation of the war."

Mr. Thornton mentions that Mr. Sumner was followed by a few other Senators, all speaking in the same sense, and that Mr. Chandler, Senator from Michigan, seemed to have been most violent against England, indicating his desire that Great Britain should possess no territory upon the American Continent, and added that the speech of Mr. Sumner was vehemently applauded by the Republican portion of the press, most of them openly proclaiming that the only satisfaction the United States Government could accept would be the cession of the British possessions on the Continent as well as the Bahama Islands.

Those who are familiar with the diplomatic correspondence which was carried on between her Majesty's Government and the United States during the Civil War, will have perceived that the American State Papers were all pervaded by the same spirit as that which dictated the speech of Mr. Sumner and the resolution of the Massachusetts Legislature. The Government of the United States, the chief Republican leaders, and the most active managers of the great political "machine," through which the national feelings and the national will were aroused and directed, had laid all their plans, and had based all their hopes, upon the supposition that the so-called "rebellion" would soon collapse, or that it would be soon suppressed. They were annoyed and offended because Europe ventured to pronounce that condition of affairs to be a state of war which they affirmed to be only an insurrection. Great Britain was selected as the chief object of their displeasure, and there was a manifest determination from the beginning, not only to exact pecuniary compensation for alleged injuries, but to inflict upon her the indignity of an apology for venturing to recognise the Confederate States as belligerents, and putting them on the same footing with the United States in respect to the obtaining of supplies. That purpose was not specifically proclaimed in any State Paper before the rejection of the Clarendon-Johnson Convention; but reading the correspondence now, and comparing its tone with the progress of the subsequent negotiations, the temper and the aim boldly avowed in Mr. Sumner's speech and in the resolution of the Massachusetts Legislature are easily discerned through the light film of diplomatic reserve which partially obscured them.

It is an admirable exhibition of principle and of moral courage to offer a spontaneous, cordial, and complete *amende* for an injury inflicted upon another, whether through ignorance or inadvertence, and the man who does so will increase his influence and the respect in which he is held, by as much as the precepts of religion are more excellent than the maxims of the world. The same law applies in this respect to the conduct of a State as to an individual. But when the responsible Government of a country has deliberately adopted a certain policy towards another country, has insisted on all occasions of remonstrance that their conduct was right in principle as well as in law, and after four or five years of complaint and petition for redress, has emphatically declined to make reparation and compensation, or to refer their conduct to the arbitration of a foreign State,* it is offering them an indignity to demand, under open menace or implied threat, that they should confess themselves in error and express their sorrow. To yield under such circumstances manifests that there has been either an unstatesmanlike rashness, precipitancy, and stubbornness in the original acts, or else a lack of nerve to maintain an attitude believed to be right.

Lord Derby's Cabinet had determined to maintain the ground taken by their predecessors in power, but they had expressed an earnest desire to meet the United States in a conciliatory spirit if the two countries could agree upon the principle of arbitration and the points to which arbitration should apply. They did not, however, remain long enough in office to impress their views and their policy upon the negotiations, and all that can be said is that the concessions they were willing to make did not go far enough to satisfy the President of the United States. It seems manifest that the Government of Lord Derby would have stood upon stronger ground, and would have been able to discuss the questions at issue more

---

* See Earl Russell's letter of August 30th, 1865, quoted above.

independently than Mr. Gladstone and his colleagues, who succeeded them. Neither the Conservative Party nor its leaders were responsible for the policy of Great Britain during the Civil War, nor were they implicated in the acts which had given offence to the United States. The warmth which had characterized Mr. Seward's official correspondence during the continuance of the war would have had no *raison d'être* when he came to negotiate with a new Cabinet, none of whose members had ever given cause of offence by disregarding his protests and complaints, or had wounded his pride by an occasional retort, extorted by the pungency of his own sometimes unguarded phrases.

There can be no doubt that the new Liberal Government was not in a favourable position to deal vigorously or independently with the claims, which the United States pressed with renewed earnestness and force as soon as it was discovered that the original offenders were again in power. It must be admitted that the course pursued by her Majesty's Government during the Civil War was neither consistent nor firm. They enunciated their policy towards the two belligerents with clearness and force; they repeatedly affirmed that the policy was right in principle and in law; they over and over again refused to reverse or to modify its general principles, and yet they did more than once yield to pressure, and on one notable occasion to an ill-concealed threat, and interfered with the alleged operations of one belligerent for the benefit and protection of the other.

I am very desirous not to make a general statement which shall convey a meaning not justified by the facts. In a previous chapter I have given actual quotations from speeches of several leading members of her Majesty's Government and from despatches of the Secretary of State for Foreign Affairs, on the subject of the neutral duties of Great Britain, in direct reference to the American Civil War. I feel sure that I am not overstating the views of her Majesty's advisers at that time in repeating that they were as follows:—"A neutral may supply either of two belligerents not only with arms and cannon, but with ships suitable to operate in war; and her Majesty's Government cannot, therefore, interfere with the dealings between British subjects and the 'so-styled' Confederate States, whether the object of those dealings be money or contraband goods, or even ships adapted for war. The seizure of the *Alabama* would have been altogether unwarrantable by law. She might have been legitimately built by a Foreign Government; and though a ship-of-war, she might have formed a legitimate article of merchandise even if meant for the Confederate States. The Foreign Enlistment Act was not meant to prohibit commercial dealings in ships-of-war with belligerent countries, but to prevent what the law regards as the fitting out, arming, or equipment of a ship-of-war within the British dominions, with the intent that she should be employed in the service of a foreign belligerent. A ship or a musket may be sold to one belligerent or the other, and only ceases to be neutral when the ship is owned, manned, and employed in war, and the musket is held by a soldier and used for the purpose of killing his enemy. There must, in fact, be a proved violation of the Foreign Enlistment Act to justify her Majesty's Government in preventing a British subject from selling a ship of any description whatever to a foreign belligerent."

In the foregoing brief synopsis I have kept closely to the spirit, indeed, I have used in the main the very words employed in the original speeches and despatches, previously quoted more at length, and it will be remembered that the Lord Chief Baron of the Exchequer, in a test case, confirmed the declarations of her Majesty's Ministers, and settled the definition of the words "fit out" and "equip," as they are, or were, used in the Foreign Enlistment Act.

Notwithstanding the clear and very definite position thus assumed by her Majesty's Government, they gave way to the pressure applied to them by the American Minister and seized the *Alexandra*, a wholly unarmed ship, and in a very incomplete condition, upon precisely the same kind of evidence which they thought insufficient in the case of the *Alabama*, and which proved to be false in every material point, when put to the test at the trial which followed. A number of other vessels unarmed, unequipped, most of them manifestly designed for trading purposes alone, and all of them clearly within the limits of legal merchandise as defined by her Majesty's Government, were interfered with or detained for inquiry upon the complaint, or to satisfy the suspicions, of the United States Consuls. But the most notable departure from the principles of neutrality enumerated in the declarations of Ministers was the seizure of the so-called "Liverpool rams."

On the 20th of August, 1863, the depositions furnished by the American Consul at Liverpool in respect to the above vessels were submitted to the law officers of the Crown. After some preliminary comments they advised as follows:—"Having regard to the entire insufficiency of the depositions forwarded to her Majesty's Government by Mr. Adams to prove any infraction of the law, we cannot advise her Majesty's Government to interfere in any way with these vessels. There is, in fact, no evidence capable of being presented to a court of justice of any intention on the part of any persons in this country, that either of these vessels should be employed in the belligerent service of the Confederate Government against the United States, even if it would have been proper (had such evidence been forthcoming) to act upon the assumption that the law recently laid down by the Lord Chief Baron in the case of the *Alexandra* is incorrect, or that his lordship's ruling is inapplicable to vessels of this description, a point on which it may be better to reserve the expression of our opinion till such a case arises."*

In consequence of the above opinion of the law officers, Earl Russell wrote Mr. Adams on September 1st, 1863, that her Majesty's Government could not interfere with the vessels, and to justify the refusal he said:—"A court of justice would never condemn in the absence of evidence, and the Government would be justly blamed for acting in defiance of the principles of law and justice, long recognised and established in this country."†
Mr. Adams replied to the foregoing on the 5th of September, and strongly remonstrated. He said:—"The fatal objection of impotency which paralyzes her Majesty's Government seems to present an insuperable barrier against all further reasoning. Under these circumstances, I prefer to desist from communicating to your lordship even such portions of my existing instructions as are suited to the case, lest I should contribute to aggravate difficulties already far too serious. I therefore content myself with informing your lordship that I transmit by the present steamer a copy of your note for the consideration of my Government," etc.‡

The above letter of Mr. Adams, with its covert threat, proved sufficient to counteract the opinion of the law officers, and overcame the objections of the Government to act without evidence. On the 8th of September Earl Russell informed Mr. Adams, in a hasty note of two and a half lines,§ that orders had been issued which would prevent the departure of the vessels, and he confirmed the statement in a long despatch under date of September 11th. In the last-mentioned despatch, which has been quoted and commented upon in a previous chapter, Earl Russell affirms most decidedly that a ship may be legally sold to one of two belligerents, "and only ceases to be neutral when she is owned, manned, and employed in war," and yet he closes his communication in the following words:—"I have to add that instructions have been issued for preventing the departure of the ironclad vessels in question from Liverpool until satisfactory evidence can be given as to their destination, or, at all events, until the in-

---

* See "British Appendix," vol. ii., pp. 336, 337.
† "British Appendix," vol. ii., p. 344.
‡ Ibid., pp. 352, 353.
§ Ibid., vol. ii., p. 355.

quiries which are now being prosecuted with a view to obtain such evidence shall have been brought to a conclusion."[*]

The simplest possible summary is all that is necessary to illustrate the vacillating policy of her Majesty's Government. They affirmed that ships of any description were legitimate articles of trade between neutrals and belligerents, and that they would not interfere with such trade unless a clear violation of the Foreign Enlistment Act could be *proved*. They stated that there was *no such proof in the case of the ironclad vessels*, and yet when pressed they seized the ships—what for? Not to bring their builders or alleged owners to trial, but *in order to gain time for the purpose of making inquiries, and thus discovering evidence* against them.

When Mr. Seward perceived that there was a limit to the fortitude of her Majesty's Government, and that it was possible to obtain from them in practice more than they would admit in principle, the diplomatic difficulties were greatly moderated. The representatives of the United States had only to urge with vehemence in order to obtain, and each successive concession thus yielded under pressure made the following attack more easy, and the succeeding victory more complete.

But if her Majesty's Government disparaged their prestige and weakened their position by preaching one doctrine and practising another, they still further contributed to strengthen the claims and pretensions of the United States by extraordinarily indiscreet and seemingly thoughtless admissions. In a despatch to Lord Lyons, dated March 27th, 1863, Earl Russell reported to her Majesty's Minister at Washington the purport of an official conversation between himself and Mr. Adams, in which he says:—"I admitted that the cases of the *Alabama* and *Oreto* were a scandal."[†]

Now, the cases of the *Alabama* and *Oreto* could only have been scandalous from one of two points of view: either the Foreign Enlistment Act did not give her Majesty's Government sufficient power to fulfil their neutral duties, in which case the United States had a clear right to ask for its amendment, or, the law being strong enough, her Majesty's Government had administered it so inefficiently as to admit of its open violation, in which latter case the United States could justly complain that no effort had been made to enforce its provisions or to punish the offenders. Earl Russell did not mean to admit the former hypothesis, because in the very

[*] "British Appendix," vol. ii., pp. 358–60.

[†] See "Document" presented to Parliament, "The *Alabama*, North America (no. 1), 1864," pp. 2, 3.

despatch above quoted he wrote thus:—"I said (to Mr. Adams) that the Cabinet were of opinion that the law was sufficient;" and he could hardly have meant to admit the latter, because down to the very close of the war her Majesty's Government invariably refused to prosecute the Confederate agents or the builders of the ships, on the plea that there was no proof that the law had been violated by any of them.

More than one member of the Government permitted still another unguarded expression to fall from his lips or from his pen. It was that the *Alabama* had "escaped," or, to be more precise in the expression, they spoke frequently of the "escape of the *Alabama*." Now, I have always understood that to fly from the consequences of breaking a criminal statute does not purge the offence, and that the offender may be arrested and punished whenever he can be laid hold of. The *Alabama* did not go out of the port of Liverpool of her own volition. If her departure was illegal, it was effected by persons who were then and afterwards within the reach of the law, and yet no one has ever been called to account in respect to her movements. We can, therefore, only class the phrase used by Earl Russell, and the admissions of other Ministers, among those unfortunate expressions which slip from the tongue in an unguarded moment, which can never be recalled or explained, but which rise up in future judgment against the speaker, often to his embarrassment, sometimes to his shame, and to the serious detriment of the country he represents. The admissions were carefully noted by Mr. Adams, and were effectively used afterwards in pressing the "*Alabama* Claims." Even the Solicitor-General, when speaking as a politician in defence of the Government, and not with the caution of a lawyer, said on one occasion that "we (the Government) strained the law" in the proceedings against some of the ships, which served as an encouragement to Mr. Adams in urging a further and continuous process of straining. Other unhappy slips of the tongue and of the pen might be culled from the speeches and despatches of her Majesty's Ministers during the Civil War, but the foregoing are sufficient to demonstrate the advantage which accrued to the United States from such unguarded expressions.

But the British Ministers of that day still further compromised the country, and supplied Mr. Seward with plausible data for the allegations of unfriendly neutrality to the United States which are so prominently set forth in the claims and in the "Case" laid before the Tribunal of Arbitration, by speeches both in and out of Parliament, which certainly did greatly offend the North and did arouse a hope of "recognition" at the

South. The stab at the North about fighting for "empire" and not upon the question of slavery in Earl Russell's speech at Newcastle has already been quoted in another connection. In the same speech his lordship said:—

"But I cannot help asking myself frequently, as I trace the progress of the contest, to what good end can it tend? Supposing the contest to end in the reunion of the different States; supposing that the South should agree to enter again the Federal Union with all the rights guaranteed to her by the Constitution, should we not then have debated over again the fatal question of slavery?... But, on the other hand, supposing that the Federal Government completely conquer and subdue the Southern States— supposing that be the result after a long military conflict and some years of Civil War—would not the national prosperity of that country be destroyed?... If such are the unhappy results which alone can be looked forward to from the reunion of these different parts of the North American States, is it not then our duty... is it not the duty of men who wish to preserve in perpetuity the sacred inheritance of liberty, to endeavour to see whether this sanguinary conflict cannot be put an end to?"*

In a speech delivered in the House of Lords, February 5th, 1863, Earl Russell said:—"There is one thing, however, which I think may be the result of the struggle, and which, to my mind, would be a great calamity— that is, the subjugation of the South by the North." After some comments he added:—"But there may be, I say, one end of the war that would prove a calamity to the United States and to the world, and especially calamitous to the negro race in those countries, and that would be the subjugation of the South by the North."†

Mr. W. E. Gladstone, the Chancellor of the Exchequer, said in a public speech at Newcastle, October 7th, 1862:—"We may have our own opinions about slavery; we may be for or against the South; but there is no doubt that Jefferson Davis and other leaders of the South have made an army. They are making, it appears, a navy, and they have made what is more than either—they have made a nation. [Loud cheers.] ... We may anticipate with certainty the success of the Southern States so far as regards their separation from the North. [Hear, hear.] I cannot but believe that that event is as certain as any event yet future and contingent can be."‡

Lest it may be thought that the foregoing was one of those bursts of exuberant eloquence which escape from an orator of ardent temperament

---

* Quoted in "United States Case," pp. 23, 24.
† Ibid., p. 24.
‡ "United States Case," p. 24.

when free from the restraints and responsibilities of office, here is an extract from a long speech by the same distinguished gentleman, in the House of Commons, delivered June 30th, 1863, while he was still a member of the Government:—"Why, sir, we must desire the cessation of this war. No man is justified in wishing for the continuance of a war unless that war has a just, an adequate, and an attainable object, for no object is adequate, no object is just, unless it is also attainable. We do not believe that the restoration of the American Union by force is attainable. I believe that the public opinion of this country is unanimous upon that subject. [No.] Well, almost unanimous. I may be right or I may be wrong—I do not pretend to interpret exactly the public opinion of the country. I express in regard to it only my private sentiments. But I will go one step further, and say I believe the public opinion of this country bears very strongly on another matter upon which we have heard much, namely, whether the emancipation of the negro race is an object that can be legitimately pursued by means of coercion and bloodshed. I do not believe that a more fatal error was ever committed than when men—of high intelligence I grant, and of the sincerity of whose philanthropy I, for one, shall not venture to whisper the smallest doubt—came to the conclusion that the emancipation of the negro race was to be sought, although they could only travel to it by a sea of blood. I do not think there is any real or serious ground for doubt as to the issue of this contest."*

The foregoing extracts are not now selected by me from the speeches of Mr. Gladstone with the purpose of showing the bias or the opinions of a member of her Majesty's Government in reference to the American Civil War; they are copied *verbatim* from the "Case" presented to the Tribunal of Arbitration on behalf of the United States, and they were quoted in that document with the avowed intent of demonstrating to the arbitrators that the Government of Great Britain did not think the United States would succeed, nor did they wish them to succeed, and the inference that the counsel for the United States wished to establish was that, in consequence of those unfriendly convictions and wishes, the Confederates were encouraged to obtain the supplies in England which enabled them to prolong the war.

It is proper to mention that some years after the war Mr. Gladstone made an explanation of the sentiments contained in his various speeches, and he categorically denied that his sympathies were with the South, stating that in point of fact his leanings were towards the North. Of course,

* Quoted in "United States Case," p. 25.

those explanations must be taken as decisive in regard to the private feelings of the right honourable gentleman, but in an historical narrative the narrator must state the meaning that was commonly attached to the speeches of responsible statesmen at the time they were delivered, and he must describe the effect then created without reference to the explanations, which, coming long after the events, have no practical importance. If Mr. Gladstone, speaking as a Minister of the Crown in 1862 and in 1863, thought it advisable to sum up in eloquent language the achievements of the Southern leaders, and to express the belief that their final success was an event as certain as any occurrence yet future and contingent could be—if he could say officially from his place in the House of Commons that the restoration of the American Union by force was not attainable, and therefore the war against the South was without a just or adequate object; and, moreover, that it was a fatal error to attempt the emancipation of the negro race by travelling through "a sea of blood"—it matters very little at this late day whether he was giving utterance to an irrepressible feeling of sympathy for the South, or was only expressing an abstract opinion upon the result of the war and the inadequacy of the object which impelled the North to wage it.

The compilers of the "United States Case," in the printed argument laid before the Tribunal of Arbitration at Geneva, make the following comment upon the several speeches quoted above:—"It is scarcely too much to say that his" (Mr. Gladstone's) "language, as well as much of the language of other members of her Majesty's Government herein quoted, might well have been taken as offensive";* and they allude elsewhere to the speeches of Ministers as manifesting a partiality to the South which they allege caused her Majesty's Government to relax the restrictions which should have been imposed upon the Confederate agents. In support of the foregoing allegation the following very pointed·statement is made:—"The United States summon no less illustrious a person than the present Prime Minister of England" (the Right Hon. W. E. Gladstone) "to prove not only that the insurgents were engaged in the year 1862 in making a navy, but that the fact was known to the gentlemen who then constituted her Majesty's Government."†

The foregoing comments are sufficient to settle the interpretation that was put upon Mr. Gladstone's speeches by the people of the North. There

---

* See "United States Case," House of Commons Blue Book, "North America (no. 2), 1872," p. 24.
† "United States Case," p. 58.

can be no doubt that at the South they were received as evidence that some of her Majesty's Ministers at least sympathized with the Confederate cause, and they did arouse hopes of some sort of intervention which would contribute to its success. Every Southerner believed with Mr. Gladstone that the war of coercion was without a just or adequate object, although all of them did not follow him to the conclusion that the object was unattainable. He carried the entire South with him when he eloquently affirmed his belief that "a more fatal error was never committed than that of seeking the emancipation of the negro race by coercion and bloodshed," even though the hot sun of the Carolinas or of Louisiana did not inspire any representative Southerner to describe the way by which the North was seeking to accomplish it in the glowing metaphor of "a sea of blood." As, therefore, both parties in the late Civil War put the same interpretation upon the speeches at the time they were delivered, and one of them at least retained the impression up to the date of the Geneva Arbitration, it does not seem presumptuous to affirm that the language fairly implied the meaning attached to it.

It is, therefore, embarrassing to be told, years after the event, that both sides were mistaken, and that the speaker meant quite a different thing. Such a declaration upsets all definite rules of interpretation, and drives one to the conclusion that when oratory leaves the strict line of argument and soars into the higher atmosphere of eloquence and metaphor, the words are only mystic oracles, which, like the notes of an Æolian harp, delight the ear with their harmonious melody, but do not convey to the senses a distinct tune. In fact, if the declaration is to be taken as generally applicable to the speeches of great public orators and statesmen, it will be necessary in the future for each speaker to supply the shorthand writers with the key to his meaning, which might be put in a note at the foot of the "report" in the next morning's papers. Thus would be obtained a double advantage. The reader would not be mystified, and the speaker would avoid the trouble of a future explanation.

It seems impossible to doubt the opinion previously expressed that the Conservative Government of 1866–68, composed chiefly of the late Earl of Derby, Mr. Disraeli, and Lord Stanley, could have negotiated for a settlement of the "*Alabama* Claims" with a much better chance of arriving at a fair, equitable, and friendly result than the Cabinet which succeeded them. Neither of the Conservative statesmen mentioned above had given any outward manifestations of sympathy with either side, and had not irritated Mr. Seward, or wounded the susceptibilities of the North, by speeches which were taken to be offensive and were at least indiscreet.

They would no doubt have been held to be responsible for the policy of their predecessors, but the negotiations would in all probability have been carried on without any manifestations of pique on the part of the United States, and much of the harsh comment, the personal insinuations, and the sarcastic criticisms which appear in the "United States Case" would have had no standing-place in that document, as they would have been wholly inapplicable to Ministers who had given no cause of offence. But the conditions under which the negotiations were resumed after the Liberal Party came back into power, with Mr. Gladstone as Prime Minister, and with other members of the Cabinet who administered the Government during the Civil War for his colleagues, rendered it almost certain that the United States would not only urge their claims with some asperity, but would insist upon such concessions as would involve a confession of error and an apology; and they succeeded in extorting both after a long and weary discussion.

The rejection of the Clarendon-Johnson Convention was officially notified to Lord Clarendon on the 4th of May, 1869. About the same time Mr. Hamilton Fish relieved Mr. Seward as Secretary of State at Washington, and Mr. John Lothrop Motley succeeded Mr. Reverdy Johnson as United States Minister to Great Britain. It appears that Mr. Motley arrived in London on the 31st of May, 1869; and on the 10th of June he called on Lord Clarendon "to make known to him the general tenor of his instructions."[*] In the interview which followed, Mr. Motley explained the reasons which led to the rejection of the Claims Convention by the Senate of the United States. He said that owing to an accident the Convention had been published in the United States prematurely, and that in consequence it had been unfavourably received by all classes and parties in the country long before it came under the notice of the Senate. Moreover, he said that the time at which it was signed was inopportune, as the late President and his Government were virtually out of office, and their successors could not be consulted on the subject. Finally, he said, the Convention was further objected to because it embraced only the claims of individuals, and had no reference to those of two Governments on each other, and that it settled no question and laid down no principle. Mr. Motley furthermore said that "in the present state of excitement which existed in both countries, his Government was of opinion that to reopen the question would be inexpedient, as it could not be approached with the calm delib-

---

[*] Lord Clarendon to Mr. Thornton, "British Case," Appendix, vol. iv., "North America (no. 1), 1870," p.1.

eration which was essential to its satisfactory solution; and he wished, therefore, to defer the discussion of the subject."

Lord Clarendon replied that her Majesty's Government were willing to comply with the wishes of the United States in respect to deferring the discussion,* but he did not consider that there was any great excitement in England on the subject, and he thought it would be very objectionable to postpone a settlement indefinitely, "and to treat the matter as a quarrel held in suspension, to be revived only when circumstances might make it the interest of either party to do so." Mr. Motley replied that Lord Clarendon need be under no such apprehension, as his Government merely desired that a definite time should be allowed for angry feelings to subside.

After the foregoing conversation there was no further discussion of the subject until October 15th, 1869, when Mr. Motley communicated verbally to Lord Clarendon the contents of a despatch he had received from Mr. Fish, which reopened the whole subject of the "*Alabama* claims," and on the next day he forwarded to him a copy of the despatch, which was dated September 25, 1869.† Considering that Mr. Motley had been instructed to propose a postponement of the discussion on the express plea that his Government wished to reopen the subject after calm deliberation, and when there had been time for all angry feeling to subside, Lord Clarendon no doubt expected to find in Mr. Fish's first despatch a plain, dignified, moderate, and friendly statement of the "claims." He doubtless hoped that all merely sentimental grievances would be omitted, that the insinuations, irritating epithets, and figures of rhetoric which marred the force and weakened the effect of Mr. Seward's State Papers would be eliminated, and that he would have to deal with practical demands based upon a clear unimpassioned statement of facts, well within the range of plausibility, even if not capable of "technical proof" in every particular. These expectations were disappointed, and the British Foreign Minister discovered that Mr. Fish's long and elaborate despatch was a mere recapitulation of the arguments previously used by Mr. Seward, stated somewhat less offensively, but retaining most of the insinuations and many of the exaggerations which there had been ample time to examine and to test.

The sentimental grievance crops up in the very first page of the despatch. After sketching the origin of what he calls the "domestic insur-

---

* Lord Clarendon to Mr. Thornton, "British Case," Appendix, vol. iv., "North America (no. 1), 1870," p. 2.

† For Mr. Fish's despatch see "British Case," Appendix, vol. iv., "North America (no. 1), 1870," p. 3.

rection," Mr. Fish says:—"In such a contest, the Government of the United States was entitled to expect the earnest goodwill, sympathy, and moral support of Great Britain." After expressing the "painful astonishment" which the manifest absence of that sympathy produced, Mr. Fish gives an elaborate *rechauffée* of Mr. Seward's complaints against Great Britain, beginning with the allegation that the Declaration of Neutrality and the admission of the South to belligerent rights were premature and unfriendly to the United States, that they gave encouragement to the "insurgents," and enabled them to prolong the contest and to inflict incalculable injury upon the United States, for which they had a right to claim compensation from her Majesty's Government.

This part of the despatch does not much affect the object of the present narrative, and as the complaint, together with the reply of Earl Russell to it, have both been stated in a previous chapter, it might be left without further notice here. But Lord Clarendon, in his answer, gave some additional reasons why the complaint was in itself unreasonable, and why the grounds upon which it was advanced were untenable, and a synopsis of what his lordship said in reply will help to illustrate the manner in which the so-called "*Alabama* Claims" were brought before a Tribunal of Arbitration.

Lord Clarendon said that at the time when the Queen was advised to issue the Proclamation of Neutrality hostilities had actually begun, that the Confederate States had established a *de facto* Government, with all the machinery of civil and military power; that Fort Sumter had fallen, and the Confederate troops were in occupation of the Shenandoah valley, and were threatening Washington; that the Confederate President had called for a levy of 32,000 troops, to which the seceded States had promptly responded; that the Federal President had called for 75,000 volunteers, and then for 42,000 more; that as fast as the regiments could be armed they were marched to the defence of Washington, and that the contending armies were, indeed, "face to face."* In respect to the operations at sea, he said that "on the 17th of April the Confederate President had issued a Proclamation offering to grant letters of marque, and two days after the Federal President had declared the Southern ports to be in a state of blockade; that one or more British ships had actually been captured while attempting to run the blockade; that Confederate privateers were already at sea; that one had been captured on the 8th of May by the United States

---

* Lord Clarendon's despatch and inclosure containing his comments will be found in Appendix to "British Case," vol. iv., "North America (no. 1), 1870," pp. 11–20.

ship *Harriet Lane;* that a few days after the American barque *Ocean Eagle,* of Rockland, Maine, was captured by the Confederate privateer *Calhoun,* of New Orleans, and that at the same port the *Sumter* was fitting out for her cruise.

Lord Clarendon especially drew attention to the following facts. He said:—"Mr. Seward, writing at the time, and previously to the Queen's Proclamation" (May 4), "characterized the proceedings of the Confederates as 'open, flagrant, deadly war,' and as 'civil war' (Congress Papers, 1861, p. 165); and in a communication to M. de Tassara, the Spanish Minister, referred to the operations of the Federal blockade as belligerent operations which would be carried on with due respect to the rights of neutrals. Judge Betts, in the cases of the *Hiawatha*, etc., said:—'I consider that the outbreak in particular States, as also in the Confederate States, was an open and flagrant civil war.' It was also judicially decided by the Supreme Court of the United States, in the case of the *Amy Warwick* and other prizes, that 'the proclamation of blockade was in itself official and conclusive evidence that a state of war existed which demanded and authorized such a measure.' "* He furthermore cited a joint resolution of the United States Congress in July, 1861, approving and confirming the war measures of the President, in which resolution the "domestic insurrection" of Mr. Fish is called the "present deplorable Civil War," and "this war."

In view of all the foregoing, Lord Clarendon said:—"The date at which the Civil War actually commenced has, therefore, been fixed by the published despatches of the Secretary of State, by proceedings in Congress, by the formal judgment of the United States prize-courts, as well as by the universal assent of all the neutral Powers concerned," and he expresses a very justifiable surprise that Mr. Seward's threadbare complaint of British recognition of an accomplished and admitted fact should be revived four years after the close of the war.

In the memorandum forwarded to the British Minister at Washington, Lord Clarendon remarked upon the claims for "vast national injuries" advanced by Mr. Fish,† and he furnished Mr. Thornton with an extract from a speech delivered at Bristol (England) by Mr. Lawrence, the editor of the second annotated edition of "Wheaton." Mr. Lawrence was an American, and he was speaking to an English audience just about the time when Mr.

---

* See, for Lord Clarendon's remarks, "British Case," Appendix, vols. iii., iv., "North America (no. 1), 1870," p. 11, etc.

† "British Case," Appendix, vol. iv. (no. 1), 1870, p. 19.

Fish's despatch was delivered to Lord Clarendon. He said:—"As far as respects the complaint founded on the recognition of the belligerent rights of the Confederates, I cannot use too strong language in pronouncing its utter baseless character. No tyro in international law is ignorant that belligerency is a simple question of fact. With the late Sir Cornewall Lewis we may ask, if the array of a million of men on each side does not constitute belligerency, what is belligerency? But what was the Proclamation of the President, followed up by the condemnation of your ships and cargoes for a violation of the blockade which is established, but a recognition of a state of war? At this moment the United States, in claiming the property of the late Confederate Government, places before your tribunals their title on the fact of their being successors of a *de facto* Government. I repeat that, however valid our claims against you on other grounds, there is not the slightest pretext for any claim against you based on the public admission of a notorious fact, the existence of which has been recognised by every Department of the Federal Government."

The foregoing is the language of the American editor of the standard American work on international law.

But Mr. Seward had apparently stamped his own peculiar views upon the State Department, and his successor was not equal to the effort of repudiating them. In reference to the despatch of Confederate cruisers from British ports, Mr. Fish writes quite in the vein and temper of Mr. Seward, and with very nearly the same recklessness and exaggeration. We find in the official communication which had been held back to give time for calm deliberation such expressions as follow:—"Great Britain … *permitted* armed cruisers to be fitted out"—"the Queen's Government … *suffered* ship after ship to be constructed in its ports to wage war against the United States"—"many ships were, with ostentatious publicity, being constructed"—"*permission* or negligence which enabled Confederate cruisers from her ports to prey," etc.—"Great Britain alone had founded on recognition a systematic maritime war"—"suffering the fitting out of rebel cruisers."

Anyone reading the despatch from which the foregoing extracts are taken, having himself no knowledge of the facts, would suppose from the language used, that fleets of Confederate cruisers had been built, armed, and equipped in England and despatched from British ports. All who have read the foregoing pages of this work, will perceive how little of substantial truth there was in such broad assertions, and will admit the fitness of Earl Russell's comment, that many of the allegations of those who represented the United States were rather "figures of rhetoric" than plain statements of fact.

In reference to the supplies furnished to the South by British subjects, Mr. Fish described the poverty of the South thus:—"We reflected that the Confederates had no ships, no means of building ships, no mechanical appliances, no marine, no legal status on the sea, no open seaports, no possible courts of prize, no domestic command of the instruments and agencies of modern maritime warfare"; and he then implies that the entire maritime force of the Confederate States was obtained in some sort of illicit way from Great Britain, with the connivance, if not with the direct consent, of her Majesty's Government. The poverty of the Southern States in respect to naval resources at the beginning of the war was not overdrawn by Mr. Fish; but what are the facts in regard to the manner and source from which their wants were supplied? In the "United States Case" presented to the Tribunal of Arbitration, claims are made against Great Britain for alleged depredations of ten Confederate vessels in addition to the *Alabama*, the *Florida*, the *Shenandoah*, and their tenders. Every one of the ten were either built or bought within the Confederacy; they were fitted out, armed, and manned at Confederate ports; all of them sailed from Confederate ports on their first cruises, and at least three of them, the *Nashville*, the *Tallahassee*, and the *Chickamauga*, returned in safety to Confederate ports when they had accomplished the purpose for which they had been despatched. The foregoing facts could have been known to anyone who chose to inquire, and it is really marvellous that the State Department at Washington should have advanced claims against Great Britain, based upon statements which her Majesty's Government could so easily disprove.

Mr. Fish laid great stress upon the indirect injury to American commerce.* He said:—"Our merchant-vessels were destroyed piratically by captors who had no ports of their own ... and whose only nationality was the quarter-deck of their ships," etc. "Indirectly," he said, "the effect was to increase the rate of insurance in the United States ... to take away from the United States its immense foreign commerce, and to transfer this to the merchant-vessels of Great Britain."† In proof of the foregoing, he said that "while in the year 1860 the foreign merchant tonnage of the United

---

* Mr. Fish's despatch, "British Case," Appendix, vols. iii., iv., "North America (no. 1), 1870," pp. 3–10.

† Ibid., p. 5.

States amounted to 2,546,237 tons, in 1866 it had sunk to 1,492,923. This depreciation," he continued, "is represented by a corresponding increase in the tonnage of Great Britain during the same period to the amount of 1,120,650 tons." After a further remark to the effect that commerce was "abstracted" from the United States and "transferred" to Great Britain, he closes that part of the subject with the following startling and sensational statement:—"Thus, in effect, war against the United States was carried on from the ports of Great Britain by British subjects in the name of the Confederates."

After so long a summary of grievances it might surely be supposed that Mr. Fish would have put the demands of the United States in some definite shape, and that he would have suggested some practical mode of adjusting the differences between the two countries, but he did not. On the contrary, he instructed Mr. Motley to inform Lord Clarendon that what he had written was not in the nature of a claim, nor did the United States then make a demand against her Majesty's Government on account of the injuries sustained, nor did they then propose or desire to set any time for a settlement.* They were willing "to leave that question, and also the more important question of the means and methods of removing the causes of complaint, and of restoring the much-desired relations of perfect cordiality, etc., to the consideration of her Majesty's Government."

It must have somewhat embarrassed Lord Clarendon and his colleagues to know how to deal with the foregoing complaints and charges, direct and implied, all of which were unpleasantly familiar to them, and which in Mr. Seward's time they had so strongly repelled; and it was rather awkward to be asked to suggest the means and method for removing the causes of complaint, and for settling the account for damages, when they had already declared that they had given no just cause of complaint, and had declined to "make reparation and compensation for the captures made by the *Alabama*, or to refer the question to any foreign state."†

It would be useless to trace the further progress of the negotiations in detail. There were other questions besides those pertaining to the Confederate cruisers, such, for example, as the relations of the United States towards the British Possessions in North America, and Naturalization Laws and the fisheries, all of which gave occasion for correspondence and discussion.

• Mr. Fish's despatch, "British Case," Appendix, vols. iii., iv., "North America (no. 1), 1870," p. 10.

† Earl Russell's despatch, August 30th, 1865, quoted previously.

In January, 1871, Sir E. Thornton (the British Minister at Washington) informed Mr. Fish that he had been directed by Earl Granville* to propose to the Government of the United States the appointment of a Joint High Commission, which should be composed of members to be named by each Government, the Joint Commission to sit at Washington, and to treat of and discuss the mode of settling all questions which had reference to the fisheries and to her Majesty's possessions in America.

Mr. Fish replied, January 30th, 1871, that he had submitted the proposition to the President, and was instructed to say that in the President's opinion the Joint High Commission would fail to re-establish the sincere, lasting, and substantial friendship between the two countries which he (the President) desired, unless the differences which arose from the acts committed by the Confederate cruisers, and which had given rise to the claims generically known as the "*Alabama* Claims," should be also submitted to the Commission.† Mr. Fish added that if her Majesty's Government would accept that view, and would agree that the "*Alabama* Claims" should also be treated of by the proposed High Commission, he was instructed by the President to say that the United States would with much pleasure appoint High Commissioners on their part to meet those appointed by her Majesty's Government at the earliest practicable moment. The proposal to include the "*Alabama* Claims" in the subjects to be referred to the Joint High Commission was promptly accepted by Earl Granville, who informed Sir E. Thornton on the 23rd of February, 1871, that Lord de Grey and the other British Commissioners had already left England.

A brief recapitulation is necessary to a clear and complete understanding of the conditions under which the so-styled "*Alabama* Claims" were at last submitted to arbitration. When the Liberal Government went out of office in 1866, the position was this:—Earl Russell had categorically declined "either to make reparation and compensation for the captures made by the *Alabama*, or to refer the question to any foreign State";‡ and his successor, Lord Clarendon (in the same Cabinet), in closing the correspondence with Mr. Adams on the subject, maintained that the British Government "had never deviated from the obligations imposed upon them by international law."§ When the late Earl of Derby came into power

---

* The same Cabinet, under Mr. W. E. Gladstone as Premier, was in office, but Earl Granville had succeeded the Earl of Clarendon as Foreign Secretary.

† For the full particulars see "Parliamentary Blue Book," "Correspondence respecting Joint High Commission," etc., "North America (no. 1), 1871," pp. 3–5.

‡ Earl Russell to Mr. Adams, August 30th, 1865, quoted on pp. 331, 332.

§ His letter of December 2nd, 1865, quoted on p. 334.

the discussion was re-opened, and Lord Stanley, who was Foreign Secretary in his father's Cabinet, stated that "although her Majesty's present advisers could not abandon the ground taken by their predecessors so as to admit the liability of Great Britain for the claims then and now put forward, yet they would be glad to settle the question, and were willing to adopt the principle of arbitration if the points to which arbitration should apply could be agreed upon." The Stanley-Johnson Convention was the result of the foregoing proposal; but the restrictions which were imposed upon the inquiry into the "*Alabama* Claims" did not satisfy the President of the United States, and in consequence the Convention was never referred to the Senate for confirmation. When the Liberal Party resumed office in 1868, the Claims were again pressed, and another agreement was made between the two countries, commonly known as the Clarendon-Johnson Convention. By the terms of this latter Convention, her Majesty's Government consented to enlarge the inquiry into the "*Alabama* Claims" so as to meet as nearly as possible the views of the President of the United States; but, nevertheless, the Convention was rejected by the Senate, in consequence of the opposition of Mr. Charles Sumner and other extreme men, who manifestly wished to humiliate Great Britain by extorting an admission that she had committed an error in permitting the Confederates to trade with British subjects on terms of equality with the United States.

After the rejection of the Clarendon-Johnson Convention the subject was again held in abeyance for some time, and when it was reopened by Mr. Fish, although Lord Clarendon repeated the arguments advanced against the claims on former occasions, and with even greater force on some points, yet it appears from this time to be manifest that her Majesty's Government were worn out with the toils and vexations arising from the controversy. They were fast losing their often-avowed consciousness of right, and also their fortitude in resisting the claims, whose justice they had always heretofore repelled. The indiscreet speeches during the war, and the heedless admissions which had been drawn from several of the Ministers at various times, now rose up in judgment against them. Those fatal ebullitions of fancy or of feeling, and those unguarded slips of the pen, had from the very first furnished topics of angry comment in the American press; they had been the inspiring theme of many orations, spoken, indeed, within the halls of Congress, but really meant for "Bunkum"; they had found their way into the very heart of society at the North, and the "*Alabama* Claims" had thus grown beyond the dimensions and importance of an ordinary inquiry affecting only certain commercial interests, or certain abstract principles of public law, and had come to be looked upon in the light of a grievance, more or less sentimental perhaps, but none the less real, and which could not have been removed without such an *amende* as would gratify the pride, and so relieve the minds of the Northern people from the feeling of mortification which had aroused both their jealousy and anger. When, therefore, Sir Edward Thornton informed Earl Granville that the President thought there could be no adjustment of the questions between the two countries, which could establish a sincere, substantial and lasting friendship, unless the differences "growing out of the acts committed by the several vessels which have given rise to the claims generically known as the *'Alabama'* Claims were also settled," her Majesty's Government probably perceived that it would be necessary either to concede the point, or to keep open a cause and source of international irritation, to the existence of which they must have felt that their own indiscretions had largely contributed.

Few, if any, will now say that the determination of the Cabinet then in power to yield was not dictated by prudence and worldly wisdom, but no one who reads the history of those times, and examines the diplomatic correspondence, can doubt that it must have cost the individual members of the Ministry some sacrifice of personal dignity and independence to make declarations and concessions which implied that they had framed their original policy hastily, and had pursued it with unreasoning stubbornness. Since the origin of the *Alabama* grievances no new fact had come to light, and no new principle had been discovered, which could have affected, or which did affect, the view her Majesty's Government took of their international duties; and as they changed their attitude only after their position had been rendered intolerable by reason of persistent remonstrances and long-continued reiterations of complaints, accompanied with many implied threats, it cannot be said that they were spontaneous advocates of a new and beneficent mode of settling international differences, nor can they claim the merit of having voluntarily set the example of substituting arbitration instead of war as the means of composing international jealousies.

The President's refusal to agree to any Commission to treat on other questions unless the "*Alabama* Claims" were also submitted for settlement was notified to Sir E. Thornton on the 30th of January, 1871, and he must have communicated the fact to Lord Granville by telegraph, because on the 1st of February he informed Mr. Fish that he had been "authorized to state that it would give her Majesty's Government great satisfaction if the claims commonly known by the name of '*Alabama* Claims' were submitted to the consideration of the same High Commission," etc.*

Mr. Gladstone's Cabinet, having thus determined to abandon the position they had always heretofore maintained, acted with promptness and without reserve in the subsequent negotiations. The British Commissioners had all left England by the 18th of February, and the following extract from their instructions will show that they were fully authorized to make the apology the United States had from the very beginning determined to exact:†—"For the escape of the *Alabama* and consequent injury to the commerce of the United States, her Majesty's Government authorize you to express their regret in such terms as would be agreeable to the United States and not inconsistent with the position hitherto maintained by her Majesty's Government as to the international obligations of neutral nations." As her Majesty's Government had hitherto maintained that they had been guilty of no default in the practice of their neutrality, that the *Alabama* was a legitimate object of mercantile traffic, and that there was no evidence that anyone connected with her had violated the law, it is difficult to penetrate the cause of their regret at that particular time, or to perceive why they did not express it at an earlier date.

Everybody laments the sufferings and losses produced by war, no matter who are the sufferers, and her Majesty's Government had often declared their hope and desire that the sanguinary struggle might soon cease; but they had always during the continuance of the war, and for years afterwards, refused to make the least concession that would imply an acknowledgment of responsibility for the acts of any Confederate cruiser, and yet they had so weakened their position by indiscreet speeches and admissions, that at last they were forced to express regrets in such a form and in such a connection as naturally to admit their default. To say that they regretted the "escape" of the *Alabama* and the consequent injuries to the commerce of the United States, etc., looks very like an admission that they should have prevented her departure, or punished the implicated parties, and cannot but excite surprise that they did not frankly say so years before.

Notwithstanding the seeming confession of guilt implied in the manner of expressing their regret, her Majesty's Government strenuously

---

* "North America (no. 1), 1871," vol. iv., p. 4.

† For Earl Granville's letter of instructions see Parliamentary Document, "North America (no. 3), 1871," in Appendix to "British Case," vols. iii., iv., pp. 1–4.

maintained in their "Case" before the Tribunal of Arbitration that Great Britain was not responsible for the acts of the *Alabama*, whatever they may have been. The general review of the allegations and arguments of the United States in respect to the *Alabama* and *Florida* occupies pp. 72 to 88 of the British "Counter Case," and the final sentence is in these words following:—"Her Majesty's Government again submit that neither in respect of the *Alabama* nor *Florida* is Great Britain chargeable with any failure of international duty for which reparation is due from her to the United States."

It is very difficult to furnish a commentary upon the conduct of the British Ministry who managed the *Alabama* negotiations, which shall be clear, and at the same time fair, without frequent repetitions or recapitulations of what has been said before. I have tried to refrain from suggesting any inferences, and from indulging in any criticism, except when the actual language of Ministers or extracts from official documents have been quoted, so that each reader might see for himself whether the facts justify the deductions. A man must have profited little from the lessons of life if he has not learned to keep his passions and prejudices in subjection to his judgment, and if he cannot state the conduct of others who may have inflicted injury upon the cause in which he was interested, without tampering with the facts or suggesting unfair inferences.

The Joint High Commissioners met and held their first conference in Washington on the 27th of February, 1871, and after producing their respective full powers, they appointed Lord Tenterden, Secretary to the British Commission, and Mr. Bancroft Davis, Assistant-Secretary of State of the United States, to perform the duties of Joint Protocolists, and agreed upon the subjects for discussion.* Conferences were held from time to time, and protocols were drawn up recording the progress made in the negotiations. At the conference on the 3rd of May, 1871, it was determined to embody in a single protocol a general statement containing an account of the negotiations upon the various subjects contained in the Treaty in the order in which the subjects were to stand in that document.† On the 4th of May the Joint High Commissioners met to consider the statement, in respect to which it is only necessary to say that the "*Alabama* Claims" take precedence of all other subjects.

It appears from the statement that at the beginning of the negotiations the American High Commissioners recapitulated the statements previ-

* "North America (no. 3), 1871," p. 5.
† Ibid., p. 8.

ously made by Mr. Seward and Mr. Fish.* They said that the United States had sustained great wrong and injury to their commerce and material interests "by the course and conduct of Great Britain during the recent rebellion"; that the *Alabama* and other cruisers "which had been fitted out, or armed, or equipped, or which had received augmentation of their force in Great Britain or her colonies," had inflicted heavy direct losses by the capture and destruction of a large number of vessels with their cargoes; that a heavy national expenditure had been incurred in the pursuit of these cruisers, and that there had been great indirect loss to the United States, in the transfer of a large part of the American commercial marine to the British flag. They said that the claims for private property destroyed already amounted to $14,000,000, without interest, and the "amount was liable to be greatly increased by claims which had not been presented," and "that the cost to which the Government had been put in the pursuit of the cruisers could be ascertained by certificates of the accounting officers," etc. Finally, "they hoped that the British Commissioners would place on record an expression of regret by her Majesty's Government for the depredations committed," etc., and proposed that the Joint High Commission "should agree upon a sum which should be paid by Great Britain to the United States, in satisfaction of all the claims and interest thereon."

The British Commissioners were not disposed to reply in detail to the foregoing statements, but were content to repeat the denial of any responsibility on the part of Great Britain for the acts of the Confederate cruisers. They expressed the hope that there would be no necessity for a lengthy controversy, and proposed to submit the whole question, both as to law and fact, to arbitration. The Commissioners of the United States said that "they could not consent to submit the question of liability of her Majesty's Government to arbitration, unless the principles which should govern the arbitrators in the consideration of the facts could be first agreed upon."† The British Commissioners replied "that they should be willing to consider what principles should be adopted for observance in the future; but they were of opinion that the best mode of conducting an arbitration was to submit the facts to the arbitrator, and leave him free to decide upon them after hearing such arguments as might be necessary." The American Commissioners replied "that they were willing to consider what principles should be laid down for observance in similar cases in

---

* For "Statement" see "Parliamentary Documents, North America (no. 3), 1871," p. 8, etc.

† "North America (no. 3), 1871," p. 9.

future, with the understanding that any principles that should be agreed upon should be held to be applicable to the facts in respect to the "*Alabama* Claims*.*" The British Commissioners replied "that they could not admit that there had been any violation of existing principles of international law, and that their instructions did not authorize them to accede to a proposal for laying down rules for the guidance of the arbitrator, but that they would make known to their Government, the views of the American Commissioners on the subject."

The question was at once referred to the home Government, and the British Commissioners were instructed to say "that her Majesty's Government could not assent to the proposed rules as a statement of principles of international law which were in force at the time when the '*Alabama* Claims' arose; but that her Majesty's Government, in order to evince its desire of strengthening the friendly relations between the two countries, etc., agreed that, in deciding the questions between the two countries arising out of those claims, the arbitrators should assume that her Majesty's Government had undertaken to act upon the principles set forth in the rules which the American Commissioners had proposed."

It was manifest that the United States would not be content with a mere diplomatic expression of regret. Their purpose was to make sure of a verdict in their favour, and to secure the award of substantial damages; and it was, therefore, necessary to create a new law, which should be applied to rights and obligations defined and ordained by a pre-existing law. By agreeing to be judged by the new rules, her Majesty's Government virtually consented to a verdict for the United States, and placed Great Britain in a very anomalous position. They denied the prior existence of the rules, and yet consented that they should be the measure of their past obligations. They affirmed to the very last that they had not deviated in any particular from the duties imposed upon them by international law, and had incurred no liability to the United States; and yet they consented to be judged by a set of new rules so broad and indefinite as to render a judgment against them certain.

If we are asked to admit that this was a great and generous concession made in the interests of peace, and in obedience to the kindly and noble precept which commands us to do what is right, though the heavens fall, we are forced to reply that the date and circumstances of the surrender alike oppose that view. So far as the questions at issue were affected either by the specifications of law or the principles of equity, there had been not the slightest change since the day when Earl Russell had emphatically refused to admit any liability whatever, or to make any compensation; and throughout the "Case" presented to the Tribunal of Arbitration on behalf of Great Britain, it is argued with force and persistency, and the highest American authorities are quoted to prove, that her Majesty's Government had violated no international duty. The conclusion is, therefore, irresistible that the members of the British Ministry were conscious of their former vacillation; and perceiving how much they had weakened their own position, and given plausibility to the claims of the United States by their own indiscretions, they thought it prudent to silence further complaints by concessions which would yield to the United States the substantial fruits of victory, while they themselves seemingly maintained the attitude of a vigorous defence.

But her Majesty's Government, having determined to yield, do not appear to have paid much heed to the language in which the rules were expressed, nor did they take the least pains to fix upon them a common interpretation. In the proceedings before the Tribunal of Arbitration, the United States plainly declared that they regarded the rules as no more than a statement of previously established rules of international law. In the British "Counter-Case" it is admitted that certain expressions employed in the rules belong to a class in common use among publicists to define the duties of neutrality, but the construction put upon those expressions by the United States for the purposes of the arbitration is strongly opposed.*

For example, in the British Case it is contended that the phrase "base of naval operations" denotes the use of neutral territory by a belligerent ship as a point of departure, where she may await, and from which she may issue to attack her enemy, whereas the United States contended that Great Britain made her territory a base of naval operations for the Confederate States by the mere fact of having permitted their cruisers to obtain occasional supplies of coal at their ports. The meaning attached to the words "specially adapted to warlike use" and "due diligence" were prominent subjects of controversy in the arguments before the Tribunal, and the general objections of the British representatives to the American interpretation of the rules is thus stated in the British Counter Case:—— "Her Britannic Majesty's Government observes with sincere regret that, as in other particulars, so more especially in this, the Government of the United States, instead of accepting in a fair and reasonable sense rules which the two Powers have engaged to observe towards one another, and to recommend for adoption to other States, seems on this occasion to have

---

* These rules are given at the end of the chapter, p. 588.

considered how they might be turned to the greatest advantage in the present controversy, and with that view to have strained the construction of them to the very utmost. The undue extension which it is proposed to give to the first rule does not accord with its plain and natural meaning, was never contemplated by the Government of her Britannic Majesty, and is altogether rejected by Great Britain."*

The simple fact is that her Majesty's Government gave way to the United States, and agreed to the three rules hastily, and without fully appreciating the extent to which it would afterwards be attempted to apply the principles of the rules in determining the liability of Great Britain. A half hour's discussion at Washington before the fatal Treaty was signed would have saved much argument before the arbitrators, and would probably have saved to Great Britain a large portion, if not the whole, of the £3,000,000 indemnity.

On the 6th of May, 1871, the Joint High Commission met for the last time before the signing of the Treaty.† The business of the Commission was merely to confirm the general protocol of the conference held on the 4th of May, and then followed the customary exchange of friendly congratulations. The British Commissioners said "it had been most gratifying to them to be associated with colleagues who were animated with the same sincere desire as themselves to bring about a settlement equally honourable and just to both countries ... and they would always retain a grateful recollection of the fair and friendly spirit which the American Commissioners had displayed."

Her Majesty's Commissioners had no doubt yielded the concessions they were instructed to make with affability and grace, and in the expectation that all cause for acrimony and recrimination had been removed, and that the case before the arbitrators would be conducted in a friendly spirit, their complimentary farewell was the natural outcome of their inward satisfaction. The United States Commissioners, on the other hand, having virtually obtained in respect to the "*Alabama* question" all that their Government had been vainly contending for during the preceding eight or nine years, were naturally in exuberant good-humour, and were doubtless quite sincere in saying that "they were gratefully sensible of the friendly words expressed by Lord de Grey ... and that they had been impressed by the earnestness of desire manifested by the British Commissioners to reach a settlement worthy of the two Powers who had com-

---

• "British Counter-Case," p. 17.
† "*Alabama* Claims—North America (no. 3), 1871," p. 15.

mitted to this Joint High Commission the treatment of various questions of peculiar interest, complexity, and delicacy."

It has been necessary in previous chapters to comment upon the peculiar harshness of tone and the angry spirit which pervades the "United States Case" in the proceedings before the arbitrators, and anyone who cares to read the above-mentioned document will be surprised to perceive how little the whole procedure resembles the friendly reference of a dispute to the impartial judgment of a disinterested tribunal. A large portion of the reply of her Majesty's Government to the "Statement of Claims" on the part of the United States is in the nature of a defence or a remonstrance against the insinuations, the depreciation of English laws and institutions, and the disparaging comparisons between the conduct of Great Britain and other countries, with which that statement bristles.

The courtly congratulations and gratifying compliments exchanged at Washington in May, 1871, were forgotten—at least, they were not permitted to lessen the vigour or to blunt the sharpness of the attack at Geneva—and the contrast between the suave parting of the Joint High Commissioners, when they had agreed to refer the questions at issue to friendly arbitration, and the ill-disguised irritation on one side, and scarcely suppressed disappointment and mortification on the other, furnish a melancholy example of the utter inadequacy of polite phrases to convey any substantial meaning.

The Treaty for the settlement of the "*Alabama* Claims" and other questions was signed at Washington, May 8th, 1871, and the ratifications were exchanged June 17th, 1871. The preamble of Article I. sets forth very prominently "the regret felt by her Majesty's Government for the escape, under whatever circumstances, of the *Alabama* and other vessels from British ports, and for the depredations committed by those vessels." In Lord Granville's original instructions to the British Commissioners they were authorized to express regret for the escape of the *Alabama* alone, but in the Treaty that regret is made to include "other vessels."

Her Majesty's Government never admitted, except in an indiscreet conversation of one of the Cabinet, that even the *Alabama* had "escaped," until the Joint Commission was about to meet. Up to the very close of the arguments before the Tribunal of Arbitration the British representatives contended that even in respect to the *Florida* "there was no reasonable ground to believe that she was intended to cruise against the United States," and they strongly urged that there was no ground for suspicion in respect to the *Georgia* and *Shenandoah;* indeed, in respect to the last-named vessel they say that it is not even pretended that the United States consular authorities called the attention of her Majesty's Government to her, or that anyone suspected at the time of her departure from London that she would pass into the Confederate naval service. It must, therefore, have been careless on the part of her Majesty's Government to permit the expression of regret in respect to the *Alabama* to be so extended in the very preamble of the Treaty as to include "other vessels"—a very indefinite expression. To admit an escape certainly seemed to imply the acknowledgment of some negligence in permitting the escape. At any rate, the United States made good use of the admission in that sense.

By the conditions of the Treaty, Great Britain and the United States agreed to refer all the claims "generically known as the '*Alabama* Claims,'" to a Tribunal of Arbitration to be composed of five arbitrators, one to be named by each of the contracting Powers, one by his Majesty the King of Italy, one by the President of the Swiss Confederation, and one by his Majesty the Emperor of Brazil. The several Powers named appointed the following arbitrators:—Great Britain, Sir Alexander Cockburn, Baronet; the United States, Charles Francis Adams, Esq.; Italy, his Excellency Count Frederic Sclopis; the Swiss Confederation, M. Jacques Staempfli; Brazil, his Excellency Marcos Antonio d'Araujo, Viscount d'Itajubá. The five arbitrators met at Geneva on the 15th of December, 1871, exchanged their respective powers, and declared the Tribunal of Arbitration to be duly organized.* The High Contracting Parties were represented by agents, to wit, Great Britain by Lord Tenterden, and the United States by John C. Bancroft Davis, Esq., and there were also counsel, whose office it was to argue the cases of their respective Governments.

In the very nature of things it was manifest that the British and American arbitrators would cancel each other's votes on most, if not all, crucial points. It is hardly possible to conceive that Mr. Adams would be induced to abandon the position he had taken throughout his long controversial correspondence with Earl Russell on the subject of the claims, or that he would be converted to the views of their own conduct which her Majesty's Ministers had previously maintained by any fresh exposition of the subject. It was equally unlikely that Sir Alexander Cockburn would be convinced by the arguments of the counsel for the United States that her Majesty's Government, the law officers of the Crown, and the Lord Chief Baron of the Court of Exchequer, had misinterpreted the Foreign Enlist-

---

* "Proceedings of Tribunal of Arbitration at Geneva—North America (no. 2), 1873." After several adjournments the Tribunal met June 15, 1872, and pronounced judgment September 14, 1872.

ment Act, and that the British authorities had neglected to perform their neutral duties in accordance with international law.

The judgment of the Tribunal of Arbitration therefore depended mainly upon the view which the three remaining arbitrators might take, and it must be admitted that those distinguished statesmen were in a somewhat embarrassing position. If the whole subject-matter of the controversy had been submitted to them, both as regards law and fact, and they had been asked to decide in accordance with the principles and rules of international law which were binding upon all nations during the time when the events upon which the claims of the United States were based occurred, their office would have been simple enough. But they found themselves in the position of having to assess the amount of liability Great Britain had incurred under three new rules of very indefinite signification, and which they soon perceived the two contending parties construed very differently. They were, in fact, required not to give judgment upon the rules of international law as commonly received, but to declare a new code, which, according to the interpretation of those who represented the United States, would render the position of neutrals in case of war between two great naval Powers simply intolerable. They perceived, however, that Great Britain had virtually confessed that she owed both reparation and compensation to the United States by admitting that the "*Alabama* and other vessels" had escaped from her jurisdiction, and by expressing regret for the injury they had inflicted; and it must have appeared to them that all previous contentions to the contrary had been abandoned by Great Britain, and that their only course was to judge between the parties according to the conditions agreed upon between them, and to keep the damages down to a reasonable figure.

The United States appeared before the Tribunal with all the advantages of a diplomatic triumph in their favour, and could also point to such a plain confession of default on the part of their opponents, as to make it well-nigh certain that the judgment would in the main be favourable to them. It is therefore greatly to be regretted that their "Case" was not drawn up in the friendly spirit which appears to have possessed the Joint High Commissioners in their deliberations; on the contrary, it seems to have been written on the model of Mr. Seward's most acrimonious despatches, bears evidence of pique and irritation which is strikingly out of harmony with the character of the proceedings, and manifests the purpose throughout to obtain a specific present advantage, and to secure a pecuniary profit, rather than the desire to found an honourable precedent for the settlement of future international disputes, and to establish new rules for the guidance of neutrals which both England and America could recommend to other Powers.

But if the statement of the "United States Case" is open to censure in its general features, the specific claims are set out in a still more objectionable manner. Special failures of duty are alleged against Great Britain, in respect to a number of vessels, and then she is charged indiscriminately with all the losses occasioned by those vessels, and the cost which the United States incurred in their pursuit. In addition to the losses interest is claimed on the amount, which is calculated at seven per cent. per annum, and so little care was taken to verify the accounts, that when the specific items were submitted to inspection, it was discovered that the date from which interest was charged was, in a large proportion of the alleged losses, long antecedent to the dates when they were stated to have occurred.*

The claims made by the United States may be classed under two general heads, viz., "Claims for Private Losses," and "Claims for National Loss and Expenditure." Under the former they included (1) claims for the value of ships freighted with cargo destroyed by Confederate cruisers, for the consequent loss of freight, and the value of the cargoes; (2) claims for vessels in ballast; (3) claims by owners of whaling vessels destroyed, for the value of the vessels themselves, for the oil actually on board, and for the prospective catch of fish—in fact, for speculative earnings; (4) claims by American insurance companies, for insurance on ships, cargoes, freights, and profits, alleged to have been lost by the destruction of the vessels; (5) claims for captains' wages, personal effects taken or destroyed, and personal damages.

The United States appear to have exercised no sort of discrimination or oversight in testing the accuracy of private claims, but presented them just as they were handed in by the persons who alleged that they were interested in the property destroyed. Everyone knows that not much reliance can be put upon the estimate of the interested parties in respect to the value of lost property they are seeking to recover, and a responsible Government should at least test the accuracy of the calculations of claimants before adopting them as the basis of a national claim.

During the Franco-Prussian War of 1870 some British vessels were sunk in the Seine by the German military forces. The owners sent in a claim for £20,270.† The German Government was perfectly willing to pay the actual loss incurred, but thinking the amount asked exorbitant, they

---

* "British Counter-Case," p. 133.

† Ibid., p. 134.

referred the claim to her Majesty's Government for investigation, who directed the Board of Trade to make the necessary scrutiny. After due examination the Registrar of the Court of Admiralty reported that the owners were only entitled to £6,899, which the German Government paid, thus saving about two-thirds of the claim by the very honourable and friendly intervention of the Government whose subjects were the claimants. The British Government in like manner referred the claims of the United States to a Committee appointed by the Board of Trade. A few extracts from the reports of the Committee will demonstrate how little pains the United States took to keep their demands within just limits.*

The Committee report thus:—"We find shipowners putting forward claims for full freights and earnings without any deductions whatsoever, so that they are, in effect, demanding profits at a rate exceeding 200 per cent., and sometimes exceeding 2,000 per cent.... We find the owners of whaling vessels demanding the whole value of their ships and outfits, although they have received more than $700,000 from insurance companies, who at the same time, and in addition, put forward a claim for the same amount. We find the charterer claiming for the loss of the charter party or his profits thereon, whilst the shipowner demands the freight in full; and finally, we find merchants claiming profits on their goods at the rate of 30 and 40 and even 50 per cent. per annum, without making any allowance for freight and for charges at the port of destination." In regard to the claims on behalf of whale-ship owners for prospective earnings, the Committee report:—"The total claim in respect of the whaling and fishing vessels amounts to about $8,500,000, about half of which is demanded for the loss of prospective earnings, without any deductions whatever"; and they very justly add that such claims are perfectly illusory, and "can be proved, as will be shown hereafter, to be equivalent to claiming, over and above the whole capital invested in those speculative adventures, a profit on such capital at a rate exceeding 300 per cent. per annum."

Again, the Committee state that neither the English nor American Courts have ever allowed a claim for loss of wages by the master in cases of collision or capture; but, irrespective of that, they say "it must be observed that the claim of the master for loss of wages when advanced at the same time, as it invariably is in the present case, with a claim by the shipowner for full freight, is not less unjust than the claim by the owner for the amount of his loss when followed immediately by the claim of the insurance company for the very same amount, for it is out of the gross

* The reports are printed in full in the Appendix to "British Case," vol. vii.

freight that the wages would have been paid, and without such payment the gross freight could not have been earned."*

A few items taken from the claims for personal effects, etc., will show what license the United States allowed such claimants. Ebenezer Nye, master of the *Abigail,* of 310 tons, claimed for upwards of $16,000, or about £3,200, for the loss of personal effects on board that vessel; the master of the *Rockingham,* of 976 tons, claimed for loss of personal effects, $8,054, or £1,600; a passenger by the *Winged Racer* claimed $10,000 for loss of office as Consul, and $1,015 for loss of personal effects; the master and mate of the *Crown Point,* of 1,100 tons, each advanced claims for $10,000.

But if the United States were careless in accepting and presenting extortionate and unjust claims on behalf of private individuals, they were none the less heedless of accuracy, and indifferent to criticism, in regard to the claims for national losses. For example, they claimed for the value of the war-steamer *Hatteras,* sunk by the *Alabama,* which afforded her Majesty's Government the opportunity to prove that the engagement took place so near to a powerful United States squadron that she could not have been destroyed except for want of proper support. They claimed for the value of the revenue-cutter *Caleb Cushing,* which claim the British "Counter-Case" argues ought certainly to be disallowed, because that vessel was cut out of the fortified harbour of Portland, in the State of Maine, by boats sent from a small fishing schooner, captured by the *Florida* and commissioned as a tender.†

The claims for expenditure alleged to have been incurred in the pursuit of Confederate cruisers were also submitted to the scrutiny of the practical and painstaking Committee of the Board of Trade, and they found it necessary to point out that the accounts upon which that description of claims were based contained "many obvious errors, many discrepancies which there were no means of reconciling, and a great number of charges which, in the absence of explanations, cannot but be deemed excessive." The United States alleged that the sailing-ship *Sheppard Knapp* was wrecked while in pursuit of Confederate cruisers, and she is entered in the claims. In reference to her, the report of the Committee states as follows:‡—"The whole amount of the *Sheppard Knapp*'s outfit is charged,

---

* The report states that in five cases—the *Alert, Covington, Catherine, General Williams,* and *Gipsey*—the owners give credit for money received from the underwriters, but in all other cases they believe no such credit was given.

† "British Counter-Case," p. 137.

‡ Appendix to "British Case," vol. vii., p. 90.

although in the official account of her loss, in the report of the Secretary of the United States Navy to Congress on the 7th of December, 1863, p. 556, it is stated that "her battery (11 guns) and appointments, ordnance, yeoman's and masters' stores, instruments and charts, provisions and clothing, spars, sails, running and standing rigging, anchors and chains, everything portable and of value to the Government, has been saved. The only loss is the hull and the use of the ship."*

As an example of the excessive charges in the claims for expenditure, the following will suffice:—"For example," the reports says, "the charges under the head of medicine and surgery amount to $28,664.24. The Medical Director-General of her Majesty's Navy states that £2,500 (about $12,000) would probably cover the charge for medicines and medical stores for 7,600 men for 303 days in her Majesty's Navy. And this appears to have been the total of the complements of the United States cruisers."

Further extracts from the Board of Trade reports, and further examples from the United States claims, are unnecessary. Those who are curious on the subject will find ample evidence in the British "Counter Case," and in the "Appendix to the British Case," vol. vii., that the American Government showed little, if any, desire to seek fair and just compensation, and he will be forced to conclude that the purpose was to present as big a bill as possible, in order to allow for a probable large deduction. It is hardly possible to calculate what the claims of the United States would have amounted to if they had been allowed in their entirety. The amount claimed under the head of "Expenditure incurred in pursuit of Confederate vessels" alone was $7,080,478.70;† and who can tell what figures the double claims for ships, cargoes, and insurance would have reached, or what amount would have expressed the prospective catch of the thirty-eight whale-ships destroyed by the *Shenandoah,* and the fourteen by the *Alabama?*

The best evidence that the claims were preposterously excessive is to be found in the fact that the United States have not been able to find claimants to whom they have been willing to pay more than about one half of the moderate amount awarded by the Tribunal in gross eleven or twelve years ago, and there has been more than one discussion in Congress as to how the remainder should be disposed of. A member of the House of Representatives is reported to have said that in his opinion it ought to be handed back to Great Britain.

---

* Quoted from report, "Counter-Case," p. 137.
† Appendix to "British Case," vol. vii., pp. 63, 111.

The Treaty of Washington and the award of the Tribunal are too long to be given in full in this work. It is hoped that so much of the former as pertains to the "*Alabama* Claims" has been sufficiently explained. Both documents are easily accessible to all who care to consult them. The actual decision of the Tribunal in respect to each ship for whose operations the United States claimed damages was as follows:—

The *Alabama.*—"Great Britain has in this case failed, by omission, to fulfil the duties prescribed in the first and the third of the rules established by the Sixth Article of the Treaty of Washington." The *Florida.*—"Great Britain has in this case failed, by omission, to fulfil, etc., in respect to the first, second and third of the rules," etc. The *Shenandoah.*—"Great Britain has not failed by any act or omission to fulfil, etc., during the period of time anterior to her entry into the port of Melbourne, but Great Britain has failed, etc., under the second and third rules aforesaid, in the case of this same vessel, from and after her entry into Hobson's Bay, and is therefore responsible for all acts committed by that vessel after her departure from Melbourne," etc.

In respect to the vessels called the *Retribution, Georgia, Sumter, Nashville, Tallahassee* and *Chickamauga,* the decision was "that Great Britain has not failed by any act or omission," etc., and in respect to the *Sallie,* the *Jefferson Davis,* the *Music,* the *Boston* and the *V. H. Ivy,* respectively, the Tribunal decided unanimously "that they ought to be excluded from consideration for want of evidence." The Tribunal also decided that the vessels captured by the *Alabama* and *Florida,* and which were commissioned as auxiliary vessels, must follow the lot of their principals.*

It will be seen, then, that the United States lodged claims in respect to fourteen vessels (irrespective of the auxiliaries), and that Great Britain was declared to be at fault in respect only to three, and it is, moreover, important to note that in the three cases in which she was judged to have failed in her duties, the failure of default was in each case stated to be, not by reason of any act at variance with the principles of international law as commonly understood, but for omission to fulfil the duties prescribed by two or three of the new rules established by the Treaty—rules which are of course binding upon no other Powers.

Let us for a moment reflect upon the consequences of the foregoing decision, supposing that the rules laid down in the Washington Treaty are adopted as international law. The *Shenandoah,* a merchant screw-steamer,

* For the award respecting money indemnity, etc., see p. 588.

built, however, with arrangements suited for carrying troops, sailed from London, ostensibly on her regular voyage to Bombay, and left London without suspicion and without any intimation to her Majesty's Government that she might ultimately fall into the hands of a belligerent. Many hundred miles from the British coast she was transferred to a Confederate officer, who took possession of her with a staff of officers, and regularly and lawfully commissioned her as a Confederate ship-of-war. She at once proceeded on a cruise, made several captures, and in course of time arrived at the British colonial port of Melbourne, in the Antipodes.

The Tribunal of Arbitration have decided that up to the date of her arrival at Melbourne the *Shenandoah* was a legitimate national cruiser, and that Great Britain was not in any respect liable for her acts, notwithstanding her British origin. But after her departure from that port it was discovered that some fifteen or twenty men had joined and gone to sea in her, in spite of the vigilance of the local police, who had been directed by the Governor to prevent any attempt to increase the crew. The commander of the *Shenandoah* stated officially that the men got on board secretly, and were not discovered until the ship was at sea, and as she was lying in a large bay and was receiving coals and other supplies which required the constant passage of many boats between her and various points on the shore, it is not difficult to perceive that a few men could have got on board and concealed themselves without the possibility of detection by the limited water-police of a colonial port. The Tribunal of Arbitration have, however, declared that from the date at which it was discovered that fifteen or twenty idle and adventurous seamen at Melbourne smuggled themselves on board the *Shenandoah,* the second and third rules of the Treaty were aroused into action, and the British Government became pecuniarily responsible for every act of war committed by her. That is to say, because the police of a distant colonial port have proved to be unsuspecting or inefficient, or have been deceived by a ruse, the mother country is at once saddled with an indefinite responsibility.

Let us now apply the consequences of the foregoing decision prospectively to the United States. Suppose that Great Britain and France should some day have the misfortune to fall out and go to war with each other. After the beginning of hostilities one of the steam-packets employed in the trade between New York and the Brazils sails from that port for Rio de Janeiro, having fulfilled every legal requirement at the port of departure. Instead of going direct to Rio, she proceeds to an uninhabited Cay on the Bahama Banks, where she is handed over to a French naval officer, who brings with him a staff of officers, a few guns, a supply of small arms, with other stores, shipped from New Orleans, and a number of seamen, and commissions her as a French ship-of-war.

The French officer wishes to have a dash at British commerce, and he runs to the northward, along the American coast, burning and scuttling a few Liverpool or Bristol ships, until he finds himself short of fuel and other supplies. He is now off the New England coast, and, shunning the large seaports for prudential reasons, he slips into some quiet nook, say Provincetown, at the back of Cape Cod, or one of the small harbours in the Martha's Vineyard Sound. There he begins to take in such supplies as can be got. The British Consul, if there is one, notifies the local authorities that the Frenchman is no better than a "pirate," and that if they don't mind he will infringe the neutrality of the port. The mayor, or the United States marshal, or both, are quite willing to do what is right in the matter, and strict orders are given that no American citizen must enlist on the strange craft, and the local constables are strictly enjoined to keep their eyes open.

The crew of the Frenchman meanwhile mix with the groups of seafaring men whom they meet along the shore, and tell them that their ship is a fine vessel, that there are twenty or thirty Americans on board who are well satisfied with the fare, the treatment, and the chances of prize-money. The cod-fishing season has been dull, and the men have no employment. A few of them think it would be a fine thing to have a cruise in the natty craft they have been admiring, and which, in spite of her tri-colour flag, looks every inch a New York ship; so they slip on board while the marshal and mayor are asleep, and the constables are looking after other matters, and are concealed by their confederates. The next day the French commander, ignorant of the addition to his crew, pays his bills, bids a suave "good-bye" to the friends he has made on shore, and steams away in search of more British ships.

Her Majesty's Consul has all this time been fretful, suspicious, and inquisitive. Before the Frenchman has been gone twenty-four hours he discovers, no matter how, that a number of men whom he used to see lounging about the foreshore, or smoking their pipes on the jetties, have disappeared, and some man who was disappointed in getting on board supplies him with evidence that the absentees have gone off in the Frenchman. The fact is duly reported to her Majesty's Minister at Washington, and is notified to the home Government, and then formally to that of the United States. The French cruiser is fortunate: she picks up a good many prizes, costly steamers, rich with the freights of India, the gold of Australia, and the corn of Chili and California. By-and-by there is peace: France and England shake hands across the Channel. Her Majesty's Government compile a list of the captures of British ships by the "American piratical cruiser," refer the list to the Board of Trade to assess the loss, and the bill, say for £2,000,000 or £3,000,000, is forwarded to Washington with the following "N.B." at foot:—"In accordance with the duties prescribed by the rules established in the Sixth Article of the Treaty of Washington."

Such would be the legitimate, the logical, the unavoidable consequences of enforcing the three rules of the Treaty of Washington as they were construed by the United States and confirmed by the decision of the Tribunal of Arbitration.

One of the most striking examples of the effort made by the United States to extend the meaning and to strengthen the application of the rules of the Treaty is furnished by their claim in respect to the *Sumter.* That vessel, it will be remembered, ran out of the Mississippi and began her cruise in June, 1861. During her very successful foray through the West Indies, she touched at various ports, and was permitted to receive coal as follows:—"Cienfugos, 100 tons; Curaçoa, 120 tons; British island of Trinidad, 80 tons; Paramaribo, 125 tons; Maranham, 100 tons. From Maranham she proceeded to the French island of Martinique, where she took on board, by the written permission of the Governor, a sufficient supply to carry her across the Atlantic to Cadiz."*

Of the prizes captured by the *Sumter* during the above West India cruise, eleven were taken before she put in at Trinidad, *none from the date of leaving Trinidad to that of her arrival at Paramaribo,* two between Paramaribo and Maranham, and three after leaving Martinique.†

It will be seen that the *Sumter* not only received a less quantity of coal at Trinidad than at either of the Spanish, Dutch, Brazilian, and French ports mentioned above, but she did not take a single prize while consuming the eighty tons she was permitted to receive there; yet the United States asked the arbitrators to declare that Great Britain had "failed to fulfil the duties set forth in the three rules in Article VI. of the Treaty of Washington," etc.; and in considering the amount to be awarded to the United States, they asked that "the losses of individuals in the destruction of their vessels and cargoes by the *Sumter,* and also the expenses to which

---

* See "British Counter-Case," pp. 67, 68, and Semmes's "Adventures Afloat."
† See list in Appendix to "United States Case," vol. iv., p. 473.

the United States were put in the pursuit of that vessel, may be taken into account."*

The *Sumter* went from Cadiz to Gibraltar, where she was laid up and finally sold, and she never entered any other British port as a Confederate cruiser. What the United States asked the arbitrators to do was simply to declare that if a belligerent ship-of-war is permitted to purchase 80 tons of coal in a neutral port, the neutral nation becomes chargeable with all the damage she may subsequently inflict upon the other belligerent.

Throughout the case of the United States, the contention appears to be that whenever a Confederate cruiser was permitted to buy in a British port what is called "an excessive supply of coal," Great Britain was thereby permitting her territory to be used as a "base of naval operations," and made herself liable under the rules of the Treaty to make good the injury inflicted upon the United States by that cruiser thereafter. International law permits a neutral to sell to a belligerent vessel whatever she may require to renew her sailing or steaming power, but not arms or munitions of war, or anything else that will add to her purely warlike force. In the British "Counter-Case," it is contended that the consent of nations has drawn that line and no other, and that there is no such thing known to international law as "an excessive supply of coal." In the British "Counter-Case" it was shown that if the Confederate ships were permitted to buy coal in British ports, the Federal cruisers got very much more, and therefore the United States had no just cause of complaint. To which the United States rejoined that it was Great Britain, and not themselves, who were on trial.

When it is considered that the two great maritime Powers were engaged in a friendly arbitration, which it was hoped would settle principles tending to lessen the unnecessary burdens of war, such quibbling as the foregoing is as lamentable as it is unworthy. To put the case briefly, and from the point contended for by the United States, if Great Britain is ever again engaged in war, and a British man-of-war should go into some port in Alaska, or should touch at one of the Florida Cays, and buy eighty tons of coal, the United States would be responsible for every dollar's worth of damage she might inflict upon her enemy's commerce afterwards, because it must be borne in mind that the *Sumter* was originally fitted out at a Confederate port, and never entered a British port until after she had been fully recognised as a national ship-of-war.

---

* "United States Case," p. 89.

Does any sane man suppose that any nation, even including the two who were parties to the Treaty, will ever adopt the rules of the Treaty of Washington as the common law of neutral duties? The United States would be the very first to discard them.

There is no reason to doubt that the Executive Government of the United States has always been willing to comply with its neutral duties, but the number of vessels armed, equipped, even officered and manned in American ports for belligerents, to wit, for the French Republic of 1792 and the South American States, and the histories of the Lopez expedition against Cuba, the various filibustering expeditions of Walker, the operations of the Cuban Junta, and the Fenian raids, all combine to prove how powerless the United States are to prevent infringements of their neutrality.

The United States have enormous coast-lines on the two great oceans. They have no navy to speak of, an army in its grand total not equal to a single European corps d'armée, no national police at all, and a population especially averse to State interference in matters of local trade, and particularly inclined to encourage adventurous enterprises. There are places—they may be counted by hundreds—along the coast of the United States where a belligerent cruiser could enter and replenish her contraband stores and increase her crew without the least danger of interference, and yet the United States have proposed, and have obtained the sanction of a Court of Arbitration to, an extension of the principles of international law, involving responsibilities and liabilities which would make the position of a neutral but little less onerous than that of a belligerent. And what have the Unites States gained in return? A transient diplomatic triumph and a paltry $15,500,000, an amount which cannot cover the regret every American must feel who reads the exorbitant and ill-considered claims that were presented to the arbitrators, and who learns from the British "Counter-Case" how largely and for what reasons those claims were reduced in amount.

If the principles contended for by the United States were to be generally adopted, neutrals would be obliged to prohibit all traffic with belligerents, and to exclude all belligerent vessels from their ports. Powers like Great Britain, France, and the German Empire have possibly the police organization and the military and naval force necessary to guard all points and to enforce their prohibitions, but the United States and many other Powers are manifestly unequal to such a task, and they could not isolate their whole population from contact with maritime belligerents by any legislative or administrative restrictions.

The extension of belligerent rights which the United States claimed and practised during the Civil War in respect to the search of neutral vessels on the high seas and of blockade, would be favourable to Great Britain with her numerous and powerful marine, and the broad interpretation of neutral duties prescribed in the rules of the Treaty of Washington would work to her advantage if she should be again drawn into a great war. But the United States as a neutral would be simply ruined by the application of those rules to them as a neutral Power. American ships could not approach the hemisphere in which either belligerent was situated without the certainty of search and capture, and they would incur incalculable damages for violations of their neutrality, which they could only prevent by openly espousing the cause of one of the belligerents, which, under all the circumstances, would probably be the safest and the cheapest course.

The "*Alabama* Claims" afforded a favourable opportunity for establishing a new and philanthropic method of settling international disputes, and they might have been the means of defining the relative rights and duties of belligerents and neutrals, so as to have greatly simplified the very complex and elastic code commonly called international law, and to have relieved some of the doubts and embarrassments of neutrals. But neither Power approached the subject in the right spirit. Great Britain yielded reluctantly, after years of opposition; the United States pressed their claims angrily, and demanded exorbitant and impossible concessions. At last, when the two Powers agreed to refer their differences to arbitration, they went before the Tribunal without any common understanding of the rules they had bound themselves to be judged by, and they wrangled over their meaning during the whole hearing of the cases, Great Britain protesting to the last that the United States sought to give them an interpretation not contemplated by her Britannic Majesty's Government at the ratification of the Treaty.

The "Geneva Arbitration" must therefore be recorded in history as a great international fiasco. It is thought by some to have saved the cost and peril of a war between Great Britain and the United States. This is important, if true, and no one is now disposed to be critical on that point, or desires to begrudge it the credit of having done that much in the cause of peace; but it was not the means of founding any new law, or clearly defining any old one. It laid down no general principle whatever, and the rights of belligerents and the duties of neutrals remain in the fog which has enveloped them ever since strong maritime Powers first began to enforce the one and exact the other—for that is the process by which "international law" became the "code of nations."

No one who has had occasion to consult the standard authorities in respect to the rights and duties of belligerents and neutrals, or to search for precedents, is likely to attempt a dogmatic exposition of the law. It has, however, been commonly agreed heretofore that there can be no such thing as contraband goods on board of a neutral ship, when she is bound from one neutral port to another. The United States, previous to the Civil War, always contended for that doctrine, but during that great struggle their anxiety to isolate the South caused them to lose sight of every consideration but that of a present advantage. They stopped on the high seas, boarded, searched, and captured, neutral ships while sailing between neutral ports hundreds of miles from the blockaded coast, and have thus established precedents which will give them much trouble whenever they may occupy the position of a neutral during a war between two strong maritime Powers.

THE RULES PRESCRIBED IN ARTICLE VI. OF THE TREATY.

NOTE FOR PAGE 572.

"A neutral Government is bound—

"First,—To use due diligence to prevent the fitting out, arming, or equipping, within its jurisdiction, of any vessel which it has reasonable ground to believe is intended to cruise or to carry on war against a Power with which it is at peace; and also to use like diligence to prevent the departure from its jurisdiction of any vessel intended to cruise or carry on war as above, such vessel being specially adapted, in whole or in part, within such jurisdiction, to warlike use.

"Secondly,—Not to permit or suffer either belligerent to make use of its ports or waters as the base of naval operations against the other, or for the purpose of the renewal or augmentation of military supplies or arms, or the recruitment of men.

"Thirdly,—To exercise due diligence in its own ports and waters, and, as to all persons within its jurisdiction, to prevent any violation of the foregoing obligations and duties."

NOTE FOR PAGE 581.

The award, in respect to money indemnity, etc., was rendered in the following words:—

"The Tribunal, making use of the authority conferred upon it by Article VII. of the said Treaty, by a majority of four voices to one, awards to the United States a sum of 15,500,000 dollars in gold as the indemnity to be paid by Great Britain to the United States for the satisfaction of all the claims referred to the consideration of the Tribunal, conformably to the provisions contained in Article VII. of the aforesaid Treaty."

CHAPTER XIII

Position of the Confederate Agents at the end of the War.—Financial difficulties.—The United States and the property of the Confederate Government.—Proceedings against Messrs. Fraser, Trenholm and Co. by the United States Government.—Presidents Lincoln and Johnson.—The "reconstruction" of the Southern States.—Political condition of the United States at the present day.

———

Although the shifts to which the fiscal agents of the Confederate Government were driven in their efforts to supply the ever-increasing wants of the country, and the condition of the Confederate finances in Europe at the close of the Civil War, are not perhaps subjects of much historical importance, yet a narrative whose purpose it is to reveal the means by which aggressive operations against the Federal Government were organized abroad, would scarcely be complete without some explanation of the peculiar and perplexing position in which the representatives of the Confederate States in Europe were placed by the sudden and complete overthrow of the authority under which they had been acting.

While Mr. Davis and his Cabinet could maintain their position in Richmond, they fulfilled all the practical requirements of a *de facto* Government, and were recognised as such by foreign Powers. Even the United States were compelled to exhibit a marked distinction between their practice and their theory, and were driven by force of circumstances to treat in Virginia with men on terms of entire equality, who in Washington they denounced as "traitors" and "rebels."

In ordinary international wars the defeat of the vanquished may be so crushing as to wholly disorganize the political institutions of the States, or even to effect an entire change in them, as was the case with France at the close of the Franco-German war. But in all modern contests between different countries there has remained at the close of the struggle a vested sovereignty in the people of the defeated States, which the conquerors themselves have acknowledged, and they have been permitted to decide upon the authority who should act for them in pledging the national faith, and thus arranging the conditions of peace. But when General Lee was forced to abandon his lines around Richmond, the Executive Government of the Confederacy was compelled to retire with him or to quickly follow, and when the armies under Lee and Johnston surrendered, and the officers and men dispersed to their homes under parole, there was no longer a common central authority to whom the several States could refer. Indeed, after Mr. Davis and his Cabinet were driven from Richmond they never found a resting-place in which they could remain long enough to examine the condition of affairs and to reorganize further resistance. President Davis was soon captured; the Vice-President, Mr. Stephens, and the Secretary of the Navy, Mr. Mallory, were shortly afterwards arrested; Mr. Benjamin, who was the Secretary of State, and General Breckenridge, the War Secretary, happily escaped and got out of the country; and thus it will be perceived that the civil organization of the Confederate States was destroyed simultaneously with the military power which gave it vitality.

The politicians in Mr. Lincoln's Cabinet, and the Republican senators who had professed extreme views on the question of secession, had now the opportunity to enforce their favourite theory—a theory so often and so vehemently enunciated by Mr. Seward in the declarations that "the integrity of the Republic is unbroken," the so-called Civil War "is only an insurrection," the Southern people "are rebels," and the Government at Richmond "represents merely a domestic faction."

The Southern States were without a common rallying point, and were thus deprived of the strength which results from union, even if they had not been too thoroughly exhausted to make any further resistance. The people in the conquered States had no other resource than to submit, and the victors, with an external manifestation of clemency, imposed conditions in the way of test oaths, political disabilities, alien governors, universal negro suffrage, and executive interference with elections, which have left a permanent stain upon the political institutions and the political integrity of the whole country.

By the conditions under which the military leaders of the South had surrendered, the whole population actually in arms against the United States were protected against any civil prosecution, and it would have been so manifest a violation of those conditions to proceed against any of them by indictment for "treason," that the extreme men in the North were forced to abandon that purpose. Reasonable men also perceived that it would not be either rational or just to prosecute mere civilians for alleged offences which had already been condoned in respect to the military forces of the Confederacy. It is well known that several prominent leaders of the Republican party were desirous to act with extreme rigour, and were disposed to treat the vanquished Southerners with all the penalties commonly inflicted upon traitors and rebels, but their hot tempers and harsh counsels were not suffered to prevail, and they were forced to exhaust their malice in vituperative speeches, which I refrain from quoting, having no wish to revive animosity on the one side, or to provoke a blush on the other.

The civil as well as the military and naval representatives of the Confederate States abroad were excluded from "pardon," under the so-called Amnesty Proclamations, which were issued immediately after the war, and none of them could have returned to the United States without the certainty of arrest, imprisonment, or, under the most favourable circumstances, the alternative of taking what has not been inaptly called the "iron-clad oath." The course to be followed by officers, whether of the civil or military service of the Confederate States, at home, was plain. As sensible men, they could only submit to the requirements of the situation, and look for consolation to the future, with its cheering promises of recuperative energy, wealth, and freedom. The representatives of the Confederate Government abroad were in a different position. Their duties had compelled them to enter into large business transactions with persons in many branches of trade, who had always acted with scrupulous fidelity in the fulfilment of their engagements, and who had undertaken large contracts for forward delivery upon the personal guarantee of those whom they knew were authorized to pledge the credit of the Government.

I suppose it is hardly necessary to demonstrate that contracts made by the representatives of the Confederate Government were valid in law, and that there was the same reciprocal obligation to fulfil them as existed between the agents of the United States and the tradespeople with whom they had contracted business engagements. It is sufficient to state that when the sudden collapse of the Civil Government at Richmond was known in Europe, the very best legal advice was sought, and the opinion of eminent counsel was that the acts of all Confederate agents duly appointed by the proper authority at Richmond, and which had been done within the limits of their prescribed power, would be recognised and confirmed by the English Courts; and that no Confederate agent, and no person who had dealt with him, could be held to a responsibility greater either in kind or degree towards the United States than that which the Confederate States could have exacted. The foregoing opinion appeared to be in accordance with common-sense and common notions of equity, and it was afterwards confirmed by the judgments of the Courts, when the United States attempted to seize property alleged to have been acquired by the Confederate Government, without acknowledging and paying the claims or liens of those who were in possession.

There were two fiscal agencies of the Confederate States in Europe during the Civil War. The commercial house of Fraser, Trenholm and Co. were the bankers, or, as they were officially called, the "Depositories," of the Treasury. At a very early period of the war, one or two sums of money were remitted to special purchasing agents for specific purposes, and were at once expended for these purposes; but as soon as Messrs. Fraser, Trenholm and Co. received their official appointment, all remittances, whether in cash sterling or produce, were made to them, and they were instructed to place the funds to the credit of the several Departments, and to pay the drafts of the purchasing agents in Europe, as well as bills drawn by the heads of departments in Richmond, or their representatives elsewhere. Messrs. Fraser, Trenholm and Co. opened a special set of books for the record of their financial transactions with the Confederate States, and those books contained a complete register of all the funds the Treasury Department was able to place in Europe by export from home.

During the year 1862, General Colin J. McRae was sent to Europe as a special agent of the Treasury, his functions being to regulate the disbursement of the so-called "Erlanger Loan," and to negotiate the sale of Treasury Bonds. The heads of the several departments sent drafts upon him to meet the wants of their purchasing agents, which he had to honour from the above-mentioned sources, and his office was also to do all that was possible to keep the bankers in funds.

After the fall of Fort Fisher, about the middle of January, 1865, intercourse with the Confederate States was cut off through the sea-ports. There were, it is true, one or two shoal bays on the coast of Texas into which supplies might still have been sent, but then there was but little chance of the Trans-Mississippi States holding out if the military power of the Confederacy elsewhere was once destroyed; and as the strategic points on the banks of the Mississippi were in possession of the United States, and numerous gunboats patrolled its waters from the mouth of the Ohio to New Orleans, no quantity of supplies sufficient to justify the cost and risk of transport could have been got across, even if they could have been safely landed on the Texan shore. The financial agents of the Confederate States saw that remittances must cease after the capture of Fort Fisher, which closed the last port from which shipments could be made, and they warned those who were charged with the duties of purchasing and forwarding to contract their operations, and to prepare for a final settlement.

Before the end of 1864 the net proceeds of the "Erlanger Loan" had been exhausted, and the supply of funds from the sale of bonds, never very large, had wholly ceased after the fall of Fort Fisher, partly because they could not probably have been sold except at a nominal price, but chiefly because the fiscal agent, foreseeing that the end was close at hand, felt restrained from offering them. General McRae was therefore reduced to great financial straits, and was only able to meet the most pressing and urgent wants by means of the funds accruing from the forced sale of several ships, and the transfer of those funds to the Treasury Department, which, under the circumstances, was an absolute necessity.

Messrs. Fraser, Trenholm and Co., the bankers of the Government, were in no better plight at the close of the war than the special fiscal agent of the Treasury. They had throughout the war used their own commercial credit without stint to sustain the Government, and were nearly always under advances, at least to the War Department. During the last three or four months of the struggle, the Richmond authorities sent several agents to the Bahamas, Cuba, and Texas, with urgent instructions to hurry in supplies, and drafts from those agents came upon the bankers at Liverpool at the last moment, in many cases without advice, and when they were well-nigh overwhelmed by the requirements of the local agents.

At the time when hostilities actually ceased and the authority of the United States over the whole country was resumed, the Confederate finances in Europe were in a condition of actual depletion. The only Department which had a balance in the hands of the bankers was that of the navy; but that balance was not sufficient to make good the deficits in other accounts. Messrs. Fraser, Trenholm and Co., acting with their accustomed liberality and public spirit, informed me that they would pay any liabilities of the Navy Department for which I had given a personal pledge, but they thought that I should make the best practicable arrangements with contractors, so as to leave as much as possible for transfer to the general account. The justice as well as the liberality of this proposition was so apparent that I cheerfully accepted it, and the final statement of account exhibited a considerable amount still to the credit of the Navy Department, which helped to reduce the general balance against the defunct Government.

In those painful settlements I happily experienced the advantage as well as the satisfaction which results from dealing exclusively with persons of the first respectability, because I had no difficulty in effecting arrangements with those who were still under contract with the Navy Department through me which they were good enough to say were satisfactory. In several important cases it was not possible to pay in full, but such settlements were made as, by leaving the property in possession of the contractors, apparently secured them from ultimate loss, although they might have difficulty and delay in realizing, as the goods, from their nature, would be difficult of sale in ordinary times of peace.

The arrangements for the War Department were not so satisfactory, because the operations had not only been on a larger scale, but it had also been necessary to employ a great many agents, who were stationed at distant points, and could not therefore keep the bankers and the general fiscal agent of the Treasury regularly and accurately informed of their prospective wants.

It is generally known that the United States took possession of all the property of the Confederate Government which could be identified, and which was within the Southern States at the close of the war. The authorities at Washington did not permit any perplexing questions of private claims, by reason of loans to the Confederate Government or other liens based upon dealings with a Confederate agent, to deter them from seizing and appropriating cotton or military stores, or any other property in which it was possible to trace a Confederate title.

Mr. Seward was not content to base the claims of the United States upon the plea that they had succeeded by right of conquest to the title of the Confederate Government, but he took the position that Mr. Davis and his Cabinet having been "merely the representatives of a domestic faction," never did have the status of a *de facto* Government, and therefore all transactions with them were illegal, null and void. In the Southern States, and in regard to the claims of persons to property within the conquered territory, and therefore within the power of the Federal Government, it was possible to enforce the foregoing pretensions, but Mr. Seward soon attempted to apply the same principle in Europe. The Consuls appear to have been instructed to bring suits against the fiscal agents of the Confederate Government and to attach all property which they had reason to believe belonged to that Government. A direct straightforward courteous inquiry from the United States Minister, or from any other representative whom Mr. Seward had chosen to appoint for the purpose, formally and officially addressed to either of the fiscal agents, or to either of the chief practical agents of the Confederate Government, would have been met by a prompt and equally straightforward reply, and all questions of right and title to property could have been satisfactorily settled without unnecessary loss to individuals, and without sacrifice of dignity on the part of the United States.

Within about three months after the surrender of General Lee, a case involving the title to some alleged Confederate property was brought before the late Vice-Chancellor Sir W. Page Wood (afterwards Lord Hatherley). That learned and most conscientious judge laid down the rule, that "whenever a Government *de facto* has obtained possession of property, as a Government, and for the purposes of the Government *de facto,* the Government which displaces it succeeds to all the rights of the former Government and to the property they have so acquired." The Vice-Chancellor then proceeded to say, in effect, that the Confederate States had been a *de facto* Government, that British subjects had the right to deal with that Government while it existed, and that the United States could have no greater or more exclusive interest in the property than the Government which they had displaced originally possessed, and he gave judgment accordingly.

The foregoing principle being thus authoritatively enunciated and settled, I will undertake to say that all of the official representatives of the late Confederate Government in Europe would have accepted it, and would have loyally assisted any reputable and duly authorized agent of the United States in winding up affairs so as to secure to that Government their just rights. But it did not suit Mr. Seward's purpose to proceed in accordance with Vice-Chancellor Wood's interpretation of the law. He manifestly wished not only to get possession of the Confederate property, but to punish those who had dealt with the "insurgents." Persons whom no one knew anything about were sent to England to spy out the land, and to discover if there was any Confederate property within reach. Arrangements were made with those persons that they were to receive a portion of the property which might be recovered through their efforts.* The

* See "Executive Document, No. 304, House of Representatives, 40th Congress, 2nd Session."

persons referred to were soon in consultation with the Liverpool Consul, and it was generally known that they were travelling about the country and making inquisitorial inquiries into the alleged transactions of various tradespeople with the late Confederate agents.

It will, I think, be admitted that these were not dignified proceedings, and it is at least doubtful whether any respectable Government ever before attempted to settle important matters by such means. Mr. Seward could hardly have supposed that any Confederate agent who had due regard for his own personal honour, or who retained any loyal feeling of obligation to those who had come into business relations with him, would either approach or permit himself to be approached by those "commission agents." I wish to cast no reflection upon them personally, but their office was one that would not have tempted a representative of the Confederate Government to join in their explorations.

It is worthy of mention that the plan of getting possession of Confederate property through such means did not result in much pecuniary profit. By a return published in the Congressional Document referred to above, it appears that the gross proceeds of the property thus obtained in England during the years 1866–67 amounted to $144,157.15—the greater portion of which accrued from the sale of the *Shenandoah,* which realized $108,632.18—against which are charged disbursements to the amount of $90,308.76. Some of the items in the disbursements are interesting as well as curious. One person received in fees as counsel $10,000, another styled "special counsel" is credited with $17,339 and a third, mentioned as "special agent," got $11,963. One of the items is sufficiently important to be quoted in full. It runs thus:—"1867, August 5th, paid Barings, for advances, £6,600 (including 150,000 francs deposited by the United States as security for costs in suit against Arman, in France)=$45,265.04."

The suit against M. Arman has been mentioned in a previous chapter. He would have been glad to effect a compromise with the United States to avoid the trouble and expense of a law-suit, but the representatives of that Government were instructed to proceed against him upon the principle that the Confederate States had no legal right to the money paid to him, and therefore could give him no title, and they appear to have sought to recover the whole amount it was supposed that he had received on account of the Confederate ships. The French Court gave judgement in favour of M. Arman, and the United States were subjected to the additional mortification of having to get an advance of 150,000 francs from Messrs. Baring to deposit as security for M. Arman's costs, a requirement very unusual, if not unprecedented, in respect to a Sovereign State.

Very shortly after the close of the war, the United States Consuls in England began, in compliance with their instructions, to harass persons supposed to have Confederate property in possession by attachments, etc.; and they instituted a suit against General McRae, the general fiscal agent of the Treasury, the object being to draw from him a statement of account and payment of any balance in hand. The position assumed by the United States in the above process, and the answer of General McRae, were such that the Court dismissed the suit, and no further proceedings were taken against him. A corresponding suit was instituted against Messrs. Fraser, Trenholm and Co., and was continued for several years.

While these various proceedings were in progress, an arrangement was come to between Mr. F. H. Morse, the United States Consul in London, and Messrs. Fraser, Trenholm and Co., which it was hoped would result in a full exposition of the financial condition of the Confederate States at the close of the war, and would also enable the United States to obtain possession of the proceeds of all property of the Confederacy in excess of the legitimate liens against said property. By the terms of that agreement, Messrs. Fraser, Trenholm and Co. were to submit the whole of their books and accounts with the Confederate Government to official inspection, and they were to give a statement of all property of that Government which was then in their possession, or which might at any time thereafter come into their hands. The property was to be sold to the best advantage, the United States giving full titles; and the proceeds were to be appropriated, first in payment of the claim of Messrs. Fraser, Trenholm and Co. for over-advances to the Confederate States, which it was agreed should be fixed at £150,000, although they alleged it to be much more; and all in excess of that amount was to be paid over to the United States. Mr. Morse produced official letters from Mr. Seward and from the Secretary of the United States Treasury, which the solicitors of Messrs. Fraser, Trenholm and Co. thought contained full authority to him to make the arrangement; and there can be no doubt that if it had been carried out, there would have been a fair, open, and perfectly trustworthy settlement of affairs, and the United States would not only have obtained an account of the Confederate property remaining abroad at the close of the war, but they would have received the net proceeds without vexing so many persons with costly legal proceedings, and placing themselves often in undignified positions before the Courts of England and France.

As a part of the agreement with Mr. Morse, Messrs. Fraser, Trenholm and Co. undertook to lay the proposed arrangement before the practical agents of the several Departments of the Confederate Government, and to represent to them the propriety of assisting in bringing about a satisfactory settlement. When the scheme was mentioned to me, I consented to render every possible assistance; and I believe all the principal agents of the Confederate Government would have acted in the same spirit. No one had any other wish or purpose than to protect those who had fair and legitimate liens upon the property; and if the United States had been willing to acknowledge those liens, a large quantity of goods and materials could have been collected, which, if openly sold without doubt as to title, would have realized, together with the proceeds of the steamers built or building under the McRae contract, a sum sufficient to have left a much larger balance to go into the United States Treasury than found its way there through the means actually adopted.

Before the arrangements between Mr. Morse and Messrs. Fraser, Trenholm and Co. could be got into working condition, Mr. Seward telegraphed Mr. Adams, the United States Minister in London, "to disavow and reject" it *in toto.* It appears from a lengthy document issued for the information of the House of Representatives in Washington,[*] that there was some jealousy between certain Consuls and other agents of the United States abroad, and such representations were made to Mr. Seward in respect to Mr. Morse's arrangement that he determined to annul it, and as I do not wish to take any part in a family quarrel, I refrain from any comments, further than to say that Messrs. Fraser, Trenholm and Co. could not possibly have concealed any of their dealings with the Confederate Government, even if they desired to do so, because the United States had already obtained an order from the Court of Chancery for an examination of their books by an official accountant, and a close and thorough inspection was made of all their transactions and accounts with the Confederacy during the entire period of the war, under the supervision and direction of the Solicitors of the United States; and thus Mr. Seward knew, or could have known, every penny of public funds that came into their hands as the bankers of the Confederate Government, and could have known to whose order, or on whose behalf, it had been paid out. The United States Government must, then, have been perfectly well aware that the finances of the Confederate Government abroad were exhausted at the close of the war, and their further proceedings against the bankers of the defunct Confederacy can hardly be attributed to any other motive than one of revenge.

---

[*] See "Executive Document, No. 63, House of Representatives, 39th Congress, 2nd Session."

After repudiating the Morse arrangement Mr. Seward directed the Liverpool Consul to prosecute the suits against Messrs. Fraser, Trenholm and Co.; and that unhappy firm was pursued with relentless zeal, and was so persistently involved by their persecutors in Chancery and other proceedings, that it was hardly possible for the partners to give due attention to their private business, and finally their financial credit was affected, and they were reduced to commercial ruin.

I feel that I can speak impartially of those matters, because no United States official ever gave me the least personal trouble or annoyance after the war, and except for my voluntary offer to assist in bringing the "Morse arrangement" to an equitable settlement, I should never have come in contact with any one of them at that time. In consequence of my consent to assist in the above settlement, Mr. Consul Morse called on me in London, and said that his only wish was to effect an equitable arrangement which would secure the rights of his Government without detriment to just private claims, and without the irritation and expense necessarily caused by litigation; and there can be no reason to doubt that Mr. Morse was both sincere and disinterested in his efforts, because by the arrangement with Messrs. Fraser, Trenholm and Co. he was sacrificing the importance as well as the profits which would have been attached to his office as a prosecuting agent of those national claims.

The foreign policy of the United States during the war was conducted in a spirit which brought some discredit upon American institutions, and the country was not placed in a worthy position before foreign courts of law by their representatives after the war. These convictions have been forced upon me by the necessary perusal of a large portion of the diplomatic correspondence and the reports of the legal proceedings which the United States initiated in England and France.

In composing the difficulties at home, after the cessation of hostilities, the ruling powers seemed equally regardless of ultimate consequences, or the effect of their action upon the national character. The evil consequences of the war are mainly due to the ill-advised measures of reconstruction adopted by the politicians at Washington, because the Southern people, properly so called, had no voice in the matter at all. The union between the several States of the South was not complete, and the various Administrative Departments of the new Confederacy were not yet fully organized, when hostilities began, and such preparations for the great struggle as it was possible to make were effected under the pressure of daily increasing demands, with which it was never possible to keep pace. Hence the Confederate Government was ever enduring an extreme tension, and the fortitude, patience, and endurance of the Southern people were put to a test from which there was no relief, but, on the contrary, a ceaseless and ever increasing strain. Weeks, often months, were required to collect materials for a single battle; and whether the issue of each succeeding struggle was victory or defeat, the exhaustion of supplies was equally thorough. Thus it was nearly always impossible for the Confederate armies to follow up a victory; and when they met with a serious check or repulse, the disaster was only short of being a crushing and perhaps irretrievable catastrophe from want of energy in the victor, or his ignorance of the actual destitution of the vanquished. The poverty of the South in respect to military resources, the great extent of the country (poorly provided with roads), the scattered population, and the difficulty of transport—all combined, not only to make the labour of collecting and maintaining troops in the field very arduous, but appeared from the beginning to render final success well-nigh hopeless in the minds of those whose judgment was superior to their enthusiasm.

All who have studied the facts impartially will probably admit that the successful resistance of the South for four years was a surprising effort, never excelled, if it has been equalled, in any great historic struggle of which we have a trustworthy record.

Experiments have demonstrated that rigid objects subjected to a breaking strain generally give way at last with a repulsive energy commensurate with the tenacity of their resistance, and either fly into fragments, or leap asunder with a vicious sweep that makes the near neighbourhood dangerous. At any rate, the final rupture is always complete, thorough, and irremediable. It was so when General Lee's grasp upon the defences of Richmond was torn adrift. The wrench vibrated to the very heart of the Confederacy, and the whole fabric fell at once into chaos.

The most lamentable event which could have happened for the South, and indeed for the whole country, did unhappily occur in the assassination of President Lincoln almost immediately after the cessation of active hostilities. Mr. Lincoln had all the prestige of success to strengthen his position, and he had also the entire confidence of the great mass of the Northern people. He was naturally of a kindly disposition, and had on many occasions openly and frankly declared that all he wanted was to "restore the Union." Even during the heat and passion of the war he had expressed many generous hopes for the final restoration of brotherly feeling between the dissevered sections of the country, and his first utterances after receiving the news of General Lee's surrender appear to indicate that he rejoiced rather that a fratricidal strife was ended than that an enemy had been beaten. Looking, then, to his temperament; to the genuine, even though somewhat grotesque, *bonhomie* of his character; the prestige of his position, and his personal popularity, it is well-nigh certain that if he had been spared, the so-called "reconstruction" of the Southern States would have been effected in far less time, and with few, if any, of the evil consequences which now unhappily remain as mementoes of that unquiet period.

Upon the death of Mr. Lincoln, the Vice-President, Mr. Andrew Johnson, of Tennessee, succeeded to the higher office; but he brought to the management of affairs neither Mr. Lincoln's qualities nor his influence. The new President was a Southern man who had taken the side of the Federal Government against his own State, and he appeared at first desirous to manifest a persecuting zeal against the Southern people equal to the bitterest Party leaders at the North. His earlier proclamations and personal speeches exhibited a purpose to act with great rigour—indeed, some of his expressions can hardly be described as less than sanguinary. Afterwards he relented, and seemed very desirous to ameliorate the harsh and ruinous measures that Congress was forcing upon the South; but the extreme men had then got complete control. The majority of the Northern people had gone back to their private business and to their pleasures, and the chief politicians of the dominant Party were masters of the situation.

The President had lost the popularity which his "loyalty" during the war had won for him at the North. He was very naturally distrusted at the South, and the Republican members of Congress who controlled the Government treated him with a degree of contempt which at last found visible and startling expression in a serious but futile effort to remove him from office by impeachment. It was soon manifest that Mr. Johnson could do nothing to modify the scheme of "reconstruction" proposed by the leading Republican senators, who were supported by a large majority in the House of Representatives. His subsequent zeal in opposing the will of Congress was almost as unfortunate for the South as his earlier purposes promised to be threatening and disastrous, because it stimulated his opponents to act with increased energy and rigour, in order to gratify their ill-will to him.

It can hardly now be doubted that if the best men at the South, whose personal honour was unimpeachable, and whose influence with the white people, and with the impressionable and docile negroes, was paramount, had been invited to take the lead in the pacification of the country and the rearrangement of the State Governments, there would have been far less confusion, less pecuniary loss, and fewer bitter memories. Mr. Alexander H. Stephens was, from personal qualities and public services, the foremost man in Georgia. He was originally opposed to the secession of the Southern States,* a fact well known at the North; but when the Convention, elected by the people of Georgia to determine the action of that State passed the "Ordinance of Secession," he yielded his will to that of the majority, and became Vice-President of the Confederate States.

Can anyone doubt that if the people of Georgia had been permitted to elect Mr. Stephens to the office of Governor, or if the United States had appointed him to that office provisionally, at the close of the war, the pacification and the "reconstruction" of that important State would have been effected without violence or local resistance? Is it not absolutely certain that the people of Virginia would have welcomed General Lee with enthusiasm as their Governor? and will anyone now venture to affirm that either of those men (General Lee or Mr. Stephens) would have failed to use their influence and their power in complete harmony with the purpose to restore, not only the political, but the fraternal union of the States? The history of their lives before and after the Civil War, the services of both to the whole Union in former times, and the eulogies pronounced upon Mr. Stephens in the United States Congress on the occasion of his death (within the current year, 1883), furnish a sufficient answer.†

But what are the facts in regard to the "reconstruction of the South"? Mr. Alexander H. Stephens was arrested and taken away from his home under some vague charge of treason, and General Lee was saved from a like indignity only because the terms of his military surrender afforded a clear and explicit protection against civil prosecution. The leaders—and, indeed, all the prominent men in the South—were disfranchised and disqualified from holding any public office. The external forms of public elections were permitted, but they were carefully guarded and regulated by the Federal authorities. The management of the elections and of affairs generally was given over to needy adventurers from Northern States, who entered into association with the "residuum" of the local white population; and they contrived, with the support of the Party politicians at Washington, to thrust the freedmen into a position for which they were not in the least degree fitted, and which produced an antagonism of races,

---

* He thought secession inexpedient, but did not deny the right of the Southern States to secede.

† Distinguished men from other Southern States might be mentioned who would have acted in harmony with Mr. Stephens and General Lee.

the unhappy effects of which will be felt for many a day to come. White men with neither property nor experience, aliens who had no local interests and no local ties, and negroes who could neither "read, write, nor cipher," were elected to the State Legislatures, and were entrusted with the delicate and important office of readjusting the shattered foundations of society, and the bankrupt finances of great commonwealths.

The result was to impose the burden of intolerable taxation upon thousands who held all the property which the ravages of the war had spared, but who had had no voice in the election of their so-called representatives, and the manufacture of State Bonds whose proceeds were in great part squandered; and a further and more unhappy effect was that of creating a stinging sense of injustice, and a consciousness of improper administration, which at first aroused feelings of dismay and aversion, and has at last taken in some States the practical but lamentable form of "repudiation."

Confessions made by leading politicians at the North have established the fact that the "reconstruction" policy of the ruling faction was based upon the expectation of securing the votes of the Southern States to the Republican Party, and thus to insure a continued lease of power. But the very same men have acknowledged that the result has not been satisfactory. The intolerable nuisance and shame of "carpet-bag" governors and ignorant, thriftless legislators drove the unquiet spirits of the South into a condition of "veiled rebellion," which the more orderly, who longed for repose, and perceived its necessity, could not prevent. As the political disabilities of the whites were removed, or the disqualifying Acts were permitted to lapse, the superior race assumed its natural ascendency, and the pliant blacks were taken like sheep to the polls, and voted against the very Party who claimed their gratitude for giving them their freedom and the protection of the franchise.

We have the highest possible authority for believing that afflictions are ultimately beneficial to those who are duly "exercised thereby." Surely the American States, from the great lakes of the North to the Gulf of Mexico, and from the tide-waters of the Atlantic to the golden gates of San Francisco, were scourged and chastened by that terrible Civil War. But what has been the effect upon the political institutions of the country? The populous commercial cities of the North are held in the grasp of corrupt associations, and the representatives of the people in Congress, the executive officers of the several States, and the highest members of the national Government, are spoken of with suspicion, if not with contempt, by the very people who, by the theory of the Constitution, have the right, and therefore the responsibility, of choosing their own rulers.

At the South the condition of affairs is, if possible, even worse. The necessities of the "reconstruction" period have produced a large class of professional Party whips and "manipulators," in whose hands the docile negro, vain of his franchise, as children with a new toy, is nothing more than clay to the potter. Flattered, cajoled, sometimes threatened, he for the present helps to swell the great Democratic majorities in the Southern States; but to-morrow, or the day after, he may be sent flying like a shuttlecock to the other existing Party. To-day he votes taxes by thousands of dollars to meet the interest on State Bonds, and to-morrow, under a change of influences, he votes for repudiation, but is known in the new political phraseology of the period by the euphemistic title of a "readjuster." Can anyone acquainted with the history of Virginia, that grand old Commonwealth, "the mother of Presidents," the birthplace of Washington, Patrick Henry, Jefferson, Madison, the Lees, and other founders of the great Republic, believe that the present policy of "readjusting" the State debt is the true popular will? Does anyone doubt that the present condition of affairs in Virginia is the result of an arrangement between the leaders of the ruling Party at Washington and the men—some ambitious and some unscrupulous—who have been bred since the war, and who have sold, not their own birthright, but that of their State, for Federal office, or Federal favour of some sort?

The politicians whom the people of the North were content to trust with the important duty of reuniting the dissevered States do not appear to have looked very far into the future. The more violent spoke and acted with bitterness and precipitancy, and they carried their measures for the reconstruction of the vanquished States by appeals to the prejudices of the moderate men of their party, and by exciting the fear of open resistance, or perhaps even a renewal of the war by the Southern people. They deliberately set on foot a system of managing the elections throughout the South by the direct interference of the central power at Washington, and with the purpose to maintain a particular party in office, they bargained with the least reputable and most ignorant of the Southern population, and have thus extended and confirmed over the whole country a system of interference in the management of elections, and of trade and barter in respect to the public offices, which had indeed begun to prevail even before the Civil War in the large cities, but whose baneful effects had not yet depraved the rural districts and the least populous States.

It is a remarkable fact that the political leaders who directed and controlled the executive and legislative powers of the United States at the end of the Civil War wholly neglected to define the rights and privileges of the individual States by a specific declaration. The pretence that the war upon the South was fought in the interest of the negro, or to effect his freedom, will hardly now be affirmed by any one who is acquainted with the history of its origin. The object of the Federal Government, and of the States which supported it, was to prevent the dissolution of the Union, and the principle involved was that no State should retire or secede from the National League without the consent of the others.

It is admitted, even by the majority of those who were most strongly opposed to the doctrine of State Rights, that the Constitution was at least vague on that point. It remains in the same condition now. So great was the desire of the politicians to reconstruct the Union in a manner which should serve their party purposes, that they either forgot or were heedless of the real end for which so much blood and treasure had been expended, and although they introduced "amendments" in the Constitution to clearly define and secure the designs which were then uppermost in their minds, they left the relations of the States towards each other, and towards the general Government, in the precise condition which those questions occupied on the morning when the echoes of Beauregard's guns at Charleston aroused the whole country, and involved the rival sections in a fratricidal struggle.

It was manifestly impossible for a new country like the United States to wait for the gradual growth of a Constitution like that of Great Britain. When the American colonies achieved their independence, and formed a union or federation for purposes of mutual protection and mutual profit, it was no doubt necessary to draw up a formal agreement to define the conditions of the Union, and the powers of the central or general authority. The result of the Civil War has been to prove that in a great democratic confederation, the interpretation of the written document which prescribes the relative rights and duties of the several parties rests practically with the majority, and the minority have no right of appeal, and no tribunal to which they can appeal. So long as political parties are distributed with a near approach to equal proportions in the different States, such Constitutional documents answer well enough, but when questions arise which affect the States differently, and a large group is disposed to follow one policy, and the smaller and weaker group is impelled to a different course, then the meaning of the compact, or constitution, or Articles of Confederation, or whatever the document may be called, will be determined by that combination of States which compose the majority.

The political corruption which has become so lamentably apparent since the war, and the obscurity which exists in the national Constitution on some important points, are doubtless subjects of serious and earnest thought to all Americans whose patriotism rises above party, and who think the United States have a higher and more important mission than to populate a continent, to grow big crops of corn and cotton, and to accumulate great wealth.

The injuries inflicted upon each other by the North and the South during the heat and passion of the struggle were deep, but many of the most violent spirits have already disappeared, and their bitter memories are happily buried with them. Those who remain of the generation who took part in the war are conscious of a yearly increase of brotherly feeling, and perceive with satisfaction a growing tendency in both sections of the Union towards a mutual reconciliation. If the young men who have sprung into manhood since the Presidential Election of 1860 will heartily unite in efforts to restore the pristine purity of the Government, and the primitive simplicity of its Republican form, the restored Union may have a more glorious future than could have been attained by that which was dissolved in 1861, and the joy and pride of belonging to it will render the right of secession a question of no importance.

NOTES

ORN stands for *Official Records of the Union and Confederate Navies,* Washington, D.C., 1894–1922.

page 15   Texas seceded on February 1, 1861; Arkansas on May 6; and North Carolina on May 21; Tennessee on June 24. West Virginia, formed out of the pro-Union western counties of Virginia, declared its independence of the mother state in June, 1861, and was admitted to the Union on June 20, 1863. The border slave-holding states, Missouri, Kentucky, Maryland, and Delaware, never joined the Confederacy.

page 18   "As early as April, 1861, it was determined to send an agent to England ..." This was probably Major Caleb Huse, although Benjamin Moran, secretary in the American Embassy in London, says in his diary that Dudley Mann, Confederate agent, called on the Embassy on April 18.

page 33   The ship which Semmes was outfitting was a packet-boat renamed the *Sumter.* This was the first government-owned warship of the Confederacy. Only privateers, commissioned after Davis's proclamation offering letters of marque to privately owned vessels was issued on April 17, 1861, were at sea before the *Sumter* sailed on June 30.

page 58   Ports used by blockade runners. The advantages of using Bermuda, Nassau, and Havana can readily be seen; yet Matamoras, Mexico, was the most useful of all ports, for it is at the mouth of the Rio Grande opposite Brownsville, Texas. Cotton was shipped there by rail, wagon, and barge to be exchanged for cargoes of much-needed manufactured goods. Since Matamoras was on Mexican soil, ships under foreign flag could run in and out of there with impunity.

page 76   The Confederate loan in Europe (sometimes called the Erlanger loan). In September, 1862, Emil Erlanger, head of the Paris banking firm of that name, proposed to Slidell to float a large loan for the Confederacy with cotton as collateral. The Confederate Congress rather reluctantly approved the loan on January 29, 1863, and authorized General Colin McRae and James Spence to supervise the handling of the bonds. On March 19, $15,000,000 worth of Confederate 7-per-cent bonds were placed on the market in several European financial centers. The loan was heavily oversubscribed by eager speculators, among whom were W. E. Gladstone and the Duc de Morny. The Confederates constantly had to switch money from one source to another to meet interest payments and prop up the sagging value of the bonds. Toward the end of the war the bonds decreased tremendously in price; after Appomattox they became worthless. An interesting sidelight on this financial transaction is the fact that Erlanger's daughter married Slidell's son—against the protests of both parents.

page 81   Terceira is one of the Azores Islands.

page 110   The *M. (Florida)*. The "M" Stands for *Manassas,* the second of this ship's three successive names.

page 128   The seizure of the *Florida* in a neutral port. Professor James R. Soley, Massachusetts-born naval historian, specialist in international law, and assistant Secretary of the Navy from 1890 to 1893, in 1883 wrote of Collins's act that "the capture of the *Florida* was as gross and deliberate a violation of the rights of neutrals as was ever committed in any age or country. It is idle to attempt to apologize for it or to explain it; the circumstances were such that the question does not admit of discussion. All that can be said is that it was the independent act of an officer, and that it was disavowed by the Government. In the words of the Secretary of State, it 'was an unauthorized, unlawful, and indefensible exercise of the naval force of the United States within a foreign country, in defiance of its established and duly recognized Government.' "

page 189   Semmes's description of the *Alabama;* cf. also text on p. 43. The U.S. Navy was in possession of a detailed description of the *Alabama* some time before November, 1862. Captain Hager, whose ship, the *Brilliant,* had been burned by Semmes, surveyed the *Alabama* with an expert's eye and wrote this fairly accurate description of her for the November 1, 1862, issue of *Harper's Weekly:*

> The *Alabama* was built at Liverpool, or Birkenhead, and left the latter port in August last; is about 1,200 tons burden, draught about fourteen feet; engines by Laird & Sons, of Birkenhead, 1862. She is a wooden vessel, propelled by a screw, copper bottom, about 210 feet long, rather narrow, painted black outside and drab inside; has a round stern, billet head, very little shear,

flush deck fore and aft; a bridge forward of the smoke stack carries two large black boats on cranes amidships forward of the main rigging; two black quarter boats between the main and mizen masts, one small black boat over the stern, on cranes; the spare spars, on a gallows between the bridge and foremast, show above the rail. She carries three long thirty-two pounders on a side, and is pierced for two more amidships; has a one hundred-pound rifled pivot gun forward of the bridge, and a sixty-eight pound pivot on the main deck; has tracks laid forward for a pivot bow gun, and tracks aft for a pivot stern chaser—all of which she will take on board to complete her armament. Her guns are of the Blakely pattern, and manufactured by Wesley & Preston, Liverpool, 1862. She is bark-rigged; has very long, bright lower masts, and black mast-heads; yards black, long yard-arms, short poles (say one to two feet), with small dog-vanes on each, and a pendant to the main; studding-sail booms on the fore and main, and has wire rigging. Carries on her foremast a square foresail; large try-sail with two reefs, and a bonnet top-sail with two reefs, top-gallant sail and royal. On the mainmast a large try-sail with two reefs and a bonnet. No square mainsail bent, top-sail two reefs, top-gallant sail and royal. On the mizenmast, a very large spanker and a short three-cornered gaff top-sail; has a fore-and foretop-mast stay-sail and jib; has had no stay-sail to the main or mizen-mast bent or royal yards aloft. Is represented to go thirteen knots under canvas and fifteen under steam. Can get steam in twenty minutes, but seldom uses it except in a chase or an emergency. Has all national flags, but usually sets the St. George's cross on approaching a vessel. Her present complement of men is one hundred and twenty, all told, but is anxious to ship more. Keeps a man at the mast-head from daylight to sunset. Her sails are of hemp canvas, made very roaching; the top-sails have twenty cloths on the head and thirty on the foot. General appearance of the hull and sails decidedly English. She is generally under two top-sails, fore and main try-sails; fore-and foretop-mast stay-sails; sometimes top-gallant sails and jib, but seldom any sails on the mizen except while in chase of a vessel. She is very slow in stays; generally wears ship. She was built expressly for the business. She is engaged to destroy, fight, or run, as the character of her opponent may be. She took her armament and crew and most of her officers on board near Terceira, Western Islands, from an English vessel. Her crew are principally English; the officers chivalry of the South. All the water consumed on board is condensed. She has eight months' provisions, besides what is being plundered, and has about four hundred tons of coal on board.

page 274   M—— is probably the Duc de Morny (see text on p. 294).

page 319   "A great majority of the people of England sympathized with the South." This is true about the upper-class people Bulloch met, but it can hardly be said that a majority of the people of England favored the South. Many of the workingmen and middle-class people did not.

page 342   The confidential clerk who stole—and copied—some of the correspondence of M. Voruz was an Alsatian named Petermann, who professed to favor the Union cause. He took the papers to the American Legation in Paris where he offered them for sale for 20,000 francs—but settled for 15,000.

page 344   The *Tuscaloosa*, originally named the *Conrad*, was one of the four captured American ships which the Confederates armed and commissioned at sea to raid Yankee commerce. She was taken by the *Alabama* in the South Atlantic on June 21, 1863. During her brief career she made but one capture and was seized by the British at the Cape of Good Hope on December 27, 1863.

page 346   "Mr. Eustis being present." This was George Eustis, Slidell's secretary.

page 365   Bulloch suppresses much of the story of the purchase of the *Stonewall* from the Danish government. It is told in detail in ORN, I, 719ff. Since the intermediary, Henri A. de Rivière, was an irresponsible soldier of fortune, Bulloch was probably ashamed of his connection with such a person, especially since he knew that De Rivière had secretly opened one of the bilgecocks of the ship on its trial run for the Danes, making the ironclad so sluggish that the Danish government was glad to be rid of her. De Rivière then persuaded Caleb Huse to go to Denmark with him. It was because of this that Bulloch and Huse broke their longstanding friendship.

page 382   Craven was court-martialed and sentenced in December, 1865, to two years suspension from duty on leave pay, but Gideon Welles set the verdict aside.

page 383   Captain Page was an elderly, honest, and apparently capable naval officer, but his excessive caution undoubtedly delayed the arrival of the *Stonewall* in America. He wasted six weeks going to Paris to consult Slidell about what to do. He was ordered to cross the Atlantic at once and attack Sherman's supply bases in South Carolina. Yet he wasted still more time getting under way so that he did not reach Nassau until May 6, 1865, nearly a month after Appomattox.

page 411   "I find it difficult to account for the unwillingness of the men to ship for the *Shenandoah*." Bulloch seems to forget that the *Alabama* had been sunk on June 19 that year (1864) and that word of the capture of the *Florida* had reached Europe by this time.

page 412   Irvine S. Bulloch was James D. Bulloch's younger half-brother.

page 420   Bulloch's dates are incorrect. Lee evacuated Petersburg and Richmond on April 2, 1865, and surrendered the Army of Northern Virginia to Grant at Appomattox Court House on April 9. Bulloch surely knew the correct dates at this time; perhaps he was relying on memory.

page 421   "President Johnson has formally declared the war to be at an end." This was not actually done until April 2, 1866, when Texas was specifically exempted; peace was not proclaimed there until August 20, 1866.

page 435   "The behaviour of the *Shenandoah*'s crew in preserving their discipline ... etc." All but five of the officers of the *Shenandoah* (Bulloch's half-brother among them) signed a petition to the commander urging him to put ashore at Cape Town rather than go on to Liverpool and run the risk of capture on the way. There was a near mutiny on the ship. (ORN, I, 3, 779ff.) The crew, however, signed a petition supporting Captain Waddell.

page 439   American ships destroyed by Confederate cruisers of English or French origin. According to J. T. Scharf's *A History of the Confederate Navy,* published in 1887 (after Bulloch had written his book), 249 Union-owned vessels with a total value of $8,639,999.82 were destroyed.

page 451   "Two armour-cased vessels were built in Charleston." These were the *Chicora* and the *Palmetto State,* which made a desperate but unsuccessful attempt to drive away the Federal blockading fleet on January 31, 1863.

page 490   The secret mission Bulloch refers to was the sending of the *Georgia* in February 1864 to meet the *Rappahannock* off the Atlantic coast of Morocco about forty miles south of Mogador. There the *Georgia* was to transfer her guns, ammunition, and part of her crew to the *Rappahannock.* But that luckless ship was held in Calais until the war was over.

page 495   Lt. James A. North. Although Bulloch carefully refrains from saying anything about the internal feuds among the Confederate agents stationed in Europe, much bickering went on. When Bulloch was made a commander, North complained to Richmond about his promotion. Even Bulloch himself was not above petty jealousy. A careful reading of the text indicates that he resented it whenever the power to obtain ships in Europe was entrusted to anyone but him. His annoyance with Matthew Fontaine Maury is easily seen. And after four years of close friendship with Major Caleb Huse, Bulloch quarreled with him about handling the negotiations with Denmark to get the *Stonewall* away from Copenhagen. (See note for p. 365.)

page 510   The British Proclamation of Neutrality was issued on May 13, 1861; it was officially published in the London *Gazette* on May 14.

page 514   Bulloch's book from here on is devoted largely to a discussion of the *Alabama* Claims. A brief summary of this famous case of international arbitration can be found in the Eleventh Edition of *The Encyclopedia Britannica*, vol. I, pp. 464–65, "ALABAMA" ARBITRATION. See also *The Alabama Arbitration* by Thomas W. Balch, Philadelphia, 1900.

page 521 James Spence, author of *The American Union*, was a trader on the Liverpool Cotton Exchange. His book, strongly pro-Southern, was widely read in England and was published in translation in several European countries. He later helped the Erlangers float the European Confederate bond issue of 1863.

page 534 "Two blockade runners, built ... in England but taken to Wilmington." These were the *Chickamauga* and the *Tallahassee*.

INDEX

A Note on the Type

The principal text of this Modern Library edition
was set in a digitized version of Janson,
a typeface that dates from about 1690 and was cut by Nicholas Kis,
a Hungarian working in Amsterdam. The original matrices have
survived and are held by the Stempel foundry in Germany.
Hermann Zapf redesigned some of the weights and sizes for Stempel,
basing his revisions on the original design.